Pickett's Charge at Gettysburg

A Guide to the Most Famous Attack in American History

James A. Hessler and Wayne E. Motts

cartography by Steven A. Stanley

photography by Karl Stelly, Steven Stanley, James Hessler & Michael Waricher

Library of Congress Control Number: 2015933139.

ISBN 13: 978-1-61121-200-6

Second edition, first printing

SB

Published by
Savas Beatie LLC
989 Governor Drive, Suite 102
El Dorado Hills, CA 95762

Mailing address:

Savas Beatie LLC
P.O. Box 4527
El Dorado Hills, CA 95762
Phone: 916-941-6896
(E-mail) editorial@savasbeatie.com

Savas Beatie titles are available at special discounts for bulk purchases worldwide by corporations, government agencies, institutions, and other organizations. For more details, please contact Special Sales, P.O. Box 4527, El Dorado Hills, CA 95762, or you may e-mail us at sales@savasbeatie.com, or visit our website at www.savasbeatie.com for additional information.

Title Page Images: 1883 Cyclorama of the "Battle of Gettysburg"
by Paul Philippoteaux.

This book is dedicated to all of those who served at Gettysburg on July 3, 1863. It is also dedicated to Gettysburg's Licensed Battlefield Guides for keeping these stories alive.

Table of Contents

Pickett's Charge: Introduction

"So much has been said and written about the battle of Gettysburg that it would seem that little of interest could be added." – Colonel Richard Penn Smith, 71st Pennsylvania (1887). [1]

If Colonel Smith were still with us today, he would undoubtedly be startled to see the volumes of words that continue to be added about Gettysburg.

Assuming that Gettysburg is the most written about battle in American history, then Robert E. Lee's July 3 assault, popularly known as "Pickett's Charge," may be the most studied single action during this battle. There is something about this charge that still emotionally connects with Gettysburg enthusiasts like no other aspect of the battle. On the 150th anniversary of the charge on July 3, 2013, an estimated 15,000 visitors (more than the number that made the actual charge) recreated the march to Cemetery Ridge while as many as 25,000 people watched from the Union lines. [2] Why? Perhaps because there is something inexplicable, tragic, and yet still inspiring about the notion of a legendary general ordering thousands of his men to march across nearly one mile of open ground in what appears to the untrained eye to be an almost suicidal charge.

This book is not an attempt to provide a detailed military micro-history of the attack since many other works have already accomplished that task. Yet for those who study the battle through a myriad of resources, there is no more important reference than the battlefield itself. But in an ever increasing field of Gettysburg literature that includes a number of walking tour guides, it is surprising that no one has yet produced a tour guide to this seminal attack. As a result, the battlefield and the monuments placed here by the veterans have never been fully used to tell the story of this attack and defense.

Contrary to the views of some who regard this action as a simple frontal assault, there are still a number of mysteries and unanswered questions associated with it. Many of those questions can be best answered, or at least debated, with a thorough understanding of the ground upon which this charge occurred. But unfortunately most Gettysburg visitors consider the attack from a narrow viewpoint of the ground between the Virginia State Memorial and the "High Water Mark" area on Cemetery Ridge. Many visitors "walk the charge" by dutifully following the National Park Service's mowed path that leads from the Virginia monument straight to "the Angle," probably unaware this was not the direct route followed by Maj. General George Pickett's Division during the course of the attack. General Lee's attack was considerably broader in scope than this, and an understanding that his Army of Northern Virginia's active operations extended from beyond the Fairfield Road to the Peach Orchard gives both novices and dedicated Gettysburg students a better understanding of what Lee tried, and ultimately failed, to accomplish.

The traditional interpretation of Pickett's Charge (notwithstanding the popular name) fosters a very "Pickett-centric" reading of the day's actions. Much of the ground upon which Brig. General Johnston Pettigrew and Maj. General Isaac Trimble's Confederate divisions fought has been lost to modern development. Likewise, the ill-fated support provided by the two brigades under Brig. General Cadmus Wilcox and Col. David Lang is given scant, if any, historical scrutiny. Some histories barely even acknowledge their

presence. Some readers will criticize our frequent use of "Pickett's Charge" rather than the name preferred by hard-core enthusiasts: "The Pickett-Pettigrew-Trimble Charge." The latter is more accurate but the former is more popular and has a long history of its own. Our use of the popular, and easier to say, version does not indicate that Pettigrew and Trimble (and Wilcox and Lang) will be absent from these pages.

On the other side, the defense of Maj. General George Meade's Army of the Potomac was more extensive than simply the several hundred yards surrounding the so-called "Copse of Trees." The traditional focus on Brig. General Alexander Webb's brigade at the Angle has also shortchanged the contributions of Union artillery from as far away as Little Round Top and the stoic defense provided by others such as Brig. General Alexander Hays's division or Col. Norman Hall's brigade. The Army of the Potomac's successful defense of Cemetery Ridge comprises a considerable portion of this book, and unlike many other books on this topic ours should not be considered "Confederate-centric."

Last, and certainly not least, history is about the people who made events happen. In addition to military strategy and monuments history, readers will find numerous stories about individual participants, both well-known and lesser-known players, throughout this work. We believe that some of these stories have seldom, if ever, been told in other books.

Our goal is to provide the reader and battlefield-walker a better understanding of the people and scope of the Pickett-Pettigrew-Trimble-Wilcox-Lang Charge and Meade's defense while also examining many of the more colorful and controversial aspects of the story. When completed, it is hoped that Gettysburg enthusiasts will better appreciate this action as being much more than a simple frontal assault by one Virginia division upon an otherwise unremarkable clump of trees.

James A. Hessler and Wayne E. Motts

February 2015

Acknowledgments

A project of this size could not be completed without the help and support of many friends, family, and colleagues.

Colleagues at several institutions generously provided their time, access, and permission to use their materials: Ben Neely and Tim Smith at Adams County Historical Society, John Heiser at Gettysburg National Military Park (including information on the return of several monuments to their original positions as part of the Ziegler Grove rehabilitation), and Matthew Turi at Wilson Library, University of North Carolina at Chapel Hill. The staffs at Cornell University Libraries, Minnesota Historical Society, National Civil War Museum, and VMI also provided material. Thanks also to Martha Brogan for material related to John Blinn.

A special thanks to Gettysburg Licensed Battlefield Guide Jim Clouse. He is the keeper of the Association of Licensed Battlefield Guides' library and this work would have been considerably more difficult to complete without his thankless efforts in keeping the library stocked and organized.

Access to private collections was graciously provided by Erik Dorr at the Gettysburg Museum of History (including Fred Pfeffer's collection of relics found on the

battlefield), Robert K. Krick for the Coupland R. Page Memoir, Sam Magruder for the William T. Magruder Family Archives, and Ed and Faye Max for Winfield S. Hancock's correspondence and several images from their collection.

From the beginning we expected this book to rely heavily on visuals. In addition to Steve's efforts, we are indebted to Michael Waricher and Karl Stelly for providing most of the modern photography included here. Michael has also done extensive photographic research in Gettysburg National Military Park's archives and assisted in locating many of the historical images used here.

Although it is often said that authors should not have friends read their manuscript, that does not hold true in Gettysburg which is home to the country's foremost concentration of experts on this great battle. Several friends took time out from their battlefield studies to read early drafts, make corrections, and offer useful suggestions. We expected no less from them but we offer our gratitude to Bob George, Chris Army, Steve Mock, and fellow Gettysburg Licensed Battlefield Guide John Zervas.

Gettysburg's Licensed Battlefield Guides, of which Wayne and Jim are proud members, have kept many of the stories told within these pages alive for generations of visitors. The Orders of Battle include here were a combined long-time effort of Wayne's and fellow Battlefield Guides John Volbrecht and Ed Guy.

In addition to those Guides who are not named elsewhere, we would also like to thank Sue Boardman for providing access to her extensive photo collection, Christina Moon for research assistance, Phil Lechak for assistance in distributing updates to the ALBG membership, and Jack Drummond for editorial comments.

This book initially sprouted from a conversation between Jim and Eric Lindblade questioning why no one had ever written a tour guide for Pickett's Charge. Completing this was a rough patch at times but it is finally done.

Thanks to Garry Adelman, Director of History and Education for the Civil War Trust. At his request, we served as historians and content contributors to the Trust's Gettysburg Battle App Guide for mobile devices. It was that project that helped renew our interest to finish this book after our initial enthusiasm had waned.

Additional suggestions, transcriptions, and research were provided by Kendra Debany (including access to her research on several local farms), Randy Drais (for his insights on Pickett's "Lost Report"), Steve Floyd (for sorting through Vermont's monuments history), Ben Dixon, Bryce Suderow, Mark H. Dunkelman, and Tonia "Teej" Smith.

Esteemed historians Scott Hartwig, Jeff Wert, and Carol Reardon graciously read a preview in order to provide comments for the dust jacket.

Ted Savas, Sarah Keeney, and the team at Savas Beatie were a pleasure to work with once again. Ted supported us as always with enthusiasm and the time needed to complete this, even when deadlines were missed. A special thanks to Mary Gutzke for her thorough editing work.

Jim would like to thank his wife Michele and children Alex and Aimee for tolerating all of the frustration that the author exhibits while writing and re-writing. Michele again volunteered her scarce time to assist in proofing and indexing (on Valentine's Day 2015!) in order to push this across the finish line. Perhaps one day they will even read these words! Wayne Motts was a mentor of mine when I became a

Licensed Battlefield Guide in 2003 and I have always considered him the world's foremost authority on Pickett's Charge. I was thrilled when he agreed to this project and the book is immeasurably better because of his involvement. Steve's maps and layout provided the visuals that a book of this nature requires and it was a pleasure to finally work together after many years as friends.

Wayne wishes to thank his co-author, friend, and colleague Jim for allowing him to be part of this great project, and for all the effort he put forth in the completion of the volume. His dedication, knowledge, and expertise truly made this work the best of a combined effort. Wayne also wishes to note the maps and layout work done by Steven Stanley which have greatly contributed to the book. Wayne is grateful for the support of his wife Tina, daughter Brittney, and son-in-law Michael in all his historical endeavors including this book.

Steven would like to thank his lovely wife, Kyrstie, for her love and support through all the late nights and moments of frustration while working on this project. Also I would like to thank both Jim and Wayne for bringing him into this project and for their patience while the maps were being created. It truly was a pleasure working with both of them.

Touring the Fields of "Pickett's Charge"

This book consists of four comprehensive tours of Gettysburg National Military Park and landmarks associated with the action that occurred on July 3, 1863. The two major National Park avenues (West Confederate and Hancock Avenue) used in these tours are one-way to vehicular traffic, therefore the book is laid-out in the physical order an actual battlefield visitor would experience while traveling on these roads. Each tour includes a series of detailed maps (along with numbered "stop signs" indicating current and nearby positions) and photographs to assist the reader and battlefield walker.

We have endeavored to follow an accurate chronology of events as much as possible, but the terrain has occasionally forced us to deviate from this plan. As a result, it may be helpful to inform the casual reader how each tour aligns with the basic sequence of events that occurred on that hot summer day.

Our tours begin with the army that was on the offense: Robert E. Lee's Army of Northern Virginia. The first tour primarily consists of the Confederate positions along Seminary Ridge (modern West Confederate Avenue) and the Peach Orchard. This tour primarily discusses Lee's strategy and Confederate troop placements. General Lee's activities began pre-dawn on July 3 as Lee planned his attack and continued up through the commencement of the Confederate artillery assault (sometimes referred to as "the cannonade") which began at around 1:00 p.m. in the afternoon.

While there is debate over the exact times that events occurred, and we enthusiastically tackle those types of disputes in this work, Lee's great cannonade (and the return fire of the Union artillery) is generally believed to have lasted for about two hours until approximately 3:00 p.m. The Confederate infantry, thought to be about 12,500 strong, then stepped off from Seminary Ridge. Portions of three Confederate divisions spearheaded the main attack. On the Confederate left (the first positions you will encounter when traveling on West Confederate Avenue), the Southerners consisted of men

from several states and were led by Generals J. Johnston Pettigrew and Isaac Trimble. The second tour is a walking tour of "Pettigrew-Trimble's Charge" from the North Carolina State Memorial toward the northern end of Cemetery Ridge.

At the same time, to the right of Pettigrew and Trimble, a fresh Confederate division commanded by Maj. General George Pickett also launched their attack. Our third tour is again a walking excursion and begins near the modern Virginia State Memorial as we trace the march of Pickett's Virginians to Cemetery Ridge. With slightly less than one mile to march, the Confederates were hit by long-range artillery fire and were increasingly subjected to Yankee rifle-musket fire while en route. Yet they still continued forward.

Additional attention is also given throughout the text to the two brigades that were led by Brig. General Cadmus Wilcox and Col. David Lang. These men had fought heavily on July 2, and the survivors were assigned the role of protecting Pickett's right flank on July 3. For reasons that are not completely clear, they started forward about 20 minutes after Pickett and were decimated by Federal artillery before being forced to withdraw.

We then move to the defense for the fourth and final tour. This segment provides a comprehensive overview of the Army of the Potomac's lines primarily along modern Hancock Avenue. General George Meade's men withstood withering Confederate artillery fire for much of the afternoon, returned cannon fire themselves, and after 3:00 p.m. watched and waited as Lee's infantry advanced across the undulating but open ground. As the Confederate foot soldiers came into closer range, Federal regiments on the far left and right enveloped both of the Southern flanks and decimated the attackers with rifle-musket fire.

The weakened Confederates continued to press their advance, and their efforts converged along a roughly 400 yard front ranging from the area known today as the Copse of Trees to the Abraham Bryan farm. Only a small number of Southerners briefly pierced the Union lines, but by 4:00 p.m. they were repulsed with heavy losses. General Meade's army had successfully defeated Lee's forces, and the final tour tells this story primarily (but not exclusively) from the victors' point of view.

Readers are encouraged, of course, to complete all four of the tours sequentially. However, each tour is also designed to be taken individually so one is not totally dependent upon completing any other.

Other actions that occurred on this day, including morning combat at Culp's Hill and afternoon cavalry fights at East Cavalry and South Cavalry fields, also contributed to the battle's outcome and Lee's ultimate decision to retreat. These episodes are discussed within this book but are outside the scope of our tours.

Finally, we also emphasize that the reader does not need to be present at the Gettysburg battlefield in order to enjoy this book. Walking the terrain is only one of our goals. The stories, maps, and photographs were selected so a user can appreciate and understand these tours from any location. GPS coordinates and elevations were plotted for each tour stop using Google Earth as an aid not only to those walking the field but also for those who may want to "follow along" at home on their computer or other devices.

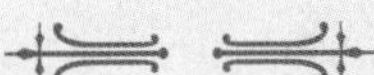

TOUR ONE
Confederate Battle Line

"The attack of Pickett's division on the 3d has been more criticized, and is still less understood, than any other act of the Gettysburg drama . . . it was not ordered without mature consideration and on grounds that presented fair prospects of success."

— **Colonel Armistead Long**[1]

General Robert E. Lee's Headquarters

GPS: 39°50'5.75"N, 77°14'42.34"W; Elev. 562 ft.

For our first tour stop proceed to General Robert E. Lee's headquarters. This stone house is located approximately 0.5 miles west of Gettysburg's town square on the north side of the Chambersburg Pike (modern Route 30 West.) This was the residence of a widow named Mary Thompson during the battle but was commandeered by General Lee and his staff during the evening of July 1, after fighting had swirled around the property earlier that day. Both the home and surrounding land served as Lee's headquarters for the remainder of the battle.

The Thompson house operated in recent years as a privately-owned museum and was encircled by other commercial properties. In July 2014, the Civil War Trust, America's largest nonprofit organization devoted to Civil War battlefield preservation, announced their intention to acquire and preserve the 4.01-acre site by returning it to its 1863 appearance beginning in 2015.

Mrs. Thompson's house as it appeared at the time of the battle.
Image courtesy of Library of Congress

If there is no available public parking at the headquarters when you are taking this tour, then please use public parking at the nearby Lutheran Theological Seminary and Seminary Ridge Museum. If you park at the Seminary and walk to Lee's headquarters, this will give you an excellent opportunity to see the Seminary grounds, Schmucker Hall (which we will discuss briefly before our next tour stop), and Thompson's property on the south side of the Chambersburg Pike where an upturned cannon today commemorates Lee's headquarters.

Always be careful of vehicular traffic.

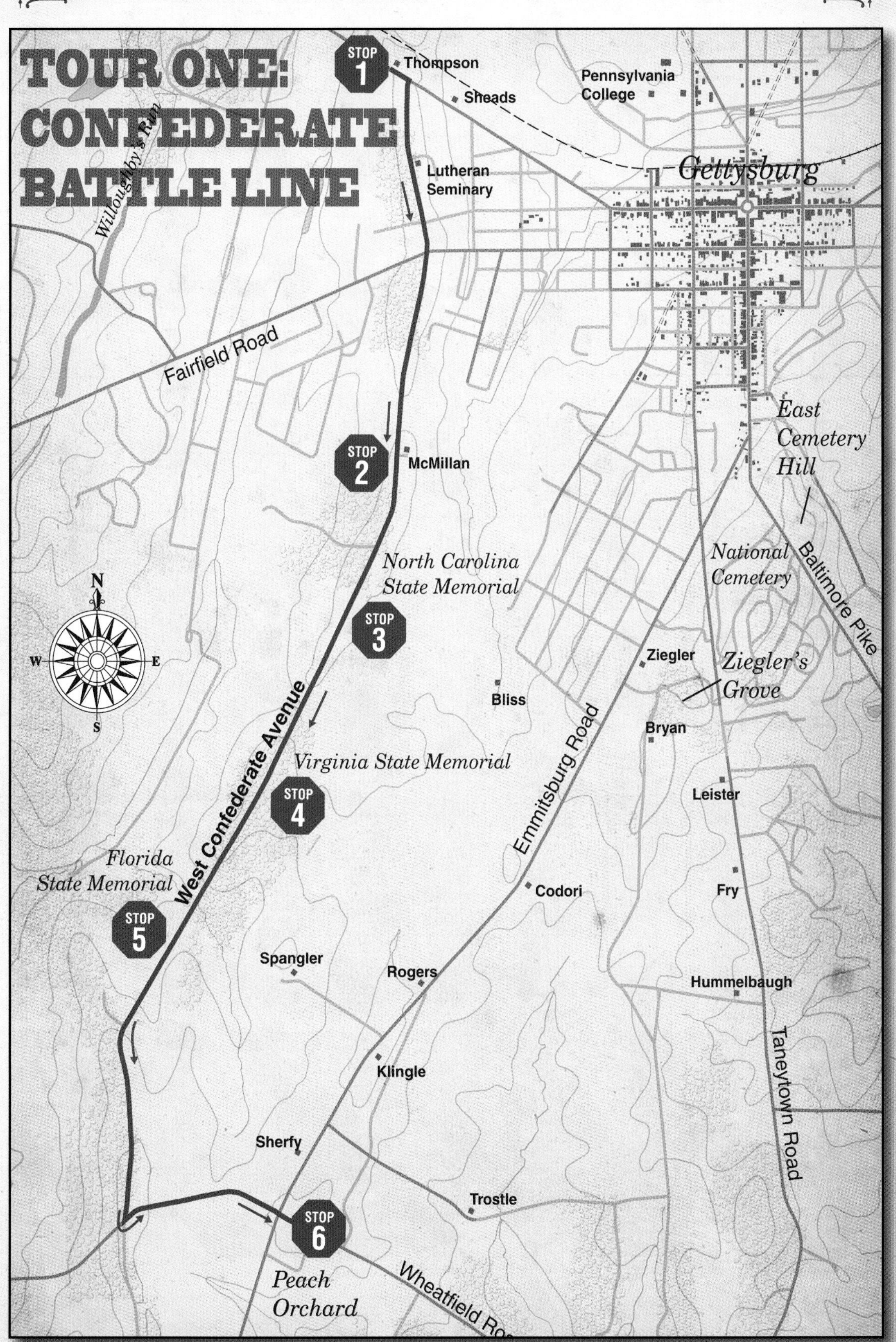
TOUR ONE: CONFEDERATE BATTLE LINE
STOP 1
Thompson
Sheads
Pennsylvania College
Willoughby's Run
Lutheran Seminary
Gettysburg
Fairfield Road
East Cemetery Hill
STOP 2
McMillan
North Carolina State Memorial
National Cemetery
Baltimore Pike
N
W
E
S
STOP 3
Ziegler
Ziegler's Grove
Bliss
West Confederate Avenue
Emmitsburg Road
Bryan
Virginia State Memorial
STOP 4
Leister
Florida State Memorial
Codori
Fry
STOP 5
Spangler
Rogers
Hummelbaugh
Klingle
Taneytown Road
Sherfy
Trostle
STOP 6
Peach Orchard
Wheatfield Ro

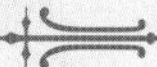
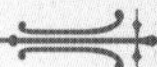

Gen. Robert E. Lee.
Image courtesy of Library of Congress

Confederate General Robert E. Lee was in a dilemma on July 3, 1863.

When Lee launched his Northern invasion that summer, he apparently hoped to avoid an offensive engagement. He wrote in his battle report, "It had not been intended to fight a general battle at such a distance from our base, unless attacked by the enemy."[2] This intention to fight a defensive battle, if possible, undoubtedly suited Lee's senior subordinate, Lt. General James Longstreet. According to Longstreet, by mid-1863 "the war had advanced far enough for us to see that a mere victory without decided fruits was a luxury we could not afford. Our numbers were less than the Federal forces, and our resources were limited while theirs were not." [3] General Longstreet believed the one-sided Confederate victory at Fredericksburg in December 1862, in which Union leadership ordered their men to make numerous futile frontal assaults against Longstreet's entrenched position, had shown the "advantage of receiving instead of giving attack." Heavy losses from offensive operations would deplete Southern manpower to such an extent that "we should not be able to hold a force in the field to meet our adversary." Although Lee reportedly later characterized any pre-campaign "promise…not to fight a general battle" as "absurd," Longstreet insisted he and Lee had agreed on fighting a defensive battle "in a position of our own choosing" as the "ruling idea of the campaign." [4]

Any hopes for fighting a defensive battle were dashed, however, by the Confederate victory of July 1, 1863. General Lee had not planned to fight a battle at Gettysburg on that day, but Maj. General Henry Heth's Division of Lt. General A. P. Hill's Third Corps unexpectedly collided with Union Brig. General John Buford's cavalry division and Maj. General John Reynolds's infantry I Corps in the fields west of Gettysburg. As the day progressed, Hill's men were joined by Confederate Lt. General Richard Ewell's Second Corps and succeeded in defeating the Federal I and XI Corps (who had reinforced Reynolds's corps north of the town in the afternoon). After retreating through the town, however, the Northern forces rallied by nightfall on the heights of Cemetery Hill and Culp's Hill south of Gettysburg. Although Lee and his generals may not have yet fully realized it, their July 1 victory had ironically only served to drive the Union forces into a stronger defensive position.

In the process of scoring this fruitless victory, Lee had also allowed his army to be drawn away from his communication and supply lines which had been west of the South Mountain range. (These mountains are clearly visible from Gettysburg on the western horizon.) That evening on Seminary Ridge, General Longstreet arrived and allegedly proposed that the Confederate army move farther south toward Washington, locate a

strong defensive position, and force the Yankees into making a presumably futile attack. Lee disappointed Longstreet by rejecting this proposal: "No, the enemy is there [on Cemetery Hill], and I am going to attack him there." [5] Longstreet found Lee to be uncharacteristically agitated, in part due to the absence of J. E. B. Stuart's cavalry, which had lost contact with Lee's main body during the march north. As a result of Lee's insistence on attacking, Longstreet properly deferred to his commanding officer and returned to his bivouac in order to prepare for the following day's offensive operations. [6]

Lee later elaborated on his desire to renew the attack:

> [F]inding ourselves unexpectedly confronted by the Federal Army, it became a matter of difficulty to withdraw through the mountains with our large trains. At the same time, the country was unfavorable for collecting supplies while in the presence of the enemy's main body… A battle thus became, in a measure, unavoidable. Encouraged by the successful issue of the engagement of the first day, and in view of the valuable results that would ensue from the defeat of the army of General Meade, it was thought advisable to renew the attack. [7]

On July 2, Lee launched his main attack by directing Longstreet's First Corps to partially envelop the Army of the Potomac's left flank "which he was to drive in" and also to "endeavor to gain a position from which it was thought that our artillery could be brought to bear with effect." [8] Both Generals Ewell and Hill were essentially ordered to cooperate and prevent Federal reinforcements from being sent against Longstreet, and take advantage of any opportunities that might present themselves. After some delays in getting into position, Longstreet finally began his attack at 4:00 p.m., commencing three hours of epic fighting at locations that have since taken on legendary status: Little Round Top, the Peach Orchard, Devil's Den, and the Wheatfield. Longstreet gained some ground, notably capturing the elevation known as the Peach Orchard along the Emmitsburg Road from Union General Daniel E. Sickles's III Corps. However, the attack petered out along General Hill's front, as two brigades in R. H. Anderson's Division (commanded by Generals William Mahone and Carnot Posey) barely engaged the enemy. Ewell's Second Corps meanwhile succeeded in capturing the lower summit of Culp's Hill on the Union right flank in an early evening assault, but daylight faded before they could take the summit and the nearby Baltimore Pike.

Despite some serious failures by the Confederates to coordinate their attacks, and despite the fact Meade's army still held Cemetery Hill and Cemetery Ridge, in Lee's words, "These partial successes determined me to continue the assault next day." Lee further wrote:

> The result of this day's operations induced the belief that, with proper concert of action, and with the increased support that the positions gained on the right would enable the artillery to render the assaulting columns, we should ultimately succeed, and it was accordingly determined to continue the attack. [9]

"We have not been so successful as we wished," was Longstreet's rebuttal. [10] But Lee was encouraged that Longstreet's capture of the Peach Orchard and surrounding ground

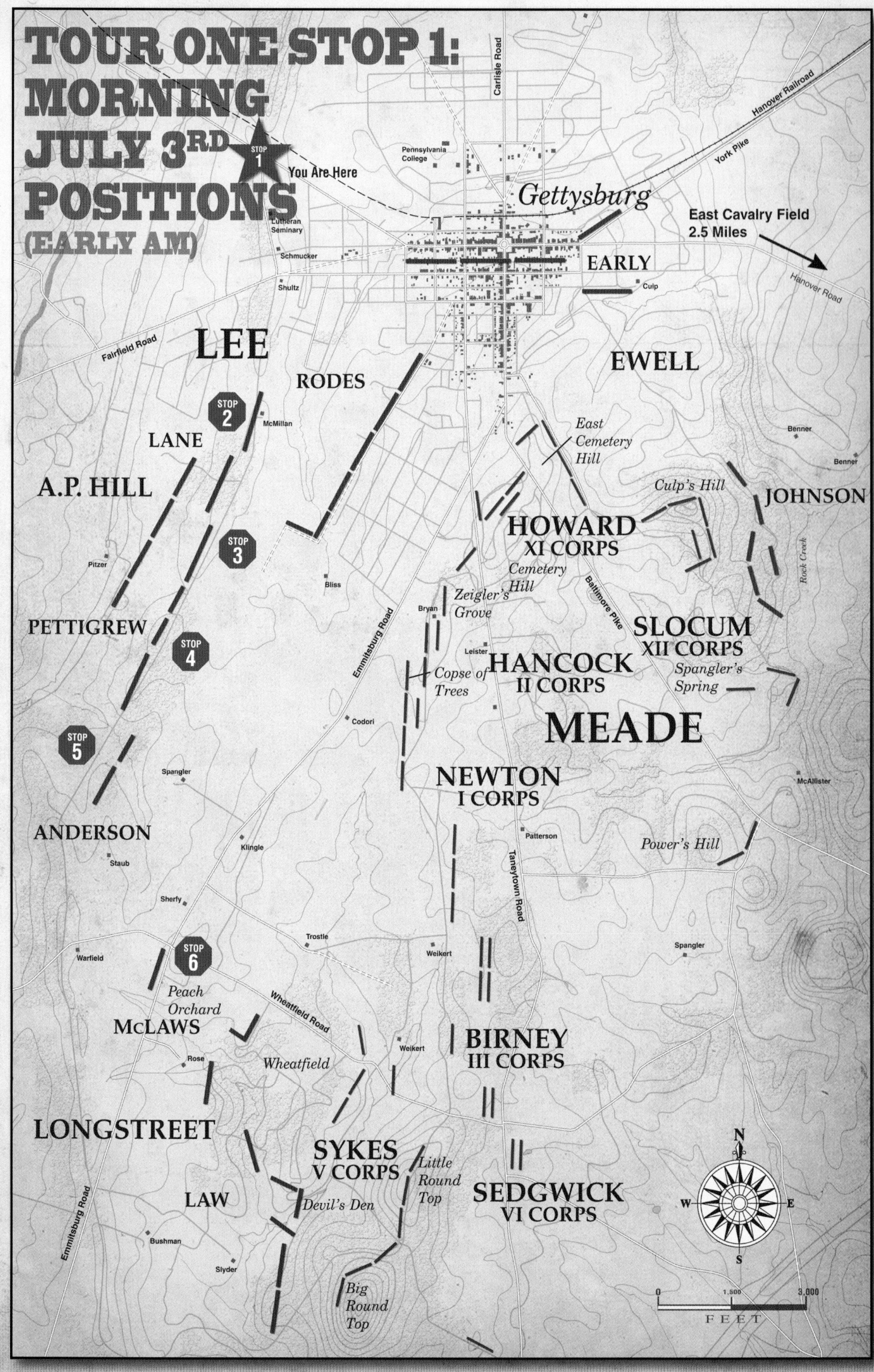

TOUR ONE STOP 1: MORNING JULY 3RD POSITIONS (EARLY AM)
STOP 1
You Are Here
Gettysburg
Carlisle Road
Hanover Railroad
York Pike
Pennsylvania College
Lutheran Seminary
Schmucker
Shultz
East Cavalry Field 2.5 Miles
Hanover Road
EARLY
Culp
Fairfield Road
LEE
RODES
EWELL
STOP 2
McMillan
LANE
A.P. HILL
East Cemetery Hill
Benner
Benner
Culp's Hill
JOHNSON
HOWARD
XI CORPS
STOP 3
Pitzer
Bliss
Cemetery Hill
Zeigler's Grove
Baltimore Pike
Rock Creek
Bryan
Emmitsburg Road
PETTIGREW
STOP 4
SLOCUM
XII CORPS
Leister
HANCOCK
II CORPS
Copse of Trees
Spangler's Spring
Codori
MEADE
STOP 5
Spangler
NEWTON
I CORPS
McAllister
ANDERSON
Klingle
Staub
Patterson
Power's Hill
Taneytown Road
Sherfy
Trostle
Spangler
Warfield
STOP 6
Weikert
Peach Orchard
Wheatfield Road
McLAWS
Weikert
BIRNEY
III CORPS
Rose
Wheatfield
LONGSTREET
SYKES
V CORPS
Little Round Top
SEDGWICK
VI CORPS
LAW
Devil's Den
Emmitsburg Road
Bushman
Slyder
Big Round Top
N
W
E
S
0
1,500
3,000
FEET

would provide sufficient artillery positions from which to converge fire onto Cemetery Hill and support further offensive operations. In addition, after two days of fighting, Lee's army had badly damaged at least three of the Army of the Potomac's infantry corps (Reynolds's I, Sickles's III, and Oliver Howard's XI) and inflicted casualties on nearly all of the others.

However, it was also apparent from Lee's reports, and reiterated in comments he made after the war, that success on July 3 would require better coordination between his infantry and artillery leaders. Given this need, it may be appropriate to criticize Lee for neglecting to bring his senior leaders together on the night of July 2 in order to clearly communicate his intentions for July 3. [11] Rather than July 3 being a desperate assault as is often portrayed, Lee's decision to continue the attack was the only viable alternative that allowed him to remain on the field. If he disengaged without fighting, he would have bled his army for two days while having accomplished nothing of strategic value. Had he not attacked on the third day, Lee would still have been face to face with the Northern army while in enemy territory. The initiative would have been handed to General Meade. Lee also had his supply trains and communication lines to protect and an army that still required food, water, and other supplies. Lee considered his army unable to simply sit and wait indefinitely, and since he clearly still believed himself capable of winning another battle, retreat did not seem to enter his mind as an option. Believing his forces could still successfully carry Cemetery Ridge, Lee reacted characteristically on July 3: he was going to continue the attack. Lee was confident his men would win the day with proper coordination.

Lee initially claimed his "general plan [was] unchanged" on the third day --- implying either another attack on the Union flanks or at least the same ultimate objectives as the prior day. "Longstreet, re-enforced by Pickett's three brigades, which arrived near the battle-field during the afternoon of the 2d, was ordered to attack the next morning, and General Ewell was directed to assail the enemy's right at the same time." [12]

Unfortunately, the Army of the Potomac's XII Corps stole the initiative from Lee and began the fighting at Culp's Hill around 4:30 a.m. before Longstreet was ready to again hit the Union left. Lee implied in his post-battle report that Longstreet bore some responsibility for this. "General Longstreet's dispositions were not completed as early as was expected, but before notice could be sent to General Ewell, General [Edward] Johnson had already become engaged, and it was too late to recall him." [13]

Presumably hoping to avoid a repeat of the futile July 2 assaults against Little Round Top, Longstreet claimed to have sent scouts out during that evening to explore the possibility of maneuvering around the Round Tops. [14] Longstreet admitted in his battle report that he was planning to "pass around the hill occupied by the enemy on his left, and to gain it by flank and reverse attack. This would have been a slow process, probably, but I think not very difficult." [15]

Longstreet later elaborated, "On the next morning he [Lee] came to see me, and fearing that he was still in his disposition to attack, I tried to anticipate him by saying: 'General, I have had my scouts out all night, and I find that you still have an excellent

opportunity to move around to the right [sic-left] of Meade's army and maneuver him into attacking us.'" To Longstreet's disappointment, Lee replied much as he had on the evening of July 1, pointing with his fist at Cemetery Hill, "The enemy is there, and I am going to strike him." [16]

In his memoirs, Longstreet labeled Lee's proclamation that Longstreet was not ready "as early as was expected" as being "disingenuous."

> He did not give or send me orders for the morning of the third day, nor did he reinforce me by Pickett's brigades for morning attack…In the absence of orders, I had scouting parties out during the night in search of a way by which we might strike the enemy's left, and push it down towards his center. I found a way that gave some promise of results, and was about to move the command, when he rode over after sunrise and gave his orders. [17]

Several accounts challenge Longstreet's assertion that orders had not been given to attack early in the morning. General Ewell stated in his report, "I was ordered to renew my attack at daylight Friday morning." [18] Walter Taylor, who it must be noted was one of Longstreet's bitter postwar critics, wrote in 1877 that Ewell ordered his men "to attack at an early hour, anticipating that Longstreet would do the same. Longstreet delayed. He found that a force of the enemy, occupying high ground on their left, would take his troops in reverse as they advanced." [19] Artillerist E. Porter Alexander wrote that he received orders late on July 2 for an attack to be "renewed as soon as Pickett arrived, and he was expected early" and accordingly began to put his First Corps batteries in position at 3:00 a.m. [20]

It is difficult at this date to determine the extent to which Lee's intentions for July 3 were miscarried, misinterpreted, or misrepresented. It was certainly not Lee's style at Gettysburg to issue specific and detailed orders. Since Lee did not confer with Longstreet on the evening of July 2, perhaps Lee simply issued orders to renew the attack early on July 3, in which case Longstreet may have felt a turning movement was perfectly within his latitude to execute. Perhaps more specific instructions from Lee were miscarried and never reached Longstreet. Ultimately, all we can say is that Pickett's men were not in position to attack at the earliest possible hour. [21]

It should also be understood that Longstreet's proposed turning movement around the Round Tops was not without considerable risks. Several brigades of the VI Corps and artillery were posted behind the Round Tops and to the Taneytown Road in order to block just such an attempt by the Confederates. The Union V Corps also still remained within supporting distance. Since Pickett was not yet ready, the brunt of any morning attack would have forced Generals McLaws and Hood's battered divisions to over-extend Lee's already stretched battle lines. You will have an opportunity later in this tour guide to journey to the seldom visited Howe and Wright Avenues within Gettysburg National Military Park to assess Longstreet's chances of success for yourself.

Probably now realizing uncoordinated flank attacks had failed on the second day, Lee halted Longstreet's plans and instead began to search for an alternative. After making

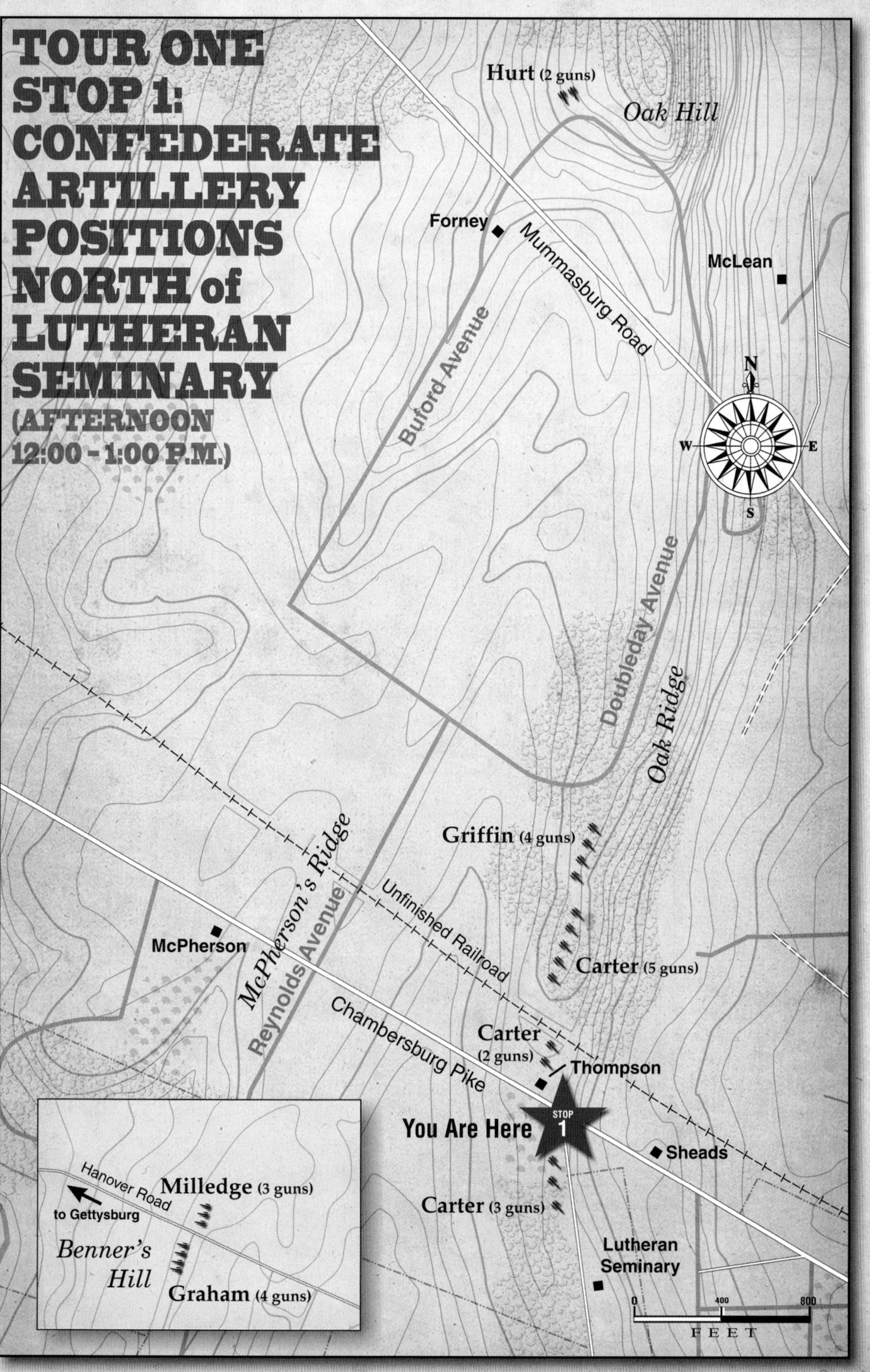

TOUR ONE
STOP 1:
CONFEDERATE
ARTILLERY
POSITIONS
NORTH of
LUTHERAN
SEMINARY
(AFTERNOON
12:00 - 1:00 P.M.)
Hurt (2 guns)
Oak Hill
Forney
Mummasburg Road
McLean
Buford Avenue
N
W
E
S
Doubleday Avenue
Oak Ridge
Griffin (4 guns)
McPherson's Ridge
Unfinished Railroad
McPherson
Reynolds Avenue
Carter (5 guns)
Chambersburg Pike
Carter
(2 guns)
Thompson
STOP
1
You Are Here
Sheads
Hanover Road
to Gettysburg
Milledge (3 guns)
Benner's
Hill
Graham (4 guns)
Carter (3 guns)
Lutheran
Seminary
0
400
800
FEET

a reconnaissance of the enemy's position, at some point in the morning Lee determined to instead attack the Union army's left center. [22] Lee was likely encouraged by the brief success of Brig. General Ambrose R. Wright's Brigade who practically reached that point in the late afternoon of July 2 before being forced to withdraw due to lack of support. Wright's attack clearly showed that the desired position could be reached. [23]

Longstreet wrote, "I felt then that it was my duty to express my convictions," and "pointing to Cemetery Hill," Longstreet told his commander:

> General, I have been a soldier all my life. I have been with soldiers engaged in fights by couples, by squads, companies, regiments, divisions and armies, and should know as well as anyone what soldiers can do. It is my opinion that no 15,000 men ever arrayed for battle can take that position. [24]

But General Lee was not deterred and "ordered me [Longstreet] to prepare Pickett's Division for the attack." [25] Longstreet stressed that Lee "was impatient of listening, and tired of talking" so Longstreet turned his attention toward organizing the assault. [26]

Colonel Armistead Long, Lee's military secretary, claimed the decision was reached during a consultation with several members of the Confederate high command and Longstreet's only offered objection was, "the guns on Round Top might be brought to bear on his right." Colonel Long claimed he rebutted Longstreet with the untenable suggestion that the Confederate batteries could suppress the Little Round Top artillery. "This point being settled, the attack was ordered, and General Longstreet was directed to carry it out."[27]

Much ink has been spilled debating the objective of Lee's attack. Was it the "Copse of Trees," the larger Ziegler's Grove, or Cemetery Hill itself? Lee stated in his report only that the attack was "directed against the enemy's left center." [28] Longstreet reported the assault was to be "made directly at the enemy's main position, the Cemetery Hill" and the "center of the assaulting column would arrive at the salient of the enemy's position." [29]

Some historians point out that Lee's objective was not the "Copse" (a term used to refer to a small thicket of trees) but rather the much larger and more important Cemetery Hill. The nearby Ziegler's Grove then served as a more prominent and visible guiding landmark than the smaller Copse. As an ultimate objective, this theory has much merit since Cemetery Hill — both as an artillery position and the "hook" in Meade's fishhook-shaped line — was arguably the most important point of the entire Union battle line at Gettysburg. The loss of Cemetery Hill would have certainly required Meade to at least abandon his position. Conversely, the Copse of Trees on Cemetery Ridge had no military significance whatsoever.

Yet Longstreet wrote that the "center" of his assault would "arrive at the salient" which implies that he intended to break through near the Copse of Trees and the area known today as the Angle. His troop dispositions— placing a second supporting line behind Pettigrew's right and not his left— also supports this premise. Also note that many of the Confederates in Long Lane, directly opposite and closest to Cemetery Hill, did not participate in the attack, while much of Longstreet's First Corps (particularly Brig. General

James Kemper's Brigade) would have to cover a considerable distance under fire and with their flanks exposed if they were expected to strike Cemetery Hill.

Trees were not Lee's military objective but were more likely merely guiding landmarks to the troops while advancing under fire. Colonel Armistead Long described the attack's goal as follows:

> Cemetery Ridge, from Round Top to Culp's Hill, was at every point strongly occupied by Federal infantry and artillery, and was evidently a very formidable position. There was, however, a weak point upon which an attack could be made with a reasonable prospect of success. This was where the ridge, sloping westward, formed the depression through which the Emmitsburg road passes. Perceiving that by forcing the Federal lines at that point and turning toward Cemetery Hill the right would be taken in flank and the remainder would be neutralized, as its fire would be as destructive to friend as foe…General Lee determined to attack at that point. [30]

As with so many aspects of this battle, the debate continues, but a strategy in which Lee hoped to strike the Federal defenses near the Angle (rather than launch a direct frontal assault on the elevated and fortified Cemetery Hill), split the Union lines, and then turn toward Cemetery Hill seems as logical as any.

Curiously, Lee originally seems to have still intended for Lafayette McLaws and John B. Hood's divisions of Longstreet's First Corps (both of which had fought heavily the previous day and were not in an advantageous position to assault the Federal "left center") to participate and be reinforced by George Pickett's fresh division as the attacking column. But Longstreet convinced his commander that Hood and McLaws were needed to anchor Longstreet's right flank and could be "attacked in reverse" by Federal forces on the elevated Round Tops, so Lee decided that Longstreet would instead be "re-enforced by Heth's Division and two brigades of Pender's" from A. P. Hill's Third Corps. [31] It appears clear from the participant accounts that these portions of Hill's Third Corps were directly placed under Longstreet's supervision for the upcoming assault.

General Hill was then "directed to hold his line with the rest of his command, afford General Longstreet further assistance, if required, and avail himself of any success that might be gained." [32] Two brigades from R. H. Anderson's Division (under Cadmus Wilcox and David Lang) were later added to protect Pickett's right flank, bringing the total in the attack force to 11 brigades with an estimated strength of perhaps 12,500 men. (This is a generally accepted number today and we will discuss this in greater detail later.) General Hill's Corps thus was intended to play a dual role: to participate directly with Longstreet and to take advantage of any success with additional support. Not chosen to directly engage were two relatively fresh brigades in Anderson's Division under Brig. General William Mahone and Carnot Posey.

The final critical component of Lee's plan was the use of artillery. Infantry alone was not expected to carry the day. Lee wrote:

> A careful examination was made of the ground secured by Longstreet [the Peach Orchard], and his batteries placed in positions, which, it was believed, would enable them to silence those of the enemy. Hill's artillery and part of Ewell's was ordered to open simultaneously, and the assaulting column to advance under cover of the combined fire of the three. *The batteries were directed to be pushed forward as the infantry progressed, protect their flanks, and support their attacks closely.* [Emphasis added.]

Note that in addition to the massive cannonade which would precede the attack, Lee also intended for the guns to move forward with the infantry and serve as protection for the flanks. [33] This aspect of the plan is often lost on Gettysburg students. In sum, Longstreet, Hill, and Ewell's engaged artillery would exceed 150 and perhaps 160 field pieces. But with a few exceptions, Ewell's positioning north and east of town would prove to make poor use of the Second Corps artillery.

Knowing the outcome in hindsight, history has been very harsh on Robert E. Lee's decision to launch this frontal assault at Gettysburg. It should be remembered, however, that there were precedents for such successful attacks. Almost exactly one year earlier, during the Seven Days' Battles, Lee launched a series of massive and ultimately triumphant attacks against a portion of the Union army at Gaines's Mill. More recently, on the afternoon of July 1 at Gettysburg, Col. Abner Perrin's South Carolina brigade overran Union I Corps positions near the Lutheran Theological Seminary. Both victories had come at heavy costs, but they demonstrated that frontal assaults could work under the right combination of tactics, leadership, terrain, artillery support, luck, and enemy performance.

On the other hand, Lee also ordered some of these same men to attack Malvern Hill a few days after Gaines's Mill. Poor Confederate execution and murderous Federal artillery caused that attack to end in bloody failure. Lee also undoubtedly remembered his own success, and the part that his artillery played, in defending against the Union's headlong attacks at Fredericksburg in December 1862.

Lee knew that he was taking a great risk in ordering this July 3 charge. But with proper coordination between Longstreet, Hill, their artillery, and use of the ground gained by Longstreet on July 2, Lee obviously believed that this climactic assault on Cemetery Ridge could succeed.

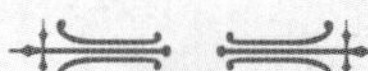

THE ROLE OF CONFEDERATE GENERAL J. E. B. STUART'S CAVALRY

While we consider Lee's strategy on July 3, the intended role of Maj. General J. E. B. Stuart's cavalry also needs to be contemplated. Stuart's objectives are one of the numerous contentious issues surrounding Lee's third day goals. Many participants and historians have championed the notion that Stuart's horsemen were part of a coordinated effort to penetrate the Union rear while Generals Pickett, Pettigrew, and Trimble pierced Meade's center. If true, then the addition of cavalry to the infantry and artillery assault would make Lee's final Gettysburg attack a very complex combined operation using every element of his army.

Gen. J.E.B. Stuart.
Image courtesy of Library of Congress

On the afternoon of July 3, General Stuart and portions of his cavalry division positioned themselves on the Confederate's left flank approximately 3.5 miles east of Gettysburg. Stuart's horsemen collided with elements of Union Brig. General David M. Gregg's division and a brigade under Brig. General George A. Custer on what is now known as "East Cavalry Field." After several hours of dismounted and mounted fighting, the day culminated with Confederate Brig. General Wade Hampton leading an epic mounted charge toward the Hanover Road that was met head-on by Custer's Michigan Wolverines and other Union forces. The Southerners were grudgingly forced to abandon the field and the Federal cavalry scored a victory by virtue of having held their ground.

But what were Stuart and his men doing out there?

A commonly purported theory is that Lee intended for Stuart to attack the Federal rear while Longstreet's infantry successfully broke the Union left-center on Cemetery Ridge. This idea was initiated by battle participants on both sides, and later grabbed by many historians, due to both a genuine lack of clarity regarding Stuart's objectives and also as a means of elevating the significance of the action in which they had proudly participated.

"Stuart's object was to gain position where he would protect the left of Ewell's Corps," wrote Stuart's adjutant general Maj. Henry B. McClellan in his postwar memoirs, "and would also be able to observe the enemy's rear and attack it in case the Confederate assault

on the Federal lines were successful. He proposed, if opportunity offered, to make a diversion which might aid the Confederate infantry to carry the heights held by the Federal army." [1]

This version was similarly perpetuated by Northern veterans such as Lt. William Brooke-Rawle (later a captain and brevet lieutenant colonel) who fought in the 3rd Pennsylvania Cavalry. Brooke-Rawle survived to become a prominent and influential postwar chronicler of the fighting at East Cavalry Field. He described Stuart's role as:

> …occupying the elevated ground east of Gettysburg, from which, while protecting the left of Lee's army, he could command a view of the routes leading to the rear of the Army of the Potomac, and could, at the same time, be in position to move out at the proper moment, and there attack it, simultaneously with the grand assault which was to be made upon Cemetery Ridge from the other side…That this was his purpose he [Stuart] tells us almost in so many words. [2]

But accounts such as McClellan and Brooke-Rawle's were given years after the battle, when memories were often unintentionally flawed or intentionally distorted to further personal agendas. Did either Lee or Stuart provide contemporary confirmation, "in so many words" or otherwise, that Stuart's was a coordinated effort with Longstreet's infantry assault? The short answer: No.

General Lee's July 31 report does not even hint at any expected cooperation between Stuart and Longstreet. [3] His January 1864 report, which noted the "embarrassment" suffered by the Confederate army due to Stuart's missing cavalry, added little regarding July 3. "The ranks of the cavalry were much reduced by its long and arduous march, repeated conflicts, and insufficient supplies of food and forage, but the day after its arrival at Gettysburg it engaged the enemy's cavalry with unabated spirit, and effectually protected our left." [4] Flank protection was a classic use of cavalry, although Lee's statement that Stuart effectively "protected our left" is mildly misleading since General Gregg's cavalry never made any hostile moves toward the Confederate left. Lee's statement, however, suggests that he simply intended Stuart to perform standard protective service on the flanks.

General Stuart's report provided greater details:

> On the morning of July 3, pursuant to instructions from the commanding general (the ground along our line of battle being totally impracticable for cavalry operations), I moved forward to a position to the left of General Ewell's left, and in advance of it, where a commanding ridge completely controlled a wide plain of cultivated fields stretching toward Hanover, on the left, and reaching to the base of the mountain spurs, among which the enemy held position…[I] hoped to effect a surprise upon the enemy's rear, but Hampton's and Fitz. Lee's brigades, which had been ordered to follow me, unfortunately debouched into the open ground, disclosing the movement, and causing a corresponding movement of a large force of the enemy's cavalry. [5]

So the only instructions from Lee that Stuart acknowledged was the move onto Ewell's left. General Wade Hampton similarly wrote, "On the morning of July 3, I was ordered to…

endeavor to get on the right flank of the enemy." [6] Lee's report implied a defensive role, Hampton's suggested an offensive intent (getting on the enemy's right flank rather than the Confederates' left), and Stuart added the perfectly characteristic caveat that he "hoped to effect a surprise upon the enemy's rear." Stuart may have indeed been hoping to "surprise" the Northern rear, but what is entirely lacking is any substantial evidence that Lee ordered Stuart to strike in conjunction with any success by Longstreet's infantry. Some historians have supposed that this lack of supporting documentation proves an intentional conspiracy of silence, however a lack of documented evidence may simply indicate no proof for anything else. [7]

After arriving on East Cavalry Field via a turnoff from the York Pike, Stuart's forces concentrated around an elevation known as Cress Ridge and the John Rummel farm. The east-west Hanover Road was visible about 1.5 miles south of Stuart's position. Stuart was guilty of some embellishment when he described Cress as "a commanding ridge [that] completely controlled a wide plain of cultivated fields stretching toward Hanover" but there is no doubt from this point that Stuart enjoyed an excellent view of the surrounding countryside.

Control of the Hanover Road would certainly have given Stuart greater command of eastern approaches to the Union's right flank and also cut off Hanover as an avenue of escape if Meade chose to use it. But also in front of Stuart was the Low Dutch Road that intersected the Hanover Road and then continued roughly 2.3 miles southwest toward the Baltimore Pike. If Confederates reached the Baltimore Pike they then would have been in the rear of Meade's army. Henry McClellan observed: "The roads leading from the rear of the Federal line of battle were under his [Stuart's] eye and could be reached by the prolongation of the road by which he had approached. Moreover, the open fields, although intersected by many fences, admitted of movement in any direction." [8]

By the afternoon of July 3, only two major roads into and out of Gettysburg remained behind Union lines: the Baltimore Pike and the Taneytown Road. The Baltimore Pike was Meade's most important escape route from Gettysburg because it was an improved road and was essentially

The Michigan Cavalry monument located on East Cavalry Field. Image courtesy of Steven Stanley

Meade's road to Washington. In order for Stuart to gain access to the Army of the Potomac's rear, Stuart would have had to gain control of at least three roads (the Hanover Road, Low Dutch Road, and the Baltimore Pike) with his own exhausted and damaged command over a distance of three to four miles. If Stuart was supposed to harass an already retreating Union army, then his men would have had to contend with additional Federal cavalry along the Baltimore Pike. If Stuart was supposed to actually attack Cemetery Ridge in reverse while Longstreet attacked the front, then he again would have been required to fight both enemy cavalry and infantry while riding several miles north along the pike. The first scenario would have been difficult; the second scenario highly unlikely. [9]

Unfortunately for Stuart, General Gregg had already realized the strategic importance of this Hanover / Low Dutch Road intersection (despite requests from the Union high command to move away from it). Gregg ensured that his small command was reinforced by the newly appointed General Custer and together Gregg and Custer were well-positioned to block any Confederate attempts into the rear of Meade's army.

Stuart's ability to effectively "surprise" the Yankees was further compromised by the exhausted condition of his men and horses. His ride north, compounded by a series of detours, had covered roughly 200 miles in eight days. It also included seven military actions, ranging in scale from skirmishes to battles. By the time they debouched east of Gettysburg during the late morning of July 3, some exhausted troopers were nearly asleep in the saddle. [10]

Stuart's four brigades (commanded by Brig. General Wade Hampton, Brig. General Fitzhugh Lee, Col. John Chambliss, and the brigade of Brig. General Albert Jenkins who was wounded on July 2) should have amounted to approximately 6,000 troopers. But the shoddy condition of both men and horses greatly reduced the strength of many of the regiments. Stuart's exact strength on July 3 is unknown, but historians have estimated anywhere from 2,500 to 3,400 effectives. Stuart's men and animals were far from peak strength. [11]

Stuart's personal movements on Cress Ridge have further added to the debate. According to Henry McClellan, Stuart ordered an artillery piece pushed "to the edge of the woods and [Stuart] fired a number of random shots in different directions, himself giving orders to the guns." These artillery rounds and the appearance of Wade Hampton and Fitz Lee's men in the open ground to Stuart's left seemingly announced his position to the Federal cavalry. (In reality, Gregg had also received dispatches from Union observers on Cemetery Hill indicating a mass of enemy horsemen were moving toward the Confederate left.) McClellan was puzzled by Stuart's actions:

> I have been somewhat perplexed to account for Stuart's conduct in firing these shots; *but I suppose* [emphasis added] that they may have been a prearranged signal by which he was to notify General Lee that he had gained a favorable position; or, finding that none of the enemy were within sight, he may have desired to satisfy himself whether the Federal cavalry was in his immediate vicinity before leaving the strong position he then held. [12]

McClellan's memoirs are often cited by supporting historians as proof of a coordinated

plan between Lee, Longstreet, and Stuart, yet even a cursory reading of McClellan's words clearly indicates that McClellan was only guessing at Stuart's reasons for firing the cannon shots. According to Union artillerist Alexander Pennington, McClellan told Pennington in a postwar conversation, "Stuart looked in every direction but could find no sign of our [Federal] troops, so he ordered a gun out and ordered it to be fired in different directions in hopes of getting an echo or a reply from one of our guns, and then through his glass locate the smoke." [13]

Even more problematic for proponents of the coordinated effort theory is the distance over which Lee would have supposedly recognized a series of signal shots from Stuart. Depending on where exactly Lee expected to be positioned at the moment the alleged signal shots were fired, the sounds would need to have been recognized over a minimum distance of at least four air miles and also would need to have been differentiated from the hundreds of other sounds of battle in the air. In a word: preposterous.

Finally, one needs to remember Robert E. Lee's management of this battle. He did not give precise orders of the type which would have been necessary if Longstreet and Stuart's men were expected to attack the Federal front and rear simultaneously. Lee knew such an attack could not be perfectly coordinated over these distances. Lee did not yet know exactly how the afternoon infantry attack would unfold when Stuart was sent onto his left flank. Lee did not even know what time the attack would commence. Lee left that detail to General Longstreet who left that detail to artillery Col. Edward Porter Alexander. There was no way in which Lee could have precisely told Stuart when to attack and there was only a general understanding where to attack.

Stuart's cavalry played an important role on July 3 as did the Federal horsemen under Gregg and Custer who stopped him. Stuart's defined role was, as cavalry was often used, to guard the Confederate left flank and harass the enemy in the event of their retreat. After that, Stuart's aggressive nature was probably looking for any additional opportunity to reach the rear of the Yankee army. We might expect as much from Stuart, but there is no existing evidence to support any conclusion that Stuart was another planned or coordinated element of "Pickett's Charge." Whatever the goal was, all of Stuart's intentions were ultimately rendered academic at the hands of Generals Gregg and Custer.

Although a tour of East Cavalry Field is outside the scope of this work, the reader is encouraged to later take the opportunity to visit that fascinating yet overlooked portion of Gettysburg National Military Park. To reach East Cavalry Field from Stuart's perspective, drive approximately 2.8 miles east from Gettysburg's town square on the York Pike (modern Route 30 East.) Turn right when you reach Cavalry Field Road. Proceed southeast on this winding road for roughly 1 mile. Shortly after passing the historic Isaac Miller farm on your left, you will reach the narrow entrance to East Cavalry Field. By entering the field from this point you will have approximated Stuart's own approach. The Hanover Road is visible in the distance but also try to gain an appreciation of the distances Stuart would have needed to cover in order to reach the more distant Baltimore Pike beyond.

The Confederate Left Flank (David McMillan Farm)

GPS: 39°49'25.39"N, 77°14'41.51"W; Elev. 561 ft.

From General Lee's headquarters, drive south along Seminary Ridge and through the grounds of the Lutheran Theological Seminary.

You may wish to stop and visit the Seminary Ridge Museum in historic Schmucker Hall. The "Old Dorm" of the Lutheran Seminary is typically associated with the first day's battle that occurred on and near this ridge, including Union Brig. General John Buford's use of the building's cupola as an observation point while he awaited reinforcements from Maj. General John Reynolds's I Corps of infantry.

The "Old Dorm" of the Lutheran Seminary at sunset. Image courtesy of Michael Waricher

However, the building also has a rich battle-related history as a field hospital and was one of the first buildings put to such use at Gettysburg. Among the patients treated here afterwards were Confederate Generals James Kemper and Isaac Trimble. Both men were seriously wounded leading troops on July 3 but each survived the war. General Kemper was said to be "well attended to by female sympathizers." General Trimble's leg was amputated as a result of his wound. He was initially treated in the town but was relocated here and

complained that one particular guard "takes every occasion to vex us." Likewise it was recorded that Trimble's "audacity often tried the patience of the hospital attendants." [1] The Seminary Ridge Museum tells the story of this building's service as a hospital and the patients who were treated here.

After you depart the Seminary, cross the Fairfield Road. Drive south on modern West Confederate Avenue and notice that you will pass several Confederate artillery positions. After traveling approximately 0.75 miles from Lee's headquarters, please stop near the David McMillan house (a prominent white house on the left side of West Confederate Avenue.) Please note that it is now a privately owned residence and you should not approach the house or block entry ways. Park your vehicle in one of the available public parking spaces on the right side of the avenue.

The white house located on the eastern side of West Confederate Avenue was the home of David McMillan and his family during the 1863 battle. Note the orchard which has been replanted by the National Park Service opposite the house. David McMillan's large fruit orchards dated back to the 1840s, and when he saw troops approaching his property on July 1 he hurriedly chopped down his fences with an axe in order to facilitate the soldiers' movements and presumably avoid their trampling his fields and valuable trees. McMillan's daughters also provided water to Union troops who hurried by during the first day's fighting. The nearby McMillan Woods sheltered portions of Pettigrew's Division

The David McMillian house. Image courtesy of James Hessler

(probably parts of Brockenbrough and Davis's brigades) prior to the Confederates' July 3 charge.

Tree removal in this area during 2010 and 2011 revealed approximately 300 yards of Confederate earthworks and artillery lunettes on the reverse slope across the avenue from the McMillan house. The McMillan family recorded that many of their personal belongings such as furniture, clothing, and books were used and buried under earthworks near the house. [2] Please do not disturb these historic landmarks. It is interesting to observe that these surviving earthworks were constructed on the reverse (western) slope of the ridge and not along the more heavily visited modern West Confederate Avenue or eastern slope.

Visitors to Gettysburg frequently view Pickett's Charge from the relatively narrow perspective of the area between the Virginia State Memorial on Seminary Ridge and "The High Water Mark" on Cemetery Ridge. In reality, Lee's July 3 assault covered a much broader area. Much of Lt. General A. P. Hill's engaged Third Corps artillery line began near the Fairfield Road in what would prove to be a futile attempt to overwhelm Union batteries on Cemetery Hill and northern Cemetery Ridge. As we will see, the left flank of Hill's infantry was also positioned near here during the early afternoon of July 3.

STOP 2a Hill and Ewell's Artillery

GPS: 39°49'32.90"N, 77°14'41.79"W; Elev. 562 ft.

Numerous markers today denote Confederate battery positions that spanned the ground between the Fairfield Road, the David McMillan farm, and the modern Virginia State Memorial. There were all or parts of 19 batteries approximating 63 guns actively engaged in this sector on July 3.

Gen. A. P. Hill.
Image courtesy of Library of Congress

The National Park Service's tree removal project in 2010 and 2011 helped improve visitor access to several of these battery monuments on the western side of modern West Confederate Avenue. Still, not all of these tablets are easy to locate. Can you find the stone wall on the reverse slope of Seminary Ridge and the nearby tablet to Hurt's Battery of the Hardaway Alabama Artillery, McIntosh's Battalion?

The artillery in this vicinity can be confusing to interpret because several of these batteries have duplicate tablets on both sides of the avenue, several other markers commemorate batteries that fought here on July 2 but not July 3, and at least one battery served here on July 3 but is not marked. We will examine these shortly.

Confederate artillery along West Confederate Avenue. Image courtesy of James Hessler

To start, it is worth recalling whom these batteries belonged to and how their placement aligned with General Lee's grand strategy.

While one of Longstreet's First Corps artillery subordinates, Col. Edward Porter Alexander, is primarily remembered as leading the third day's Confederate artillery efforts, most of the cannons in this sector were actually under the control of Col. R. Lindsay Walker, who commanded the Artillery Reserve in General Hill's Third Corps. This fact helps illustrate that participation from much more than Longstreet's First Corps was essential to the success of this attack. Unfortunately, because Colonel Alexander produced a substantial amount of post-battle writing and analysis, his efforts often overshadow his Third Corps counterparts.

Colonel Walker said little about the July 3 activity in his post-battle report, but described his firing as "incessant" from about 1:00 p.m. until the infantry advanced. "This fire having been continued so long and with such rapidity, the ammunition was almost exhausted." [3]

Major William T. Poague commanded an artillery battalion in General Hill's Third Corps. Poague wrote that his orders were to open upon the enemy's position following the signal from two cannon shots on the Confederate right. As soon as the Southern infantry charged and "reached the crest" the artillery was "to proceed as rapidly as possible to the summit with all my guns, and there be governed by circumstances." Despite contemporary evidence to the contrary, Poague added in his memoirs, "Not a word was said about following the infantry as they advanced to the attack." [4]

From these positions parallel to Cemetery Ridge, Lee's artillery would have been able to concentrate heavy fire onto the northern extension of Cemetery Ridge, including the western face of Cemetery Hill. However, it should be remembered that with Lee's army on the exterior of Meade's so-called "fishhook," the Confederates' chances of success were greatly dependent upon their converging fire onto Cemetery Hill from multiple directions (west, north, and east). This was, in fact, the only real advantage Lee's exterior lines offered.

This 1905 photograph shows the Confederate Whitworths in the wrong location along West Confederate Avenue. Image courtesy of GNMP

In addition to the firepower from A. P. Hill's Corps, additional cannons from General Richard Ewell's Second Corps were also expected to contribute. On the Confederate far left flank, near Benner's Hill, possibly as many as seven pieces may have shelled Cemetery Hill from the northeast. [5]

Nearly two miles away, two long-range Whitworths (from Hill's reserve) were also moved by General Hill's orders to Oak Hill, "a commanding point north of the railroad cut, to enable them to enfilade the enemy's position. They fired, it is believed, with effect from this point." [6] Their positions are readily visible today near the modern Eternal Light Peace Memorial. However, there were no other suitable positions north and east of Gettysburg from which Ewell's artillery could be effectively brought to bear.

Roughly one mile south of Oak Hill, near the railroad cut and Chambersburg Pike, Lt. Colonel Thomas Carter, commanding the artillery battalion attached to Robert Rodes's Second Corps division, moved 10 pieces into action. Carter wrote:

> On Friday, July 3, ten rifled guns were posted on the high ridge on the right and left of the railroad cut, and their fires directed on the batteries planted on the Cemetery Hill. This was done to divert the fire of the enemy's guns from Hill's and Pickett's troops in their charge across the valley, and also to divert their fire from three batteries of the First Virginia Artillery, under Captain Dance, and temporarily in my command. These three batteries had been ordered to fire, in conjunction with a large number of guns on their right, on a salient part of the enemy's line prior to

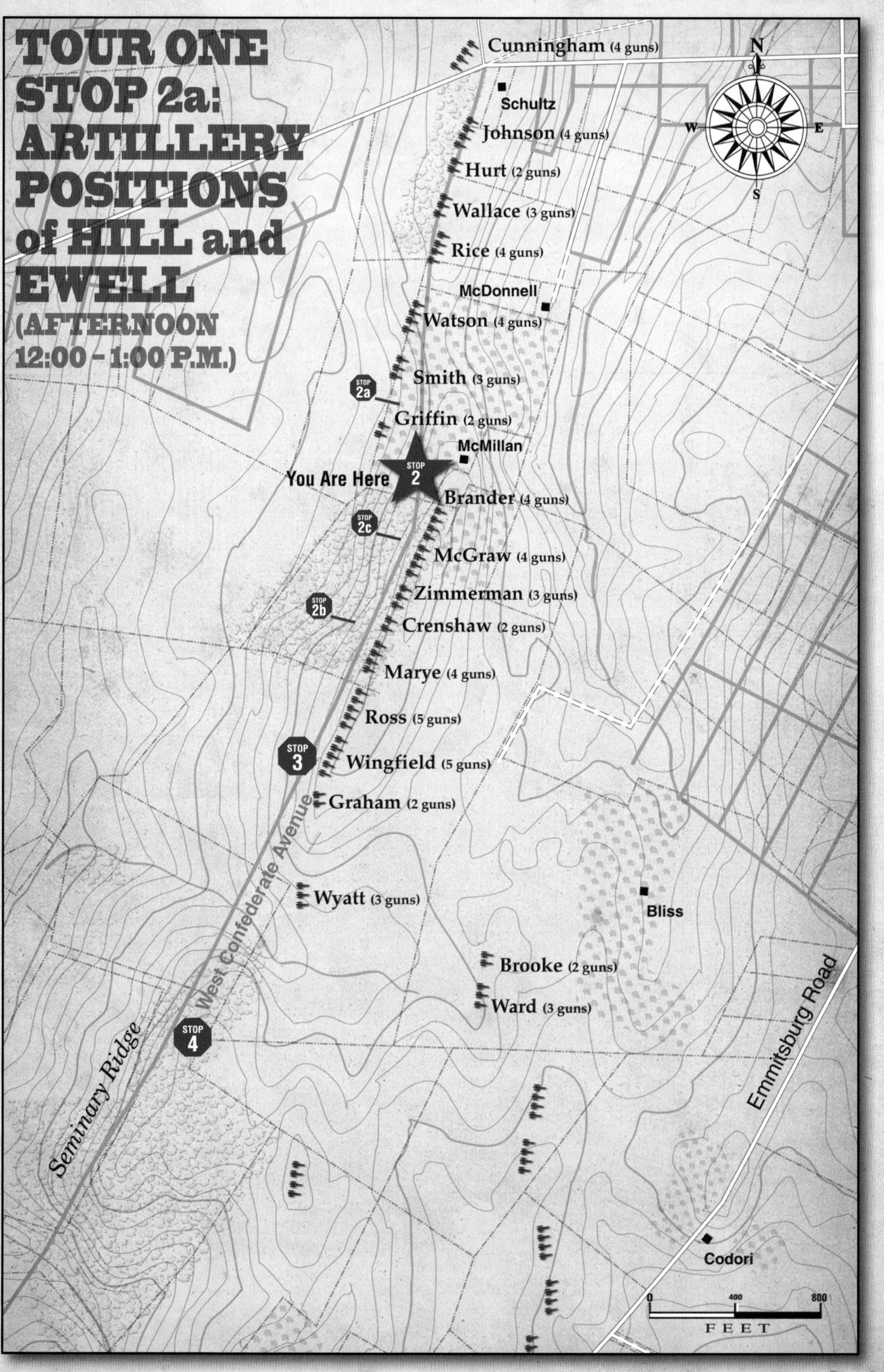
TOUR ONE STOP 2a: ARTILLERY POSITIONS of HILL and EWELL (AFTERNOON 12:00 – 1:00 P.M.)
Cunningham (4 guns)
Schultz
Johnson (4 guns)
Hurt (2 guns)
Wallace (3 guns)
Rice (4 guns)
McDonnell
Watson (4 guns)
Smith (3 guns)
STOP 2a
Griffin (2 guns)
McMillan
You Are Here
STOP 2
Brander (4 guns)
STOP 2c
McGraw (4 guns)
Zimmerman (3 guns)
STOP 2b
Crenshaw (2 guns)
Marye (4 guns)
Ross (5 guns)
STOP 3
Wingfield (5 guns)
Graham (2 guns)
West Confederate Avenue
Wyatt (3 guns)
Bliss
Brooke (2 guns)
Ward (3 guns)
STOP 4
Seminary Ridge
Emmitsburg Road
Codori
N
S
E
W
0
400
800
FEET

the charge of infantry. [7]

There is evidence that four additional and often overlooked guns also added to the mix near Carter's pieces and the railroad cut. Henry McClellan on J. E. B. Stuart's staff placed Capt. Wiley H. Griffin's 2nd Maryland (Baltimore Light) Battery of four cannons on East Cavalry Field and many battle histories have followed suit. [8] However, several accounts placed this battery "to the left of the Cashtown Pike." One battery member even described them as slightly under the fire of the Whitworths on Oak Hill. [9]

In summary, 16 Confederate guns were in action around Oak Hill and the unfinished railroad cut. Another seven fired from Benner's Hill, putting as many as 23 of Ewell and Hill's cannons into service northwest and northeast of today's West Confederate Avenue line. Although Carter claimed some success in his actions, this relatively small number dispersed over such a wide area demonstrates that Lee's artillery was unable to effectively converge their fire from multiple directions. This caused Pettigrew and Trimble's divisions to march directly into some still-formidable Union cannon fire later in the afternoon. In hindsight, First Corps artillerist Colonel Alexander considered this inability to be a "phenomenal oversight" and one of the principal reasons for the attack's failure. [10]

Although lacking in their ability to strike from multiple directions, Hill and Ewell's artillery were more successful in concentrating along Seminary Ridge (modern West Confederate Avenue) demonstrating the topographical value of this long flat ridge.

As stated previously, 63 cannons stretched from the intersection of modern Seminary Ridge Avenue and the Fairfield Road (beginning with Cunningham's Powhatan Artillery of Dance's Battalion), past the McMillan house and the modern North Carolina State Memorial. But finding all of the correct July 3-related positions is complicated by the existence of duplicate tablets and several that commemorate July 2 actions or inactive batteries. The table on the next page highlights the battlefield tablets to be ignored in our study of July 3 positions.

Note that both Lewis and Maurin's batteries were held in reserve south of McMillan Woods on July 3. This suggests that the area south of the woodlot was viewed as a relatively safe harbor from enemy fire.

There is nothing on West Confederate Avenue to denote the three 3-inch ordnance rifles of Capt. Benjamin Smith's Third Richmond Howitzers from Dance's Battalion in Ewell's Artillery Reserve. Although often cited as having four guns in action, Sergeant William S. White wrote that only three were engaged and the fourth was sent to the rear due to a shortage of ammunition and men. John Bachelder's 1876 troop position map places Smith to the right (south) of Watson's battery and near the McMillan house. [11] The tablet for Smith's battery is instead located on Seminary Ridge Avenue.

As you continue south along West Confederate Avenue, notice the tablets do not always represent precise positions occupied. For example, both Brooke and Ward's batteries were engaged elsewhere and withdrew afterwards to a position "near here." We also see that several batteries withheld shorter-range howitzers in the event that the enemy were

Extraneous Artillery Monuments/Tablets on West Confederate Avenue

South of the Fairfield Road, East Side of West Confederate Avenue to McMillan House

Danville (VA) Artillery, Rice's Battery	Duplicate marker across West Confederate Ave.
Johnson's (VA) Battery	Duplicate marker across West Confederate Ave.
2nd Richmond (VA) Howitzers, Watson's Battery	Duplicate marker across West Confederate Ave.
Donaldsonville (LA) Artillery, Heth's Division Artillery, Garnett's Battalion, Maurin's Battery	One 10-pounder Parrott and two 3-inch rifles engaged on July 2
Lewis's (VA) Artillery, Heth's Division Artillery, Garnett's Battalion, Lewis's Battery	Two 3-inch rifles and two Napoleons engaged July 2

McMillan House to North Carolina State Memorial

Huger (VA) Artillery, Heth's Division Artillery, Garnett's Battalion, Moore's Battery	One 10-pounder Parrott, one 3-inch rifle, two Napoleons, Inactive
Norfolk (VA) Light Artillery Blues, Heth's Division Artillery, Garnett's Battalion, Grandy's Battery	Two 3-inch rifles, two 12-pounder howitzers, Inactive

to counterattack, reinforcing the notion that Lee's army would not have been utterly defenseless if Meade had attempted an assault following the charge.

When we add the 63 Seminary Ridge artillery pieces from Hill and Ewell's corps to the 23 on Benner's Hill and near Oak Hill, 86 cannons were engaged by the Confederate Second and Third Corps on July 3. As we shall see, this was actually more than the number that participated in Longstreet's First Corps. [12]

A. P. Hill's Infantry Left Flank

GPS: 39°49'16.95"N, 77°14'44.21"W; Elev. 574 ft.

After Lee decided to focus the third day's attack on the Yankees' "left center," Lee decided to "re-enforce" Longstreet with General Henry Heth's Division and two brigades of Dorsey Pender's Division of Hill's Corps.

Heth's Division was commanded by General James Johnston Pettigrew. His two left brigades, probably portions of those under Col. John Brockenbrough and Brig. General Joseph Davis, occupied the McMillan woodlot and surrounding area prior to the charge. (We will discuss more about Pettigrew's deployments at our next tour stop.)

One of the greatest tactical challenges facing Generals Lee and Longstreet was the question of how the Southern attackers were going to protect their flanks as they advanced across nearly a mile of ground to strike the Union lines. General Longstreet later asserted that he took great care in placing his troops prior to the attack; but one has to wonder about the breakdowns that occurred on both the left and the right sides of the Confederate line. Here

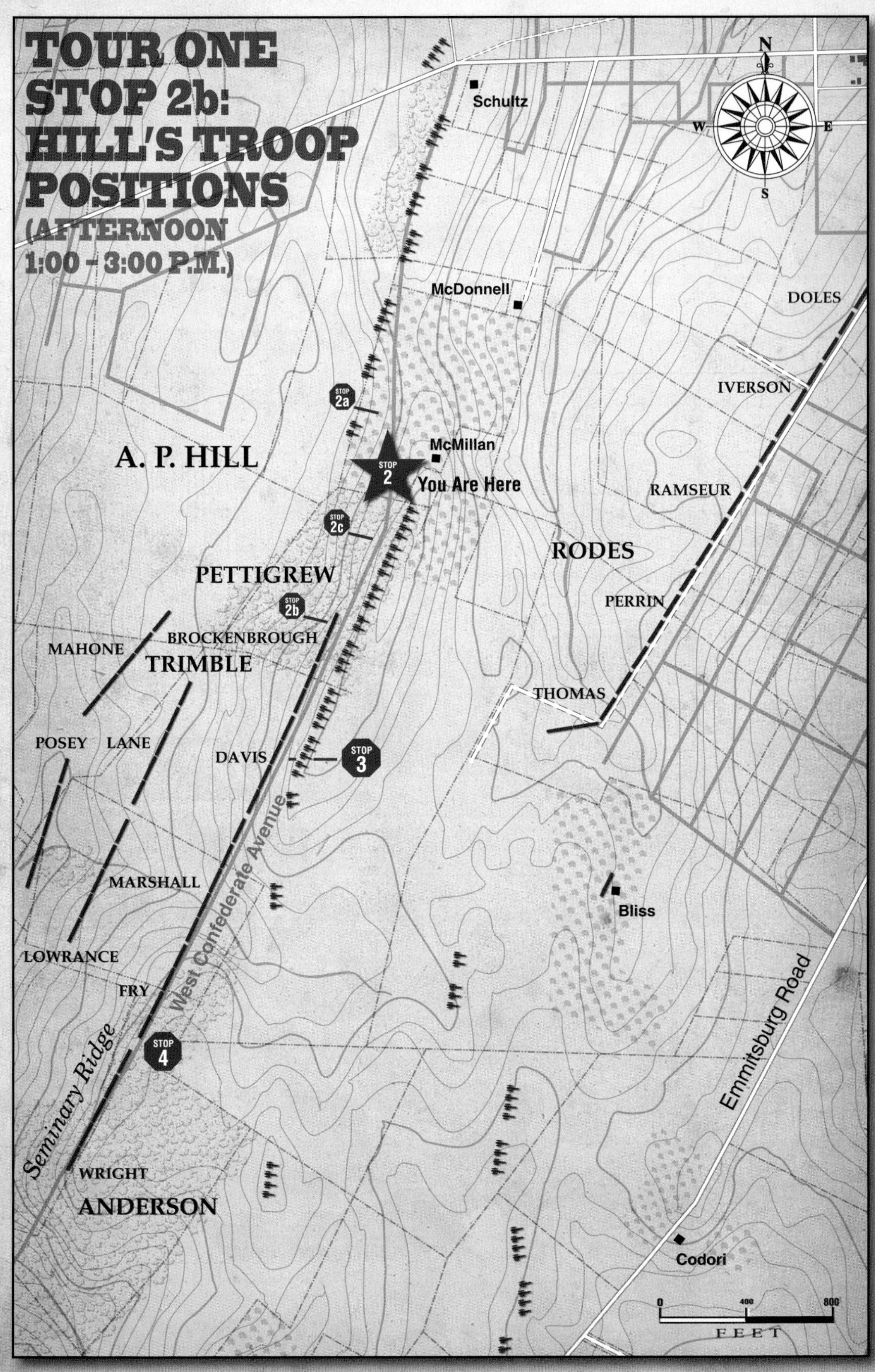
TOUR ONE
STOP 2b:
HILL'S TROOP
POSITIONS
(AFTERNOON
1:00 - 3:00 P.M.)
N
W
E
S
Schultz
McDonnell
DOLES
IVERSON
STOP 2a
A. P. HILL
McMillan
STOP 2
You Are Here
RAMSEUR
STOP 2c
RODES
PETTIGREW
STOP 2b
PERRIN
MAHONE
BROCKENBROUGH
TRIMBLE
THOMAS
POSEY
LANE
DAVIS
STOP 3
West Confederate Avenue
MARSHALL
Bliss
LOWRANCE
Emmitsburg Road
FRY
STOP 4
Seminary Ridge
WRIGHT
ANDERSON
Codori
0
400
800
FEET

on the left, the selection of Col. John Brockenbrough's Brigade as the attack's left flank, with no supporting brigade in Brockenbrough's immediate rear, was certainly questionable. Perhaps the failure to place any troops behind Brockenbrough was unintentional. Brigadier General James Lane, in Trimble's command, noticed Pettigrew's command was "much larger" than Trimble's "and there was consequently no second line in rear of its [Pettigrew's] left." [13] Whether this was the result of sloppy staff work or negligence by Generals Lee, Longstreet, and Hill, this failure to adequately support the flanks would prove to have dire consequences.

Gen. Isaac Trimble.
Image courtesy of Library of Congress

Virginia native John M. Brockenbrough was 32 years old at Gettysburg. He had been in command of his brigade, as a colonel rather than a brigadier general, since the wounding of Brig. General Charles Field at Second Manassas in August 1862. Although Field's Virginians were battle-hardened veterans, they seemed to regress under uninspired leadership and lax discipline from Brockenbrough. They saw minimal action in the Antietam campaign and became disoriented in foliage at Fredericksburg. [14] Brigadier General Henry Heth took command and led the brigade into Chancellorsville. Colonel Brockenbrough was back in charge when Heth replaced the promoted A.P. Hill as division commander. Problems began to publicly surface after Chancellorsville when the results of a court martial in the 40th Virginia, Brockenbrough's original regiment, noted the "very reprehensible example set" by the regiment's officers. [15]

There were further accounts of bad behavior during the march into Pennsylvania. The brigade fought, some believe ineffectually, during the afternoon of July 1. While fighting near the McPherson farm, they advanced cautiously against the 150th Pennsylvania, failing to exploit a gap in the Union line and temporarily buying time for the Union infantrymen to re-position themselves and mount an effective defense. [16] Confederate Brig. General A. M. Scales reported that he twice came upon a Confederate line in his front who were "halted and lying down." Finally, the "officers on this part of the line informed me that they were without ammunition, and would not advance farther." [17] After the war, Scales told historian John Bachelder that these were Brockenbrough's men and Scales had "ordered my men to march over them." From this point, Brockenbrough's men probably observed the fight on Seminary Ridge and then followed in Scales's wake to pick up Federal prisoners along the way. [18] General Heth acknowledged in his report, "the enemy was steadily driven before it at all points, excepting on the left, where Brockenbrough was held in check for a short time," although Heth then quickly added (in the overly laudatory nature of many official reports), "but finally succeeded in driving the enemy in confusion before him. Brockenbrough's Brigade behaved with its usual gallantry, capturing two stand of colors and a number of prisoners." [19]

According to one of General Pettigrew's staffers, the brigade had been "so badly handled that it was in a chronic state of demoralization and was not to be relied upon; it was virtually of no value in a fight." [20] One has to be careful when assessing postwar criticisms directed at Brockenbrough's July 3 performance. As Virginians attached to Pettigrew's Brigade, they became a natural source for veterans from other states to censure when too much attention was directed at the supposed gallantry of Pickett's Virginians. Nevertheless, most historians concede that Brockenbrough did not perform well on either day engaged at Gettysburg.

Estimates of the brigade's strength on July 3 vary. Some studies estimate less than 600 in the ranks, [21] and Col. Robert Mayo of the 47th Virginia may have reported as few as 200 muskets. Whatever the actual number, they were clearly well below average strength and according to Mayo, "was nothing more than a line of skirmishers." [22] Yet it was Brockenbrough's Brigade among all others who were selected as the Confederates' left flank on July 3. Brockenbrough's left flank was roughly 25 yards north of where the modern McMillan Woods campground road intersects with West Confederate Avenue.

Prior to the charge, Brockenbrough apparently split his brigade into two wings. The 55th and 47th Virginia regiments were on the left and placed under the command of Colonel Mayo. Brockenbrough would lead the 40th and the 22nd Battalion on the brigade's right. Some historians debate whether or not Brockenbrough was even on the field leading his men in the July 3 attack. Colonel W. S. Christian of the 55th Virginia wrote: "Colonel Brockenbrough came to me and said he intended to divide the brigade and said that the 55th and 47th [left] must move only at the orders of Colonel Mayo of the 47th, and that I must consider myself under the command temporarily of Colonel Mayo." Christian's account indicates Brockenbrough was present and giving orders. [23] It is unclear why Brockenbrough created such an arrangement. He may have needed his two wings to navigate obstacles at Long Lane and the Bliss farm. Or he may have hoped for greater individual oversight of the brigade amidst the allegations of poor conduct. Unfortunately, if greater oversight was intended, then Brockenbrough would fail again on July 3. [24]

When Davis's men (to Brockenbrough's right) stepped off around 3:00 p.m., Brockenbrough's right wing moved forward but his left did not budge. Colonel Mayo was nowhere to be found. Observing a rapidly increasing gap between the brigade's two wings, Colonel Christian rode over to confer with another officer. The left remained idle while they waited for any word from the absent Colonel Mayo. It was finally suggested that perhaps Mayo had been killed by artillery fire. (Was Mayo even on the field? He would later file the brigade's report in place of Brockenbrough and only recorded, "we were the last to advance.") Orders were then given to advance the two left regiments, but it was already too late. Christian remembered: "We were a long ways behind and had to run to catch up with the rest of the brigade." [25] So began the advance of Lee, Longstreet, and Hill's critical left flank as the assault marched toward Cemetery Ridge.

Pender's Division Tablet

GPS: 39°49'17.80"N, 77°14'44.66"W; Elev. 572 ft.

- Major General William Dorsey Pender was mortally wounded on July 2. General Pender was highly regarded within the Confederate army and his absence was surely a loss to the Confederate cause on July 3. How would his division have performed this day had they been united under his command?
- Two brigades of his division were ordered to report to General Longstreet on the morning of July 3 and were placed behind General Pettigrew's right during the assault. These brigades were under the command of Maj. General Isaac Trimble. Pender's remaining brigades stayed in Long Lane and while engaged with Union skirmish lines west of Cemetery Hill were not otherwise involved in the assault.

LONGSTREET'S COMMAND OF HILL'S TROOPS

Did Longstreet, as commander of the overall attack, exert proper care in placing the troops in Hill's Corps? Or was this expected to be General Hill's responsibility? Brigadier General James Lane, who commanded Pender's half-division until the assignment was given to General Trimble, specifically reported that he was ordered by Hill to report to Longstreet and it was Longstreet who directed his troop placements. "I was ordered by General Hill…to move in person to the right, with the two brigades forming my second line, and to report to General Longstreet as a support to Pettigrew. General Longstreet ordered me to form in rear of the right of Heth's division, commanded by General Pettigrew." [1]

Longstreet wrote in his memoirs:

> He [Lee] knew that I did not believe that success was possible; that care and time should be taken to give the troops the benefit of positions and the grounds; and he should have put an officer in charge who had more confidence in his plan. Two-thirds of the troops were of other commands, and there was no reason for putting the assaulting forces under my charge…Knowing my want of confidence, he should have given the benefit of his presence and his assistance in getting the troops up, posting them, and arranging the batteries; but he gave no orders or suggestions after his early designation of the point for which the column should march. [2]

Longstreet was unenthusiastic. (One might also ask if Longstreet's lack of enthusiasm manifested itself in lowering the morale of his men, but there is no evidence of this.) [3] The majority of the attack's objective was primarily opposite Hill's front. Three of the four participating divisions (Heth, Pender, and Anderson) were in Hill's Corps. Yet Lee's selection of Longstreet to lead this assault either speaks well of Lee's continued confidence in Longstreet or to Lee's relative lack of confidence in the untested and possibly unwell General Hill. However, Longstreet's assertion that Lee "should have given the benefit of his presence" in posting the troops exhibits a lack of acknowledgement by Longstreet of how Lee managed his army during the Gettysburg campaign.

Lee expected reasonable coordination among his subordinates. There is no evidence to indicate that Longstreet and Hill openly communicated and cooperated with each other on this day. Their past antagonism that had caused Hill to be transferred away from Longstreet following the Seven Days was reportedly not a factor. Longstreet's staffer Thomas Goree insisted that the Longstreet – Hill relations "were strained for a short time only, and they were warm friends until the day of General Hill's death," while historian Douglas Southall Freeman described them as "not cordial and may not even have been genuinely co-operative in spirit." Did each officer assume the other was attending to the details? Did Hill feel that it was no longer proper for him to manage brigades now assigned to Longstreet? Did Hill neglect to do so in a display of ego? [4] Longstreet wasn't admitting to anything afterwards and Hill didn't survive the war to give his side of the story.

Did General Lee closely supervise to ensure that such cooperation occurred? Apparently not and so it is justifiable in hindsight to criticize Lee for his lack of oversight, especially given the coordination needed between Longstreet, Hill, and the artillery. Lee was, by most accounts, within visible sight of operations. (The same cannot be said of General Hill. Where exactly was he on this day?) Porter Alexander thought the troop arrangements must have met with Lee's approval since he was riding the lines between 11:00 a.m. and 12:00 p.m. and "his not interfering with it stamps it with his approval." [5] But Lee, right or wrong, left the details to his subordinates during this battle and Longstreet surely knew this. Longstreet was the designated leader of the forces used in this attack, despite his personal misgivings, and was ultimately responsible for correcting or failing to correct any formations. [6]

When you are finished at the McMillan farm, return to your vehicle and continue south along West Confederate Avenue. After approximately 0.4 miles, you will see the large North Carolina State Memorial on the left. Although this is a popular stop for visitors, there is usually adequate parking available on the right side of the road. Exit your vehicle and walk down the footpath toward the North Carolina monument. You will also see the smaller Tennessee State Memorial nearby.

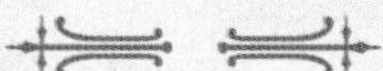

Pettigrew and Trimble's Battle Line (North Carolina State Memorial)

STOP 3

GPS: 39°49'5.93"N, 77°14'50.03"W; Elev. 561 ft.

The next stop is at the North Carolina State Memorial. This memorial commemorates all of the North Carolina infantry, cavalry, and artillerymen who fought at Gettysburg. It was sculpted by Gutzon Borglum, the same man who carved Mount Rushmore. Borglum used photographs of actual Confederate veterans to model the faces of the soldiers. [1] Observers often comment that the memorial is visually similar to the famous photograph of Marines raising the flag on Iwo Jima. However, any similarity is purely coincidental as this monument was dedicated in July 1929, well before World War II.

The North Carolina monument is located near what was the approximate center of General Pettigrew's infantry lines on July 3. Although some histories emphasize Virginia's role in the great charge at the expense of other states, North Carolina, Mississippi, Tennessee, and Alabama also contributed foot soldiers to this attack as part of Pettigrew and Trimble's commands. (Along with soldiers from Florida and Alabama who participated in Lang and Wilcox's brigades.) Likewise, while history has remembered the name "Pickett's Charge," more than half of the soldiers in this assault were part of General Hill's Third Corps and not under General Pickett.

An undated photograph of the North Carolina Monument with crews working in the background.
Image courtesy of Garry Adelman

After Lee decided to "re-enforce" Longstreet with General Henry Heth's Division and two brigades of Dorsey Pender's Division of Hill's Corps, "General Hill was directed to hold his line with the rest of his command, afford General Longstreet further assistance, if required, and avail himself of any success that might be gained." [2]

General Hill similarly reported, "I was directed to hold my line with [General R. H.]Anderson's division and the half of Pender's (now commanded by General Lane)," and later added that General Anderson "had been directed to hold his division ready to take advantage of any success which might be gained by the assaulting column, or to support it, if necessary." [3] A letter reprinted in the Southern Historical Society Papers in 1916 from Hill's adjutant, Colonel (then Major) William H. Palmer alleged that Hill "begged General Lee to let me [Hill] take in my whole Army Corps. He [Lee] refused, and said what remains of your corps will be my only reserve, and it will be needed if Gen'l Longstreet's attack should fail." [4]

Col. Birkett Fry.
Image from *Miller's Photographic History of the Civil War*

Since General Heth had been wounded on July 1, command of his division was given to one of his brigade commanders, the scholarly and well-educated Brig. General Johnston Pettigrew. General Pettigrew hailed from a wealthy North Carolina family and was one day short of what would be his thirty-fifth, and final, birthday. Major William Poague called Pettigrew "a fine officer, polished gentleman and always handsomely dressed." Pettigrew was a soldier and leader of great potential, but he was unaccustomed to leading an entire division into combat. [5]

Colonel Birkett Fry, who would command Archer's Brigade in Pettigrew's new division on this day, remembered:

> During the forenoon of the 3d, while our division was resting in line behind the ridge and skirt of woods which masked us from the enemy, Generals Lee, Longstreet and A.P. Hill rode up, and, dismounting, seated themselves on the trunk of a fallen tree some fifty or sixty paces from where I sat on my horse at the right of our division. After an apparently careful examination of a map, and a consultation of some length, they remounted and rode away. Staff officers and couriers began to move briskly about, and a few minutes after General Pettigrew rode up and informed me that after a heavy cannonade we would assault the position in our front, and added: "They will of course return the fire with all the guns they have; we must shelter the men as best we can, and make them lie down." [6]

Command of the mortally wounded Pender's half division was initially given to one of Pender's brigadiers, General James Lane. No sooner had Lane reported to Longstreet and received his orders to "form in rear of the right of" Pettigrew's Division than Lane was

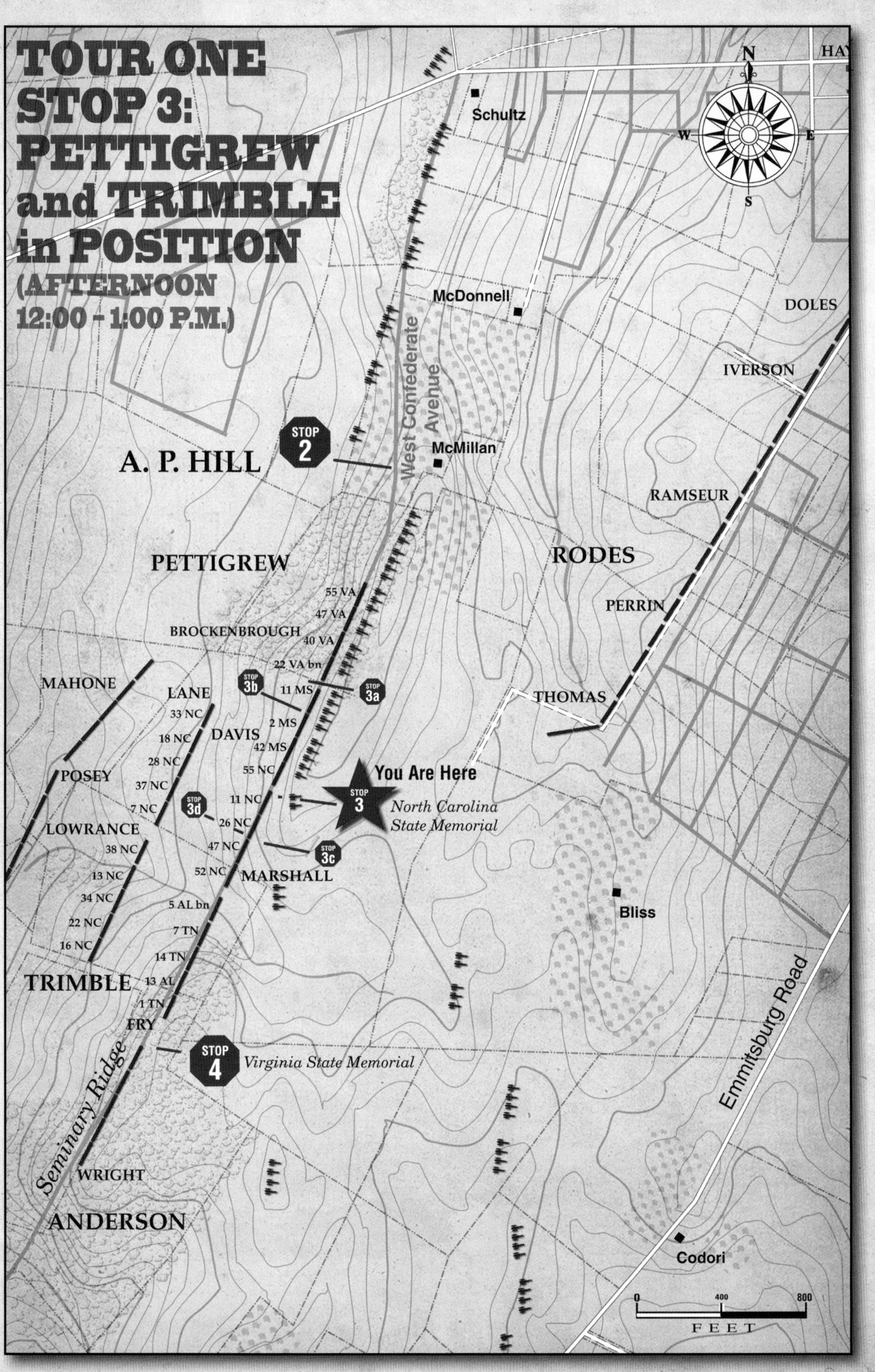
TOUR ONE
STOP 3:
PETTIGREW
and TRIMBLE
in POSITION
(AFTERNOON
12:00 - 1:00 P.M.)
N
W
E
S
Schultz
McDonnell
DOLES
IVERSON
West Confederate Avenue
STOP 2
A. P. HILL
McMillan
RAMSEUR
PETTIGREW
RODES
55 VA
47 VA
40 VA
BROCKENBROUGH
PERRIN
22 VA bn
11 MS
STOP 3b
STOP 3a
MAHONE
LANE
THOMAS
33 NC
2 MS
18 NC
DAVIS
42 MS
28 NC
55 NC
POSEY
You Are Here
37 NC
STOP 3
11 NC
North Carolina State Memorial
7 NC
STOP 3d
26 NC
LOWRANCE
47 NC
38 NC
STOP 3c
13 NC
52 NC
MARSHALL
34 NC
5 AL bn
Bliss
22 NC
7 TN
16 NC
14 TN
TRIMBLE
13 AL
1 TN
FRY
STOP 4
Virginia State Memorial
Emmitsburg Road
Seminary Ridge
WRIGHT
ANDERSON
Codori
0
400
800
FEET

replaced by 61-year-old Maj. General Isaac Trimble. [7] A native of Virginia, the aggressive Trimble (whom Stonewall Jackson had once referred to as one of the most "fancy" dressers in the army) had ridden north with Lee's army as a supernumerary, or senior officer without a command. He had initially attached himself to General Ewell where he reportedly tried Ewell's patience with an overabundance of unsolicited advice. [8] According to Trimble, he had heard that both Generals Heth and Pender were wounded and applied to Lee for command of one of the divisions. This arrangement probably satisfied General Ewell.

The morning sun embracing the North Carolinians. Image courtesy of Steven Stanley

Although Trimble was a soldier of great experience, he too was at a disadvantage on July 3 because Pender's men were by his own admission "entire strangers" to him. [9]

Casualties likewise caused several further command changes at the brigade level. Since Pettigrew was substituting for Heth, command of Pettigrew's Brigade was given to 24-year-old Col. James Marshall, normally commander of the 52nd North Carolina. The VMI graduate was the grandson of former Chief Justice of the U.S. Supreme Court John Marshall. At the institute, Marshall's "oration gave evidence of a vigorous mind, and promise of a good speaker" but like so many young Southern men he became "fired with patriotic zeal to battle for the Southern cause." Marshall had been colonel of the 52nd since the spring of 1862. [10]

To Marshall's right, Brig. General James Archer had been captured on July 1, so his brigade was now led by Col. Birkett Fry. [11] In Trimble's back line, Brig. General A.M. Scales's battered brigade was now commanded by Col. William Lowrance of the 34th North Carolina. [12] In summary, both of the Confederate divisions on the left and three of the six

brigades were led by replacements on July 3.

One of the few aspects that historians can agree upon was Pettigrew and Trimble's brigade formations. Colonel John Brockenbrough's small Virginia brigade formed the left of Pettigrew's line. To Brockenbrough's right was Brig. General Joseph Davis's Brigade (another victim of heavy July 1 action.) Davis was the 38-year-old nephew of Confederate President Jefferson Davis and had been narrowly confirmed as a general in September 1862 without having yet led troops in combat. General Davis was put in command of this brigade in January 1863. They were the second largest brigade in Heth's (Pettigrew's) Division, comprised of three Mississippi regiments (the 2nd, 11th, and 42nd) and the 55th North Carolina.

Next in line to the right (and advancing from the general vicinity of the North Carolina monument) was Pettigrew's North Carolina brigade under the command of Colonel Marshall. Finally, Archer's Brigade under the command of Colonel Fry formed the right of the attack and probably ended the division near the fence line currently situated just north of the Virginia State Memorial.

As Trimble's demi-division formed the second line, Lowrance's Brigade was on the Confederate right behind Fry. General Lane, having returned to command his brigade after being replaced by Trimble, formed on Lowrance's left. Lane's left extended behind at least part of Davis's Brigade, but as noted previously there was no support behind Brockenbrough's left. [13]

The selection of Heth's Division and half of Pender's has puzzled many historians given that Heth's men in particular had seen heavy combat on July 1. Captain George Wilcox, of the 26th North Carolina later observed:

> If I am not mistaken Pickett's men were fresh and had hardly fired a gun till that charge, their ranks were full and well officered. Pettigrew's men were just the reverse; anyone who knows anything about it can imagine the very great disadvantage that Pettigrew's men labored under in the front line with Pickett's and it always seemed strange to me that they were put there in that condition. [14]

While Heth's Division was well below par, the brigades of Generals Carnot Posey and William Mahone in R. H. Anderson's Division were nearby and had been comparatively unused. What did General Mahone's Brigade accomplish at Gettysburg? Unlike the lengthy official reports of his peers, Mahone summed up his brigade's activity for the entire battle in only "a few brief remarks" and reported only 102 casualties, of which 39 were "missing."[15] Posey's report is equally brief and his casualties have been estimated at 112. [16] Private A. T. Watts in Posey's 16th Mississippi was on the skirmish line and wrote concisely in a postwar account: "We supposed that Anderson's Division would be in the assault, and prepared to fall into line when they reached our position; but we were ordered to remain on the line we then held." [17]

It is also a mystery as to why only half of Pender's Division was selected to participate in the attack while Pender's two remaining brigades under Col. Abner Perrin and Brig.

General Edward Thomas remained nearby in Long Lane. Although Perrin's Brigade had seen action on the afternoon of July 1, Thomas had escaped relatively unscathed. Perrin reported that he spent July 3 in "the heaviest skirmishing I have ever witnessed" but Thomas's report is silent on his July 3 activities. [18] Thomas's Brigade strength was about 1,248 men and suffered "only" 264 casualties during the campaign, suggesting at least another 1,000 soldiers could have better assisted Pettigrew and Trimble. [19]

Some writers have proposed that Perrin and Thomas were, in fact, intended by Lee to actively support Pettigrew's left and these arrangements were somehow botched by either Longstreet or Hill. William Swallow, a controversial figure who claimed to be attached to Lee's army and also corresponded with prominent individuals like John Bachelder and James Kemper, wrote in a published postwar account that these two brigades "were placed on the left flank of the assaulting column, covering the advance of Pettigrew's Division." [20]

Generals Lee and Trimble reviewed Trimble's men prior to the assault. Lee reportedly noted the condition of Lowrance's men, many of whom had been decimated by Federal artillery fire near the Chambersburg Pike and Lutheran Seminary on July 1, and commented, "Many of these poor boys should go to the rear, they are not able for duty." Lee then added that the attack "must succeed" before riding away. [21] This account dramatically portrays the seeming desperate need that Lee must have felt for his attack to prevail. Yet if Lee was so concerned about the chosen men's condition, then why did Generals Lee, Longstreet, Hill, Anderson, Pettigrew, and Trimble all neglect to propose any alternatives from the fresher and nearby Thomas, Posey, or Mahone? Clearly Lee did not believe better options were available.

While awaiting their orders to attack, a captain in the 7th North Carolina observed "a fox, doubtless alarmed for its safety came at full speed from the direction of the enemy's line, and in its attempt to pass our line was surrounded, and Major Turner dispatched it with his sword. This incident is thrown in to show the make-up of the Confederate soldier, and that no danger however great deterred him from the enjoyment of a little sport." [22]

On the right flank of Pettigrew's line, Colonel Fry was directed by Pettigrew to locate General Pickett and to determine the dress (or alignment) in the advance. Fry found Pickett "in excellent spirits," engaged in "pleasant" small talk, and "expressed great confidence in the ability of our troops to drive the enemy after they had been 'demoralized' by our artillery." General Richard Garnett soon joined and it was agreed Garnett would dress on Fry's command. Returning to Pettigrew, Fry then understood that his brigade "should be considered the center" in the upcoming assault. [23] This understanding that Fry was considered the center may actually be the key to accepting why Longstreet placed troops behind Pettigrew's right (instead of his left). Longstreet seemingly expected this end of Pettigrew's line to strike the key point in the enemy's defenses and he wanted to be prepared with an attack in depth. [24]

Brockenbrough's Brigade Tablet

STOP 3a

GPS: 39°49'9.18"N, 77°14'50.39"W; Elev. 564 ft.

- The tablet marks the approximate July 2 evening position of Brockenbrough's Virginians (on the reverse slope of the ridge) and should not be confused with where they aligned on July 3. Their left during the July 3 assault has been estimated as being approximately 25 yards north of where the McMillan Woods campground road intersects with West Confederate Avenue.

11th Mississippi Infantry Regimental Monument

GPS: 39°49'7.83"N, 77°14'51.23"W; Elev. 563 ft.

- It is extremely rare for individual Confederate regiments to be honored with monuments at Gettysburg. The 11th Mississippi Regiment actually has two monuments, both of which were erected in 2000 by the 11th Mississippi Memorial Association. We will see the other monument when we visit the Union lines near the Abraham Bryan farm on Cemetery Ridge.
- The 11th Mississippi formed the left flank of Brig. General Joseph Davis's Brigade. The 11th was the only regiment under Pettigrew not engaged on July 1. This battlefield monument counts 393 combatants. [25]
- Company "A" was the famous "University Greys" which at one time had consisted of over 100 students from the University of Mississippi. Only about 33 remained in the ranks when July 3 started and only 31 would make the fateful charge. [26]

The 11th Mississippi Monument in fall.
Image courtesy of Steven Stanley

Tennessee State Memorial

GPS: 39°49'3.68"N, 77°14'52.39"W; Elev. 561 ft.

- The Tennessee monument was dedicated in 1982 and was the last Confederate state monument placed on the field. [27]

The Tennessee State Memorial honors the men from Tennessee.
Image courtesy of James Hessler

- Three Tennessee regiments – the 1st, 7th, and 14th – participated in this attack as part of General James Archer's Brigade. Archer had been captured on July 1, so his brigade was under temporary command of Col. Birkett Fry. The brigade was primarily located further to the right (south) and ended about where the fence line sits just north of the Virginia State Memorial.

Lieutenant General Ambrose P. Hill Headquarters Marker

GPS: 39°49'4.14"N, 77°14'53.20"W; Elev. 562 ft.

- Prior to Gettysburg, General A. P. Hill was one of the most successful division commanders in Lee's army. He was rewarded with a promotion to lieutenant general and command of the new Third Corps in May 1863 during the reorganization caused by Thomas J. "Stonewall" Jackson's death.
- Hill's Third Corps initiated the first contact with Federal forces on July 1 and many of his brigades saw heavy combat during the three days. Yet there are almost no accounts of Hill exerting any personal leadership and this absence from the historical record has allowed him to escape much of the scrutiny that has been

directed at his peers James Longstreet and Richard Ewell. Poor health may have contributed to Hill's lackluster Gettysburg performance.

- According to Lee's report, after Longstreet was "re-enforced" by Heth's Division [Pettigrew] and two brigades of Pender's [Trimble], "General Hill was directed to hold his line with the rest of his command, afford General Longstreet further assistance, if required, and avail himself of any success that might be gained." There is no evidence that Hill asserted any oversight of these troops during the July 3 attack.
- Hill's headquarters may have been at the Emanuel Pitzer farm (now the large modern farm buildings visible behind the marker.) The Army of Northern Virginia Corps Headquarters markers were placed on the field in 1921. Take care in assuming their accuracy since there is no verifiable documentation to support the correctness of the other markers for Generals Longstreet and Ewell.

STRENGTH OF PETTIGREW AND TRIMBLE'S DIVISIONS?

Estimates of all July 3 Confederate infantry strength, including Pettigrew and Trimble's, are purely speculative, and can cause heated arguments amongst Gettysburg students. There is no precise method to accurately calculate the number of Southern forces in Pickett's Charge.

To start, remember that Confederate reporting procedures make it difficult to ascertain the exact number of men who went into action and the resulting casualties. Prior to Gettysburg, it was common for Lee's commanders to list their starting strength along with the subsequent casualties in their after-action reports. These casualty totals typically included men who were only slightly wounded and therefore still fit for duty. General Lee was worried that Union authorities could exploit this information to estimate his army's total strength, and was also concerned that large published casualty lists were detrimental to civilian morale.

Lee therefore issued General Order Number 63 on May 14, 1863, to address this situation. Lee's officers were requested "to insure the immediate suppression of this pernicious and useless custom" of reporting "the number of men taken into action." Regarding the definition of a "casualty," it was ordered that "future reports of the wounded shall only include those whose injuries, in the opinion of their medical officers, render them unfit for duty." [1]

The challenges of assessing July 3 strengths are further compounded by the fact that reports seldom broke down casualties by day. At full strength, Pettigrew's command would have mustered slightly more than 7,000 men. But all four of his brigades fought and bled on July 1 and we do not know how many of the first day's casualties returned to the ranks two days

later. In cases where daily estimates are available (such as in Brockenbrough's Brigade and the 26th North Carolina) suggestions are that July 1 casualties alone were as high as 50% in some commands. However, since the four brigades combined to average "only" 53% casualties for the entire battle, Pettigrew's overall July 3 starting strength must have been higher than 50% of his available total. (Otherwise we would have to assume that nearly all reported casualties were from July 1 only.) Lee and Trimble's observations confirm that notable numbers of July 1 walking wounded returned to the ranks. Using the admittedly ungrounded but reasonable estimate that July 1 unfit for service casualties in Heth's (Pettigrew's) Division were between 25% - 30%, with some brigades suffering more and some less, then Pettigrew should have had roughly 5,000 men available on the third day. [2]

Trimble's two brigades should have mustered about 3,100 men if fully complemented. Trimble allows for slightly different math to estimate strengths because battle accounts all suggest that Scales's Brigade (Lowrance) fought more severely on July 1 than did Lane. Therefore, Lane should have been closer to full strength on July 3. General Lane acknowledged that the majority of his casualties were incurred on July 3 as "our loss on the 1st and 2d being but slight." If we place Lane's July 1 unfit for service casualties at a low 10%, then nearly 1,500 men stood ready on July 3. [3]

Colonel Lowrance took over for Scales on the evening of July 1 and counted "in all about 500 men…without any field officers…and but few line officers, and many companies were without a single officer to lead them or to inquire after them. In this depressed, dilapidated, and almost unorganized condition, I took command of the brigade." [4] Lowrance would have us believe only about 37% of the men remained, but if we assume some soldiers returned in the morning of July 3, and if we then land on a high-side estimate of only 60% in the ranks on the third day (i.e. 40% July 1 casualties), then Lowrance led perhaps 800 men into the charge. This would then total 2,300 men under Trimble's command. [5]

Pettigrew and Trimble's Division Strength Estimates

	Total K	Total W	Total MC	Total Casualties	Starting (Jul. 1) Strength	Total Casualty %	Total KIA %	July 3 Strength Estimates Using Range Estimates of July 1 Losses 10%	20%	30%	40%
Pettigrew (Marshall)	412	978	229	1,619	2,580	62.75%	15.97%	2,322	2,064	1,806	1,548
Davis	308	717	200	1,225	2,305	53.15%	13.36%	2,075	1,844	1,614	1,383
Brockenbrough	41	106	67	214	972	22.02%	4.22%	875	778	680	583
Archer (Fry)	69	219	396	684	1,197	57.14%	5.76%	1,077	958	838	718
Heth's (Pettigrew) Division	**830**	**2,020**	**892**	**3,742**	**7,054**	**53.05%**	**11.77%**	**6,349**	**5,643**	**4,938**	**4,232**
Lane	178	376	238	792	1,734	45.67%	10.27%	1,561	1,387	1,214	1,040
Scales (Lowrance)	175	358	171	704	1,351	52.11%	12.95%	1,216	1,081	946	811
Pender (Trimble) Division	**353**	**734**	**409**	**1,496**	**3,085**	**48.49%**	**11.44%**	**2,777**	**2,468**	**2,160**	**1,851**

This analysis would then make 7,300 men available to Pettigrew and Trimble on July 3, plus or minus several hundred. This is only an attempt to make a reasonable high-side estimate and does not assume all 7,300 men marched toward Cemetery Ridge on the afternoon of July 3. There is little doubt that hundreds of men were lost prior to the charge due to cannon fire, heat, and perhaps even a reconsideration of their motivation. Therefore,

making another arbitrary 10% haircut would give us approximately 6,600 men available to make the charge. Other historians have arrived at, and will continue to arrive at, different estimates. It is worth reminding the most die-hard Gettysburg student, again, that precise numbers will never be known. [6]

Such estimates of paper strength and losses are further complicated, however, by the distances on the ground and presumed tactics. Since Pettigrew's line was the front and clearly the longer of the two, how long of a "line" did Pettigrew's Division form? Assuming Brockenbrough's left started near the center of McMillan Woods and Fry's right ended short of the modern Virginia State Memorial, then Pettigrew's entire line from left to right covered between 800 to 1,000 yards. If Pettigrew had deployed a tight formation (one man per every two feet of line) with double ranks, then there was (and is today) only enough room to deploy between 2,500 – 3,000 men in Pettigrew's main formation!

Trimble's line falls more easily into the available terrain constraints. If we assume his shorter line was perhaps 650 yards in length, then he should have generally had room to deploy about 2,000 men in double formation. Granting that Pettigrew shuffled several hundred men onto a skirmish line, and Brockenbrough's Brigade was lagging from the beginning, and that escalating casualties would have quickly made the problem academic (with lines closing to fill in gaps created by losses), one begins to appreciate why several Union accounts described three apparent Confederate battle lines. There simply does not appear to have been enough room for only two traditionally deployed lines, unless one easily accepts the notion that Pettigrew went into action with a shockingly low 2,500 men.

Return again to your vehicle and drive approximately 0.4 miles to the equally impressive Virginia State Memorial. After parking your vehicle, proceed into the field to the east of the monument in order to obtain a clear view of the attack's objective: Cemetery Ridge.

Virginia State Memorial

GPS: 39°48'50.79"N, 77°15'1.22"W; Elev. 574 ft.

There was initially resistance, from veterans on both sides, to mark and commemorate Confederate battle lines on the field. The Virginia State Memorial was the first Southern state monument placed at Gettysburg. It was dedicated in June 1917, nearly fifty-four years after the battle. Lee sits mounted on his horse Traveller, forever looking across the fields of Pickett's Charge. [1]

The Virginia State Memorial as seen in this aerial view from 1941.
Image courtesy of GNMP

It is believed that Robert E. Lee watched much of the afternoon's action from near here while seated on a large oak stump. Colonel J. Thompson Brown, Ewell's acting artillery chief, observed Lee holding Traveller's reins in his left hand and supporting his bowed head with his right hand. Brown assumed that Lee was praying.[2] One can see why this would have been considered a suitable observation point. Longstreet, in fact, believed that he did not have the authority to call off the attack because Lee was in such close proximity and could presumably see everything that Longstreet could.

This is also an appropriate location for Virginia's memorial because General George Pickett's three Virginia brigades (under the commands of Generals James L. Kemper, Richard B. Garnett, and Lewis A. Armistead) started their legendary attack from points to the south and east of this memorial.

General Pickett's Division had been in the rear of the Confederate army during the march to Gettysburg, having been ordered to remain at Chambersburg to destroy railroads and other public property until relieved during the night of July 1. They started toward Gettysburg around 2:00 a.m. on the morning of July 2. The Virginians arrived west of Gettysburg during the afternoon hours, having marched roughly 24 miles in 12 hours. Pickett rode in advance to communicate with Longstreet, "who had signified his desire to have our command up before making any attack with his corps." Staff officer Walter Harrison reported

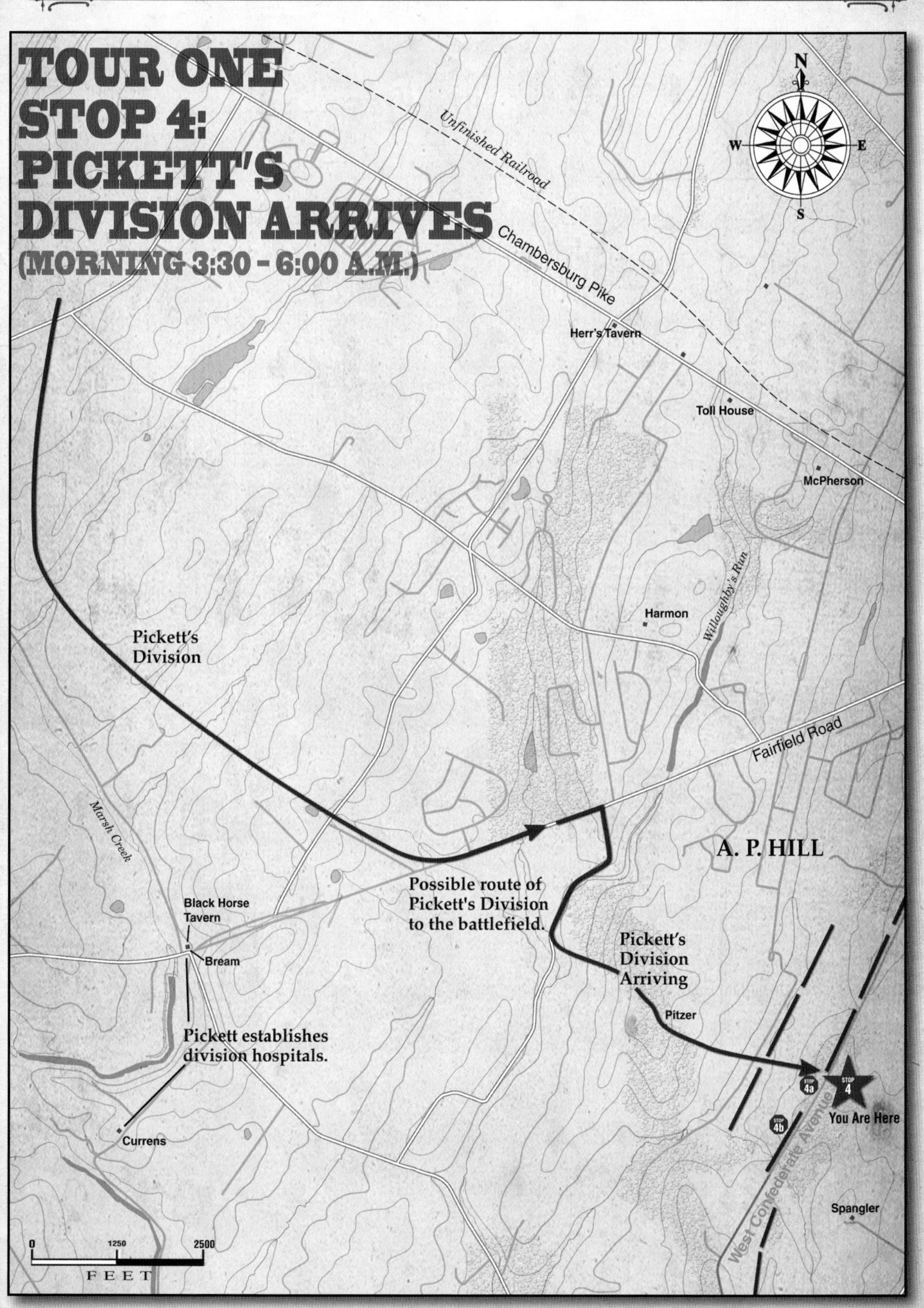
TOUR ONE
STOP 4:
PICKETT'S
DIVISION ARRIVES
(MORNING 3:30 - 6:00 A.M.)
Unfinished Railroad
Chambersburg Pike
Herr's Tavern
Toll House
McPherson
Harmon
Willoughby's Run
Pickett's Division
Fairfield Road
Marsh Creek
A. P. HILL
Possible route of Pickett's Division to the battlefield.
Black Horse Tavern
Bream
Pickett's Division Arriving
Pitzer
Pickett establishes division hospitals.
Currens
STOP 4a
STOP 4
You Are Here
STOP 4b
West Confederate Avenue
Spangler
0
1250
2500
FEET
N
S
E
W

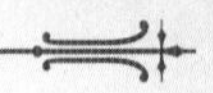

The Virginia State Memorial.
Image courtesy of Steven Stanley

to Lee with instructions that two hours of rest would be needed before the division would be ready for action. Lee replied, "Tell General Pickett I shall not want him this evening, to let his men rest, and I will send him word when I want them." Harrison relayed Lee's message to Pickett and "we turned in for a quiet night's rest, with the fairest prospect of bloody work in the morning." Some men second-guessed this decision. [3]

As Longstreet's only unengaged division, Pickett's thus became a logical choice to participate in Lee's attack of the third day. Lee wrote that he had intended for Pickett to participate in the morning attack, reporting: "Longstreet, re-enforced by Pickett's three brigades…was ordered to attack the next morning, and General Ewell was directed to assail the enemy's right at the same time." [4] Longstreet, however, insisted that he received no orders for Pickett to be ready for a morning attack. [5]

Whoever's version was accurate, Pickett's Division was simply not yet on the field and ready for action when Ewell became engaged at Culp's Hill around 4:30 a.m. Both Col. William Aylett (53rd Virginia) and Maj. Joseph Cabell (38th Virginia) reported that the division moved out from camp about four miles west of Gettysburg at 3:00 a.m. [6] Walter Harrison wrote that they hit the road "just a little before daylight," arrived near Seminary Ridge, cleared some obstructions, and awaited further orders "by about seven o'clock." [7] As is often the case with reconstructing Confederate movements and strategy at Gettysburg, we find discrepancies with what Lee apparently intended (Pickett to be ready for an early morning attack) and what actually transpired.

From a point near the Virginia monument, one can easily see the areas that later became known as the Angle and the Copse of Trees approximately one mile east of us.

Longstreet reported, "the center of the assaulting column would arrive at the salient of the enemy's position, General Pickett's line to be the guide and to attack the line of the enemy's defenses." [8] Given Longstreet's dispositions of Fry and Lowrance's brigades, it seems apparent that he considered the point where Pettigrew's line met Pickett's to be the center which would arrive at the Federal "salient," although this would cause some confusion in execution as Pickett's men would oblique to the left to reach the salient while Pettigrew's men would march relatively straight forward (and were in some accounts told to dress to the right.)

Pickett's Division arrived on the Emanuel Pitzer farm by 9:00 a.m. "in high spirits and in good condition." [9] *(To see this beautiful farm, return back to West Confederate Avenue. Walk through the woods on the west side of the avenue. You will cross a horse trail and then reach a fence which runs parallel to West Confederate Avenue. The large modern farm visible to the west sits on the wartime site of the Pitzer residence.)* After halting for a period of time, Pickett's men then traveled via a farm lane to the Spangler woodlot just south of the Virginia monument. [10] James Kemper's Brigade led the march, so he continued south past Henry Spangler's farm buildings and into line beyond Spangler's farm lane. Richard Garnett's Brigade was next, so his men lined up to the north of Spangler's lane and in front (east) of the woodlot. Lewis Armistead's Brigade was last in line. The men "felt the gravity of the situation," recalled Col. Rawley Martin, "for they knew well the metal of the foe in their front; they were serious, resolute, but not disheartened." [11]

According to Walter Harrison, Armistead was going to move on Garnett's left and continue the division line but was unable to do so because Garnett's left already slightly overlapped Pettigrew's right. Armistead inquired as to what he should do, and as Pickett was unavailable, Harrison requested assistance from Longstreet. General Longstreet did not appear to be in good humor and replied sharply, "General Pickett will attend to that, sir." Longstreet then quickly reconsidered and continued, "Never mind, colonel, you can tell General Armistead to remain where he is for the present, and he can make up the distance when the advance is made." Armistead's Brigade ended up being 100-200 yards behind Garnett as a result. [12] While it is unclear where precisely Garnett's left and Kemper's right ended, their two brigades may have comprised a front of 1,000 or 1,100 yards.

By late morning, Pickett's Division was in position behind the Confederate artillery and awaited their fate. A corporal in the 7th Virginia called the heat "excessively oppressive," and numerous accounts described the suffering caused by the high temperatures and sunstroke. [13] The mood was also remembered as being generally grim, particularly amongst those who had an opportunity to view the Yankee defenses. "The strength of position of the enemy was frightful to look at," observed Walter Harrison. [14]

Poague's Lunettes

GPS: 39°48'51.26"N, 77°15'2.23"W; Elev. 573 ft.

This brief stop refers to the howitzers that sit just west of West Confederate Avenue behind the Virginia monument.

- The howitzers in these lunettes represent guns that belonged to Virginian William T. Poague's artillery battalion, Pender's Division, Hill's Corps.
- Due to their short range, they would not have been effective in the great cannonade that preceded the attack and did not actively participate. They were instead intended as a defensive measure in the event that Meade's forces launched a counterattack.
- These guns are sometimes erroneously pointed out as representing the so-called "missing" howitzers that were promised to support Colonel Alexander but were moved by General William Nelson Pendleton. Those pieces were intended by Alexander to move forward with Pickett's infantry but could not be located when it was time to attack.

Pickett's Division Tablet

GPS: 39°48'46.99"N 77°15'5.74"W; Elev. 563 ft.

- Major General George Pickett's Division arrived at Gettysburg with three infantry brigades under the commands of Brigadier Generals Richard B. Garnett, Lewis A. Armistead, and James L. Kemper. Major James Dearing commanded Pickett's four artillery batteries of 18 cannons.
- Pickett had been promoted to command this division in October 1862. This was the division's first major engagement together with Pickett at the head.
- The total force (including artillery) may have been as high as 6,200 although several contemporary accounts suggested that the aggregate rank and file strength on that day was as low as 4,700. This made Pickett's Division small by Confederate standards but still very large when compared to any individual division in the Army of the Potomac.

MAJOR GENERAL GEORGE PICKETT

Major General George Pickett was a colorful and dashing member of Lee's army, the kind of leader who added an aura of romance and excitement to the Civil War but whose flamboyance would be impossible to fathom in the modern military. In appearance, Pickett is best remembered for his long hair often worn in perfumed ringlets. "In memory I can see him," Longstreet recalled, "of medium height, of graceful build, dark, glossy hair, worn almost to his shoulders in curly waves…as he gallantly rode from me on that memorable 3d day of July, 1863, saying in obedience to the imperative order to which I could only bow assent, 'I will lead my division forward, General Longstreet.'" [1] Longstreet's staff officer Moxley Sorrel described:

Gen. George Pickett.
Image courtesy of Library of Congress

> A singular figure indeed! A medium-sized, well-built man, straight, erect, and in well-fitting uniform, an elegant riding-whip in hand, his appearance was distinguished and striking. But the head, the hair were extraordinary. Long ringlets flowed loosely over his shoulders, trimmed and highly perfumed; his beard likewise was curling and giving out the scents of Araby. [2]

George Pickett was born of a good Richmond pedigree in 1825, making him 38 years old at Gettysburg. His uncle had helped him get an appointment to West Point in 1842 where he graduated last in his class of 1846. [3] While West Point grades were seldom a predictor of battlefield success, it is worth noting that Moxley Sorrel also later recalled that Longstreet always "made us give him [Pickett] things very fully; indeed, sometimes stay with him to make sure he did not get astray." [4]

Most Civil War officers' resumes were filled with years of mundane prewar garrison duty on the frontier, and Pickett was no exception. But he also had several notable encounters that gained national attention. During the Mexican-American War, Second Lieutenant Pickett showed great bravery (and received a brevet promotion to captain) during the battle of Chapultepec, when he took the colors from wounded Lt. James Longstreet and carried them over the fortress parapet. [5] In 1859, Pickett led a small infantry garrison on San Juan Island (today part of Washington State) that successfully participated in a standoff against 1,000 British forces and three warships in a boundary dispute over the shooting of a pig. (The event appropriately became known as the Pig War.) Pickett famously exclaimed during the episode, "We'll make a Bunker Hill of it!" but diplomacy eventually prevailed.

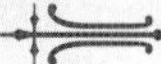

Pickett also married twice during this period. An 1851 marriage ended when his wife died in childbirth later that year. A second marriage to an Indian woman also ended when she died in childbirth in 1856 or 1857. When Pickett returned east, he left his surviving half-Indian son James with a friend and the boy was later put in care of a white farmer couple. Pickett never returned for his child, although he reportedly left financial support and third wife LaSalle Corbell Pickett later corresponded extensively with the son. James Pickett became an artist, never married, and died in 1889.[6]

George Pickett resigned from the U.S. Army in support of his native Virginia and the Confederacy when the Civil War broke out. Colonel Pickett made brigadier general in February 1862 and led his new brigade capably in action at Williamsburg and Seven Pines before being shot in the shoulder at Gaines's Mill. Pickett was away from the army for three months to recover.[7]

When he returned in late September 1862, Pickett was quickly promoted to major general in command of a division in Longstreet's newly created First Corps. Some have speculated Pickett's promotion was due to the influence of his friend Longstreet. Their personal relationship certainly did not hurt Pickett's cause, but he also had seniority and a good record as a brigadier. General Lee endorsed the promotion, which would be Pickett's last within the Army of Northern Virginia.[8] Unfortunately, Pickett's Division saw no real combat at Fredericksburg and was detached with Longstreet foraging during the Chancellorsville campaign.

Moxley Sorrel recalled Pickett as being "very friendly, was a good fellow, a good brigadier. He had been in Longstreet's old Army regiment, and the latter was exceedingly fond of him."[9] But if Pickett enjoyed the friendship of General Longstreet, the same cannot be said for his relationship with Robert E. Lee. Although there is some debate amongst historians over the level of Lee and Pickett's frigid feelings for each other, the record seems to provide ample suggestions that their relations were less than cordial.

They were complete contrasts in style: the duty-bound and frosty Lee vs. the self-indulgent and emotional Pickett. Whatever the extent of their personal issues, the problems appear to predate Gettysburg. In January 1863, Lee criticized the condition and discipline of Pickett's men to Longstreet. In February, Pickett's men were detached to guard Richmond and stayed away throughout Longstreet's spring Suffolk campaign. Some have suggested that detaching officers was a favorite tactic of Lee's to rid himself of problems. Pickett sent several testy dispatches that spring, complaining about travel restrictions and also about the apparent refusal of Lee's headquarters to answer his inquiries. [10] On the march into Pennsylvania, female admirers asked for a lock of Lee's hair. Lee declined but suggested that Pickett "would be pleased to give them one of his curls." The sensitive Pickett was reportedly not amused to be the butt of Marse Robert's joke. [11]

Several accounts suggest that by the end of the war the Lee-Pickett relationship had completely broken down. War Department clerk John Jones wrote in 1864 that it was "possible" Pickett "may have…criticized Lee." [12] Eppa Hunton was the colonel of the 8th

Virginia at Gettysburg. He observed in 1904: "Pickett had lost caste entirely with General Lee. I cannot tell exactly what the trouble was. It is reported that he abused and criticized Lee on the [Appomattox] retreat for not surrendering, and condemned him severely for continuing the war. I cannot say that this is true, or whether General Lee was visiting discipline upon Pickett for his loss of Five Forks and Sailor's Creek…" [13] Confederate cavalier John Mosby likewise wrote of bad blood between the two Virginians.

Part of Lee's issues may have been Pickett's well-known romantic escapades. Prior to the Gettysburg Campaign, the widower fell in love with Virginia teenager LaSalle "Sallie" Corbell, who may have met Pickett when she was as young as four. [14] Sorrel recalled that Pickett fell "in love with all the ardor of youth" and he would sometimes leave his command to spend nights with Sallie. On one occasion, Pickett asked Sorrel for permission to leave because Longstreet was "tired of [dealing with] it." Sorrel refused "but Pickett went all the same, nothing could hold him back from that pursuit…I don't think his division benefited by such carpet-knight doings in the field." [15]

Pickett and Sallie were married in November 1863. (Lee did not attend the ceremony and instead sent a fruitcake as a gift.) Eppa Hunton recalled, "Pickett was a gallant man. Up to the time he was married, I had the utmost confidence in his gallantry, but I believe that no man who married during the war was as good a soldier after, as before marriage….marriage during the war seemed to demoralize them." [16]

Much of Pickett's reputation as a swashbuckling scion of the Old South, and a supposed favorite of Lee's, comes to us from LaSalle's writing and speaking engagements conducted decades after his death. Unfortunately, many of her yarns are generally considered historically unreliable such as the popular story that Pickett's West Point appointment was secured by Abraham Lincoln. Her tall tale that Lincoln then paid a visit to the Pickett household in Richmond during the closing days of the war is equally dubious. [17] Likewise, modern research has even cast some doubts on her touching story that Pickett handled the funeral arrangements for Longstreet's children who died of disease during the winter of 1862.[18]

Lee may not have appreciated Pickett's emotionally crying out, "I have no division!" following the repulse of July 3. However, other officers (such as Cadmus Wilcox) were also reported to be in a similar condition following the debacle. [19] Pickett probably did not help his cause when he questioned Lee on July 8 about being assigned to guard Union prisoners on the retreat from Gettysburg. [20] Pickett's mortification at being assigned guard duty was shared by his men. Charles Loehr said the order "was but little relished by the men, most of them considering it as almost a disgrace to act as provost guard; however, orders must be obeyed." [21]

Much has also been made of Pickett's missing official report of the battle, although his was not the only one omitted from publication. It reportedly complained about a lack of support (which was not uncommon in Civil War battle reports), but Lee asked for it to be resubmitted, cautioning, "we have the enemy to fight, and must carefully, at this critical moment, guard against dissensions which the reflections in your report would create. I will,

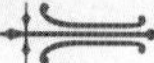
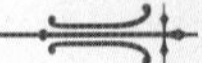

therefore, suggest that you destroy both copy and original, substituting one confined to casualties merely."[22] Who exactly Pickett blamed is debatable, but perhaps Lee considered the contrast between Pickett's apparent willingness to criticize others while Lee had openly accepted the blame himself.

Pickett's post-Gettysburg career is perhaps best remembered for his disastrous defeat at Five Forks in April 1865 which occurred while he was several miles in the rear enjoying a shad bake. Pickett was reportedly relieved of command several days later following another rout at Sailor's Creek. Lee allegedly passed Pickett and coldly scoffed, "I thought that man was no longer with the army." Yet there is historical controversy around even this. Walter Taylor, Lee's chief of staff, wrote after the war that he issued orders for Lee relieving Pickett, but no copies of this order survive. As late as April 11, 1865, Pickett was still signing documents as "Maj. Genl. Comdg." It has been speculated that in the chaos of the Army of Northern Virginia's final days, the relief order never reached Pickett. Taylor later explained that although Pickett was relieved of his division command, he was not dismissed from the army, and thus explains why he was still present at Appomattox.[23]

LaSalle's always questionable recollections are the source of a frequently quoted postwar anecdote concerning "Pickett's Charge." Mrs. Pickett claimed that while attending a dinner in Canada, General Pickett was asked by dignitaries as to who was responsible for the Gettysburg defeat. "With a twinkle in his eye," George Pickett replied, "I think the Yankees had a little something to do with it."[24]

Yet another often-repeated conclusion to the Lee-Pickett saga occurred in March 1870. (Although like so many aspects of Pickett's legend, this too is debated by scholars.) Confederate cavalryman John Mosby arranged a meeting in Richmond between Pickett and a dying Lee. Mosby alleged that the meeting was "cold and formal, and evidently embarrassing to both commanders." Mosby and Pickett departed after only a few minutes. Pickett reportedly spoke very bitterly of Lee, calling him "that old man" and exclaiming that Lee "had my division massacred at Gettysburg." Mosby replied, "Well, it made you immortal."[25]

George Pickett died July 30, 1875. He is buried in Richmond's Hollywood Cemetery near about 2,000 of Gettysburg's Confederate dead, many presumably being from his own division, who had been reinterred there in 1872.

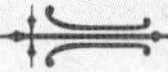

STRENGTH OF PICKETT'S DIVISION?

How many infantrymen were in Pickett's Division and how many actually participated in the charge? As with assessments of Pettigrew and Trimble's strength, the answer is uncertain. In addition to the reporting challenges noted previously, the problem also exists because some Confederate muster rolls are missing and all reconstructions require a degree of mathematical guesswork to arrive at their totals. Even Lee's officers could not agree on the aggregates within the army. [1]

One source of confusion arises from the habit of some researchers to include artillery strength when assessing Pickett's overall manpower. Our question attempts to identify the number of infantrymen who stepped off from Seminary Ridge and literally made the charge. Our desire to exclude artillerymen from the total is in no way dismissive of their service, but their inclusion simply does not represent those whom we traditionally consider as having actually marched across the mile of open ground to Cemetery Ridge.

Another source of confusion exists, as researcher John Busey noted, because Confederate officers often interchangeably reported strengths as "effectives," "men," and "rifles" to generally represent the enlisted men. [2] This observation was certainly true in Pickett's Division. General Pickett himself wrote on June 21: "I have now only three brigades, not more than 4,795 men." [3] Pickett's staff officer Walter Harrison wrote that there were only 4,481 "muskets" and an "aggregate effective strength" of 4,700 "rank and file." [4] Arthur Fremantle described the division as a "weak one (under 5,000), owing to the absence of two brigades." [5] Longstreet thought in *Annals of the War*, "the real strength of Pickett's Division was 4,500 bayonets." [6] Captain Robert Bright on Pickett's staff believed: "forty-seven hundred muskets, with officers added, five thousand strong."[7] David Johnston, 7th Virginia, wrote in his postwar reminiscences of "about 4,700 men, which included the General's staff, and regimental officers." [8] It has been proposed that the Confederates, primarily using Walter Harrison as their source, intentionally under-estimated their strength in order to inflate their post-battle valor. This rationale does not explain, however, examples such as General Pickett's June 21 estimate.

The three brigade monuments on the battlefield for Garnett, Kemper, and Armistead add up to 4,705 men present. (Armistead's Brigade monument adds to 1,650, Garnett's to 1,480, and Kemper's to 1,575.) Garnett's Brigade was the only one of Pickett's brigades to estimate their combat strength via an official report. Major Charles Peyton of the 19th Virginia filed for the deceased General Garnett and stated that their command went into action with 1,427 men. [9] This is actually even lower than Garnett's tablet total of 1,480 men. If we assume, as a mere statistical exercise and nothing else, that the other two brigade tablets are also approximately 4% higher than what would have been reported, then we would expect 4,516 men to have been reported for the entire division. In Garnett's case at least, a radically higher total then must assume that both Major Peyton and the source for the battlefield

monuments were drastically wrong.

The field returns for Lee's army suggest potentially higher numbers for the division. The July 20 field returns count 3,733 officers and men present for duty. [10] If we add the 2,863 casualties noted in General Longstreet's report then we achieve an estimated total of about 6,596 men in action at Gettysburg (the sum of July 20 rolls + reported casualties.) [11] But as Busey noted, reliance on the returns yield their own problems and the methodology used above would undoubtedly double-count some unknown number of wounded who were included in Longstreet's initial casualty total but had returned to duty by July 20. [12]

Amongst modern historical studies, George Stewart's once-considered-definitive *Pickett's Charge* (1959) accepted approximately 4,700 in the ranks. [13] But more recent studies routinely bias toward higher totals.

Pickett's Division Strength Estimates

Source:	Official Reports	Battlefield Tablets	Busey Strengths & Losses	Busey Nothing But Glory
Kemper	NA	1,575	1,634	1,781
Armistead	NA	1,650	1,950	2,188
Garnett	1,427	1,480	1,459	1,851
Pickett's Infantry	NA	4,705	5,043	5,820
Dearing's Artillery	NA	NA	420	430
Pickett's Division Total	**NA**	**NA**	**5,463**	**6,250**

The influential John Busey and David Martin, in their *Regimental Strengths and Losses* (2005, 4th Edition), estimated 5,944 men present and 5,474 engaged under Pickett at Gettysburg. However, in detail, the engaged strength represents only 4,528 enlisted infantrymen. The remainder were comprised of 526 officers and 420 artillerymen. If we subtract the artillerymen, then this again would imply roughly 5,054 officers and infantrymen engaged in the charge. [14] Gettysburg National Military Park historian Kathy Georg Harrison estimated "some 5,800 infantrymen strong, *including* [emphasis added] those on detail as teamsters, drovers, cooks, aids, and ambulance drivers." The addition of artillery brought Pickett's total to "over 6,200 men." [15] As part of Harrison's work, researcher John Busey then revised his totals to 5,830 infantry, 430 artillerymen, and 6,260 total engaged under Pickett.[16] Numerous historical studies have since accepted roughly 5,830 "men on the battle line" as the engaged July 3 infantry strength although Harrison initially included those on support detail in this total. [17]

Measurements on the field are another factor to consider. The distance from Garnett's approximate left, past the Spangler farm, and stretching toward the Sherfy farm to equate Kemper's right flank is between 1,100 to 1,300 yards. Using a 1,100 yard combined front would allow for 3,300 men in two ranks. Armistead's starting position from the Spangler farm lane to the corner of Spangler's woodlot is about 500 yards, or about room for 1,500 men. Such distances would suggest about 4,800 men in the ranks when combining the three brigades. Adding at least another 300 men in skirmish lines (a 1,100 yard front would permit

about 275 skirmishers at 5 pace intervals) would bring the total to about 5,100. [18]

Unfortunately, the honest answer is that no one will ever know exactly how many of Pickett's men participated in the charge. Whether the starting total was 5,830 or closer to the original suggestions of only 5,000 infantrymen, we must then also deduct several hundred from this total due to various detachments for support roles, stragglers, and casualties from the cannonade and oppressive heat. David Johnston of the 7th Virginia felt confident that "not less than 300 of Pickett's men were killed or injured by artillery fire." [19] When all factors are considered, the number of infantrymen who physically stepped off from Seminary Ridge with Pickett that afternoon was probably under 5,000 men.

It is also worth remembering that two of Pickett's brigades, commanded by Micah Jenkins and Montgomery Corse, were detached from the division and deprived Lee of approximately 3,700 additional men at Gettysburg. [20] Pickett complained to Lee's headquarters on June 21:

> I have the honor to report that in point of numerical strength this division has been very much weakened…I have now only three brigades, not more than 4,795 men, and unless these absent troops are certainly to rejoin me, I beg that another brigade be sent to this division ere we commence the campaign. I ask this in no spirit of complaint, but merely as an act of justice to my division and myself, for it is well known that a small division will be expected to do the same amount of hard service as a large one, and, as the army is now divided, my division will be, I think, decidedly the weakest. [21]

Pickett was wasting his energy in complaining to Lee, given that Lee had been futilely trying to get President Davis and the Richmond authorities to return all detached troops, including Pickett's, to the army. On June 29, Walter Taylor advised Pickett on Lee's behalf: "I am directed by the commanding general to say that he has repeatedly requested that the two brigades be returned, and had hoped that at least one of them (Corse's) would have been sent to the division ere this. There is no other brigade in the army which could be assigned to the division at this time." [22] We know that even at reduced strength, Pickett's men did at least briefly penetrate the Union defenses. Gettysburg students are left to ponder: Would the addition of 3,700 presumably fresh men have had any material impact on the outcome of July 3? Like most historical "what ifs," we will never know, but their absence certainly did not help their cause.

From the Virginia Monument, we will continue to drive south on West Confederate Avenue for roughly another 0.5 miles.

You will pass a War Department tablet on your right to Brig. General Edward Perry's Florida Brigade. General Perry was absent at Gettysburg due to illness and his brigade was commanded by Col. David Lang. Farther on is the Florida State Memorial and shortly afterwards you will see another War Department tablet dedicated to the Alabama brigade commanded by Brig. General Cadmus Wilcox. As both Wilcox and Lang's brigades will be discussed at this stop, you may choose to park your vehicle at either monument.

Note, however, these monuments were placed here to conform with the heavily trafficked West Confederate Avenue and do not represent the positions that Wilcox and Lang's men actually occupied prior to the assault. To obtain their actual perspectives, you may choose to walk about 620 yards east from here toward the Emmitsburg Road. The Henry Spangler farm buildings will be on your left as you walk. If the ground conditions are not conducive to walking in the fields themselves, as an alternate route you may elect to walk along the Spangler farm lane itself before veering into the fields south of the Spangler property. Note that while the Spangler farm is National Park Service property, it is also used as a private residence. Please do not approach the house and respect the privacy of the residents.

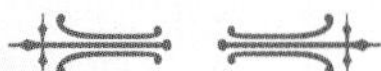

Support of Wilcox & Lang's Brigades

(Wilcox Brigade Tablet and Florida State Memorial)

GPS: 39°48'32.62"N, 77°15'17.41"W; Elev. 537 ft.

One of the greatest tactical challenges facing General Longstreet was the protection of his flanks as his attacking force advanced over nearly one mile of open ground. General Kemper's Brigade on the right of Pickett's Division line was forced to significantly expose their right flank to Union fire after crossing the Emmitsburg Road at distances beginning at

The Florida State Memorial on West Confederate Ave. Image courtesy of Karl Stelly

roughly 1,000 yards but soon diminished to as little as 300-400 yards as they veered north toward the salient target.

To protect Pickett's right, General Longstreet wrote that General Cadmus Wilcox's Brigade (another contribution from A. P. Hill's Third Corps) "was ordered to move in rear of his [Pickett's] right flank, to protect it from any force that the enemy might attempt to move against it." [1] In addition to Wilcox, General Hill added still more support under Col. David Lang's Florida brigade. Neither Wilcox nor Lang was optimistic of their chances for success. Lang believed, "what Anderson's Division had failed to do on the 2nd, Pickett could not do 24 hours later." [2]

General Wilcox's Brigade had seen heavy combat on July 2, and according to Wilcox his men had not eaten since the previous morning. Wilcox reported that prior to the charge, they spent much of the day posted about 200 yards west of the Emmitsburg Road in support of Alexander's First Corps artillery (which was to Wilcox's front and stretched beyond his brigade line.) During the cannonade, Wilcox's men were exposed to enemy fire "but suffered comparatively little, probably less than a dozen men killed and wounded. The brigade lying on my right (Kemper's) suffered severely." When the order was given for Pickett to advance, Kemper's Brigade marched over Wilcox's men, who were ordered to lie down to allow for Pickett's troops to pass them. [3]

Colonel Lang meanwhile reported that his Floridians were ordered to assume position on Wilcox's left and conform to Wilcox's movements. [4] The brigade had fought heavily over nearly much of the same ground on July 2, and may have had as few as 400 men still in the ranks on July 3. Like Wilcox's Alabamians, Lang's men hunkered down west of the Emmitsburg Road with little shade during the cannonade that preceded the charge. [5]

Wilcox and Lang's men are often forgotten participants in the great charge, yet their involvement was no less than that of Pettigrew, Trimble, and Pickett's men. What was their combined strength on July 3? A full complement would have brought a maximum of 2,468 men into action but both had suffered casualties on July 2. Wilcox wrote in his report that he mustered "about 1,200" on July 3. [6] Since a stake has also been placed in the ground estimating 400 Floridians were present for duty, then we can best estimate this combined force at 1,600 men. [7]

Wilcox and Lang's Brigades Strength Estimates

	Total K	Total W	Total MC	Total Casualties	Starting (Jul. 2) Strength	Total Casualty %	Total KIA %	July 3 Strength Estimates Using Range Estimates of July 1 Losses 10%	20%	30%	40%
Wilcox	78	443	257	778	1,726	45.08%	4.52%	1,553	1,381	1,208	1,036
Lang	80	228	147	455	742	61.32%	10.78%	668	594	519	445
Anderson's Division	**158**	**671**	**404**	**1,233**	**2,468**	**49.96%**	**6.40%**	**2,221**	**1,974**	**1,728**	**1,481**

Although Longstreet's report implies that Wilcox's movements were part of a preplanned attempt to protect Pickett's flanks, there is evidence to suggest that Longstreet only considered this option after the charge had already begun.

According to both Capt. Robert Bright of Pickett's staff and E. P. Alexander, Pickett

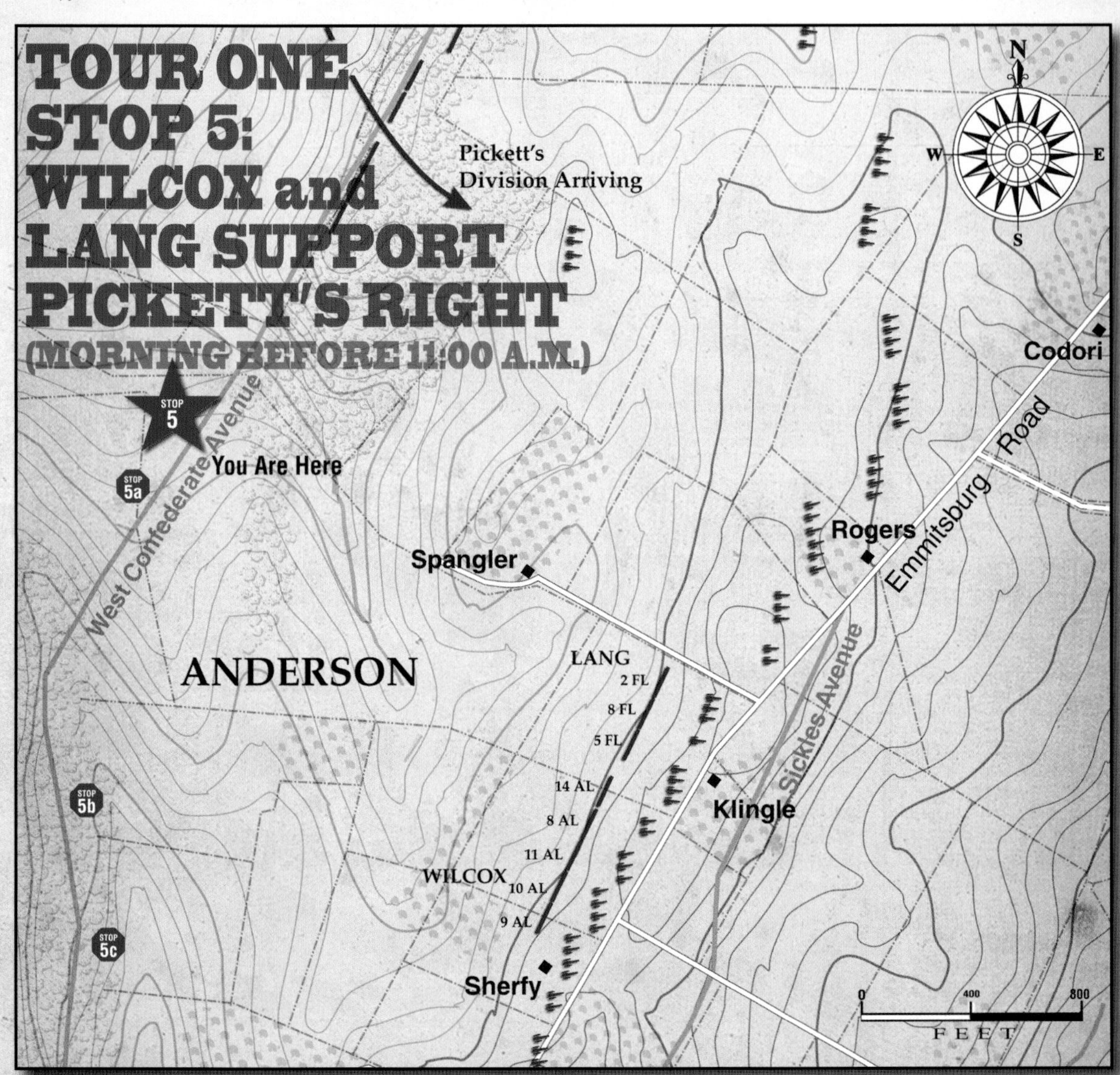

was riding behind his advancing infantry and noted that Pettigrew's left was "crumbling away." [8] Pickett sent Captain Bright to Longstreet with a message that the Union position could be carried but not held without reinforcements. As Bright rode back, he passed a number of unwounded men heading for the rear, which he claimed were from Pettigrew's command. Bright found Longstreet sitting on a fence. They were joined by British military observer Lt. Colonel Arthur Fremantle, who told Longstreet, "I wouldn't have missed this for anything." Longstreet laughed in reply, "The devil you wouldn't! I would like to have missed it very much; we've attacked and been repulsed. Look there!" Longstreet then told Fremantle that Pickett's Division had already carried the enemy's works but had been forced to retire. [9]

After commenting, "The charge is over," Longstreet then instructed Bright to "ride to General Pickett, and tell him what you have heard me say to Colonel Fremantle." But as Bright started off, Longstreet curiously called out to Bright again: "Tell General Pickett that

Wilcox's Brigade is in that peach orchard [pointing], and he can order him to his assistance." Bright then added in a postwar account: "Some have claimed that Wilcox was put in the charge at its commencement…but this is a mistake." [10]

Wilcox, whom it should be pointed out was later amongst Longstreet's many postwar Southern detractors, said he did not receive his orders to advance until "more than twenty or thirty minutes" after Pickett's own movements began. Both Captain Bright and Wilcox described three messengers (with Bright being the last of the three) being sent to Wilcox in rapid succession. By the time Bright reached Wilcox (one wonders how much time had elapsed since Longstreet's original request) an exasperated Wilcox raised both hands and said, "I know. I know." [11] According to an 1877 account by Wilcox, Pickett was already "several hundred yards" ahead by this point. [12]

Colonel Lang curiously reported that his order to advance came "soon after General Pickett's troops retired behind our position." One wonders if the increasing number of walking wounded and stragglers were so abundant that Lang mistakenly assumed Pickett's entire division had retired. Lang started his brigade forward with Wilcox "under a heavy fire of artillery." [13] In any event, one lieutenant in the brigade observed, "Knowing what we had to encounter, the order to advance was not obeyed with the same alacrity as" July 2. [14]

Confederate artillerist E. Porter Alexander wrote in 1877 that Wilcox attacked "a little before" Pickett's repulse. [15] His 1880s *Battles and Leaders* version, elaborated that as Wilcox advanced "only disorganized stragglers pursued by a moderate fire were coming back. Just then, Wilcox's Brigade passed by us, moving to Pickett's support. There was no longer anything to support, and with the keenest pity at the useless waste of life, I saw them advance. The men, as they passed us, looked bewildered, as if they wondered what they were expected to do, or why they were there." Alexander called it "at once both absurd and tragic." [16]

Pickett's Division had veered toward the left (toward the Angle) as they approached Cemetery Ridge. Due to the combination of elapsed time, smoke, and chaos, Wilcox and Lang did not conform to these movements, and instead steered straight ahead. Wilcox wrote:

> As they [Wilcox's men] came in view on the turnpike, all of the enemy's terrible artillery that could bear on them was concentrated upon them from both flanks and directly in front, and more than on the evening

The Wilcox Brigade Tablet just south of the Florida State Memorial. Image courtesy of Karl Stelly

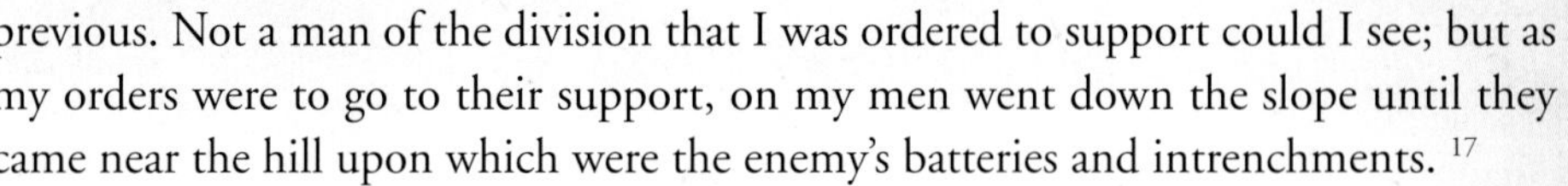

previous. Not a man of the division that I was ordered to support could I see; but as my orders were to go to their support, on my men went down the slope until they came near the hill upon which were the enemy's batteries and intrenchments. [17]

Numerous questions remain unanswered. Did Longstreet intend for Wilcox to move simultaneously with Pickett? Why was there a delay? If the delay was intentional, then why did someone not better guide Wilcox toward Kemper's right? Why did Longstreet instruct Bright to order Wilcox forward if Longstreet truly thought the charge had failed? Would better coordination between Pickett and Wilcox have made any difference on the outcome? While these questions will never conclusively be answered, it becomes apparent that a lengthening list of Confederate "what ifs" and failures impacted their execution of Lee's intended attack.

Before proceeding, we have now covered all of Lee's utilized infantry on July 3. (Additional Confederate infantry in Longstreet's First Corps was positioned south of us but was not engaged as part of this assault.) If we accept our estimates of 7,300 combined for Pettigrew/ Trimble, 5,000 for Pickett, and 1,600 for Wilcox/ Lang, we then achieve a grand total of 14,000 soldiers available to make the assault. If we then take a 10% haircut deduction to allow for cannonade and heat casualties, we then arrive at an estimated 12,500 men who "made the charge" from all of the combined commands.

Florida State Memorial

GPS: 39°48'36.33"N, 77°15'14.51"W; Elev. 526 ft.

- Visitors are sometimes surprised to see that Florida was one of the states fighting for the Confederacy at Gettysburg. Only three Confederate infantry regiments represented the sparsely populated Florida at Gettysburg.
- Brigadier General Edward Perry's Brigade was temporarily commanded by Col. David Lang because Perry was sick. The brigade's position on July 3 was several hundred yards east of the monument and near the Emmitsburg Road.
- A large number of the 2nd Florida and the regimental colors were captured on July 3. Colonel Lang reported 455 casualties out of 700 engaged during the entire battle.
- Private Lewis Powell of the 2nd Florida was wounded and captured at Gettysburg. (Accounts vary on whether he was wounded on July 2 or July 3.) Powell escaped from a Baltimore hospital and eventually became involved with John Wilkes Booth's plot to assassinate President Lincoln. On the night Lincoln was murdered, Powell (who also used the alias Lewis Payne / Paine) nearly stabbed Secretary of State William Seward to death. Powell was captured and hanged with the remaining conspirators.

- The monument was dedicated on July 3, 1963, the centennial of the brigade's ill-fated participation in Pickett's Charge.

From here, return again to your vehicle and drive another 0.5 miles toward the intersection of West Confederate Avenue and the Millerstown Road. Prior to the intersection, you will pass tablets and cannons that are intended to mark the locations of several Confederate First Corps artillery battalions that participated in the assault. As we have seen previously, however, if you read the tablets you will note that these are not the actual points from which these batteries bombarded Cemetery Ridge on the afternoon of July 3. For now, you may simply wish to read these tablets as you will have a better opportunity to examine the positions themselves at our next stop. The Eshleman marker in particular does offer an excellent view toward the Sherfy farm and Emmitsburg Road.

Dearing's Artillery Battalion

GPS: 39°48'17.88"N, 77°15'22.16"W; Elev. 571 ft.

- Pickett's Division artillery consisted of a battalion of four batteries (18 cannons) and was commanded by 23-year-old Maj. James Dearing. The bright young Major Dearing had been at the top of his West Point class before being forced to resign in April 1861 when his home state of Virginia seceded.

A 1936 view of Confederate artillery on West Confederate Ave. near Pitzer's Woods. Image courtesy of GNMP

- Dearing's guns were not located here during the battle on July 3 but were instead placed close to the Emmitsburg Road near the Rogers farm (which no longer stands.)
- On the morning of July 3, Major Dearing had ridden out on the skirmish line to get a closer look at the enemy's position, when a courier arrived with a message from General Lee. Dearing was flattered that General Lee apparently wished to consult him regarding his observations, but was instead disappointed to receive Lee's message: "Major Dearing, I do not approve of young officers needlessly exposing themselves; your place is with your batteries." [18]
- Dearing was appointed a brigadier general on April 29, 1864, but his appointment was never confirmed by the Confederate Congress. He was mortally wounded on April 6, 1865, and died on April 22. It is sometimes said that he was the last general killed or to die of wounds during the Civil War, but as his commission had not yet been confirmed he was technically only a lieutenant colonel at the time of his death. [19]

Eshleman's Artillery Battalion

GPS: 39°48'10.85"N, 77°15'21.71"W; Elev. 583 ft.

- Major Benjamin Franklin Eshleman commanded one of the two artillery battalions in Longstreet's Corps Artillery Reserve. (Colonel E. Porter Alexander commanded the other battalion.)
- Eshleman was born in Lancaster County, Pennsylvania. He had moved to New Orleans, Louisiana, early in life and elected to fight for his adopted southern state.
- Eshleman's battalion was dubbed the Washington (Louisiana) Artillery and consisted of ten guns. These batteries were not located here on July 3, but were instead north of the Sherfy property and opposite the Klingle farm. Two cannons from Capt. Merritt B. Miller's battery fired the signal shots that preceded Pickett's Charge.

A closeup view of the Louisiana State Memorial. Image courtesy of Steven Stanley

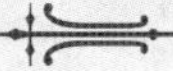

- The nearby Louisiana State Memorial (dedicated in 1971) shows a female "Spirit of the Confederacy" soaring over a fallen member of the Washington Artillery.[20] As the monument is near positions occupied by Longstreet's infantry during their attack of July 2, many observers fail to realize that this particular memorial is actually more representative of Louisiana's artillery contributions to July 3.

CONNECTED WITH THE REBEL ARMY

Most Gettysburg students are familiar with the stories of Wesley Culp and Henry Wentz – Gettysburg youths who moved South prior to the war and returned as members of Lee's army during the battle. Culp and Wentz were not, however, the only local men to fight for the Army of Northern Virginia at Gettysburg.

Francis W. (or "Frank") Hoffman was the second son born to Gettysburg carriage maker Charles W. Hoffman and his wife Sarah Ann. Frank was born in 1842 and spent his formative years living with his family, which included at least three other brothers, in a two-story dwelling on the north side of Chambersburg Street. In 1856, Charles Hoffman relocated his family to Virginia when Frank was about 14. The property was not actually sold until 1860 to Eliza Harper, who owned it during the battle. [1]

Now a transplanted Southern boy, Frank enlisted in the Confederate service in July 1861 as a member of Company A, 38th Battalion Virginia Light Artillery, commanded by Capt. Robert Stribling. Hoffman served with Stribling's battery throughout the war, and since he was present on all rolls there is nothing to indicate that he was not with the battery at Gettysburg. [2]

Stribling's battery was attached to Maj. James Dearing's Battalion, Pickett's Division, as the Fauquier Artillery. Their battlefield marker is inaccurately located on West Confederate Avenue. Stribling's true position was slightly north and west of the Rogers farm along the Emmitsburg Road. Their plaque reads:

> July 3. Advanced to the front about daybreak. Later in the morning took position on the crest of ridge west of Emmitsburg Road and near the Rogers House. Drove back with a dozen well directed rounds a strong line of skirmishers whose fire wounded a few men and horses. Bore a conspicuous part in the cannonade preceding Longstreet's assault. But its ammunition being exhausted about the time the assault began and repeated efforts to obtain a fresh supply proving fruitless the Battery was withdrawn.

Although the battery's losses were not reported in detail, estimates are one man killed and four wounded out of 135 engaged. [3]

Frank was actually not the only Hoffman fighting for the Confederacy during this

campaign. His older brother (by two years) Robert N. had enlisted in the 2nd Virginia, but was detailed to drive cattle and probably experienced the battle from the relative safety of a supporting role. Ironically, Robert Hoffman was a member of the same regiment and company ('B') as Gettysburg's most noteworthy wayward son: Wesley Culp. [4]

It would seem that father Charles also proclaimed some allegiance to the Confederates. A Gettysburg *Compiler* newspaper account from June 1862 reported that he had been arrested by John Geary's command near Linden, Virginia, "and sent to Washington. It is said he has been connected with the rebel army, and has three sons in that army." [5]

Frank Hoffman was seriously wounded in 1865 by a bullet in the throat and captured by Federal forces. The wound was believed to be mortal. About six months after the war ended, his father received a letter from Frank stating that he was alive but too weak to get himself home. Charles journeyed to a Fort Monroe hospital and retrieved his son. Recovery was slow and Frank was "a complete wreck" until several years later, in a violent coughing fit, he coughed up the musket ball. This immediately sent Frank on a "rapid recovery" into a "hearty man." Hoffman married in 1869 and spent the majority of his life as a farmer in Culpeper County before dying in 1920. [6]

Turn left when you reach the intersection of West Confederate Avenue and the Millerstown Road. Longstreet's forces, specifically the battered divisions of Generals Lafayette McLaws and John Bell Hood (who was seriously wounded on July 2 and was replaced in command by Evander Law), occupied positions south of this point on July 3. Several of Lee's staff officers insisted Lee intended for them to participate in the July 3 attack, a decision Longstreet considered impracticable as their presence was necessary to provide a right flank for the Army of Northern Virginia. Not only was their presence required to defend against Union infantry near the Round Tops, but Federal cavalry in Judson Kilpatrick's division was also active beyond Longstreet's right.

Proceed east along the Millerstown Road for approximately 0.4 miles. You will pass the historic Warfield residence on your right. As you reach the Emmitsburg Road, you will see the Sherfy residence on your left. Carefully cross the Emmitsburg Road and park near the Peach Orchard on the right, observing that the National Park Service prohibits parking too close to the Emmitsburg Road for safety reasons.

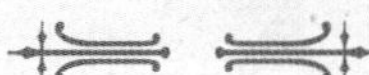

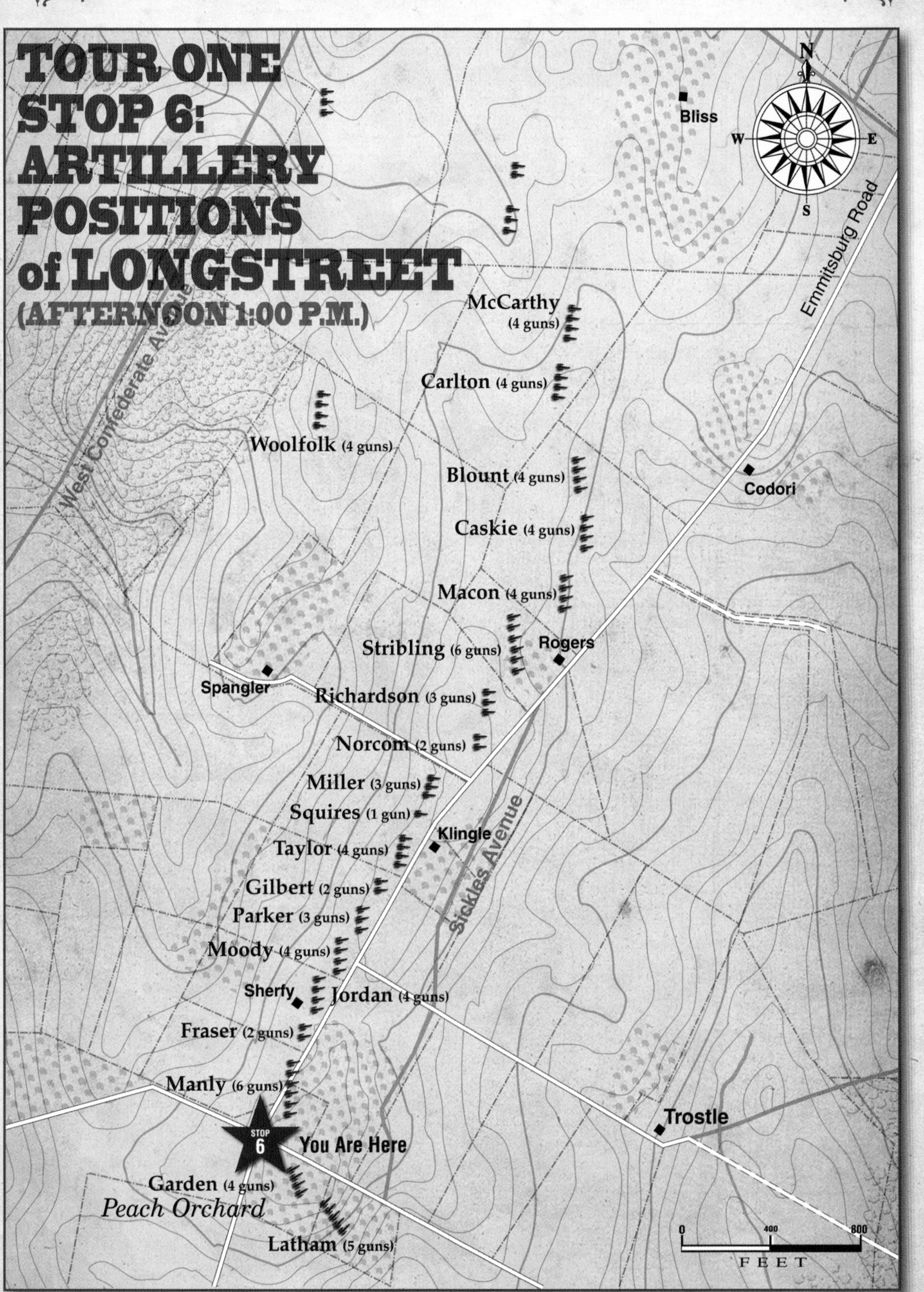
TOUR ONE
STOP 6:
ARTILLERY
POSITIONS
of LONGSTREET
(AFTERNOON 1:00 P.M.)
N
W
E
S
Bliss
Emmitsburg Road
West Confederate Avenue
McCarthy (4 guns)
Carlton (4 guns)
Woolfolk (4 guns)
Blount (4 guns)
Codori
Caskie (4 guns)
Macon (4 guns)
Stribling (6 guns)
Rogers
Spangler
Richardson (3 guns)
Norcom (2 guns)
Miller (3 guns)
Squires (1 gun)
Klingle
Taylor (4 guns)
Sickles Avenue
Gilbert (2 guns)
Parker (3 guns)
Moody (4 guns)
Sherfy
Jordan (4 guns)
Fraser (2 guns)
Manly (6 guns)
Trostle
STOP 6
You Are Here
Garden (4 guns)
Peach Orchard
Latham (5 guns)
0
400
800
FEET

The Peach Orchard

GPS: 39°48'3.51"N, 77°14'56.06"W; Elev. 585 ft.

Although this area is normally remembered as part of Union General Daniel E. Sickles's advanced line that was captured by Longstreet's First Corps on July 2, the Peach Orchard was actually held by the Confederates through July 3. The orchard's occupation by Lee's army was a key strategic reason that encouraged Lee to continue the fighting on July 3. Lee referred to "the increased support that the positions gained on the right would enable the artillery to render the assaulting columns" when "it was accordingly determined to continue the attack." [1]

If you stand in the Peach Orchard today and look north toward Cemetery Hill, you can readily see how Lee hoped to use this point to converge artillery fire onto Cemetery Hill. Since most of the Confederate guns were located north of the Joseph Sherfy house and on the west side of the Emmitsburg Road, you may want to take a few moments to cross the Emmitsburg Road (being extremely careful for oncoming traffic) and walk north toward the Spangler or Rogers farm sites in order to truly appreciate what the Confederate fields of fire were like on July 3.

General Longstreet's First Corps Artillery Reserve was commanded at Gettysburg by Col. James Walton. Colonel Walton (who had been born in New Jersey) was 50 years old in 1863. His reserve consisted of two battalions under the command of Col. Edward Porter Alexander and Maj. Benjamin Eshleman. Colonel Alexander is generally best known to Gettysburg students for seemingly commanding Longstreet's corps artillery at Gettysburg. This job was actually still held by Walton, although it was Alexander who maintained true tactical field control of Longstreet's long arm. Longstreet later attempted to clarify this confusion, and smooth Walton's ruffled feathers, by describing Alexander's role as:

> *[S]pecial service* [emphasis in original], after seeing that the batteries were most advantageously posted, was to see that field artillery was ready to move with General Pickett's assault, and to give me the benefit of his judgment as to the moment the effect of the artillery combat would justify the assault. I regard Colonel Alexander's position on the 3d as that of an engineer staff officer, more than one exercising any authority in a manner calculated to place you [Walton] in an improper light. [2]

Alexander had rolled his batteries into the orchard following the bloody fighting of July 2. "It was evident," a disappointed Alexander wrote, "that we had not finished the job, and would have to make a fresh effort in the morning." After receiving "a fresh horse, affectionate congratulations on my safety, and…something to eat" from his "faithful" servant, Alexander then sought out Longstreet for orders. "They were, in brief, that our present position was to be held and the attack renewed as soon as Pickett arrived, and he was expected early." [3]

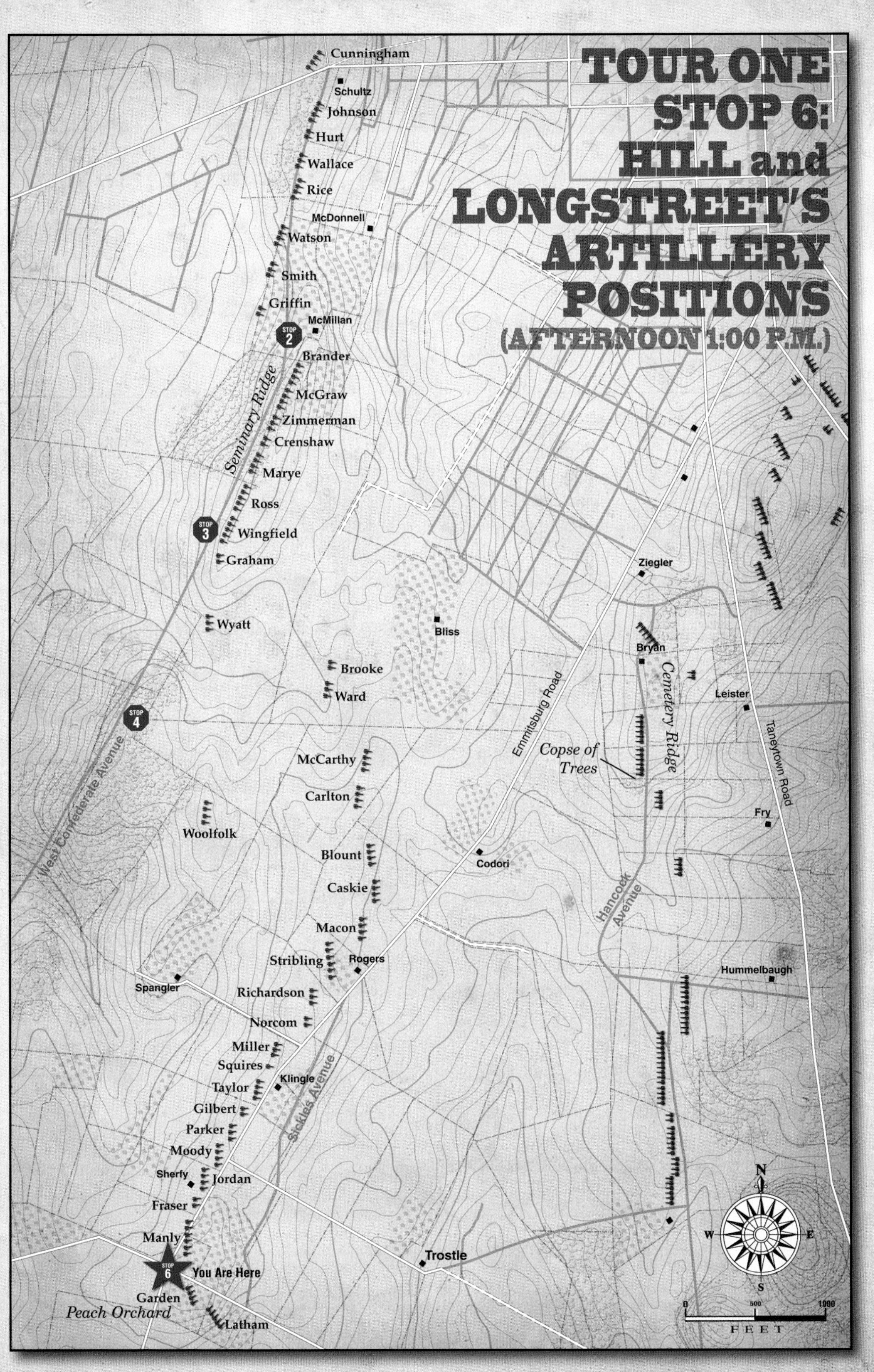

TOUR ONE STOP 6: HILL and LONGSTREET'S ARTILLERY POSITIONS (AFTERNOON 1:00 P.M.)
Cunningham
Schultz
Johnson
Hurt
Wallace
Rice
McDonnell
Watson
Smith
Griffin
McMillan
STOP 2
Brander
Seminary Ridge
McGraw
Zimmerman
Crenshaw
Marye
Ross
STOP 3
Wingfield
Graham
Wyatt
Ziegler
Bliss
Bryan
Brooke
Ward
Cemetery Ridge
Leister
STOP 4
Emmitsburg Road
Taneytown Road
West Confederate Avenue
McCarthy
Copse of Trees
Carlton
Fry
Woolfolk
Blount
Codori
Caskie
Hancock Avenue
Macon
Stribling
Rogers
Hummelbaugh
Spangler
Richardson
Norcom
Miller
Squires
Klingle
Taylor
Sickles Avenue
Gilbert
Parker
Moody
Sherfy
Jordan
Fraser
Manly
Trostle
STOP 6
You Are Here
Garden
Peach Orchard
Latham
N
W
E
S
0
500
1000
FEET

Colonel Alexander lay down for sleep on the field around 1:00 a.m. on July 3. He was awake by 3:00 a.m. and began to put his batteries in position, including the recently arrived Washington Artillery. At daylight, Alexander was panicked to realize he had placed about 20 guns in such an alignment that they were in danger of being enfiladed from Cemetery Hill. He was able to rectify his mistake before the Federals opened fire and caused any serious damage. [4]

Brigadier General William N. Pendleton, the Army of Northern Virginia's artillery chief, reported:

> By direction of the commanding general, the artillery along our entire line was to be prepared for opening, as early as possible on the morning of the 3d, a concentrated and destructive fire, consequent upon which a general advance was to be made. The right, especially, was, if practicable, to sweep the enemy from his stronghold on that flank. Visiting the lines at a very early hour toward securing readiness for this great attempt, I found much (by Colonel Alexander's energy) already accomplished on the right. Henry's battalion held about its original position on the flank. Alexander's was next, in front of the peach orchard. Then came the Washington Artillery Battalion, under Major Eshleman, and Dearing's battalion on his left, these two having arrived since dusk of the day before; and beyond Dearing, Cabell's battalion had been arranged, making nearly sixty guns for that wing, all well advanced in a sweeping curve of about a mile. In the posting of these there appeared little room for improvement, so judiciously had they been adjusted. To Colonel Alexander, placed here in charge by General Longstreet, the wishes of the commanding general were repeated. [5]

According to Alexander, "Early in the morning General Lee came around, and I was then told that we were to assault Cemetery Hill, which lay rather to our left." This required Alexander to change gun positions again while the enemy took a few occasional shots. With Dearing's artillery now added in, Alexander estimated that by 10:00 a.m. perhaps 75 guns "in what was virtually one battery, so disposed as to fire on Cemetery Hill and the batteries south of it, which would have a fire on our advancing infantry." [6]

Most of the batteries that Alexander commanded were not in the Peach Orchard itself. Latham and Garden's two batteries (from Maj. M. W. Henry's Battalion, Hood's Division) of nine cannons were amongst Sherfy's peach trees. The rest of Alexander's line extended north from the Peach Orchard along the Emmitsburg Road ridge toward the Rogers farm. North of Rogers' property, the artillery continued toward the point of woods and the modern Virginia State Memorial. Counting the nine in the Peach Orchard, 73 cannons were under Alexander during the afternoon of July 3. [7]

With our earlier total of 86 cannons active in Ewell and Hill's Corps, we can calculate that the Confederates engaged approximately 159 field pieces during the entire action on July 3.

"It had been arranged that when the infantry column was ready," wrote Colonel

Alexander, "General Longstreet should order two guns fired by the Washington Artillery. On that signal all our guns were to open on Cemetery Hill and the ridge extending toward Round Top, which was covered with batteries. I was to observe the fire and give Pickett the order to charge." [8] Longstreet wrote the order (addressed to Colonel Walton) to begin the assault around 1:00 p.m.:

> Colonel- Let the batteries open. Order great care and precision in firing. When the batteries at the Peach Orchard cannot be used against the point we intend to attack, let them open on the enemy's on the rocky hill. [9]

Captain William Miller Owen of the Washington Artillery wrote that he received the message from a courier at about 1:30 p.m. The first signal gun fired, but the second delayed due to a failed friction primer. "Finally a puff of smoke was seen at the Peach Orchard, then came a roar and a flash, and 138 [sic] pieces of Confederate artillery opened upon the enemy's position, and the deadly work began with the noise of the heaviest thunder." [10]

The Peach Orchard sector south of the Wheatfield Road was generally devoid of Confederate infantry on July 3. The remnants of William Barksdale's Brigade were deployed on a skirmish line several hundred yards to the east, roughly halfway between the Emmitsburg Road and the Trostle farm. West of the Emmitsburg Road, the right of Wilcox and Kemper's brigades reached nearly to the north side of the Sherfy farm.

General Pickett may have spent portions of the afternoon in this area. A colonel in Kershaw's 7th South Carolina, posted near the Emmitsburg and Wheatfield Roads intersection, wrote that he saw Pickett nearby. A major commanding Henry's two batteries

The Sherfy barn on the Emmitsburg Road. Image courtesy of Steven Stanley

here stated "positively and solemnly as a fact" that Pickett and staff were near here before and after the charge. [11] While Pickett was not expected to "lead" his charge as a division commander, if these allegations are true, ask yourself if this was an ideal location from which to oversee the movements of his three brigades.

The Joseph Sherfy house on the west side of the Emmitsburg Road was present at the time of the battle. The barn, however, is not original. On the morning of July 3, as Lee, Longstreet, and their staffs rode through this area while on reconnaissance, an errant Federal shell aimed in their direction ignited the Sherfy barn. Tragically, an unknown number of wounded, primarily from Sickles's Union III Corps (including the distinctly uniformed Zouaves of the 114th Pennsylvania) had earlier sought refuge in the barn and were unable to escape the inferno. Some accounts from Parker's Virginia Battery suggest that they ordered a cease-fire in order to rescue as many wounded Yankees as possible. Those who were unable to escape, "must have perished miserably in the flames," wrote British military observer Arthur Fremantle. Too badly burned to be identified, they were later only recognized by their Zouave uniforms. Decades later, speaking at the dedication of the 114th Pennsylvania regimental monument, Capt. A. W. Givin reminded the veterans of "that sickening sight that met your gaze as you advanced to where the old barn stood, to find it in ashes, and the charred remains of many of your companions." [12] The famed 20th Maine Regiment bivouacked in this area shortly after the battle concluded. "There lay the remnants too terrible to describe of officers and men- rebel and union- half burned or with roasted heads," wrote the regiment's commander, Col. Joshua Chamberlain. [13]

This concludes our first tour of the Confederate positions along Seminary Ridge (West Confederate Avenue) and the Peach Orchard. Hopefully you have gained a better appreciation for the theater of Lee's operations on the afternoon of July 3, 1863. Much more than a traditional "Pickett-centric" view from the Virginia State Memorial, a straight line drawn from Oak Hill (position of the Whitworths) to the Peach Orchard encompasses nearly 3 miles. The combined infantry front was more than one mile in length. Lee and his subordinates intended for this to be a broad attack but at the same time were handicapped by their inability to coordinate movements between two infantry corps (Longstreet and Hill) and batteries from both corps across such an extended front.

You now have three additional tours to choose from. The next tour, number 2 (Pettigrew-Trimble Charge) will allow you the opportunity to walk from the North Carolina State Memorial to Cemetery Ridge and follow the approximate route of Generals Pettigrew and Trimble's forces. Or you may proceed to tour number 3 which will trace the final march of Pickett's Division. Tour number 4 will provide you a thorough examination of General Meade and the Army of the Potomac's defensive lines along Cemetery Ridge.

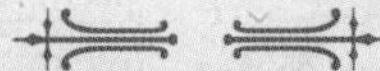

TOUR TWO

Pettigrew-Trimble Charge

"*For the honor of the good Old North State, forward!*"

– Brigadier General James Johnston Pettigrew[1]

North Carolina State Memorial

GPS: 39°49'5.93"N, 77°14'50.03"W; Elev. 561 ft.

This next tour will allow you to walk the charge of Pettigrew and Trimble's divisions.

Return to the North Carolina State Memorial and walk east from this point toward Cemetery Ridge. If you are taking this tour with a partner and have multiple vehicles, before beginning you may want to park one vehicle at our final stop near the Abraham Bryan farm on Cemetery Ridge. Otherwise, please remember that you will also have to walk back here upon completion of this tour. The one-way walking distance is approximately 1,200 yards.

Please note that the National Park Service does not routinely maintain a mowed path here as they do along the route of Pickett's Division and you will encounter high grass and some potentially rough patches. Be mindful of natural resources. If you encounter any farmer's planted crops along the way, do not walk into these fields and damage the produce. Although the ground looks flat and open from this vantage point, you will encounter both rolling and wet terrain. The authors recommend that you wear long pants, proper footwear, sun protection, tick repellent, and bring adequate water for your journey.

Prior to the charge, Pettigrew and Trimble's commands were located on the west slope of Seminary Ridge, or west of today's West Confederate Avenue. [2] Colonel Fry recorded that shortly after conferring with Pickett and Garnett, "the two divisions moved forward about a hundred paces, and the men lay down behind our lines of batteries." [3] After the cannonade, which Colonel Fry "justly described as the most terrible of the war," General Pettigrew started the charge by riding in front of Marshall's Brigade and calling out, "for the honor of the good Old North State, forward!" [4] One captain in Trimble's ranks recalled, "company commanders were instructed to inform their men of the magnitude of the task assigned to them, and also to caution their men to keep cool, preserve the alignment, press steadily to the front, and gain the enemy's works." [5]

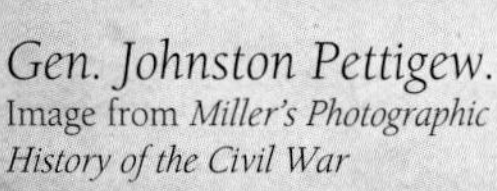

Gen. Johnston Pettigew.
Image from *Miller's Photographic History of the Civil War*

As Pettigrew and Trimble's men descended the eastern slope of Seminary Ridge, the terrain afforded little protective cover from Union artillery fire. "The ground over which we had to pass was perfectly open," wrote Pettigrew staffer Louis Young, "and numerous fences, some parallel and others oblique to our line of battle, were formidable impediments in our way. The position of the enemy was all he

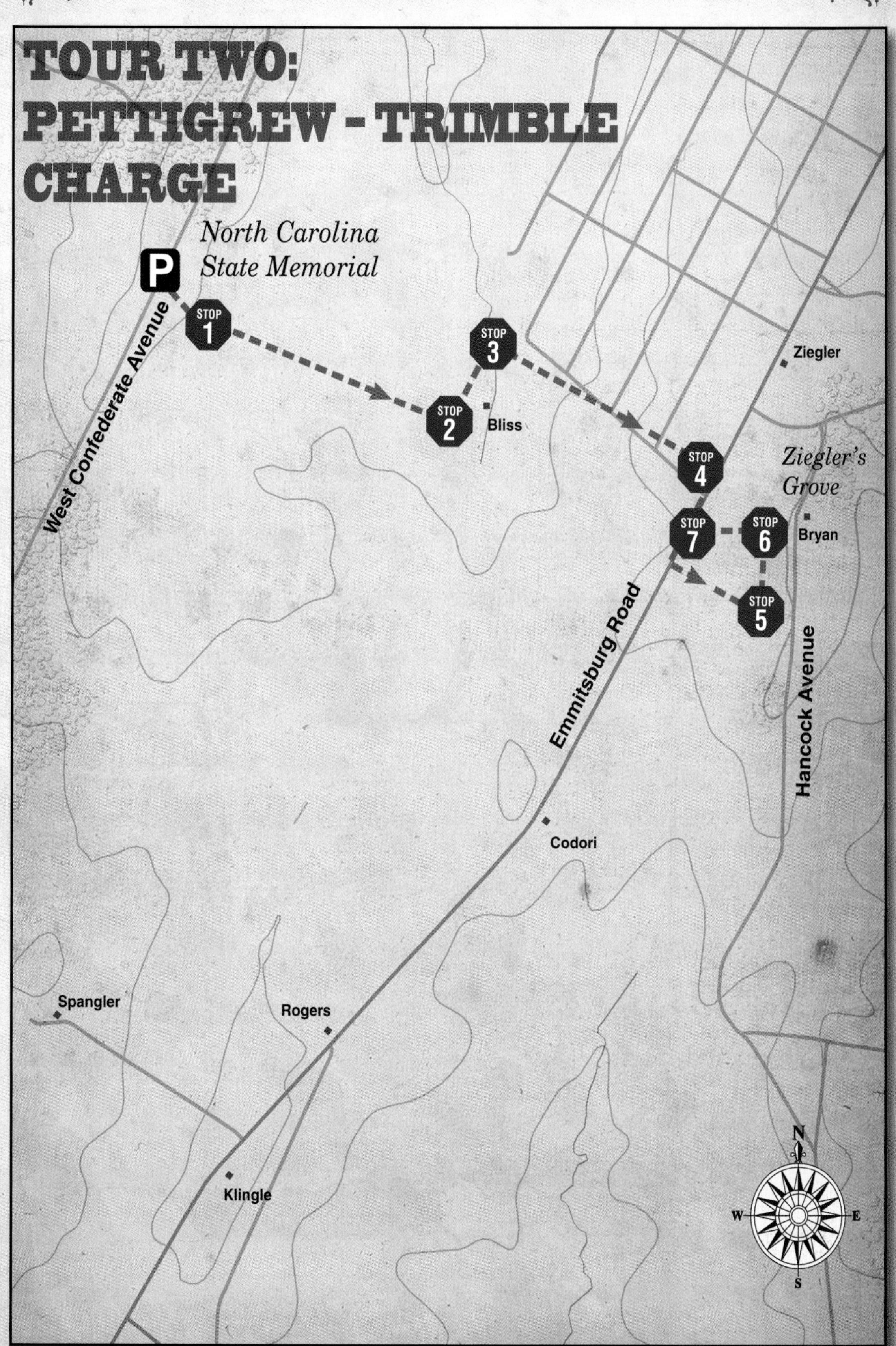
TOUR TWO:
PETTIGREW - TRIMBLE
CHARGE
North Carolina
State Memorial
P
STOP 1
STOP 2
STOP 3
STOP 4
STOP 5
STOP 6
STOP 7
West Confederate Avenue
Bliss
Ziegler
Ziegler's
Grove
Bryan
Emmitsburg Road
Hancock Avenue
Codori
Spangler
Rogers
Klingle
N
W
E
S

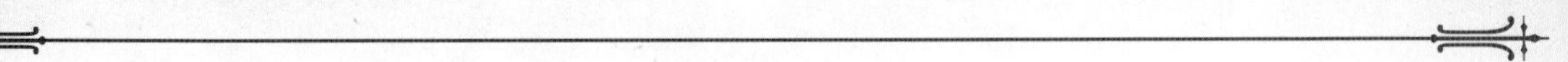

could desire." [6] General Lane described the charge being "made down a gentle slope, and then up to the enemy's lines, a distance of over half a mile, denuded of forest, and in full sight of the enemy, and perfect range of their artillery." [7]

Confederate accounts on this part of the field generally agree that they were hit with minimal artillery fire until about halfway to the enemy's line. [8] Colonel Fry wrote that the men sprang up with "cheerful alacrity," and the long line advanced. They were soon hit with a storm of shot and shell but moved steadily forward, quickly closing gaps and preserving their alignment. [9]

If Pickett understood that his division was to dress (align to the left) upon Fry, as Fry claimed, then Pettigrew's men appear to have understood they were to dress (align to the right) on Pickett. General Davis and Maj. John Jones of the 26th North Carolina both reported that they kept dressed to the right, and Jones commented, "there was some confusion in the line, owing to the fact that it had been ordered to close in on the right on Pickett's Division, while that command gave way to the left." [10] Although Davis did not acknowledge it in his report, his brigade appears (along with Brockenbrough) to have not stepped off on time. The reason for the delay is unclear but Pettigrew sent an aide to spur them into motion. Davis's men, however, came out of the woods with an "impetuous rush" and quickly caught up with Marshall's troops on their right. [11]

As noted previously, Brockenbrough's Brigade also did not move when planned. Pettigrew's aide was told by the general not to bother journeying over to get them started.[12] General Davis uncharitably told historian John Bachelder in 1891 that Brockenbrough's men simply "refused to advance." [13] However, eventually Brockenbrough's men did get started due to the initiative of subordinate officers.

Pettigrew and Trimble's men advanced across these fields as seen from the perspective of the North Carolina State Memorial. Image courtesy of Karl Stelly

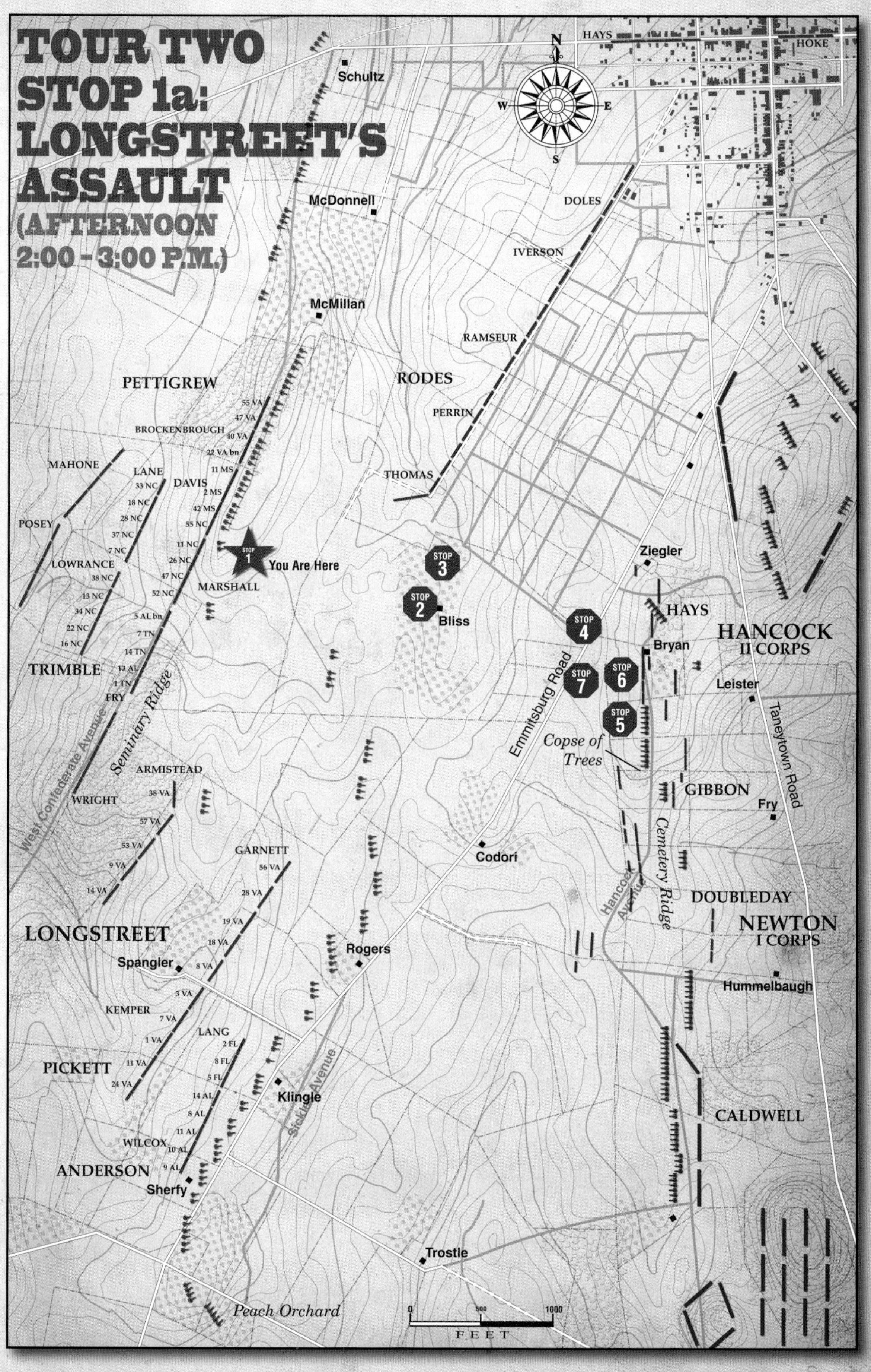
TOUR TWO
STOP 1a:
LONGSTREET'S
ASSAULT
(AFTERNOON
2:00 - 3:00 P.M.)
N
S
E
W
HAYS
HOKE
Schultz
McDonnell
DOLES
IVERSON
McMillan
RAMSEUR
RODES
PETTIGREW
PERRIN
BROCKENBROUGH
MAHONE
LANE
DAVIS
THOMAS
POSEY
LOWRANCE
MARSHALL
You Are Here
STOP 1
STOP 2
STOP 3
STOP 4
STOP 5
STOP 6
STOP 7
Bliss
Ziegler
HAYS
Bryan
HANCOCK
II CORPS
Leister
TRIMBLE
FRY
Seminary Ridge
West Confederate Avenue
Emmitsburg Road
Copse of Trees
Taneytown Road
ARMISTEAD
WRIGHT
GIBBON
Fry
Cemetery Ridge
GARNETT
Codori
Hancock Avenue
DOUBLEDAY
NEWTON
I CORPS
LONGSTREET
Rogers
Spangler
Hummelbaugh
KEMPER
LANG
PICKETT
Klingle
Sickles Avenue
CALDWELL
WILCOX
ANDERSON
Sherfy
Trostle
Peach Orchard
0
500
1000
FEET

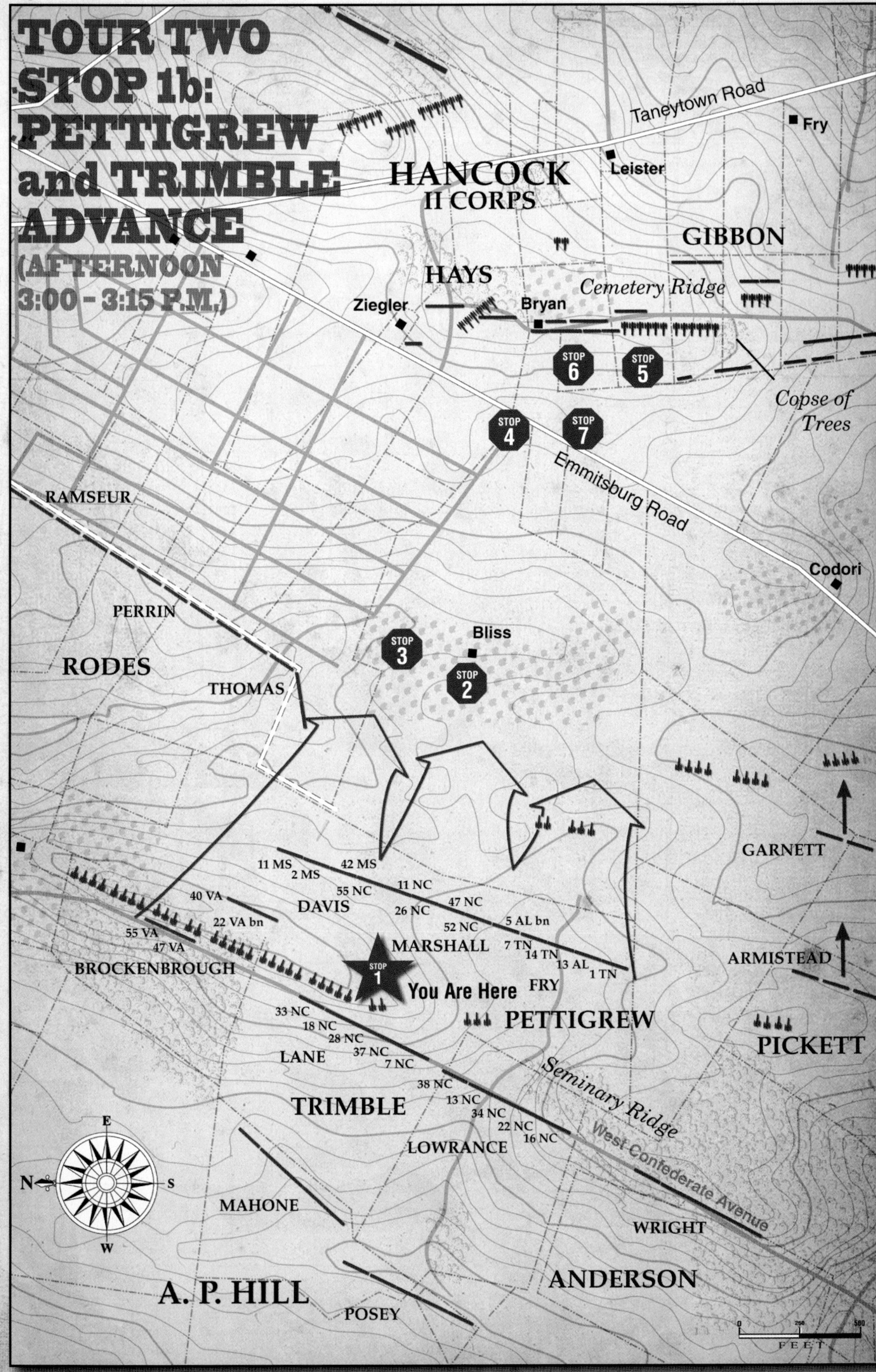

TOUR TWO
STOP 1b:
PETTIGREW
and TRIMBLE
ADVANCE
(AFTERNOON
3:00 - 3:15 P.M.)
Taneytown Road
Fry
Leister
HANCOCK
II CORPS
GIBBON
HAYS
Cemetery Ridge
Ziegler
Bryan
STOP 6
STOP 5
Copse of Trees
STOP 4
STOP 7
Emmitsburg Road
RAMSEUR
Codori
PERRIN
STOP 3
Bliss
STOP 2
RODES
THOMAS
GARNETT
11 MS
2 MS
42 MS
55 NC
11 NC
40 VA
DAVIS
26 NC
47 NC
22 VA bn
52 NC
5 AL bn
55 VA
47 VA
MARSHALL
7 TN
14 TN
13 AL
1 TN
ARMISTEAD
BROCKENBROUGH
STOP 1
You Are Here
FRY
33 NC
18 NC
28 NC
PETTIGREW
PICKETT
LANE
37 NC
7 NC
Seminary Ridge
38 NC
13 NC
TRIMBLE
34 NC
22 NC
16 NC
West Confederate Avenue
LOWRANCE
E
N
S
W
MAHONE
WRIGHT
ANDERSON
A. P. HILL
POSEY
0
250
500
FEET

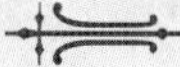
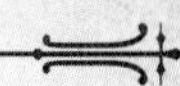

Bliss Farm

GPS: 39°48'58.98"N, 77°14'31.41"W; Elev. 560 ft.

Walk approximately 540 yards east from the North Carolina State Memorial. You will come to a seemingly empty field that upon closer inspection contains several reminders of the William Bliss farm that once stood here.

The 60 acre William Bliss farm had the unfortunate fate of being caught between the two armies on July 2 and July 3. Sharpshooters from both sides exchanged occupancy of Bliss's large barn and the farmstead may have changed hands as many as ten times over the course of two days. The Bliss barn was a large Pennsylvania "bank" barn, so named because an earthwork "driveway" extended from the ground to the second floor. "Mr. Bliss was like many other farmers who give more attention to the architecture and pretentiousness of their barns than they do their houses," observed Charles Page of the 14th Connecticut. [1] Major John Hill of the 12th New Jersey later recalled that the barn "was a large building…It afforded a good shelter for sharpshooters. Any mounted officer riding along our lines was shot at continually." [2]

The Bliss house site (marker to the center of Bliss house shown above and inset) looking southeast toward the Union lines. Image courtesy of Steven Stanley; Image courtesy of James Hessler (inset)

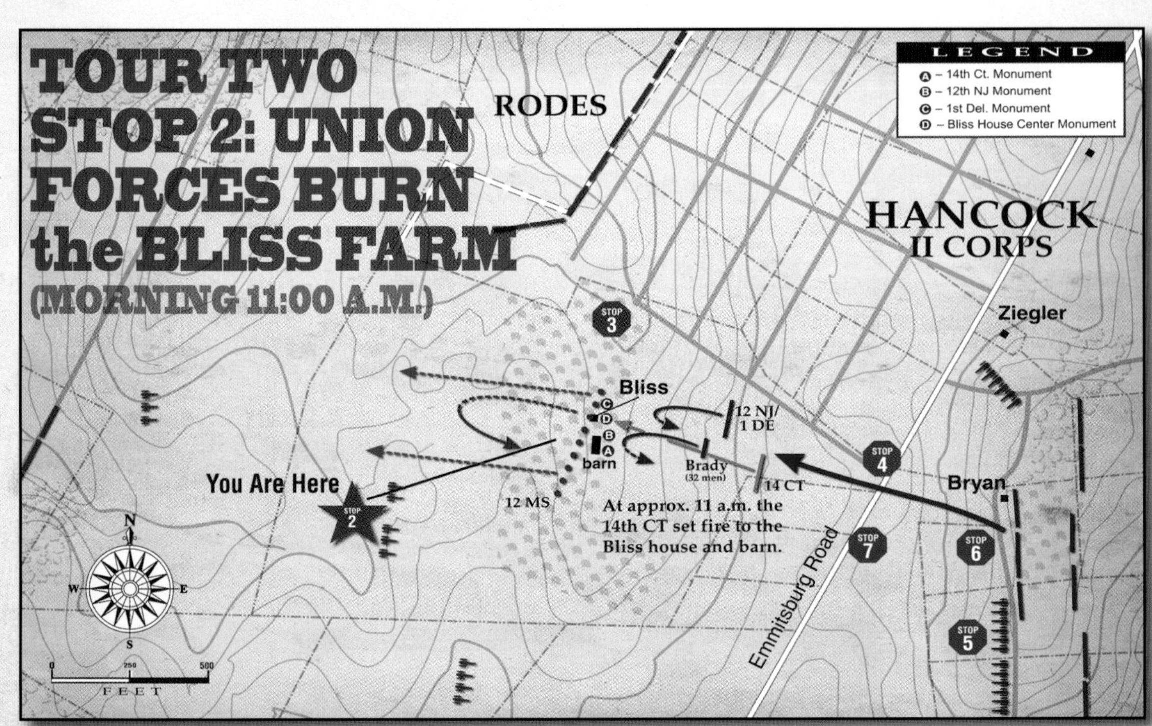

Elements of Alexander Hays's division of the Union II Corps and A. P. Hill's Confederate Third Corps fought for control of the property since the morning of July 2. During Longstreet's July 2 assault on the Union left flank, Brig. General Carnot Posey's Brigade failed to move beyond the Bliss farm, which helped to stall A. P. Hill's intended support of Longstreet's attack. [3]

General Posey's men held the farm in the early morning hours of July 3. They were "more pertinacious in their assault," wrote General Hays, and were inflicting casualties on Union skirmishers and artillerymen. A detachment of about 200 men from the 12th New Jersey were ordered to re-take the buildings. They chased Posey's men away before a spirited countercharge by more than 400 men of Col. Abner Perrin's Brigade drove the Yankees out.[4] The tensions also set off sporadic artillery fire from both sides. Finally, a detachment of 60 men from the 14th Connecticut captured the farm one more time. [5] Here they received new orders from General Hays: "About 11 a.m. an entire lull occurred, which was continued until nearly 2 p.m. Anticipating the movement of the enemy, I caused the house and barn in our front, which interrupted the fire of our artillery, to be burned."[6] Major Hill of the 12th New Jersey recalled Hays as saying, "that barn costs us too many men, it must be destroyed." [7]

If the Confederates had been able to exert better control of this area and the knoll to the east then it might have been more difficult for the Federals' 8th Ohio to advance beyond the Emmitsburg Road and outflank Pettigrew's left flank during the charge. [8]

Bliss Farm Monuments

(12th New Jersey, 14th Connecticut, & 1st Delaware)

GPS: 39°48'59.56"N, 77°14'30.96"W; Elev. 560 ft.

- Contrary to popular notion, not all Union monuments were placed on Cemetery Ridge where the army formed their main "line of battle." These smaller monuments at the Bliss farm commemorate their roles in the skirmishing on July 2 and July 3. On the morning of July 3, the 12th New Jersey briefly recaptured the farm from Confederate soldiers prior to the buildings being burned by the 14th Connecticut.

The 12th NJ Monument on the Bliss Farm. Image courtesy of Karl Stelly

- Many Union regiments have multiple monuments at Gettysburg. The 12th New Jersey, 14th Connecticut, and 1st Delaware all have larger monuments on North Hancock Avenue denoting their roles in the repulse of Pettigrew and Trimble's assault.
- The larger 12th New Jersey monument on North Hancock Avenue includes a bas-relief that is intended to visualize the regiment's activities at the Bliss barn.[9]
- The marker that notes the alleged "center of the house" is believed to be inaccurate. The large ditch nearby may have, in fact, been the remains of the house's cellar.[10]
- The large earthen mound near the 14th Connecticut is what remains of the ramp leading into the "bank barn."[11]
- When the veterans of the 12th New Jersey decided to erect a monument on the Bliss farm, the land was already owned by the veterans of the 14th Connecticut for their monument. The Connecticut veterans would not sell any portion of their land but instead agreed to allow their former comrades from New Jersey the right to place a monument on Connecticut's plot of land free of charge.[12]

A burnt barn beam from the Bliss farm with bullet embedded. Image photographed by Karl Stelly, image courtesy of Erik Dorr, Gettysburg Museum of History

The Bliss buildings would have still been smoldering several hours later when

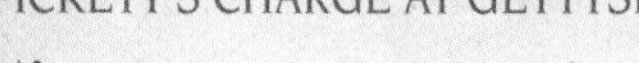

During the tenure of Camp Colt, located on Pickett's Charge field, the Bliss farm was used as a tank training grounds. Here a Renault tank is driving over the Bliss barn site. Image courtesy of GNMP

portions of Davis, Marshall, and Lane's brigades passed through here during the main assault on Cemetery Ridge. Yet, Confederate accounts curiously do not describe what should have been a memorable image. [13] Perhaps Southern perspectives were similar to those echoed by Major Hill of the 12th New Jersey. He wrote that once the assault began "we were kept too busy to pay any further attention to the barn." [14] The buildings did temporarily disrupt Marshall's Brigade alignment as the North Carolinians had to move around the structures and then redeploy in the low area east of the farm.

The left of Pettigrew's line was increasingly exposed to Federal artillery from Cemetery Hill and the northern extensions of Cemetery Ridge. Major Thomas Osborn, commanding the Union XI Corps Artillery Brigade wrote:

> The left of the charging column rested on a line perpendicular to our front, then stretching away to the right beyond our view, thus offering an excellent front for our artillery fire. We used, according to distance, all descriptions of projectiles. The whole force of our artillery was brought to bear upon this column, and the havoc produced upon their ranks was truly surprising.
>
> The enemy's advance was most splendid, and for a considerable distance the only hindrance offered it was by the artillery, which broke their lines fearfully, as every moment showed that their advance under this concentrated artillery fire was most difficult; and though they made desperate efforts to advance in good order, were unable to do so, and I am convinced that the fire from the hill was one of the main auxiliaries in breaking the force of this grand charge. [15]

"I moved forward to the support of Pettigrew's right," wrote Gen. James Lane, "through the woods in which our batteries were planted, and through an open field about a mile, in full view of the enemy's fortified position, and under a murderous artillery and infantry fire." [16] Straggling and walking wounded returning back to Seminary Ridge increased while in this vicinity but Pettigrew and Trimble's main line pressed forward.

Long Lane

GPS: 39°49'5.30"N, 77°14'25.52"W; Elev. 555 ft.

Note the modern housing and streets that are laid out roughly 200 yards northeast of the Bliss farm site. The street farthest to the west of the housing follows much (but not all) of the original Long Lane. The post and rail fence just behind (west of) these homes marks the original portion of Long Lane which ran onto the Bliss property. [1]

Colonel Brockenbrough's Brigade, which had already started the charge lagging behind the rest of Pettigrew's line, probably did not advance beyond Long Lane. [2] General Thomas, stationed in Long Lane, told General Lane on the following day that Brockenbrough "did not advance beyond the road." [3] Louis Young noted shortly afterward: "Under this fire from artillery and musketry, the brigade on our left, reduced almost to a line of skirmishers, gave way. Pettigrew's and Archer's brigades advanced a little further." [4]

Major John McLeod Turner of the 7th North Carolina, in Lane's Brigade, recalled that as soon as they had cleared their own artillery batteries: [5]

> We were met by crowds of stragglers coming to the rear, and in such numbers that I ordered my men to charge bayonets in order to compel them to go around the

The fence line running back to the modern homes follows Long Lane. Image courtesy of Karl Stelly

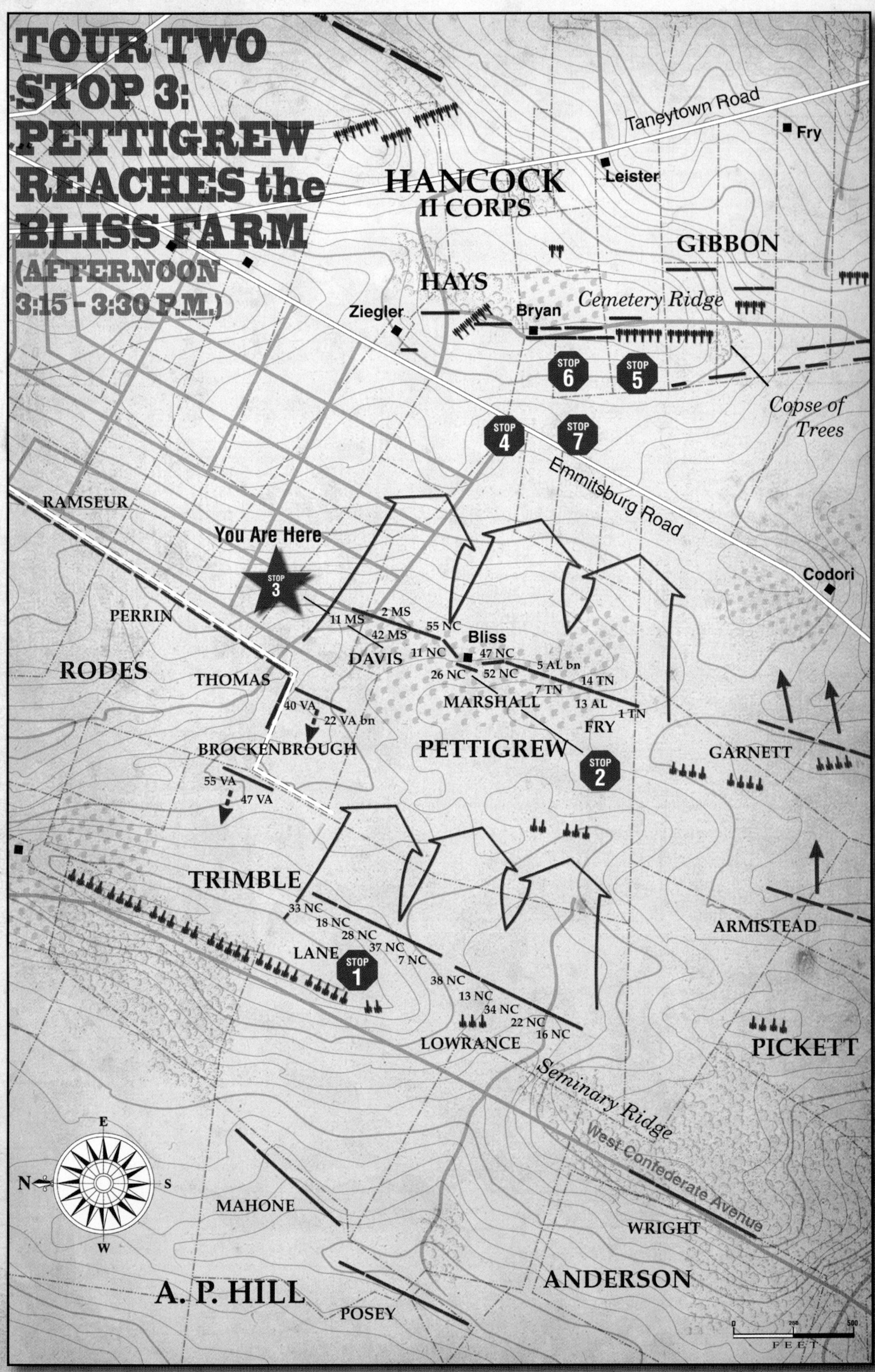

TOUR TWO
STOP 3:
PETTIGREW
REACHES the
BLISS FARM
(AFTERNOON
3:15 - 3:30 P.M.)
Taneytown Road
Fry
Leister
HANCOCK
II CORPS
GIBBON
HAYS
Cemetery Ridge
Ziegler
Bryan
STOP 6
STOP 5
Copse of Trees
STOP 4
STOP 7
Emmitsburg Road
RAMSEUR
You Are Here
STOP 3
Codori
PERRIN
11 MS
2 MS
42 MS
55 NC
Bliss
DAVIS
11 NC
47 NC
RODES
THOMAS
26 NC
52 NC
5 AL bn
14 TN
7 TN
MARSHALL
13 AL
1 TN
40 VA
22 VA bn
FRY
BROCKENBROUGH
PETTIGREW
STOP 2
GARNETT
55 VA
47 VA
TRIMBLE
33 NC
18 NC
28 NC
37 NC
7 NC
LANE
STOP 1
ARMISTEAD
38 NC
13 NC
34 NC
22 NC
16 NC
LOWRANCE
PICKETT
Seminary Ridge
West Confederate Avenue
E
N
S
W
MAHONE
WRIGHT
ANDERSON
A. P. HILL
POSEY
0
250
500
FEET

flanks of our regiment to prevent their breaking our line; these men were from Brockenbrough's Brigade.[6]

In some of the more fantastical eyewitness accounts written at Gettysburg, Col. W. S. Christian, commanding Brockenbrough's 55th Virginia, claimed: "We remained out in that field until all the troops on our right had fallen back. We saw that the whole attack had miscarried." Some unknown officer begged "us to stand firm" while efforts were made to renew the charge. "We stood there to be shot at, and that was about all that we did, and did not retire until after the retreat had become general." [7]

Colonel Robert Mayo, 47th Virginia, likewise wrote, "We succeeded however in holding the enemy in check until everything on our right had given way. Our brigade was the last to leave the field…after the flags of every other brigade had disappeared. We halted, at General Thomas's Brigade which during the entire fight, had occupied a position, about midway between our line and the enemy's, and waited to see if the Yankees would pursue us." [8]

While Pickett, Pettigrew, Trimble, Wilcox, and Lang's men crashed into Cemetery Ridge, portions of five additional brigades remained in Long Lane, roughly midway between the two armies. Half of Pender's Division (the brigades under Brig. General Edward L. Thomas and Col. Abner Perrin), along with portions of Robert Rodes's Division (the brigades of Brig. Generals Stephen Ramseur, Alfred Iverson, and George Doles as well as the 5th Alabama regiment) sat here in relative idleness. Some excuses may be made for Iverson's and Perrin's brigades, as both had been hurt on July 1, but several of these brigades still had as much potential strength as any in Heth's Division would have had that morning.

Confederate Strength Estimates In and Around Long Lane

Brigade	Engaged Strength	Estimated Casualties	Available?
Thomas	1,248	264	984
Perrin	1,882	647	1,235
Ramseur	1,027	275	752
Iverson	1,384	903	481
Doles	1,322	219	1,103
5th Alabama	317	209	108
Total	**7,180**	**2,517**	**4,663**

The above table is not intended to be an exhaustive study of the troop strength in Long Lane, but merely represents potential maximum power that may have been available to Lee and was ultimately not used. [9] General Rodes, for example, insisted that he had "not over 1,800 men" in position and we also know that the 5th Alabama was skirmishing in town before being moved to Long Lane. [10] But even deducting half of the strength in this table would still have left nearly 2,400 infantrymen halfway between Seminary and Cemetery Ridges.

Their intended roles are unclear. Were they to be reinforcements, part of General

Hill's orders to take advantage of any Confederate success? Were they supposed to remain behind as a reserve in case the assault met with disaster? Or were they forgotten, as one more example of the Confederate communication breakdowns that plagued Lee's army throughout the battle? "Logic dictates that they were held back because they were much closer to the objective and could advance faster than either Pickett's or Pettigrew's and Trimble's men," argued historian Richard Rollins in favor of the theory that these men were part of a so-called "second wave" intended to strike the Federal defenses immediately after Longstreet punched a hole in it. [11] Yet it must be noted that contemporary Confederate accounts, notably the official battle reports, are strikingly absent on this point.

General Thomas wrote almost nothing of his brigade's role in his miniscule report, commenting only that he was "directed to take position in the open field, about 300 yards in front of the enemy's line, on the right of General Ewell's corps. Here we remained until the night of July 3." [12] General Lane added in an 1877 newspaper account that Thomas could see "everything that was going on the left" from "his position in the road." [13]

Colonel Abner Perrin described more activity, but also failed to mention any intent to join Pettigrew's charge. "Early next morning (the 3d), the heaviest skirmishing I have ever witnessed was here kept up during the greater part of the day. The enemy made desperate efforts to recapture the position, on account of our skirmishers being within easy range of their artillerists on the Cemetery Hill, but we repulsed every assault, and held the position until ordered back to the main line at Gettysburg." [14] Charles Page of the 14th Connecticut did note that "flanking fire" from Thomas and Perrin's brigades "located in 'Long Lane'" harassed Union soldiers on the Bliss property prior to the barn's burning. [15]

Despite the fact that it was not mentioned in any reports, at least two accounts suggest Thomas's 35th Georgia may have played some role in the day's action. Their postwar regimental history alleged, "When the grand charge was made some brigade in its advance passed near Thomas' Brigade and seemed disposed to stop; but that it might have no excuse for halting, General Thomas ordered his brigade forward. The Thirty-Fifth being near him heard the command and led by Colonel McCulloch, participated in that ever memorable charge of Picket [sic] and Heth." Likewise, a captain's field diary claimed that Thomas joined Pettigrew in charging "the enemy's battery at 5 o'clock. They charged under one of the most galling fires that ever came from an enemy's line, but were repulsed and had to retreat under the same fire." [16]

General Robert Rodes, whose performance throughout the battle has been questioned by a number of historians, had two of his brigades (Daniel and O'Neal, with the exception of the 5th Alabama) detached to support the Southern offensive on Culp's Hill:

> This order [removal of Daniel and O'Neal] left me powerless to do more than hold my position, unless the enemy should be very much weakened in my front, for I had now remaining but a single thin line, composed of two small brigades, about the third of another, and one regiment (the 5th Alabama) of O'Neal's Brigade (in all, not over 1,800 men), facing what I believed then and now to be the most impregnable portion of the enemy's line of intrenchments.

The gallant men and officers of this line held their new position all day on July 3, under a sharp and incessant fire from the enemy's sharpshooters and an occasional artillery fire. The enemy made, during the day several ineffectual efforts, by advancing heavy lines of skirmishers, equal almost, if not fully, to my main line, and using their artillery, to dislodge them from their position.

On the 3d, my orders were general, and the same as those of the day before, and accordingly, when the heavy cannonade indicated that another attack was made from the right wing of our army, we were on the lookout for another favorable opportunity to co-operate. When the sound of musketry was heard, it became apparent that the enemy in our front was much excited. The favorable opportunity seemed to me close at hand. I sent word to Lieutenant-General Ewell by Major [H. A.] Whiting, of my staff, that in a few moments I should attack, and immediately had my handful of men, under Doles, Iverson, and Ramseur, prepared for the onset; but in less than five minutes after Major Whiting's departure, before the troops on my immediate right had made any advance or showed any preparation therefor, and just as the order forward was about to be given to my line, it was announced, and was apparent to me, that the attack had already failed. [17]

In the end, we do not know why these forces did not join in the great charge. The most logical answer is that they were opposed by a strong Union skirmish line. The removal of the wounded Pender, the momentary ascension to command by Lane, and his subsequent replacement by the newcomer Trimble may also have contributed to Thomas and Perrin's lack of inclusion.

Given that Rodes's men had seen heavy combat on July 1, were below the formidable heights of Cemetery Hill, were ordered to send two brigades over to Culp's Hill, and moved the 5th Alabama into town, it is plausible that Rodes simply was not counted on to play a major role on July 3. Perhaps, as Rodes wrote, he was given "general" orders to be "on the lookout for another favorable opportunity" which unfortunately for the Southerners was only fleeting.

Although the weight of evidence speaks poorly for a coordinated "second wave," General Hill was told to take advantage of any successes, Pickett's men would wonder why "the rest of the army did not come," General R. H. Anderson was about to move two more of his brigades forward until halted by Longstreet, and Lee complained of an overall lack of support. Certainly there are indications that Lee hoped for a stronger attack force than he was given and at the very least one may question why Thomas and Perrin's brigades did not immediately support Pettigrew's troublesome left flank. We will return to the question of reinforcements later, but from this point try to envision as many as 3,000 - 4,000 more infantrymen in the attack and ask yourself if it would have made any difference in the outcome.

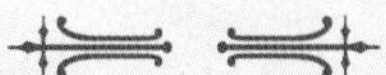

8th Ohio Regimental Monument

GPS: 39°48'57.78"N, 77°14'13.35"W; Elev. 587 ft.

Continue to walk toward the Emmitsburg Road which (depending on your current position) is roughly 400 yards from the Bliss site.

Longstreet's inability to protect his flanks reached a bloody climax along the front of the 8th Ohio Regiment.

The Buckeyes were part of Col. Samuel Carroll's First Brigade in Brig. General Alexander Hays's Third Division of the II Corps. Lieutenant Colonel Franklin Sawyer commanded the regiment at Gettysburg. During the late afternoon hours of July 2, the 8th Ohio was ordered to advance into the Emmitsburg Road, beyond the remainder of the division, in order to drive out "a nest of Rebels" who had taken position there and were harassing Hays's men. After accomplishing this mission, Colonel Sawyer said that his men took down much of the remaining fencing and strung it along the road as a makeshift barricade. The pickets and skirmishers then took positions "lying down several rods in front of the road where there was a slight ridge. The rest took to the road again."

The 8th Ohio regimental monument stands out amongst the colors of fall. The Bliss farm site is in the mid-background. Image courtesy of Michael Waricher

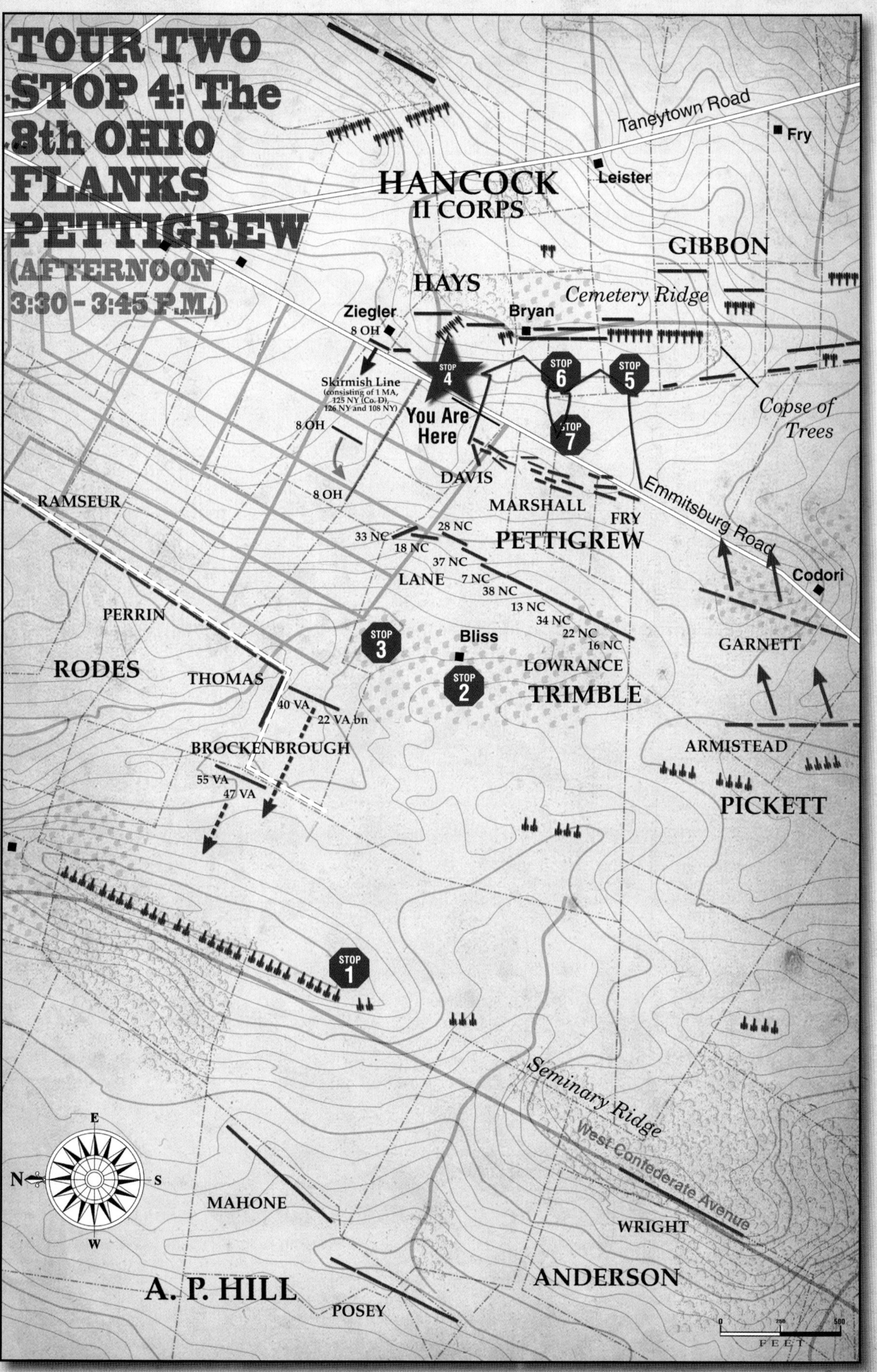
TOUR TWO
STOP 4: The 8th OHIO FLANKS PETTIGREW
(AFTERNOON 3:30 - 3:45 P.M.)
Taneytown Road
Fry
Leister
HANCOCK
II CORPS
GIBBON
HAYS
Cemetery Ridge
Ziegler
Bryan
8 OH
STOP 4
STOP 6
STOP 5
Skirmish Line
(consisting of 1 MA, 125 NY (Co. D), 126 NY and 108 NY)
You Are Here
8 OH
STOP 7
Copse of Trees
DAVIS
8 OH
RAMSEUR
MARSHALL
FRY
Emmitsburg Road
33 NC
28 NC
18 NC
PETTIGREW
37 NC
LANE
7 NC
38 NC
Codori
13 NC
34 NC
22 NC
16 NC
PERRIN
STOP 3
Bliss
GARNETT
RODES
THOMAS
STOP 2
LOWRANCE
TRIMBLE
40 VA
22 VA bn
BROCKENBROUGH
ARMISTEAD
55 VA
47 VA
PICKETT
STOP 1
Seminary Ridge
West Confederate Avenue
E
N
S
W
MAHONE
WRIGHT
ANDERSON
A. P. HILL
POSEY
0
250
500
FEET

The regiment then remained here that evening while the balance of Carroll's brigade was moved to support General Howard on East Cemetery Hill. "A gloomier night than was now experienced by us can scarcely be imagined," Sawyer recalled. "We were a good way in advance of our division, without any direct support." During the cannonade on the afternoon of the third, the 8th was then stuck between the batteries of these two great armies. "Fences, trees, and even buildings, are riddled and swept away by this storm of iron hail." [1]

"We found ourselves," Pvt. Thomas Galway wrote, "a single regiment of less than three hundred men, two hundred yards in front of the main Federal position. Seemingly a forlorn position for us but, as it turned out, destined to play an unexpectedly vital part" in the defense of Meade's army. [2]

William Tipton photo of Co. G & I, 4th Ohio monument with the Bryan barn and Ziegler's Grove tower in background. Image courtesy of GNMP

It is interesting to contemplate the extent to which Sawyer's men were exposed to fire from Confederates in the Long Lane vicinity. Sawyer recalled that near daylight on July 3, they noticed enemy activity "along a lane in [the regiment's] front" which caused a renewal of the day's skirmishing and continued up until about the time that the Bliss buildings were burned.[3] While Sawyer described a slight protective ridge to the 8th's front (something clearly not evident today due to the existing modern development) and his regiment would have also received some shelter from the sunken Emmitsburg Road, it is less clear as to what comparable terrain protection was available to the Southern skirmishers. Even after the 2003 demolition of the "Home Sweet Home Motel" on these grounds, it is obvious that decades of postwar development have had an adverse impact on battle interpretation in this area.

As noted previously, Colonel Brockenbrough's Brigade was on the left of Pettigrew's line and was either faltering or already in retreat. Sawyer described his movements in his report:

> I advanced my reserve to the picket front, and as the rebel line came within about 100 yards, we poured in a well-directed fire, which broke the rebel line, and it soon fled in the wildest confusion. Being relieved from this direction, I changed

> front forward on the left company, thus presenting our front to the left flank of the advancing rebel column. Our fire was poured into their flank with terrible effect for a few minutes before the Second Brigade at the battery opened, but almost instantly on the fire from the front, together with the concentrated fire from our batteries, the whole mass gave way, some fleeing to the front, some to the rear, and some through our lines, until the whole plain was covered with unarmed rebels, waving coats, hats, and handkerchiefs in token of a wish to surrender. [4]

Sawyer later elaborated that as Brockenbrough approached, most of the 8th Ohio joined the picket line and the Buckeyes then did a "left wheel…and formed facing the line of the rebel left flank, which was now seen passing between us and the Bliss premises." Sawyer said the initial Rebel fire was brisk and often terrific "mostly from unseen foes," a possible reference to enemy troops in Long Lane, "but our fire apparently caused Brockenbrough to draw off to his right, and we certainly drove out the skulking fellows who had first fired upon us. At all events there was now no way of retreat- we must take our chances where we stood- our blood was up, and the men loaded and fired and yelled and howled at the passing column." [5]

Private Thomas Galway recorded, "from the first it was easy to see the difference between the mettle of these men and those of Pickett's glorious column. Two or three times Pender's [Trimble's] line hesitated" as Federal artillery bursts "were now actually tearing their ranks to pieces…We so galled them with our fire that a panic soon took hold of them and they fled, back to the low ridge." [6]

As nearby Union artillery on the slopes of Cemetery Ridge joined Sawyer's regiment in pouring "a sheet of flame" into the faltering Confederates, the Yankees could hear shouts of "Close up!" ringing out from inside the growing dust clouds. "Above the turmoil of battle we could hear curses, shouts, shrieks, and could see hats, guns, legs, arms and mutilated carcasses hurled out [of the dust cloud] into the less murky atmosphere." Sawyer and his officers "watched this scene in utter amazement- not a word was spoken- we stood with bated breath." [7] On another occasion Sawyer described, "Arms, heads, blankets, guns, knapsacks were thrown and tossed into the clear air. Their track, as they advanced, was strewn with dead and wounded." [8]

Although some of Brockenbrough's officers left fanciful accounts suggesting that they actually reached the Federal lines, the evidence suggests they did not advance beyond the Bliss property. Captain Dunaway, Brockenbrough's Brigade adjutant, added: "I feel no shame in recording that out of this corner the men, without waiting for orders turned and fled, for the bravest soldiers cannot endure to be shot at simultaneously from front and side. They knew that to remain, or to advance, meant wholesale death and captivity." [9]

Once Colonel Brockenbrough's Brigade had been disposed of, the left flank of Davis's Brigade became Sawyer's next target as soon did Lane's Brigade in the rear line. Although the 8th Ohio has historically received the lion's share of accolades for raining lead on Pettigrew and Trimble's disintegrating left, they were assisted by portions of several other regiments and skirmishers, including the 108th and 126th New York, 1st

Massachusetts Sharpshooters, and Woodruff's battery.[10]

Combined with the fire that George Stannard's Vermont brigade was meanwhile pouring into Kemper's right flank on the other end of the field, the Federals had succeeded in catching both of Longstreet's flanks in a double envelopment. Defeat was officially in progress for Lee's Army of Northern Virginia.

"Almost as suddenly as the fray commenced- it slackened, ceased," said Colonel Sawyer. The dust clouds lifted and "the western slope of Cemetery Ridge for hundreds of yards was covered with the rebel dead and dying." The regiment was then nearly overwhelmed by more Rebels, this time being those "who came down upon us" to surrender. "We had no trouble with them – they took kindly to the situation." Sawyer initially reported bagging about 200 prisoners although he later inflated this number. He also reported 102 casualties but later added that an additional eight had been wounded. These 110 casualties on approximately 209 engaged would give the 8th Ohio a casualty rate in excess of 50%, a high but worthy price to pay for their role in stopping the assault. [11]

The 8th Ohio's regimental monument has the distinction of being the farthest forward (west of the Emmitsburg Road) of any Union regiment engaged in the July 3 defense. This was obviously a source of pride to Sawyer and his veterans. [12] The monument's position is generally considered inaccurate as a representation of where the regiment helped repulse Pettigrew's left. The monument states that the 8th "took this position" on July 2 and "held it" through Longstreet's July 3 assault. Sawyer stated at the monument dedication (September 1887) that the memorial is situated where they had placed the

regimental "headquarters" on the afternoon of July 2 after capturing the road but the fighting afterwards "was considerably in advance and to the west of this point." [13]

Others have argued that the monument should actually be several hundred feet north of the present site. Colonel Carroll stated in his report that the 8th Ohio had relieved several companies of the 4th Ohio from skirmish duty on July 2. The 4th Ohio's often overlooked monument, with the inevitable "advanced to this position" inscription, is approximately 340 feet northeast of the 8th Ohio monument, albeit on the opposite (east) side of the Emmitsburg Road.

Several of the veterans contended there was a deep cut in the Emmitsburg Road about 500 feet north of the 8th's monument and that this point approximated the regiment's center. Colonel Carroll's report also stated that the brigade's line on July 2 was between Woodruff's battery on the left and the Taneytown Road on the right which would also be inconsistent with the monument's current position. [14] A site 500 feet north of the present monument would roughly place the regimental center between the current and long-standing "General Pickett's Buffet" restaurant and the neighboring establishment on modern Steinwehr Avenue. The precise location of the 8th Ohio may seem trivial to casual observers, but understanding their correct position allows for a better understanding of the length of Pettigrew and Trimble's battle lines and a greater appreciation of the true scope of this attack.

Confederates from Pettigrew and Trimble's divisions moved from right (west) to left (east) in the mid distance toward waiting Union forces along Cemetery Ridge on the left. Image courtesy of Michael Waricher

Colonel Sawyer survived the war and was later awarded a brevet promotion to brigadier general before dying in 1892. His reputation was slightly sullied when Carroll filed a drunkenness charge (not altogether uncommon in the Civil War) against him following the New York City draft riots. [15] This perception must have stuck to Sawyer, because historian John Bachelder remarked at an 1885 reunion, "Col. Sawyer was reeling drunk and did not know where he was." Sawyer hotly denied the charge, telling Bachelder in reply: "As for being drunk the charge is wholly untrue. I [drank] no liquor nor do I believe ate a mouthful while we were at that point, and I must say Colonel that I think you did me a great wrong in making the charge." [16] Likewise, the Army of the Potomac's II Corps historian Francis Walker wrote: "So audacious was the action of this regiment as to give rise to an absurd report among those who witnessed it, but did not know the 8th Ohio, that its commander was intoxicated." Those who knew the regiment, however, appreciated "this was the very sort of thing" that they were likely to do in such an emergency. [17]

26th North Carolina Regimental Monument

GPS: 39°48'48.82"N, 77°14'8.29"W; Elev. 600 ft.

After carefully crossing the Emmitsburg Road, you can imagine the relentless fire that awaited the remaining Confederate soldiers from Union troops on their left and from the stone wall roughly 200 yards to their front. A modern monument to the 26th North Carolina sits just on our side of the farthest stone wall near an area sometimes referred to as the "Inner Angle."

The monument to the 26th North Carolina was placed here in 1986 and represents the farthest point reached by the regiment, and by extension Pettigrew's Division, during the assault. However, the monument is most likely inaccurately located. The North Carolinians probably crashed into the stone wall about 200 yards farther north, nearer the Bryan farm and opposite the 12th New Jersey's monument. That vicinity would be more consistent with their flag's capture by the New Jersey troops and also by the 26th's position on Marshall's left center. The 26th's monument location is probably due to a popular misconception that Arnold's battery hit the remnants of the 26th during the close of fighting. The case has been made convincingly that the 26th could easily have been confused in the chaos with the 16th North Carolina regiment who was posted on the right of Lowrance's Brigade line. [1] Symbolically, this monument helps define the postwar debate over which state -- North Carolina or Virginia -- advanced the farthest during the charge. Did Virginia deserve the credit for Armistead's breaking through the Union defenses? Or

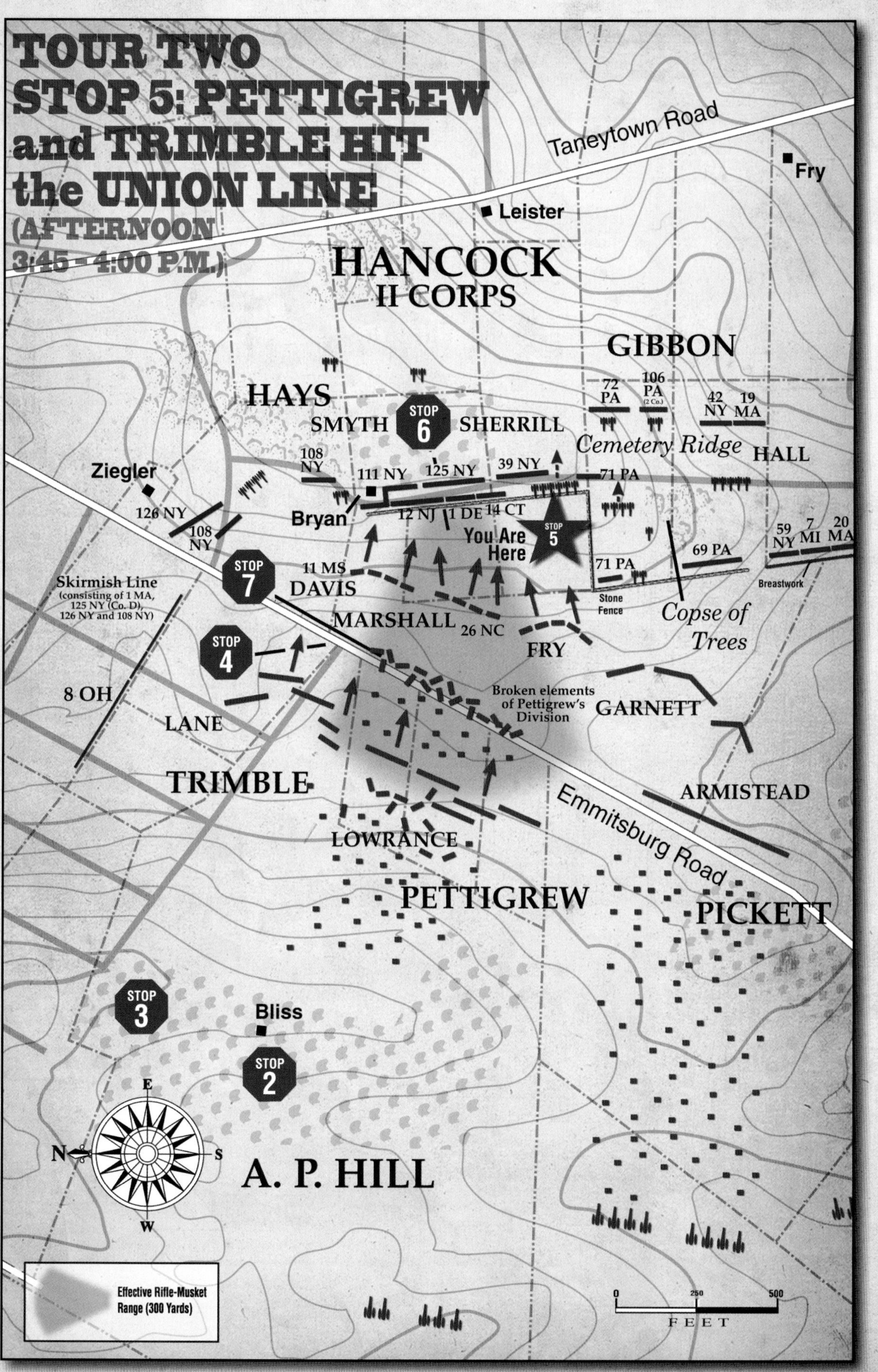
TOUR TWO
STOP 5: PETTIGREW and TRIMBLE HIT the UNION LINE
(AFTERNOON 3:45 - 4:00 P.M.)
Taneytown Road
Fry
Leister
HANCOCK
II CORPS
GIBBON
HAYS
SMYTH
STOP 6
SHERRILL
72 PA
106 PA (2 Co.)
42 NY
19 MA
Cemetery Ridge
HALL
108 NY
111 NY
125 NY
39 NY
71 PA
Ziegler
126 NY
108 NY
Bryan
12 NJ
1 DE
14 CT
You Are Here
STOP 5
59 NY
7 MI
20 MA
69 PA
71 PA
11 MS
DAVIS
STOP 7
Skirmish Line (consisting of 1 MA, 125 NY (Co. D), 126 NY and 108 NY)
Breastwork
Stone Fence
Copse of Trees
MARSHALL
26 NC
FRY
STOP 4
8 OH
Broken elements of Pettigrew's Division
GARNETT
LANE
TRIMBLE
ARMISTEAD
Emmitsburg Road
LOWRANCE
PETTIGREW
PICKETT
STOP 3
Bliss
STOP 2
E
N
S
W
A. P. HILL
Effective Rifle-Musket Range (300 Yards)
0
250
500
FEET

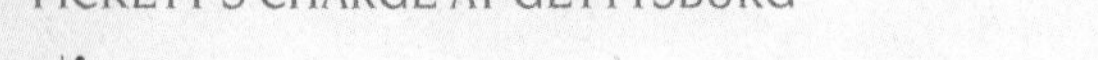

The 26th North Carolina advance marker for July 3. Image courtesy of Michael Waricher

did Pettigrew's men warrant more praise for advancing further up Cemetery Ridge? In any event, the 26th sacrificed more than 600 men in total casualties at Gettysburg. [2]

Pettigrew and Trimble's commands were brutalized by a heavy fire of musketry and canister as they approached and attempted to cross the Emmitsburg Road. The terrain was particularly cruel to Pettigrew and Trimble. Not only were they marching straight into artillery fire, but the northeast axis of the Emmitsburg Road meant that they had to cross the road at ranges of 150-250 yards from the Union lines. This was at shorter distances than which Pickett's men crossed and easily within the effective range of Yankee gunfire. It was miraculous that any of these soldiers succeeded.

Brockenbrough's Brigade had already retired and Davis's Brigade was likewise struggling from Yankee fire into their fearfully exposed left. Davis's troops were also pounded with double shots of canister from Lt. George Woodruff's 1st U.S. Artillery, Battery I, located north of the Bryan farm near Ziegler's Grove. Lieutenant Tully McCrea of the battery's right section recalled that each gun had "forty rounds of canister" and Davis's men "got the most of it." Yet some of Davis's boys still managed to reach the Bryan barn before either being shot down or forced to surrender. General Davis, however, managed to personally escape unscathed while every other field officer in the brigade was either killed, wounded, or captured. Davis reported that there "was nothing left but to retire to the position originally held, which was done in more or less confusion." [3]

Colonel James Marshall remarked to a nearby officer, "We do not know which of us will be the next to fall," and was instantly killed by two bullets to the forehead. Marshall

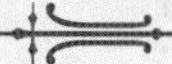

was one of only three Confederate brigade commanders to lose his life in the attack, yet he has escaped much of the historical spotlight that has shown on Pickett's generals Garnett and Armistead. Pettigrew's staffer Louis G. Young said that "no danger or difficulty seemed to him too formidable" and at Gettysburg "he manifested skill and dashing bravery. Great is the country's loss when such are taken from it." Marshall's burial location is unknown. [4]

On Pettigrew's far right, Lt. Colonel S. G. Shepard, in Archer's 7th Tennessee, wrote, "The enemy held their fire until we were in fine range, and opened upon us a terrible and well-directed fire. Within 180 or 200 yards of his works, we came to a lane enclosed by two stout post and plank fences. This was a very great obstruction to us, but the men rushed over as rapidly as they could…" Shepard observed the enemy's "first line of which was composed of rough stones," an apparent reference to the stones that ran north of the Copse of Trees. The Federals seemingly abandoned this line, "but just in rear was massed a heavy force." By the time they reached "this work", Shepard's own lines "had become very much weakened; indeed, the line both right and left, as far as I could observe, seemed to melt away until there was but little of it left." [5]

Col. James Marshall.
Image courtesty of the Virginia Military Institute Archives

Colonel Birkett Fry, commanding Archer's Brigade, suffered a thigh wound as he approached the wall. Fry was so confident of victory that he still urged his men forward. "Go on; it will not last five minutes longer!" His men disappeared into the dense smoke that now enveloped the field. Over the roar of gunfire, Fry heard Pettigrew calling to "rally them on the left… At length the firing ceased, and cheer after cheer from the enemy announced the failure of our attack." [6]

If Pettigrew's men made it this far in relatively large numbers and in something still resembling formations, the same was probably not true for Trimble's two battered brigades. Trimble later admitted:

> We marched 3/4 mile under a terrible fire passed the first line & reached a point some 200 yards from the breast works – here the men broke down from exhaustion & the fatal fire & went no further but walked sullenly back to their entrenchments. It was a mistake to charge batteries & lines over so great a distance every yard exposed to a hot fire. [7]

Trimble later elaborated that upon reaching the Emmitsburg Road "men in squads were falling back on the west side of the Emmitsburg Road. By this I inferred that Pickett's Division had been repulsed, and if so that it would be a useless sacrifice of life to continue the contest. I, therefore, did not attempt to rally the men who began to give back from the fence." [8]

Pettigrew staffer Louis Young bluntly recalled: "The supports under Maj. General Trimble did not reach as far as we had." [9] Major McLeod Turner, in the 7th North Carolina, admitted that his men struggled to bypass the Emmitsburg Road fences. Turner and some men passed through the fence on the right of his line, but after he was shot down about ten yards beyond the road, his men "returned to and laid down in the Pike, as did the entire regiment." [10]

Some participants maintained that portions of Trimble's command successfully advanced beyond the Emmitsburg Road. Lieutenant Colonel Jos. Saunders of the 33rd North Carolina was among those who insisted "we overtook the first line (Pettigrew's) and the two lines then became one and the advance was continued." Lieutenant Thomas Molloy of the 7th North Carolina added that his regiment reached the road as "an organized body. About half of the men and most of the officers crossed this fence, and some of them I think reached the works." [11]

General Lane, who by this point had moved his men forward in a futile attempt to protect Pettigrew's left, reported that they "advanced to within a few yards of the stone wall, exposed all the while to a heavy raking artillery fire from the right. My left was here very much exposed, and a column of the enemy's infantry was thrown forward in that direction, which enfiladed my whole line. This forced me to withdraw my brigade, the troops on my right having already done so." Under Trimble's direction they reformed behind the Confederate artillery. [12]

Feisty old General Trimble, who had spent much of the campaign looking for his opportunity to fight the hated Yankees, suffered a leg wound which necessitated amputation.

The Bryan farm where the left of Pettigrew's Division reached on July 3.
Image courtesy of Michael Waricher

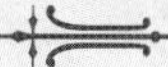

Fearing the effects that travel might have on him, he was left behind when Lee's army retreated from Gettysburg. Trimble was medically treated at several locations, including the Lutheran Seminary field hospital, before becoming a prisoner of war. [13]

Captain James Harris in Lane's 7th North Carolina wrote, "To remain and be captured, or run the gauntlet of the enemy's batteries and escape, was our only alternative and the latter, (the bravest act of the day), was resorted to, every man going to the rear as fast as his well-nigh exhausted nature would admit." [14]

The loss of flags on a Civil War battlefield was typically viewed as a disgrace to the surrendering regiment. However, a theory has been proposed that the opposite should be true in an assault such as this. The capture of one's colors meant that the regiment advanced close enough to the Union lines to be unable to save their flags. Based on this measure, Pettigrew's Division performed well on July 3. Pettigrew's men lost nine flags to regiments that were generally to their front, while another was lost to an unidentified Union conqueror, and only three (the 2nd Mississippi, 11th North Carolina, and 7th Tennessee) were saved. In contrast, only five of Trimble's 10 flags are confirmed to have been captured, a lower ratio than either Pickett or Pettigrew's flags, again suggesting that Trimble's men did not approach the enemy's works as nearly as the others. [15]

FARTHEST TO THE FRONT AT GETTYSBURG

General George Pickett and Virginia's reputation will always benefit from his men being the only semi-organized body of troops to breach the Union works. If only other Southern troops had performed as well, many argued, then surely Lee would have been victorious on July 3. Captain Robert Bright of Pickett's staff was a token example of this approach when he complained about "our left being exposed by the retreat of Pettigrew's command" after Pettigrew "broke all to pieces" and abandoned the field in great disorder. [1]

Eppa Hunton survived his tenure in Pickett's Division and served several postwar terms in the United States Congress and Senate. Hunton wrote in his memoirs:

> The North Carolinians maintain that their division also reached the line of the enemy, but from the evidence on the subject that is a mistake. The North Carolinians were very brave and heroic in the war, and I would not derogate from their bravery for any consideration, but still it is a truth of history that they gave way before Pickett's men got to the enemy's lines, and left Pickett's three depleted brigades entirely without support. Before I was wounded and left the field, I saw that the North Carolina division under Pettigrew was disintegrating, and there is no question at all, in my mind, that these North Carolinians never reached the enemy's line. [2]

It must be noted that such scorn was not always from partisan Virginians. General Ambrose Wright was a Georgian in Hill's Third Corps who had no state loyalty to the Old Dominion or organizational allegiance to Longstreet's First Corps. His men had come close to Cemetery Ridge on the prior day but were unable to hold their position without support. Wright observed: "On the left Pettigrew's line wavers- it pauses- all is lost- it falls back- it runs. Some of the officers attempt to rally their men, but a great many are scampering away in front of their men; helter skelter, pell-mell, here they come." [3]

Correspondents and early biographers also contributed greatly to fanning the sectional flames. Among the earliest, correspondent Jonathan Albertson wrote in the July 23 Richmond *Enquirer* that in contrast to Pickett's "splendid division," Pettigrew's lacked the "the firmness of nerve, and steadiness of tread which so characterized Pickett's men." While Pickett's "brave Virginians" planted "their banner[s] in the enemy's works," Pettigrew's were "all over the plain, in utmost confusion…Their line is broken; they are flying apparently panic stricken to the rear." [4]

This common theme would be consistently repeated elsewhere. Edward Pollard, editor of the Richmond *Examiner*, published several Southern-based war histories. In Pollard's *The Second Year of the War* (published in 1864), Pickett's Virginians were in the "advance" and carried the enemy's works but Pettigrew "faltered, and that gallant commander in vain strove to rally the raw troops." [5] In Pollard's 1867 work, appropriately titled *The Lost Cause*, Lee witnessed the North Carolinians fall "back in confusion, exposing Pickett's Division to attack both from front and flank. The courage of Virginians could do no more. Overwhelmed, almost destitute of officers, and nearly surrounded, the magnificent troops of Pickett gave way." [6]

Such imagery was not limited to Southern pens. Northern historian William Swinton's influential *Campaigns of the Army of the Potomac* made similar accusations against Pettigrew, while "Pickett's Division remained alone a solid lance-head of Virginia troops, tempered in the fire of battle." [7] When General Pickett died in 1875, the New York *Times* produced an error-filled obituary where his Virginians were "unsupported in the advantage gained, for General Pettigrew's line had been broken, and his men were flying panic stricken to the rear."[8]

Following Robert E. Lee's death in 1870, the efforts of several prominent Virginians (led by former General Jubal Early) popularized the *Southern Historical Society Papers* as a forum to re-fight battles such as Gettysburg. Although best remembered for their efforts to perpetuate the so-called "Lost Cause" and portray Lee as a nearly-peerless battlefield warrior and Christian, as a byproduct the Virginians had a venue to publish their often highly biased reminiscences. Pickett and his men were often notably absent as contributors during the peak 1870s and 1880s, but Lee's old staff (many of whom publicly held Longstreet responsible for the defeat) enthusiastically participated. Walter Taylor created a stir, but reflected the prevailing sentiments, when he wrote in 1877:

The assaulting column really consisted of Pickett's division…while Heth's division

> moved forward on Pickett's left in echelon, or with the alignment so imperfect and so drooping on the left as to appear in echelon, with Lane's and Scales' brigades in rear of its right…It is needless to say a word here of the heroic conduct of Pickett's division; that charge has already passed into history as "one of the world's great deeds of arms." While, doubtless, many brave men of other commands reached the crest of the height, this was the only organized body that entered the works of the enemy. Much can be said in excuse for the failure of the other commands to fulfill the task assigned them. [9]

In contrast, Pettigrew and Trimble's aging survivors were less successful in coordinating their efforts. While Virginia-based historians essentially ignored the fact that Pettigrew's faltering began with his only Virginia brigade, Brockenbrough's, this was not lost on the Tar Heels. Captain Benjamin Little, 52nd North Carolina: "Even if some brigade to our left did give way under a pressure that could not be resisted, or otherwise, it was not a brigade of North Carolinians." [10] William McLaurin of Lane's Brigade observed, "the shafts of distraction were hurled at" Pettigrew's men on account of Brockenbrough. Lieutenant Colonel John T. Jones of the 26th North Carolina argued that Pettigrew would have held their works if Brockenbrough had not given way. [11]

One of North Carolina's most enthusiastic defenders was former staff officer William R. Bond. In 1888, Bond wrote (with subsequently revised and expanded editions) an angry tome entitled, *Pickett or Pettigrew?* Bond railed on what was already being popularly called "Pickett's Charge" and set out to right "the trash which passes for Southern history." Bond challenged the popular image of heroic fighting by Armistead's men inside the Angle as nothing more than a myth. It "is no exaggeration to say that they [Pickett's Virginians] did not kill twenty of the enemy at Gettysburg." To have Pickett's Virginians imply cowardice upon any other state was the equivalent of "a lion barked at by a cur." [12]

North Carolina did not form their own literary and historical society until 1900 (with William Bond as an active member.) By 1904 they had adopted the unofficial motto: "First at Bethel, Farthest to the front at Gettysburg and Chickamauga, Last at Appomattox." [13]

Southern literature continued to champion the "Lost Cause," of which "Pickett's Charge" was now inexorably entangled, long after the warriors were gone. Most notably, William Faulkner's 1948 novel *Intruder in the Dust* declared, "For every Southern boy fourteen years old…there is the instant when it's still not yet two o'clock on that July afternoon in 1863." Faulkner's George Pickett "with his long oiled ringlets…[is] looking up the hill waiting for Longstreet to give the word and it's all in the balance, it hasn't happened yet, it hasn't even begun yet…This time. Maybe this time with all this much to lose." Generals Garnett, Kemper, Armistead, and even Wilcox were there too for Faulkner…but no Pettigrew or Trimble. [14]

William Faulkner's South largely does not exist anymore and increasing generations of battlefield students come to Gettysburg having never read *Intruder* but are instead schooled on Ken Burns, *The Killer Angels*, and the motion picture *Gettysburg*. Save for an outburst or two by Trimble and Pettigrew, those stories also belong to dashing and fiery Virginians

such as Pickett, Kemper, and Armistead. While not always historically accurate, Virginia has defeated North Carolina in popular media to an extent in which they could never defeat the Yankees.

Virginia's victories in the court of popular imagination are further secured on the battlefield itself. The well-preserved ground over which Pickett's brigades marched stands in contrast to the modern development that has obliterated much of Pettigrew and Trimble's assault. Thanks to the efforts of early historians such as John Bachelder and Paul Philippoteaux's Cyclorama painting, the Angle and the High Water Mark have all cemented the charge as being "Pickett's Charge" from an interpretative perspective. Battlefield visitors not only cannot help but view the charge from Pickett's viewpoint, they almost have no choice.

However, both North Carolina and Mississippi have scored modest counterstrikes on the battlefield as modern scholars attempt to present a more balanced perspective with the "Pickett-Pettigrew-Trimble Charge." The Inner Angle wall which Pettigrew and Trimble nearly, but failed to, penetrate is approximately 80 yards east of the Angle which Armistead crossed, giving visitors the impression that Pettigrew had to cross a greater distance than did Pickett. (In reality, most of the commands had to cover approximately 1,200 yards, plus or minus, with Kemper having crossed the greatest distance at about 1,500 yards.) Advance markers placed to the 26th North Carolina (1986) and 11th Mississippi (2000) are also 25-30 yards farther east of Armistead's mortal wounding memorial. These monuments now give supporters from three states the opportunity to boast of their accomplishments: Virginia may have broken the Union lines, but North Carolina and Mississippi visibly advanced "farther."[15]

To many modern historians, unburdened by the sectional rivalries of 1863, the question over who was "farthest at Gettysburg" is essentially meaningless. Louis Young fought under Pettigrew and appreciated the dangers that all of the commands shared:

> This repulse, to judge from results, was fatal to our campaign in Pennsylvania, and the troops engaged in the charge of the 3d July are blameable for having retired without orders; but you will perceive that they had to pass through a most trying ordeal, and it must remain always a sealed question, whether or not Cemetery Hill could have been taken with the forces engaged. [16]

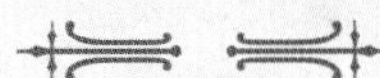

11th Mississippi Advance Monument

STOP 6

GPS: 39°48'55.10"N, 77°14'7.82"W; Elev. 600 ft.

Approximately 215 yards north of the 26th North Carolina monument you will find an advance marker to the 11th Mississippi infantry.

There are two monuments to the 11th Mississippi: one on West Confederate Avenue, and the second one here to commemorate their repulse near the Bryan farm. Both were dedicated in the year 2000 by the 11th Mississippi Memorial Association.

This memorial is unique, along with the 26th North Carolina's advance marker and General Armistead's mortal wounding monument, in denoting an advance position reached by Confederates during the charge. A supporter of the 11th Mississippi had unsuccessfully attempted to get such a position marked as early as 1939, but was rebuffed by National Park Service officials who reasoned that such monuments would both deviate from the long-standing policy of focusing on main lines of battle and would also serve as a precedent for other regiments' supporters to "confuse rather than clarify" visitor interpretation. [1]

The 11th Mississippi was on the extreme left of General Davis's Brigade and would have been severely punished by Union flanking fire after Brockenbrough's Virginia brigade fled the field. Company A famously included students from the University of Mississippi

A collection of buttons (right) retrieved near the Bryan barn (above). Barn image courtesy of Steven Stanley. Buttons image photographed by Karl Stelly; image courtesy of Erik Dorr, Gettysburg Museum of History

A drawing showing local farmer Fred Pfeffer unearthing a grave of Mississippi soldiers in 1887.
Image photographed by Karl Stelly, image courtesy of Erik Dorr, Gettysburg Museum of History

known as "The University Greys" and suffered 100% casualties in killed and wounded on July 3. Veteran Baxter McFarland wrote postwar that the entire regiment's official casualty returns of 32 killed and 170 wounded were understated. True losses, including those ascertained to be killed or wounded later, were tallied by McFarland as 103 killed and 207 wounded/captured for a total of 310 out of 350 engaged. [2]

Some of Davis's Brigade reached the Bryan barn. Portions of the 11th Mississippi were amongst those captured on the west side of the structure, and there is evidence that some Confederates may even have been north of the barn before being overwhelmed by the Yankees. [3]

While working these fields in May 1887, local farmer Frederick Pfeffer uncovered the remains of seven soldiers "who probably fell in the front of Pettigrew's division" on the east side of the Emmitsburg Road and near the 12th New Jersey monument. According to news accounts, Pfeffer also recovered about 50 bullets along with some Mississippi buttons. The bones were reported to have been reburied. [4]

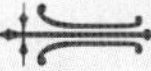

EXPECTED TO BE A BLOODY CONTEST

Confederate Capt. William Thomas Magruder was the assistant adjutant general to Brig. General Joseph Davis at Gettysburg.

Magruder was born in 1825 in Upper Marlboro, Maryland. He was accepted to West Point from his home state and graduated in 1850. Young Lieutenant Magruder then served 11 years out west fighting Indians (killing at least "one with his own hands") in then-remote locations such as Minnesota, Kansas, New Mexico, and California. [1]

Capt. William T. Magruder.
Image courtesy of William T. Magruder Family Archives

Magruder was a captain in the U.S. Army when the Civil War erupted. He served in the Virginia Peninsular Campaign, not as a Confederate but as a member of the Army of the Potomac. Magruder was, in fact, active in the Northern army for nearly the first 15 months of the war. In August 1862, however, he took a leave of absence and resigned his U.S. Army commission on October 1. Magruder reported for duty in the Southern army in November 1862, although his rank on Davis's staff was not confirmed until May 1863. Magruder was the last U.S. Army officer and West Point graduate to resign and join the Confederacy. [2]

Captain Magruder carried a field diary to Gettysburg. On July 3, he recorded "heavy cannonading commenced at daylight" and continued his entries up until the early afternoon:

> Major Genl [sic] Pickett is to charge the enemy batteries on the heights south of Gettysburg, supported by Heth's division. It is expected to be a bloody contest [.] God, Liberty + the Independence of the South.

Before entering into the assault against his former comrades in the Army of the Potomac, Magruder made a plea to

FRIDAY, JULY 3, 1863.

Capt. Magruder's pocket watch and his diary entry for July 3.
Images courtesy of William T. Magruder Family Archives

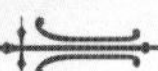

"take care of my wife and child should I fall," but his last recorded words were, "This is to be a terrible blow for the redemption of my native land- Maryland." [3]

As the remnants of Pettigrew's assault crossed the Emmitsburg Road and stalled under the Federal fire, Magruder called out, "Men, remember your mothers, wives, and sisters at home and do not halt here!" Some of the men took Magruder's encouragement and continued forward, but the captain himself was fatally struck in the shoulder while east of the road. [4]

Captain W. D. Nunn of the 11th Mississippi was a friend of Magruder's and was also wounded nearby. He crawled over to Magruder, whose last thoughts were of his wife and child and asked Nunn to notify them of his fate. Magruder gave Nunn several personal belongings, including his diary, coat, and watch. Nunn died in a field hospital on July 13 but succeeded in getting Magruder's belongings to his family, although the handsome timepiece temporarily went missing following Nunn's death as the widow Mary Magruder had to advertise in the newspaper for the watch's safe return. It was also reported afterwards that Mrs. Magruder "never ceased to do all in her power" to send supplies and comfort to Southern prisoners of war at Fort Delaware. [5]

Captain Magruder's final resting place is unknown.

A rare 1866 painting by artist George Leo Frankenstein looking north on the Emmistburg Road from near the Codori farm. On the far left of the image is the David Ziegler farm (white), then the Bryan tenant house (red), and on the far right the Bryan barn (white). Image courtesy of the Special Collections, Musselman Library, Gettysburg College

Camp Colt and Other Developments

GPS: 39°48'53.46"N, 77°14'15.06"W; Elev. 585 ft.

Re-tracing your steps approximately 185 yards from the 11th Mississippi monument back toward the Emmitsburg Road, you will find a lone tree that was planted to commemorate Camp Colt which once stood in this vicinity.

Long after Gettysburg's guns fell silent, the fields of the July 3 attack were converted into use for a variety of government and agricultural purposes. Our current generation of Civil War devotees, what some have dubbed as "heritage" enthusiasts, strive to preserve battlefields in conditions as near their wartime appearance as possible. Historically, this was not always the case as each generation has established their own definitions of appropriate remembrance.[1] Numerous terrain changes have encroached on the field and each modification has increasingly altered our ability to interpret this battle. Nowhere is this more evident than on Pettigrew's left flank and in the area defended by General Hays's Union division, now the scene of mid-twentieth century housing and fast food restaurants.

Structures that stood near this site such as the Abraham Bryan tenant house and the David Ziegler farm are long gone, as is the original woodlot known as Ziegler's Grove. The current Long Lane only partially follows its wartime trace. In the late 1860s, a horse track was built west of Long Lane, altering the terrain on the left of Pender's Division. [2]

Post Civil War intrusions on the fields of Pickett's Charge as viewed from the Pennsylvania State Monument. Image courtesy of GNMP

In 1913, the "Great Camp" covered much of the area west of the Codori farm and between Long Lane and the Bliss farm. This camp was created to temporarily house the estimated 50,000 or so veterans who attended the battle's 50th anniversary celebration. The fields of "Pickett's Charge" have also been home to the Gettysburg Electric Trolley, which existed from 1893 to 1916, and the Harrisburg and Reading Railroad line.

In 1917, the U.S. Army established a training camp on these grounds. The site was

A World War II P.O.W. camp was located on the fields of Pickett's Charge during 1944. Image courtesy of GNMP

dubbed Camp Colt in 1918 to train the fledgling Tank Corps during World War I. A young Capt. Dwight D. Eisenhower commanded Camp Colt. The camp stayed in service until dismantled in 1919. You can read a wayside exhibit on the west side of the Emmitsburg Road near the 8th Ohio monument. The post-World War II housing development that still stands west of the Emmitsburg Road, "Colt Park," was named for Camp Colt. The housing makes it impossible to visualize the thousands of armed combatants who once fought on this ground. The grading that comes along with such development makes it nearly impossible to re-create the knolls and ravines that once existed here.

In 1944, a German POW camp was built along the west side of the Emmitsburg Rood, just south of Long Lane and the old Home Sweet Home Motel. The main body of prisoners arrived in June 1944 and were put to "critical" work as civilian laborers on farms and in packing plants due to local manpower shortages. They earned $1.00 per hour (with $0.10/hour credited to their personal accounts and the remainder to the U.S. Government to pay for food and housing). Two escapees created a stir when they used a tube under the Emmitsburg Road to escape on July 5. This camp is sometimes erroneously referred to as "Camp Sharpe," a

The battle's 50th anniversary "Great Camp" as shown in this map (left) and panoramic view (below). Map image courtesy of GNMP; panoramic image courtesy of LOC

series of more permanent POW structures that were erected near Pitzer's Woods on West Confederate Avenue. The tent encampment along the Emmitsburg Road was primarily moved to Camp Sharpe in November 1944 "following the close of fruit and vegetable season." At its peak, Gettysburg housed at least 400 German prisoners of war. [3]

Not only are we unable to view much of the terrain across which Pettigrew, Trimble, and Hays's men fought and died, but these changes helped perpetuate a more "Pickett-centric" view of the charge which subliminally encourages visitors to focus on the Virginia monument, the Angle, and the Copse of Trees. Although this view shed has been improved by the 2003 demolition of the Home Sweet Home Motel from the field next to the 8th Ohio monument, a clearer view of the Pettigrew-Trimble ground would give us a much better appreciation for the size and scale of Lee's July 3 assault.

The Home Sweet Home Motel (middle distance) was built in the area where the 8th Ohio flanked the Confederates on July 3.
Image courtesy of GNMP

Camp Colt Tree

GPS: 39°48'53.46"N, 77°14'15.06"W; Elev. 585 ft.

- The large tree and plaque on the east side of the Emmitsburg Road were placed in 1954 to honor Eisenhower and Camp Colt.
- Eisenhower and his wife purchased a farm south of town in 1950 and used the property as a residence for the remainder of their lives.

■ President Eisenhower would play tour guide for visiting dignitaries who wished to see the battlefield. During a 1957 tour, British Field Marshal Bernard Montgomery caused a sensation by telling news reporters that Lee and Meade both should have been "sacked" for their Gettysburg performance. (Lee for failing to "press his advantages" and Meade for not having "control of the situation.") Ike mused about Pickett's Charge: "Why he [Lee] wanted to charge across that field I'll never know…I guess he got so mad he wanted to hit them with a brick." Montgomery called the attack "absolutely monstrous" and devised his own alternate strategy. "I would have thrown a right hook around Little Round Top where you had plenty of cover." When asked by newsmen if he agreed with his British friend's criticisms, the President wisely laughed, "Oh no you don't get me into that." [4]

President Eisenhower and Field Marshall Montgomery at the Virginia State Memorial with the press and Press Secretary James Hagerty (right). Image from Paul Roy (Ziegler Studio), Courtesy of the Eisenhower National Historic Site

You have now completed a walking tour of the Pettigrew-Trimble attack. You should have a better appreciation of the distance and open terrain which was contested by these two armies on July 3, 1863. You have also hopefully noted that, unlike on the portion of the field covered by Pickett's men, this area has been encroached by considerable modern development which has eliminated our ability to re-create some of the positions occupied by both Confederate and Union soldiers.

At this point you may elect to move on to Tour 3 ("Pickett's Charge"). Or if you proceed to Tour 4 to study the Union defense of Cemetery Ridge, you may even want to skip ahead to Stop U10 ("The 'Inner Angle' and the Abraham Bryan Farm") to specifically read about the experiences of Brig. General Alexander Hays's II Corps division in repulsing Pettigrew and Trimble's assault.

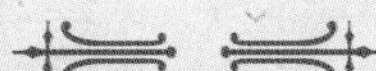

TOUR THREE
Pickett's Charge

"I was convinced that he would be leading his troops to needless slaughter."

– Lieutenant General James Longstreet.[1]

Point of Woods

GPS: 39°48'47.20"N, 77°14'55.67"W; Elev. 562 ft.

This tour will allow you to walk in the footsteps of General Pickett's Virginia Division. Walking this ground will give you the best appreciation for the experiences endured by the men of the Army of Northern Virginia on July 3.

To begin, return to the Virginia State Memorial and park your vehicle in designated areas. As we noted during the Pettigrew - Trimble tour, if you are taking this tour with a partner and have multiple vehicles, before starting you may want to park one vehicle near the end point at the High Water Mark on Cemetery Ridge. Otherwise, please remember that you will also have to walk back here upon completion of this tour. The walking distance from the Virginia memorial to the High Water Mark is roughly 1,400 yards.

Due to the popularity of this walk, the National Park Service does typically maintain mowed paths along the route traversed by Pickett. When possible, please remain on these paths. Our tour will, however, occasionally take you off of these paths and you may encounter high grass, potentially rough patches, and wet terrain. Exercise good judgment when determining whether a route is appropriate for you. Be respectful of natural resources. You may encounter farmers' planted crops along the way. Do not walk into and damage these fields.

You will enjoy this experience more if you are properly prepared. The authors recommend that you wear long pants, appropriate footwear, sun protection, and bring adequate water for your journey.

After parking your vehicle, walk east down the sidewalk (the Spangler woodlot will be on your immediate right and the Virginia monument will be behind your left shoulder) for approximately 170 yards until you reach a point where the woods form a right angle.

This point where the Spangler woods forms a right angle is often referred to as the "point of woods." The left of Colonel Alexander's artillery line ended near here, although the presence of several cannons maintained by the National Park Service immediately in front of this point is misleading. In reality, Alexander's guns were probably on the ridges about 100 yards or more to the east, in something of a "line" that curved in a southeast to northwest direction from the Emmitsburg Road. The closest battery to this point was probably Woolfolk's Ashland (Virginia) Artillery. It is also believed that Colonel Alexander and General Longstreet observed much of the afternoon's activities from near this point. The left of General Armistead's Brigade extended into these woods.

Shortly before the great cannonade commenced, Colonel Alexander took position near here on the left of his line to observe the effects of his fire. [2] Shortly thereafter, Alexander received a surprising note from General Longstreet:

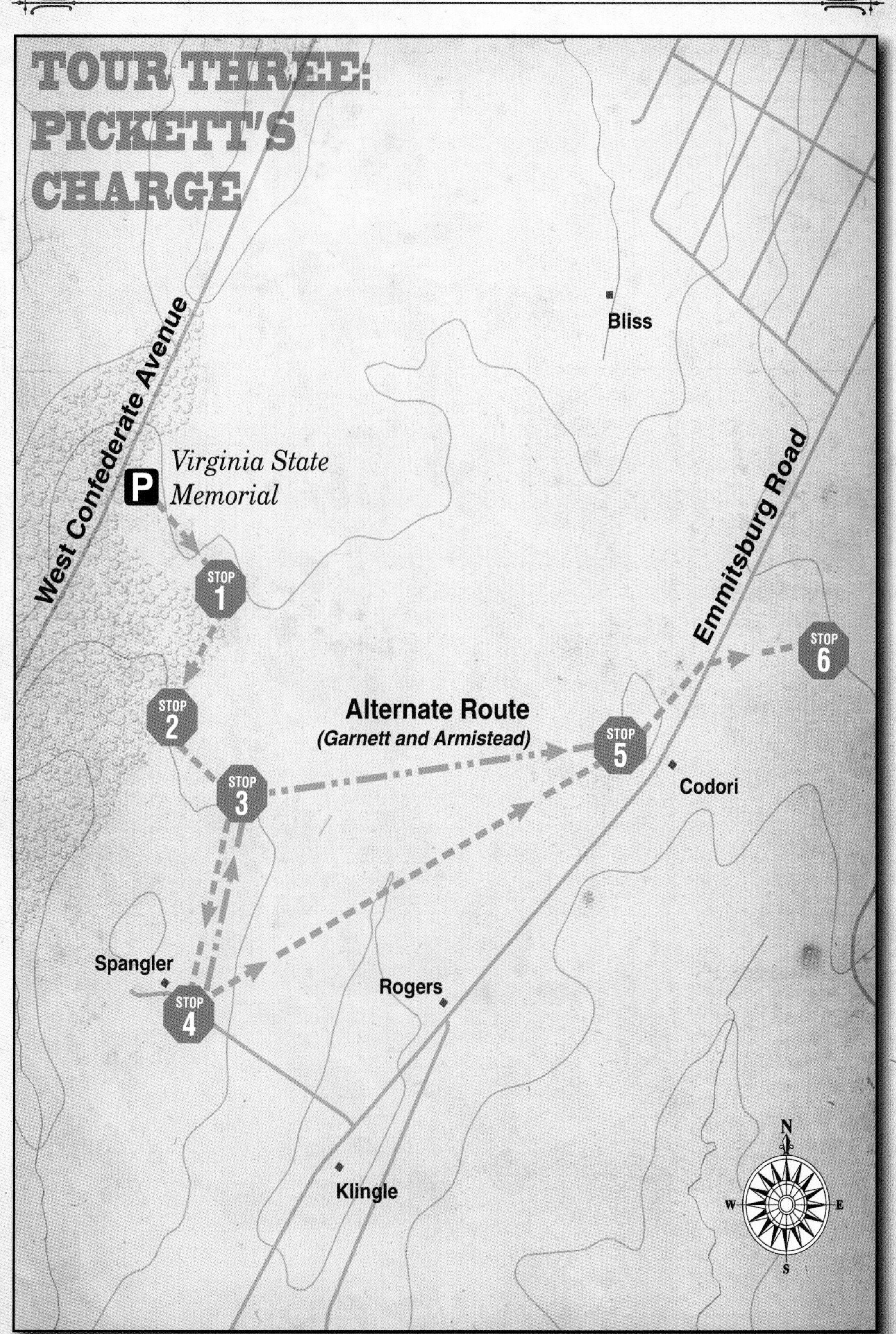
TOUR THREE: PICKETT'S CHARGE
West Confederate Avenue
Virginia State Memorial
P
Bliss
Emmitsburg Road
STOP 1
STOP 2
STOP 3
STOP 4
STOP 5
STOP 6
Alternate Route
(Garnett and Armistead)
Codori
Spangler
Rogers
Klingle
N
W
E
S

> Colonel: If the artillery fire does not have the effect to drive off the enemy or greatly demoralize him, so as to make our efforts pretty certain, I would prefer that you should not advise General Pickett to make the charge. I shall rely a great deal on your good judgment to determine the matter, and shall expect you to let General Pickett know when the moment offers. [3]

Gen. James Longstreet.
Image courtesy of Library of Congress

The artillery colonel was understandably "startled…If that assault was to be made on General Lee's judgment it was all right, but I did not want it made on mine." [4] Longstreet has been criticized by many for apparently attempting to defer responsibility for the attack onto his subordinate. Yet Longstreet was acting within the intent, if not the spirit, of the day's objectives: the infantry's advance would depend on the artillery's success or lack thereof. "When he [Alexander] could discover the enemy's batteries silenced or crippled," Longstreet later wrote, "he should give notice to General Pickett." [5] Still, Longstreet's attempts to direct Alexander to "not advise" Pickett to charge speaks poorly of Longstreet's character when, by his own admission, he did not feel that he had the authority to cancel the attack himself. [6] Alexander replied:

> General: I will only be able to judge of the effect of our fire on the enemy by his return fire, for his infantry is but little exposed to view and the smoke will obscure the whole field. If, as I infer from your note, there is any alternative to this attack, it should be carefully considered before opening our fire, for it will take all the artillery ammunition we have left to test this one thoroughly, and, if the result is unfavorable,

On July 3, Generals Lee and Longstreet had this perspective of Pickett's Charge from near the point of woods. Image courtesy of Karl Stelly

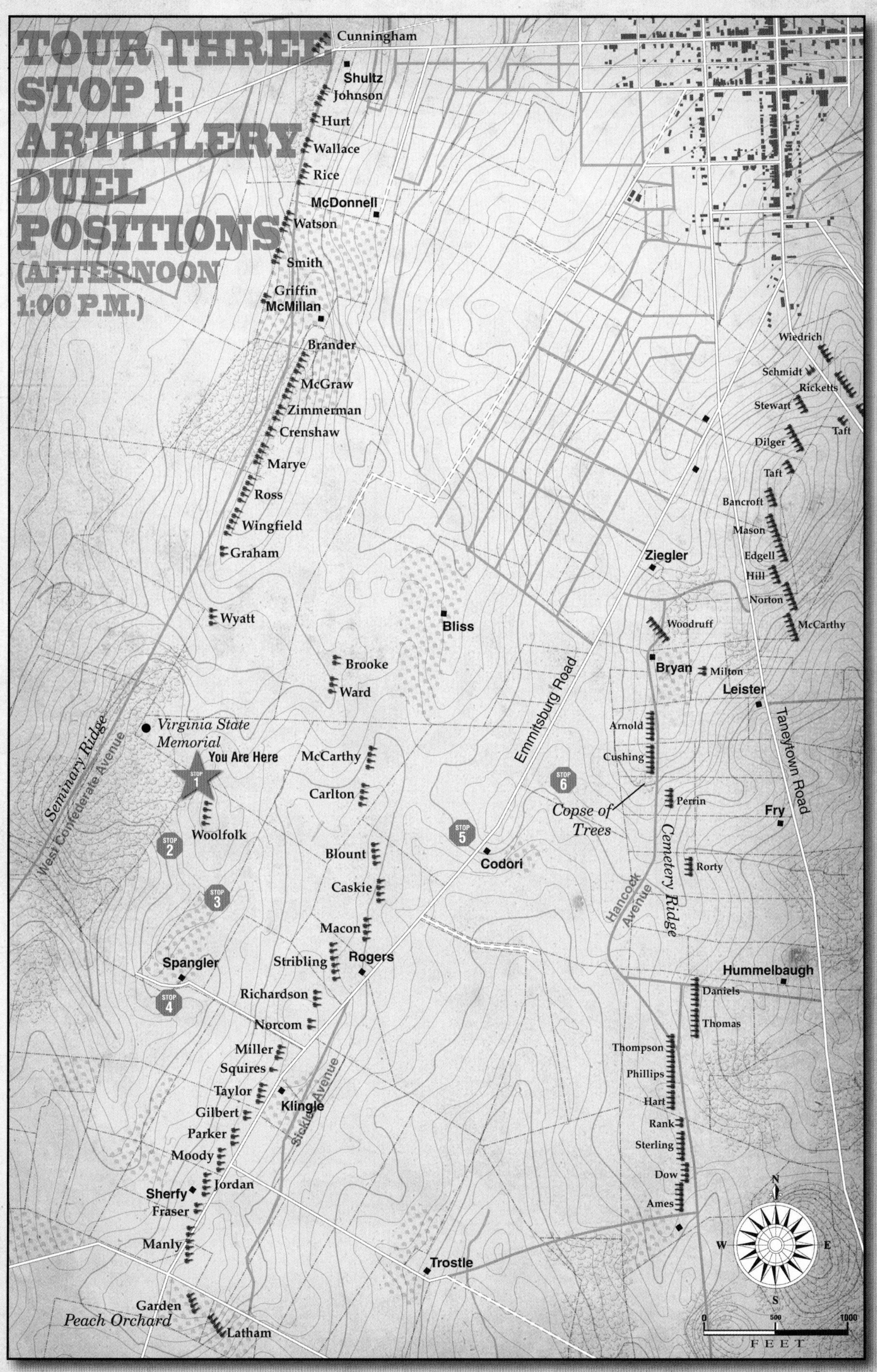
TOUR THREE
STOP 1:
ARTILLERY
DUEL
POSITIONS
(AFTERNOON
1:00 P.M.)
Cunningham
Shultz
Johnson
Hurt
Wallace
Rice
McDonnell
Watson
Smith
Griffin
McMillan
Brander
McGraw
Zimmerman
Crenshaw
Marye
Ross
Wingfield
Graham
Wyatt
Brooke
Ward
Bliss
Ziegler
Woodruff
Bryan
Milton
Leister
Wiedrich
Schmidt
Ricketts
Stewart
Taft
Dilger
Taft
Bancroft
Mason
Edgell
Hill
Norton
McCarthy
Emmitsburg Road
Taneytown Road
Virginia State Memorial
You Are Here
Seminary Ridge
West Confederate Avenue
McCarthy
Carlton
Woolfolk
Arnold
Cushing
Copse of Trees
Perrin
Fry
Blount
Codori
Caskie
Rorty
Hancock Avenue
Cemetery Ridge
Macon
Spangler
Stribling
Rogers
Hummelbaugh
Daniels
Richardson
Thomas
Norcom
Miller
Squires
Taylor
Klingle
Sickles Avenue
Gilbert
Parker
Moody
Jordan
Sherfy
Fraser
Manly
Thompson
Phillips
Hart
Rank
Sterling
Dow
Ames
Trostle
Garden
Peach Orchard
Latham
N
W
E
S
0
500
1000
FEET

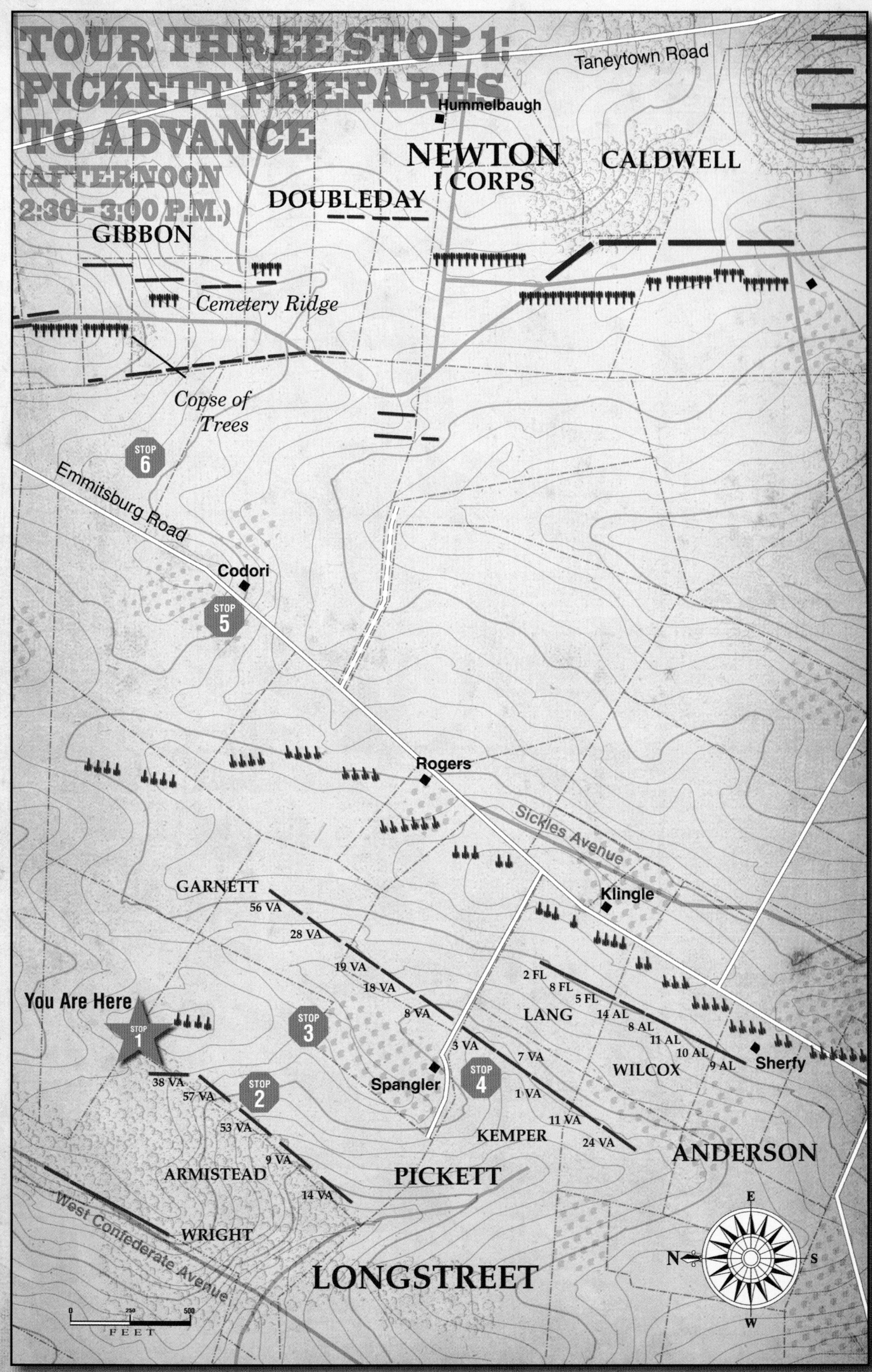
TOUR THREE STOP 1: PICKETT PREPARES TO ADVANCE
(AFTERNOON 2:30 - 3:00 P.M.)
Taneytown Road
Hummelbaugh
NEWTON
I CORPS
CALDWELL
DOUBLEDAY
GIBBON
Cemetery Ridge
Copse of Trees
STOP 6
Emmitsburg Road
Codori
STOP 5
Rogers
Sickles Avenue
Klingle
GARNETT
56 VA
28 VA
19 VA
18 VA
8 VA
2 FL
8 FL
5 FL
LANG
14 AL
8 AL
11 AL
10 AL
9 AL
Sherfy
You Are Here
STOP 1
STOP 3
3 VA
7 VA
WILCOX
38 VA
57 VA
STOP 2
Spangler
STOP 4
1 VA
53 VA
11 VA
KEMPER
24 VA
ANDERSON
9 VA
ARMISTEAD
PICKETT
14 VA
West Confederate Avenue
WRIGHT
LONGSTREET
E
N
S
W
0
250
500
FEET

> we will have none left for another effort. And even if this is entirely successful, it can only be so at a very bloody cost. [7]

Longstreet apparently regained his sense of his own responsibilities and soon sent yet another note clarifying his intentions:

> Colonel: The intention is to advance the infantry if the artillery has the desired effect of driving the enemy's off, or having other effect such as to warrant us in making the attack. When the moment arrives advise General Pickett, and of course advance such artillery as you can use in aiding the attack. [8]

"I hardly knew whether this left me discretion or not," Alexander later recalled, "but at any rate it seemed decided that the artillery must open." Alexander discussed the increasingly sorry state of affairs with General A.R. Wright. "It is not so hard to go there as it looks," Wright cautioned. "The trouble is to stay there. The whole Yankee army is there in a bunch." A still anxious Colonel Alexander then sought out General Pickett who, in contrast to Wright, seemed "very sanguine, and thought himself in luck to have the chance." [9]

Col. Edward Porter Alexander.
Image from *Miller's Photographic History of the Civil War*

Artillery chief General Pendleton had previously given Alexander the use of nine shorter range howitzers from Hill's artillery. Alexander had them set aside in order to be used during the general advance. Colonel Alexander soon sent a courier to locate them so "that they might lead in the advance for a few hundred yards before coming into action." The howitzers could not be found. It was later learned that General Pendleton "had sent for a part of them" and the remainder had been moved into a nearby hollow to protect them from enemy fire. [10] General Pendleton has been criticized by some commentators for moving the guns, although directing them out of the line of fire was a logical tactic and it seems unlikely that nine howitzers would have changed the day's fortunes. The real significance is that it illustrates another example of communication breakdowns in Lee's army.

When the batteries opened shortly after 1:00, "every gun was at work…the grand roar of nearly the whole artillery of both armies burst in on the silence, almost as suddenly as the full notes of an organ would fill a church." Contrary to myth, Robert E. Lee had not specifically designated the artillery assault to be a lengthy one. Alexander had decided to "give Pickett the order to advance within fifteen or twenty minutes after it began," but could not find the opportunity as it "seemed madness to launch infantry into that fire, with nearly three-quarters of a mile to go at midday under a July sun." [11] As a result, the minutes ticked away while the Confederates expended their ammunition. [12]

Despite the seeming "madness," after (by his later estimates) approximately thirty minutes Alexander felt that "something had to be done" [13] so he sent a note directing Pickett to "come at once, or I cannot give you proper support, but the enemy's fire has

not slackened at all. At least 18 guns are still firing from the cemetery itself." [14] Thus was Alexander's dilemma. Despite the fact that Union artillery fire had not slackened, Pickett had to come forward while there was still sufficient Confederate ammunition to support him. [15]

Seemingly miraculously, within minutes of sending this dispatch to Pickett, the Federal fire began to lessen and "the guns in the cemetery limbered up and vacated the position." Studying the situation with his field glass, Alexander watched some enemy batteries limber up and leave. Alexander watched and waited in vain for their replacements. "But the fresh ones not promptly appearing, I said, 'If they don't put fresh batteries there in five minutes this will be our fight.'" Still observing Cemetery Ridge, "there was not a single fresh gun replacing any that had withdrawn." Alexander then fired off a second note to Pickett: "For God's sake come quick. The eighteen guns are gone; come quick, or my ammunition won't let me support you properly." [16]

General Pickett apparently received Alexander's first note and took it to Longstreet. "General, shall I advance?" Longstreet recalled: "I was convinced that he would be leading his troops to needless slaughter, and did not speak. He repeated the question, and without opening my lips I bowed in answer. In a determined voice Pickett said: 'Sir, I shall lead my division forward.'" [17]

Longstreet then mounted and rode to an observation point, most likely at the point of woods, from which to watch the advance. He also paid a visit to Alexander, who expressed to Longstreet that he was "feeling then more hopeful, but afraid our artillery ammunition might not hold out." Longstreet replied, "Stop Pickett immediately and replenish your ammunition." Alexander explained that it would take too long to resupply and there was very little left anyways. "I don't want to make this attack," Longstreet told his subordinate. "I would stop it now but that General Lee ordered it and expects it to go on. I don't see how it can succeed." Alexander listened, "but did not dare offer a word. The battle was lost if we stopped." [18]

As noted previously, a key component of Lee's artillery plan was for the Confederate batteries to move forward with the infantry and provide covering fire all the way to Cemetery Ridge. As Pickett and Pettigrew's divisions stepped forward, Alexander began to ride down the lines and round up those cannons that had enough ammunition (decided as having more than 18 rounds available) to follow Pickett. Alexander selected between 15 and 18 guns. [19] "Meanwhile, the infantry had no sooner debouched on the plain than all the enemy's line, which had been nearly silent, broke out again with all its batteries." Alexander had gambled and lost in assuming that the Union artillery had withdrawn from Cemetery Ridge. Instead, "a storm of shell began bursting over and among our infantry." [20]

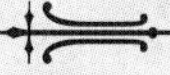

A MOST TERRIFIC ARTILLERY DUEL

It can be fairly stated that Lee's artillery failed to achieve their objectives on July 3. Lee had required his "long arm" to suppress the enemy's artillery fire and retain enough ammunition to support the attacking infantry. Neither goal was fulfilled. Lee's artillery chief, General William N. Pendleton, reported on the numerous problems associated with keeping the batteries resupplied:

> Proceeding again to the right, to see about the anticipated advance of the artillery, delayed beyond expectation, I found, among other difficulties, many batteries getting out of or low in ammunition, and the all-important question of supply received my earnest attention. Frequent shell endangering the First Corps ordnance train in the convenient locality I had assigned it, it had been removed farther back. This necessitated longer time for refilling caissons. What was worse, the train itself was very limited, so that its stock was soon exhausted, rendering requisite demand upon the reserve train, farther off. The whole amount was thus being rapidly reduced. With our means, to keep up supply at the rate required for such a conflict proved practically impossible. There had to be, therefore, some relaxation of the protracted fire, and some lack of support for the deferred and attempted advance. [1]

Major James Dearing, commanding Pickett's Division artillery, similarly wrote: "About this

Confederate artillery in position in front of the point of woods. Image courtesy of Karl Stelly

time my ammunition became completely exhausted, excepting a few rounds in my rifled guns, which were used upon a column of infantry which advanced on General Pickett's right flank. I had sent back my caissons an hour and a half before for a fresh supply, but they could not get it." [2]

General Ambrose Wright watched in amazement as "our artillery now ceased firing, and upon inquiry, I learned they had exhausted their ammunition! And at such a time!" As he watched the Federal artillery pour fire into Pickett and Pettigrew, "My God! All is as silent as death along our whole line of artillery." [3]

The situation was the same along A. P. Hill's front. Colonel R. Lindsay Walker reported that Hill's batteries "kept up an incessant fire from about 1 p.m. to the time of the advance of the infantry. This fire having been continued so long and with such rapidity, the ammunition was almost exhausted."[4]

The expenditure of ammunition prevented the Confederate batteries from moving forward with Longstreet's assaulting infantry. This would have been a difficult maneuver even under the best of circumstances: Lee's artillerymen would have been required to suppress the Federal batteries' fire, limber up, move forward, unlimber, and then effectively fire over the heads of their own infantry. Nevertheless, this appears to have been the plan and was not materially accomplished. Major B. F. Eshleman of the Washington (Louisiana) Artillery was one of several officers who understood this when he wrote:

> It having been understood by a previous arrangement that the artillery should advance with the infantry, I immediately directed Captain Miller to advance his and Lieutenant Battles' batteries. Captain Miller having suffered severely from the loss of men and horses, could move forward only three pieces of his own battery and one of Lieutenant Battles' section. Then, with one piece of Major Henry's battalion, under the direction of Major [J. C.] Haskell, he took position 400 or 500 yards to the front, and opened with deadly effect upon the enemy. With the exception of these five guns, no others advanced.[5]

Given that the Confederates obviously suffered from an inadequate supply of ammunition to sustain a prolonged barrage, was the cannonade the long, protracted, and intense assault that has been typically portrayed? Alexander estimated that the Confederates had 100-150 rounds per gun when the invasion started. This total presumably included rounds that were farther back with the ammunition trains as well as those attached to the batteries themselves. If we assume the majority of the engaged cannons fired two shots per minute, then they each would have expended 100 rounds in less than one hour. [6]

How long did the artillery assault last? The traditional view is that it lasted for nearly two hours, popularized in part because several leaders noted comparable times in their battle reports. A representative sample of 79 participant accounts was compiled by author John Michael Priest.[7] 34% (27) noted a cannonade of approximately 1.25 hours or less. 54% (43) remembered the bombardment as lasting between 1.5 to 2 hours. 11% (9) claimed that it lasted for greater than 2 hours. While there is clearly a range of potential answers, the majority of the eyewitnesses thought that it was between 1.5 to 2 hours, as noted in the chart on the next page.

An interesting trend from Priest's data was that Federal accounts skewed toward 90 minutes or greater (78%), while roughly half of the Confederate recollections were 1.25 hours or less. Clearly

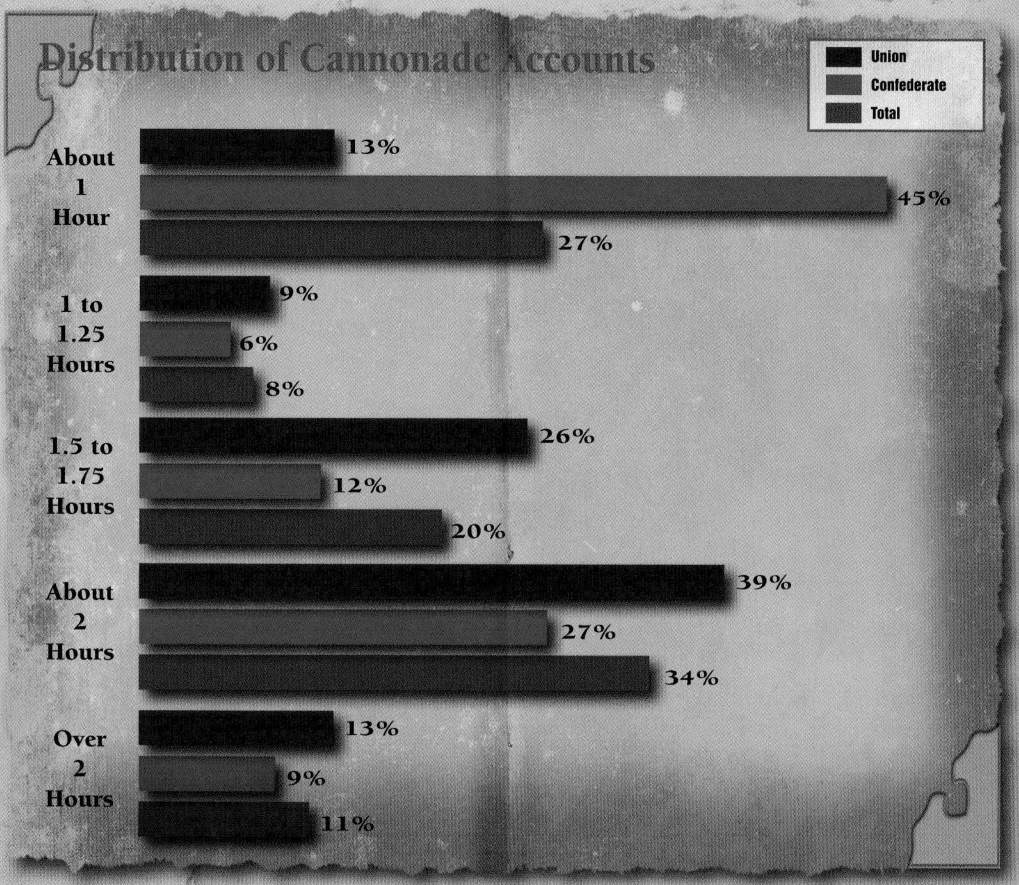

Distribution of Cannonade Accounts

	Union	Confederate	Total
About 1 Hour	13%	45%	27%
1 to 1.25 Hours	9%	6%	8%
1.5 to 1.75 Hours	26%	12%	20%
About 2 Hours	39%	27%	34%
Over 2 Hours	13%	9%	11%

the Northerners had a longer perception of receiving fire than their Southern opponents had of giving it. Time was simply not as precisely measured in that era, and many recollections are similar to those of Capt. A. N. Jones in the 7th Virginia who wrote on July 5: "At 3:00 p.m. the artillery opened...*I suppose it was about* [emphasis added] 4:00 p.m. when the order to charge the enemy was given." [8]

Amongst Northern accounts, General Meade reported that it opened at 1:00 p.m. and continued "over two hours." Hancock also wrote that it started at about 1:00 p.m. and the enemy advanced "after an hour forty-five minutes." General Hunt recorded a 1:00 p.m. opening, he ordered his own batteries to cease fire around 2:30 p.m., and the Confederates advanced at nearly 3:00 p.m. [9] Lieutenant Colonel Freeman McGilvery thought 90 minutes. [10] Local college professor Michael Jacobs timed the cannonade as beginning at 1:07 p.m. and the Confederates were "seen to appear" from the woods of Seminary Ridge at 2:30 p.m. [11]

On the Confederate side, Col. Henry Cabell commanded the artillery battalion for General McLaws's Division and supported the common view, writing that it "opened about 1 p.m. For over two hours the cannonading on both sides was almost continuous and incessant, far, very far, exceeding any cannonading I have ever before witnessed." [12] General Longstreet recalled in *Battles and Leaders*: "For an hour or two the fire was continued." [13] At the opposite end of the spectrum, Major Eshleman

of the Washington Artillery thought the infantry moved forward "about thirty minutes after the signal guns had been fired." Eshleman also thought it "a most terrific artillery duel," which it most surely was during those first thirty minutes. [14]

Colonel Alexander's recollections are the most problematic for historians to tackle because Alexander was tasked with determining when Pickett should advance and we assume that Alexander would have been aware of the elapsed time. In *Battles and Leaders*, Alexander said that it started at "exactly" 1:00 p.m. After 25 minutes, he wrote Pickett urging, "If you are coming at all you must come at once." Five minutes later, Federal batteries seemingly slackened and began to withdraw from the cemetery. Another five minutes elapsed and Alexander wrote again, "For God's sake, come quick." At 1:40, Longstreet arrived and was angry to learn that there was inadequate remaining ammunition. During this conversation, Alexander tells us, "Pickett's Division swept out of the wood..." Alexander then engaged in several activities such as riding with General Garnett briefly, and selecting 15-18 guns to advance with the infantry. [15]

All we can say with relative certainty is the signal guns erupted shortly after 1:00 p.m., the heaviest firing lasted around an hour, some firing occurred for at least another 30 minutes afterward, and (most importantly) the Confederate batteries expended much of their ammunition before they could overpower their opponents.

A final failure of the Confederates was their inability to use their exterior lines to advantage. General Pendleton reported:

> So mighty an artillery contest has perhaps never been waged, estimating together the number and character of guns and the duration of the conflict. The average distance between contestants was about 1,400 yards, and the effect was necessarily serious on both sides. With the enemy, there was advantage of elevation and protection from earthworks; but his fire was unavoidably more or less divergent, while ours was convergent. His troops were massed, ours diffused. We, therefore, suffered apparently much less. Great commotion was produced in his ranks, and his batteries were to such extent driven off or silenced as to have insured his defeat but for the extraordinary strength of his position. [16]

But Alexander understood that Lee's army had failed to converge their fire onto Cemetery Hill:

> The artillery of Ewell's corps, however, took only a small part...as they were too far away on the other side of the town. Some of them might have done good service from positions between Hill and Ewell, enfilading the batteries fighting us. The opportunity to do that was the single advantage in our having the exterior line, to compensate for all its disadvantages. But our line was so extended that all of it was not well studied, and the officers of the different corps had no opportunity to examine each other's ground for chances to cooperate. [17]

A small number of Confederate guns ultimately moved forward during the late stages of the attack but provided inadequate firepower to help the infantry. Alexander noted "the few guns" advancing from the center, but specifically identified nine cannons, five under Maj. John Haskell (of Henry's Battalion) near the Peach Orchard and four from Miller and Norcom's (under Lt. Henry Battles) batteries to their left. Haskell recalled that he moved about 300-500 yards and opened fire

on enemy infantry that was threatening Pickett's right. But the Federals then revealed a large number of guns, later estimated to have been more than 20, who returned fire and quickly forced Haskell to withdraw. Battles and Miller's four guns suffered similar fates. [18]

How many Confederate pieces actually advanced to support the charge? Alexander's accounts vary, but the official reports of Henry Cabell (9), Mathis Henry (1), and Benjamin Eshleman (4) combine to suggest as many as 14 ineffectually pressed forward.

With Lee's long arm having failed to break the enemy's defenses, and unable to retain sufficient ammunition to support the attacking infantry, the order to move forward passed from Alexander to an unenthusiastic Longstreet and finally to a hopeful General Pickett.

Armistead's Brigade

STOP 2

GPS: 39°48'41.13"N, 77°14'59.73"W; Elev. 551 ft.

If you look south from the "point of woods," you will notice there is a swale that sits immediately in front of the Spangler woodlot. This area sheltered General Armistead's Brigade during the cannonade and prior to the charge. You may want to walk 200-300 yards south from this point in order to better understand the terrain that Armistead's soldiers encountered on that hot afternoon.

As General Pickett's Division arrived near Spangler's woods during the late morning, Brig. General James Kemper's Brigade led the march and formed their line on the other side (south) of the Spangler farm lane. Brigadier General Richard Garnett's Brigade was next and they formed on the north side of the Spangler farm lane perhaps 150-200 yards in front (east) of where we now stand.

Near our current position, Brig. General Lewis Armistead's Brigade formed behind Garnett. Armistead's double-ranked line stretched south for roughly 500 - 600 yards from the northeast corner of Spangler's woods. The 38th Virginia was the extreme left of Armistead's line and enjoyed "partial shelter" in Spangler's woods. Armistead's remaining regiments (the 57th, 53rd, 9th, and 14th Virginia) were formed in the low ground in front of the trees. [1]

The War Department marker for Armistead's Brigade along West Confederate Avenue is seen here in this Tipton image from 1911.
Image courtesy of GNMP

Note as you walk into this low ground that your view of Cemetery Ridge quickly disappears. The typical enlisted man in Armistead's Brigade would have seen little of what awaited him on Cemetery Ridge. General Lee has been heavily criticized for ordering his men to seemingly attack "across a mile of open ground" but in reality he may have counted on the protection of numerous swales to temporarily shield his infantry as they attacked. [2]

Participants remembered that General Armistead bravely reassured his men during the cannonade prior to the grand assault. Lieutenant Colonel Rawley Martin of the 53rd Virginia observed Armistead pacing up and down in front of the troops. "Men, remember what you are fighting for," encouraged Armistead. "Remember your homes, your firesides, your wives, mothers, sisters and your sweethearts." Martin thought, "Such an appeal would have made those men assault the ramparts of the infernal regions." [3]

As the cannonade ceased, a courier from General Pickett reached Armistead. The command "Attention, battalion!" soon rang out as the men rose to their feet and aligned. Before departing, Armistead challenged Leander C. Blackburn, the color sergeant of the 53rd Virginia, "Sergeant, are you going to put those colors on the enemy's works today?" Blackburn, who had been appointed on June 1, 1862 and would have carried the flag during the attack of Armistead's Brigade at Malvern Hill, replied: "I will try, sir, and if mortal man can do it, it shall be done." Undoubtedly impressed by Blackburn's moxie, Armistead took a flask from his pocket and offered the soldier a drink. [4]

During the artillery barrage, Armistead's Brigade formed inside and along the woodline.
Image courtesy of James Hessler

Lieutenant John Lewis, of the nearby 9th Virginia, later recalled:

> If I should live for a hundred years I shall never forget that moment or the command as given by General Lewis A. Armistead on that day. He was an old army officer, and was possessed of a very loud voice, which could be heard by the whole brigade, being near my regiment. He gave the command, in words, as follows- 'Attention, second battalion! Battalion of direction forward; guides center; march!'...He turned; placed himself about twenty paces in front of his brigade, and took the lead. His place was in the rear, properly. After moving he placed his hat on the point of his sword, and held it above his head, in front of him. [5]

It was approximately 3:00 p.m. when Armistead's Brigade moved forward at "quick time."

ARMISTEAD AND HANCOCK

Gen. Lewis Armistead. Image courtesy of Army Heritage and Education Center

Lewis Armistead was born on February 18, 1817 in New Bern, North Carolina. The Armisteads were an illustrious military family, having produced several officers. Their most famous member was George Armistead, who defended Fort McHenry in Baltimore from the British in September 1814.

With such bloodlines, it should be no surprise that Lewis Armistead pursued a military career of his own. However, he almost did not make it. Young Lewis was appointed to West Point in 1833, but he did not graduate. His career there was cut short by the often repeated story that he broke a mess hall plate over Jubal Early's head after a parade ground insult. [1] He returned to the army in 1839 after an uncle successfully petitioned the secretary of war and secured a direct commission for Lewis. What followed was a lengthy and often mundane army career that took him to the swamps of Florida, out west to Oklahoma Territory, and to war in Mexico. [2]

Much has been made of the prewar friendship between General Armistead and Union General Winfield S. Hancock because it was featured prominently in the classic novel *The Killer Angels* and motion picture *Gettysburg*. The novel and film are heavily fictionalized but have successfully reached larger audiences than any other Gettysburg works. As a result, some historians are often frustrated by their tremendous influence on many visitors and students of the battle. There is ample evidence to confirm that the two officers were indeed friends from the old army, as were many opposing officers at Gettysburg. They were likely aware that they were facing each other on July 3, but there are no

contemporary accounts to indicate that the two were emotionally pining for each other during the battle as they do in the popular novel and film. These men had been hardened by two years of war.

There are no known surviving papers of General Hancock's that speak of this friendship, however Mrs. Almira Hancock wrote of the relationship. Armistead did leave his prayer book with Mrs. Hancock, which carried the inscription, "Lewis A. Armistead. Trust in God and fear nothing." [3]

One of the most memorable aspects of their novelized portrayal was at a going-away party held in California at the war's outset. In *The Killer Angels*, a tearful Armistead told Hancock, "Win, so help me, if I ever lift a hand against you, may God strike me dead." [4] This adds to the impression that the two men were nearly brothers and increases the tragedy of their competing roles at Gettysburg.

However, as recorded by Mrs. Hancock, Armistead actually hoped to be struck dead "if I am ever induced to leave my native soil." [5] The actual quote is quite a different interpretation of Armistead's motives from the more popularly quoted fictional version.

Lewis Armistead had written in December 1861:

> I have been a soldier all my life. I was an officer in the army of the U.S., which service I left to fight for my own country and for and with my own people - and because they were right and oppressed. [6]

Almira Hancock and Armistead's own words tell us that he was a dedicated Confederate who was committed to his home state more than his ties to the old prewar army.

THE SON OF A BRAVE SOLDIER

While General Armistead's story remains of great interest to Gettysburg scholars, few realize that his only surviving child was also at Gettysburg serving as his father's aide-de-camp.

Lewis Armistead's family life was indeed a tragic one. The 46-year-old had lost two wives, a young daughter, and an infant son to disease while pursuing his pre-Civil War military career at frontier outposts.

Walker Keith Armistead was General Armistead's only child to reach adulthood. Walker, who went by the name "Keith" since an uncle and grandfather also shared the same name, was born in 1844 to Lewis and his first wife Cecilia. (Cecilia Armistead died in December 1850, one day after Keith's sixth birthday and eight months after daughter Flora had also died.) [1]

Keith Armistead was a student in the North when the war broke out, but he journeyed to Richmond shortly before his father arrived there on September 15, 1861. In April 1862, Keith requested an endorsement from Robert E. Lee to obtain a cadetship and Confederate officer training. While admitting their acquaintance was of "recent date," Lee praised the "the independence and manliness displayed by him in supporting himself…by manual labor while at school in the North" and also "his successful efforts in making his way through the enemy's lines to Virginia." Referring to Keith's father,

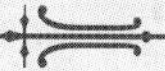

Lee added, "I know him to be the son of a brave soldier and worthy man." Unfortunately his officer aspirations were temporarily unsuccessful and Keith instead enlisted as a private in the 6th Virginia Cavalry in May 1862. [2]

Due to a vacancy, General Armistead applied for his son to be appointed as his aide-de-camp in February 1863. Keith Armistead was appointed as a 1st lieutenant on his father's staff to date from April. As a result, father and son served together at Gettysburg. [3]

Sergeant Major Coupland R. Page was a courier for Confederate artillery chief William N. Pendleton at Gettysburg. Following the cannonade on July 3, Page was delivering a message when he passed by Pickett's "splendid" division and spotted both Armisteads mounted together. Page knew Keith, whom he called "a charming fellow," and young Armistead called out, "Good bye, old fellow!" Page replied, "God bless you, Keith!" [4]

Keith Armistead survived Pickett's Charge. We do not know how he reacted to losing his father on that day, but Keith's staff assignment also died with General Armistead. General Lee continued to monitor Keith's progress, telling Keith's grandmother, "I have taken much interest in him from the beginning of his career; his amiable disposition, setting aside other considerations, having attracted me towards him." Lee had hoped Keith would accept a position with the army's Chief of Ordnance, but young Armistead preferred to remain in the ranks instead. Lee added, "I think the position of a private soldier in the Confederate army is the most honorable in the service." Keith returned to the 6th Virginia Cavalry and survived the war. [5]

In 1871, he married a granddaughter of noted Massachusetts statesman Daniel Webster. The Armisteads settled in New England where he held mundane peacetime occupations such as general manager for an animal protection organization and the official reporter for Massachusetts higher courts. Keith Armistead died in 1896 at the age of 51, leaving behind his widow and two sons. [6]

(CONFEDERATE.)

A

W. Keith Armistead
1 Lt.

Appears on a

Register

of Appointments, Confederate States Army.

State Va.
To whom report Genl. L. A. Armistead
Date of appointment Apr. 30, 1863.
Date of confirmation Apr. 30, 1863.
To take rank Feb. 19, 1863.
Date of acceptance May 17, 1863.
Delivered Genl. R. E. Lee
Secretary of War J. A. S.
Remarks: Aides de Camp with the rank of 1 Lt.

Out of Commission by the death of Genl. Armistead

Confed. Arch., Chap. 1, File No. 86, page 159

Geo. S. Preston
(635) Copyist.

A page from Keith Armistead's service record.
Image courtesy of National Archives

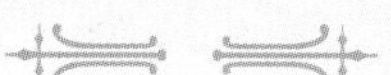

Garnett's Brigade

GPS: 39°48'37.56"N, 77°14'51.39"W; Elev. 560 ft.

As you walk forward from Armistead's swale, within about 200 yards, you should pass into another slight depression which was probably the point where Brig. General Richard Garnett deployed his brigade during those early afternoon hours.

Gen. Richard Garnett.
Image courtesy of the National Civil War Museum, Harrisburg, PA

Brigadier General Richard Brooke Garnett was 45 years old at Gettysburg, having been born November 21, 1817, at the family plantation in Essex, Virginia. After several attempts, he received an appointment to West Point in 1837. An average student, like many of his contemporaries, he graduated 29th out of 52 in the Class of 1841. [1]

There is a historical debate over what General Garnett physically looked like. The most frequently reproduced images of him show a dark haired officer with a beard. However, some believe these images to be his cousin Robert S. Garnett. (Cousin Robert served in the Mexican War and also joined the Confederacy. He holds the dubious distinction of being the first Confederate general killed in the Civil War at the battle of Corrick's Ford on July 13, 1861.) The debate even led to a 1987 court case between dueling sides of the Garnett family tree but remains inconclusive. [2]

Although Garnett's pre-Civil War career exhibited much of the characteristic tedium that accompanied long stints of garrison duty out west, at least one interesting personal fact emerges from that period. In April 1855, an Oglala Lakota woman named Looks at Him (alternatively referred to as Looking Woman) gave birth to Garnett's son near the confluence of Saline Creek and the Laramie River. "Billie" Garnett would become a distinguished scout and interpreter in the Old West and witnessed the death of Chief Crazy Horse in September 1877. Although Richard essentially abandoned his offspring to continue his army career, Billie was recognized as such by the general's descendants. [3]

Garnett was described as "a strong friend and supporter of the Federal Union" who had even made a public address in its favor. [4] But when the unpleasantness erupted between the states, Garnett was commissioned a lieutenant colonel in Cobb's Georgia Legion. Colonel Thomas Cobb thought Garnett "a perfect gentleman" and "an excellent officer." Garnett was promoted to brigadier general by November 1861 and (unfortunately) placed under Stonewall Jackson in command of Jackson's old Stonewall Brigade. At the battle of Kernstown on March 23, 1862, Garnett ordered a retreat when his men were running low

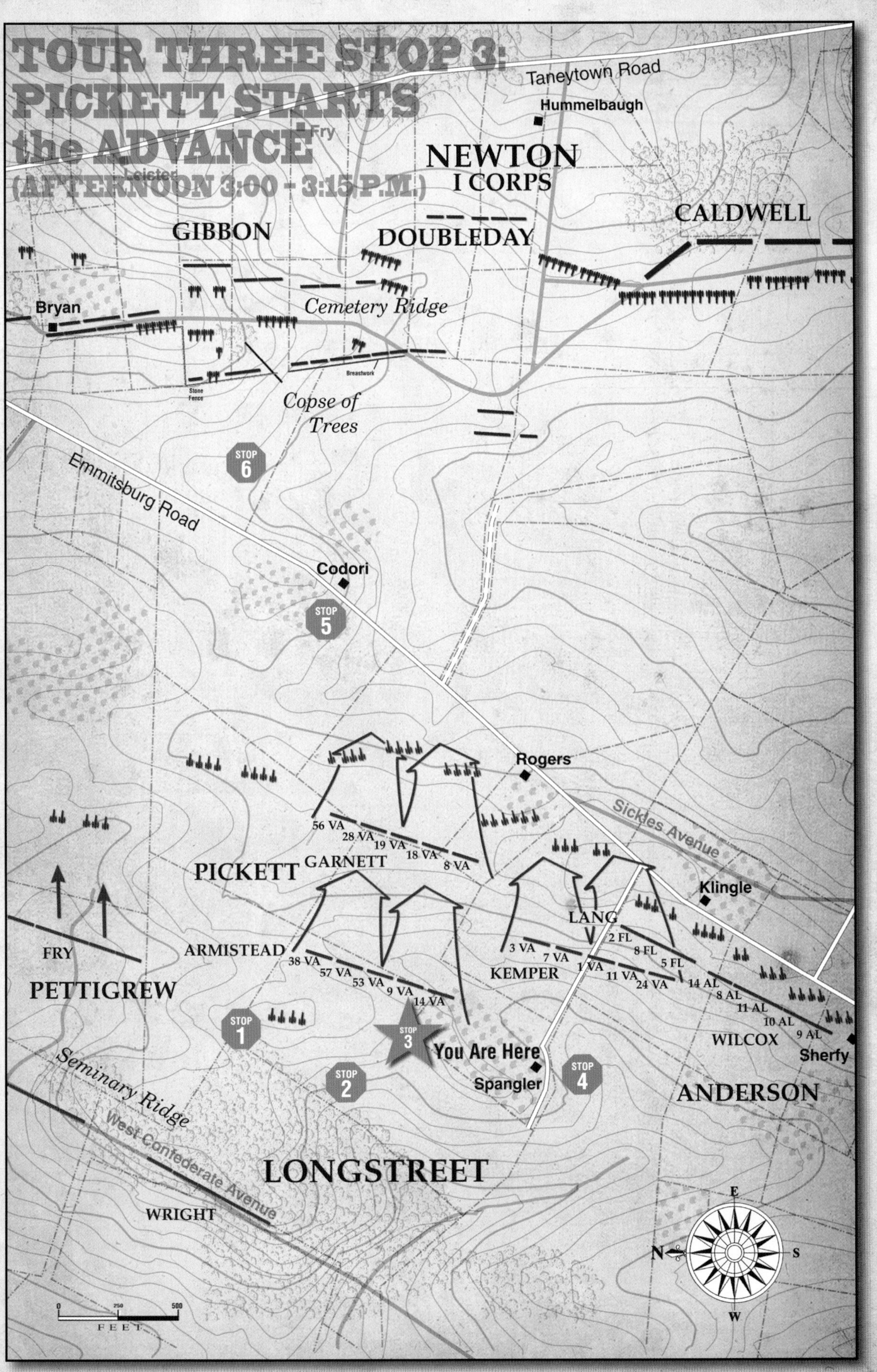
TOUR THREE STOP 3:
PICKETT STARTS
the ADVANCE
(AFTERNOON 3:00 - 3:15 P.M.)
Taneytown Road
Hummelbaugh
Fry
Leister
NEWTON
I CORPS
CALDWELL
GIBBON
DOUBLEDAY
Bryan
Cemetery Ridge
Breastwork
Stone Fence
Copse of Trees
STOP 6
Emmitsburg Road
Codori
STOP 5
Rogers
Sickles Avenue
56 VA
28 VA
19 VA
18 VA
8 VA
GARNETT
PICKETT
Klingle
LANG
2 FL
8 FL
5 FL
ARMISTEAD
38 VA
57 VA
53 VA
9 VA
14 VA
3 VA
7 VA
1 VA
11 VA
24 VA
KEMPER
14 AL
8 AL
11 AL
10 AL
9 AL
WILCOX
Sherfy
FRY
PETTIGREW
STOP 1
STOP 3
You Are Here
STOP 2
Spangler
STOP 4
ANDERSON
Seminary Ridge
West Confederate Avenue
LONGSTREET
WRIGHT
E
N
S
W
0
250
500
FEET

on ammunition. Justified or not (and Garnett was supported by his subordinates), Jackson ordered Garnett relieved of command and brought up on charges of misconduct. An equally outraged Garnett demanded a court of inquiry. After only one day, in which several historians have deemed Garnett to have held the upper hand against mighty Stonewall, the trial was suspended and never reconvened. By September of that year Garnett was reassigned to temporary command of Pickett's Brigade and led them (Pickett being wounded and absent) during the Maryland campaign. "While he was not a man of much mental force," wrote a colonel in the 8th Virginia, "he was one of the noblest and bravest men I ever knew." [5]

Curiously, Garnett apparently did not hold a grudge against Jackson. He wept so bitterly over Jackson's casket that Jackson's staffer "Sandie" Pendleton asked him to serve as a pallbearer. Garnett agreed and joined Longstreet, Ewell, and others in this honor. [6] Yet Pickett's staff officer Walter Harrison wrote:

> [T]o the brave, proud, and sensitive spirit of Garnett, it [Kernstown] was a cruel blow, from the effects of which his heart was never relieved until its last throb at Gettysburg…His peculiar sensitiveness suffered under this supposed imputation at Kernstown, and he was ever thereafter anxious to expose himself, even unnecessarily, and to wipe out effectually by some great distinction in action, what he felt to be an unmerited slur upon his military reputation. [7]

Garnett would ride his horse "Red Eye" during Pickett's Charge (not that he was alone as probably at least 15 other men did so) because he had been kicked in the ankle by a horse during the march north; probably on June 20. Garnett wrote to a female friend

Cemetery Ridge as viewed from Garnett and Armistead's approach.
Image courtesy of Karl Stelly

shortly afterward, in his last known correspondence, that the leg was "still quite sore" and was "improving slowly." He was confined to an ambulance and thought it might be "a week or more" before he could even ride. [8]

There is also debate over Garnett's physical condition and attire on the day of his death. E. P. Alexander wrote in *Battles and Leaders* that Garnett "was a warm personal friend…I rode with him a short distance, and then we wished each other luck and a good-bye, which was our last." Alexander should therefore have been in a position to note that Garnett was "just out of the sick ambulance, and buttoned up in an old blue overcoat." Other accounts repeated this, but Capt. Henry T. Owen, of the 18th Virginia, countered that it was much too hot to wear an overcoat and Garnett was instead wearing "a fine, new gray uniform" that he recently acquired in Richmond. [9]

Major Charles S. Peyton, of the 19th Virginia, took command of Garnett's Brigade after the general's battlefield death and filed the brigade's report. Peyton described the Virginians' morning activities:

> Notwithstanding the long and severe marches made by the troops of this brigade, they reached the field about 9 a.m. in high spirits and in good condition. At about 12 m. we were ordered to take position behind the crest of the hill on which the artillery, under Colonel [E. Porter] Alexander, was planted, where we lay during a most terrific cannonading, which opened at 1.30 p.m., and was kept up without intermission for one hour.
>
> During the shelling, we lost about 20 killed and wounded…At 2.30 p.m., the artillery fire having to some extent abated, the order to advance was given, first by Major-General Pickett in person, and repeated by General Garnett with promptness, apparent cheerfulness, and alacrity. The brigade moved forward at quick time. The ground was open, but little broken, and from 800 to 1,000 yards from the crest whence we started to the enemy's line. [10]

A position that was roughly 200 yards in front of Armistead, behind Alexander's artillery, and 800-1,000 yards from Cemetery Ridge would have placed Garnett's men on a line roughly perpendicular to the Spangler farm buildings. As you may note, there was no protective cover for Garnett's men. "All along the line men were falling from seeming sunstroke with dreadful contortions of the body," recalled the 19th Virginia's Lt. William Wood, "foaming at the mouth, and almost lifeless. Some were possibly shamming but much, real, downright suffering from the sun's hot rays was experienced." [11]

Before continuing your walk toward Cemetery Ridge, you may choose to detour about 275 yards south and west to visit the historic Henry Spangler farm. This will provide you with a considerably better perspective of the positions occupied by Kemper's Brigade, as well as those of Wilcox and Lang.

Henry Spangler Farm

GPS: 39°48'30.24"N, 77°14'59.04"W; Elev. 556 ft.

Kemper's Confederates formed on the Henry Spangler farm prior to the charge.
Image courtesy of James Hessler

The Henry Spangler farm is situated approximately 300 yards west of the Emmitsburg Road. It was built circa 1820 and sold to Spangler in 1862. The home has been significantly altered since 1863. Most notably, in 1880 a brick second story was added to the stone summer kitchen and the entire structure was attached to the original log house.[1] The existing barn is also a replacement for the one that stood here during the battle.

Brigadier General James Kemper's Brigade was posted on this property prior to the charge. Kemper's men had little protection from both enemy artillery and the heat of the mid-day sun. "We suffered considerable loss before we moved," wrote Capt. John Holmes Smith, in the 11th Virginia. Smith estimated that his company lost 10 out of 29 men before the charge even started. The regiment's adjutant, Lt. Hilary V. Harris, wrote that the cannon fire "was kept up almost constantly for two hours. It was terrific and we lost a good many men from it as we had no shelter except the slight crest of a hill." [2] In addition to the lack of cover, when standing on this property, one might be impressed by the distance that Kemper's Brigade needed to travel to reach the area near the "Copse of Trees." While

Garnett and Armistead's brigades had roughly 1,000 and 1,200 yards to cover respectively, Kemper's men would have crossed a distance of approximately 1,400 yards to reach the enemy's works.

Kemper's right stretched south for several hundred yards toward the Sherfy farm. Participant accounts clearly indicate that they were placed behind Alexander's batteries which were along the Emmitsburg Road ridge. Prior to the assault, both Lang and Wilcox's brigades would have been in front (east) of Kemper's line, with Lang's left roughly in front of the 1st Virginia in Kemper's center. [3]

Kemper's Brigade "arrived at the scene of operations about 11 o'clock in the morning," wrote Col. Joseph Mayo, 3rd Virginia, and formed in line of battle behind Eshleman's artillery battalion with their left connected to Garnett and skirmishers "thrown out about 50 paces in front." [4] Mayo claimed, "General Lee passed in front of us, coming from the right, and a little while afterwards every man in the ranks was made to know exactly what was the work which had been cut out for us." The boys stacked arms and were allowed some rest, "but one thing was especially noticeable; from being unusually merry and hilarious they on a sudden had become as still and thoughtful as Quakers at a love feast." Mayo chatted with Col. Waller Tazewell Patton, 7th Virginia. "This news has brought about an awful seriousness with our fellows, Taz." Patton replied somberly, "Yes, and well they may be serious if they really know what is in store for them. I have been up yonder where Dearing [artillery] is, and looked across at the Yankees." [5]

Gen. James Kemper. Image courtesy of Army Heritage and Education Center

The subsequent artillery fire was "terrific" and lasted "nearly two hours." David Johnston in the 7th Virginia watched several men get killed or wounded, including one who was lifted three feet into the air by a single shot. "It was as if we were placed where we were for target practice for the Union batteries." [6] Colonel Mayo recalled "fearful havoc was made in our lines" and the 3rd and 7th Virginia regiments on the left and left center suffered "with particular severity. Many too were completely prostrated by exposure to the blazing sun in the open field. At 3 o'clock the firing ceased and the advance was ordered." [7]

Charles Loehr wrote, "the shells fell thickly in the line of battle" and his 1st Virginia "suffered severely." Loehr thought "the very ground shook." [8] John Dooley of the same regiment freely admitted that the men were "frightened out of our wits" while the earth exploded around them. When the order to rise up was finally given, many fainted "from the heat and dread." Although the Rebels were ordered to "sweep from our path anything in the shape of a Yankee," there was no optimism about doing so under such adverse conditions. Enthusiasm simply "*ain't there* [emphasis in original]." [9]

General Kemper described his command's actions in an 1886 letter:

Reaching the ridge on which our artillery was posted and being posted, we were

> directed to choose positions behind the ridge, and near its crest, and to cause the men to lie down as a precaution against the enemy's artillery…Very soon after the fire of the artillery ceased, a young officer of Pickett's staff galloped to my position and said, 'General Pickett orders you to advance your brigade immediately.' That was the only order I received during the battle, and on receiving it I looked up and saw that Garnett and Armistead were already in line and apparently ready to advance. [10]

Colonel Mayo recalled that one of the last shots of the cannonade hit two men laying near him, causing "earth mixed with blood and brains" to strike Mayo's shoulder. Soon after, and contrary to Kemper's assertion that the attack orders were delivered by a staff officer, Mayo recalled, "General Pickett came riding briskly down the rear of the line, calling the men to get up and prepare to advance, and 'Remember Old Virginia.'" [11] Johnston claimed Pickett rode near him and yelled, "Up, men, and to your posts! Don't forget today that you are from old Virginia!" [12]

Over on the Union side of the field, General Winfield S. Hancock has been singled out for dramatically riding along his lines during the cannonade. But an equally courageous ride by another notable leader occurred along Kemper's front. "Just before the artillery ceased General Longstreet rode in a walk between the artillery and the infantry," recalled Capt. John Holmes Smith of the 11th Virginia, "in front of the regiment toward the left and disappeared down the line. He was as quiet as an old farmer riding over his plantation on a Sunday morning, and looked neither to the right or left." [13]

Looking south in Henry Spangler's fields. Kemper's men suffered severely here from heat and artillery fire. Image courtesy of James Hessler

You may begin to walk from this point toward Cemetery Ridge if you wish to approximate Kemper's march, or return to the vicinity of Stop PC3 to trace Armistead and Garnett's assault. The National Park Service maintains fences throughout these fields but you will find some occasional openings that will allow you to pass without having to climb these enclosures.

About half-way across the field, you will come upon a monument that commemorates the July 2 skirmish line of the 1st Massachusetts Infantry Regiment. No Union forces

occupied this area on July 3, although portions of Alexander's batteries were along this ridge during the artillery fighting. You may want to stop here for a moment to view the monument and the surrounding terrain. Keep in mind that smoke, dust, and the general chaos of battle would have obscured the sight lines that exist today.

At a standard "quick time" rate of approximately 85 yards per minute, Pickett's men might have reached here in as little as 5-6 minutes from stepping off. Images courtesy of Karl Stelly

Emmitsburg Road (West Side) Across from Codori Farm

GPS: 39°48'43.35"N, 77°14'23.47"W; Elev. 578 ft.

As you walked from the Spangler woodlot to this point, you were approximating the route followed by Garnett and Armistead's brigades. (Note that while many park visitors often walk directly from the Virginia monument to the Angle, no troops actually traveled such a route on July 3.) Kemper's Brigade would have crossed the road to the south of us in the vicinity of the Daniel Klingle farm. Kemper's advance was by a series of alternate moves by the left flank and then by the front. [1]

Rawley Martin of the 53rd Virginia described the "tramp, tramp" sound the men made in the tall grass as they moved forward. Federal batteries were hitting Confederate targets across much of the field. Martin thought the Yankee batteries opened at a distance of about 1,100 yards, "hissing, screaming shells break in their front, rear, on their flanks, all about them." [2] Major Joseph Cabell, 38th Virginia, wrote that after crossing about half of the field, they were "subjected to a severe enfilading fire from the right" and "until nearly to their works, grape and canister were poured onto us from the right and front." Cabell's line was "steady and unbroken" except for gaps that were quickly closed up. [3]

"All during this time the line was exposed to a terrible fire," wrote Charles Loehr of

As you walk in the footsteps of Pickett's men, you will notice the dips and swells in the ground. At times you will lose sight of the Codori farm (above) and of Cemetery Ridge. These dips offered the Confederates a brief reprieve from Union guns. Image courtesy of Karl Stelly

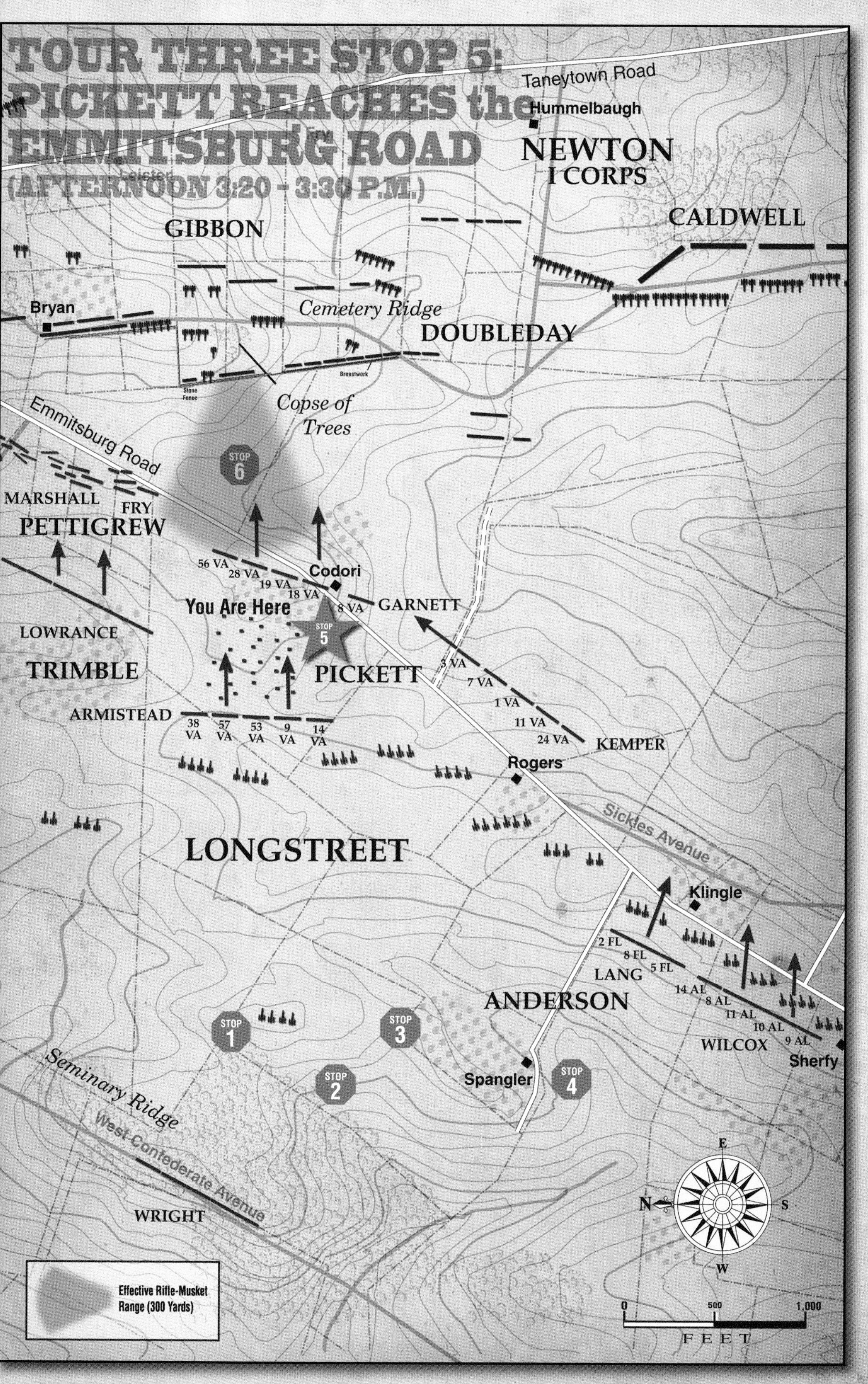
TOUR THREE STOP 5: PICKETT REACHES the EMMITSBURG ROAD
(AFTERNOON 3:20 - 3:30 P.M.)
Taneytown Road
Hummelbaugh
NEWTON
I CORPS
CALDWELL
GIBBON
Bryan
Cemetery Ridge
DOUBLEDAY
Breastwork
Stone Fence
Copse of Trees
Emmitsburg Road
STOP 6
MARSHALL
FRY
PETTIGREW
56 VA
28 VA
19 VA
18 VA
8 VA
Codori
GARNETT
You Are Here
STOP 5
LOWRANCE
TRIMBLE
PICKETT
3 VA
7 VA
1 VA
11 VA
24 VA
KEMPER
ARMISTEAD
38 VA
57 VA
53 VA
9 VA
14 VA
Rogers
LONGSTREET
Sickles Avenue
Klingle
2 FL
8 FL
5 FL
LANG
14 AL
8 AL
11 AL
10 AL
9 AL
ANDERSON
WILCOX
Sherfy
STOP 1
STOP 2
STOP 3
STOP 4
Spangler
Seminary Ridge
West Confederate Avenue
WRIGHT
E
N
S
W
0
500
1,000
FEET
Effective Rifle-Musket Range (300 Yards)

the 1st Virginia, "but the line would close up as the men fell" and continue to oblique left.[4] "I remember I saw a shell explode amidst the ranks of the left company of the regiment on our right," James Crocker of the 9th Virginia recalled. "Men fell like ten-pins in a ten-strike." [5] Lieutenant John Lewis, also of the 9th Virginia, wrote that they started to take fire about 200 yards into the advance:

> Crash after crash came the shot and shell. Great gaps were being made in the lines only to be closed up; and the same steady, move forward; the division was being decimated. Its line was shortening, but as steady as ever, the gallant Armistead still in the lead, his hat working down to the hilt of his sword, the point having gone through it. [6]

Just to the west of the Emmitsburg Road opposite the Codori farm, you will see a large orchard that has been replanted by the National Park Service and is intended to represent a Codori orchard that stood here during the battle. However, period maps and photos are not in agreement on whether Codori's orchard sat west or east of the house in 1863. [7]

Charles Loehr, on Kemper's skirmish line, recalled one of his comrades, M. J. Wingfield (nicknamed "Monk"), turning when about half way across the field, "Where are our reinforcements?" None were "in sight" except Pickett's brigades "and now subject to a storm of shells, tearing great gaps into the lines." Monk realized, "We are going to be whipped, see if we don't." Those were Monk's last words as a bullet struck him only minutes later. [8]

Joseph Mayo, in General Kemper's Brigade, recalled that as they approached the Emmitsburg Road, Pickett directed them to keep a proper interval with Garnett. Kemper then went to "see what troops those were coming up behind us," discovering them to be Armistead's. "At the same moment I saw a disorderly crowd of men breaking for the rear," with Pickett and staff officers "vainly trying to stop the rout." Federal cannon were "double-stocked" and "literally riddling the orchard on the left of the now famous Codori house, through which my regiment and some others passed." Remarking to a nearby captain that things were "pretty hot," the captain replied: "It's redicklous, Colonel; perfectly redicklous. [sic]"[9]

By now you should greatly appreciate the fact that the ground over which this assault occurred is not flat but is actually rolling with a large number of elevations and swales. Just west of the replanted orchard, there is a large drop that may have allowed Garnett and Armistead's men one final opportunity to re-form before reaching the Emmitsburg Road.

The Emmitsburg Road in 1863 was an unimproved road and was more narrow and sunken than what you see today. The arrival of Pickett's Division at the road would have changed the nature of the attack dramatically. The fences and the road itself became obstacles for the attackers to cross under fire. The Virginians now also increasingly moved within range of the Yankees' rifle muskets. It is roughly 400 yards from the Emmitsburg Road at the Codori farm to the monuments that approximate the Union's defensive position, and even closer where the road angles to the northeast. Things were about to get even more dangerous for Pickett's men.

Nicholas Codori Farm

GPS: 39°48'38.86"N, 77°14'25.93"W; Elev. 572 ft.

- The Nicholas Codori property witnessed some of the battle's most epic fighting on July 2 and July 3 as large bodies of infantry maneuvered through here on both days. Pickett's Division passed on both sides of the house while en route to Cemetery Ridge.
- Like many property owners on the battlefield, Nicholas Codori lived in town and leased the farm to tenants. He did not reside on the property that so famously bears his name today.

The Nicholas Codori farm as viewed from the east side of the Emmitsburg Road.
Image courtesy of Michael Waricher

- Codori became a successful butcher and was later described as "the leading and best-known butcher in this section of the country." He was also considered a "prudent" investor who placed his "surplus means" into real estate investments such as this one. Unfortunately, Codori met a gruesome demise in July 1878 at the age of 70 while working fields near the Bliss farm. He was accidentally thrown by his horse team in front of a mower and suffered a severed foot and groin injury. He died several days later as a result.
- The house was present at the time of the battle, although the two-story brick addition was added to the rear in the 1870s. The current barn is a replacement. Evidence indicates that the barn that stood during the battle was smaller and white.[10]

Daniel Klingle Farm

GPS: 39°48'22.31"N, 77°14'46.42"W; Elev. 584 ft.

- Farther south down the road, you will see the restored Daniel Klingle house. Klingle's home was a wartime structure and has recently been returned to its original log exterior by the National Park Service. [11] The existing barn is a post-battle building.
- General Kemper's Brigade had to execute a series of moves by their front and left flank to reach their objective on Cemetery Ridge. Kemper's right probably crossed the road in the vicinity of the Klingle farm. Portions of Wilcox and Lang's brigades also passed through here approximately 20 minutes later in their ill-conceived attempt to protect Kemper's right flank.
- Across the road and just north of the Klingle farm once stood the home of Peter and Susan Rogers. The now-forgotten one-story log home was riddled with shot and shell, and the property was covered with dead bodies. [12]

EMMITSBURG ROAD FENCES

The presence and impact of the post and rail fences along the Emmitsburg Road are just one of the many battle details that can create endless debates amongst Gettysburg students. Many battlefield visitors have tried to visualize Pickett and Pettigrew's men scrambling over these sturdy fences under a withering enemy fire. There is even a popular notion, perpetuated several years ago by a television documentary, that these fences were such an obstacle that they actually played a decisive part in the charge's outcome.

There is no doubt that fences existed in July 1863. Nor should there be any doubt that they were subjected to a heavy fire of bullets and artillery projectiles on both July 2 and July 3. Southerner William Swallow graphically wrote, "some slabs were so completely perforated with bullet holes that you could scarcely place a half inch between them." One 16- foot piece of fence rail was found to contain 836 bullet or shrapnel holes. Swallow believed that this particular rail was located where Lowrance's Brigade had reached the road. [1]

Numerous eyewitness accounts attest to the suspense and the length of time required to climb the fences. Not only would attack formations have nearly collapsed, but the soldiers would have also provided increasing target density as they slowed and bunched near these obstacles. William Swallow wrote:

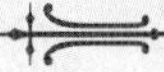

Scores of the survivors often related their anxious suspense and the length of time it seemed to climb up to the top of the fence. As soon as the top of the fence was lined with troops the whole line tumbled over, falling flat into the bed of the road, while the enemy's bullets buried themselves into the bodies of the falling victims. [2]

"At the Emmitsburg Road, where the parallel fences impeded the onward march," Rawley Martin observed, "large numbers were shot down on account of the crowding at the openings where the fences had been thrown down, and on account of the halt in order to climb the fences. After passing these obstacles, the advancing column deliberately rearranged its lines and moved forward." [3] Lieutenant V. A. Tapscott of the 56th Virginia wrote, "the crossing of the second road [sic] broke up the line, and it was not compact after that, yet we went forward all the same to the rock fence, and I was surprised to find but few friends in sight in getting there." [4]

James Francis Crocker remembered going "over the double fences." [5] Lieutenant J. Irving Sale of the 53rd Virginia described trying to crawl between two fence rails while the sounds of "ping-ping" struck the wood. His head got stuck between two rails and he was horrified by the thought "that I might be killed and left hanging there dead." [6]

Several accounts suggest that Union skirmishers used the road and fences as fortifications against attack. Joseph Mayo in Kemper's Brigade described "the Emmitsburg Road, along which, behind piles of rails, the enemy's strong line of skirmishers was posted." [7] Major Charles Peyton, in Garnett's Brigade: "The brigade moved in good order, keeping up its line almost perfectly, notwithstanding it had to climb three high post and rail fences, behind the last of which the enemy's skirmishers were first met and immediately driven in." [8] In Union Brig. General Alexander Webb's brigade, several soldiers who were on the skirmish line confirmed that they had built a temporary breastwork of rails and "the fence on the Emmitsburg Road to our left was mostly destroyed, but on our immediate front almost intact." [9]

General Webb stated in a postwar interview that when the Confederates "reached the Emmitsburg Road, it was noticed that the fences on both sides were great obstacles to them, and being oblique to the lines the men, after facing them, took directions normal to the fence at times which caused a confusion which was not easily repaired by the officers in command." [10]

We will never know with certainty how decisive a factor these fences were. Fences were among the many obstacles that a Civil War soldier was likely to encounter on the battlefield. They certainly disrupted the Confederate advance and formations, as noted in many of the above accounts, but given the large number of soldiers who did proceed beyond the road, it seems that they only served as a temporary barrier to overcome. "There were two fences at that road," recalled Lt. John Lewis of the

A fence post from the Emmitsburg Road with bullet embedded. Images photographed by Karl Stelly; images courtesy of Erik Dorr, Gettysburg Museum of History. The misspellings on the card (at right) are part of the original display.

9th Virginia, "but they were no impediment." [11] Lieutenant William Wood, 19th Virginia: "Over the fence we scramble. We bound diagonally across the Emmitsburg Pike and feel that the hill has fallen." [12]

There is a general perception that the fences would have been removed by Union skirmishers as the road angles toward the town and closer to the Union lines. On the 8th Ohio front, Col. Franklin Sawyer recalled in a postwar account that the road was "fenced on both sides with the old-fashioned stake and rider-rail fence" as of the afternoon of July 2. But when his regiment occupied the road and drove out some Confederate skirmishers, they dismantled the fences and piled them into a "barricade" which presumably still stood on July 3. [13]

Stout fences, similar to those that slowed the Confederate troops, line the Emmitsburg Road today with the Nicholas Codori farm in the background. Image courtesy of Michael Waricher

On the other hand, we have the postwar account of Maj. McLeod Turner of the 7th North Carolina in Lane's Brigade under Trimble:

> This road known as the Emmitsburg Pike, had a post and rail fence on either side; the first, I ordered the men to rush up against and push down, which they did, but having to run up out of the road they did not succeed in a like attempt on the second, and seeing that we were losing time, I climbed over on the right and my men were following me rapidly. [14]

Likewise, a surgeon in the 108th New York recorded that the road was "bounded on both sides, in our front, by a straight rail fence, the double posts of which were firmly planted in the earth. These could not be thrown down without taking them slowly to pieces- consequently they had to climb those two fences & reform in the open field which gently sloped up to our position."[15]

In fact, more than one battlefield visitor has dismissively asked, "Why didn't the Confederates simply knock the fences down?" Fences were not intended to come down easily. Participant accounts demonstrate that it was not as simple to remove a Pennsylvania farmer's sturdy fence from both sides of a sunken road while under heavy rifle and artillery fire as many an armchair warrior has often assumed.

Emmitsburg Road (East Side) West of Stone Wall

STOP 6

GPS: 39°48′46.01″N, 77°14′12.37″W; Elev. 585 ft.

Now cross the Emmitsburg Road. Be careful of oncoming traffic in both directions. The National Park Service routinely places strategic gaps in the fence line along this road and you are requested to cross at one of these breaks. Once you have crossed the road, proceed into the large open field that is on the west side of the stone wall that was defended by Northern soldiers.

You should now be across the Emmitsburg Road, north and east of the Codori farm. You may note that the National Park Service mows a path from the road to the Angle. It is roughly 250 yards from the east side of the Emmitsburg Road to the stone wall and the Angle. The final charge up this slope was met by a barrage of bullets and canister.

After crossing the Emmitsburg Road, follow the mowed path up to the Union lines at the stone wall.
Image courtesy of Karl Stelly

As Pickett's Division bunched into this area, they were taking infantry and artillery fire both in their front and their right flank. Garnett's men were still ahead of Armistead and some accounts indicate that Garnett told his men to not return fire and to keep moving at a quickstep. Major Charles Peyton wrote that General Garnett "ordered the brigade forward, which it promptly obeyed, loading and firing as it advanced…under a galling fire both from artillery and infantry, the artillery using grape and canister. We were now within about 75 paces of the wall, unsupported on the right and left, General Kemper being some 50 or

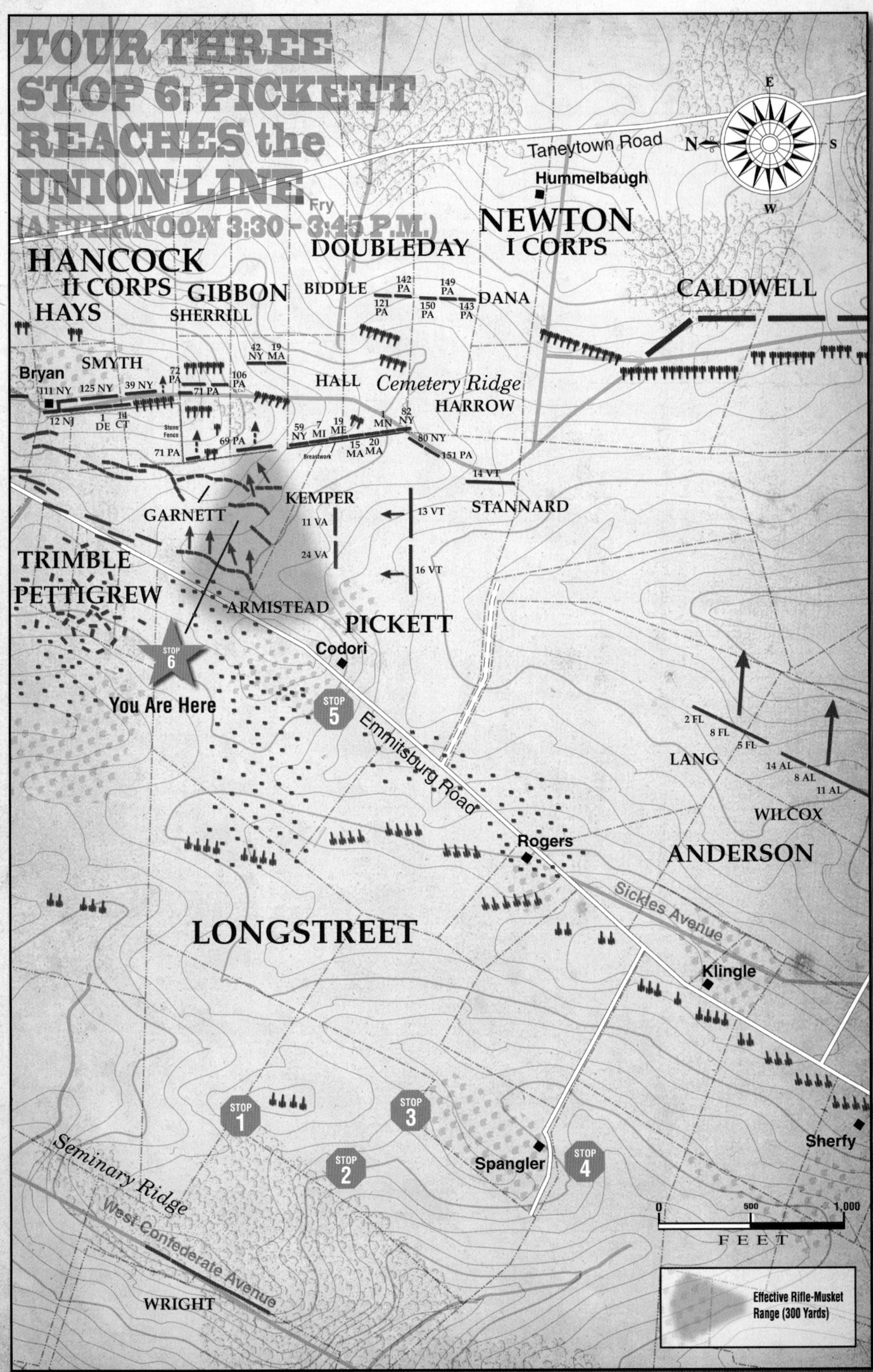
TOUR THREE
STOP 6: PICKETT REACHES the UNION LINE
(AFTERNOON 3:30 - 3:45 P.M.)
Taneytown Road
Hummelbaugh
Fry
NEWTON
I CORPS
DOUBLEDAY
HANCOCK
II CORPS
HAYS
GIBBON
SHERRILL
BIDDLE
DANA
CALDWELL
142 PA
149 PA
121 PA
150 PA
143 PA
SMYTH
Bryan
111 NY
125 NY
39 NY
72 PA
106 PA
71 PA
42 NY
19 MA
HALL
Cemetery Ridge
HARROW
12 NJ
1 DE
14 CT
Stone Fence
71 PA
69 PA
59 NY
7 MI
19 ME
1 MN
82 NY
80 NY
151 PA
15 MA
20 MA
Breastwork
14 VT
STANNARD
KEMPER
13 VT
11 VA
24 VA
16 VT
GARNETT
TRIMBLE
PETTIGREW
ARMISTEAD
PICKETT
Codori
STOP 6
You Are Here
STOP 5
Emmitsburg Road
2 FL
8 FL
5 FL
LANG
14 AL
8 AL
11 AL
WILCOX
ANDERSON
Rogers
Sickles Avenue
LONGSTREET
Klingle
STOP 1
STOP 3
STOP 2
STOP 4
Spangler
Sherfy
Seminary Ridge
West Confederate Avenue
WRIGHT
0
500
1,000
FEET
Effective Rifle-Musket Range (300 Yards)
E
N
S
W

60 yards behind and to the right, and General Armistead coming up in our rear." [1] Peyton added:

> Our line, much shattered, still kept up the advance until within about 20 paces of the wall, when, for a moment, it recoiled under the terrific fire that poured into our ranks both from their batteries and from their sheltered infantry. At this moment, General Kemper came up on the right and General Armistead in rear, when the three lines, joining in concert, rushed forward with unyielding determination and an apparent spirit of laudable rivalry to plant the Southern banner on the walls of the enemy. His strongest and last line was instantly gained; the Confederate battle-flag waved over his defenses, and the fighting over the wall became hand to hand, and of the most desperate character; but more than half having already fallen, our line was found too weak to rout the enemy. We hoped for a support on the left (which had started simultaneously with ourselves), but hoped in vain. [2]

Joseph Mayo claimed that when "within only a few steps of the stone fence" he managed to shake General Garnett's hand and congratulate him "on being able to be with his men." [3] First having escaped Stonewall Jackson's censure and then having been injured by a horse's kick, Garnett's road to Cemetery Ridge had been a difficult one. Many soldiers, almost too many, claimed to have seen him meet his demise and some of those accounts vary greatly.

Approaching the Angle from the perspective of Pickett's men. Image courtesy of Michael Waricher

"There was scarcely an officer or man in the command whose attention was not attracted by the cool and handsome bearing of General Garnett," wrote Major Peyton of the 19th Virginia, "who, totally devoid of excitement or rashness, rode immediately in rear of his advancing line, endeavoring by his personal efforts, and by the aid of his staff, to keep his line well closed and dressed. He was shot from his horse while near the center of the brigade, within about 25 paces of the stone wall." [4]

Colonel Birkett Fry, leading the brigade to Garnett's left, wrote: "I heard Garnett give a command to his men which amid the rattle of musketry I could not distinguish. Seeing my look or gesture inquiring he called out, 'I am dressing on you.' A few seconds after he fell dead." [5]

Captain John Jones and a Pvt. Robert Irvine both claimed to have been present when Garnett was killed instantly by a minie ball through the brain and fell from his horse. Irvine saw that a bullet had entered just above and behind the general's left ear. Irvine claimed to recover Garnett's watch and gave it to an adjutant before both were forced to run for their lives. Irvine placed this "within fifteen or twenty paces of the stone wall" and a little to the right of the Angle. [6]

Private James Clay, in the 18th Virginia, was struck down when about 100 yards from the clump of trees. "The last I saw of General Garnett he was astride his large black horse in the forefront of the charge and near the stone wall…General Garnett was waving his hat and cheering the men on to renewed efforts against the enemy." Garnett's horse soon "came galloping toward us with a huge gash in his right shoulder, evidently struck by a piece of shell." Two Federal soldiers told Clay, "our brigade general had been killed, having been shot through the body at the waist by a grapeshot." [7] Yet at least one other account insisted

On July 3, 2013, approximately 20,000 people recreated Pickett's Charge during the battle's 150th anniversary commemoration. Image courtesy of Michael Waricher

that his horse went down with him. [8]

Near the Emmitsburg Road, wrote William Swallow (who did not personally observe the moment), "the brave General Garnett, of Virginia, rode along his line covered with blood, with his head bowed almost to his horse's neck. In a moment the General and his horse fell to the ground riddled with bullets in all parts of their bodies." [9]

Whatever the exact cause of Garnett's death--whether he fell due to canister or to a bullet in the head--his body was never identified. If he was seemingly visible to nearly everyone at the time of death then his corpse disappeared immediately afterwards. Pickett staff officer Walter Harrison later claimed to know "about the spot where Garnett fell." Union General Henry Hunt later told Harrison that he made a "diligent search in person, for Garnett's body, the day after the battle, but could not identify it. He remained unrecognizable by any one, among the many dead, and was doubtless buried in the trenches near the spot where he fell." [10] Private Clay recalled that the general "wore a uniform coat, almost new, with a general's stars and wreath on the collar, and top boots, with trousers inside, and spurs. It is therefore inexplicable that his remains were not identified." [11] But if Garnett had been killed by a head wound, stripped of his uniform by scavengers, and then had his corpse subjected to the elements for even as little as twenty-four hours, then there should be no real mystery as to why his body was not recognized amongst the heaps of dead. All that remained was his inscribed sword that reappeared in a Baltimore shop years later. [12]

A National Park Service marker in front of the Angle at the stone wall.
Image courtesy of Karl Stelly

According to Rawley Martin, Armistead's soldiers had advanced thus far with their rifles on their shoulders having not fired a shot. Several accounts stated that Armistead rushed forward in response to an appeal from General Kemper. By some versions, Kemper approached on horseback and called out: "Armistead, I am going to charge those heights and carry them and I want you to support me." To which Armistead replied, "I'll do it! Look at my line. It never looked better on dress parade." [13] Such postwar quotations might be apocryphal, but they defy the popular impression that Pickett's men were beleaguered and on the defensive from enemy fire. Kemper and Armistead believed that they might succeed up until nearly the very end.

After conferring with Armistead, General Kemper returned to his own men. Colonel Joseph Mayo recalled Kemper rising "in his stirrups and pointing to the left with his sword" shouting, "There are the guns boys, go for them!" [14] By this time, Pickett's Division was threatened not only on their front but also on their right flank from Stannard's Vermonters.

Captain John Holmes Smith of the 11th Virginia, Kemper's Brigade, remembered that at a distance of "several hundred yards" from the enemy's lines "we rushed towards the works, running, I may say, almost at top speed, and as we neared the works I could see a good line of battle, thick and substantial, firing upon us." Smith described the enemy's defenses as a "hasty trench and embankment" and his own regiment "was a mass or ball, all mixed together, without company organization." Smith suffered a flesh wound in the leg but kept fighting, as did Lt. Hilary Harris who had picked up the regiment's colors and was struck several times but unharmed. Harris told his father several days later, "there were but few left to reach the enemy's works and we so weak that although the enemy broke we could not hold them." [15]

An enemy ball hit General Kemper in the groin and ranged up into his body. Calling the wound "excruciatingly painful," Kemper later wrote:

> I think I was shot from my horse about the instant at which the general rout began. I know that I was then near enough to the enemy's line to observe the features and expressions on the faces of the men in front of me, and I thought I observed and could identify the soldier who shot me. Quickly after I fell, a federal officer with several men took possession of me, placed me on a blanket, and started to carry me (as the officer said) to a federal surgeon, when some of my men came up and firing across my body, recaptured me and carried me in the same blanket to our own rear. [16]

Kemper's wound was erroneously believed to be mortal, but it did prove to be painful for the remainder of his days. Too badly injured to be removed with Lee's retreating army after the battle, he would spend some time in captivity before being exchanged for General Charles Graham from Sickles's III Corps who was captured on July 2. [17] James Kemper's postwar career included a stint as post-Reconstruction governor of Virginia in the 1870s before dying in 1895.

With both Generals Garnett and Kemper down, the moment now belonged to Armistead. Waving his hat on his sword, which soon cut through the hat and caused it to slip down to the hilt, Armistead urged his men onward: "Forward, double quick!" The double quick soon turned into a run. [18] Armistead's Brigade now closed the gap with Garnett's disorganized men.

At about this time, the 53rd's color sergeant Leander Blackburn was mortally wounded. Corporal James Carter momentarily grabbed the flag, but another man, John B. Scott took it from him and dashed forward until he was killed. Robert Tyler Jones now seized the flag but was shot in the arm. Jones held onto the colors and leapt onto the stone wall where he momentarily waved them triumphantly. But he was shot again and fell severely wounded. Lieutenant Hutchings Carter was the last to grab the flag, and soon went

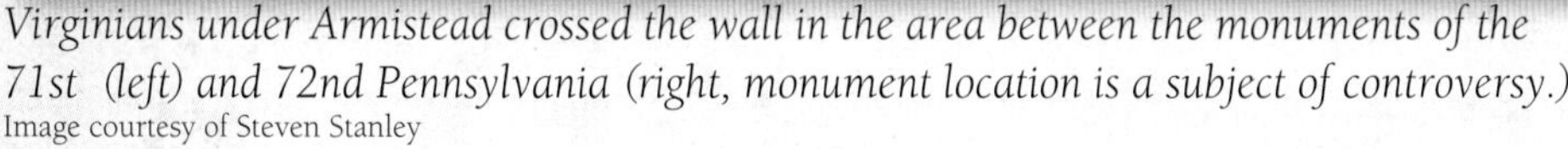

Virginians under Armistead crossed the wall in the area between the monuments of the 71st (left) and 72nd Pennsylvania (right, monument location is a subject of controversy.)
Image courtesy of Steven Stanley

over the wall with Gen. Armistead. It had taken five men to carry the 53rd Virginia's colors less than one mile. The flag was captured and Lieutenant Carter was lucky to survive; he counted 17 bullet holes in his clothes but was not even wounded. [19]

Lieutenant John Lewis of the 9th Virginia described these final chaotic moments:

> Within 800 yards of the Federal works Garnett's Brigade gave their usual yell and strike the double quick. At 100 yards they deliver their fire and dash at the works with the bayonet. Kemper's Brigade takes up the yell, fire, and dashes at them with the bayonet. Armistead, who is a little to the left and rear catches the enthusiasm, joins the yell, and, on the run, Armistead fell back to the rear to give his brigade a chance to fire. They fire and rush at the works and to the assistance of Garnett and Kemper. There are shouts, fire, smoke, clashing of arms. [20]

Whether by chance or intent, Armistead found a relative opening at the stone wall between the 71st and 69th Pennsylvania regiments. When the 71st withdrew from the area now known as the Angle, Armistead's men gained a momentary foothold on the west side of the wall. However, Union fire was still heavy and many of the Virginians momentarily took cover on this side of the wall to return fire. This probably lasted for several moments when, according to the 53rd Virginia's Rawley Martin, Armistead turned to Martin and said, "We can't stay here!" upon which Martin replied, "We'll go forward then!" Armistead then climbed the wall and with a wave of his sword shouted, "Boys! Give them the cold steel! Who will follow me?" Over the wall went Armistead and perhaps 100-150 men. The charge's climactic moment had arrived. [21]

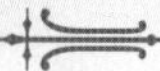

TO DIE IN A FOREIGN LAND

As Confederate casualties increased between the Emmitsburg Road and the stone wall, Pickett's Division lost three promising young officers whose lives had all followed remarkably similar roads to Gettysburg.

Lewis B. Williams, Robert C. Allen, and Waller Tazewell Patton were all Virginia natives who had attended VMI together. They graduated in the same small class on July 4, 1855. The men then all pursued occupations as lawyers prior to the Civil War. When military duty called, they all ended up commanding regiments in Pickett's Division during Pickett's Charge and all three were killed or mortally wounded on this day.

Lewis B. Williams (left), colonel of the 1st Virginia (Kemper's Brigade), was 29 years old at Gettysburg. He had graduated VMI with excellent academic standing and held the highest military office in his class. After graduation, he taught mathematics and tactics for three years before pursuing law. The bachelor served with other Virginia regiments early in the war, but was elected colonel of the 1st Virginia in April 1862. He was wounded and taken prisoner at Williamsburg. [1]

Williams was mounted on his horse "Nelly" during the charge. Somewhere near the Codori house, he took a ball in the shoulder, fell from his horse onto his own drawn sword and was killed. The riderless horse was later caught by a member of Dearing's artillery battalion. His body was eventually reburied in Richmond's Hollywood Cemetery. [2]

Image from *Opening Celebration of the 1st VA Regiment Armory, Richmond, VA, May 29, 1914*

Robert C. Allen (top next page) was a colonel in the 28th Virginia (Garnett's Brigade.) He had celebrated his 29th birthday less than two weeks earlier. Allen's father was a lawyer and US congressman. He too had pursued a law career following VMI and married the daughter of a judge in 1861. [3]

Allen had been a member of the 28th Virginia since May 1861. He was considered a strict disciplinarian, which was essential to making his citizen soldiers combat-ready, but was not always appreciated by the rank and file themselves. He fought in numerous battles and was wounded when a shell struck his shoulder at Gaines's Mill. His brother was killed in the same battle. [4]

The suggestions that Allen may have been a bit of a martinet would seem to be confirmed by Eppa Hunton's memoirs. Hunton had led Pickett's Brigade at Second Manassas and blamed Allen for botching an attack after Allen allegedly refused to advance his regiment on verbal orders, insisting instead that all orders be made in writing. "I ought to have court-martialed Colonel Allen," wrote

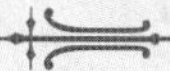

Hunton. "He lost his prestige with the brigade; his regiment became dissatisfied with him, and General Garnett thought seriously of disbanding the regiment, but at Gettysburg Allen led his regiment with heroism, and was killed in that great battle." [5]

Allen reached near the stone wall at Gettysburg with his men before being shot in the head and shoulder. A soldier who was with him claimed that the colonel was brought into the Union lines as a prisoner. Allen asked the soldier, "Whar is the colors? [Sic]" and promptly died. Allen's burial place is unknown. [6]

The final member of this trio was Col. Waller Tazewell Patton (bottom right). He was slightly younger than his two classmates. Born July 15, 1835, Patton was 27 years old at Gettysburg. His great-grandfather was Revolutionary War hero General Hugh Mercer and it was no surprise that Patton pursued a military education. [7]

Patton had served with distinction throughout the war and made colonel in June 1862. He was then wounded at Second Manassas. Patton must have been held in some esteem: he was elected to the Virginia State Senate while serving with the army despite not having an opportunity to even canvass his district during the election. [8]

Courtesy of the Virginia Military Institute Archives

Colonel Patton led the 7th Virginia (Kemper's Brigade.) He was shot in the jaw at the Emmitsburg Road and left behind when Lee's army retreated. Taken to Pennsylvania (later Gettysburg) College's field hospital, he was kindly attended to by a nurse from Baltimore. Patton could only communicate by writing on a slate due to his injury. "Tell my mother that I am about to die in a foreign land," he wrote shortly before his death, "but I cherish the same intense affection for her as ever." Federal officers who saw what he had written were astonished that he described Pennsylvania as a foreign land. Patton died at the hospital on July 21, days after his 28th birthday, and was eventually reinterred at the Stonewall Confederate Cemetery in Winchester, Virginia. He was buried next to his brother who also died during the war. [9]

The military tradition continued in the Patton family. Colonel Waller Tazewell Patton is perhaps best remembered as the great-uncle of World War II General George S. Patton.

Courtesy of the Virginia Military Institute Archives

ELLIOTT BURIAL MAP

The "Elliott Burial Map" was created to show the locations of Union and Confederate mass graves (as well as dead horses) on the field after the battle. Although it is generally believed to greatly over-estimate the number of burials, the general patterns are assumed to be accurate. One of the heaviest concentrations of graves on the map are situated in the field immediately east of the Emmitsburg Road and west of the stone wall held by the Federal army. This confirms that large numbers of Confederate infantry crossed the Emmitsburg Road before meeting their demise. It is unlikely that soldiers killed west of the road would have had their decomposing corpses dragged across the sunken road for burial.

Image courtesy of Library of Congress

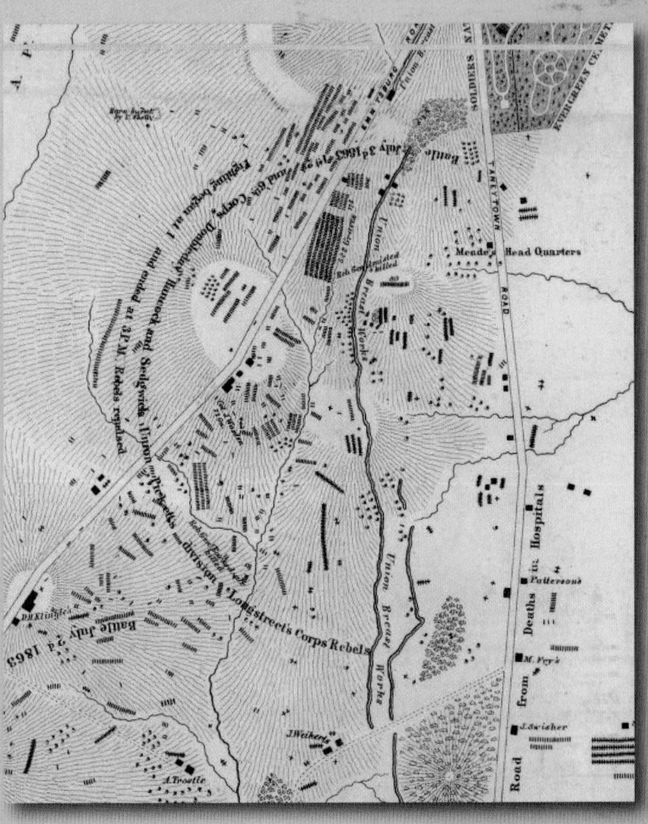

WHERE WAS PICKETT?

Battlefield visitors, past and present, upon hearing the tale of "Pickett's Charge" often ask about General Pickett's actions and where he was physically located during the attack. A popular assertion, supported by few definitive facts, is that General Pickett reached an observation point near the Nicholas Codori farm along the Emmitsburg Road. When asked about this afterwards, Union General Webb laughed and replied, "let us be kind to him, he is said to have been hidden from us by the Codori House and barns." [1]

But Pickett's actual whereabouts were controversial enough that they were debated by the battle's veterans. It was repeatedly noted that, unlike most other mounted officers, neither Pickett nor his staff were killed or wounded. The same could not be said for Generals Pettigrew and Trimble, both of whom were wounded while leading their men. [2] Eppa Hunton wrote in his memoirs:

> Did Pickett go with his division in the charge? The evidence is pretty strong on both sides of that question. No man who was in that charge has ever been found, within my knowledge, who saw Pickett during the charge. One of my soldiers…told me that he was detailed to carry water to Pickett and his staff during the fight at Gettysburg. I asked him where were Pickett and his staff? He said they were behind a lime-stone ledge of rocks, about 100 yards in the rear of the position that we held just prior to the charge…I understand a Confederate surgeon says that he had his field hospital behind this ledge of rocks, and that Picket was there during the charge of his division. Another strong argument on that side of the question consists in the fact that neither Pickett nor any of his staff was killed or wounded, and not one of their horses was killed or wounded, whereas every man who was known to have gone into that charge, on horse-back, was killed or wounded, or had his horse killed…On the other hand, several of his staff say that he did go into the charge. But how far he went, or how near he was to his division, they have not informed us; General Lee met General Pickett after the charge and said, "You and your division have covered yourselves with glory"; I leave this question to be determined according to the feelings and judgment of every man who reads what I have said. [3]

Hunton's recollections were seemingly supported by a 1904 account of Dr. Clayton Coleman, in Kemper's Brigade, who described being several hundred yards in rear of the Confederate lines during the cannonade. "Upon arriving at the edge of woods," he saw General Pickett and staffer Walter Harrison standing behind a tree, holding their horses. "Just then a shell exploded in the tree behind which Major Harrison was standing, a few feet above his head, when both he and General Pickett mounted their horses and rode rapidly to rear." Apparently not having any postwar ax to grind, Clayton asked that his account not be publicized. [4] Needless to say, Harrison did not recall such an episode in his memoirs *Pickett's Men: A Fragment of War History.*

Major Kirkwood Otey, in the 11th Virginia, "never heard a positive statement as to where General Pickett was in that charge; never heard him located or placed…" Otey was wounded and helped to a field hospital in rear. While there, he saw some of Pickett's staff drawing whiskey from a surgeon's wagon and assumed that their general must be nearby. [5]

Colonel David Aiken, in Kershaw's 7th South Carolina, and Maj. John Cheves Haskell, in Henry's artillery battalion, both placed Pickett and staff during the assault. The division commander was not cowering behind the Confederate lines but was in fact well to the right and rear of his attacking force. They claimed that Pickett and staff spent nearly all of the afternoon near the Sherfy peach orchard and the Wheatfield Road and Emmitsburg Road intersection. Aiken alleged that Pickett was drunk, while Haskell described Pickett and staff as being in "great confusion." Haskell also thought it odd, as did others, that Pickett and staff all survived the day unscathed. [6] While some might argue that the elevation along the Emmitsburg Road offered an ideal vantage point for Pickett to view and coordinate movement, it would have been near impossible for Pickett to manage his entire line from that point, particularly given the clouds of dust and smoke that surely enveloped the field. The roughly 1,500 yards from the Sherfy farm to area in front of the Angle and Copse of Trees would have challenged the ability of active staff officers to deliver quick and timely messages.

Moxley Sorrel of Longstreet's staff was sent to locate Pickett and discuss threats to his flank.

Sorrel wrote only that he "did not meet" Pickett, yet was able to locate both Garnett and Armistead. This implies, but is nowhere near conclusive, that Pickett was not where Sorrel might have expected him to be. [7]

"When the advance commenced," wrote Lt. Colonel Rawley Martin of the 53rd Virginia, "General Pickett rode up and down in rear of Kemper and Garnett, and in this position he continued as long as there was opportunity of observing him. When the assault became so fierce that they had to superintend the whole line, I am sure he was in his proper place." According to Martin, the members of Pickett's staff held a postwar meeting in Richmond, and after comparing recollections, published a statement that Pickett "was in the division throughout the charge; that he made an effort to secure reinforcements when he saw his flanks were being turned, and one of General Garnett's couriers testified that he carried orders from him almost to the rock fence." [8]

Pickett's staff officers were publicly in agreement that their leader was in a proper position behind his men and advanced as the troops did. Captain Robert Bright wrote in 1891:

> I have nothing to guide me as to the farthest point General Pickett reached in person…[at the Emmitsburg Road Pickett sent Bright to Longstreet requesting assistance] when I returned to General Pickett with General Longstreet's answer, I found General Pickett between the Emmitsburg Road and Cemetery Heights. Then three of us, one directly after the other, were sent to urge General Wilcox to bring his brigade to our assistance. On my return I found him near the descent of the last hill, facing the Federal works.

Artist Paul Philippoteaux depicted General Pickett and staff near the Codori farm in his Gettysburg Cyclorama painting. Image courtesy of Steven Stanley/GNMP

Bright's final sighting of Pickett "was near the last valley in front of Cemetery Ridge." [9] Although this description is imprecise, it suggests that the mounted Pickett was perilously close to the Union

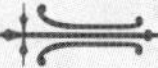

lines at a time when troops such as Stannard's Vermonters were in front of the Union works pouring a deadly flank fire into Pickett's men. Such accounts were clearly at variance with the assertions of Aiken and Haskell that Pickett and staff remained stationary near the Peach Orchard.

Bright offered a slightly revised account in 1904 (and reprinted in *Confederate Veteran*): "I found General Pickett in front about three hundred yards ahead of the artillery position, and to the left of it, and some two hundred yards behind the command, which was then at the stone wall over which some of our men were going…He had remained behind to watch and protect that left, to put in first help expected from infantry supports, then to break the troops which came around his flank with the artillery; all had failed." [10] Such distances, if accurately remembered, would have placed Pickett's final position at the Emmitsburg Road or perhaps slightly east of it.

It is clear from primary accounts that wherever Pickett was, he did not "lead" the charge that bears his name in the traditional sense. Nor should he have. His proper place as a divisional commander was in rear of his men and in a position from which he could observe, supervise, and coordinate movements to the best that such activities were possible on a Civil War battlefield. Lieutenant W. Stuart Symington of Pickett's staff argued that his commander ended up "much closer than was prudent or necessary for a Major General commanding an assault." Major Edmund Berkeley of the 8th Virginia: "I have been often asked if Pickett was in the charge. I have always replied that he was not and in my opinion, if [he] had been would have been out of his proper place." [11]

General Pickett was active enough to have sent a staffer (Bright) to Longstreet requesting flank support and then sent several couriers to Wilcox. Those were proper activities for the division commander. On the other hand, there is no conclusive evidence that he was in position to give any direction to Kemper, Garnett, and Armistead once the charge started. The hasty final consultation between Kemper and Armistead near the Emmitsburg Road suggests that Pickett's brigadiers were on their own. There also remains the thorny fact that the mounted Pickett and his staff suffered no casualties, making Bright's assertion that Pickett reached "the last valley in front of Cemetery Ridge" unlikely.

George Pickett was active in this charge. But his legacy is sometimes confronted by the fact that his peers, Pettigrew and Trimble, and all three of his subordinate brigadiers became casualties in the grand assault while he and his staff officers did not. It might be unfair to compare him negatively to Pettigrew and Trimble as they may have exposed themselves inappropriately (due to their ranks) to danger. Nevertheless, martyred leaders such as General Armistead provide the real inspiration of the July 3 assault: waving his word while leading his men into the teeth of Union canister and muskets. Pickett was, in comparison, a participant in "Pickett's Charge," disappearing from much of the historical record until he afterwards greeted Lee with the emotional, "General Lee, I have no division now." [12]

At this point, we have completed tours of the Confederate positions on Seminary Ridge, and the routes of Pickett, Pettigrew, and Trimble's commands.

As General Pickett once reportedly said that "the Yankees had something to do with" the outcome, we will now turn our attention to the Union defense against Longstreet's Assault. The tour of the Union battle line will begin at General Meade's headquarters. Return to your vehicle and drive to the Lydia Leister farm which served as Meade's command post.

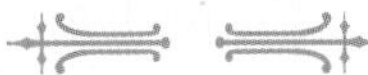

TOUR FOUR
Union Battle Line

"If Lee attacks tomorrow, it will be in your front."

— Major General George Meade. [1]

General George Meade's Headquarters

GPS: 39°48'51.92"N, 77°13'55.61"W; Elev. 566 ft.

Major General George Meade's headquarters are located on the west side of the Taneytown Road at the intersection of Hunt Avenue. If traveling from the north (from the town of Gettysburg), the building will be on the right side of the Taneytown Road. If driving from the south, the building will be on your left (approximately 0.1 miles north of the Taneytown Road entrance to the National Park Service Museum and Visitor Center.)

Park in the lot designated for the National Cemetery and walk south on the paved sidewalk for about 220 yards.

This modest farm was owned by the widow Lydia Leister, who purchased the property in 1861. Leister was about 52 years old in 1863. Her husband James had died in 1859, leaving the illiterate woman with five children who by 1863 ranged in age from six to 24 years old. She fled the property by heading south of town on July 1. [2]

When Maj. General George Meade arrived at Gettysburg near 1:00 a.m. on the morning of July 2, the Leister farm must have been identified as an excellent location for

A colorized 1903 photo of the Lydia Leister house. Image courtesy of Library of Congress

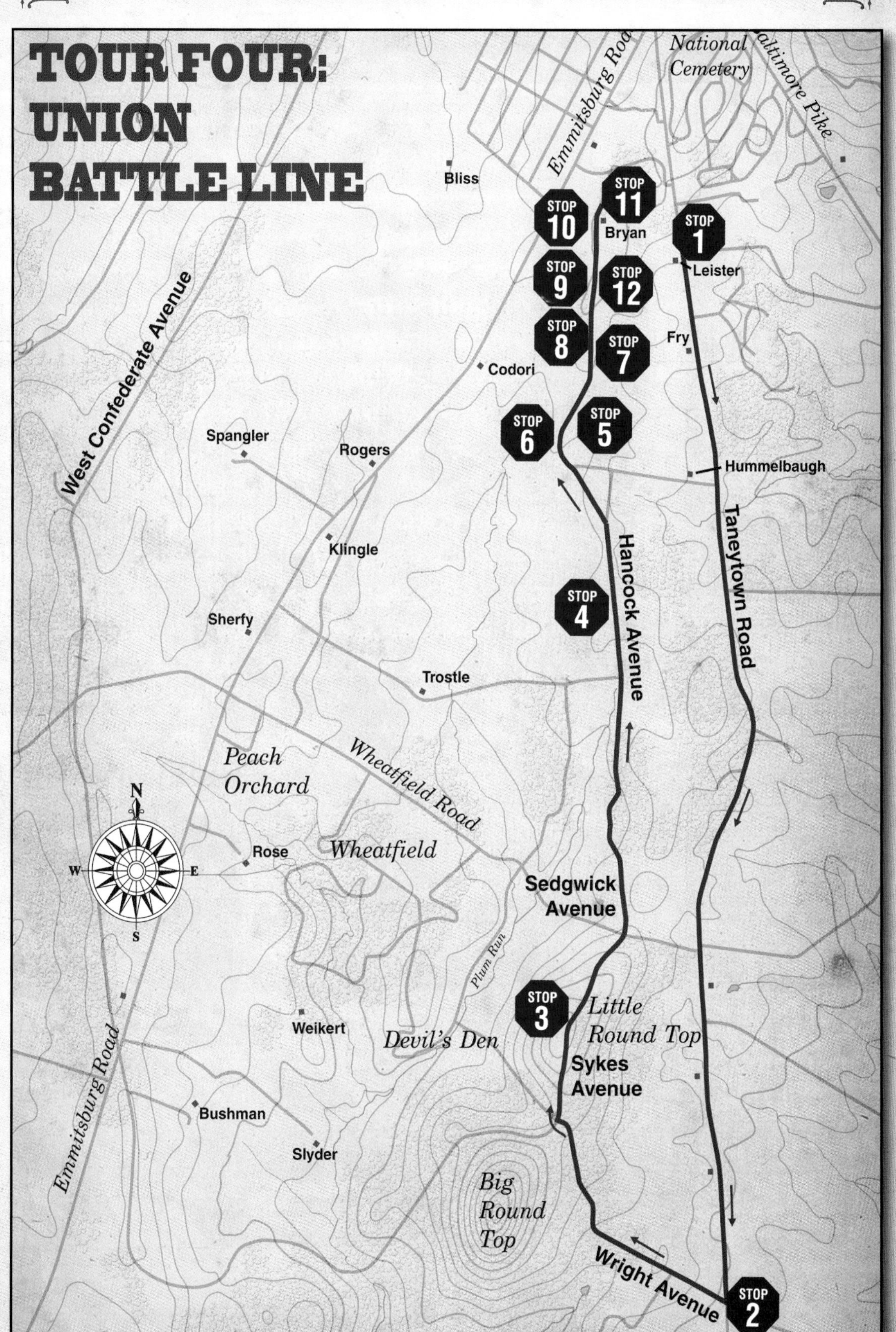
TOUR FOUR: UNION BATTLE LINE
National Cemetery
Emmitsburg Road
Baltimore Pike
Bliss
Bryan
Leister
Fry
Codori
Hummelbaugh
Spangler
Rogers
Klingle
Sherfy
Trostle
West Confederate Avenue
Hancock Avenue
Taneytown Road
Peach Orchard
Wheatfield Road
Wheatfield
Rose
Sedgwick Avenue
Plum Run
Little Round Top
Sykes Avenue
Devil's Den
Weikert
Bushman
Slyder
Emmitsburg Road
Big Round Top
Wright Avenue
STOP 1
STOP 2
STOP 3
STOP 4
STOP 5
STOP 6
STOP 7
STOP 8
STOP 9
STOP 10
STOP 11
STOP 12
N
S
E
W

army headquarters. Although the so-called "fishhook" would not take shape until later that day, from this location Meade was in close proximity to the already occupied Cemetery Hill and Culp's Hill. If you look to the south you can see how Meade had a line of sight to signal officers on Little Round Top. The portion of Cemetery Ridge immediately west of here would soon be defended by Hancock's II Corps. The Taneytown Road remained a key thoroughfare behind Union lines (although often overshadowed historically by the improved Baltimore Pike) and the placement of headquarters here on the reverse slope of Cemetery Ridge facilitated troop movements and communications throughout Meade's interior lines.

Gen. George G. Meade.
Image courtesy of Library of Congress

After the brutal fighting of July 2, General Meade's Army of the Potomac still held Cemetery Ridge from the Round Tops on the left to Cemetery Hill in the near center, and to Culp's and Wolf's hills on the right. General Meade had written a message for General in Chief Henry Halleck at 8:00 p.m. on the second, stating: "I shall remain in my present position to-morrow, but am not prepared to say, until better advised of the condition of the army, whether my operations will be of an offensive or defensive character." [3]

That evening, the recently appointed Meade (who had complained that his predecessor Joe Hooker too often kept subordinates uninformed) summoned his senior leaders to army headquarters at the Leister farmhouse. After some discussion, including concerns about their still-vulnerable flanks, the generals voted on whether to remain in their present position and whether to attack or await Lee's attack. The Union generals agreed, as XII Corps commander Henry Slocum famously voted, to "stay and fight it out." [4] (Ironically, Meade was criticized by some as being indecisive for meeting with his subordinates while Lee has been criticized for not meeting with his subordinates.)

Among the attendees was Meade's friend and II Corps division commander John Gibbon. General Gibbon technically should not have been present, but he was invited as part of the ongoing confusion over whether or not General Hancock was commanding more than just his II Corps. According to Gibbon, as he was departing the meeting, Meade said, "If Lee attacks tomorrow, it will be in your front." When Gibbon inquired why, Meade replied, "Because he has made attacks on both our flanks and failed, and if he concludes to try it again it will be on our center." Gibbon responded: "Well, general, I hope he does, and if he does, we shall whip him." [5]

Meade's testimony before the Joint Committee on the Conduct of the War contradicted Gibbon's oft-quoted recollections predicting an attack on the center. Meade testified:

The strong attack of the enemy that day upon my left flank, and their persistent

> efforts to obtain possession of what is called Round Top Mountain, induced the supposition that possibly, on the next day, a very persistent attack might be made, or that a movement, upon their part, to my left and rear might be made to occupy the lines of communication I then held with the Taneytown road and the Baltimore pike. [6]

Although the decision to "stay and fight" turned out to be the correct one, the Union generals' resolution to await attack essentially shifted the burden of responsibility to Lee, who was loathe to sit idly in enemy country. That burden was further pressed upon the Confederates when Slocum's Union XII Corps began shelling the Southerners at Culp's Hill during the early morning hours of July 3. Lee was denied his preferred renewal of coordinated flank attacks when Richard Ewell's forces became engaged here before Longstreet was ready to assault the Union left. The Confederates eventually withdrew from Culp's Hill by noon.

Meade continued to ponder and plan from these headquarters, but the morning of July 3 was not quiet. Not only did the heaviest sustained fighting of the entire battle rage on the Union right at Culp's Hill, but skirmishing (accompanied by some artillery fire) had also occurred at the Bliss farm opposite the Union left center.

Shortly before noon, soon after the Culp's Hill fighting had ended, General Gibbon invited Meade join him in a meal of rooster stew that had been appropriated from some unlucky farmer. Several II Corps officers (notably Generals Hancock, Gibbon, and Lt. Frank Haskell) were the primary guests at Gibbon's headquarters in the field just south of Leister's house. General Newton of the I Corps was also in attendance and chided Gibbon as "this young North Carolinian." The dining table was a mess chest. Chairs were scarce and many of the officers were seated on the ground, but as the ranking officer Meade enjoyed the luxury of a cracker box to sit on. The men smoked cigars afterwards and discussed what Lee's next movements might be. As noted previously, Gibbon's recollections were that Meade had already predicted an assault on the Union center, but according to Haskell, "General Meade still thought that the enemy would attack his left again today towards evening; but he was ready for them. General Hancock thought that the attack would be upon the position of the II Corps." Haskell also noted that Hancock would again assume command of his corps and Gibbon would return to commanding his own division. (The extent of Hancock's authority over the entire Union left being yet another later point of contention.) [7]

After eating, Meade then rode down his lines and briefly joined General Gouverneur K. Warren, Chief Engineer of the Army of the Potomac, on Little Round Top. By this point, the enemy was clearly massing their troops and artillery and most felt sure an attack was soon to follow. [8] Meade had a dispatch sent to General in Chief Henry Halleck in Washington at 12:30 p.m.:

> At the present moment all is quiet. Considerable firing, both infantry and artillery, has taken place in various parts of our line, but no development of the enemy's intentions. My cavalry are pushing the enemy on both my flanks, and keeping me advised of any effort to outflank me. We have taken several hundred prisoners since morning. [9]

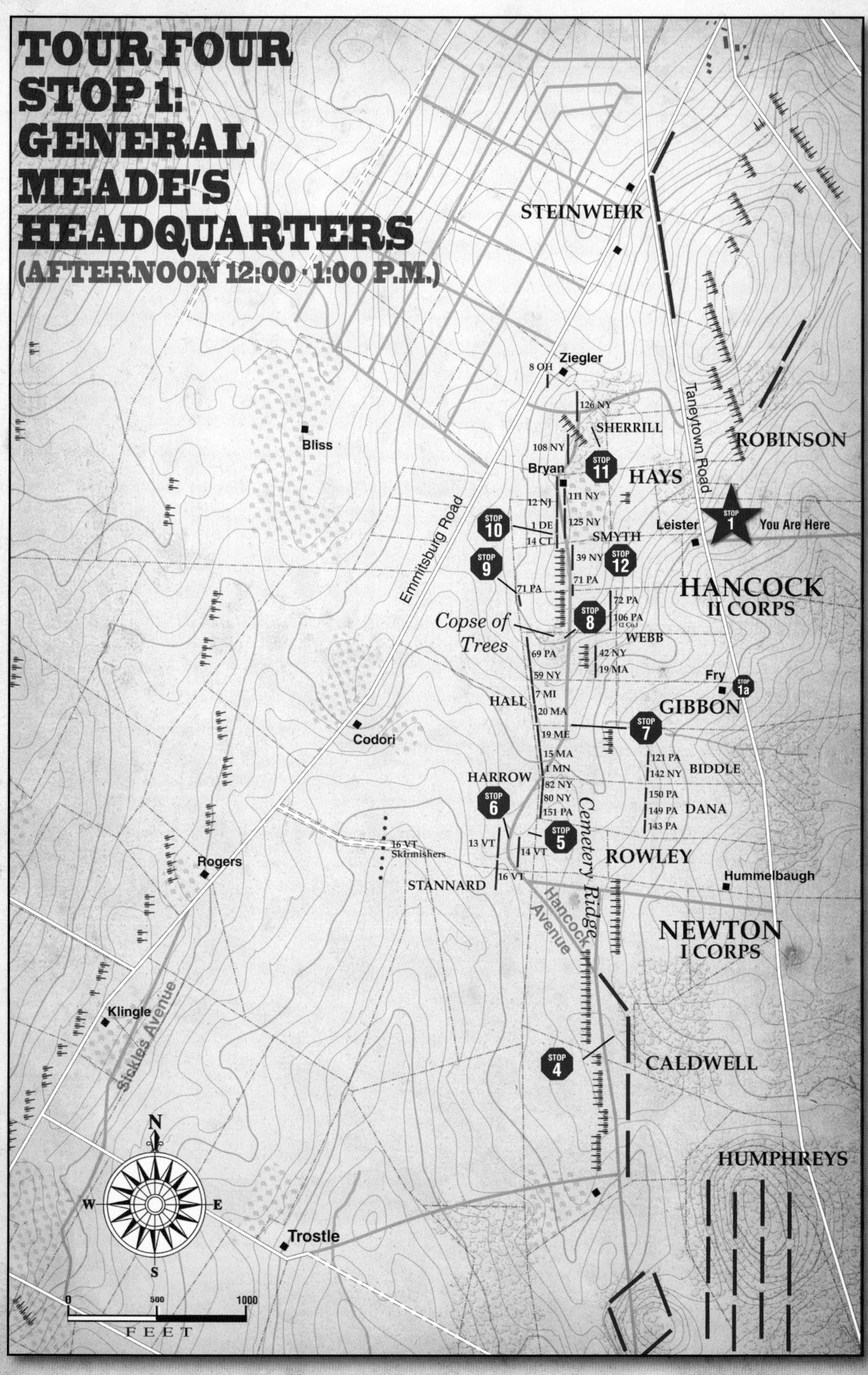

TOUR FOUR
STOP 1:
GENERAL
MEADE'S
HEADQUARTERS
(AFTERNOON 12:00 - 1:00 P.M.)
STEINWEHR
Ziegler
8 OH
126 NY
SHERRILL
108 NY
STOP 11
Bryan
HAYS
Taneytown Road
ROBINSON
Bliss
111 NY
12 NJ
STOP 10
1 DE
125 NY
14 CT
SMYTH
Leister
STOP 1
You Are Here
Emmitsburg Road
STOP 9
39 NY
STOP 12
71 PA
71 PA
HANCOCK
II CORPS
72 PA
106 PA
(2 Co.)
STOP 8
Copse of
Trees
WEBB
69 PA
42 NY
19 MA
59 NY
Fry
STOP 1a
7 MI
HALL
20 MA
GIBBON
STOP 7
Codori
19 ME
15 MA
121 PA
142 NY
BIDDLE
1 MN
HARROW
82 NY
80 NY
150 PA
STOP 6
151 PA
149 PA
DANA
Cemetery Ridge
143 PA
STOP 5
13 VT
16 VT
Skirmishers
14 VT
ROWLEY
Rogers
STANNARD
16 VT
Hummelbaugh
Hancock
Avenue
NEWTON
I CORPS
Klingle
Sickles Avenue
STOP 4
CALDWELL
N
W
E
S
HUMPHREYS
Trostle
0
500
1000
FEET

Back at Gibbon's headquarters, most of the officers had departed by 12:30 but Gibbon's staff stayed and dozed in the heat, until "the distinct sharp sound of one of the enemy's guns, square over to the front, caused us to open our eyes and turn them in that direction, when we saw directly above the crest the smoke of the bursting shell, and heard its noise." Shells quickly began to fall in on this side of Cemetery Ridge. General Gibbon's groomsman started to bring Gibbon his horse when a shell struck and killed him. [10]

It must have appeared that the overshooting Confederate shells were targeting the army's headquarters. A shell burst in the yard among the staff horses, another tore up the steps of the Leister house, another carried away the porch supports, still another passed through the door, and Meade was barely grazed by a solid shot that whizzed by him as he stood in the open doorway. To "avoid flying splinters of wood or falling timber," Meade and his staff withdrew to the fenced yard between the house and the Taneytown Road. He watched with amusement as several staff officers were congregating on the sheltered side of the house and "pleasantly" reminded them that no one place was safer than any other. [11]

Casualties amongst the horses were a sad but inevitable result of the raining shells. One man saw his horse badly wounded and rushed into the house to find a pistol and put the poor creature out of its misery. Unfortunately, he was a poor shot and put two bullets into another officer's uninjured horse before the owner stopped him. [12] Mrs. Leister later counted 17 dead horses in her yard. Although she received some recompense afterwards when she sold their bones, their presence corrupted her water supply and killed her "best peach tree" when five horse carcasses were burned too close to it. [13]

Still centrally located, Meade and his staff were able to distribute orders to several Union commanders. Slocum was to strengthen the line to his left while several brigades in the army's I, III, and VI corps were ordered to move into supporting distance of Hancock's II Corps. [14]

But as no staff officers from the other corps were able (or willing?) to reach this point, headquarters was eventually transferred "to a barn several hundred yards down the Taneytown Road." A shell fragment reportedly struck and wounded chief of staff Dan Butterfield while here, and after remaining a "short time," Meade and his staff then moved to Slocum's headquarters on Powers Hill. Meade soon decided to issue orders to cease the Union's return artillery fire. [15] Although the Confederate overshots are generally acknowledged as contributing to Lee's overall failure, they momentarily succeeded in disrupting Meade's headquarters communications, as artillery commander Henry Hunt and others noted the difficulty in locating Meade during this time.

Meade would return here after the day's actions concluded, but as the farm was now in use as a field hospital, the victorious Meade and staff spent the night of July 3 and morning of July 4 sleeping "among the rocks in the open" field about a quarter of a mile down the Taneytown Road. There was no rest for the weary, however, as it started to rain sometime after 2:00 a.m. [16]

General Meade then relocated to new headquarters on the Baltimore Pike from July

4 until his departure on the morning of July 7. The precise location of the new headquarters was a mystery until 1987. Esteemed historian William A. Frassanito discovered that photographer Frederick Gutekunst had captured an image of the probable site on about July 15, although it had been confusingly labeled as Meade's headquarters "during the last two days of the battle." Frassanito identified the Gutekunst image as the wartime home of the widow Mary Pfeffer, situated on the east side of the Baltimore Pike, about 650 yards southeast of East Cemetery Hill. Although not conclusive, evidence strongly suggested that the Pfeffer property was the one later commandeered by General Meade. [17]

Lydia Leister returned soon afterwards to find her modest home nearly devastated. She later told a correspondent that she was sorry she had not stayed home as "she lost a heap." In addition to the dead horses that littered her yard, her bed linen, clothes, meat, wheat, apple trees, and fences were all casualties of war. At least two shells had damaged the house. The correspondent noted, "This poor woman's entire interest in the great battle, I found, centered in her own losses. What the country lost or gained, she did not know nor care, never having once thought of that side of the question." [18] Leister continued to own this property until it was acquired by the Gettysburg Battlefield Memorial Association in early 1888. She then moved into town on property near the Dobbin House and lived in Gettysburg until her death in 1893. [19]

You may want to take a few moments to view the large Peter Fry (Frey) farm that is approximately 400 yards south of the Leister farm and on the same side of the Taneytown Road. The Taneytown Road entrance to the National Park Service visitor center is only about 100 yards from and opposite the Fry farm. As there is not an opportunity to park your vehicle along the road near the Fry farm, we would encourage you to take a few minutes to walk there. If not, then please proceed to your vehicle and continue south along the Taneytown Road toward the Army of the Potomac's extreme left flank.

Peter Fry (Frey) Farm

GPS: 39°48'39.53"N, 77°13'52.94"W; Elev. 538 ft.

- Much of the surrounding farm area, including the Copse of Trees, was owned by Peter Fry at the time of the battle. The house along the Taneytown Road is original but the barn is post-battle. "The roof of the house was torn up and the stone wall broken in one place & the stones thrown upon the floor," recalled an assistant surgeon in the 108th New York. [20]
- Given that it was located on the reverse slope of Cemetery Ridge, behind Hancock's lines and just south of Meade's headquarters, it was logical that this farm would be used as a field hospital for Hancock's II Corps. However, the 108th New York assistant surgeon described it as only a temporary hospital from which surgeons

would apply light dressings and superintend removal of patients to an operating hospital farther to the rear. [21]

- Fry leased the property to tenants and did not live here in 1863. It is sometimes erroneously identified as the battle residence of African-American Basil Biggs, but Biggs did not purchase the property until 1865. Biggs lived on a farm west of town near Marsh Creek during the battle. Basil Biggs became noteworthy later in 1863 because he was amongst those employed in the exhumation of the Northern dead from the battlefield for reburial in Gettysburg's National Cemetery. [22]

Now continue driving south on the Taneytown Road for approximately two miles. You will reach two of the least visited avenues in Gettysburg National Military Park. You may want to turn left and park in the roundabout at the end of Howe Avenue. If you are driving a large vehicle, then you should instead turn right and carefully park along the right side of Wright Avenue. Although you will encounter minimal traffic along these avenues, continue to be mindful of opposing traffic on the Taneytown Road or along Wright Avenue if you elect to stop there.

Wright and Howe Avenues

GPS: 39°47'2.64"N, 77°13'48.72"W; Elev. 498 ft.

James Longstreet's postwar accounts have helped perpetuate the misconception that Meade's extreme left was unguarded on July 3, and that Lee's best chance for victory lie in Longstreet's proposed turning movement around the Round Tops. "On the next morning he [Lee] came to see me, and fearing that he was still in his disposition to attack, I tried to anticipate him by saying: 'General, I have had my scouts out all night, and I find that you still have an excellent opportunity to move around to the right of Meade's army [sic-Longstreet's right or Meade's left] and maneuver him into attacking us.'" To Longstreet's disappointment, Lee replied, allegedly pointing with his fist at Cemetery Hill: "The enemy is there, and I am going to strike him." [1]

Where and how Longstreet intended for Lee's army to "move around to the [Confederate] right" is unclear. For example, which roads did he intend for the Confederates to use? Was he planning for McLaws and Hood's divisions to march from Devil's Den and the Peach Orchard past Big Round Top? Any such movements near the Yankees' left would not only have been plainly visible to Union forces on the Round Tops, but any attempted turns toward the Taneytown Road could have been at least temporarily blocked by portions of the Union VI Corps who were stationed behind the Round Tops. These troop positions can be viewed from the intersection of modern Wright and Howe Avenues with the Taneytown

The colorful 5th Wisconsin monument sits at the east end of Howe Avenue. Image courtesy of Michael Waricher

Road. Note the open ground to the south which Longstreet's forces would have crossed as they maneuvered into Meade's rear. No element of surprise would have existed for the Southern army.

On the morning of July 3, Brig. General Horatio Wright, commanding the First Division of the VI Corps, proceeded here with Brig. General David Russell's brigade and Col. Lewis Grant's brigade of Brig. General Albion Howe's division. [2] Russell and Grant's brigades combined for an estimated strength of 3,400 men. [3] (Ironically, Howe's division was positioned near what is today Wright Avenue and Wright's men were around modern Howe Avenue.) Two batteries from the V Corps Artillery Reserve provided additional support. Ultimately nothing came of Longstreet's proposed turning movement and the troops here were relatively unengaged, although Grant reported that they were subject to the enemy's overshooting artillery during the afternoon. [4] Howe's deployment, incidentally, gave him the unique distinction of having infantry on both extreme flanks of the army. Grant's brigade was here on the Union left and his other brigade under Brig. General Thomas Neill defended the far right near Wolf's Hill.

Unfortunately, the lack of visitation to this area deprives battlefield stompers of the opportunity to view one of the most picturesque portraits on any monument at Gettysburg: the lion on top of the 1st Vermont Brigade monument. Since the Vermonters were positioned to block any Confederate attempts to turn the Union left flank, the veterans who placed this memorial believed that "the enemy would have found a 'lion in his path' had he made the anticipated movement." Although it was originally hoped that this monument would be placed at "the highest point on Sedgwick Avenue" to the lion's "right and rear he hears the roar of the conflict preceding and during Pickett's charge, and is ready to spring to that point if necessary." The lion was designed by Boston artist Charles Wellington Reed. He was a Medal of Honor recipient for bravery with the 9th Massachusetts Battery on July 2 at Gettysburg.[5]

The 1st Vermont Brigade Monument on Wright Avenue. Image courtesy of Steven Stanley

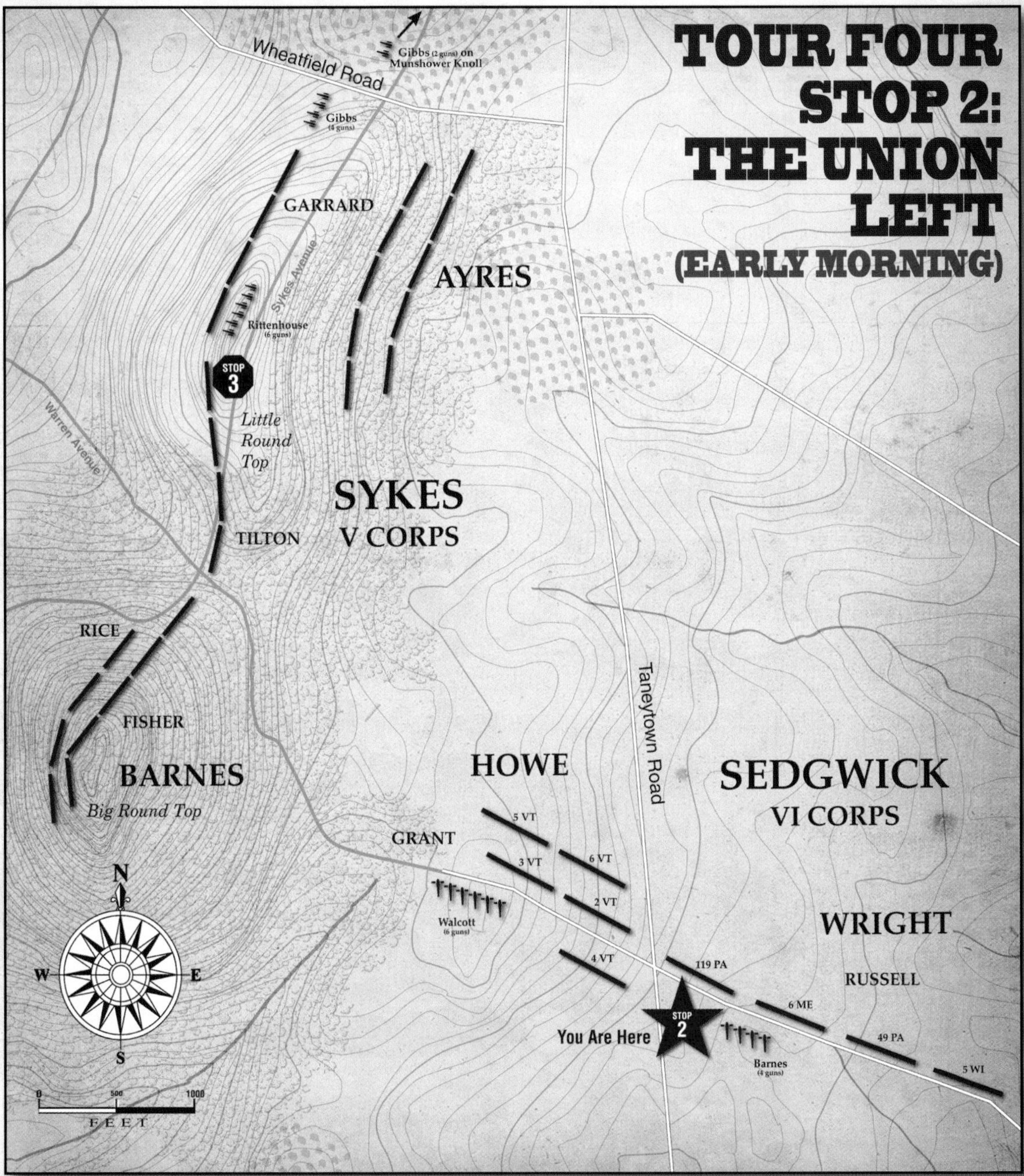

TOUR FOUR STOP 2: THE UNION LEFT (EARLY MORNING)

From one of the least visited battlefield locations to the most visited. After traveling for approximately 0.5 miles on Wright Avenue, turn right onto Sykes Avenue and proceed to the summit of Little Round Top. Parking is easily visible although not always easily obtained on busy afternoons.

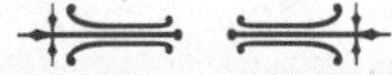

Little Round Top

GPS: 39°47'31.61"N, 77°14'12.00"W; Elev. 665 ft.

Although Little Round Top is best remembered for the heroic defense on July 2 by Col. Strong Vincent, Joshua Chamberlain, Patrick O'Rorke, and numerous others, the hill still played a key strategic role in the Union defense of July 3. Little Round Top's primary value was as an ideal observation point, as Gen. Gouverneur Warren understood, from which to view operations on Longstreet's right. As Lee reported, the continued presence of a Federal force occupying these "high, rocky hills on the enemy's extreme left," caused Longstreet to deem "it necessary to defend his flank and rear with the divisions of Hood and McLaws." [1]

Little Round Top was not the stronghold for Union artillery that it has often been portrayed as. The crest runs in a north-south direction, making it easier for an occupying force to fire to the west than to the north. [2] Although there is no contemporary evidence to prove that these guns participated in the cannonade prior to the attack, [3] Lt. Benjamin Rittenhouse (commanding Hazlett's battery on the summit) enfiladed Pickett's infantry with artillery fire as the Confederates were on the march. But his success diminished as Pickett approached Cemetery Ridge and Rittenhouse could not turn all of his guns to the

View of the fields of Pickett's Charge from Little Round Top with Gen. Warren's statue in the foreground. Federal artillery here fired at Pickett's troops as they advanced from upper far left to right in the photo.
Image courtesy of Karl Stelly

northwest to effectively hit his opponents. Lieutenant Rittenhouse remembered:

> I watched Pickett's men advance, and opened on them with an oblique fire, and ended with a terrible enfilading fire. Lt. Samuel Peebles pointed the first or right piece, and Sgt. Timothy Grady the second piece—both splendid shots. When the enemy got a little more than half way to our lines, I could only use these two pieces, as the others could not be run out far enough to point them to the right. [4]

Despite this flaw, several Confederate accounts confirm that Rittenhouse did cause damage in Pickett's ranks. Colonel Mayo in Kemper's Brigade recalled the charge as being made "under a galling flank fire from the Round Top." [5] Major Peyton of the 19th Virginia reported that Garnett's command "suffered but little from the enemy's batteries…with the exception of one posted on the mountain, about 1 mile to our right, which enfiladed nearly our entire line with fearful effect, sometimes as many as 10 men being killed and wounded by the bursting of a single shell." [6]

Little Round Top also served as an observation point for several senior members of the Army of the Potomac on July 3. Brigadier General Henry Hunt, Union artillery chief, reported that he had just finished inspecting Rittenhouse's guns and was still on Little Round Top when the cannonade opened up "at about 1 p.m." [7]

No less than General Meade himself also took advantage of the visibility offered from the high ground. A member of the 146th New York said that Meade and his staff, "with the Signal Corps, were there all day, occupying a rocky pen directly in the line" held by the regiment. [8] Note that the 146th New York's regimental monument states that Meade observed "from this position…for a time" on July 3. Meade later told the Joint Committee on the Conduct of the War that "as soon as" Longstreet's assault was repulsed, he immediately went to "the extreme left of my line, with the determination of advancing the left and making an assault upon the enemy's lines." [9]

Continue along Sykes Avenue to the intersection of the Wheatfield Road. Sykes Avenue will become Sedgwick Avenue. Continue along this route past the intersection of United States Avenue. You are now on Hancock Avenue. A number of monuments including those commemorating several artillery batteries will appear on your left. You may elect to park along the right side of Hancock Avenue at any point between here and the large Pennsylvania State Memorial.

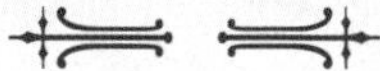

Lieutenant Colonel Freeman McGilvery's Artillery Line

GPS: 39°48'15.09"N, 77°14'4.83"W; Elev. 563 ft.

Lieutenant Colonel Freeman McGilvery, whose stoic defense on this part of the field helped plug a large hole in the Union battle line on July 2, commanded portions of several Federal batteries near here during the cannonade and Longstreet's assault of July 3.

After the heavy combat of July 2, McGilvery "ascertained the whereabouts of all my batteries, and early on the morning of July 3 brought them into line on the low ground on our left center, fronting the woods and elevated position occupied by the enemy along the Gettysburg and Emmitsburg road, a point at which it was plain to be seen they were massing artillery in great force." McGilvery wrote that his left "rested on an oak wood," which would have been near the George Weikert farm and modern United States Avenue. [1]

According to McGilvery's post-battle report, he commanded 39 guns. [2] However, this was not a completely static line as all or part of several batteries moved in and out during the course of the day. He also had several of these batteries only temporarily assigned to him. As a result, there is not complete historical agreement on what the exact alignment was during the cannonade or the Confederate assault. [3]

An astute observer may quickly realize there are monuments to more than 39 cannons along this avenue. The artillery markers and monuments between modern United States and Pleasonton Avenues commemorate the following units:

Federal Artillery Monuments and Markers on Hancock Avenue
(Designation and Commander as Inscribed)

Between United States and Pleasonton Avenues (South to North to 148th PA Infantry)	# Engaged and Type
Battery G (Ames), 1st New York Light Artillery (Capt. Nelson Ames)	Six 12-pounder Napoleons
Dow's 6th Maine Battery (Lt. Edwin Dow)	Four 12-pounder Napoleons
2nd Connecticut Light Battery (Capt. John Sterling)	Four 6-pounder James Rifles and Two 12-pounder Howitzers
1st Volunteer Brigade, Artillery Reserve (Lt. Col. Freeman McGilvery)	War Department Marker
New Jersey Light Artillery, 2nd Battery (Capt. Judson Clark)	Six 10-pounder Parrotts
3rd Pennsylvania Heavy Artillery, Battery H (Capt. William Rank)	Two 3-inch Rifles
15th Battery, New York Light Artillery (Capt. Patrick Hart)	Four 12-pounder Napoleons

The line continues after the monument to the 148th Pennsylvania Infantry Regiment.

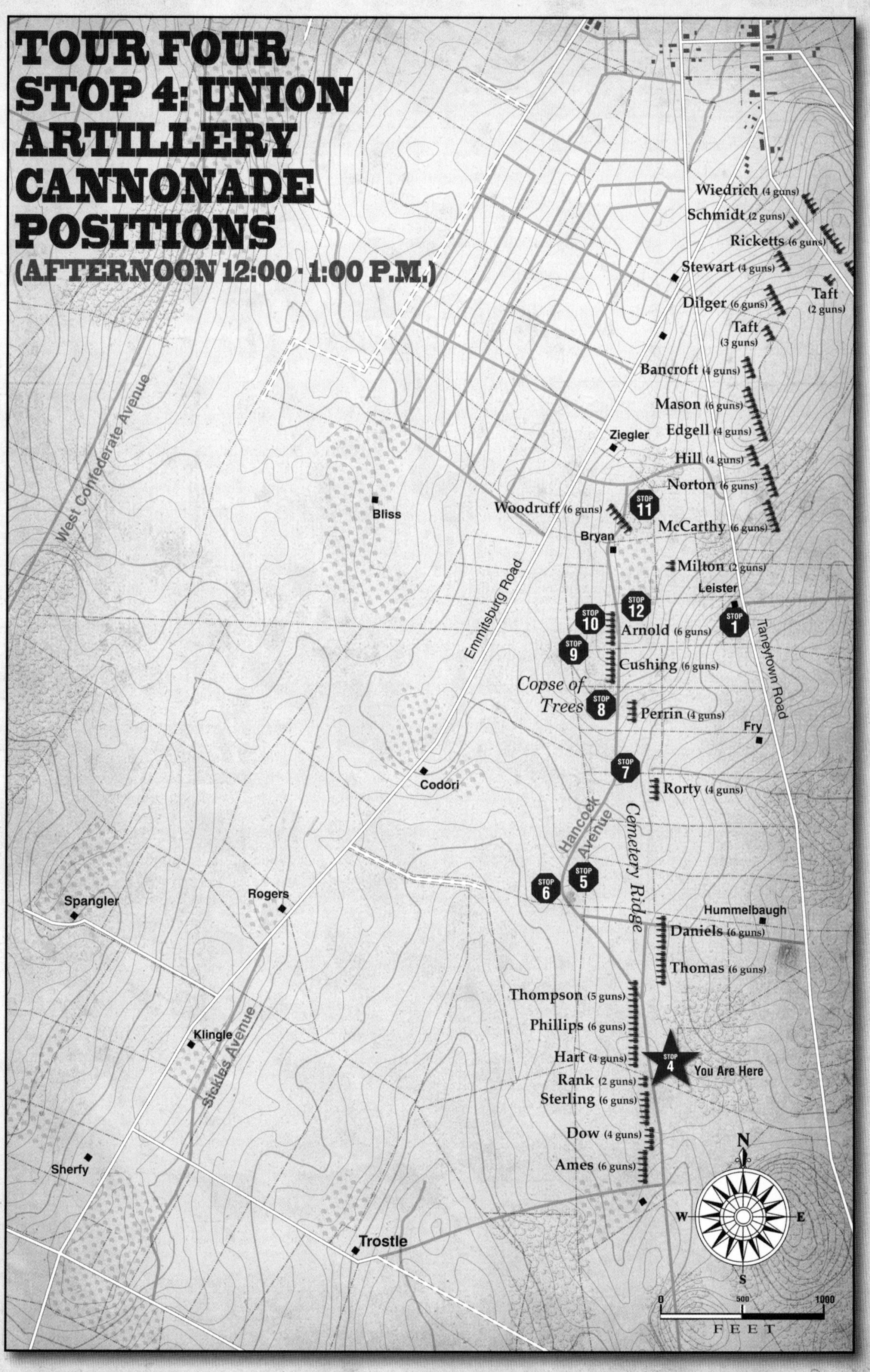
TOUR FOUR
STOP 4: UNION
ARTILLERY
CANNONADE
POSITIONS
(AFTERNOON 12:00 - 1:00 P.M.)
Wiedrich (4 guns)
Schmidt (2 guns)
Ricketts (6 guns)
Stewart (4 guns)
Taft (2 guns)
Dilger (6 guns)
Taft (3 guns)
Bancroft (4 guns)
Mason (6 guns)
Edgell (4 guns)
Ziegler
Hill (4 guns)
Norton (6 guns)
Woodruff (6 guns)
STOP 11
McCarthy (6 guns)
Bliss
Bryan
Milton (2 guns)
Leister
West Confederate Avenue
Emmitsburg Road
STOP 12
STOP 10
Arnold (6 guns)
STOP 1
Taneytown Road
STOP 9
Cushing (6 guns)
Copse of Trees
STOP 8
Perrin (4 guns)
Fry
STOP 7
Codori
Rorty (4 guns)
Hancock Avenue
Cemetery Ridge
STOP 6
STOP 5
Spangler
Rogers
Hummelbaugh
Daniels (6 guns)
Thomas (6 guns)
Thompson (5 guns)
Phillips (6 guns)
Klingle
Sickles Avenue
Hart (4 guns)
STOP 4
You Are Here
Rank (2 guns)
Sterling (6 guns)
Dow (4 guns)
Ames (6 guns)
Sherfy
N
W
E
S
Trostle
0
500
1000
FEET

Federal Artillery Monuments and Markers on Hancock Avenue
(Designation and Commander as Inscribed)

Between United States and Pleasonton Avenues (South to North after 148th PA Infantry)	# Engaged and Type
5th Battery E, Massachusetts Light Artillery (Capt. Charles Phillips)	Six 3-inch Rifles
Battery B, 1st Pennsylvania Light Artillery (Capt. James Cooper)	Four 3-inch Rifles

We now pass several infantry monuments on the west side of Hancock Avenue, including the 1st Minnesota Infantry Regiment monument, as we proceed past the Pennsylvania State Memorial.

Federal Artillery Monuments and Markers on Hancock Avenue
(Designation and Commander as Inscribed)

Between United States and Pleasonton Avenues (South to North after 1st MN Infantry)	# Engaged and Type
C&F Independent Pennsylvania Artillery, "Hampton's Battery" (Capt. James Thompson)	Five 3-inch Rifles
Battery C, 4th United States Artillery (Lt. Evan Thomas)	Six 12-pounder Napoleons
1st Regular Brigade, Artillery Reserve (Capt. Dunbar Ransom)	War Department Marker
9th Michigan Battery (Battery I, 1st Michigan Light Artillery) (Capt. Jabez Daniels)	Six 3-inch Rifles

Clearly not all of these batteries were located here throughout July 3. Note, for instance, that Cooper's battery did not arrive here until 3:00 and Ransom's marker commemorates several batteries that were not on this part of the field.

East of Hancock Avenue and in front of the Pennsylvania memorial is a monument to Hexamer's Battery A, 1st New Jersey. The battery was commanded at Gettysburg by 1st Lt. Augustin Parsons. Although it is in a relatively prominent position near the heavily visited Pennsylvania monument, it is probably in the wrong location. The relevant battle reports suggest that this battery arrived about 3:00 p.m. into a position several hundred yards north of here. [4]

Portions of at least two additional Union batteries, two guns in each of Lt. John Turnbull's 3rd U.S. and Lt. Richard Milton's 9th Massachusetts, were nearby during the morning but departed by early afternoon. [5] Captain Judson Clark's 1st New Jersey Light Artillery had seen heavy service near the Peach Orchard on July 2 and probably unlimbered to Sterling's right on July 3 but was unengaged. [6]

Army of the Potomac artillery commander Henry Hunt described his early activities on July 3:

> I had just finished my inspection, and was with Lieutenant Rittenhouse on the top of Round Top, when the enemy opened, at about 1 p.m., along his whole right, a furious cannonade on the left of our line. I estimated the number of his guns bearing on our west front at from one hundred to one hundred and twenty. I have since seen it stated by the enemy's correspondents that there were sixty guns from Longstreet's, and fifty-five from Hill's corps, making one hundred and fifteen in all. To oppose

these we could not, from our restricted position, bring more than eighty to reply effectively. Our fire was well withheld until the first burst was over, excepting from the extreme right and left of our positions. It was then opened deliberately and with excellent effect. [7]

In his post-battle writings, General Hunt varyingly estimated the overall number of Federal guns that participated in the great cannonade as being between 75 and 80. Although historians will never know the precise number, since the Army of the Potomac's artillery commander did not know, a comprehensive modern study placed the number at 78 total cannons engaged during the cannonade (from Little Round Top to Cemetery Hill). In this specific area under our study (from Ames to Daniels's batteries), the same analysis estimated that 26 pieces participated in the cannonade, primarily under orders from General Hancock. [8]

Regardless of the exact number of field pieces engaged, the accounts of Lt. Colonel McGilvery and Brig. General Hunt both indicate that Lee's massive artillery cannonade had little effect on the Federal batteries here. "At about 12.30 o'clock the enemy opened a terrific fire upon our lines with at least one hundred and forty guns. This fire was very rapid and inaccurate, most of the projectiles passing from 20 to 100 feet over our lines." For those shots that did not pass overhead, McGilvery "had a slight earthwork thrown up" in front of his guns "which proved sufficient to resist all the projectiles which struck it." [9]

General Hunt was in motion during much of the barrage, but ultimately observed a considerable portion from a position behind McGilvery. Although he called the scene "indescribably grand…covered with smoke, through which the flashes were incessant," General Hunt likewise thought the spectacle to be more visually epic than effective. "In fact, the fire was more dangerous behind the ridge than on its crest…Most of the enemy's projectiles passed overhead, the effect being to sweep all the open ground in our rear, which was of little benefit to the Confederates – a mere waste of ammunition." [10]

WHO ORDERED THE CEASE-FIRE?

On the Confederate side of the field, Colonel Alexander claimed that he delayed Longstreet's advance because the Federals' return fire did not provide a suitable opportunity for Alexander to give the order. Given that Longstreet had described his intent "to advance the infantry if the artillery has the desired effect of driving the enemy's off," at least one historian has raised the interesting question as to what would have happened if the Union artillery had simply not stopped firing from Cemetery Ridge? Would Pickett, Pettigrew, and Trimble's forces have still marched forward? Would uninterrupted enemy fire have given Longstreet the latitude to call off the attack? [1]

Ultimately, several Union officers claimed credit for originating the idea to stop the artillery fire. Henry Hunt could be expected to have responsibility for the directive. In his official report, he wrote:

> As soon as the nature of the enemy's attack was made clear, and I could form an opinion as to the number of his guns, for which my position afforded great facility, I went to the park of the Artillery Reserve, and ordered all the batteries to be ready to move at a moment's notice, and hastened to report to the commanding general, but found he had left his headquarters. I then proceeded along the line, to observe the effects of the cannonade and to replace such batteries as should become disabled. About 2.30 p.m., finding our ammunition running low and that it was very unsafe to bring up loads of it, a number of caissons and limbers having been exploded, I directed that the fire should be gradually stopped, which was done, and the enemy soon slackened his fire also. [2]

In his later *Battles and Leaders* account, Hunt jumbled the order of events and elaborated on his intentions. In this version, he rode along the lines and discovered his own ammunition running low. He *then* hastened to "advise" Meade of the need for "its immediate cessation and preparation for the assault that would follow." With Meade's headquarters having been abandoned, Hunt ended up searching the cemetery for his missing commander, but instead found XI Corps commander Gen. Oliver Howard who agreed with him. Hunt then rode south again along the lines back toward the Union left and ordered the guns to cease fire. "This was followed by a cessation of that of the enemy, under the mistaken impression that he had silenced our guns, and almost immediately his infantry came out of the woods and formed for the assault." He then met up with Henry Bingham of Hancock's staff near the Taneytown Road, who carried an order from Meade to cease firing, "so I had only anticipated his wishes." [3] Hunt later learned that General Warren had come to the same conclusion from Little Round Top and had also sent Meade a similar message to cease fire. [4] In Meade's published *Life and Letters*, it was Meade who determined and decided to give orders to stop the artillery assault, although the editors (Meade's son and grandson) acknowledged that Hunt also came to the decision independently. [5]

Major Thomas Osborn, commanding the XI Corps artillery, claimed that he initiated the suggestion to stop firing during conversation on Cemetery Hill with Generals Hunt, Howard, and Carl Schurz. "It was conceded by all that the mass of Lee's army was concentrated behind Seminary Ridge and in front of Meade's left wing...We also believed that Lee's primary object was to drive the guns off of Cemetery Hill." According to Major Osborn, he made the proposal that the Federal batteries should stop firing to which Generals Hunt and Howard agreed. Hunt then gave the order and said he would ride down the line and stop all firing. Whether the idea originated with Meade, Hunt, Warren, or Osborn, the episode proves once again that success has many authors. [6]

HOW LITTLE AN INFANTRY OFFICER KNOWS ABOUT ARTILLERY

As trained artillerists, both General Hunt and Lt. Colonel McGilvery had issued orders for their subordinates to conserve ammunition through controlled counter-battery fire. Hunt had given "instructions to the batteries and to the chiefs of artillery not to fire at small bodies, nor to allow their fire to be drawn without promise of adequate results; to watch the enemy closely, and when he opened to concentrate the fire of their guns on one battery at a time until it was silenced; under all circumstances to fire deliberately, and to husband their ammunition as much as possible." Hunt claimed that his intent was to create a "cross-fire" to break the enemy's infantry formations. [1]

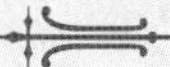

Unfortunately for Hunt, Maj. General Winfield S. Hancock had others ideas. Hancock had been given temporary command of the field on July 1, which he relinquished when the senior Maj. General Henry Slocum arrived at Gettysburg. During the late fighting of July 2, Meade had ordered Hancock to take command of the III Corps in place of the wounded Maj. General Daniel E. Sickles. Meade implied in his report that this arrangement continued on July 3, stating that Hancock commanded an ambiguous "left center" and that Brig. General John Gibbon had Hancock's II Corps. Gibbon, on the other hand, wrote that at 1:00 p.m., Hancock "resumed command of the corps" and Gibbon "returned to my division." [2]

Gen. Henry Hunt.
Image courtesy of Library of Congress

Although Hancock did not state it in his own report, in an account written more than a decade later and after Meade's death, Hancock laid claim to command of the "left center of our army, composed of three corps." [3] Whether or not Hancock believed such an arrangement existed in 1863, he was at least operating under the presumption that defense was the responsibility of the infantry and their commanders. Hancock also did not consider Hunt to possess the official authority of an army's artillery commander, terming his actions "without authority, merely officious." Hancock argued that Meade, in fact, fought Gettysburg without an artillery commander, and was instead "regulated by the will of the different commanders of the Army of the Potomac." [4] In 1887, Hancock's friend and II Corps historian, then Brevet Brig. General Francis Walker claimed to "have had much correspondence and conversation" with the since-deceased Hancock and argued that Hancock "knew that by both law and reason the defense of Cemetery Ridge was entrusted to him," subject to Meade's orders and not "to the discretion of one of General Meade's staff-officers." Walker argued that Hunt's desire for full ammunition chests did not adequately consider the morale effect on nearby infantry. "Every soldier knows how trying and often how demoralizing it is to endure artillery fire without reply." [5] Finally, Hancock may have simply thought it sufficient to retain only shorter-range canister for the forthcoming infantry assault. [6]

Hancock ordered his own II Corps Artillery Brigade under Capt. John Hazard, who was closer to the Copse of Trees, to return fire. Noticing an inactive battery nearby from the army's artillery reserve, which was not under his normal line command, General Hancock sent orders to "open fire at once; so that it would appear to the enemy that that [sic] point was strongly defended." When this order was "not obeyed" and the fiery infantry commander was informed that Hunt had given orders not to shoot, Hancock "then rode to the battery myself, and was actually compelled to threaten force…I would have been held responsible in the event of the loss of the line, while the chief of artillery of the army would have had no responsibility in that event." [7] Other participants, such as the veterans of Thompson's battery, recalled that Hancock's orders were intended to counteract the "demoralizing" effect on "the whole line of battle" that was resulting from Hunt and McGilvery's refusal to engage the enemy. [8]

If Hancock indeed commanded the entire left of Meade's army, then this fact had clearly not been communicated to McGilvery and his batteries. "About one-half hour after the commencement,"

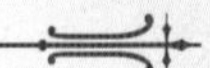

wrote McGilvery, "some general commanding the infantry line ordered three of the batteries to return the fire. After the discharge of a few rounds, I ordered the fire to cease and the men to be covered." [9] McGilvery later allegedly called Hancock "unnecessarily excited." Captain Patrick Hart of the 15th New York Battery proudly proclaimed that he refused a direct order from Hancock to open fire, although his after-action report indicated that he did briefly obey Hancock's instructions until "after firing a few rounds Major [sic] McGilvery ordered me to cease firing." [10]

Captain Charles Phillips of the 5th Massachusetts Battery likewise admitted that he was forced to open counter-battery fire on Hancock's conflicting orders, "but in the thick smoke probably did very little damage. By your [McGilvery's] orders, we soon ceased firing." [11] Phillips later called it all a "foolish cannonade" [12] and quipped sarcastically that Hancock showed "how little an infantry officer knows about artillery." A private in the battery agreed that Phillips's reaction was "exactly what the rank and file thought." [13] Not every artilleryman ridiculed Hancock's objectives however. Thompson's battery men "were only too glad for the chance, for it is much easier to fight than lay idle under such a storm of shot, shell, and missiles." [14]

Gen. Winfield S. Hancock.
Image courtesy Ed and Faye Max Collection

Since Hunt and McGilvery's orders to conserve ammunition had been (primarily) observed by those batteries along McGilvery's front, these guns were finely positioned to enfilade Kemper's right flank and then to later hit Wilcox and Lang head on. "The execution of the fire must have been terrible," McGilvery wrote, "as it was over a level plain, and the effect was plain to be seen. In a few minutes, instead of a well-ordered line of battle, there were broken and confused masses, and fugitives fleeing in every direction." [15] Captain Phillips observed that when "Longstreet reached our lines, the bushes and trees on our right concealed his troops" so that "we could not fire with very good effect, but this was merely during the last 50 yards or so of his charge. During the greater portion of it he was entirely exposed to our fire." [16] The damage would have been equal, if not more severe, when Wilcox and Lang frontally approached near the end of the attack. "My men falling all around me with brains blown out," recalled a lieutenant in Lang's 5th Florida, "arms off and wounded in every description." [17]

On one point both Hancock and Hunt seemed to agree: there was a noted lack of comparable fire from the II Corps batteries as Longstreet's troops approached. But not surprisingly both men differed on the cause. "No attempt was made to check the advance of the enemy until the first line had arrived within about 700 yards of our position," Hancock thundered in his report, "when a feeble fire of artillery was opened upon it, but with no material effect, and without delaying for a moment its determined advance." [18] Hunt, the more prolific writer of the two and eager to defend any perceived besmirches on his reputation, countered:

> I had counted on an artillery cross-fire that would stop it before it reached our lines, but, except for a few shots here and there, Hazard's [II Corps] batteries were silent until the enemy came within canister range. They had unfortunately exhausted their long range projectiles during the cannonade, under the orders of their corps commander, and it was too late to replace them. Had my instructions been followed here, as they were by McGilvery, I do not believe that Pickett's Division would have reached our line. We lost not only the fire of one-third of our

guns, but the resulting cross-fire, which would have doubled its value. [19]

The upshot of all this was that Hancock and Hunt developed a mutual dislike for each other, and neither officer would be shy about criticizing the other, directly or indirectly, ever again. Later that afternoon, after being wounded in the groin, Hancock still found time to criticize the handling of the artillery by complaining to Meade "that the twelve guns on my salient had been removed by someone, whom I call upon you to hold accountable, as without them, with worse troops, I should certainly have lost the day." [20]

Although Hunt ended the war with a brevet rank of major general, he reverted to a postwar rank of colonel of the 5th U.S. Artillery. Hancock appears to have ignored the customary courtesy of postwar officers to address each other by their highest attained ranks and instead referred to Hunt as "Col. Hunt," a fact that was indignantly noted by Hunt. Hancock went to his grave insisting that he simply outranked Hunt at Gettysburg and that the defense of Cemetery Ridge was his responsibility. For his part, Hunt wrote Gen. William T. Sherman in 1882 that Hancock suffered from "an aggravated form of the military disease described...as 'pruriency of favor-not earned' the characteristic symptom being 'self-puffing' to the malignant exclusion of others...and he resorts to defamations which sinks sometimes to calumny." [21]

Hancock Avenue veers to the left past the Pennsylvania State Memorial. About 270 yards (0.2 miles) past the state monument, you will see several monuments on the right side of the avenue dedicated to Vermont troops.

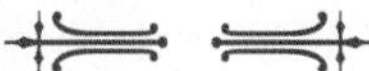

Stannard's Brigade Counterattacks

GPS: 39°48'33.96"N, 77°14'10.93"W; Elev. 563 ft.

This portion of the Union defensive works was assigned to Brig. General George Stannard's Third Brigade of Vermonters from the Third Division of I Corps. Stannard's men had enlisted for nine month terms in the fall of 1862 and their service was set to expire within one month. The brigade was also new to the Army of the Potomac, having been sent from the defenses of Washington to reinforce Meade's army only days before the battle. Stannard noted during the march north, "many of the men fell out. The great proportion after we left Frederick. I think whiskey the cause. They marched until this time first rate. They count their time by days. Consequently they do not have any heart in their work. Officers as little as men." [1]

On July 3, Stannard fought with his 13th, 14th, and 16th Vermont regiments. Two

additional regiments, the 12th and 15th Vermont, were detached to guard the corps supply wagons. [2] Prior to the Confederates' approach, the 16th manned Stannard's skirmish line. The 16th's commander, Col. Wheelock Veazey, described his line as "extending from a little to the right of the brick house [the Codori house] on the Pike in our front, a short distance along the Pike and then along the bottom of the ravine or slope out towards Round Top and connecting on the left with the line of the 5th Corps." [3] Veazey also observed a curious effect of the great cannonade:

> My men were lying flat down, and most of the fire with that of our own artillery which was on the crest in our rear passed over us. I lost several men, however, by it. This continued about 2 hours. The effect of this cannonading on my men was the most remarkable ever witnessed in any battle, many of them, I think, the majority fell asleep. It was with the greatest effort only that I could keep awake myself, notwithstanding the cries of my wounded men. [4]

As Kemper's Brigade approached from the west, first crossing near the Klingle farm and then passing by the Codori farm, they made inviting targets to Stannard's troops, who by this time had moved into positions west of modern Hancock Avenue and in advance of the line of Union monuments. Looking across this field, you can imagine the exposure that Kemper's right flank must have presented.

After Veazey's 16th Vermont was pulled in from the skirmish line and placed in the rear of the other Vermont regiments, Kemper initially appeared headed toward the front of the 14th Vermont (on Stannard's left). According to General Stannard, "the enemy came within 100 yards or thereabout" when the 14th's colonel "in order to change his line, had a part of his regiment raise up. That being discovered the rebels halted," and Stannard "immediately ordered a fire from both" the 13th and 14th regiments. The rebels then "immediately changed direction by their left flank," to Stannard's right, and kept moving under fire for the entire distance. "When past our front they changed direction again by the right flank, and marched direct to the attack of our lines." [5]

To the Vermont observers, it appeared that their fire was causing Kemper's men to diverge or crowd toward the Copse of Trees. Naturally, some Confederate accounts saw it quite differently. Colonel Joseph Mayo claimed that when "within a hundred yards of his [the enemy's] works, our men poured into the enemy one well-directed volley and then at the command of General Kemper rushed with a cheer upon the works, closely followed by the noble brigades of Garnett and Armistead. The entrenchments were carried, the enemy was driven from his guns." Mayo also wrote that portions of the 11th and 24th Virginia regiments "were thrown back at right angles to our line" to protect their right and rear, but such coverage must have been nominal at best. [6]

With Kemper having primarily passed his lines and again moving forward, Stannard now saw an even greater flanking opportunity. "Forming in the open meadow in front of our lines," the 13th and 16th regiments "changed front forward on first company" with the 16th forming on the left of the 13th, at right angles to the main Union line and again facing Kemper's new right. (The 16th's left may have been nearly as far out as the Codori

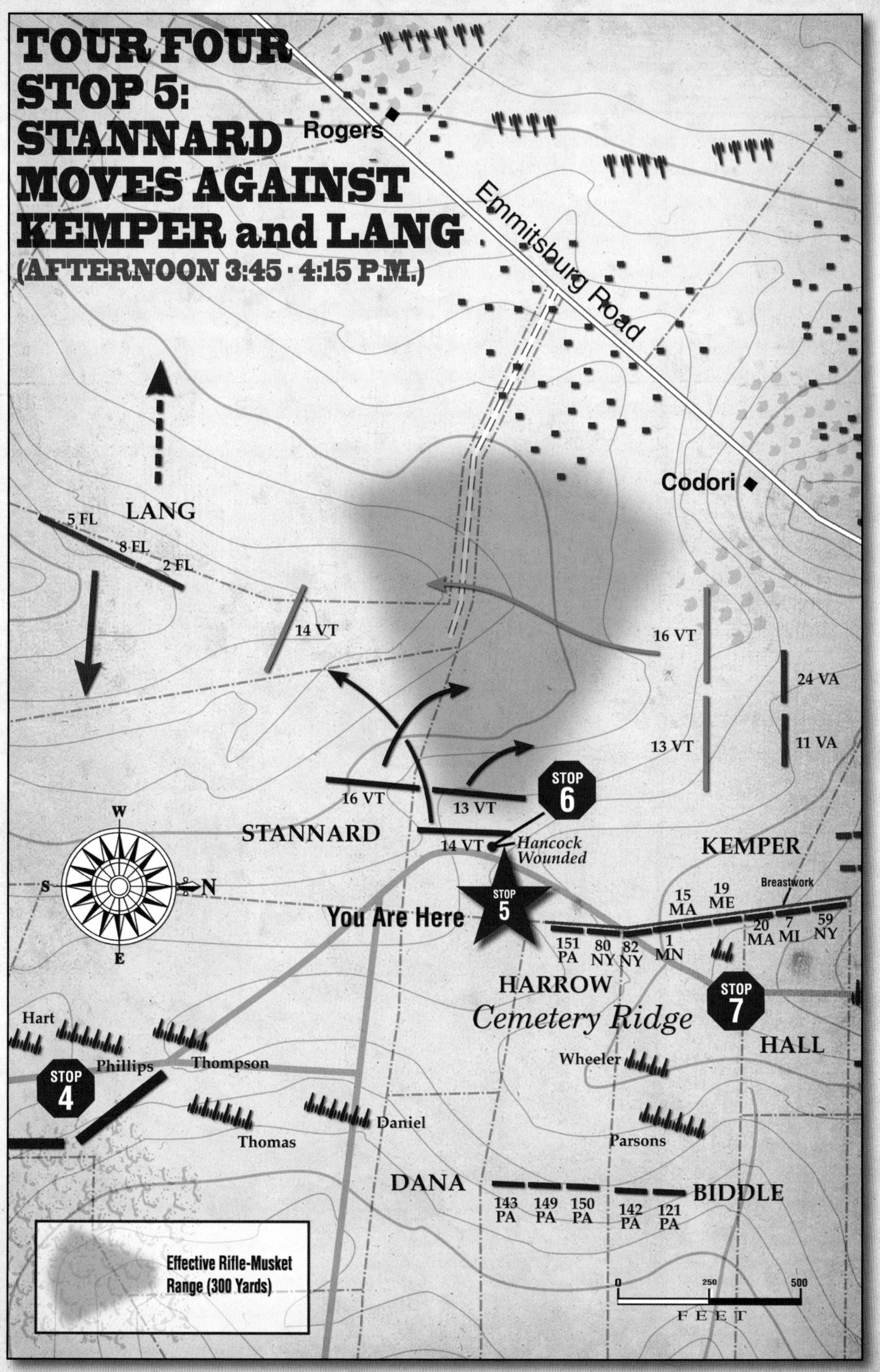
TOUR FOUR
STOP 5:
STANNARD
MOVES AGAINST
KEMPER and LANG
(AFTERNOON 3:45 - 4:15 P.M.)
Rogers
Emmitsburg Road
Codori
LANG
5 FL
8 FL
2 FL
14 VT
16 VT
24 VA
13 VT
11 VA
16 VT
13 VT
STOP 6
STANNARD
14 VT
Hancock Wounded
KEMPER
W
S
N
E
STOP 5
You Are Here
Breastwork
15 MA
19 ME
20 MA
7 MI
59 NY
151 PA
80 NY
82 NY
1 MN
HARROW
STOP 7
Cemetery Ridge
HALL
Hart
Phillips
Thompson
STOP 4
Wheeler
Daniel
Thomas
Parsons
DANA
BIDDLE
143 PA
149 PA
150 PA
142 PA
121 PA
Effective Rifle-Musket Range (300 Yards)
0
250
500
FEET

The Vermont State Memorial (center) stands along Hancock Avenue. Image courtesy of Michael Waricher

buildings.) The Vermonters poured in a very "destructive fire at short range, which the enemy sustained but a very few moments before the larger portion of them surrendered and marched in- not as conquerors, but as captives." [7] It was the most difficult maneuver performed by any regiments in Meade's army during this assault, but Stannard successfully managed to place "the rebels under flank fire the whole length of their lines." [8] Stannard's aide Lt. George G. Benedict wrote that the Confederates "began to break and scatter" in "less than five minutes" and "in ten more it was an utter rout." [9] Colonel Veazey of the 16th wrote:

> [W]e charged forward on the enemy and completely destroyed their lines. Very many of the enemy were killed, but more were captured and probably still more ran away, except on their right which was particularly exposed as the left of my regiment extended across their line. [10]

Hardly had Kemper been brushed aside when Wilcox and Lang's brigades appeared in their ill-conceived attempt to support Pickett's right. But instead of following Kemper, Wilcox and Lang headed straight for McGilvery's artillery and Stannard's left. General Stannard was in the process of ordering "my two regiments the 13th and 16th back to the original position" when this new threat appeared. Stannard then ordered Colonel Veazey's 16th "to move down in our front upon their flank again." [11] In laymen's terms, the 16th essentially pivoted to face south, remained at a right angle to the main Union line and now poured a destructive fire into Lang's left. (Contrary to Stannard's recollections, Colonel Veazey later wrote that the whole idea was his and he actually had to convince a skeptical Stannard to perform the maneuver.) [12] The 14th then opened fire along their front. This

fire "decimated" the Rebels who, in Stannard's words, "were scooped almost en masse into our lines." [13] Veazey recorded "killing or capturing all that did not run away." [14] The scene was unforgettable to Stannard, who had suffered a painful but non-mortal thigh wound: [15]

> I will state that the heavens were completely filled with missiles of death, of all kinds and descriptions, that ever was invented to be projected from the cannon's mouth. It beat everything that I ever saw or read of. [16]

From the Southern perspective, flight was a better alternative than death or being "scooped" into the hated Yankees' lines. "To remain in this position unsupported by either infantry or artillery," wrote Colonel Lang, "with [enemy] infantry on both flanks and in front and artillery playing upon us with grape and canister, was certain annihilation." Lang ordered a retreat, but lost a large portion of the 2nd Florida and their colors to capture. [17] These men had utterly failed to provide any protection for Pickett's flank.

Only days earlier, Stannard had questioned the "heart" of his men. Now they had earned his respect. "I will here state with much pleasure; that my men at this time had been out of rations for two days, and not a murmur did I hear; thereby showing their true courage and manhood." [18]

Vermont State Memorial

GPS: 39°48'33.96"N, 77°14'10.93"W; Elev. 563 ft.

- Although this 1889 state monument honors all of the Vermont troops who fought in the Gettysburg campaign, not just those of Stannard's brigade, it was decided to place General Stannard, Vermont's "most distinguished soldier," at the top of the column. [19]
- Stannard lost his right arm in 1864, and although this wound occurred after Gettysburg, the missing arm was included here because it was thought that it would help underscore the sacrifices of heroes like Stannard. [20]

13th Vermont Regimental Monument

GPS: 39°48'34.77"N, 77°14'10.51"W; Elev. 565 ft.

- The monument is unique in honoring a junior officer, Lt. Stephen Brown (commander of the regiment's Company K.)
- Brown was arrested for allowing his men to fill water canteens while on the march and his sword was taken away from him. Reinstated in time for the action on July

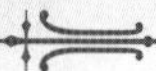

3 but unable to locate his sword, Brown raced into the Confederate masses with his men and demanded their surrender while swinging a camp hatchet. (See the hatchet that rests near Brown's foot.) [21]

- Can you find the three position markers for the 13th Vermont?

16th Vermont Regimental Monument

GPS: 39°48'31.75"N, 77°14'11.72"W; Elev. 560 ft.

- This monument was dedicated in 1892 and originally placed about 1,000 feet south and west of its present position near the northern end of the Codori thicket. The memorial was moved to the current location in 1907 to be nearer the other Vermont monuments on the more heavily trafficked Hancock Avenue. Note the inscription: "Rallied here and assaulted his [Pickett's] flank to the right 400 yards - then changing front charged left flank of Wilcox's and Perry's brigades. At this point captured many hundred prisoners and two stands of colors." This caption actually refers to the original and not the current position. [22]
- Colonel Veazey received a Medal of Honor for his role here and later served on the Vermont Monument Commission that placed this and other memorials. [23]

Proceed approximately 120 yards southwest from the Vermont State Memorial toward a small knoll and tree on the west side of Hancock Avenue. Next to the tree is a small and easily overlooked memorial commemorating the wounding of Maj. General Winfield Hancock on the afternoon of July 3.

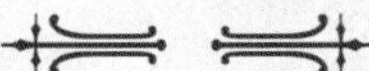

Monument to the Wounding of Major General Winfield Hancock

STOP U6: GPS: 39°48'31.57"N, 77°14'13.45"W; Elev. 560 ft.

Although Maj. General Winfield S. Hancock's afternoon began with a lunch near Meade's headquarters, the Army of the Potomac's II Corps commander was characteristically aggressive during the afternoon assault. He rode along his lines to steady his men during the cannonade (having allegedly and famously said, "There are times when a corps commander's life does not count!"), gave orders to artillery commanders (sometimes in conflict with General Hunt), and observed Stannard's opportunities to outflank the Confederates (and

by some accounts originated the idea himself.) [1]

Although varying accounts of Hancock's wound were published, Lieutenant Benedict of Stannard's staff insisted his version was true and accurate. According to Benedict, it happened shortly after Stannard had ordered the 13th and 16th regiments out to hit Kemper's right flank. Hancock and an orderly were momentarily speaking to Stannard:

> The din of artillery and musketry was deafening at this time, and I did not hear the words that passed between the two generals. But my eyes were upon Hancock's striking figure - I thought him the most striking man I ever saw on horseback, and magnificent in the flush and excitement of battle - when he uttered an exclamation and I saw that he was reeling in the saddle. [2]

Both Hancock and his staff officer C. H. Morgan wrote that it occurred when Hancock was "turning towards the clump of trees" and away from Stannard. [3] Benedict and another officer caught Hancock as he fell from his horse. Joined by Stannard, they examined the "profusely" bleeding "upper thigh" wound. Hancock "was naturally in some alarm for his life" and exclaimed, "Don't let me bleed to death," and "Get something around it quick." They cut off a portion of Hancock's pants, tied Stannard's handkerchief around the gash, and the men were able to comfort Hancock by assuring him that an artery had not been severed. [4]

Still, the wound was described as an "ugly one and ghastly to see. An onlooker has compared it to the stab of a butcher's knife." [5] Hancock refused to be removed from the field so a doctor soon arrived and removed several small pieces of wood and a bent ten-penny nail. [6] It was initially thought Hancock must have been the victim of an artillery shell filled with nails, and it was only after a hole was later discovered in the pommel of his saddle that they realized the source of the wood and the nail. [7]

Tough as nails himself, Hancock stayed to observe the repulse of Pickett's attack. John Vanderslice picturesquely described Hancock as "lying upon the front line in a reclining position, with the blood gushing from a wound in the groin, directed the battle." [8] Staff officer Captain H. H. Bingham arrived with word that Hancock's old friend Armistead had been wounded and with the Rebel's personal effects. [9] Despite the painful wound and general good feelings that should have resulted from the seeming victory, Hancock still managed to fire off a note to Meade's headquarters that was sprinkled with some testiness as he demanded that "someone" be held "accountable" for the removal of artillery on his salient. Hancock added :

> I have never seen a more formidable attack, and if the Sixth and Fifth Corps have pressed up, the enemy will be destroyed. The enemy must be short of ammunition, as I was shot with a ten penny nail. I did not leave the field till the victory was entirely secured and the enemy no longer in sight. I am badly wounded, though I trust not seriously. [10]

An officer delivered this note to Meade who replied, "Say to General Hancock that I regret that he is wounded, and that I thank him, for the country and for myself, for

A circa 1889 photo of the Hancock Wounding Monument with sign board in the background. Image courtesy of GNMP

the service he has rendered today."[11] Hancock was finally moved to a field hospital, then to Westminster, Maryland, on to Baltimore, and finally Philadelphia to recover. While there, Mrs. Hancock complained that "gay bands of music" and cheering crowds would pass his hotel nightly with no signs of recognition "but heaping upon General Meade's family the entire honor of that victory…This oversight, though deeply felt by him, he considered very natural." [12]

Unfortunately, the wound did not heal well. Almira Hancock called his convalescence "slow, weary." He later told Benedict that he suffered "immense pain" for weeks until a doctor finally probed him again (reportedly while having him assume the position of being in the saddle) and found a minie ball between six and eight inches from the surface along with still more wood embedded in his thigh. Hancock wrote his chief of staff, William Mitchell, on August 24: "I had an ounce and ninety grains of lead taken out of my leg on Saturday last. It was an elongated ball and in my leg to the depth of six inches. It was only found the day before and it had to be cut out. I expect to get well now soon." [13] Hancock returned to duty by 1864 but he remained only a shadow of the energetic and aggressive officer who thundered up and down Cemetery Ridge. Gettysburg had been his finest hour on any battlefield.

This small monument was dedicated in 1888 to presumably mark the site on which Hancock's wounding occurred. Although it had once been contemplated to place Hancock's equestrian monument nearby, [14] that memorial was instead placed on East Cemetery Hill.

Is the wounding monument in the correct location? General Hancock returned to the field with historian John Bachelder and others on November 19 and 20, 1885, less than three months before his death. [15] Hancock was, characteristically, somewhat critical of the conditions of the field. Notably, he believed that "Hancock Avenue" had resulted in the cutting of some timber and undergrowth in this vicinity. [16] Regarding the alleged site of his wounding, he wrote to former aide Francis Walker on December 12, 1885:

> I was shot from my horse when leaving the Vermont position by its right, along the high ground, proceeding directly towards the clump of timber…The place where I was shot, as at present marked, is not very accurately indicated. I saw no great boulder in the neighborhood. Lying on my back and looking through the remains of

> a very low, disintegrated stone wall, I could observe the operations of the enemy and give directions accordingly; and the Vermont troops, obeying my orders, proceeded close to my left, along that wall, towards the right. In lying down my head was to the south and my feet to the north. From where my horse fell I was carried a few yards to the spot upon which I lay down. [17]

William Tipton photographs from the period show a sign board placed in this position near two boulders and a small tree. By 1888, the monument appears to have been placed in the same location. A large graded mound was added underneath the monument that reduced the prominence of the rocks and today gives the misleading impression that Hancock was struck while on a small knoll. [18] Although memories can fail, if Hancock was correct in dismissing the presence of boulders then the current monument is inaccurately located. Conversely, if the Hancock monument is accurate then the placement of the Vermont monuments behind his are misleading because they give the impression he was on Stannard's left when struck despite the fact that he was moving right toward the Copse of Trees at the moment of impact. [19]

Did you know that in an 1893 monument dedication, colorful Union General Daniel E. Sickles proposed that the Northern army's position should be designated as "Hancock Ridge" instead of "Cemetery Ridge"? Sickles's suggestion has never been put to use. [20]

This monument, dedicated in 1888, marks the position of Hancock on July 3 when he was wounded. Or does it? Image courtesy of Steven Stanley

Traveling north again along Hancock Avenue, numerous monuments are located prior to reaching the Copse of Trees.

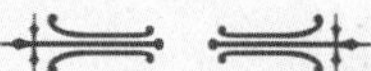

Monuments South of the High Water Mark

GPS: 39°48'37.14"N, 77°14'9.87"W; Elev. 572 ft.

Brigadier General John Gibbon Statue and "The Gibbon Tree"

GPS: 39°48'39.64"N, 77°14'7.41"W; Elev. 580 ft.

Gen. John Gibbon.
Image courtesy of Library of Congress

Brigadier General John Gibbon was a distinguished figure during the Gettysburg campaign and the American Civil War.

Gibbon was born in Philadelphia in 1827, the son of a prominent doctor. The family relocated to North Carolina in 1838 when his father accepted a position with the U.S. Mint. [1] Gibbon graduated from West Point in 1847 (the same class as Confederate General A. P. Hill) and authored the influential *Artillerist's Manual* which was used by artillery officers on both sides during the war.

When North Carolina seceded from the Union, John Gibbon remained a loyal member of the U.S. Army. Like many American families, Gibbon's was divided by this war. With official communications cut off with the South, Gibbon lost contact with his family. "When I next heard," Gibbon later recalled, "all of my three brothers were in the Southern army and I saw none of them until after the war." [2]

Gibbon's brothers cast their loyalties with the South, despite that all were born in Pennsylvania and had their own ties to the North. Oldest brother Lardner Gibbon (right, image from *Bulletin of the International Bureau of the American Republics*) was in the U.S. Navy from 1837 to 1857 and served on an expedition

to South America. (Lardner was the maiden name of the boys' mother Catherine.) Lardner was appointed to the Confederate army in July 1861 from North Carolina as a captain of artillery. He was on leave during the Gettysburg campaign and resigned in August 1863. [3] John Gibbon apparently did not hold a grudge against Lardner. After the war, John wrote Secretary of State William Seward requesting amnesty for his formerly rebellious brother. "I know him to be loyal to the Union." Lardner later moved back to Philadelphia and died there in 1910. [4]

Robert Gibbon (right, from *Clark's NC Regiments,* Vol. 2) was also older than John, born in 1822. He graduated from Yale Medical School in 1847. Robert put his medical schooling to use and was appointed a surgeon in the 28th North Carolina. By 1864, he was the senior surgeon in Lane's Brigade. [5] Robert Gibbon was a doctor after the war and died in 1898. He is buried in North Carolina.

Youngest brother Nicholas Gibbon (bottom right, from *Clark's NC Regiments,* Vol. 2), born in 1837, attended school in Philadelphia at Jefferson Medical College. He was a captain in the 28th North Carolina and in April 1863 became acting brigade commissary. [6] Despite his medical schooling, Nicholas became a farmer after the war and died in 1917.

Robert and Nicholas Gibbon may have been at Gettysburg fighting against their brother and their former home state. While muster records are incomplete, both men were present with Lee's army before and after this campaign so we have nothing to indicate they were not at Gettysburg.

John Gibbon fought in nearly all of the major campaigns of the Eastern Theater prior to Gettysburg. In 1862, Gibbon commanded a brigade from Wisconsin and their distinctive black Hardee hats resulted in their being nicknamed "The Black Hat Brigade." Later that year, their solid performance at the battle of South Mountain caused Union General Joseph Hooker to exclaim that the men "fought like iron," giving birth to the "Iron Brigade." [7]

General Gibbon commanded the Second Division in Hancock's Corps at Gettysburg. He attended the council of war at Meade's headquarters on the night of July 2, and his division bore much of Longstreet's attack on July 3. Gibbon was wounded during the assault. He was a staunch Meade supporter and vigorously defended General Meade from criticism during the postwar years.

Gibbon's career was equally noteworthy after Gettysburg. He attended the Soldiers National Cemetery dedication in November 1863 with Frank Haskell and witnessed Lincoln's "Gettysburg Address." He served throughout the remainder of the war and was present at Appomattox.

Like many career army officers, Gibbon served in the West after the Civil War. He commanded one of the army columns in the 1876 campaign against the Sioux which

This 1906 William Tipton photo looks south along Hancock Avenue at it's (then) intersection with Harrow Avenue. Note the "Gibbon Tree" on the right of the photo. Image courtesy of GNMP

resulted in George Armstrong Custer's death at the battle of the Little Bighorn in Montana. Gibbon has been criticized by some historians for appearing unwilling to engage the hostiles with his small command, but his arrival on the field may have helped save the remainder of Custer's 7th Cavalry. In August 1877, Gibbon fought the Nez Perce at the battle of the Big Hole (again in Montana.) Gibbon initially surprised the tribe's village but was eventually pinned down by warrior gunfire and had to be relieved by troops under another Gettysburg veteran, Oliver Howard, after the Native Americans withdrew from the field.

John Gibbon died in 1896 and is buried in Arlington National Cemetery.

Gettysburg monuments to five prominent Pennsylvania generals, including Gibbon, were originally proposed in the early 1900s. Those commemorating Generals Andrew Humphreys, Alexander Hays, and John Geary were placed, but memorials to Samuel Crawford and Gibbon were not. This statue, sculpted by Terry Jones, was dedicated on July 3, 1988, the 125th anniversary of the battle.

Battlefield lore tells us that the large tree on the west side of Hancock Avenue, slightly southwest of Gibbon's statue and across from the memorial to Lt. Gulian V. Weir's Battery C, 5th U. S. Artillery, is not only a witness tree but is also the tree near which General Gibbon stood when he was wounded on July 3, 1863. As a result, it is sometimes referred to as "The Gibbon Tree." [8]

Gibbon's various postwar accounts were not overly specific on his location at the time of being struck. By his telling, he was riding all over his divisional line trying to throw troops into various gaps. In 1866, he wrote, "When I was struck I was trying to get the 19th Maine to swing to the right and take the enemy in flank. Just previous to this I looked to the left and saw some troops leaving a line of breastworks just on the right of a little clump

of trees, rode down and induced them to go back." [9] In a later account, he similarly stated, "I galloped back to my own division and again attempted to get the left of that to swing out. Whilst so engaged, I felt a stinging blow apparently behind the left shoulder." Soon faint and weak from blood loss, Gibbon turned over command to Brig. General William Harrow. [10]

During the assault, the 19th Maine was posted roughly in the center of General Harrow's brigade line, south of the Copse of Trees, and just to the north of Stannard's brigade. For comparison's sake, their regimental monument is currently situated about 100 yards north of this tree.

General Hancock, in his 1885 visit, noted that Hancock Avenue and the passage of time had changed the appearance of this part of the field. Near the Vermont position, he observed: "The 'Avenue' has evidently cut off some of the fringe of timber and undergrowth in that direction, and the railroad cutting, has done the same on the opposite side." [11] Hancock further added:

> Some of those trees have evidently been cut down, however, since the date of the battle and since my former visit there nineteen years ago, notably one which General Stannard and others pointed out as the place where General Gibbon was shot, sometime before I was struck. [12]

Given Hancock's observation and the tree's distance from the 19th Maine monument, it is not definitively known that the existing tree is actually "The Gibbon Tree." However, as a presumed witness tree, it is still one of a diminishing number of remaining survivors to the great battle.

1st Minnesota Secondary Monument (July 3)

STOP 7b

GPS: 39°48'37.84"N, 77°14'9.91"W; Elev. 573 ft.

The 1st Minnesota has long been one of the best-known regiments on the field due to the desperate counterattack of eight companies on July 2 that produced more than 80% losses. This attack is commemorated by the regiment's prominent monument located approximately 1/3 mile to the south. But it is often forgotten that the regiment has a secondary monument just south of the Copse of Trees to memorialize the role the 1st Minnesota's remnants played in repulsing Pickett's Division on July 3. Both the primary and secondary monuments were dedicated in 1893. [13]

The regiment was commanded on July 3 by Capt. Nathan Messick of Company G, who took charge after Col. William Colvill was wounded on July 2 and all other senior officers were also incapacitated. The 36-year-old Messick was a veteran of the Mexican War,

where he had served in the 4th Indiana under Col. Willis A. Gorman, who would later become the first colonel of the 1st Minnesota. Messick was a shoemaker when he enlisted in the 1st Minnesota in 1861, and he quickly gained a reputation for gallantry when he personally protected the regiment's colors at First Manassas. [14]

Perhaps Messick and his men thought they had earned some rest after Gettysburg's bloody second day. Captain Messick had been wounded twice himself. The roughly 47 survivors had moved to their right after fighting and slept on their arms that night. Although there is some lack of clarity regarding their July 3 strength (aided by erroneous assumptions that only the 47 men remained in line) they were probably joined by an additional 60-70 comrades who were detached on July 2, bringing the July 3 muster to slightly over 100 men.[15]

According to the battered Minnesotans' regimental history, they were posted "early in the morning…on what is now 'Hancock Avenue,' about 400 feet to the left of 'high water mark'…Soon after sunrise… [the regiment] was moved up to its place in Harrow's Brigade line…The regiment's position was on the crest of the ridge – the line running north and south- a little south of the clump of trees." Upon their arrival, the men built a crude line of miniature breastworks behind which they might find "some shelter from the storm." The regiment lay behind this makeshift barricade all afternoon and throughout the cannonade. "The air seemed to be filled with the hissing, screaming, bursting missiles," one participant remembered, "and all of them really seemed to be directed at us." The historian recalled that the 15th Massachusetts was in line to the 1st Minnesota's left; note that the monuments' positions are reversed. [16]

Capt. Nathan Messick.
Copy Image of Nathan Messick by John J. Phillips, courtesy of Minnesota Historical Society

Captain Henry Coates wrote that the Confederate infantry then "marched resolutely in the face of a withering fire up to our lines, and succeeded in planting their colors on one of our batteries." As the Rebels reached the Union's stone wall, Coates implied an orderly movement "by the right flank to oppose them, firing upon them as we approached, and sustaining their fire, together with the fire of batteries which they had brought up to within short range. The fighting here was desperate for a time."[17] The Minnesotans were more likely part of the mad scramble made by Harrow and Hall's brigades to shore up Webb's wavering defenses at the Copse and Angle. "Whether the command to charge was given by any general officer I do not know," one man remembered. "My impression then was that it came as a spontaneous outburst from the men, and instantly the line precipitated itself upon the enemy." [18]

However it came about, the 1st Minnesota once again found itself in the thick of combat. "Closing on them with a rush and a cheer; there was shooting, stabbing, and clubbing, for there was no time to reload." [19] When it was all over, there was little left to do but accumulate the spoils of war. A private in Company C was credited with capturing the colors of the 28th Virginia (Garnett's Brigade) and Coates made

the unlikely claim that his shell of a regiment captured about 500 prisoners. [20]

The victory was marred by the loss of the newly appointed temporary commander, Captain Messick. He had been instantly killed by a shell fragment that struck him near the right eye and exited the back of his head sometime between 2:45 - 3:00 p.m. [21]

His sword and pocket book (containing $15.00) were said to have been taken from his corpse within 15 minutes of his death. His body was carried to the rear, where his personal cook stayed with him and saved the captain's shoulder straps for Messick's wife. He was then buried in the early morning hours of July 4 on the Jacob Schwartz farm. (His body was wrapped in a tent and a towel was placed over his face.) Messick left a grieving widow and four young daughters at home. His remains were later moved to the Minnesota plot in the Gettysburg National Cemetery where he rests today. [22]

20th Massachusetts Regimental Monument

STOP 7c

GPS: 39°48'41.17"N, 77°14'10.18"W; Elev. 580 ft.

This regiment was commanded by Col. Paul Joseph Revere, grandson of Paul Revere. Colonel Revere was mortally wounded on July 2, and died two days later. Lieutenant Colonel George Macy then took command until he was wounded on July 3. Also among the regiment's losses was 2nd Lt. Sumner Paine. The 18-year-old Paine commanded Company A and was one of the youngest officers in charge of men at Gettysburg. [23]

Lt. Sumner Paine.
Image courtesy of Harvard University Archives, HUP Cartes-de-visite

Sumner Paine was the son of an affluent and privileged Boston family. His father was a wealthy lawyer and his great-grandfather was Robert Treat Paine, one of the signers of the Declaration of Independence. As a youth, Sumner traveled with his family through Europe, was a scholar in Latin School, and entered Harvard College in July 1861. He was said to learn with "great ease" and quickly rose to the top of his class. [24]

A strong desire to participate in the war caused him to terminate his studies, and he enlisted in the 20th Massachusetts in May 1863. He joined the regiment immediately prior to the battle of Chancellorsville and took command of Oliver W. Holmes's company after Holmes was wounded. [25]

During the fighting on July 3, Paine was struck in the leg by a Confederate ball. The blow forced him down to one knee, but he continued to wave his sword and urge his men forward. Paine was then heard to exclaim, "Isn't this glorious!" just before a Confederate

shell struck and killed him. [26]

Despite Paine's youth, Capt. Henry Abbott declared, "Paine was one of the finest officers I have ever seen." [27] He was originally buried along Rock Creek, but was later reinterred in the Massachusetts plot of Gettysburg's National Cemetery. [28]

The regiment's unique 18-ton "pudding stone" monument was transported to Gettysburg from Roxbury, Massachusetts. The boulder was said to be a landmark on the town's playground where the soldiers had once played when children. [29] Just south of the Copse of Trees, there is another iron marker denoting that the 20th was among the numerous regiments who crowded in toward the trees as the fight reached its climax.

19th Massachusetts Regimental Monument

GPS: 39°48'41.39"N, 77°14'7.50"W; Elev. 581 ft.

Attached to Col. Norman Hall's brigade, regimental commander Col. Arthur Devereux had been watching events unfold "when I saw that Webb could not sustain the shock with his front line. I saw that the 69th PA were apparently run over, but not retreating. The 71st PA were giving ground rapidly." After observing Webb's vain attempts to get the 72nd Pennsylvania to attack, Colonel Hall "did the true soldierly act" by refusing his right which unfortunately also opened a gap on his front. According to Devereux, "just then Hancock came riding furiously up. I halted him, pointing out the enemy's colors crossing the stone wall and asked permission to put my men in there." Hancock's "prompt direction was 'To get in God Damn quick.'" [30]

Colonel Devereux would claim credit for capturing four Southern regimental colors. One of the flags was the 14th Virginia (Armistead's Brigade) by Joseph H. DeCastro. Corporal DeCastro was an 18-year-old Boston native and former reform school resident whose father hailed from Spain. (His mother was from Maine.) [31]

Near the Copse of Trees "we met them breast to breast," wrote Devereux. Corporal DeCastro was one of the regiment's color-bearers and knocked down the Virginia color-bearer with the staff of the Massachusetts state colors. DeCastro snatched the 14th Virginia's flag from the enemy's hands, broke back through the lines, thrust the prize into Devereux's hand, and dashed back into action without saying a word. [32]

DeCastro was awarded a Medal of Honor in 1864 for his bravery, although the citation erroneously credited him with capturing the 19th Virginia's flag. DeCastro is believed to be the first Medal recipient of Hispanic descent. [33]

Like most Massachusetts monuments, the 19th's is fairly simple: adorned by a cartridge box, knapsack, and bugle. It is also one of the regiments further represented by a series of iron signs south of the Copse of Trees.

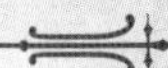

The High Water Mark is readily identifiable by a small grove of trees surrounded by an iron fence on the west side of Hancock Avenue. A large monument inscribed like a tablet and two bronze cannons sit in front of the trees and facing the avenue.

Copse of Trees / High Water Mark and 69th Pennsylvania Regimental Monument

GPS: 39°48'45.42"N, 77°14'10.65"W; Elev. 590 ft.

With the possible exception of Little Round Top, no area on the field receives as much visitation as the area surrounding the "High Water Mark" and "The Angle." The numerous monuments, cannons, and flank markers create what Gen. Alexander Webb once called "these cities of the dead" to commemorate those who fought here. [1]

The High Water Mark of the Rebellion Monument next to the Copse of Trees.
Image courtesy of Michael Waricher

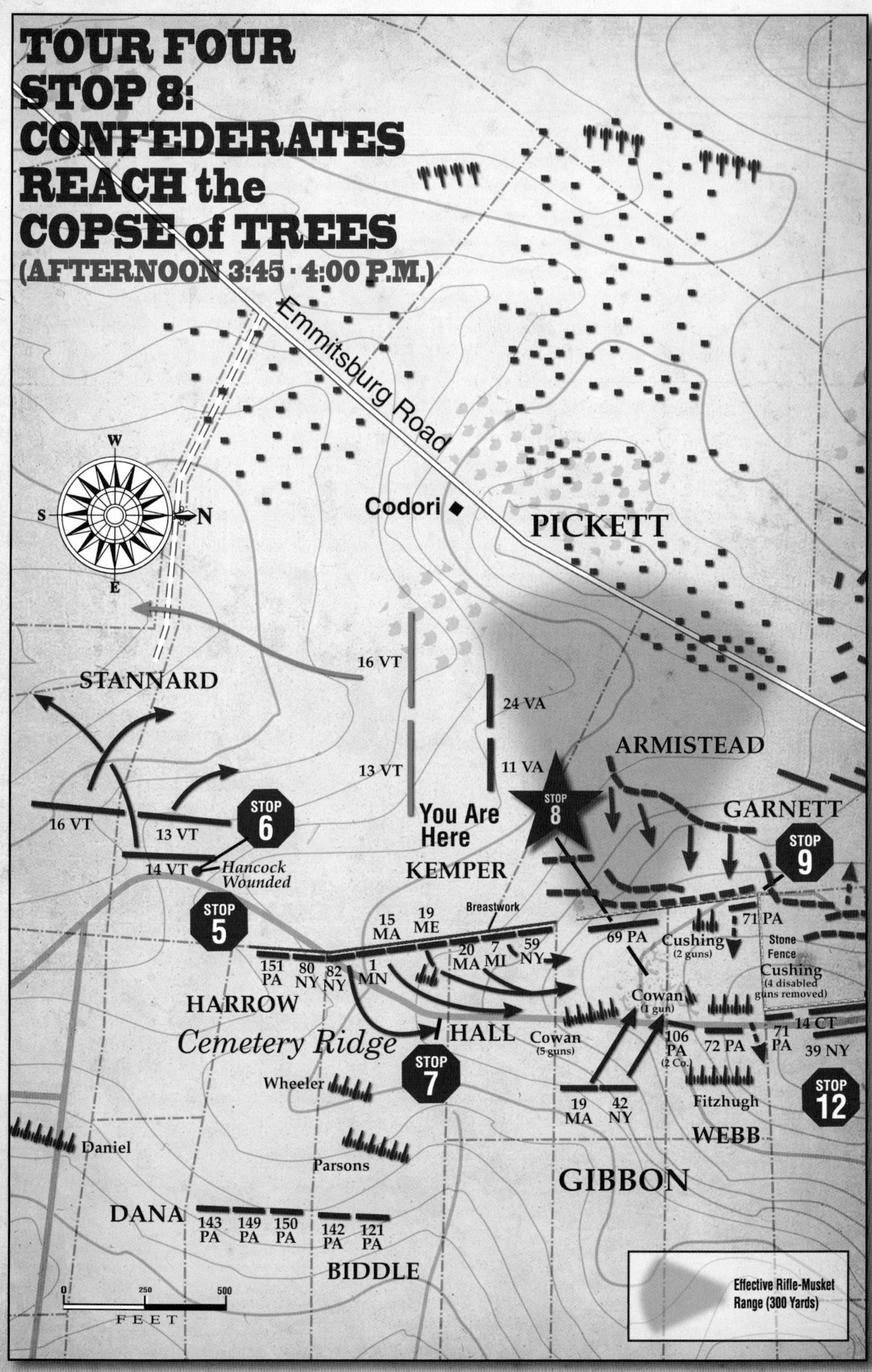
TOUR FOUR
STOP 8:
CONFEDERATES
REACH the
COPSE of TREES
(AFTERNOON 3:45 - 4:00 P.M.)
Emmitsburg Road
W
S
N
E
Codori
PICKETT
STANNARD
16 VT
24 VA
13 VT
11 VA
ARMISTEAD
GARNETT
16 VT
13 VT
STOP 6
You Are Here
STOP 8
STOP 9
14 VT
Hancock Wounded
KEMPER
STOP 5
Breastwork
15 MA
19 ME
69 PA
71 PA
Cushing (2 guns)
Stone Fence
Cushing (4 disabled guns removed)
151 PA
80 NY
82 NY
1 MN
20 MA
7 MI
59 NY
Cowan (1 gun)
HARROW
Cemetery Ridge
HALL
Cowan (5 guns)
106 PA (2 Co.)
72 PA
71 PA
14 CT
39 NY
STOP 7
Wheeler
19 MA
42 NY
Fitzhugh
STOP 12
WEBB
Daniel
Parsons
GIBBON
DANA
143 PA
149 PA
150 PA
142 PA
121 PA
BIDDLE
0
250
500
FEET
Effective Rifle-Musket Range (300 Yards)

As Pickett's men advanced across the field under a storm of artillery and gunfire, these trees may have served as a logical guiding point, although it is questionable that they were prominent enough to be officially designated as a target. An officer in the 72nd Pennsylvania later described the trees as "a clump of saplings, not over 30 paces in depth" and a common postwar description was "they stood out in relief from the ridge and afforded a most excellent target for the concentrated fire of the enemy's artillery." [2] Nevertheless, the work of prominent post-battle historian John Bachelder and other efforts such as Paul Philippoteaux's cyclorama painting have helped establish this area as a key, and perhaps decisive, point in the battle. Note that the open books on the monument refer to "Longstreet's Assault" and not "Pickett's Charge."

During the battle, this vicinity was defended by newly promoted Brig. General Alexander Webb's Second Brigade of John Gibbon's Second Division in Hancock's II Corps. As General Webb noted in his report, the relative concentration of the Confederate artillery fire on Webb and Hall's brigade fronts "had plainly shown…that an important assault was to be expected." [3] At the onset of the assault, Webb's 69th Pennsylvania was at the stone wall near the Copse of Trees, the 71st Pennsylvania to their right at the Angle, the 72nd Pennsylvania were "held in reserve under the crest of the hill," and eight companies of the 106th Pennsylvania were supporting General Howard on the Federal right, while two companies remained on skirmish duty. [4]

At the trees, Col. Dennis O'Kane's 69th Pennsylvania was a regiment of primarily Irish immigrants from Philadelphia. Colonel O'Kane was born in Ireland, but had immigrated to Philadelphia in the early 1840s with his wife and young children. Prior to the war, he was a working-class tavern keeper in the streets of South Philadelphia and served in the militia. The Irishmen of the regiment were reportedly showered with bricks and stones from residents of their adopted city while marching off to war and the ethnic discrimination continued within the Army of the Potomac. [5]

The 69th was positioned behind the low stone wall. Captain Andrew Cowan described it as "partly demolished" and it may have stood no more than two feet in height. A member of Brown's Rhode Island battery said that the wall was topped by post and rails, while along General Harrow's front the wall was replaced by a rail fence. [6] There was a small opening in the wall on the regiment's left and their line then ran north for perhaps 250 feet. The 69th's right probably ended at least 120 feet from the Angle. A gap between the 69th's right and the left of the 71st Pennsylvania at the Angle would be partially filled by Cushing's battery. The ground in front of the wall was littered with the refuse of Wright's failed attack on July 2, including equipment and decaying bodies whose stench were becoming increasingly unbearable in the July sun. The men of the 69th and other Union regiments used their time prior to the Confederate arrival to collect spare guns and ammunition from the dead. One Pennsylvanian said, "almost every man had from two to five guns loaded that were not used until Pickett got within fifty yards of the wall." [7]

The ground surrounding the Copse of Trees was not the well-manicured lawn that you see today. In addition to the litter from these two large armies, numerous trees and

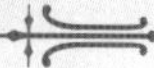

growth had been cleared by the Army of the Potomac to open fields of fire for their artillery. These trees were not removed and were instead generally left where they fell. Colonel Theodore Gates, commanding a so-called demi-brigade in the I Corps referred to this felled timber as "the slashing." This slashing would prove to be both an obstacle and a protective barrier to both armies. [8]

General Webb observed that Union artillery fire "opened great gaps" on the onrushing Confederates, "but steadily they advanced in four solid lines, right on, up to my works and fence." [9] Webb had ordered the men to hold their fire until the enemy had crossed the Emmitsburg Road, and Colonel O'Kane had added to wait until they "could distinguish the whites of their eyes." O'Kane further declared that since "we were upon the soil of our own state" any man who hesitated in his duty should be killed by his comrades "on the spot." As Pickett's men crowded into the field east of the Emmitsburg Road and surged toward the stone wall, some sporadic shooting occurred before the 69th was finally permitted to open fire. This "threw their front line into confusion, from which they quickly rallied and opened their fire upon us." Some number of Virginians dropped behind the brushy knoll in front of the 69th's left front (still visible today) but others withstood the volleys and continued to press forward. The enemy gained a foothold at the wall in front of the trees as a disorganized mob. [10]

Captain Andrew Cowan's 1st NY Independent Battery had been unlimbered behind the 69th. As bodies increasingly massed into their front, Cowan's battery fired double canister into the crowd. Cowan recalled:

> A good many of those two companies of the 69th ran away. Officers among them, as I saw plainly and cursed them…One of them was a Captain. He ran like a turkey, with his sword tucked under his arm, and his face distorted with fear. Corporal Plunkett, near me was raging mad and swore at them like a pirate. I saw him pick up

from the ground a Dutch coffee pot by the handle and smash it on the head of one of the runaways. The bottom broke in but that fellow went on running with the tin pot down on his ears…I can still see that fellow running away with the coffee pot, down over his ears. [11]

Cowan's criticism was somewhat misguided since not only was the 69th taking enemy fire in their front, but Cowan's canister was also subjecting them to friendly fire in their backs. In addition to the lethal artillery fragments, Cowan's fire was also kicking up nearby stones as projectiles. [12] The predicament was the same on the right of the regiment's line. Private Anthony McDermott thought that Cushing's two guns at the wall "done [sic] more harm in that position to us than they did the enemy" as they only fired two or three rounds and "one of those rounds blew the heads off two privates of the company 'I'."[13]

The situation certainly seemed dire as Armistead's men were now surging over the wall on the 69th's right. Webb claimed the Southerners "shot my men when their muskets touched their breasts." [14] Somebody ordered the three right companies of the 69th to change front and pull back from the wall at a right angle. Company F hesitated, possibly because their captain was shot in the head and killed before he could execute the maneuver. "The men were pretty much fighting at will," wrote Captain Cowan. Private McDermott recalled that the enemy "rushed in on the rear of our main line, and it looked as though our regiment would be annihilated, the contest here became a hand to hand affair." Large portions of the 69th's Company F were killed, wounded, or captured in the melee. [15]

Colonel Dennis O'Kane was among the casualties. He was mortally wounded in either the chest or abdomen and died for his adopted country on July 5. Private (later Lieutenant) McDermott said that O'Kane fell "like a soldier in great glee…he was not an

A panoramic view of the Copse of Trees, Cushing's battery, and the Angle.
Image courtesy of Steven Stanley

educated man, and was gruff in his speech, but with all he had a heart as tender as a woman's and above all things he despised a coward." His body was returned to Philadelphia where the funeral was held on July 9. [16]

Although the 69th Pennsylvania was, for the most part, gamely holding their ground at the trees, General Webb's defense had reached a critical moment. History has given Webb's brigade the lion's share of the credit for "stopping" Pickett. But to Webb's left, Col. Norman Hall "saw that a portion of the line of General Webb on my right had given way, and many men were making to the rear as fast as possible, while the enemy was pouring

The monument to the 69th Pennsylvania with the Copse of Trees in the background.
Image courtesy of Michael Waricher

over the rails that had been a slight cover for the troops." Hall found what he only knew as "two regiments that could be spared from some command there" but they hesitated so Hall was "forced to" move his own brigade "by the flank under a heavy fire. The enemy was rapidly gaining a foothold; organization was mostly lost; in the confusion commands were useless…" Fighting the natural urges of the men to fall back, Hall and his staff officers "crowded [his men] closer to the enemy and the men obliged to load in their places. I did not see any man of my command who appeared disposed to run away, but the confusion first caused by the two regiments above spoken of so destroyed the formation in two ranks that in some places the line was several files deep." [17]

Lieutenant Frank Haskell claimed the idea for reinforcements as his own. Galloping past Webb's left, he found Hall who, with sword in hand, was "cool, vigilant." Haskell

shouted: "Webb is hotly pressed and must have support, or he will be overpowered. Can you assist him?" Hall quickly gave the order and hurried to Webb's aid. "Hall's men are fighting gallantly side by side with Webb's before the all-important point." [18]

Next to Hall, Brig. General William Harrow could see "the crest of the hill occupied by the right of Colonel Hall and the left of General Webb seemed to be the point to which their main attack was directed." Harrow also joined Hall in moving to their right, with "the whole command meeting the shock from the enemy's heaviest lines and supports near the crest of the ridge. Here the contest raged with almost unparalleled ferocity for nearly an hour [sic], when the enemy was routed and fled in disorder…It would be gross injustice to claim a greater share of this triumph for one brigade of the division to the exclusion of another. It was a common struggle and a common success." [19]

A man in Harrow's 15th Massachusetts said, "we ran in all in a huddle and took a position immediately to the left of the Copse of Trees, and opened fire as best we could, the enemy was safely layed [sic] down behind the wall, having planted their flag in the stones and poured a deadly fire into us from behind it." After perhaps five minutes of fighting a private in the regiment cried out, "For God's sake let us charge, they'll kill us all if we stand here!" Rushing toward the wall "in a mass" caused the Rebels to jump up and run. The Yankees then unloaded a volley upon which "nearly all [Confederates] lay down again and cried out to us to stop firing and let them come in." [20]

Colonel Theodore B. Gates, commanding the 80th New York and 151st Pennsylvania regiments (often called a "demi-brigade"), added the fury of the Union I Corps to the brawl. "The men were now within quarter pistol range, and the fence and fallen trees gave the enemy considerable cover." Gates also ordered an advance and his regiments pushed their way through "the slashing" and to the wall "cheering as they went, and the enemy broke and hastily retreated in great disorder, while we poured into their broken line a heavy and continuous fire. This concluded the fighting at this point, and left us in undisputed possession of the contested ground." [21]

The support from the numerous regiments in Gates, Harrow, and Hall's commands finally caused the Confederate resistance to crumble. Still, it is Dennis O'Kane's Irishmen from Philadelphia, the 69th Pennsylvania, who are most remembered for defending the Copse of Trees. Their monument's inscription, just west of the trees, simply says it all: "This position was held by the 69th PA. Vols." The monument also notes: "A number of Confederate flags were picked up on this front after the battle." The 69th, despite being in the thick of the repulse, was credited with no flag captures. They were, according to Private McDermott, "kept busy looking after our wounded and burying the dead." McDermott described with disgust how one soldier with a "42" on his cap "ran past me [and] seized" a flag that stood against the wall. The Confederate trophies which surely littered the ground along this front were picked up by men from other regiments "who wandered over the field from curiosity." [22]

1st Rhode Island Artillery, Battery B

GPS: 39°48'44.17"N, 77°14'7.48"W; Elev. 591 ft.

The 1st Rhode Island Artillery, Battery B, is often referred to as "Brown's Battery" because it was commanded at Gettysburg by Lt. Thomas Fred Brown. But Brown was wounded on July 2, so this battery was led by Lt. Walter Perrin on July 3. [23]

The battery, only four Napoleons remaining, was posted on July 3 in the open ground just south of the Copse of Trees and slightly west of modern Hancock Avenue. The battery monument, however, is just east of the avenue. [24] Perrin's men took heavy fire during the cannonade and a Confederate shell hit the muzzle face of one gun while being loaded. Cannoneer No. 1 William Jones had the top of his head cut off by a shell fragment. No. 2 Alfred Gardner's left arm was nearly severed. Gardner exclaimed, "Glory to God! I am happy! Hallelujah!" He then passed along a final message for his wife that he died happy. [25]

The remaining members of the battery tried loading another projectile but it got stuck in the dented muzzle. The gun was displayed afterwards, with the shell still in the muzzle, in Washington, D.C.. It was then turned over to the state of Rhode Island in the 1870s, where it has been displayed in the State House as the "Gettysburg Gun." [26]

Perrin's battery was withdrawn during the cannonade, under Captain Hazard's orders, and replaced by Cowan's battery. The battery claimed two members killed on July 3 (Jones and Gardner), 15 wounded (one mortally), and one man was believed to have deserted. Lieutenant Perrin had his horse disemboweled by a Confederate artillery shell but Perrin was fortunately not mounted at the time. Another officer of Battery B, 2nd Lt. Joseph Milne, was mortally wounded on this day, but he was on detached duty with Cushing's battery and therefore not included in Battery B's losses. [27]

The Rhode Island men returned to this area shortly after Longstreet's Assault had been repulsed and buried their dead. A grave was dug for Jones and Gardner "near a clump of bushes at the left of the gap in the wall." The gap is presumably a reference to what has become known as "Brown's Gate," an opening in the stone wall that Brown's battery had passed through during the evening of July 2. [28]

Cowan's 1st New York Independent Battery

STOP 8b

GPS: 39°48′44.43″N, 77°14′8.26″W; Elev. 595 ft.

Captain Andrew Cowan's 1st New York Independent Battery had initially unlimbered farther to the Federal left, under orders to support General Abner Doubleday's I Corps division. "The field in front of me was so smoky I could not see far," Cowan recalled. As Perrin's Rhode Island battery withdrew due to casualties and low ammunition, a staff officer arrived and told Cowan to report to General Webb. Cowan considered himself under Doubleday's orders and, apparently like many men on the field, did not know the newly appointed Webb. "While doubting for an instant, I looked toward the higher grounds and at the point where you have my battery [monument] placed, saw a General waving his hat to me." Cowan knew that he risked disobeying Doubleday's orders but went anyways "as I must be needed there." [29]

An early 1900s Tipton photo of Cowan's battery. Image courtesy of GNMP

In the mad gallop toward the trees, Cowan said that his leading piece passed the trees and came into battery too close to Cushing's left gun—at an interval of only six or seven yards. Nearby Federal batteries were still in action as Cowan unlimbered and opened with shell. [30]

> The rebel skirmishers had just commenced firing, and their second line was advancing from the woods. The artillery fire was quite accurate and did much execution; still, the rebel line advanced in a most splendid manner. I commenced firing canister at 200 yards, and the effect was greater than I could have anticipated. [31]

While Cowan's men were loading up their canister, Gen. Henry Hunt rode up and proceeded to empty his pistol into the advancing foes, all the while emotionally shouting: "See 'em! See 'em! See 'em!" (General Webb later mocked Hunt, "He looked so funny picking at them; I did not need his little pistol.") An enemy bullet struck Hunt's horse in

the head and the mount fell to the ground, pinning him beneath it. The artillery chief was pulled out, quickly given another steed, and before riding away warned Cowan that he would "kill our men" in front of the battery by inadvertently hitting them with canister. Hunt's admonishments proved accurate as some of the 69th Pennsylvania were later killed by Cowan's friendly fire. [32]

Despite Cowan's deadly canister and the volleys from Webb's infantry, Pickett's men still gained a momentary hold on the stone wall. "I fired canister low, and my last charge, two rounds in each of the six guns was fired when the advance of the enemy in my front was but ten yards distant, and while they had possession of our guns on my right [Cushing]." [33] Some Southerners, possibly members of the 14th Virginia, came over the wall yelling: "Take the guns!" [34]

> My last charge (a double-header) literally swept the enemy from my front, being fired at less than 20 yards. The infantry in front of five of my pieces, and posted behind a slight defense of rails, some 10 yards distant, turned and broke, but were rallied, and drawn off to the right of my battery by General Webb in a most gallant manner. It was then I fired my last charge of canister, many of the rebels being over the defenses and within less than 10 yards of my pieces. They broke and fled in confusion. [35]

After grudgingly ordering his men to roll the guns to a knoll about fifty yards in their rear following the final discharge, Cowan concluded his day by disabling several Confederate batteries that had been advanced to distances of approximately 1,300 yards. Cowan reported five killed and six wounded - low by infantry standards but testimony that his battery had been in the thick of the fight. In typical official report braggadocio, he added, "My battery was the only remaining one on this part of the hill." [36]

"In my front, it is no exaggeration to say 'the dead lay in heaps.' Our own soldiers covered the ground where my battery fought and beyond the wall the canister had done terrible execution." Cowan buried the Rebel officer who had shouted "Take the guns!" alongside artillery Capt. J. M. Rorty and other Union officers. [37]

General Webb was grateful for Cowan's services, but when his staff prepared Webb's battle report they misidentified Cowan's battery as Wheeler's New York battery. When Cowan later learned of the "injustice" that Webb had "done us," he wrote the general who assured Cowan it was simply an error. Webb had the report corrected "in soldierly language" in 1885; note in Webb's published report that references to Wheeler are bracketed by "[Cowan]." Webb continued to show his support and friendship for Cowan by writing to him on New Year's Day nearly annually until Webb's death. [38]

The battery's memorial, dedicated in 1887, is noteworthy for at least one reason. Look closely at the bas-relief, depicting "Double Canister at Ten Yards." The Confederate flag in the relief is the first to be depicted on a monument at Gettysburg. [39]

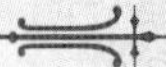

JOHN BACHELDER AND THE HIGH WATER MARK

John Bachelder was the most prominent nineteenth century historian in chronicling and memorializing this battlefield. Born in 1825, Bachelder did not serve during the war, but was a New Hampshire artist who aspired to study and eventually publish a history of a decisive battle. [1]

> At the commencement of the war I determined to attach myself to the army and wait for the great battle which would naturally decide the contest; study its topography on the field, and learn its details from the actors themselves, and eventually prepare its written and illustrated history. [2]

Not only would the battle of Gettysburg meet his definition of a "great" battle, but his work would also help perpetuate that image to the American public. Bachelder arrived and began his work almost immediately afterwards. "When I arrived at Gettysburg the debris of that great battle lay scattered for miles around." [3] The fledgling historian soon began interviewing and corresponding with members of both armies. His surviving papers are required reading for any serious Gettysburg student.

Bachelder ultimately fulfilled some of his artistic and commercial aspirations. He published popular guidebooks, created his own "isometric" aerial drawing of Gettysburg, commissioned an artist to paint "The Repulse of Longstreet's Assault," and issued a set of troop position maps. Bachelder failed, however, to use his vast accumulated research to write a comprehensive battle history. He instead completed a dry and rudimentary volume that essentially copied large extracts from the government's compiled Official Records of battle reports.

He was also a seminal figure in the early memorialization of the postwar battlefield. From 1880 to 1881 and 1883 to 1894 Bachelder served as a director of the Gettysburg Battlefield Memorial Association (GBMA) and was also Superintendent of Tablets and Legends from 1883 to 1887. He thus had major influence in determining where monuments were placed on the field and ensured that those monuments met his definition of historical accuracy. His strong opinions sometimes butted heads with participants who did not always agree with his interpretations and he was involved in several debates with veteran groups, perhaps most notably the controversy over the placement of the 72nd Pennsylvania monument. [4]

Arguably, Bachelder's most lasting contribution to history was his popularizing the "Copse of Trees" and "High Water Mark" as turning points of the battle, and, perhaps symbolically, of the entire war. As noted previously, no contemporary battle reports specifically endorsed the Copse as being the attack's objective, yet the wave of Longstreet's Assault did crest there.

According to Bachelder, in 1868 while commissioning artist James Walker's painting of "Longstreet's Assault," General Longstreet was in Walker's studio examining the work "with a sad smile" and observed, "There's where I came to grief." Bachelder then replied, "Yes, I have called your assault the 'tidal-wave,' and the Copse of Trees in the center of the picture, the 'high-water mark' of the rebellion." Longstreet seemingly agreed, "We were successful until then. From that point we retreated and continued to recede, and never again made successful headway." [5]

Mr. and Mrs. John Bachelder in Devil's Den.
Image courtesy of GNMP

The meeting in Walker's studio implies that Bachelder was already fixated in 1868 on the Copse as a "High Water Mark." Longstreet apparently agreed at the time, although he neglected to give special importance to this small thicket in his subsequent major postwar articles. In *Annals of the War*, Longstreet referenced "Cemetery Hill" as the target and the artillery was to "pour a continuous fire upon the cemetery."[6] In his *Battles and Leaders* contribution, the Southerners were to "renew the attack against Cemetery Hill." [7] He simply failed to specify the target in his memoirs, although he called Pickett's "the division of direction." [8]

Either forgetting his 1868 conversation with Longstreet, or embellishing upon it, Bachelder elaborated on his fondness for these trees in his 1894 report to the GBMA. "Soon after the close of the war," Bachelder toured the field with Pickett's staffer Walter Harrison "and we spent several hours under the shade cast by the Copse of Trees, when he explained to me what an important figure that Copse of Trees was at the time of the battle, and how it had been a landmark towards which Longstreet's assault of July 3d 1863 had been directed." Bachelder was so "impressed with its importance" that he declared "this Copse of Trees must have been the high water mark of the rebellion." Harrison agreed and from that point on Bachelder "felt a reverence for those trees." [9] Harrison, in his 1870 memoirs, dated this visit as occurring in August 1869. He omitted mentioning Bachelder or their conversation, but acknowledged "much valuable information" gained during his stay.[10] Regarding the trees, Harrison wrote:

> Upon getting in full view of the enemy's position, the line of attack was naturally directed against the highest point and apparent center of the enemy. Thus their movement across the open field was necessarily a considerable oblique to the left on their first front. A small clump of trees made the enemy's center a prominent point of direction. [11]

Bachelder continued the theme in his 1873 guidebook, *Gettysburg: What to See and How to See it.* He referred visitors to "a peculiar, umbrella-shaped Copse of Trees…From Seminary Ridge, this cuts boldly against the sky, and forms a prominent landmark, which was selected by General Longstreet to guide the direction of the column in its charge." [12]

This notion was eventually accepted wholesale by the veterans who had fought in this area on July 3: those who wanted credit for nearly capturing the Copse and those who successfully defended it. General Webb, speaking at the dedication of the 72nd Pennsylvania monument in 1883, essentially adopted Bachelder's tone verbatim: "These trees being relieved in clean outline against the sky, when seen from the Rebel line, formed an unmistakable landmark.'" Webb further fired up his old veterans: "Your clump of trees was to be taken, and to be assaulted by the flower of the Rebel host. This decision

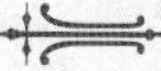

gave you your place in history; this stone wall its prominence." [13]

Bachelder's protective devotion to the "High Water Mark," he said, prevented a prior owner from cutting down the Copse. The site itself was finally acquired by the GBMA in the winter of 1881-1882. In order to protect the woods from relic hunters, Bachelder obtained the GBMA's agreement in 1887 to surround the trees with a fence. That same year, the association requested that Bachelder submit a design for a "tablet descriptive of the engagement and movements of all the commands engaged in the assault of July 3." It took more than four years for him to successfully do so, and it was not until May 1891 that he submitted a proposal for "the High Water Mark tablet to be erected at the 'Copse of Trees.'" [14]

The High Water Mark Memorial was finally dedicated in 1892, nearly 24 long years after Bachelder's supposed art studio conversation with Longstreet. Inscribed on the massive open book are the names of both the Union and Confederate units that participated in the assault, one of the few memorials on the field to honor both armies. The tablet references "Longstreet's Assault" and not the more popularly used "Pickett's Charge." [15]

John Bachelder died in December 1894, only slightly more than two years after his High Water Mark was officially memorialized. He would, no doubt, be happy today to know that his vision of the assault's key landmarks has been passed down to generations of battlefield tourists. As he once admitted, "The thought of naming the Copse of Trees the 'High Water Mark of the Rebellion' and the idea of perpetuating its memory by a monument was mine." [16]

MURDER AND MAYHEM IN THE PHILADELPHIA BRIGADE

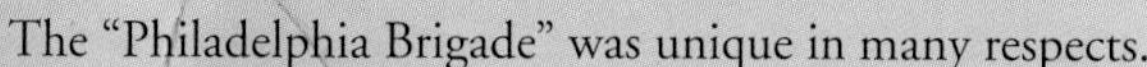

The "Philadelphia Brigade" was unique in many respects.

The only brigade in the Army of the Potomac connected to a single city, it was originally intended to represent California in the Union army. In May 1861, a number of prominent Pacific Coast citizens convinced Oregon Senator Edward Baker to raise a regiment, whom they would supply, if the regiment fought in California's name. The President and Secretary of War then authorized Baker to do so, with himself as colonel and to dub his new command the "California Regiment." [1]

Baker's California Regiment was originally intended to be recruited in New York City. A friend convinced Baker to instead recruit in Philadelphia, and ultimately only one of the regiment's ten companies hailed from New York. Thus, the "Philadelphia Brigade's" sole connection with the City of Brotherly Love is technically inaccurate. In any event, Washington must have been happy with Baker's efforts, because by October 1861, Lincoln further authorized the senator to expand to a full brigade. Three more Philadelphia regiments were re-mustered following the expiration of their original three months' service and were then attached to Baker's growing ranks. [2]

Unfortunately, Colonel Baker was killed in battle at Ball's Bluff before the month was over. (Baker was the only sitting senator killed during the war.) The state of Pennsylvania then promptly appropriated the California regiments as part of their quota and they eventually became known as the

"Philadelphia Brigade." Baker's original regiment became the 71st Pennsylvania. Note the "California Regiment" designation on the 71st's Gettysburg monument. The 2nd California was renamed the 69th Pennsylvania, the 3rd California was re-christened the 72nd Pennsylvania, and the 5th California became the 106th Pennsylvania. (The 4th California was a detached unit of artillery and cavalry.) [3]

Although the brigade was certainly combat-experienced by July 1863, some have argued theirs was a mixed record and that Lee's army actually caught a lucky break by hitting their front. [4] One enlisted man alleged that the brigade was "never…known to stand fire," and still another man remarked that the 72nd Pennsylvania did all of its fighting from the rear. [5]

The brigade started the campaign under the command of Wales native, Philadelphia lawyer, and original founder of the 69th Pennsylvania, Brig. General Joshua T. "Paddy" Owen. [6] Whether or not the brigade's spotty image was the result of stereotypical anti-Irish bigotry, the historical record does suggest that the men of the Philadelphia Brigade may have been more than a handful to manage.

While encamped in October 1862, then-Colonel Owen and the 69th's Lt. Colonel Dennis O'Kane (a former saloon-keeper and eventual regimental commander at Gettysburg) engaged in a fistfight one evening after Owen greeted O'Kane with, "Who the hell are you, you son of a bitch?" O'Kane replied, "If you call me that again I will knock you off that horse." After several soldiers broke up the ensuing scuffle, Owen placed O'Kane under arrest and filed charges including being AWOL and drunk. A court-martial exonerated O'Kane. [7]

On the eve of battle, June 28, division commander John Gibbon arrested brigade commander Owen and (temporarily) relieved him of duty. It has been speculated that Owen was finally a victim of the brigade's lax discipline, but Gibbon's precise reasons are unclear. (Owen was at Gettysburg with no assignment and would return to his command in the spring of 1864.) Owen's replacement was newly promoted Brig. General Alexander Webb. The young Webb immediately tried to instill some discipline on his new Irish charges while on the march but they were reportedly skeptical of his youth and inexperience. [8]

The drama extended to the regimental levels as well. Take, for example, the dispute between captains Bernard McMahon of the 71st Pennsylvania and Andrew McManus of the 69th Pennsylvania. McManus was spreading allegations that McMahon was "a coward." On May 27, 1863, McManus and several officers were socializing in a tent while McMahon was nearby. McManus loudly referred to McMahon as a "coward and a loafer" for perhaps as long as two hours. McMahon eventually reached his limits, entered the tent, and asked McManus if he had been talking about him. When McManus replied in the affirmative, Captain McMahon emptied his pistol into Captain McManus. [9]

A closeup of the 72nd Pennsylvania Monument.
Image courtesy of Michael Waricher

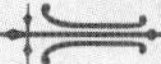

Needless to say the murder of Captain McManus caused great excitement in the brigade's camps. A court-martial, whose members included Lt. Colonel Franklin Sawyer of the 8th Ohio, was convened on June 5 and McMahon was found guilty of murder. The sentence: death by firing squad.[10] One can only imagine the less than fraternal feelings between the City of Brotherly Love's two regiments when they literally fought side by side at Gettysburg.

Captain McMahon was still under arrest at Gettysburg but was fighting with his regiment on July 3, and was among those members of the 71st who helped man Alonzo Cushing's guns. The regiment's commander, Col. Richard Penn Smith, praised McMahon's performance during the battle. McMahon had "with his cartridge box by his side and gun in hand…acted the part of a soldier and man." Smith asked for leniency. General Webb seconded the request, in part because after two months, "it would be difficult to shoot a man a long time after the crime has been committed." [11]

When the date of execution, July 21, finally arrived, General Meade suspended the sentence based on McMahon's "good conduct" in the recent battle. Judge Advocate General Joseph Holt then also recommended a full pardon due to McMahon's long service and the fact that Captain McManus's continued allegations had proven to be "unendurable provocation." President Lincoln agreed and signed McMahon's pardon on September 9. [12]

So it was that the brigade, with a new commander and bad blood between at least two of the regiments, fought at Gettysburg. The brigade performed well in repulsing Wright's Georgia brigade near the Copse of Trees on the afternoon of July 2. In the evening, however, Col. Richard Penn Smith reportedly mortified his men by quickly withdrawing his 71st Pennsylvania from Culp's Hill "against orders" (by his own admission) after exchanging only a few volleys with the enemy. [13] Given the brigade's history, one might wonder if the momentary breakthrough along their front by Pickett's men was such a surprise after all.

The Angle

GPS: 39°48'48.23"N, 77°14'10.82"W; Elev. 593 ft.

This portion of the stone wall, which forms a right angle, was manned by several companies of the 71st Pennsylvania, Colonel Baker's old "California Regiment." As occurred elsewhere along the Union battle line after the fighting of July 2, Col. Richard Penn Smith had ordered his soldiers to stockpile guns that were scattered amongst "the piles of dead men." These extra weapons were loaded and distributed along the line. Colonel Smith recalled that some men had as many as a dozen rifles at the ready, but he issued orders not to fire until the enemy had crossed the Emmitsburg Road and then to "fire and load as rapidly as possible." [1]

A portion of Lt. Alonzo Cushing's battery, probably two guns, were rolled down to

the wall in the space between the 69th and 71st as the Confederates approached. A third cannon was possibly later moved into position near the location of the 71st Pennsylvania's present regimental monument. Colonel Smith had responded to an appeal from Webb and Cushing to help man the cannons by providing approximately 50 infantrymen from the 71st. Lacking proper ammunition, they loaded at least one piece with any refuse that they could find: stones, bayonets, and broken shells. [2]

Participants and historians have long disagreed on how many companies of the 71st were aligned on the right of the 69th Pennsylvania and how many companies were deployed approximately 80 yards behind them at what is sometimes referred to as the "Inner Angle." Many studies generally accept that eight companies were deployed in the front line and two in the rear, although this is far from conclusive. Colonel Smith's official report is frustratingly brief on their overall July 3 activities: "On the 3d instant, some 50 of my men assisted in working Lieutenant Cushing's battery, while the balance were in position, protected by a stone wall from an infantry attack, engaging the enemy and scattering confusion in his ranks, taking some 500 prisoners, as many arms, and 3 stand of rebel colors." Regardless of the exact number of companies, the important points are that the entire regiment could not fit on one line. Rather than extend the right of the regiment beyond (or north of) the Angle, where they would have enjoyed minimal protection on their front and right (as well as having friendly fire in their rear), several companies were deployed at the rear Inner Angle. [3]

Whether General Armistead exploited an opportunity by design or by chaotic chance, his men surged toward two potential soft spots in the Federal line: this space between the 69th and the 71st Pennsylvania, which was defended by only the heavily-damaged portion of Cushing's battery, and the salient angle which was protected by this less than full complement of the 71st Pennsylvania. The California Regiment then assisted the Confederates' efforts by abandoning their position on the front line. William Burns of the 71st wrote: "We went down to the fence and saw the rebs advancing. It was a grand sight and worth a man's while to see it. The fight soon became awful. We mowed the rebs right and left but still they came on when we had to retreat." [4]

But did the 71st Pennsylvania fall back under orders and in good form, or was it a chaotic retreat? Accounts were conflicting since veterans seldom acknowledged panicked retreats in published reminiscences or in the friendly confines of reunions and dedication speeches. They often instead blamed such moments on "some misunderstanding" or the failure of other supports.

Although Colonel Smith was mum on the matter in his report, he claimed in an 1887 interview that he had ordered Lt. Colonel Charles Kochersperger, commanding the left wing, "when they had been pushed too hard to have time to reload, to fall back substantially on a line with the right of the regiment, and to caution his men on retiring to look out for an enfilading fire from the right of the regiment." Smith was steadfast that his men had not retreated before coming in contact with the enemy, but he also acknowledged that "overpowering numbers had forced my advanced left front back." Upon reflection, Smith added, "At no time did Pickett's men actually break through the Federal line." The

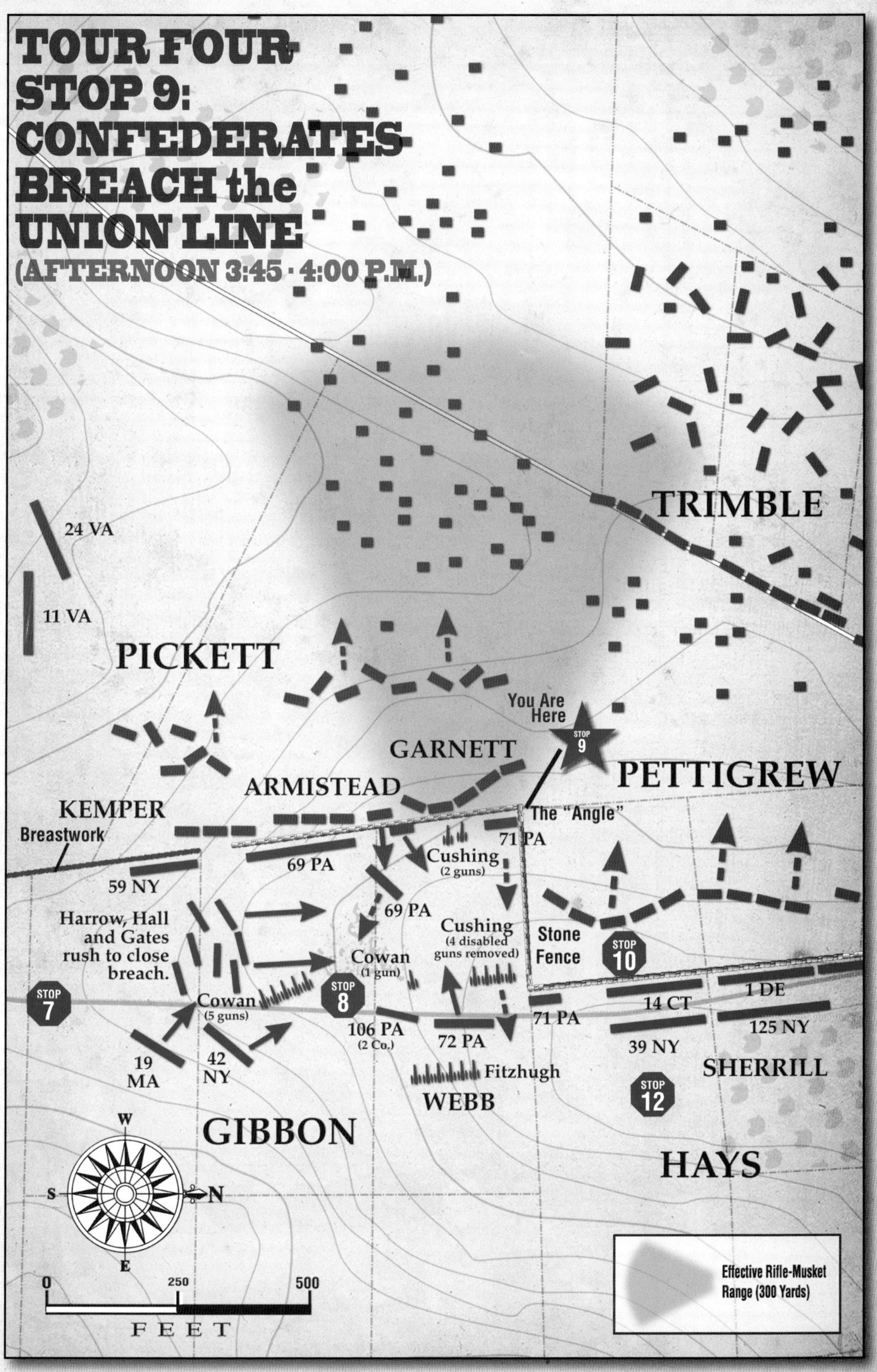
TOUR FOUR
STOP 9:
CONFEDERATES
BREACH the
UNION LINE
(AFTERNOON 3:45 - 4:00 P.M.)
TRIMBLE
24 VA
11 VA
PICKETT
You Are
Here
STOP
9
GARNETT
PETTIGREW
ARMISTEAD
KEMPER
The "Angle"
Breastwork
71 PA
Cushing
(2 guns)
69 PA
59 NY
69 PA
Harrow, Hall
and Gates
rush to close
breach.
Cushing
(4 disabled
guns removed)
Stone
Fence
STOP
10
Cowan
(1 gun)
STOP
7
Cowan
(5 guns)
STOP
8
1 DE
14 CT
71 PA
106 PA
(2 Co.)
72 PA
125 NY
39 NY
19
MA
42
NY
Fitzhugh
SHERRILL
WEBB
STOP
12
W
GIBBON
HAYS
S
N
E
0
250
500
FEET
Effective Rifle-Musket
Range (300 Yards)

The 71st Pennsylvania defended the Union line at the Angle. Image courtesy of Steven Stanley

Virginians had only momentarily pushed back the right of the 69th and left of the 71st, which allowed the right of the 71st to hit Armistead's men with a powerful enfilading fire ("more than any human power on earth could withstand") as if part of some pre-arranged trap. [5]

General Webb dryly admitted in his report, "The enemy advanced steadily to the fence, driving out a portion of the Seventy-first Pennsylvania Volunteers." But he then added the somewhat dubious claim that his men held their ground "even after the enemy were in their rear." [6] Writing to his wife a few days later, General Webb conceded that "two companies [were] driven out" and "all my artillery" was in enemy hands. [7]

Some suggested that only one company fled without orders and that wing commander Kochersperger then followed by ordering the other forward companies to fall back. [8] Private Anthony McDermott of the 69th thought that not "much more than two companies" of the 71st were "withdrawn" during the Confederate artillery fire "as that line would be enfiladed- a humane and prudent act." [9] Major Samuel Roberts of the 72nd Pennsylvania, who thought only two companies of the 71st were in front to begin with, said that they "had been forced to change position to the rear, over the open space on the right of the 69th." [10] Sergeant Major William Stockton of the 71st admitted that after the enemy passed the Emmitsburg Road's fences "they came on with a great rush. I saw one or two of our men start for the rear and I must say that, at the time, I thought it was rather cowardly." [11]

Webb's adjutant Charles Banes admitted only that "the advance companies of the 71st [were] literally crowded out of their places by the enemy." [12] But Banes must have thought more occurred than a simple "crowd[ing] out" because he also testified that "they came back. I was ordered to institute a Court Martial, but the matter was dropped, I suppose

it was dropped because we were successful. A portion of the 71st Regiment had left the line, with the exception of a few who could not get back." [13]

As this occurred nearly simultaneously with the 69th Pennsylvania's struggle to hold their ground near the trees, the Confederates obtained a momentary foothold along the wall. General Webb was horrified to watch the 71st break and Armistead's men pour over his works. Webb's predicament was further increased by his inability to rally the 72nd Pennsylvania. "When they were over the fence," he wrote his wife only days later, "the Army of the Potomac was nearer being whipped than it was at any other time of the battle. When my men fell back I almost wished to get killed. I was almost disgraced, but Hall (Col. on my left) saw it all and brought up two regiments to help me." [14]

Although Webb's brigade clearly bent, they did not break. With the added and timely support of Hall and Harrow's brigades, Pickett's remaining men never really had a chance. "I thought it was all up with us when our General (Webb) rallied the men," wrote William Burns of the 71st. "He went right in front of us and led us when we gave a yell and charged on them and drove them back with great slaughter. The rebs dropped their arms and asked for mercy. Hundreds gave themselves up. About this time the rebels opened on their own men with grape. If they had succeeded at this point it would have been all up with the USA." [15]

The 1887 dedication of the rather plain 71st Pennsylvania regimental monument was witnessed by the survivors of Webb's brigade, Cowan's battery, several hundred members of Pickett's Division who were "invited guests of the Philadelphia Brigade," and more than 2,000 local Adams County residents. The address of General W. W. Burns referred to the monument as a memento "of those who fell on both sides, and will be a guide-mark on the route to fame for the future American soldier." Burns claimed the memorial was placed on "the key of the position, and it was the fate of the war." [16]

72nd Pennsylvania Regimental Monuments

GPS: 39°48'46.75"N, 77°14'10.56"W; Elev. 594 ft.

The early days of Gettysburg National Military Park were not without controversy. Veterans routinely disagreed on whose regiment was the most deserving of battlefield accolades. These disputes often spilled into the public domain through veterans' reunions, monument dedication speeches, and published memoirs. The story of the 72nd Pennsylvania monument is unique, as any die-hard Gettysburg enthusiast knows, because their dispute with the Gettysburg Battlefield Memorial Association over the regiment's desire to place a memorial at the stone wall reached the Pennsylvania Supreme Court. The veterans eventually

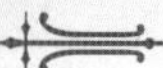

won their case and their prominent monument of a soldier swinging a clubbed musket today stands near the wall as a result. But the facts of the case and the 72nd's Gettysburg performance are not as well known as the outcome.

The 72nd Pennsylvania's beginnings had been promising enough. Known as the "Fire Zouaves" they contained representatives from almost every fire company in Philadelphia. The citizens of Philadelphia had enjoyed watching them drill and the people enthusiastically demonstrated in support when the regiment left Philadelphia and marched off to war. [17]

During the early phases of the July 3 assault, the 72nd was in a reserve position behind the Copse of Trees. [18] General Webb later testified that the 72nd "was behind the Copse of Trees, some yards, I don't remember that exact distance, but to the best of my recollection it was under cover of the crest of the hill." Since Lee's artillery assault had left little doubt as to the focal point of the attack, the 72nd was then moved to their right in order to cover the ground previously defended by Cushing's now destroyed battery. This second position is believed to be approximately marked by the 72nd's smaller 1883 monument, which sits about 15 yards west of modern Hancock Avenue. By Webb's recollections, the enemy was at this time driving in the Federal skirmishers and approaching the stone wall. [19] As the 71st Pennsylvania was forced back from the front wall near the Angle, Webb continued:

> I thought it time to advance the 72nd regiment to the wall to take advantage of the halt and confusion, and I went to their front and center and gave an order for them to move down, but not their commanding officers. They failed to move with me at that time and I passed to the left, to the right of the 69th regiment, to prevent that regiment from being forced back into the clump of trees if possible. [20]

At that point, the general historical agreement ends. Many reasons have been proposed for the 72nd's failure to charge forward with General Webb. He was new to brigade command and perhaps the men simply did not recognize him. By Webb's own admission he did not follow the regimental chain of command, but instead, "the color bearer and myself stood together, I holding onto the staff and he did not move forward with me. I ordered him forward…I know of no words said when I ordered him forward, he moved in his place but did not carry the colors out of the regimental line." [21] Lieutenant Henry Russell of the regiment claimed that:

> I told General Webb that I couldn't fire because there were men in front of me I was afraid of hurting them, and he gave a command by the right flank but it couldn't be heard…We were firing and fighting, and General Webb gave the command to charge bayonets. It couldn't be heard, I don't suppose ten feet away. [22]

As the combat in and around the angle degenerated into a "general melee" the 72nd's position certainly exposed them to a hail of bullets. [23] Major Samuel Roberts remembered "coming to a front under fire, about 60 paces from the front wall, upward of 70 of our men fell, killed or wounded. Rapid firing at close range now took place….our Color-Sergeant, had fallen, pierced by several balls…The staff had been severed by a ball a few inches below the joining of the colors." [24]

Some suggested that the regiment never advanced further beyond this point.

"They were immovable notwithstanding Webb's protests and appeals," claimed the 19th Massachusetts' Col. Arthur Devereux, and "had not advanced when the surrender came."[25] Private McDermott of the 69th Pennsylvania, who may have been motivated by a desire to prove that only his regiment had held the wall, likewise insisted that Webb was futilely "begging them to come up" and they only did so after the enemy surrendered. McDermott claimed to see only one man of the regiment at the wall. [26]

The 72nd Pennsylvania Monument with the Cordori farm in the background.
Image courtesy of Michael Waricher

The ubiquitous Lt. Frank Haskell wrote that the surviving color sergeant, "grasping the stump of the severed lance in both his hands, waved the flag above his head and rushed towards the wall." But only one man followed and the sergeant soon went down. Finally the line sprang forward and "rolls to the wall." [27]

Brigade adjutant Captain Banes stated that the regiment had not moved after Armistead came over the wall. There was some confusion in the ranks, and the men argued that Haskell's horse was crowding them out of their line. After a chaotic ten minutes of gunfire, the Confederates started to be led to the rear as prisoners. "Simultaneously, a movement, commenced, by which the men of the 72nd and those of the 3rd Brigade [Hall] all moved down. At the same time a number of men, who had not crossed before, began crossing over, threw down their arms and were taken prisoners. Still, I saw some personal conflicts going on." According to Banes, the 72nd did not have a formal battle line at the wall; a distinction that would become the crux of the court case. [28]

Naturally, the veterans of the 72nd recalled a mad rush to the wall during the final moments. "The order was now given to charge," wrote Major Roberts. "Murphy, the last of the Color-Guard…seized the colors by the remnant of the staff, and swinging his hat around his head and whirling around, joined the regiment in a dash toward the wall. In

a few minutes the fight was ended." [29] Lieutenant Russell said that eventually they fixed bayonets "and then we charged down to the enemy that were down over this wall, and drove them over that wall and captured them, and I went directly to that wall…" [30]

Sergeant Frederick Fuger of Cushing's battery was a hearty supporter of the 72nd's efforts. He testified that of the 75 to 100 dead whom he saw in the Angle, those on the Union side were "all" men of the 72nd "with part of their clothing burned, which was caused by discharge of muskets at close range." Although these bodies were in close proximity to the front wall they "fell right in their track, advancing," implying that they fell while in forward motion and not in a fixed battle line. Fuger added: "It seems to me that the monument should be placed near that spot or in other words within ten yards of that stone wall." [31]

Because of General Webb's assertion that the 72nd failed to charge under his orders, Gettysburg students often mistakenly assume that the regiment did little actual fighting. In addition to Fuger's recollections of seeing numerous dead men, it is worth noting that their estimated casualties of 192 killed, wounded, and captured were higher than the 69th and 71st Pennsylvania on both a numeric and rate basis. [32] Clearly the 72nd fought against their enemy. But the debate over whether or not they advanced toward the wall, and if they did so, was it part of an organized line of battle remained open for debate.

The regiment's first monument was dedicated in 1883. [33] Smaller and simpler in design than the latter forward monument, this memorial was erected by the 72nd's veterans and states that the regiment "held this angle" on both July 2 and 3. This monument is approximately 54 yards / 162 feet from the stone wall and would roughly be on the line that the regiment occupied when they refused to move for Webb. General Webb spoke at the dedication and assured the audience that Armistead had been greeted "from the front [by] the fire of the 72nd Regiment, perfectly organized and in line on this crest." [34] This is often inaccurately referred to as their secondary monument against the larger and later-erected "clubbed musket" monument, but actually the opposite designation was originally intended.

Trouble began in May 1887. The GBMA resolved that regiments who placed monuments on grounds owned by the Association "would be required to locate and place them in the position held by the regiment in the line of battle" although they would not be prohibited from erecting secondary or advanced markers "as the Association might determine." Although monuments had already been placed on the field that did not necessarily conform to this rule, as volume increased it had become apparent to John Bachelder that without some form of regulation, "the battlefield would look as though the troops had been scattered by a cavalry charge." [35]

About the same time, the Pennsylvania State Legislature created the Governor's Commission on Monuments and additional funds were appropriated to mark each volunteer regimental position at Gettysburg. As the 1883 monument already existed near where most believed that they had been formed prior to Armistead's breakthrough, the old veterans decided that they wanted some form of marker nearer the wall itself. But the GBMA did not believe that the regiment had actually fought there. With the initial agreement of the State Commissioners, the GBMA proposed placing the new monument into a location that was

even farther behind (east) of the 1883 monument to commemorate the first position that the regiment had occupied that day while in reserve. [36]

The veterans refused to accept this decision, arguing that the GBMA's selection was "far in the rear of where the Regiment was engaged on July 3...where the 72nd never fired a shot, nor were engaged in any contest whatever." [37]

The aging warriors were willing to conform to one GBMA rule that they must remain twenty feet away from the wall in order to avoid interloping on the original position of regiments such as the 69th Pennsylvania. But they believed that they had withstood the cannonade "sixty yards to the left and rear" before being marched by the right flank until they nearly "reached the north wall, faced to the front and engaged the foe. From that point you [the regiment] advanced fighting down to this wall having men killed and wounded in the advance." [38]

They soon convinced the State Commissioners to permit an advanced monument near the stone wall, and both the veterans and the commission considered this to be within their authority. But the GBMA refused and also thought that the final authority was theirs. "We feel that the reputation of the regiment has been assailed by the decision and consequently stand ready to defend it," wrote a representative of the veterans' group. "Had the Association even located the position" on a line near the 1883 monument "with permission to place a marker near the wall, I feel confident that all this trouble would have been avoided." [39] It should be noted here that although Gettysburg literature often portrays the ensuing court case as "the stubborn John Bachelder vs. the veterans of the 72nd Pennsylvania," there was a broader legal issue in question. Did the GBMA's charter give them the final authority or did the state's new commission have the right to determine where to place a monument with publicly appropriated funds? [40]

In December 1888, veteran John Reed was arrested for trespassing after beginning to dig a foundation near the Angle. Shortly thereafter, in January 1889, the old soldiers filed suit in Adams County Court to place their monument near the wall. The GBMA scored an early victory when the local court dismissed the complaint in their favor. But the persistent veterans appealed to the State Supreme Court in March and the state reversed the lower court. The trial then began in the fall of 1889 and testimony was taken from both sides. (Bachelder's testimony was thrown out as hearsay since he had not been present during the battle.) The final ruling in March 1891 was in the regiment's favor. The judge noted that the state had "superior authority" over the GBMA and sentimentally added that the men of the 72nd "surely...deserve" to have their position marked. The GBMA appealed the ruling but it was dismissed after only three days. Newspapers generally applauded the verdict and ridiculed Bachelder and the GBMA. [41]

On July 4, 1891, the survivors of the 72nd Pennsylvania dedicated their larger monument twenty feet from the stone wall in compliance with at least one GBMA rule. The monument's design represented "a typical soldier of the day, a youth...clothed in the uniform of which you were so proud, that of the Fire Zouaves of Philadelphia." The soldier is "clubbing his musket to illustrate the closeness of the struggle" that took place here. A reading of the dedication speeches certainly suggests that the vets were gloating over their victory. John Reed, who had been arrested for digging the foundation, was one of the speakers. The father / son judge and court master who had ruled in the regiment's favor were invited guests. [42] So the 72nd received their recognition with a prominent memorial near the wall, while the original and plain 1883 marker (in a position that most agreed had been occupied) is often neglected by visitors.

While the 72nd Pennsylvania is best remembered for not advancing under Webb's initial orders, is that worse than others who fell back, even if only temporarily, from their own positions at the wall? There is little doubt that the 72nd Pennsylvania fought hard, and perhaps even well, that afternoon. Nor is there any doubt that they suffered their fair share of killed and wounded. Did some members of the 72nd fight and die near the current monument? Yes. But did they form a "line of battle" there? That is less likely and the court's ruling was as much about the power of the Governor's Commission over the GBMA as it was about whether or not such a distinction was, and still is, important.

As an additional note, nearly 150 years later, a large windstorm blew through Gettysburg on June 25, 2013. Gusts were strong enough to topple the 1,500 pound statue from its pedestal. (It was then discovered that the statue had not been securely bolted to the pedestal.) The monument suffered some structural damage, but National Park Service officials were most concerned that the prominent statue would be missing for the following week's 150th anniversary celebrations. Although the incident caused considerable commentary, maintenance employees fortunately were able to return the statue to the pedestal the following day. [43]

Lieutenant Alonzo Cushing's Battery A, 4th U.S. Artillery

GPS: 39°48'47.32"N, 77°14'9.00"W; Elev. 600 ft.

Twenty-two-year-old Lt. Alonzo Cushing was an 1861 West Point graduate who commanded Battery A, 4th U.S. Artillery near the Angle. [44] One of the day's true heroes, Cushing refused to leave his guns despite being wounded in both the shoulder and the groin. He was finally killed by a shot through the mouth with the onrushing enemy only 200 yards away.

The battery's July 3 tale began with their involvement in the morning's skirmishing. According to Sgt. Frederick Fuger, the enemy opened fire about 8:00 a.m. and struck Cushing's limbers, blowing up three chests. The Northerners could hear the Confederates cheering and Cushing returned fire several times before all fell silent again about 11:00 a.m.[45]

Although some have labeled Lee's great cannonade as being largely ineffective, Cushing's was among those Union batteries in and around the Angle that were hit particularly

hard. Fuger called it "the most terrific cannonade I ever witnessed…The very earth shook beneath our very feet, and the hills and works seemed to reel like a drunken man." Not only were the artillerists subject to exploding shot and shell but the men were frequently hit by flying rocks as the Confederate projectiles struck the nearby stone wall.[46]

"Men and horses were being torn to pieces on all sides," remembered one soldier. "Every few seconds a shot or shell would strike right in among our guns, but we could not stop for anything." General John Gibbon was observing one of Cushing's men when an enemy shell landed under an open ammunition box, "and the poor gunner went hopping to the rear on one leg, the shreds of the other dangling about as he went." [47]

Another shell crashed into a horse, disemboweling the animal and badly injuring the driver, Pvt. Arsenal Griffin. He had been badly wounded previously in 1862 and vowed never to endure that type of pain again. Lying in agony with his abdomen shot away and entrails spilling on the ground, Griffin called out, "Good-bye boys," put his revolver to his head and shot himself. [48]

Lt. Alonzo Cushing.
Image courtesy of Library of Congress

As the Confederate infantry stepped out of the tree line nearly one mile away, General Webb warned Cushing that things were about to get even hotter. Cushing requested and received permission to "run my guns" up to the stone fence, in the space between the 69th and 71st Pennsylvania regiments. Canister was placed nearby and "in doing this we were obliged to take a closer interval, say about nine yards, owing to some obstructions toward our left" and the Angle on the right. Placing the canister so close to the guns allowed for faster reloading but was potentially dangerous because the rounds could be ignited upon impact by an enemy shell. [49]

How many of Cushing's guns were run down to the stone wall? General Webb reported: "Three of Cushing's guns were run down to the fence, carrying with them their canister." [50] He later modified his view slightly to say that, "Cushing's Battery was destroyed, leaving but one or two pieces that could be manned." [51] John Bachelder was particularly interested in this aspect of the battlefield and likewise wrote on several occasions that three of Cushing's guns were at the wall and that Armistead fell near the other three guns that remained in their original positions. [52]

Many scholars, however, support the notion that only two of Cushing's guns were at the wall. Sergeant Fuger's various accounts can be confusing on this point. He typically implied, or stated outright, that Cushing had ordered all six guns forward to the wall, but on other occasions said that they only left "room for Nos. 1 and 2 to work." [53]

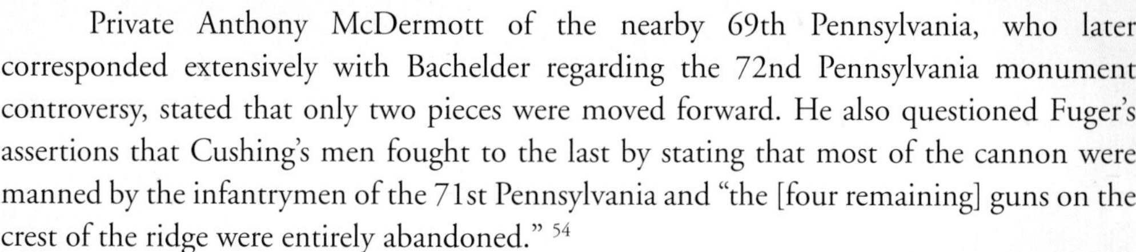

Private Anthony McDermott of the nearby 69th Pennsylvania, who later corresponded extensively with Bachelder regarding the 72nd Pennsylvania monument controversy, stated that only two pieces were moved forward. He also questioned Fuger's assertions that Cushing's men fought to the last by stating that most of the cannon were manned by the infantrymen of the 71st Pennsylvania and "the [four remaining] guns on the crest of the ridge were entirely abandoned." [54]

Regardless of how many guns were actually at the wall (we will accept two for this study) it was this seam between the 69th and 71st Pennsylvania that Armistead's men eventually exploited.

If the eyewitness accounts differed on the number of Cushing's guns that were moved forward, then the same could be said regarding the manner in which Cushing was mortally wounded and ultimately met his death.

Sergeant Fuger actively shared his recollections of the battery's actions following the war, and his stories are typically the most commonly cited accounts of Cushing's death. When the Rebels reached an estimated distance of about 450 yards, the battery opened with single charges of canister. At that time, according to Fuger, Cushing was hit in the right shoulder, and a few seconds later the young lieutenant was hit in the testicles, "a very severe and painful wound." Cushing became "very ill and suffered frightfully" but refused Fuger's suggestions to go to the rear. "No," Cushing replied, "I stay right here and fight it out or die in the attempt." [55] Cushing reportedly added to his injuries by thumbing the vent of gun number four with his bare thumb and burned it to the bone. [56]

At 200 yards, less than the distance from the wall to the Emmitsburg Road, double and triple charges of canister "opened immense gaps in the Confederate lines." When the Southerners closed to within 100 yards (about half the distance from the road) Cushing was shot through the mouth and killed instantly. "When I saw him fall forward I caught him with my arms," Fuger recalled, and "ordered several men to take his body to the rear." [57]

Yet other accounts suggested that Cushing received his initial wounds considerably earlier than Fuger indicated. Captain Cowan stated that he "saw…and spoke to" Cushing

Belt which belonged to Lt. Cushing the day he died. Detail of belt with Cushing's name penned inside.
Image courtesy of The National Civil War Museum, Harrisburg, PA

when Cowan brought his battery in near the Copse of Trees. (Cowan's right piece was only six or seven yards from Cushing's left.) Cowan recalled that Cushing was already "wounded about the legs or thighs." General Webb reported that Cushing "fought for an hour and a half after he had reported to me that he was wounded in both thighs." [58] According to Samuel Roberts of the 72nd Pennsylvania, Cushing's pants had been torn by shell, but he advanced toward Webb "and in the most nonchalant manner said: 'General, if I had some more men I could work my guns.'" Webb replied: "Some of the men here will work your guns." [59] John Bachelder apparently concluded from his studies that "a shot passed through [Cushing's] scrotum making a most painful wound. General Webb earnestly urged him to leave the field, but he refused; and with the blood oozing between his fingers as he grasped the wounded part, he continued to direct the fire of his battery." Cushing then, in Bachelder's reconstruction, obtained Webb's permission to move some pieces down to the wall and was killed thereafter.[60]

Cushing's battery in line near the stone wall at the Angle. Image courtesy of Michael Waricher

After Cushing's demise, as well as the mortal wounding of Lt. Joseph Milne who was on temporary assignment from Brown's Battery B, 1st Rhode Island, Fuger assumed command of the remaining artillerymen and continued the double and treble charges. The smoke was so dense that one could barely see a few feet away, yet to Fuger's "astonishment" Armistead's infantrymen leapt from the smoke and over the wall. The Confederates landed amongst Cushing's forward guns but "my [Fuger's] devoted cannoneers and drivers stood their ground, fighting hand to hand with pistols, sabers, hand spikes and rammers." Fuger declared "those handspikes are the finest weapons for close contact." [61]

At least one of Fuger's battery-mates admitted that he did not stand and fight. Corporal Thomas Moon was caught between two lines with infantrymen from both armies

raising their weapons so "I threw up my hands & fell among the dead men & dead horses. I do not believe I have nerve enough to let a brigade of men run over me. One man stepped on the back of my neck but I layed still." [62]

Whether or not all of Cushing's men fought to the bitter end as Fuger perpetuated is a fact that can be debated, but numerically speaking the battery certainly suffered its share of casualties. The battery's 38 estimated total losses were the highest numeric Union battery casualties and the second highest loss rate at 30.2%. However, in terms of actual men killed, the six KIAs put the battery "only" in sixth place. [63]

After the Rebel attack was ultimately repulsed, Moon was among those detailed to remove Cushing's corpse to a field hospital. Moon was on guard duty that night, but "we had nothing to guard except a few dead men that we managed to get off the field, Cushing among the rest." Few people could imagine what such a battlefield looked like in the aftermath, "the dead men & horses swelled up to bursting & their legs sticking up. I tell everyone that war is Hell." When it rained afterwards, Moon actually slept on Cushing's body to avoid getting wet. The next day, Cushing's black cook / servant, a man named Henry, assisted Moon in removing Cushing's fatigue blouse and replaced it with his dress coat. [64] Cushing was buried at West Point on July 12, nine days after his death. He was brevetted a lieutenant colonel for Gettysburg.[65]

Fuger was awarded a Medal of Honor in the 1890s, with General Webb's hearty support. [66] In 1987, Margaret Zerwekh, a woman living in Cushing's birthplace of Delafield, Wisconsin, began to lobby politicians for Cushing to receive a Medal of Honor. A Wisconsin senator nominated Cushing in 2002 and the U.S. Army approved the nomination in February 2010. The White House then granted final approval in August 2014. Since Cushing died childless and had no direct descendants, the last challenge was to determine who would receive the Medal on his behalf. The President finally presented the nation's highest military honor to a distant cousin of Alonzo Cushing (with the 94-year-old Zerwekh in attendance) on November 6, 2014, more than 151 years after he was killed in action at Gettysburg. [67]

Brigadier General Lewis Armistead Fell Here

GPS: 39°48'47.10"N, 77°14'9.38"W; Elev. 600 ft.

The image of General Lewis Armistead leading his men over the wall with his hat raised aloft on his sword remains among the most iconic and inspiring moments of the entire battle.

The withdrawal of the 71st Pennsylvania gave Armistead's men a brief safe harbor on the west side of the wall. The Virginians momentarily took cover and returned fire. After

several minutes elapsed, Armistead supposedly turned to the 53rd Virginia's Col. Rawley Martin and said, "We can't stay here!" upon which Martin replied, "We'll go forward then!" Armistead scrambled over the wall shouting, "Boys! Give them the cold steel! Who will follow me?" [68]

How many men went over the wall with Armistead? Lieutenant Tapscott in the 56th Virginia wrote that after Armistead had "stopped for a while" outside of the wall, he then "got up with his hat on his sword, and led us forward. I think in all about 150 got up and followed." [69] Sergeant Fuger of Cushing's battery thought it "about 200" men. [70] General Webb estimated that "Armistead passed over the fence with probably over 100 of his command" and that "42 of the enemy who crossed the fence lay dead." [71]

There has long been debate on whether the small monument that commemorates Armistead's mortal wounding is accurately placed. It was generally agreed that Armistead fell on or near one of Cushing's guns, but was it amongst the two (or three) guns that had been moved to the wall, or was it amongst the remainder of the battery that was still (presumably) in its original position? Lieutenant Finley of the 56th Virginia wrote that Armistead "strode over the stone fence, his hat on his sword and calling upon his men to charge. A few of us followed him until, just as he put his hand upon one of the abandoned guns, he was shot down." [72] Frederick Fuger stated that Armistead placed his hand on number three before he jumped over the wall, that Cushing fell two feet to the right of number three's handspike, and that Armistead "fell between Cushing and the wall." [73]

The monument's current placement supports John Bachelder's assertion that Armistead fell "near the three guns left at their original position of Cushing's battery," in other words those guns that were not rolled forward to the wall. [74] Several participant accounts would reasonably support this assertion. Major Samuel Roberts of the 72nd Pennsylvania said Armistead fell "a few paces to the right and rear of the right company of the 69th." [75] General Webb informed his wife on July 6, "General Armistead (an old army officer) led his men, came over my fence and passed me with four of his men." Webb was in motion himself, trying to rally his 72nd and then 69th Pennsylvania, but said that the Confederates were "but 39 paces" from him. [76]

Charles Banes testified in 1890 that "the distance from the front of the 72nd [Pennsylvania], to which Armistead fell was not over thirty-three paces, we measured it on the day of the fight." Banes was questioned regarding the proximity of Armistead's monument to where he fell. "Yes, sir, it is somewhere near it. It is as near the spot, I suppose, as you could get to it." [77]

The current monument is roughly 115 feet from the wall. Although the measurement of a "pace" is a subjective term, one pace generally approximates thirty inches or 2.6 feet. (Although some definitions stretch one pace to be as long as four to five feet.) Using the lower range estimate, 33 paces would approximate 86 feet, or less than the distance from Armistead's marker to modern Hancock Avenue. If Armistead had fallen immediately after crossing the wall, then Banes's measurements would imply that the 72nd Pennsylvania was posted closer to the wall than is the modern Armistead memorial. [78]

Sergeant Drewry B. Easley of the 14th Virginia claimed that he mounted the wall to Armistead's right, with only one cannon between them. [79]

> I forgot my company and stepped off the fence with him. We went up to the second line of artillery, and just before reaching those guns a squad of from twenty-five to fifty Yankees around a stand of colors to our left fired a volley back at Armistead and he fell forward, his sword and hat almost striking a gun.

Easley "dropped behind the gun" and returned fire for a brief period before "I ran back to the stone fence…General Armistead did not move, groan, or speak while I fired several shots practically over his body; so I thought he had been killed instantly and did not speak to him." [80]

The monument to Armistead marking where he fell inside Union lines.
Image courtesy of Steven Stanley

One point of confusion regarding Cushing's so-called "second line" of guns is that Maj. John Moore of the 99th Pennsylvania, in Sickles's III Corps, reported that during the action a "lieutenant of Battery A, Fourth U.S. Artillery, asked me to draw his pieces to the rear, to prevent them falling into the hands of the enemy, he having only 6 men and 3 horses left that were not disabled. The request was promptly complied with, and the battery removed to the rear, under cover of a hill." [81] Moore might simply have been mistaken in his report. Perhaps he misidentified the battery, but if he was correct then there was no second line for Armistead to fall near as Easley claimed.

Lieutenant Tapscott in the 56th Virginia said that he was about 100 feet to Armistead's left and nearer to the Angle himself. Armistead "was shot after he crossed, and few went any farther…I think there was a cannon near where Armistead stopped, partly across the fence, and it was this cannon that he fell by, and it was near the fence and not 300 yards away…After Armistead fell we all settled back in our places behind the fence, and did but little firing; in fact, I had no ammunition and some [men had] no guns." Tapscott claimed that they remained "fully 20 minutes" when they saw "the North Carolina troops falling back." Convinced that the attack had failed, "we had only to surrender or escape." [82]

Private Anthony McDermott of the 69th Pennsylvania left a suspiciously detailed account of Armistead's fall:

> We poured our fire upon him (the enemy) until Armistead received his mortal wound; he swerved from the way in which he winced, as though he was struck in the stomach, after wincing or bending like a person with cramp, he pressed his left hand on his stomach, his sword and hat (a slouch) fell to the ground. He then

> made two or three staggering steps, reached out his hands trying to grasp at the muzzle of what was then the 1st piece of Cushing's battery, and fell. I was at the time the nearest person to him...His men (Armistead's) threw down their arms, most of them lay down between us and the wall, to which we now returned, we sent all that surrendered to our rear. [83]

McDermott later told John Bachelder that when Armistead fell "the fighting was virtually at an end about the 'Angle', that was just previous to the coming up of Hall's regiments. In reality there was no fighting in the Angle after the enemy crossed the wall, as that spot was occupied by the Rebels from the wall *to near the crest where Armistead fell* [emphasis added], for as we returned to the wall the enemy surrendered as we approached them." [84]

General Armistead was an active Freemason, as were many prominent men of the era. While he was lying wounded on the battlefield, it was reported that he used the fraternity's "sign of distress" in order to receive prompt medical attention. [85]

Charles Banes recorded in his *History of the Philadelphia Brigade* (1876): "One of the men [of the 72nd] who was near him, asked permission of the writer to carry him out of the battle, saying, 'He has called for help, as *the son of a widow* [emphasis in original].'" [86] Banes later testified in 1890 that Armistead fell so near the front of the 72nd Pennsylvania ("not over thirty-three paces") that a member of the regiment "said that he heard a man calling for his mother, who was a widow and I saw them carrying him off the field." As three men of the regiment carried Armistead away, Banes took Armistead's revolver which was still fully loaded. [87]

Captain Henry Bingham from Hancock's staff then reportedly encountered Armistead as he was being borne from the field. Bingham wrote, "I met Armistead just under the crest of the hill, being carried to the rear by several privates." The soldiers told Bingham that they "had with them an important prisoner and designated him as General Longstreet." Seeing that the man was "an officer of rank," Bingham dismounted and the two officers exchanged introductions.

> [H]e replied General Armistead of the Confederate Army. Observing that his suffering was very great I said to him, General I am Captain Bingham of General Hancock's Staff, and if you have anything valuable in your possession which you desire taken care of, I will take care of it for you. He then asked me if it was General Winfield Scott Hancock and upon my replying in the affirmative he informed me that you [Hancock] were an old and valued friend of his, and that he desired me to say to you 'Tell General Hancock for me that I have done him and done you all an injury which I shall regret or repent (I forget the exact word) the longest day I live.' I then obtained his spurs, watch, chain, seal and pocketbook. I told the men to take him to the rear to one of the Hospitals. [88]

Captain Bingham then delivered Armistead's message and effects to Hancock, who was by this time wounded himself. [89]

There were also those who claimed that Armistead questioned his own allegiances to the Southern cause. Union General Abner Doubleday didn't profess to hear it but wrote in his memoirs that Armistead told "one of our officers… 'Tell Hancock I have wronged him and have wronged my country.'" [90] Frank Haskell also alleged that Armistead apologized for taking up arms against "my country" but that he knew he would not live to atone for that mistake. [91]

Confederate veterans were outraged when such talk was published. T. C. Holland of the 28th Virginia insisted that Armistead spoke to no one while en route to the hospital.[92] Most historians doubt that Armistead expressed full-blown contrition for participating in the Rebellion and was simply misquoted in the act of expressing regret at his friend Hancock's wounding.

Charles Loehr of the 1st Virginia would later typify the romantic portrayals of Armistead's demise when he wrote that Armistead died with "his left hand on one of the guns of Cushing's battery, and in his right hand he held his sword on which he had placed his hat. Thus a hero meets a hero's death." [93] The general's actual final hours were far less romantic.

Armistead was sent to the large George Spangler farm, located slightly more than one mile away between the Taneytown Road and the Baltimore Pike. The site had been established as a Union XI Corps hospital. The Spangler farm was deemed suitable due to the presence of a large barn and a "dry, airy knoll." However, conditions soon deteriorated due to the large numbers of men who filled the barn and tents. The wounded became so numerous that "some have yet to lie out in the open air" and suffered further misery during the heavy rain of July 4. [94]

Union XI Corps surgeon Dr. Daniel Brinton counted more than 1,000 patients on site by July 4 (other estimates were even larger) and "four operating tables were going night and day" as surgeons worked relentlessly on treatments and amputations. "Among our wounded were three Colonels, [Union] Gen. [Francis] Barlow, and Gen. Armistead of the rebel army a fine man, intelligent and refined." [95] Dr. Brinton later recalled that Armistead arrived about 4:00 p.m. on July 3 and that Brinton treated him along with another physician.

> They [the wounds] were two in number, neither of them of a serious character, apparently. The one was in the fleshy part of the arm, the other a little below the knee in the leg of the opposite side. Without being positive, I think the leg wound was in the left side. Both were by rifle balls, and no bone, leading artery or nerve was injured by either.
>
> In conversation with the General he told me he had suffered much from over-exertion, want of sleep, and mental anxiety within the last few days. His prospects of recovery seemed good, and I was astonished to learn of his death. It resulted not from his wounds directly, but from secondary fever & prostration. [96]

Armistead also reportedly pulled some raw corn from the pocket of his soiled pants

and told his physicians, "Men who can subsist on raw corn, can never be whipped." [97]

Armistead died from complications, most likely in the Spangler's summer kitchen, on the morning of July 5. [98] Private Alfred Rider, 107th Ohio, was detailed to bury the dead and told Bachelder that he interred Armistead in a "rough box" in the "Confederate part of the 11th Corps cemetery on the Spangler farm." [99] Spangler's son later told historian William Storrick that Armistead's body was "wrapped in a blanket and buried back of the barn that was filled with wounded men." Some weeks afterwards, a Dr. Chamberlain of Philadelphia disinterred and embalmed the body, thinking that Armistead's "friends would pay a good price" for it. His body was removed in October 1863 and is now buried at Old St. Paul's Cemetery in Baltimore. [100] That was the hero's death: expiring on a dirty floor, burial in a box or blanket, and having his body later disinterred by an entrepreneurial Yankee.

Friend to Friend Masonic Memorial in the National Cemetery Annex.
Image courtesy of Michael Waricher

General Armistead's memory is unique at Gettysburg. Not only does he have a highly visible monument within Union lines on Cemetery Ridge, but he is also commemorated by several other memorials. No individual Confederate soldier, not even Robert E. Lee himself, is more prolifically celebrated at Gettysburg than is Lewis Armistead.

In May 1887, a committee of veterans from the "Pickett's Division Association" appeared before the GBMA requesting placement of a monument to Pickett's Division on Cemetery Ridge. Unfortunately, the GBMA denied the request but suggested, as a compromise, that perhaps a monument could instead be placed to Armistead where the general fell. The Pickett committee was angered by their inability to secure their division monument, and almost boycotted their upcoming reunion with the Philadelphia Brigade as

a result, but the Armistead "fell here" memorial within the Angle was eventually authorized at the GBMA's July 1887 meeting. [101]

Armistead also appears in a lifelike bronze statue on the impressive but sometimes overlooked Friend to Friend Masonic Memorial. Dedicated in 1993 and located at the entrance to the National Cemetery Annex, the highly detailed sculpture depicts the encounter between Captain Bingham and the wounded Armistead. Their meeting was chosen as the subject over an initially proposed design that would have featured statues of Hancock and Armistead shaking hands. [102]

Not one, but two Armistead-related markers can be found at the Spangler farm death site. A plaque was mounted on the exterior of the Spangler summer kitchen in 1998 by the Armistead Marker Preservation Committee. (The plaque was later removed for work on the building and placed on a ground stick.) The second memorial was dedicated by the same committee in 2000 at the entrance to the Spangler farm. This tablet focuses on the Armistead-Hancock friendship and notes the Masonic aspect of the relationship. The Gettysburg Foundation, the nonprofit partner of the National Park Service at Gettysburg, purchased 80 acres of the Spangler farm in 2008 to preserve the site and reopen it for interpretation. Although the farm had served in a broader perspective as a large Union field hospital, it will undoubtedly be Armistead's memory that will attract many of the site's visitors.

While the historian's focus is often on leaders such as Armistead and Hancock, Joseph Mayo reminded us that this was a battle fought primarily by the unheralded enlisted men. "Twenty paces beyond the spot which is marked to tell where stout old Armistead fell, the foremost hero of them all, a humble private, without a name, bit the dust." A Yankee later explained to Mayo, "I tried to save him, but he would not give up, so I had to kill him to save my own life." [103]

Brigadier General Alexander Webb Monument

GPS: 39°48'46.56"N, 77°14'7.33"W; Elev. 601 ft.

Alexander Stewart Webb was born in New York City on February 15, 1835. Webb's father and grandfather were both military men. His grandfather had been wounded at Bunker Hill as a member of the Continental Army. [104]

Young Alexander was a cadet at the United States Military Academy from 1851 to 1855, graduating 13th in his class of 34. Webb developed into both a scholar and a soldier. He returned to West Point as an assistant professor of mathematics from 1857 to early 1861, and after the war returned yet again to teach geography, history, and ethics. [105] Ironically, one of Webb's West Point classmates, Union cavalry General David M. Gregg,

was protecting the approaches to the Union rear from J. E. B. Stuart's Confederate cavalry on the afternoon of July 3 while Webb defended Cemetery Ridge. [106]

Webb was assigned to artillery at the outbreak of the Civil War, but his abilities quickly elevated him to staff positions. As a result, although he had been active through many campaigns and often cited for "energy," "great coolness," and "gallantry," he had very limited experience leading men in combat prior to Gettysburg. From January until June 26, 1863, Webb was serving as an inspector general in the V Corps under General Meade where the two men clearly developed a strong relationship. [107]

The New Yorker Webb's selection to replace General Joshua T. "Paddy" Owen as commander of the Philadelphia Brigade on June 28 was undoubtedly influenced by Webb's good terms with Meade. His men were not familiar with him, and this probably contributed to the 72nd Pennsylvania's failure to heed his orders to advance on July 3. Yet overall the 28-year-old Webb more than proved himself up to the challenge at Gettysburg. [108]

Gen. Alexander Webb.
Image courtesy of Library of Congress

While General Webb's brigade did permit Pickett's forces to breach their lines during the assault, the Philadelphians held their ground in part because Webb remained on the front lines to rally his new command. Webb later said that he was sure to point his sword at the onrushing Confederates – not wave it overhead - "but pointing it to direct the fire." [109] Webb recognized and was appreciative of the fact that his line was also helped by the support that he received from others: "the enemy would probably have succeeded in piercing our lines had not Colonel [Norman] Hall advanced with several regiments to my support." [110]

Webb was wounded (alternately described as being in the leg or groin) while repulsing the charge, and he was later awarded the Medal of Honor. He believed that he held the distinction of being the only Federal general officer who fought in between both armies for a few deadly moments on that afternoon. [111]

Regarding Webb's well-deserved medal, General Meade wrote, "I know of no one general who has more claims than yourself, either for distinguished personal gallantry on that memorable field (Gettysburg), or for the cordial, warm and generous sympathy and support so grateful for a commanding general to receive from his subordinates." Meade asked Webb to consider the medal as not only a tribute to his performance on the field, but also as "reciprocation of the kindly feelings that have always characterized our intercourse both official and social." [112]

After Gettysburg, Webb temporarily replaced the wounded John Gibbon in command of the division until the spring of 1864. Webb again commanded his own brigade through the Wilderness but was shot in the head at Spotsylvania. The bullet passed through the corner of his eye and came out behind his ear. Webb recovered and returned to the army as Meade's chief of staff from January through June 1865. [113]

A 1915 Tipton photo of the Webb Monument.
Image courtesy of GNMP

Alexander Webb resigned from the army in December 1870 to accept a position as president of the College of the City of New York, a post that he held for 33 years. Webb also served on the New York Monuments Commission which was led by former Union General Dan Sickles and tasked with commemorating New York's participation at Gettysburg. [114]

Webb died on February 12, 1911 (Lincoln's birthday), and was buried on what would have been his own 76th birthday (February 15.) He was interred with full honors at West Point. [115]

General Webb's Gettysburg statue was dedicated in October 1915. The statue was erected through the efforts of friends in New York and not the Philadelphia Brigade as one might initially assume, although the Philadelphia veterans eagerly participated in the dedication ceremonies upon request. Webb was also once honored within the Park by "Webb Avenue," which was a short side avenue that looped inside of the Angle and west of modern Hancock Avenue. Supporters wanted to place a monument to him there and nearer to the stone wall that he successfully defended, but prior to his death Webb himself had requested a position east of Hancock Avenue and facing the Angle. He preferred this location as "one central point which demanded more effort and attention from him in the emergencies that arose than any other part of the arena." So this position was marked by early battlefield commissioner John P. Nicholson. [116]

The statue is meant to commemorate "both strength and courage." Although Webb stated that he wore a short shell jacket with Meade's old brigadier's shoulder straps affixed during the battle, the monument depicts him "in the full uniform of a Major General, U.S.A., the open collar gives the lungs a chance for air without as well as within. In the stalwart stand and proud pose and in the fire and resolve of the eyes there is intrepidity and alertness- a commander ready for any emergency and resolved to conquer or die." [117]

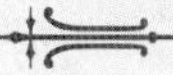

THERE WAS A GREAT BOULDER

As difficult as it may be to visualize, some Union soldiers were actually captured by the Confederates in the fighting near the Copse of Trees and the Angle.

- Private Anthony McDermott of the 69th Pennsylvania claimed that during the hand-to-hand fighting at the Copse of Trees, "Company 'F' completely hustled over the stone wall into the enemy's ranks, and all were captured." [1]
- Major Charles Peyton of Garnett's Brigade noted in his report: "Here we captured some prisoners, which were ordered to the rear without a guard." [2] Likewise, Lt. George Finley of the 56th Virginia said that within 75-100 yards of the stone wall, several Union soldiers cried out, "Don't Shoot! We surrender!" and were ordered back to the rear unescorted. [3]

Probably the best-known Union "prisoner" was Sgt. Major William Stockton, a 22-year-old former dentist from Philadelphia:

> The men who were with me stood and fought, and the enemy came in in great numbers, and, as I remember it, there was a great boulder which formed a sort of stepping stone and made it easy to get over the wall, and they appeared to mass at this place, I suppose on account of it being easier to get over, and came over the wall in overwhelming numbers. They came with such force that they seemed to rebound and go back. Like a wave receding from the shore, and as they went back they took us with them. When we got on the other side of the wall they ordered us to the rear, but I told the men to stay where they were. Then, a non-commissioned officer was ordered to take us back but he didn't do it. [4]

Although Stockton's euphemistic portrayal of surrendering – large masses of men somehow receding back across the wall like a great tidal wave—may defy the laws of physics, the "stepping stone" that he described is still actively used and visible today on the immediate west side of the wall at the Angle. The flat boulder, undoubtedly weathered by more than a century of tourists tramping over it, is sometimes referred to as the "Stockton Rock." [5]

Stockton's men then lay down and took shelter on the west side of the wall as bullets were thudding into the surrounding stones. Finally, when the would-be Southern captors had more than enough difficulties of their own to handle, Stockton and friends jumped back over the wall and ran to the safety of their Yankee colleagues. [6]

Stockton avoided captivity and survived the war, despite suffering a head wound at Spotsylvania Courthouse. Stockton held a variety of postwar occupations and was active in the veterans affairs of the old Philadelphia Brigade. The regimental association that erected the 71st Pennsylvania monument in 1887 was under his chairmanship and he also welcomed the contingent of Pickett's veterans who returned to Gettysburg during that year's reunion. A lifelong bachelor, he died in 1913. [7]

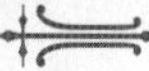

HAZARDOUS SERVICE

The comparatively high casualties suffered by those Union batteries who unlimbered along the northern extent of Cemetery Ridge speak to the lethality of Lee's attack. Several of the Union batteries in and around the Angle were assigned to Capt. John Hazard's II Corps Artillery Brigade. Hazard's command ranked first in Union artillery casualties. Their 149 numeric losses were 43 more than any other brigade, and their loss rate of 24.6% was also the highest in the army. [1] Hazard lamented the loss of several battery officers in his report:

1. Captain James M. Rorty (Battery B, 1st New York Light Artillery): Hazard reported that Rorty "had enjoyed his new position but one day" before being killed while Kemper's men temporarily overran his battery. Captain Cowan wrote that he buried Rorty on the field along with others from Cowan's battery and one Rebel officer. [2] Rorty's battery monument is well south of the Copse of Trees near the 1st Minnesota's July 3 monument.

2. Lieutenant Alonzo Cushing (Battery A, 4th U.S.): "He especially distinguished himself for his extreme gallantry and bravery, his courage and ability, and his love for his profession."

3. Lieutenant George Woodruff (Battery I, 1st U.S.): Woodruff's battery was positioned in Ziegler's Grove and their battery monument can be located there. Woodruff was mortally wounded while the Southerners were retreating and died on July 4.

4. Lieutenant Joseph Milne (detached from Brown's Battery B, 1st Rhode Island Light and serving with Cushing's battery): Milne was mortally wounded "by a musket-shot through the lungs" and lingered until July 10. "In his regiment he was noted for his bravery and willingness to encounter death in any guise." [3]

The complete story of many who served and died here will never truly be known. Private Ansel Fassett was a member of Cushing's battery during the repulse of Pickett's Charge. According to enlistment records, Fassett entered the service in October 1862 at the age of 18. He was born in Wyoming County, Pennsylvania and was a farmer. Official sources indicate that he was wounded by a shell fragment in his hip and died in a hospital on July 13. Fassett is buried today in the U.S. Regulars plot of Gettysburg's National Cemetery, under a stone that is misspelled "Amest Fassette." [4]

Pvt. Ansel Fassett.
Image courtesy Ed and Faye Max Collection

Or did Ansel Fassett survive Gettysburg? A man who insisted that he was Fassett died in California in June 1926. This Fassett asserted that he had only been briefly hospitalized and was soon discharged from the service, but unfortunately he could not remember what he had done with his papers. The government denied his pension claim and admittance to an old soldiers' home since he was unable to prove that he was a surviving veteran. The old man was forced to rent rooms and take in washing to support himself and save enough for his burial.

This Fassett's demise made the local news in Oakland, California, under the headline, "Veteran Dies Fighting to Prove He Was Alive." According to the news, Fassett's daughter arrived from Pennsylvania the day after his funeral. She had reportedly last seen her father "in the Gettysburg field hospital" (which seems unlikely since Fassett would have only been 18 or 19 years old at Gettysburg) and had come to take him home, arriving only days too late to see him. [5]

WHY DON'T THEY COME?

When Armistead came over the wall with 100-150 men against thousands of armed Yankees, many of the Southerners waited and hoped for reinforcements. None came.

Colonel Joseph Mayo of the 3rd Virginia recalled, "many an anxious eye was cast back to the hill from which we came in the hope of seeing supports near at hand and more than once I heard the desperate exclamation, 'why don't they come!' But no help came…" [1] Mayo also added, "As I gave one hurried glance over the field we had traversed, the thought in my mind was repeated at my side, 'Oh! Colonel, why don't they support us?'" [2]

But Longstreet elected not to send any remaining supports from R. H. Anderson's Division, nor from the remainder of Rodes and Pender's divisions in Long Lane:

> Major-General Anderson's Division was ordered forward to support and assist the wavering columns of Pettigrew and Trimble. Pickett's troops, after delivering fire, advanced to the charge, and entered the enemy's lines, capturing some of his batteries, and gained his works. About the same moment, the troops that had before hesitated, broke their ranks and fell back in great disorder, many more falling under the enemy's fire in retiring than while they were attacking. This gave the enemy time to throw his entire force upon Pickett, with a strong prospect of being able to break up his lines or destroy him before Anderson's Division could reach him, which would, in its turn, have greatly exposed Anderson. He was, therefore, ordered to halt. In a few moments the enemy, marching against both flanks and the front of Pickett's Division, overpowered it and drove it back, capturing about half of those of it who were not killed or wounded. [3]

Remember that Lee had reported that General Hill was "directed to hold his line with the rest of his command, afford General Longstreet further assistance, if required, and avail himself of any success that might be gained." [4] Yet it was Longstreet, and not A. P. Hill, who seemingly exercised control over R. H. Anderson's Division, whose brigades would have comprised the majority of any available reinforcements. Anderson reported:

> [A]t what I supposed to be the proper time, I was about to move forward Wright's and Posey's brigades, when Lieutenant-General Longstreet directed me to stop the movement, adding that it was useless, and would only involve unnecessary loss, the assault having failed. I then caused the troops to resume their places in line, to afford a rallying point to those retiring and to oppose the enemy should he follow our retreating forces. [5]

The performance of Brig. General William Mahone's Brigade has been something of a mystery to Gettysburg students. Despite the fact that his brigade was in a position to actively participate on

both July 2 and July 3, he reported only 102 casualties and admitted in his report that his "brigade took no special or active part in the actions of that battle beyond that which fell to the lot of its line of skirmishers." [6] At least two common soldiers in Mahone's ranks both apparently recorded that the command was ordered forward, but after advancing as far as the Confederate batteries the orders came in to halt and return to their works. It remains just part of the larger enigma of A. P. Hill's performance on July 3, but the fact remains that on both the second and third days large portions of his corps were not actively engaged. Longstreet's actions have been placed under many historical microscopes while Hill has gotten the equivalent of a free pass from many scholars. [7]

Even more curious were those Longstreet critics who insisted that McLaws and Hood's divisions (which were certainly more battered than Posey and Mahone's brigades) were to participate in the attack. Lee's staffer Walter Taylor, who was amongst Longstreet's many postwar detractors, later insisted that Hood and McLaws were still expected to move forward "in support of those of Pickett and Pettigrew." [8] Taylor added:

> The attack was not made as designed. Pickett's Division, Heth's Division, and two brigades of Pender's Division advanced. Hood and McLaws were not moved forward. There were nine divisions in the army; seven were quiet while two assailed the fortified line of the enemy. A.P. Hill had orders to be prepared to assist Longstreet further if necessary. Anderson, who commanded one of Hill's Divisions, was in readiness to respond to Longstreet's call, made his dispositions to advance, but General Longstreet told him it was of no use -- the attack had failed.
>
> Had Hood and McLaws followed or supported Pickett, and Pettigrew and Anderson have been advanced, the design of the Commanding General would have been carried out -- the world would not be so at a loss to understand what was designed by throwing forward, unsupported, against the enemy's stronghold, so small a portion of our army. [9]

Others on Lee's staff made the same accusations. Major Charles Venable and Col. Armistead Long claimed that Lee never intended for Pickett, Pettigrew, and Trimble to fight unsupported by the remainder of the army. [10] Long alleged that Pickett was to be supported by Hood and McLaws, "and General Longstreet was so ordered" by Lee verbally in the presence of Long, Venable "and other officers of the army." Venable further claimed to have brought Lee's attention to it afterwards. Lee's supposed response was: "I know it! I know it!" [11]

Longstreet publicly rebutted the accusations in 1877. "It has been absurdly said that General Lee ordered me to put Hood's and McLaws' divisions in support of Pickett's assault. General Lee never ordered any such thing." Since Taylor and friends did not specify exactly how Hood and McLaws would have physically supported such an assault, Longstreet added:

> If the reader will examine any of the maps of Gettysburg he will see that the withdrawal of these two divisions from their line of battle would have left half of General Lee's line of battle open and by the shortest route to his line of supplies and retreat. Fully one half of his army would have been in the column of assault and half of Meade's army would have been free to sally out on the flank of our column and we should have been destroyed on that field of battle beyond a doubt...The only way for those divisions to have been moved was to have attacked the heights in front. But this attack had been tried and failed the day before. If Pickett had shown signs of getting a lodgment, I should, of course, have pushed the other divisions forward to support the attack. But I saw that he was going to pieces at once. [12]

Longstreet's admission that he would have moved the other divisions forward "if Pickett had

shown signs of getting a lodgment" explains what would otherwise be a curious passage in his memoirs. In *From Manassas to Appomattox*, Longstreet wrote that the "divisions of McLaws and Hood were ordered to move to closer lines for the enemy on their front, to spring to the charge as soon as the breach at the centre could be made." [13] Taken by itself, Longstreet's memoirs could be interpreted as an acknowledgement of Taylor and Long's accusations. Yet in combination with his 1877 account, a clearer picture of his intentions emerges: Longstreet would have committed more troops along his front *if* Pickett, Pettigrew, and Trimble had been successful. Still, Longstreet's intentions notwithstanding, one is left with an unanswered question. Did Lee intend for such a piecemeal assault, or did he intend for a larger portion of his army to strike a united and simultaneous blow? In the long shadow of the postwar anti-Longstreet articles and memoirs it is impossible to know for certain.

All that we can ascertain for certain is that Pickett's men who penetrated Union lines near the Angle were on their own and incapacitated in relatively short order. Those who were not killed, wounded, or captured fled back toward Seminary Ridge. By roughly 4:00 p.m., the Confederates were in a disorganized retreat.

ONE FEMALE IN REBEL UNIFORM

It is well established that women were on the battlefield at Gettysburg and played important roles. Some stories, such as those of nurse Annie Etheridge or vivandiere Mary Tepe, are fairly well known. But although it is also generally accepted that an unknown number of women actually disguised themselves as men and fought in both armies during the war, such documented and confirmed examples at Gettysburg are scarce. [1]

One documented case of a female Confederate soldier does exist and is noted in the Official Records. Brigadier General William Hays, commanding the Union II Corps for the disabled Hancock, wrote that his command buried 1,629 bodies (387 Union and 1,242 Confederates) between July 2 and July 5. Hays added: "Remarks- One female (private), in rebel uniform." [2]

That is all that we know. We do not know who she was or where she died. It has been suggested that she was a wife of a Southern solider and that the two marched and died together in Pickett's Charge, but this legend appears to be primarily based on a romantic fictional account that appeared in an 1893 issue of *Confederate Veteran.*

Attributed to novelist Martha Caroline Keller, "The Hero of Pickett's Old Brigade" [sic] was an unnamed young soldier who enlisted with and served in the ranks with his seemingly overprotective father. But the "son" was actually the "father's" disguised wife. While marching together in the July 3 charge, a Confederate flag-bearer was shot down and the son/wife grabbed the colors. "For a moment it floats above the storm of battle…A sword pierces her, and she falls beside her husband. Both surrender life in this wonderful charge…Europe has her Joan of Arc, her Charlotte Corday, America her Mollie Pitcher, but the Confederacy has her sweet girl-hero who fell in the charge of Pickett's men at Gettysburg." [3]

Such literary imagery—the Confederacy offering up its own Joan of Arc on the fields of Gettysburg – was important to the defeated South, even if Keller did not offer a single attempt to

validate or suggest that her account was nonfictional. Still, although there is no proof to confirm the assumption that our female Rebel died fighting with her husband, it is interesting to wonder who she was and why she fought. At least one researcher has suggested that few women soldiers actually joined the armies to serve with a family member and that they were more likely recruited by the same factors that motivated men: desire to fight, adventure, duty, patriotism, and revenge against a hated foe.[4]

Continue north along Hancock Avenue. Past the Angle, you will note that the stone wall turns right (east) and then straight again (north) toward the small white house and barn that mark the Abraham Bryan farm.

The "Inner Angle" and the Abraham Bryan Farm

GPS: 39°48'48.49"N, 77°14'7.78"W; Elev. 601 ft.

The sector north of the Angle (sometimes referred to as the "Inner Angle" because it sits roughly 80 yards east of the "Outer Angle" where Armistead crossed), the Abraham Bryan farm, and nearby Ziegler's Grove were primarily defended by the II Corps division under hard-hitting Brig. General Alexander Hays.

Hays's division had manned this part of the line since July 2, although Samuel Carroll's brigade (with the exception of the 8th Ohio) was detached elsewhere on July 3. The stone wall between the Inner Angle and the Bryan farm was defended by Arnold's 1st Rhode Island Battery, the 14th Connecticut, 1st Delaware, and 12th New Jersey of Colonel Thomas Smyth's brigade. The majority of Col. Eliakim Sherrill's brigade was originally behind Smyth. Stationed north of Bryan's farm was Woodruff's battery and several additional Union regiments (Smyth's 108th and Sherrill's 126th New York, and the 1st Massachusetts Sharpshooters.)

General Hays described the ferocity and the brevity of Pettigrew's final surge:

> Their march was as steady as if impelled by machinery, unbroken by our artillery, which played upon them a storm of missiles. When within 100 yards of our line of infantry, the fire of our men could no longer be restrained. Four lines rose from behind our stone wall, and before the smoke of our first volley had cleared away, the enemy, in dismay and consternation, were seeking safety in flight. Every attempt by their officers to rally them was in vain. In less time than I can recount it, they were throwing away their arms and appealing most piteously for mercy.[1]

General Hays added in a letter dated July 4, "After cannonading us for an hour, they advanced across the plain and were met from behind our stone wall by a volley which swept them like a tornado." [2] Hays reported that his division captured "fifteen battle-flags or banners. A number of other flags were captured, but had been surreptitiously disposed of, in the subsequent excitement of battle, before they could be collected." [3]

Colonel Smyth, commanding Hays's Second Brigade, also wrote:

> As the fire of the enemy's batteries slackened, their infantry moved upon our position in three lines, preceded by skirmishers. My men were directed to reserve their fire until the foe was within 50 yards, when so effective and incessant was the fire from my line that the advancing enemy was staggered, thrown into confusion, and finally fled from the field, throwing away their arms in their flight. Many threw themselves on the ground to escape our destructive fire, and raised their hands in token of surrender. [4]

Not only was the Union infantry fire taking a heavy toll but Pettigrew and Trimble's commands paid an additional freight for marching into the teeth of Federal artillery around Cemetery Hill. General Oliver Howard observed that the Confederate left was "nearly opposite our front." The XI Corps batteries "opened fire, using shells at first. The gaps made by them seemed to have no effect in checking the onward progress of the enemy." The Rebels still "advanced steadily, gaining ground gradually toward his right. When near our line of skirmishers, the batteries opened upon them with grape and canister from the hill. The infantry also commenced firing. The enemy's lines were broken, and the plain in our

This scene from the restored 1883 Cyclorama of the "Battle of Gettysburg" by Paul Philippoteaux, shows Union artillery along the stone wall from the Inner Angle to the Bryan farm. Image courtesy of Steven Stanley/GNMP

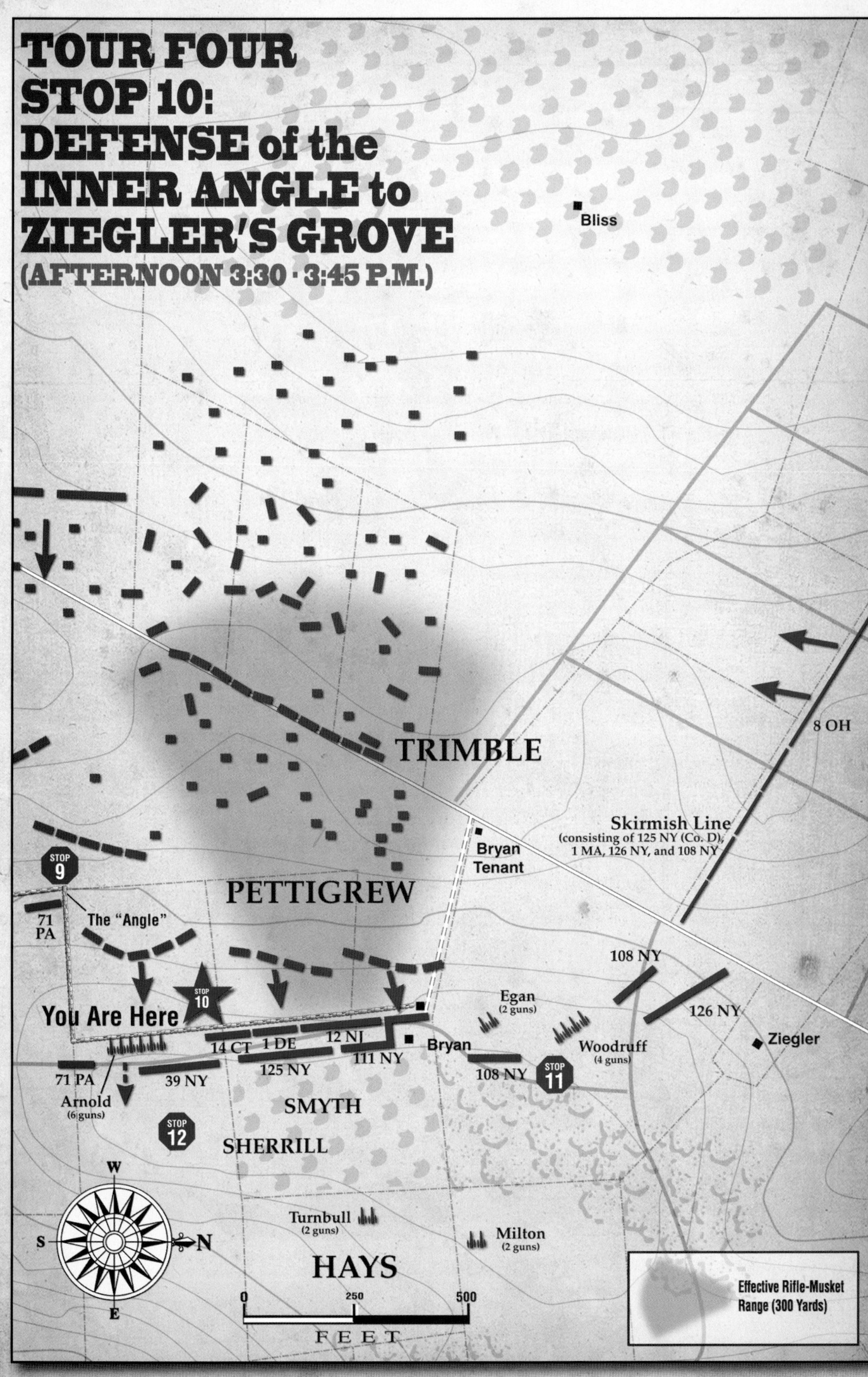
TOUR FOUR
STOP 10:
DEFENSE of the
INNER ANGLE to
ZIEGLER'S GROVE
(AFTERNOON 3:30 - 3:45 P.M.)
Bliss
TRIMBLE
8 OH
Skirmish Line
(consisting of 125 NY (Co. D), 1 MA, 126 NY, and 108 NY)
Bryan
Tenant
STOP 9
PETTIGREW
71 PA
The "Angle"
108 NY
Egan
(2 guns)
126 NY
Ziegler
STOP 10
You Are Here
14 CT
1 DE
12 NJ
Bryan
Woodruff
(4 guns)
71 PA
39 NY
125 NY
111 NY
108 NY
STOP 11
Arnold
(6 guns)
SMYTH
STOP 12
SHERRILL
W
S
N
E
Turnbull
(2 guns)
Milton
(2 guns)
HAYS
0
250
500
FEET
Effective Rifle-Musket Range (300 Yards)

front was covered with fugitives running in every direction." [5]

Howard's artillery chief, Maj. Thomas Osborn, confirmed that long distance shell was initially used on the enemy and after "about one third of the distance from Seminary Ridge to our line, their ranks had been a good deal cut out." The Southerners halted to dress lines "which were materially shortened" as "fearful artillery fire…was cutting them down by the hundreds every minute." Despite the mounting losses, there was still "no hesitation or irregularity in the movement" when the final charge was made at a double quick over about 1/8th a mile against both Yankee musketry and canister. Osborn added that Union batteries also opened fire as the Confederates retreated and "did them considerable damage," ceasing fire only when they reached the relative safety of Seminary Ridge. [6] Osborn's recollections about firing on retreating soldiers contradicts the misimpression that many battlefield visitors have over this being a "gentlemen's war."

Captain William Arnold's Battery A, 1st Rhode Island

GPS: 39°48′48.76″N, 77°14′7.63″W; Elev. 601 ft.

Captain William Arnold's Rhode Island battery of six 3-inch ordnance rifles defended the stone wall along the Inner Angle up through the great cannonade that preceded the charge. The battery's left gun was said to be at the corner of the wall itself. [7] Sergeant Major William Hincks, a Medal of Honor recipient from the nearby 14th Connecticut, later recalled that the orders to burn the Bliss barn on the morning of July 3 had been given because Rebel sharpshooters located there were "severely annoying" Arnold's battery, although at distances approaching 650 yards such shots would have been unlikely. [8]

By all accounts, this battery suffered severely during the artillery portion of the assault. Modern estimates place it as the third highest amongst all numeric Union battery casualties at 32 and fifth highest in percentage loss at 27.4%. [9] Major Charles Richardson, 126th New York, said that the battery was so disabled that several men of the 126th helped work one of the guns. [10] But whether or not the entire battery was withdrawn, and if so when, remains conjecture like so many aspects of this battle.

General Henry Hunt wrote in *Battles and Leaders* that Arnold's battery (and Brown's) were "so crippled that they were now withdrawn" about the time of the artillery cease-fire. [11] Artillerist Capt. John Hazard implied in his report that Arnold was withdrawn due to lack of ammunition during the Southerners' advance. [12] Major Theodore Ellis, commanding the 14th Connecticut, wrote on at least two occasions that he moved his regiment into Arnold's position after the battery withdrew "entirely disabled" from the field. [13]

However, the battery's withdrawal was conspicuously absent from their regimental

history to the extent that the historian also implied that they fired some of the last shots of the entire afternoon. This has caused Arnold's battery to become best remembered for a feat which they probably did not accomplish: specifically firing canister directly into the face of the 26th North Carolina Regiment.

According to battery historian and veteran Thomas Aldrich, as the 26th approached, a battery sergeant yelled to one Pvt. William Barker: "Barker, why the devil don't you fire that gun! Pull! Pull!" Barker obeyed and the "gap made in that North Carolina regiment was simply terrible." Double shots of canister hit the North Carolinians "as the last shot fired from our battery when the rebels broke in retreat." Pettigrew's Confederates had reached farther than Pickett's men, "and up to the wall running north and south in front of our battery, where they were killed and captured in great numbers, but did not cross the wall." [14]

Arnold's 1st Rhode Island battery along Hancock Avenue, the 71st Pennsylvania monument is in the middle distance. Image courtesy of Michael Waricher

Assuming that Aldrich had not simply engaged in the all too common habit of exaggerating their accomplishments, modern historians have attempted to reconcile such discrepancies by speculating that one or two guns possibly remained until nearly the end. However, as the position of the 26th North Carolina within Pettigrew's formation was believed to be farther north nearer to the Bryan barn, battle student Bruce Trinque reasonably postulated that Arnold's cannoneers actually fired upon the 16th North Carolina on the right flank of Lowrance's Brigade in Trimble's line. [15]

Artilleryman Aldrich was also clearly sensitive to allegations that the battery had been withdrawn. Some historians have placed Lt. Guilian Weir's Battery C, 5th U.S., as Arnold's replacement. Weir wrote that he had moved his battery to "the front" and "opened" with canister before following with case and solid shot. "Numbers" of the enemy surrendered with

one Rebel asking "where can I get out of this Hellish fire?" [16] However, Aldrich conceded that "one section of Weir's battery went in between Cushing and our battery just in time to fire a few shots, while the enemy were falling back." [17]

Aldrich also voiced rare criticism of Brig. General Henry Hunt's handling of the Federal artillery. As Arnold was running low on ammunition, a messenger had "great difficulty" in locating Hunt, who then ordered the man to make two unsuccessful searches for corps artillery commander Captain Hazard before finally dispatching an order to bring relief from the artillery reserves. "As far as artillery was concerned I think it was handled the poorest I ever saw in any battle…between our battery and Woodruff's on our right in Ziegler's Grove there was space enough for three batteries, and there was not one there until it was too late to be of much service as the enemy was retreating." [18]

The relatively simple battery monument was dedicated on North Hancock Avenue in October 1886. [19]

1st Massachusetts "Andrew" Sharpshooters

GPS: 39°48'49.16"N, 77°14'7.62"W; Elev. 601 ft.

Not all of the monuments along the stone wall between the Angle and the Bryan farm represent positions actually occupied by regiments during the July 3 charge.

The 240-odd yards (720 feet) from the Inner Angle to the Bryan barn is said to have comprised enough space for at least three regiments (the 14th Connecticut, 1st Delaware, and 12th New Jersey), Arnold's battery, and several companies of the 71st Pennsylvania. In the tightest possible shoulder-to-shoulder formation, the wall would have accommodated two lines of roughly 360 men each. Assuming nearly 720 total men in two lines (and ignoring any space for Arnold or others), there is not enough room for three average-sized regiments along this wall, let alone the seven monuments that are represented here today. (The seven being: Arnold's battery, 1st Massachusetts Sharpshooters, 14th Connecticut, 1st Delaware, 2nd Delaware skirmishers, 12th New Jersey, and 111th New York.)

This monument to the 1st Massachusetts Sharpshooters was dedicated in 1886. Although this position appears to have met with John Bachelder's approval as representing "one monument where we all were on the 3rd," note that the memorial states that the sharpshooters were in action "in different positions." Sculpted uniquely from Italian marble, the figure is a sharpshooter aiming his rifle at the enemy while using a crude telescope that runs the length of the barrel. The veterans considered two possible mottos for their monument's inscription before selecting, "In God We Put Our Trust, But Kept Our Powder Dry." (A better choice over the alternative: "Our aim was man. We rarely missed the mark.")[20]

The sharpshooters' Lt. Emerson Bicknell said that his men were positioned to the right and left of the 88th Pennsylvania in Ziegler's Grove, having occupied that point to discourage enemy skirmishing, "until the heavy cannonading checked sharpshooting." Note, however, that the 88th Pennsylvania's monument is several hundred yards north of this point. Bicknell observed a "shattered remnant of some regiment" who along "with many others, sought the seeming shelter of the grove" during the artillery barrage. [21] This might indeed have been a reference to the 88th Pennsylvania as their Capt. Edmund Patterson reported, "About 2 p.m. the enemy opened upon us from all sides. We were then at the foot of Cemetery Hill, and were compelled to change our position for safety during the heaviest of the fire." [22]

Just prior to the charge, Gen. Alexander Hays rounded up "all these men that lay in the grove" and formed them in line to the right of the Bryan house. As the enemy approached, the Northerners fired a left oblique before Hays "swung them down by a left wheel to the lane which then ran from the house to the Emmitsburg Road; across the lane they then fired." To Bicknell it appeared that Pettigrew's Confederates would probably have gained a foothold in Ziegler's Grove were it not for this flanking fire "which destroyed its formation and sent its shattered and disordered masses" back in retreat. Bicknell followed some of the retreating Rebels and claimed capture of 130 prisoners. [23]

Although this flank action is often portrayed as being in conjunction with the 8th Ohio's activities, Bicknell told John Bachelder in 1884 that the 8th Ohio was so far to the right as to be unaware of their presence and had "no part in the flank movement in which I took part." [24]

A second positional marker to the sharpshooters is in Ziegler's Grove several hundred yards north of this main monument and nearer to the 88th Pennsylvania. Unfortunately, that secondary marker and others were displaced in the 1960s with the construction of the Cyclorama building but will be returned to their original positions following the 2013 demolition of the Cyclorama building and subsequent rehabilitation of Ziegler's Grove.

14th Connecticut Regimental Monument

GPS: 39°48'49.78"N, 77°14'7.54"W; Elev. 601 ft.

Two companies of the regiment were actively skirmishing that morning near the Emmitsburg Road. To expose any portion of one's body was to court enemy skirmish fire. By lying down in the standing wheat and grass, the skirmishers of the 14th would speak to one another without actually seeing each other. A Corporal Huxam was not verbally replying so a comrade crawled over to him and found Huxam shot in the head. He had apparently tired of lying down and had risen to kneel behind the road's fence to take a shot

when a Rebel ball must have found him first. [25]

As noted previously, there was not enough room along this portion of the stone wall to accommodate all of the full-sized regiments who placed monuments here. In the case of the 14th Connecticut, they only brought 160-170 men to Gettysburg and with the two companies on the skirmish line and minus casualties from the various Bliss farm escapades, there were only about 100 men in a single line on the morning of July 3. [26] Further complicating matters was that when the regiment returned from their final Bliss foray, the 1st Delaware had taken their place at the wall, so the men of the 14th lay down behind the

A Confederate's view of the Inner Angle, with the monuments to the 14th Connecticut, 1st Delaware, and 12th New Jersey in the distance. Image courtesy of Michael Waricher

Delawareans during the great cannonade. They suffered little comparative loss since most of the Rebel artillery overshot them, although Arnold's battery to their immediate left was drawing considerable fire. Sergeant Major William Hincks recalled that concussion from Arnold's battery threw enough gravel on him that he could literally see, smell, and taste the powder from the charge. The stifling mid-afternoon heat caused the perspiration from his face to make mud of the ground underneath him. [27] After Arnold's battery withdrew, the 14th's Maj. Theodore Ellis wrote that he moved the regiment into that space "to fill the gap." [28]

Major Ellis described the ensuing charge:

About this time two lines of battle, extending across the plain for more than a mile,

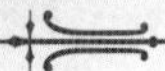

preceded by a line of skirmishers and re-enforced on the right and left by a third line, were observed to emerge from the woods, about one-third of a mile distant and running parallel to our front, and advanced steadily across the intervening plain. The spectacle was magnificent. They advanced in perfect order, the line of skirmishers firing. Our men were formed in a single line along an almost continuous line of low stone wall and fence, which offered considerable protection from the enemy's fire.

When the first line of the enemy had advanced to within about 200 yards, our fire opened almost simultaneously along our whole line. The enemy's first line was broken and hurled back upon the second, throwing that also into confusion. Detached portions of the line were rallied, and for a short time maintained their ground, but being rapidly mown down by our terribly destructive fire, they commenced falling back. A portion of this regiment then charged upon the retreating rebels, capturing five regimental battle-flags and over 40 prisoners. There also came into the lines of this regiment about 100 or more of the enemy, some of whom were wounded, and gave themselves up. [29]

The Emmitsburg Road is roughly 220 yards from the regiment's front. Orders were given not to fire until the enemy reached the road. The Northern skirmishers were driven in and then "the word 'Fire! Fire!' ran along the Union line, 'Crack! Crack!' spoke out the musketry, and the men dropped from the fence as if swept by a gigantic sickle swung by some powerful force of nature." Several of the Yankees reportedly had two breech loaders and would have a comrade load one while the other was being fired. Some of the guns even overheated and men had to pour "precious" water from canteens on them to cool them off. Very soon a shout went up amongst the regiments that the Rebel assault had been broken. [30]

Sergeant June Kimble of the 14th Tennessee left a fantastical account in *Confederate Veteran* magazine, although not the first Southerner to exaggerate his deeds in that publication, claiming that his men "stood in the works of the enemy" while "prostrated" Yankees cowered and surrendered "at our feet" as Kimble held this point for "five, perhaps ten, minutes." [31] Reminiscences from regiments such as the 14th Connecticut do not even come close to corroborating Kimble's version. [32]

Nevertheless, it is impressive enough that Pettigrew's men even made it as close as 55 to 90 yards from the Union lines. A color bearer in the Tennessee regiment planted a flag that far from the Connecticut front. Major Ellis called for someone to bring the banner in and Sgt. Major William Hincks leapt over the wall and outran several competitors to capture the flag. Although in as much danger from friendly fire as from the enemy, Hincks safely returned with the prize (after a righteous wave of his sword overhead) and later was awarded a Congressional Medal of Honor. [33]

The 14th Connecticut's Cemetery Ridge monument was dedicated in July 1884 along with the regiment's other battlefield memorials. (Recall that there is also a small monument and a "center of house" marker on the Bliss farm site.) [34]

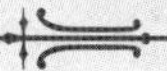

12th New Jersey Regimental Monument

GPS: 39°48'54.56"N, 77°14'7.59"W; Elev. 601 ft.

The 12th New Jersey was the largest regiment in Smyth's brigade at approximately 444 effectives. [35] Their monument is also the most distinct amongst the otherwise generally plain memorials to Smyth's regiments.

The Jersey boys were armed with old .69 caliber smoothbore muskets. The muskets only had an effective range of 100 yards and were even then highly inaccurate, but they were deadly enough at close range. They had been issued "buck and ball" cartridges of one round ball and three small buckshot. While they awaited meeting Pettigrew's forces, many soldiers loaded up to 25 buckshot into their muskets as a special surprise for their attackers. As a result, the regimental monument was dedicated in 1886 with an example of a buck and ball charge on top along with a detailed plaque representing their charge to the Bliss farm. [36]

Captain George Bowen described case, shrapnel, shot and shell cutting "great swaths through their lines" yet Pettigrew and Trimble "came as steady and regular as if on a dress parade, our guns pouring the shot into them." One plucky Confederate reached the Bryan barn when Bowen ordered a nearby lieutenant to shoot the man. The Rebel dropped and Bowen later found him with a bullet through the center of his forehead. To Bowen's left, a Confederate momentarily mounted a gun and waved his flag with a cheer before being brained by a Yankee gunner's sponge staff or rammer. [37]

As Pettigrew's column crossed the Emmitsburg Road, Smyth's brigade poured "a terrific sheet of musketry into the column before which the whole front line seems to go down." Combined with flank fire from the 8th Ohio and double canister from Woodruff's battery, one officer recalled, "in less time than I have taken to tell the story the whole of the six brigades to the left of Pickett are either prone upon the ground or fleeing in disorder." [38]

It should come as no surprise that veterans' groups often squabbled amongst themselves over whose monuments were deserving of "front line" treatment. The 12th New Jersey vets publicly emphasized that none of Hays's other regiments shared this wall with them on July 3. [39] When, in 1890, the 111th New York veterans proposed putting their monument near the New Jersey monument, Maj. John T. Hill protested that his regiment alone held this line and putting any other memorial here "will destroy the accuracy of the historical event these monuments are intended to record...and should not be permitted under any circumstances." [40] The 111th's monument was instead dedicated in 1891 farther north of this point and depicts a highly detailed skirmisher moving forward to engage the enemy. [41]

Abraham Bryan Farm

GPS: 39°48'56.02"N, 77°14'6.74"W; Elev. 601 ft.

- Abraham Bryan (alternately spelled "Brien" or "Brian") was about 61 years old and a free black man who resided with his family on this farm. Bryan owned 12 acres and lived here until 1869. [42]

The Abraham Bryan house looking west. The monument to the 8th Ohio is in the distance.
Image courtesy of Michael Waricher

- Thanks to an early Mathew Brady image, the farm was initially misidentified as General Meade's headquarters, but was in fact more likely General Hays's headquarters. [43] Not that General Hays was the type to be idly sitting in the farmhouse as Pettigrew and Trimble's assault crested only yards away.

Bryan Tenant House

GPS: 39°48'57.03"N, 77°14'12.86"W; Elev. 588 ft.

Abraham Bryan also owned a small one-story tenant house, or probably more likely a shack, that stood on the east side of the Emmitsburg Road. The fence line that sits north of the Bryan house and runs to the Emmitsburg Road is said to mark the line of the farm lane that stretched to the tenant house. [44] The tenant house stood directly in the path of Pettigrew and Trimble's assault, as well as being in close proximity to Union skirmishing activities, and was reportedly destroyed. [45]

According to the 1860 census, the Bryan tenant house was occupied by Alfred Palm, 24-year-old Margaret Divit, and their one-year-old son Joseph. Margaret's occupation was listed as "Mistress-Harlot" in census records. [46] It is not clear if the Palms occupied the tenant property at the time of the battle; in fact there is evidence to suggest that they did not.

Despite her census classification as a "harlot," much local lore has attached itself to Margaret Divit, or Margaret Palm, or Mag Palm. Local citizen David Schick recounted that Mag "lived up Long Lane, back of the old fair grounds." On one occasion she was supposedly "attacked by a group of men who made the attempt to kidnap her and take her south where they expected to sell her and derive quite a profit. She was a powerful woman, and they would have, from the sale, derived quite a profit. These men succeeded in tying Mag's hands…She was fighting them as best as she could with her hands tied. She would attempt to slow them and succeeded in one instance in catching [an attacker's] thumb in her mouth and bit the thumb off." [47]

Whether Schick's recollections were embellished or accurate, we do know that she posed for at least one photograph demonstrating how slave hunters attempted to tie her hands together. Mag's reputation as a determined resistor of slave hunters was used as the inspiration for writer Elsie Singmaster's fictional character "Maggie Bluecoat," a conductor on the Underground Railroad who wore an old War of 1812 blue coat, in the 1924 novel *A Boy at Gettysburg*. Unfortunately, fact and fiction occasionally blur and historians sometimes erroneously refer to Mag Palm as both "Maggie Bluecoat" and as a conductor leading escaped slaves to safety. [48]

Willard / Sherrill's Brigade

GPS: 39°48'55.00"N, 77°14'6.76"W; Elev. 602 ft.

This is one of two monuments to Col. George Willard's brigade on the battlefield. This War Department monument commemorates the brigade's service on July 3, while an additional memorial on Sickles Avenue near the Klingle farm marks their July 2 activities.

The brigade was comprised of the 39th (four companies), 111th, 125th, and 126th New York. All of those infantry regiments have monuments in this vicinity. They entered Gettysburg under the cloud of being dubbed the "Harper's Ferry Brigade" or "cowards" due to their having been amongst the Federal garrison that was humiliatingly captured and paroled at Harpers Ferry during the 1862 Maryland campaign.

Colonel George Willard of the 125th New York was newly appointed to brigade command prior to Gettysburg after Gen. Alexander Hays was promoted to lead the division. The brigade acquitted itself well on the late afternoon of July 2, when it was sent to stop Brig. General William Barksdale's attack against Sickles's III Corps along the banks of Plum Run. Unfortunately, Colonel Willard was killed by a Confederate shell that literally tore away

portions of his head and face. The heroic Willard's death has been unfairly overshadowed historically by the mortal wounding of Confederate General Barksdale during the same action.

Upon Willard's death, command transferred on the field to Col. Eliakim Sherrill. The fifty-year-old Sherrill had an impressive resume. He had been elected to Congress in 1847 and the New York State Senate in 1854. He raised the 126th New York at Geneva, New York, in 1862. A portrait of Colonel Sherrill can be found on the 126th's nearby monument in Ziegler's Grove. Sherrill was seriously wounded at the Harper's Ferry debacle and his 126th was sent to Chicago on parole before being exchanged. [49]

The monument to the 111th New York on the Abraham Bryan farm. Image courtesy of Michael Waricher

The brigade was badly disorganized when Sherrill replaced the fallen Willard. As shells were falling in the ranks, and Generals Hays and Hancock were nowhere in sight to provide guidance, Sherrill elected to return the brigade to its original position near here. (Lieutenant Colonel Bull of the 126th New York claimed that this decision was based on Willard's final orders but Colonel MacDougall of the 111th New York protested that this action was creating a large gap on Cemetery Ridge for the enemy to exploit.) Whatever Willard's intentions had been, the men had not gone very far when General Hancock came thundering up and launched into a profanity-filled tirade demanding to know "who was in command." Hancock then promptly put Sherrill under arrest and ordered the brigade to turn around. Although the "Harper's Ferry Cowards" had redeemed themselves in battle that day, it was a somber group that returned near the Bryan orchard and Ziegler's Grove that evening. [50]

The brigade was posted on July 3 in line behind Smyth's brigade and was probably as follows: 39th, 125th, and 111th New York extended left to right up to the Bryan buildings. North of Bryan's, the 126th New York was then posted to the far right of Smyth's 108th New York and Woodruff's battery. [51]

According to the 125th New York's regimental history, the men returned on the third

to "immediately behind the stone wall at the place occupied by the regiment during the second day. The position was directly to the left of the Bryan barn. Someone not connected with the regiment has located the position on a second line some yards to the rear of the stone wall. This error will be corrected when a monument marks – as it soon will – the true ground." A portion of the regiment spent the morning on the skirmish line where "the men hugged the ground, for the firing was hot." Around noon the skirmishers were withdrawn to a "reserve station" on the Emmitsburg Road. [52]

Captain Aaron P. Seeley, 111th New York, reported that the "regiment fell in at 3 a.m., the enemy having commenced a furious shelling upon our position at that time, which fire died away at about 9 a.m." The silence was broken about 1:00 p.m., "when there was opened upon our position a cannonading and shelling unparalleled, it is believed, in warfare. During the hottest of this fire the regiment formed and marched by the right flank up to the crest of the hill, and formed a line of battle in rear of the 12th New Jersey, who were lying under the shelter of a low stone wall. We here lay down upon the ground, the shot and shell filling the air above our heads and often striking among us." [53]

Captain Samuel Armstrong of the 125th New York's Company D was born in Maui, giving him the unusual distinction of being a Hawaiian native leading troops at Gettysburg. (Armstrong's parents were Christian missionaries in Hawaii when he was born on January 30, 1839.) He considered the cannonade "tremendous. Nothing could have been more impressive or magnificent." He then described the attacking Confederate formations as "three long lines several hundred yards apart…It was grand to see those masses coming up, and I trembled for our cause." [54]

As Pettigrew's men approached, Armstrong "saw our opportunity" and rallied about 75 men from the picket-reserve and elsewhere. He ordered them at the "double-quick" into a position along a rail fence about 60 or 70 yards from and at a right angle to the wavering Southern left. Armstrong's command "took deliberate aim and poured a murderous fire into the rebel flank." It was "a hot place" for Armstrong as his boys took fire from all directions—including from Union artillery behind them. [55]

The regimental historian noted that only the 8th Ohio "has been given the credit for the flank fire" but that the 125th was also deserving of acclaim." Hundreds of the charging [Confederate] line prostrated themselves on their backs in the Emmitsburg Road, and waved their hats and handkerchiefs in token of surrender. Some of the bravest rushed close to the main Union line, and fell a few yards away." [56]

Lieutenant Colonel James Bull of the 126th New York added: "The enemy, advancing in four lines across the flat, were subjected to a murderous fire of musketry and artillery, and were driven back in confusion, after an engagement of about an hour." [57] Although not noted in official reports, the 126th was ordered to wheel left and joined the 125th in opening an enfilading fire on the enemy's left, "who soon broke in confusion," according to Maj. Charles Richardson. The New Yorkers rushed forward and captured several colors. [58]

Tragically, Colonel Sherrill, who was still under Hancock's rebuke from the prior day, was mortally wounded during the action. As he was near the line of the 39th New York, two soldiers from that regiment carried him to the rear and the men of Sherrill's old

126th New York did not even learn about it until after the repulse. He died at the XI Corps hospital at the George Spangler farm around 8:00 a.m. on July 4. His funeral in Geneva, New York, was attended by 10,000 people. [59] Command of the brigade then fell upon Lt. Colonel Bull, the senior surviving officer and the third commander in less than 24 hours. [60]

As you pass the Bryan farm, note a woodlot of trees on the east side of Hancock Avenue and behind many of the monuments. This area has been significantly disturbed by post-battle development but during the war was the site of the larger Ziegler's Grove.

Ziegler's Grove

GPS: 39°48'58.73"N, 77°14'1.00"W; Elev. 601 ft.

The woodlot known as Ziegler's Grove was part of a 30-acre tract that was owned by David Ziegler in 1863. Like several other properties associated with the battle, Ziegler did not reside on the property that carries his name, and it was instead occupied by tenants. Some have debated whether the large and prominent Ziegler's Grove, and not the Copse of Trees, was the actual focal point of Lee's attack. Contemporary accounts can be interpreted to support either scenario.

What is clear, however, is that postwar development by private and public enterprises distorted the ground occupied by General Hays's right flank and therefore has diminished the scope of Pettigrew and Trimble's attack for modern observers. [1]

The surrounding vicinity was also labeled as the Emanuel Trostle farm on the 1868-1869 Warren Map due to the postwar Trostle residence that sat near the modern National Park Service entrance from Steinwehr Avenue (across from several fast food restaurants at the time of this writing). [2] The area was apparently already denuded of trees in 1888 when the GBMA made an effort to re-plant it. A 75-foot tall War Department observation tower was placed in Ziegler's Grove in 1896 and trees were replanted again in 1897. [3]

Yet no occupant of Ziegler's Grove was more controversial than Richard Neutra's Cyclorama Building which was located here from 1962 until it was demolished in early 2013. The building was constructed as part of the National Park Service's "Mission 66"; a project undertaken to update badly outdated NPS infrastructure. When it opened, the building was considered a significant accomplishment in providing a new home to Paul Philippoteaux's massive and historic cyclorama painting as well as a noteworthy collaboration between the National Park Service and Neutra, a famous private architect. [4]

Part of Mission 66's objectives was to make a visitor center a park's "hub" of

interpretation and to help prevent visitors from "aimlessly" driving around a park. [5] The Ziegler's Grove site was chosen to house the cyclorama painting because the position from which Philippoteaux placed the painting's viewers was just south of the building itself, the site offered a spectacular view of a crucial part of the battlefield, and it provided easy access to key attractions such as the Angle, the National Cemetery, and the then-new Visitor Center.[6] As NPS official Roy Appleman argued, "From here the most can be comprehended by the visitor if he is unable to go elsewhere." [7]

However, within only a few short decades, preservationist goals shifted toward restoring Gettysburg to as pristine of a wartime condition as possible. Buildings and utility lines that were on, or were visible from, key points of the battlefield were targeted for removal. In November 1999, the approved NPS General Management Plan included demolition of both Neutra's Cyclorama Building (which was also causing damage to the painting due to improper hanging) and the nearby Visitor Center in order to restore the grove's 1863 appearance and to provide a better home for the deteriorating painting. [8]

Philippoteaux's painting was eventually removed from public display in 2005 in order to undergo a multi-million dollar restoration. It was then relocated into the new Gettysburg Museum and Visitor Center, where it is now properly hung and reopened to the public in 2008. After considerable legal wrangling between Neutra's supporters and the National Park Service, the Ziegler's Grove building was finally demolished in March 2013.

Although the ground itself has been forever altered by these activities, the removal of this intrusion gives observers a better sense of how the area appeared during the battle.

One additional benefit of the rehabilitation of Ziegler's Grove is the planned return of several monuments to the positions that they occupied before they were moved to accommodate the Cyclorama building and accompanying parking lot. These monuments include the 90th Pennsylvania monument, Lt. Leonard Martin's Battery F, 5th U.S. Artillery (returned to its original position in September 2014), and markers to the 12th Massachusetts and 88th Pennsylvania. [9]

The view from the Ziegler's Grove tower (long gone) looking south along Hancock Avenue.
Image courtesy of Sue Boardman

Lieutenant George Woodruff's Battery I, 1st U.S. Artillery and 108th New York

GPS: 39°48'58.5"N, 77°14'04.5"W; Elev. 602 ft.

Battery I, 1st U.S. Artillery in Ziegler's Grove consisted of six 12-pounders under the command of Lieutenants George A. Woodruff and Tully McCrea. The battery's monument is of the style assigned to those of the United States Regular regiments of infantry, artillery, and cavalry on the field.

As the Rebels approached, Lieutenant McCrea "thought that our chances for Kingdom Come, or Libby Prison were very good. Now this is where our Artillery came in, saved the day, and won the battle. I have always been of the opinion that the Artillery has never received the credit which was its due for this battle. As the enemy started across the field in such splendid array, every rifled battery from Cemetery Hill to Round Top was brought to bear upon their line." [10]

The battery had smoothbores loaded with canister, so the Yankees "bided our time. When they arrived within five hundred yards we commenced to fire, and the slaughter was dreadful." Reportedly firing two rounds of canister per minute from each gun, the mounting Confederate casualties caused them to close toward the center "and by the time they reached our lines it was a mass of men without organization." McCrea admitted that the enemy reached and broke Federal lines "at one place" but "there were so few left that they were too weak to be effective, and were captured. It was the splendid work of the Artillery that saved the day and gave us the victory." [11]

Woodruff's battery and 108th New York monument in Ziegler's Grove.
Image courtesy of Michael Waricher

Lieutenant Woodruff was struck by a musket ball in the back near the charge's close and mortally wounded. McCrea and the men "knew it was the end from the nature of the wound." Woodruff was removed to a field hospital at the old Granite Schoolhouse. He died on July 4, regretting to the end that he had been shot in the back and asking his friends that it be no reflection upon his reputation. He was buried behind the schoolhouse, and his grave was marked so that it could be identified. [12]

Behind Woodruff's battery monument is a trefoil-shaped memorial to the 108th New York. The 108th had been supporting Woodruff and their monument depicts an infantryman lying in support of a battery with the inscription "it sustained a terrific fire without being able to return a shot." [13]

Brigadier General Alexander Hays Monument

GPS: 39°49'0.55"N, 77°14'4.33"W; Elev. 601 ft.

General Hays has typically received less notice from Gettysburg historians than other II Corps leaders such as Generals Hancock, Webb, and Gibbon. Ironically, while the more-heralded Webb's brigade momentarily broke at the Angle, there is no indication that Hays's men ever wavered or faltered in defending their posts north of the Angle.

Alexander Hays was a Pennsylvania native born July 9, 1819, and was just shy of his forty-fourth birthday at Gettysburg. Hays was a West Point graduate (1844) but was out of the army when war erupted in 1861. He promptly re-entered the service. [14] "When the rebellion broke upon us like a tornado," he once said, "in the desecration of our flag at Sumter, I took oath never to sheath my sword until honorable peace should restore us to one glorious Union." [15]

General Hays was commanding a brigade amongst the Washington defenses when the Gettysburg campaign opened, and he was only assigned to command the Army of the Potomac's Third Division, II Corps on June 28. [16] Hays was six feet tall, had red hair, and was reportedly both hotheaded and hard drinking. He reveled in dragging one of Pettigrew's captured flags in the dust following the Rebel repulse of July 3. An observing newsman wrote: "I reckon him the grandest view of my life. I bar not Niagara." [17]

General Hays was active throughout the battle and survived, although his horses were not so lucky. A solid shot struck his horse "Dan" while Hays was dismounted. "Noble old 'Dan' died a soldier's death," Hays observed, before directing his "servants" to dig an "honored grave" on the field for the poor animal. [18]

The defense of Cemetery Ridge may indeed have been the high point in Hays's career. When the Army of the Potomac was reorganized the following year, he was reduced to brigade command in favor of the more senior General David Birney. If Hays resented this, he had little time to reflect on it. Only 10 months after Gettysburg, Hays was shot through the head and killed while leading his men at the Wilderness. His old friend, General Ulysses S. Grant, was "visibly affected" when he learned of Hays's death. Posthumously awarded the rank of brevet major general, Hays's remains were taken to Pittsburgh where he was buried.[19]

His monument near Ziegler's Grove, while in a highly trafficked location, is not ideally situated for visitors to actually stop and ponder Hays's likeness or accomplishments. It was placed here in 1915, after five Pennsylvania division commanders were selected by the state (in 1913) to be honored. The five generals were Hays, Andrew Humphreys, John Geary, Samuel Crawford and John Gibbon. Due to the advancing ages of interested parties, diminishing funds, and the onset of World War I, only the memorials to Humphreys, Hays, and Geary were completed at that time, and General Hays did not receive a proper dedication ceremony until it was "re-dedicated" on July 3, 1982, with Hays's great-great grandson in attendance. [20]

Major General George Meade Equestrian Monument

GPS: 39°48'50.00"N, 77°14'5.21"W; Elev. 603 ft.

After returning from his brief detour to Powers Hill, Meade rode toward the front and arrived on the crest of Cemetery Ridge near the site of his modern equestrian monument.

By one account, Meade and his son met an artillery lieutenant whom Meade questioned if the enemy had "turned." The lieutenant replied, "Yes. See Hays has one of their flags," in reference to General Hays dragging a Confederate flag through the dust. "I don't care for their flag. Have they turned?" was Meade's "mighty cross" reply. According to Lt. Frank Haskell, who claimed to be nearly everywhere on the field, Meade asked Haskell in "a sharp, eager voice: 'How is it going here?'" Haskell replied that the enemy had been repulsed and "a new light began to come in his face, of gratified surprise, with a touch of incredulity…'What! Is the assault already repulsed?' his voice quicker and more eager than before." When Haskell confirmed the victory, Meade looked over the field and exclaimed, "Thank God." Near Ziegler's Grove, the victorious men began to cheer Meade and "it was one continuous ovation the whole way down" as Meade rode along his lines toward Little Round Top. [1]

Meade summarized the day in another dispatch to General Halleck that evening:

> The enemy opened at 1 p.m. from about 150 guns, concentrated upon my left and center, continuing without intermission for about three hours, at the expiration of which time he assaulted my left center twice, being upon both occasions handsomely repulsed, with severe loss to him, leaving in our hands nearly 3,000 prisoners; among the prisoners, Brigadier-General Armistead and many colonels and officers of lesser rank. The enemy left many dead upon the field and a large number of wounded in our hands. The loss upon our side has been considerable.[2]

General Meade's impressive equestrian monument was dedicated on June 5, 1896. Although Meade is often thought to be overshadowed by other generals and not given his deserved credit for leading the victory, his equestrian monument was the first of its kind on the battlefield. [3] General Hancock's equestrian monument was dedicated on Cemetery Hill the same day as Meade's, and the dual ceremonies created additional opportunities for the pomp and ceremony that Gettysburg does so well, but Meade's statue was dedicated several hours before Hancock's. Although the Gettysburg *Compiler's* coverage noted that Hancock's ceremonies were attended "by an even greater throng of people than at the Meade statue in the morning."[4]

The Meade Equestrian Monument. Image courtesy of Steven Stanley

Meade's ceremony was reportedly attended by every living Meade descendant, including his son and former aide, then Col. George Meade. The statue was covered by two large flags and was unveiled by the general's grandson. Former cavalry division commander Gen. David M. Gregg, who led Union forces at East Cavalry Field on July 3, gave the oration. General Nelson Miles, then current Commanding General of the United States Army, was also in attendance and declared, "Too much cannot be said for the patriotism and military ability of" General Meade for taking command of a "poor, defeated army" and leading it to victory. [5]

The bronze statue was sculpted by Henry Kirke Bush-Brown at a cost of $37,500. Meade sits approximately eight-tenths of a mile from General Lee's statue atop the Virginia State Memorial and is astride his beloved horse, "Old Baldy," who had been wounded in the battle. Meade feared that the old brute "will not get over it," but Baldy outlived his master until 1882. [6]

We have now concluded our tour of the Army of the Potomac's defense of Cemetery Ridge on July 3. From the far left on Wright Avenue to the extreme right of Ziegler's Grove, we have covered nearly 2.5 miles. You have experienced firsthand the fact that General Meade's army had to manage a much broader front during this attack than simply the area surrounding the Angle.

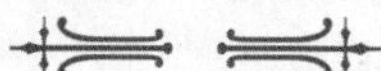

DID GENERAL MEADE COUNTERATTACK?

Many of the Confederate commanders feared that Meade might launch a devastating counterattack following the repulse of Longstreet's Assault. Colonel Edward Porter Alexander, with the years of hindsight that are often characteristic of his analysis, wrote in 1877, "I have always believed that the enemy here lost the greatest opportunity they ever had of routing General Lee's army by prompt offensive." [1] Alexander elaborated in his *Military Memoirs*:

> It must be ever held a colossal mistake that Meade did not organize a counter-stroke as soon as he discovered that the Confederate attack had been repulsed. He lost here an opportunity as great as McClellan lost at Sharpsburg. Our ammunition was so low, and our diminished forces were, at the moment, so widely dispersed along our unwisely extended line, that an advance by a single fresh corps, the 6th, for instance, could have cut us in two. Meade might at least have felt that he had nothing to lose and everything to gain by making the effort. [2]

General Lee's report (dated January 1864) tersely stated only that his "troops were rallied and reformed, but the enemy did not pursue." [3] Longstreet added:

> General Wright, of Anderson's division, with all of the officers, was ordered to rally and collect the scattered troops behind Anderson's division, and many of my staff officers were sent to assist in the same service. Expecting an attack from the enemy, I rode to the front of our batteries, to reconnoiter and superintend their operations.
>
> The enemy threw forward forces at different times and from different points, but they were only feelers, and retired as soon as our batteries opened upon them. These little advances and checks were kept up till night, when the enemy retired to his stronghold, and my line was withdrawn to the Gettysburg road on the right, the left uniting with Lieut. General A. P. Hill's right. After night, I received orders to make all the needful arrangements for our retreat. [4]

While touring the field during the battle's 25th anniversary, former Army of the Potomac Chief of Staff Dan Butterfield (who was no ally of General Meade) successfully goaded Longstreet into acknowledging that Meade's inability to successfully counterattack was "a fatal error. After the failure of Pickett's Charge – and there were some of us who expected it to fail- there were men who stood on Seminary Ridge who expected to see a general advance by the Union forces. We were for a time in great trepidation. Our lines were very thin; they were in no condition to withstand an attack if it were made with any vigor. I am convinced that had we been then vigorously attacked there would have been an end to the war." [5]

Not that every Army of Northern Virginia veteran agreed with Longstreet. North Carolinian William Bond, angry over the attention given to Pickett's Virginians, wrote that Longstreet was "evidently judging the army by his troops, some of whom are said to have been so nervous and shaky after this battle that the crack of a teamster's whip would startle them." [6]

Whether or not General Meade acted aggressively enough to "finish" Lee's battered army is one of the many contentious points of debate among battle scholars. Some historians have credited

Meade with intending a full counterattack following the Confederate repulse. However, most accounts support Meade actually ordering something closer to a reconnaissance in force. In a dispatch to General Halleck, dated July 3, 8:35 p.m., Meade wrote:

> After the repelling of the assault, indications leading to the belief that the enemy might be withdrawing, an armed reconnaissance was pushed forward from the left, and the enemy found to be in force. At the present hour all is quiet. My cavalry have been engaged all day on both flanks of the enemy, harassing and vigorously attacking him with great success, notwithstanding they encountered superior numbers, both of cavalry and infantry. The army is in fine spirits. [7]

George Meade's official report, dated October 1863, made no mention of an intended counterattack by either his infantry or cavalry. [8] When Meade testified before the Joint Committee on the Conduct of the War the following spring, he knew that he was open to criticism for his army's inability to prevent Lee's army from returning to Virginia after Gettysburg. Meade told the committee:

> As soon as the assault was repulsed, I went immediately to the extreme left of my line, with the determination of advancing the left and making an assault upon the enemy's lines. So soon as I arrived at the left I gave the necessary orders for the pickets and skirmishers in front to be thrown forward to feel the enemy, and for all preparations to be made for the assault. The great length of the line, and the time required to carry these orders out to the front, and the movement subsequently made, before the report given to me of the condition of the forces in the front and left, caused it to be so late in the evening as to induce me to abandon the assault which I had contemplated. [9]

General Hancock, who had urged the V and VI Corps to be "pressed up" while himself wounded on the field, later testified: [10]

> I think it was probably an unfortunate thing that I was wounded at the time I was, and equally unfortunate that General Gibbon was also wounded, because the absence of a prominent commander, who knew the circumstances thoroughly, at such a moment as that, was a great disadvantage. I think that our lines should have advanced immediately, and I believe we should have won a great victory. I was very confident that the advance would be made. General Meade told me before the fight that if the enemy attacked me he intended to put the 5th and 6th corps on the enemy's flank; I therefore, when I was wounded, and lying down in my ambulance and about leaving the field, dictated a note to General Meade, and told him if he would put in the 5th and 6th corps I believed he would win a great victory. I asked him afterwards, when I returned to the army, what he had done in the premises. He said he had ordered the movement, but the troops were slow in collecting, and moved so slowly that nothing was done before night, except that some of the Pennsylvania reserves went out and met Hood's Division. [11]

Meade's alternatives for converting to the offense were surprisingly limited on the afternoon of July 3. His best infantry options were Sykes's V and Sedgwick's VI Corps on the Federal left. However, both corps would need time to mobilize and since neither command was ordered to prepare to counterattack during Pickett's assault itself, time was of an even greater essence this late in the day. An assault by the V Corps would have been expected to form around the rocky Round Tops and march through the Plum Run valley to a still-occupied Houck's Ridge. Although the VI Corps was relatively combat-fresh and had nearly 24 hours to recover from its forced march of July 2, it was generally dispersed (several brigades having received orders to move toward the focal point of Longstreet's attack)

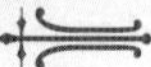

and was not in position to attack as a full corps.

Fifth Corps commander George Sykes reported no receipt of any attack orders. [12] But Brig. General Samuel Crawford, commanding the Third Division, reported: "At 5 o'clock on the 3d, I received orders from General Sykes…to advance that portion of my command which was holding the ground retaken on the left…to enter the woods, and, if possible, drive out the enemy. It was supposed that the enemy had evacuated the position." Crawford's First Brigade under Col. William McCandless advanced with skirmishers and additional support from Brig. General Joseph Bartlett's VI Corps brigade. They took some artillery fire but chased the Confederates through the Wheatfield, "completely routing" the 15th Georgia, and captured numerous prisoners. [13]

Both Crawford and McCandless's reports were generally non-specific on what stopped this pursuit, but Crawford wrote that the enemy "very greatly outnumbered us" and that the Southerners "intrenched themselves" on a second ridge. [14] However, in his testimony before the Joint Committee on the Conduct of the War, Crawford added that Meade had specifically instructed him to "clear the woods in my front; that if I found too strong a force I was not to engage them." Upon questioning from the committee as to whether there was anything to prevent "the unemployed men of the 5th and 6th corps being thrown right on the retreating enemy," Crawford answered, "Nothing at all, that I know of." [15]

General Meade did have cavalry of Brig. General Judson Kilpatrick's division working opposite the Confederate right flank and they should have been expected to support any infantry assault. In fact, some argue that this was the catalyst of the ill-fated charge led by Brig. General Elon Farnsworth's brigade.

Major General Alfred Pleasonton, commander of Meade's Cavalry Corps, has been generally remembered by history as a manipulative schemer and no friend of Meade. Pleasonton alleged in his Congressional testimony, "Immediately after that repulse, I rode out with General Meade on the field, and up to the top of the mountain, and I urged him to order a general advance of his whole army in pursuit of the enemy." After elaborating on numerous reasons why the Yankees should "have easily defeated and routed the enemy," the cavalier explained that Meade instead "ordered me to send my cavalry to the rear of the rebels, to find out whether they were really falling back." In *Annals of the War*, Pleasonton added that he even goaded his commanding officer, "General, I will give you half an hour to show yourself a great general," but to no avail. [16]

General Kilpatrick characterized his actions against the Confederate right as an "attack" based on orders that had been standing all day. He wrote, "At 8 a.m., received orders from headquarters Cavalry Corps to move to the left of our line and attack the enemy's right and rear with my whole command and the Regular Brigade." Although Brig. General George Custer's Michigan brigade was detached without Kilpatrick's approval, Farnsworth and Wesley Merritt's two brigades were still available and "at 5.30 p.m. I [Kilpatrick] ordered an attack with both brigades." [17] Kilpatrick added:

> Previous to this attack, the enemy had made a most fierce and determined attack on the left of our main line of battle, with the view to turn it. We hope we assisted in preventing this. I am of the opinion that, had our infantry on my right advanced at once when relieved from the enemy's attack in their front, the enemy could not have recovered from the confusion into which Generals Farnsworth and Merritt had thrown them, but would have been rushed back, one division on another, until, instead of a defeat, a total rout would have ensued. [18]

Kilpatrick's recollections are viewed with skepticism by some historians, given the controversies that ensued regarding General Farnsworth's death, but he did correctly highlight the lack of coordination between the Federal infantry and cavalry on the Union left. While McCandless led a moderately successful but brief reconnaissance and Kilpatrick's cavalry failed to break the Confederate right, a coordinated strike that included both cavalry and a larger portion of Sykes and Sedgwick's infantry might have turned Longstreet's right flank. But as events transpired, Law's Brigade of Hood's Division showed that they still had some fight remaining and no larger Union counterattack resulted. [19]

Meade's other choices were equally or even more problematic. Although Gen. Gouverneur K. Warren curiously characterized the battle as being "days of rest for most of" Meade's enlisted men, nearly every corps was in a varying state of disorganization. [20] Given the hard feelings that were running against the XI Corps, it is difficult to envision a scenario where Union leadership would use Howard's men to spearhead an attack. Slocum's XII Corps would have required a transfer from Culp's Hill and would have left Meade's right flank vulnerable. Part of the challenge in converting from defense to offense in diminishing daylight was the fact that no arrangements were made to give a "return thrust" while Lee's great assault was in progress. [21]

Artillery chief Henry Hunt characterized the chances of Union success as a "delusion…rash in the extreme…stark madness" as "our troops on the left were locked up. As to the center, Pickett's and Pettigrew's assaulting divisions had formed no part of A.P. Hill's line, which was virtually intact." However, Hunt based his conclusion on the questionable assumption that Lee still had 140 artillery pieces armed and ready to repulse an assault—an asset that Lee was clearly lacking only an hour earlier when he was unable to adequately support his own attack. But with all of the factors that existed late on July 3, Hunt concluded, "an immediate advance from any point, in force, was simply impracticable, and before due preparations could have been made for a change to the offensive, the favorable moment-had any resulted from the repulse- would have passed away." [22]

Finally, it is important to remember that Meade's decision-making was also influenced by his erroneous belief that Lee's army was "10,000 or 15,000" numerically superior to his own. [23] Meade was not the first army commander to suffer under this misapprehension, but he probably assumed that Lee had more available fresh troops in reserve than actually existed. Lee did have forces available (those who have been criticized for not being more actively involved in Pickett's Charge for example) to slow an enemy counterattack, but whether or not they would have repulsed a "Pickett's Charge in reverse" is simply unknowable. It did not occur because the Union generals exhibited more caution than aggression and the day ended. To quote General Warren:

> [T]here was a tone amongst most of the prominent officers that we had quite saved the country for the time, and that we had done enough; that we might jeopardy all that we had won by trying to do too much. [24]

Although viewed as a contemporary disappointment by some for seemingly failing to destroy Lee's army, Meade had in fact won a great victory. "It was a grand battle," Meade wrote his wife on July 5, "and is in my judgment a most decided victory, though I did not annihilate or bag the Confederate Army." [25]

PILES OF DEAD AND THOUSANDS OF WOUNDED

The western slope of Cemetery Ridge was strewn with the refuse of Lee's failed assault.

"Many of the retreating column lay down behind stones and hillocks," recorded the historian of the 14th Connecticut, "and even the dead bodies of their comrades, to be protected from the Union shots. Presently, as by one common impulse, bits of white cloth and handkerchiefs were waved as signals of surrender." Yankees then leapt over the wall to which "rebel wounded and unwounded in large numbers rose up and surrendered themselves." [1]

General Webb claimed that his brigade alone "captured nearly 1,000 prisoners." [2] "Of the prisoners which fell into our hands," reported General Hays, "I regret that no accurate account could be kept but by estimate, which cannot be less than 1,500."[3] Confusion reigned over who deserved credit for Confederate flag captures. "Several colors were stolen or taken with violence by officers of high rank from brave soldiers who had rushed forward and honestly captured them from the enemy," complained Col. Norman Hall, "and were probably turned in as taken by commands which were not within 100 yards of the point of attack. Death is too light a punishment for such a dastardly offense."[4] Frank Haskell wrote:

> Just as the fight was over, and the first outburst of victory had a little subsided, when all in front of the crest was noise and confusion,- prisoners being collected, small parties in pursuit of them far down into the fields, flags waving, officers giving quick, sharp commands to their men. [5]

So many Southern prisoners were being herded over the crest that several victorious Union officers mistakenly thought that the enemy had carried Cemetery Ridge. General Hancock's Chief of Staff, Lt. Colonel Morgan, actually began to order a nearby battery to limber up in retreat before he realized his mistake. Haskell observed that similar errors were made by others. [6]

Getting accurate news and casualty reports was difficult in the immediate aftermath. It was widely circulated in Northern newspapers that General Longstreet was killed or wounded and in captivity, having been mistakenly confused in some instances with the mortally wounded Armistead. "Rebel prisoners report Longstreet a prisoner. General Gibbon announced to his troops that they had captured Longstreet and a member of Kilpatrick's staff says he saw Longstreet a prisoner mortally wounded, lying in a barn…The citizens of Gettysburg affirm that Lee is certainly wounded." [7]

Dead and wounded were everywhere, a situation of horrific sights and offensive smells. Referring to the area inside the Angle, General Webb wrote to his wife, "I killed 42 Rebels inside of the fence." [8] Colonel Hall observed, "Piles of dead and thousands of wounded upon both sides attested the desperation of assailants and defenders." [9] Eventually 522 dead Confederates would be buried in a mass grave in the field between the Angle and the Emmitsburg Road. [10]

An observer attached to General Hays noted: "The field was strewn with Rebel wounded." Hospitals were overflowing on July 3. The following day, musicians were detailed with litters to bring in the wounded but "were fired upon so briskly by the Rebel sharpshooters that it was impossible to help them." The man had previously heard and disbelieved such stories "but this came under my

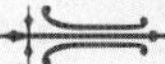

own observation. So all day Saturday the poor fellows lay there, praying for death." General Hays himself wrote that on the following morning, "I could scarcely find passage for my horse" amongst the numerous dead and wounded. Displaying an unexpected softer side, General Hays said the "shrieks" were "heart rending." [11]

"After the fight I went over the battlefield," wrote William Burns of the 71st Pennsylvania. "It was very thick with dead and wounded rebs. Bought in the wounded and lay at the fence all night. Rained during the night." Burns recorded the following diary entry for July 4:

> July 4- at stone wall all day. Rained in the morning. All quiet with us. Burying the dead. Shocking sights. This night each man slept with 3 loaded muskets at his side. A wet miserable day and night for us but a blessed day for our country. Rained all night. [12]

Several farms along the Taneytown Road were converted into field hospitals to treat the wounded of Hancock's II Corps, including the large Sarah Patterson farm. [13] The hospitals were subsequently moved farther behind the lines to farms that had open space and easier access to water. The II Corps hospital marker (completed in 1914) is located on what is now known as "Hospital Road" between the Taneytown Road and Baltimore Pike. (Not far from General Armistead's death site at the George Spangler farm.) [14] The II Corps tablet states:

> The Division Field Hospitals of the Second Corps were located at the Granite Schoolhouse but were soon removed to near Rock Creek West of the creek and six hundred yards southeast of the Bushman House. They remained there until closed August 7, 1863. These Hospitals cared for 2,200 Union and 952 Confederate wounded.

Total battle losses in Hays and Gibbon's Army of the Potomac divisions have been estimated at a combined 2,938 from all causes. [15] In Webb's brigade, Capt. William Davis (69th Pennsylvania) and Col. Richard Penn Smith (71st Pennsylvania) both estimated between 80-85% of their casualties as occurring on July 3, while Col. Norman Hall estimated 60% of his brigade's dead and injured from the third day's actions. It seems likely that at least 1,160 of Gibbon's 1,647 losses happened on July 3. [16]

Assuming that at least 60% of Hays's 1,291 losses occurred on July 3, then Hays and Gibbon combined to suffer about 1,930 of their casualties defending Cemetery Ridge from Pickett, Pettigrew and Trimble. [17]

"Our [Confederate] dead and wounded lay between the lines," wrote Pickett's staff officer Walter Harrison, "and the enemy's sharpshooters fired upon our litter-bearers whenever an attempt was made to bring off the wounded. Many were brought in after dark, but we were still in ignorance of the actual fate and condition of the great majority of our officers and men until many days after." On the morning of July 4, "we could not report an aggregate of 1,000 muskets; and this after returning to the ranks and arming all of the cooks and ambulance men…The exact number of killed, wounded, and missing, as subsequently ascertained, however, amounted to 3,393, just about three-fourths of the force carried into action." Lieutenant Hilary Harris told his father on July 7, "Our division was annihilated" and only mustered about 1,000 men as they guarded Northern prisoners on the retreat. Harris wrote that his 11th Virginia "carried in about 300 men and lost upwards of 250." [18]

Initial returns for the Army of Northern Virginia estimated that Pickett's Division alone suffered approximately 2,863 casualties with 224 killed, 1,140 wounded, and 1,499 captured/missing.[19] In his most detailed study of Pickett's casualties, researcher John Busey proposed 2,655 total losses, including 498 killed. [20]

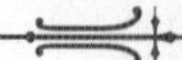

Busey's revised upward strength estimates of 6,250 (including artillerymen) caused him to arrive at a 42.5% casualty rate. (45.4% for Pickett's infantry only.) Of those categorized as wounded, 233 were mortal and subsequently died, resulting in 731 combat deaths. Finally, another 197 died in captivity, bringing the total estimated deaths in Pickett's Division to 928. [21]

There were also unreported casualties to contend with. Major Joseph Cabell, 38th Virginia, noted in his report that the "regiment lost in killed, wounded, and missing 230, besides about fifty slightly wounded, who are not reported, some of whom have returned to duty and others will do so in a few days." [22] If each regiment failed to acknowledge an additional 20% of its casualties then Pickett's total losses would easily have exceeded 50%.

Pickett's Division Estimated Casualties

	Total K	Total W	Total MC	Total Casualties
Kemper	114	223	341	678
Armistead	196	199	662	1,057
Garnett	181	213	511	905
Pickett's Infantry	491	635	1,514	2,640
Dearing's Artillery	7	8	-	15
Pickett's Division Total	**498**	**643**	**1,514**	**2,655**

Casualty rates are harder to ascertain in the other commands due to their earlier battle combat. Estimates of Heth's Division (Pettigrew) casualties were approximately 53% for the entire battle. If we assume that Pettigrew took about 5,000 men into action on July 3 and suffered at least 40% casualties (comparable to Pickett), then Pettigrew lost 2,000 men or more to death, injuries, and capture. (The previously unengaged 11th Mississippi's casualty rate has been estimated at 52.7%.) [23]

Under General Trimble, Lane's Brigade had seen minimal prior action and estimated 45.7% battle casualties. If we assume Lane and Lowrance combined to bring 2,300 men into action and suffered 45% casualties, then they lost 1,035 men. Wilcox and Lang's 1,600 men would have created 720 more casualties at the same rate. In total, it seems probable that Confederate losses attributed to this assault were at least 6,400 men. Whatever the actual numbers on both sides, they were clearly lopsided against the attackers.

Many of Pickett's wounded were treated at the division's field hospitals at Francis Bream's Mill and the John Currens farm. Sergeant D. E. Johnston of the 7th Virginia was treated at Bream's Mill and remembered "the shed in which I was placed was filled with the wounded and dying…all night long I heard nothing but the cries of the wounded and the groans of the dying." [24]

The field hospitals for Heth (Pettigrew) and Pender's (Trimble's) Divisions were scattered along the Chambersburg Pike west of Gettysburg and near the fields where they had fought on July 1. The Samuel Lohr farm was a large hospital for Heth's wounded while General Trimble and other of his casualties may have been treated at the nearby David Whisler farm. [25] Many of the injured from R. H. Anderson's Division, including Wilcox's Brigade and probably Lang's, were sent to hospitals such as the Adam Butt farm along the Fairfield Road. [26]

Generals Kemper and Trimble were among those deemed too injured to travel and did not return to Virginia with Lee's army. After spending the majority of their treatment time in the Lutheran

Seminary hospital, they were removed by train in August. The local *Adams Sentinel* reported on their departure: "We understand that General Kemper was very indignant at his removal from the comfortable quarters he had at the Seminary, where he had been so well attended to by female sympathizers, and growled at everything and everybody on his way to Baltimore." [27]

Amongst those in Pickett's Division who eventually succumbed to their wounds, 126 died in Federal field hospitals, and 50 more in Southern hospitals (including 31 who passed away near Bream's Mill.) Camp Letterman General Hospital, which was established east of town, became the final resting place of 31 men. Prisoner camps at Fort Delaware, Delaware (96), and Point Lookout, Maryland (95) claimed 191 more. Seventy of those at Fort Delaware are interred today in the National Cemetery at Finn's Point, New Jersey. Finn's Point was designated a National Cemetery in 1875 at the request of then-Virginia Governor James Kemper, who criticized the condition of the Confederate graves at Fort Delaware. The most ironic burial of all of Pickett's men may be Pvt. Howson Hall of the 3rd Virginia. He survived captivity but died in November 1864 aboard a ship en route to Georgia for exchange. Private Hall was buried at sea. [28]

In the early 1870s, the Confederate graves in and around the Gettysburg battlefield underwent a mass exhumation. The majority of the bodies were sent to Richmond. About 2,000 of Gettysburg's Confederate dead, many assumed to be from Pickett's Division, were buried amidst great ceremony as martyrs of the lost South at Richmond's Hollywood Cemetery in an area that has become known as "Gettysburg Hill." [29]

MY COUNTRY CALLED, I CAME TO DIE

Among those treated in the Union's II Corps field hospitals was Capt. John Blinn, the assistant adjutant general to brigade commander Gen. William Harrow. The young Captain Blinn, born in 1841, was an Indiana native who had once served in a cadet group unit led by future *Ben Hur* author Lew Wallace. Blinn had been wounded at Antietam and was mortally wounded on July 3 at Gettysburg while leading reinforcements into action near the Copse of Trees. He was taken to the Jacob Schwartz farm for medical treatment. [1]

Captain Azor Nickerson of the 8th Ohio was a friend of Blinn's and was recovering from his own wounds at a separate field hospital. (Like his friend Blinn, Nickerson had also been wounded at Antietam.) Nickerson learned of Blinn's status from a reverend and arranged for the two men to drink a glass of wine at the same time every morning as a sort of long distance toast. [2]

Blinn wrote his family on July 4, "Your soldier boy is wounded. But we whipped the enemy & the old flag is again victorious, glorious. My wound is a very serious one & I fear amputation may be necessary. I may die but – Mother! God give you strength & grace to bear the affliction. My country called, I came to die upon her altar. God bless you & keep you." [3]

An unpublished image of John Blinn.
Image courtesy of The National Civil War Museum, Harrisburg, PA.

Although Blinn knew that his condition might be fatal, he told the reverend that he was anxious to live until his mother, Dorthea, could arrive at Gettysburg. She left Indiana at 1:00 a.m. on July 9 and reached Gettysburg at 8:00 p.m. on July 10. She spent that evening searching in vain for her son but could not locate him until July 11. John Blinn eventually succumbed to his wounds on July 14, and his grieving mother took him home to Indiana where he is buried today. [4]

Captain Nickerson was visited one morning by the reverend with the sad news that it was no longer possible to drink his daily toast with Blinn. Nickerson survived and returned to Gettysburg later that year to witness Abraham Lincoln's Gettysburg Address. Nickerson was impressed by the President's speech, calling it "the whole matter in a nutshell." [5] After the war, he remained in the Army and went out west. His service included participation in the 1876 battle of the Rosebud as a staff officer to General George Crook.

As a postscript, Nickerson's long military career ended in disgrace. In 1880, Nickerson's wife and eight-year-old daughter went to Europe. He was placed on the Army's retired list in 1882 due to incapacity from wounds received at Antietam and Gettysburg. He had also fallen in love with his wife's dressmaker and sued his wife for divorce on the grounds of desertion. It was determined, however, that Nickerson committed fraud and perjury in his divorce filing. Although he was retired, the Army still intended to pursue a court-martial as conduct unbecoming an officer. Nickerson fled to Canada despite an order forbidding him to leave Washington. He eventually returned and was able to cut a deal with the Army allowing him to resign his commission. [6]

CONCLUSION: More Criticized and is Still Less Understood

On more than one occasion that afternoon, Robert E. Lee famously accepted the blame for the third day's failures himself. Colonel Alexander supposed that Lee came forward to rally the troops in the event of a Federal pursuit and watched Lee speak to "nearly every man who passed…'Don't be discouraged. It was my fault this time. Form your ranks again when you get under cover. All good men must hold together now.'" [1]

British military observer Arthur Fremantle thought Lee "did not show signs of the slightest disappointment, care, or annoyance" and encouraged his soldiers with words such as, "All this will come right in the end: we'll talk it over afterwards; but, in the meantime, all good men must rally. We want all good and true men just now." Lee also requested the walking wounded to "bind up their hurts and take up a musket." Lee explained to Fremantle, "This has been a sad day for us, Colonel- a sad day; but we can't expect to always gain victories." When General Wilcox reported in near tears, Lee assured him, "Never mind, General, all this has been my fault - it is I that have lost this fight, and you must help me out of it in the best way you can." [2]

According to Capt. Robert Bright, Lee advised Pickett to form "in rear of this hill

and be ready to repel the advance of the enemy should they follow up their advantage." General Pickett lowered his head: "General Lee, I have no division now. Armistead is down, Garnett is down, and Kemper is mortally wounded." General Lee replied, "Come, General Pickett, this has been my fight, and upon my shoulders rests the blame." [3]

Charles Loehr, 1st Virginia, recalled the sad return of Pickett's shattered division to Seminary Ridge:

> In straggling groups the survivors of that charge gathered in rear of Seminary Ridge, near the point from which they set out to do or die. It was a sad sight. Most of them were bleeding; numbers of them were bathing their wounds in a little creek which ran along the valley, making its clear water run red, which others used to quench their burning thirst. Some 300 or 400 men were there. General George E. Pickett was mounted, and was talking to the men here and there. Only two of the regiments had retained their colors, one of which was the 24th Virginia, and the color bearer, a tall mountaineer, named Charles Belcher, was waving it, crying: "General, let us go at them again!" Just about then General James L. Kemper was carried into the crowd, and the latter came to a halt. Then General Lee was seen to ride up, and we, as was usual, wanted to know what he had to say, crowded around him.
>
> General Pickett broke out into tears, while General Lee rode up to him, and they shook hands. General Lee spoke to General Pickett in a slow and distinct manner. Anyone could see that he, too, felt the repulse and slaughter of the division, whose remains he viewed.
>
> Of the remarks made to General Pickett by General Lee, we distinctly heard him say: "General Pickett, your men have done all that men could do; the fault is entirely my own." These words will never be forgotten.
>
> Just then, he turned to General Kemper and remarked: "General Kemper, I hope you are not seriously hurt, can I do anything for you?" General Kemper looked up and replied: "General Lee, you can do nothing for me; I am mortally wounded, but see to it that full justice is done my men who made this charge." General Lee said: "I will," and rode off.
>
> General Pickett turned to us, saying: "You can go back to the wagons and rest until you are wanted." The men then left for their wagon trains.
>
> There was little or no organization among them. Night was coming on and the writer and several of his company slept in a mill, about half way to the wagon train, getting back with those of the survivors of the Old First on the morning of the 4th. The whole command numbered hardly thirty men, rank and file. [4]

Lee's campaign reports left some indication of his immediate impressions. Lee wrote simply to President Jefferson Davis on July 4:

> The works on the enemy's extreme right and left were taken, but his numbers were so great and his position so commanding, that our troops were compelled to relinquish

> their advantage and retire. It is believed that the enemy suffered severely in these operations, but our own loss has not been light…Generals Garnett and Armistead are missing, and it is feared that the former is killed and the latter wounded and a prisoner. Generals Pender and Trimble are wounded in the leg…General Kemper, it is feared, is mortally wounded. Our losses embrace many other valuable officers and men. [5]

In Lee's July 31 "outline of the recent operations of this army," the third day's battle:

> [R]aged with great violence until sunset. Our troops succeeded in entering the advanced works of the enemy, and getting possession of some of his batteries, but *our artillery having nearly expended its ammunition* [emphasis added], the attacking columns became exposed to the heavy fire of the numerous batteries near the summit of the ridge, and, after a most determined and gallant struggle, were compelled to relinquish their advantage, and fall back to their original positions with severe loss. [6]

Lee's most detailed explanation came in his January 1864 report. In this document, Lee stated that the "main attack" had been "directed against the enemy's left center."

> His [the enemy] batteries reopened as soon as they appeared. *Our own having nearly exhausted their ammunition in the protracted cannonade that preceded the advance of the infantry, were unable to reply, or render the necessary support to the attacking party. Owing to this fact, which was unknown to me when the assault took place, the enemy was enabled to throw a strong force of infantry against our left* [emphasis added], already wavering under a concentrated fire of artillery from the ridge in front, and from Cemetery Hill, on the left. It finally gave way, and the right, after penetrating the enemy's lines, entering his advance works, and capturing some of his artillery, was attacked simultaneously in front and on both flanks, and driven back with heavy loss. [7]

Therefore, in both his July 31 and January 1864 reports, Lee implied that the attack failed because of his artillery's inability to properly support the infantry.

Although Lee never published memoirs and was reticent to publicly speak after the war, he did occasionally reveal his thoughts on Gettysburg. Responding to an inquiry in 1868, Lee wrote:

> As to the battle of Gettysburg, I must again refer you to the official accounts. Its loss was occasioned by a combination of circumstances. It was commenced in the absence of correct intelligence. It was continued in the effort to overcome the difficulties by which we were surrounded, and it would have been gained could one determined and united blow have been delivered by our whole line. As it was, victory trembled in the balance for three days, and the battle resulted in the infliction of as great an amount of injury as was received and in frustrating the Federal campaign for the season. [8]

William Allan claimed that during an 1870 conversation Lee "spoke feelingly of Gettysburg, said much was said about risky movements- Everything was risky in our

war." Lee considered himself to have been successful in drawing Federal attention away from Richmond but failed at Gettysburg due to several causes. "Stuart failed to give him information, and this deceived him into a general battle. Then he never [could] get a simultaneous attack on the enemy's position. Often thinks that if Jackson had been there he would have succeeded." [9] Allan later elaborated within the pages of the *Southern Historical Society Papers*:

> There was nothing "foolish" in Pickett's attack had it been executed as designed. Pickett carried the works before him. Had Pettigrew and Wilcox moved with him, and Hill and Ewell vigorously seconded this onset, General Lee never doubted that the Federal army would have been ruined. It was this great prize, which he believed within his grasp, that induced him to fight the battle as he did, and not to adopt the more cautious plan of merely maneuvering Meade away from his position by threatening his communications. General Lee did not consider the Federal position at Gettysburg stronger than many others that army had occupied; and the testimony of Butterfield and others shows that General Meade did not rate it highly. The notion of its great strength has grown up since the battle. [10]

Many of the subordinates who served in Lee's army did not share his reticence to re-fight Gettysburg and Pickett's Charge. Lack of support and coordination remained a common theme, but the warriors were not always in agreement regarding who was accountable for the failures.

Brigadier General John Imboden recalled (in an 1871 article) that on the night of July 3, Lee animatedly told him "in a voice tremulous with emotion": "I never saw troops behave more magnificently than Pickett's Division of Virginians did today in that grand charge upon the enemy. And if they had been supported as they were to have been- but, for some reason not yet fully explained to me, were not- we would have held the position and the day would have been ours." After a brief pause, Lee added "in a tone almost of agony: 'Too bad! Too bad! Oh, too bad!'" [11]

General Ambrose Wright, in a July 1863 letter to his wife, could not "understand why Ewell's corps and all of A.P. Hill's were not engaged in this day's fighting. I am satisfied that if they had been, our victory would have been complete." [12]

Although Pickett's original battle report was rebuffed by Lee due to allegations of inadequate support, Pickett's superior officer made similar allegations of his own. General Longstreet's July 1863 submission blamed those on Pickett's left for their repulse:

> The enemy's batteries soon opened upon our lines with canister, and the left seemed to stagger under it, but the advance was resumed, and with some degree of steadiness. Pickett's troops did not appear to be checked by the batteries, and only halted to deliver a fire when close under musket-range. Major-General Anderson's Division was ordered forward to support and assist the wavering columns of Pettigrew and Trimble. Pickett's troops, after delivering fire, advanced to the charge, and entered the enemy's lines, capturing some of his batteries, and gained his works. About the

> same moment, the troops that had before hesitated, broke their ranks and fell back in great disorder, many more falling under the enemy's fire in retiring than while they were attacking. This gave the enemy time to throw his entire force upon Pickett, with a strong prospect of being able to break up his lines or destroy him before Anderson's Division could reach him, which would, in its turn, have greatly exposed Anderson. [13]

In later years, with Longstreet's own performance under fire from his ex-colleagues due to a combination of postwar politics and his willingness to publicly question Lee's decisions, Longstreet softened his view of Pettigrew and Trimble's actions.

> It is conceded by almost, if not quite, all authority on the subject, that Pickett's charge, on the 3d, was almost hopeless. We had tested the enemy's position thoroughly on the day before, and with a much larger force than was given to Pickett. We had every reason to believe that the position was much stronger on the 3d than it was on the 2d. The troops that had fought with me the day before were in no condition to support Pickett, and, beside, they were confronted by a force that required their utmost attention. The men of Generals Pickett, Pettigrew, and Trimble, however, received and executed their orders with cool and desperate courage…The charge was disastrous, and had the Federal army been thrown right upon the heels of Pickett's retreating column, the results might have been much more serious. [14]

While it is beyond our scope to re-examine the postwar controversies that surrounded General Longstreet and the so-called "Lost Cause," suffice to say that Longstreet eventually became the day's primary villain to many Southerners who could not accept Lee's own failings. Lee's military secretary, Armistead Long, insisted, "The attack of Pickett's Division on the 3d has been more criticized, and is still less understood, than any other act of the Gettysburg drama. General Longstreet did not enter into the spirit of it, and consequently did not support it with his wonted vigor. It has been characterized as rash and objectless, on the order of the 'charge of the Light Brigade.' Nevertheless, it was not ordered without mature consideration and on grounds that presented fair prospects of success." [15]

Longstreet's most vocal postwar Lost Cause critic was Confederate General Jubal Early, who coordinated a lengthy public and private assault against the former First Corps commander. Early's infamous January 1872 address at Washington and Lee University called the July 3 attack a "miscarriage, in not properly supporting it according to the plan and orders of the commanding General. You must recollect that a commanding General cannot do the actual marching and fighting of his army. These must, necessarily be entrusted to his subordinates, and any hesitation, delay or miscarriage in the execution of his orders, may defeat the best devised schemes…A subordinate who undertakes to doubt the wisdom of his superior's plans, and enters upon their execution with reluctance and distrust, will not be likely to ensure success." [16]

While Early was vague on how specifically Longstreet had failed to execute Lee's directives, printed criticisms of Lee that were correctly attributed to Longstreet in William Swinton's *Campaigns of the Army of the Potomac* convinced Early that Longstreet "did not enter upon the execution of his plans with that confidence and faith necessary to success,

and hence, perhaps, it was that it was not achieved." [17]

Several officers persisted in the belief that Southern victory might have been attained if the Confederates had only been able to coordinate simultaneous attacks along Meade's entire line. In 1877, General Wilcox attributed defeat to "Longstreet's late attack" on July 3 (and July 2) and "Want of concert the last day. We might have, even on this day, by making a united and well directed and prompt effort, won the field." [18]

Colonel Alexander likewise acknowledged lack of coordination as a contributing factor on July 3, but did not consider it the fault of Longstreet's lack of faith.

> I attribute it partially to the fact that our staff organizations were never sufficiently extensive and perfect to enable the Commanding General to be practically present everywhere and to thoroughly handle a large force on an extended field, but principally it was due to the exceedingly difficult shape in which our line was formed, the enemy occupying a center and we a semi circumference, with poor and exposed communications along it. I believe it was simply impossible to have made different attacks from the flanks and center of the line we occupied and over the different distances which would have to be traversed and which should be so simultaneous that the squeeze would fall on the enemy at all points at the same time. [19]

Despite the practicalities of arguments such as Alexander's, many still insisted that there had been a fatal failure of obedience to Lee's grand plans. Rawley Martin of the 53rd Virginia survived the war and added in 1904, "Somebody blundered at Gettysburg but not Lee. He was too great a master of the art of war to have hurled a handful of men against an army. It has been abundantly shown that the fault lay not with him, but with others, who failed to execute his orders." [20]

If the actual participants could not agree on the causes of the outcome, then what hope do historians have?

Esteemed Southern historian Douglas Southall Freeman considered three aspects of the attack. First, Freeman asked, as have many others, "whether an attempt should have been made to break the center of the Federal position?" Freeman reminded his readers that "Lee felt at the time that the assault was in a measure unavoidable and that, if the full strength of the Army could be brought to bear, the attack would be successful." Since Lee ordered the attack under the belief that it could succeed and Freeman knew that "the responsibility was that of the commanding General," Lee likewise understood this fact when he exclaimed, "It's all my fault." [21] Clearly, however, in both planning and execution, Lee's generals failed to bring the army's "full strength" to bear on that afternoon.

Freeman's second consideration was the failure of Confederate artillery. This criticism was justified since "the reorganization of the artillery gave flexibility within a Corps, but among the Corps there was little cooperation. Pendleton had neither the prestige nor the authority to assure the employment of all the guns as one weapon under one leader. He appears in the campaign more as a consultant than as a commander." [22] Tactically,

Alexander's argument that the Southerners failed to enfilade Cemetery Hill was sound, although the terrain and positioning worked against Lee's long arm. There simply were not adequate positions north of town to hit Cemetery Hill in sufficient strength, and even if there were, three individual corps artillery commanders would have had to coordinate and communicate those efforts along an extended exterior front. Lee certainly felt that the capture of the Peach Orchard south of Gettysburg would provide sufficient ability to enfilade the Federal line, and in this the results show that Lee clearly overestimated that position's value.

The Confederate leadership's allowance of their ammunition to be depleted such that they were unable to support the advance speaks poorly for nearly all of the officers involved. It also tragically recalls a situation faced by many organizations throughout history while on the road to committing fatal mistakes. Once the wheels were in motion, no one wanted to be the individual accountable for calling it off. So the infantrymen marched forward with leaders like Longstreet and Alexander aware that there would be inadequate support while Lee claimed to be ignorant of the fact.

Regarding the infantry, Freeman argued that "tactically, in at least three respects, it was not well employed." The selection of Heth's Division (Pettigrew) was a failure of the headquarters staff and they should have been swapped with Pender's entire division while Pickett was deploying. [23] As to the faulty deployment of Trimble's brigades under Lane and Lowrance, many (including Freeman) argued that they were supposed to be en echelon, but in any event proved thoroughly incapable of protecting Pettigrew's left. (We will also add that they likewise failed to give any added weight to Pettigrew's right.) Freeman held Longstreet accountable along with both Trimble and Lane for failing to bring this to anyone's attention. Not only did Freeman also question the selection of the now often-criticized Brockenbrough as being a poor choice for the attack's left flank, but Freeman also suggested that Davis's Brigade had been too heavily damaged on July 1 and likewise should not have been placed in such a key position. [24]

General Lee has been criticized by generations of historians for ordering this frontal assault across nearly one mile of open ground against weaponry that supposedly made such maneuvers obsolete. Yet Lee obviously knew what the weaponry, the enemy, and his own army were seemingly capable of accomplishing. Critics forget that Lee's army proved twice, first with Wright's Brigade on July 2 and then with Armistead on July 3, that it was possible to reach that position. But he knew after July 2 that to maintain a foothold on Cemetery Ridge and force the Yankees to run would require more artillery and infantry coordination than existed on the second day. In hindsight, Lee's army proved incapable of achieving such coordination on any of the three days at Gettysburg. The results show that the Pickett's Charge that was executed had no chance of success, but pundits will always be left to ponder what the outcome might have been with more infantry or artillery.

In addition to the now-familiar shortcomings (the misuse or non-use of brigades under Wilcox, Lang, Posey, and Mahone, Pender's Division, and artillery) the attack also lacked any maneuver or creativity which might have fooled Meade into diverting forces away from the true objective. In execution, the Confederates' general destination was painfully

obvious. First came a cannonade that clearly telegraphed a forthcoming attack. Then followed the assault across open fields with exposed flanks. There was no demonstrating by either McLaws or Hood's divisions against the Union left or by Ewell (who was reforming after his own fighting near Culp's Hill) that might have misled the Union leadership into shifting strength elsewhere. For those who think such a scenario impossible, recall that Meade had stripped nearly all of his strength off of Culp's Hill on July 2 when the entire Confederate attack seemed concentrated against the Union left. Every Federal soldier on Cemetery Ridge knew where the Confederate thrust would land and they had time to prepare for it. Again, Lee was unable to make that united and concentrated strike against the entire Federal line as he bemoaned in postwar interviews. [25]

Finally, as Pickett reportedly said, the Yankees had something to do with it. Meade's army did not fight flawlessly at Gettysburg but they were more than good enough on July 3. Henry Hunt's artillery management overcame his misunderstanding with General Hancock and although the Federal cannon were unable to prevent Longstreet's assault from reaching Cemetery Ridge, it inflicted a fair share of damage. The Army of the Potomac did bend with the brief allowance of Armistead's men into their lines, proving again as Wright's Brigade did on the prior day that the Confederate objective could be arrived at. But the Northerners did not break and run, and with the heavy concentration of troops on Cemetery Ridge, Meade and his lieutenants had ample strength to repulse the assault and hand Lee a one-sided defeat.

Lee's assaults at Gaines's Mill during the Seven Days' Battles of the previous summer succeeded in large part because he was able to concentrate superior numbers against an isolated portion of the Union army. Lee probably hoped for similar success at Gettysburg. Recall Armistead Long's assertion "that by forcing the Federal lines at that point and turning toward Cemetery Hill the [Federal] right would be taken in flank and the remainder would be neutralized." But Meade did not give Lee that opportunity on July 3 at Gettysburg. Lee attacked a position that was easily reinforced and was unable to use his inferior numbers to isolate an equal or smaller portion of Meade's Army of the Potomac.

Although few realized it at the time, the battle of Gettysburg was over at sunset on July 3, 1863. This assault can indeed be viewed as the battle's "turning point" given that it was the outcome that convinced Lee to disengage at Gettysburg. The withdrawal through the mountain passes that Lee deemed impracticable earlier that day now became very practical during the night of July 4-5, even while burdened with the increased wounded that July 3 had created.

Meade's army pursued Lee's over the next 10 days with several engagements and skirmishes, but on July 14 the Army of Northern Virginia successfully crossed back into Virginia, near Williamsport. Heth's battered division was called upon once again, this time as a rear guard. An attack by Federal cavalry bagged several hundred prisoners and mortally wounded General Pettigrew while Lee's main body escaped across the Potomac River. Shot in the abdomen, the well-regarded Pettigrew was carried to the rear and died on July 17 (less than two weeks after his 35th birthday) near Bunker Hill, West Virginia.

Although they may have momentarily seemed broken on the afternoon of July 3, Lee's army was not defeated. Nor did Meade's army feel certain of future victory. Both commanding generals would spend the fall of 1863 refitting and maneuvering in a futile attempt to bring the other army to a decisive battle as the war continued on.

ONSLAUGHT OF PEACE

Whether or not Pickett's Charge was indeed the battle's turning point, it has become a focal point of nearly every major battle anniversary as a symbol of our reunited nation.

At the 25th anniversary in July 1888, overall Southern attendance was lower than initially expected, but "the man of all others who is never permitted to spend a moment alone is a tall soldierly-looking man with white hair and flowing gray whiskers." An ailing James Longstreet returned to Gettysburg for this anniversary, and for whatever damage his postwar actions had done to his reputation in the South, he was the town's most notable celebrity during the summer of 1888. "When it was rumored that Longstreet had arrived at the Springs Hotel hundreds at once began a pilgrimage in that direction." Longstreet dined and struck up a friendship with former Union General Dan Sickles. Longstreet also attended ceremonies on McPherson's Ridge near John Reynolds's July 1 kill-site, and at one point during the festivities so many Union veterans swarmed Longstreet that the viewing platform collapsed, sending Longstreet tumbling into the arms of his former opponents. [1]

Newsmen noted that his health was clearly failing. "Longstreet does not look strong, and his 67 years bear heavily on him. His enfeebled condition attracted attention, and he was induced to sit down. He sank into his chair with a sigh." But when given the opportunity to speak, he demonstrated that 25 years had allowed him to accept the battle's outcome as fate. "There is evidence in its plan and conduct, that the hand of God was with the cause of the Federal and against that of the Confederate army. The time and places are instances." [2]

Longstreet toured the battlefield with several former enemies such as Sickles, Dan Butterfield, and Henry Slocum. While visiting the area surrounding the Angle and Copse of Trees, Longstreet "gazed long and intently at the gloomy woods of Seminary Ridge from which Pickett and his thousands had dashed to make the memorable charge." He was gratified to learn that efforts were then underway to mark the location of Armistead's fall, and agreed with Butterfield that Meade's inability to successfully counterattack was "a fatal error." As to the miscarriage of Pickett's Charge, "Both God and reason were against it. The latter I then saw. The former I now devoutly and greatly recognize." [3]

The next major milestone came in July 1913. The battle's 50th anniversary was the largest of all Blue and Gray veteran reunions. Attendance figures are debated, but an estimated 53,000 Union and 11,000 Confederates journeyed to Gettysburg. The government created a massive encampment to house them, appropriately dubbed the "Great Camp," on ground west of the Codori farm and between Long Lane and the Bliss farm. [4]

Numerous dignitaries attended, ranging from last surviving corps commander Dan Sickles to President Woodrow Wilson. Deceased generals such as Longstreet, Pickett, Meade, and A. P. Hill were all represented by their widows and descendants. Longstreet's son, Maj. Robert Lee Longstreet, had

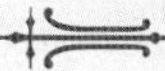

never been to Gettysburg before but "I would be derelict in memory to my father, however, did I not attend." Attesting to the "complete reconciliation" theme of the "contending forces," LaSalle Pickett was invited to participate in a ceremony honoring Gouverneur K. Warren on Little Round Top. [5]

A fight in the dining room of the Gettysburg Hotel showed that not everyone was in a fraternal mood when seven men were stabbed following "slighting remarks about Lincoln." [6] But dining hall stabbings were the rare exception. A veteran from Garnett's 28th Virginia was lost and unable to find his tent in the massive encampment. He identified his old regiment to a Union veteran and the elderly Yankee asked, "Do you know what became of your regimental flag?" The old Rebel replied, "I think some of you Yankees got it." The Northerner turned out to be a former captain in Company F of the 1st Minnesota. "We captured your flag, and we've got it now in St. Paul." The Virginian was then invited to bunk down with his former opponents for the night and observed the following morning, "I'm sorry we lost that flag, but if we had to lose it, I'm glad it was you fellows who got it." [7] The flag has since remained as a prized artifact of the Minnesota Historical Society.

Confederate and Union veterans shake hands during the 50th Anniversary commemoration. Image courtesy of Library of Congress

With Pickett's Charge now firmly established as a defining moment in the battle, it was no surprise that reenacting the charge was one of the anniversary's cornerstones. Shortly after 3:00 p.m., roughly 120 members of Pickett's Division Association marched across the field. "Its progress was slow and painful," wrote an observing newsman. Their march upslope was "in irregular columns of fours" but they were "responsive" to the commands of old W. W. Bentley of the 24th Virginia, who served as their commander. When they reached the stone wall that was "covered now with tangled vines," about 180 men of the Philadelphia Brigade Association stood to meet this "onslaught of peace." The standard bearers from both sides exchanged colors and the old men embraced to cheers. Pennsylvania Congressman J. Hampton Moore (who had not yet been born when the actual charge occurred) made a "long speech" after which the men crowded over the wall to shake hands "and the charge was over." [8]

The dedication of the Eternal Light Peace Memorial by President Franklin D. Roosevelt rightfully overshadowed all others at the 75th anniversary in 1938 but once again elderly veterans met to shake hands at the wall. By the 1963 centennial the torch had been passed from actual battle veterans to reenactors and modern military men. The 1963 highlight prior to July 3 was a "spectacular" two-hour parade through town before an audience estimated at between 35,000-50,000 people. About 1,500 "soldiers" participated in a variety of Civil War uniforms and were joined by 5,000 members of the Pennsylvania National Guard and a fly-over of Air Force jets. [9]

When July 3 arrived, the spectacle of a Pickett's Charge reenactment once again did not disappoint. Participants from 24 states included roughly 600 would-be Confederates. A "huge crowd" estimated at between 25,000-40,000 people gathered to watch a charge that included helicopters flying

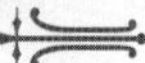

overhead, "soldiers" wearing sunglasses, and "stereophonic" sound effects. The charge itself only took about 20 minutes, and once again the Rebels failed to carry the Federals' stone wall as they instead stopped about 50 feet short to pose for photographers. The Rebels then resumed their march to the wall, handshakes were exchanged, a band played the Star-Spangled Banner, and both sides recited the Pledge of Allegiance. It was over so quickly that the thousands in the crowd "seemed at a loss as to what to do with the remainder of the afternoon." Observers thought that the event "took a good many liberties" with history but most agreed it was a "good show." [10]

It was more than a "show" for at least one spectator. In attendance was Col. Albert Fuger, an 83-year-old veteran of the Spanish American War and both World Wars. Fuger was the son of Frederick Fuger from Cushing's Battery. Journeying from their home in Maine, Fuger watched with his family and declared this as "the proudest day of my life." [11]

The 150th anniversary in July 2013 was the most observed and recorded commemoration in Gettysburg's history. The festivities ran from June 28 to July 7, and while the estimated 235,000 visitors was impressive in and of itself, this was the first milestone anniversary to be observed and recorded in the age of instant telecommunications and social media. In addition to traditional print media coverage, Gettysburg enthusiasts around the world also followed coverage via live webcasts, podcasts, cable TV, satellite radio broadcasts, and emerging social media such as Facebook and YouTube. [12]

By 2013, interpretation was expected to tell a wider story than simply the battle itself. The media relations manager for the Gettysburg Convention & Visitors Bureau observed: "For decades, people came here for military and black powder. Now they want to know about the civilians and what they endured during and after the battle." Many visitors and major media outlets also continued recent trends by focusing not on the battlefield itself, but on the large commercial reenactments that were held outside of Gettysburg National Military Park. [13]

But, as at prior anniversary commemorations, Pickett's Charge once again offered a meaningful and spectacular climax. National Park Service rangers allowed participants the opportunity to march in one of nine Confederate brigades. Although Pettigrew and Trimble's commands were remembered this time, Wilcox and Lang's were omitted under the reasoning that they were "support" and "not part of the initial assault group." [14] Where Pickett, Pettigrew, Trimble, (and Wilcox and Lang's) men had once marched and died, an estimated 15,000 men, women, and children armed with smartphones and digital cameras mixed with reenactors and rangers to make one more "assault" on Cemetery Ridge.

An estimated 20,000-25,000 people waited in the mid-day heat (afternoon temperatures were slightly lower than those recorded during the battle) on Cemetery Ridge, loosely representing Webb, Hays, and Doubleday's divisions. As has been the case at every charge since 1863, no gunshots were fired when the two sides finally met. Twelve buglers positioned along the line instead played Taps. Despite some initial trepidation from NPS officials at the prospect of successfully maneuvering such large numbers of people, the event was a success on every level. A National Park Service spokeswoman concluded, "We feel we met our goal of trying to engage visitors with the meaning of Gettysburg and why places like Gettysburg are important to save for future generations." [15]

The Gettysburg campaign has long since passed into history, but the "Pickett-Pettigrew-Trimble Charge" lives today every time someone comes to Gettysburg and looks across the fields between Seminary and Cemetery ridges, visits the High Water Mark or the Angle, remembers those who fought here, and walks the charge for themselves.

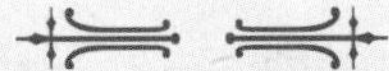

Orders of Battle

UNION INFANTRY DEFENSE [1]

I UNION ARMY CORPS
Major General John Newton

3RD DIVISION
Major General Abner Doubleday

1ST BRIGADE
Brigadier General Thomas A. Rowley

121st PA Volunteer Infantry Regiment
Colonel Chapman Biddle

80th NY Volunteer Infantry Regiment
(20th NY State Militia)
Colonel Theodore B. Gates

142nd PA Volunteer Infantry Regiment
Lieutenant Colonel Alfred B. McCalmont [2]

151st PA Volunteer Infantry Regiment
Captain Walter L. Owens

2ND BRIGADE
Colonel Edmund L. Dana

143rd PA Volunteer infantry Regiment
Lieutenant Colonel John D. Musser [3]

149th PA Volunteer Infantry Regiment
Captain James Glenn

150th PA Volunteer Infantry Regiment
Captain Cornelius C. Widdis [4]

3RD BRIGADE
Brigadier General George J. Standard [5]

13th VT Volunteer Infantry Regiment
Colonel Francis V. Randall

14th VT Volunteer Infantry Regiment
Colonel William T. Nichols

16th VT Volunteer Infantry Regiment
Colonel Wheelock G. Veazey

II UNION ARMY CORPS
Major General Winfield S. Hancock [6]

2ND DIVISION
Brigadier General John Gibbon [7]

1ST BRIGADE
Brigadier General William Harrow

19th ME Volunteer Infantry Regiment
Colonel Francis E. Heath

15th MA Volunteer Infantry Regiment
Lieutenant Colonel George C. Joslin

1st MN Volunteer Infantry Regiment
Captain Nathan S. Messick [8]

82nd NY Volunteer Infantry Regiment
Captain John Darrow

2ND BRIGADE
Brigadier General Alexander S. Webb [9]

69th PA Volunteer Infantry Regiment
Colonel Dennis O'Kane [10]

71st PA Volunteer Infantry Regiment
Colonel Richard Penn Smith

72nd PA Volunteer Infantry Regiment
Lieutenant Colonel Theodore Hesser [11]

106th PA Volunteer infantry Regiment
Lieutenant Colonel William L. Curry [12]

3RD BRIGADE
Colonel Norman J. Hall

19th MA Volunteer Infantry Regiment
Colonel Arthur F. Devereux

20th MA Volunteer Infantry Regiment
Lieutenant Colonel George Nelson Macy [13]

7th MI Volunteer Infantry Regiment
Lieutenant Colonel Amos E. Steele, Jr. [14]

42nd NY Volunteer Infantry Regiment
Colonel James E. Mallon

59th NY Volunteer Infantry Regiment
Captain William McFadden

UNATTACHED
1st MA Company of Sharpshooters (Andrew's Sharpshooters)
Captain William Plumer [15]

3RD DIVISION
Brigadier General Alexander Hays

1st Battalion, 10th NY Volunteer Infantry [16]
Major George F. Hopper

1ST BRIGADE
Colonel Samuel Spriggs Carroll

4th OH Volunteer Infantry Regiment (Companies G and I only)
Sergeant Martin Longworth [17]

8th OH Volunteer Infantry Regiment
Lieutenant Colonel Franklin Sawyer

2ND BRIGADE
Colonel Thomas A. Smyth [18]

14th CT Volunteer Infantry Regiment
Major Theodore G. Ellis

1st DE Volunteer Infantry Regiment
First Lieutenant William Smith [19]

12th NJ Volunteer Infantry Regiment
Major John T. Hill

108th NY Volunteer Infantry Regiment
Lieutenant Colonel Francis E. Pierce

3RD BRIGADE
Colonel Eliakim Sherrill [20]

39th NY Volunteer Infantry Regiment (Companies A-D)
Major Hugo Hildebrandt [21]

111th NY Volunteer Infantry Regiment
Colonel Clinton D. MacDougall [22]

125th NY Volunteer Infantry Regiment
Lieutenant Colonel Levin Crandell

126th NY Volunteer Infantry Regiment
Lieutenant Colonel James M. Bull

III UNION ARMY CORPS
Major General David Bell Birney [23]

1ST DIVISION
Brigadier General John H.H. Ward

1ST BRIGADE
Colonel Andrew H. Tippin

57th PA Volunteer Infantry Regiment
Captain Alanson H. Nelson [24]

63rd PA Volunteer Infantry Regiment
Major John A. Danks [25]

68th PA Volunteer Infantry Regiment
Captain Milton Davis [26]

105th PA Volunteer Infantry Regiment
Colonel Calvin A. Craig [27]

114th PA Volunteer Infantry Regiment
Captain Edward Bowen [28]

141st PA Volunteer Infantry Regiment
Colonel Henry J. Madill [29]

2ND BRIGADE
Colonel Hiram Berdan

20th IN Volunteer Infantry Regiment
Lieutenant William C. L. Taylor [30]

3rd ME Volunteer Infantry Regiment
Colonel Moses B. Lakeman [31]

4th ME Volunteer Infantry Regiment
Captain Edwin Libby [32]

99th PA Volunteer Infantry Regiment
Major John Moore [33]

86th NY Volunteer Infantry Regiment
Lieutenant Colonel Benjamin L. Higgins [34]

124th NY Volunteer Infantry Regiment
Captain Charles H. Weygant [35]

1st USSS
Lieutenant Colonel Caspar Trepp [36]

2nd USSS
Major Homer R. Stoughton [37]

THIRD BRIGADE
Colonel P. Regis de Trobriand

17th ME Volunteer Infantry Regiment
Lieutenant Colonel Charles B. Merrill [38]

3rd MI Volunteer Infantry Regiment
Lieutenant Colonel Edwin S. Pierce [39]

5th MI Volunteer Infantry Regiment
Lieutenant Colonel John Pulford [40]

40th NY Volunteer Infantry Regiment
Colonel Thomas W. Egan

110th PA Volunteer Infantry Regiment
Major Isaac Rogers [41]

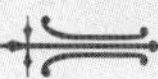

NOTES:

1. This order of battle attempts to list all Union units involved in the Union defense of Longstreet's Assault. Elements of the Third Union Army Corps brought to the center of the Union line to support the Second Corps are also listed here. Commandeers for July 3, 1863 were determined using multiple sources but most especially Edmund J. Raus, Jr. *A Generation on the March: The Union Army at Gettysburg* (Gettysburg, PA: Thomas Publications, 1996) and the *Official Records.*
2. The report of this regiment says the men of the command did "fire an occasional shot at a few sharpshooters…." The regiment occupied a second line. See the *OR,* 27/1: 326.
3. This regiment occupied a second line of battle behind the Vermont Brigade. *OR,* 27/1: 340.
4. This regiment occupied a second line of battle behind the Vermont Brigade and supported Rorty's Battery. *OR Supplement,* Part I, Reports, Vol. 5, Serial 5, 185-186.
5. Standard was wounded in leg during the attack. Ladd, *Bachelder Papers,* 3: 169.
6. Hancock was painfully wounded in the groin on July 3, 1863.
7. Gibbon was wounded in action July 3, 1863 in the left shoulder. Gibbon, *Personal Recollections of the Civil War,* 152.
8. Messick was killed in action on July 3, 1863 by a shell fragment which struck his head. *OR,* 27/1: 425; Busey, *Union Casualties at Gettysburg,* 1: 320.
9. Webb was wounded in action on July 3, 1863 by a grazing round to his thigh. Ladd, *Bachelder Papers,* 1: 19.
10. He was killed in action on July 3, 1863. *OR,* 27/1: 431.
11. Lieutenant Colonel Hesser survived the battle only to be killed in action on November 27, 1863 at Mine Run, Virginia.
12. Only companies A and B of this regiment took part in the action at Pickett's Charge. They were under the command of Captain John J. Sperry.
13. Macy was wounded in action on July 3, 1863 in the left hand. Raus, *A Generation on the March,* 39. He apparently was also wounded further up on his arm. Ladd, *Bachelder Papers,* 1: 253; Busey, *Union Casualties at Gettysburg,* 1: 209. The wound necessitated amputation of the extremity.
14. He was killed in action on July 3, 1863. *OR,* 27/1: 448. Shot in the head. Busey, *Union Casualties at Gettysburg,* 1: 259.
15. It appears that Captain Plumer commanded part of the company at Gettysburg on West Cemetery Hill while First Lieutenant Luke Emerson Bicknell led part of the company at the Bryan Farm against Pettigrew's Division. Ladd, *Bachelder Papers,* 2: 984-985; James L. Bowen, *Massachusetts in the War 1861-1865* (Springfield, MA, 1889), 864-865. According to Bicknell he took about 20 sharpshooters into action on July 3, 1863 see Edmund Rice, "Repelling Lee's Last Blow," *Battles and Leaders of the Civil War,* 3: 391-392.
16. This unit acted as the provost guard for the Third Division, Second Corps and took Confederate prisoners on July 3, 1863.
17. Eight companies of the 4th Ohio remained on East Cemetery Hill during the July 3 action. Captain Peter Grubb, commanded companies G and I of this regiment. These troops were left on West Cemetery Hill and participated in the repulse. Grubb was wounded in action on July 2. *OR,* 27/1: 460-461; Raus, A *Generation on the March,* 98; Busey, *Union Casualties at Gettysburg,* 2: 725. On July 3, Sergeant Longworth apparently commanded the two companies of skirmishers. Richard A. Baumgartner, *Buckeye Blood: Ohio at Gettysburg* (Huntington, WV, 2003), 87.
18. Colonel Smyth received a wound during the cannonade July 3, 1863. Ladd, *Bachelder Papers,* 1: 407.
19. Smith was killed in action by cannon fire on July 3, 1863. *OR,* 27/1: 469; William P. Seville, *History of the First Regiment of Delaware Volunteers* (Baltimore, MD, 1986), 82. Leadership of this regiment on July 3, 1863 is disputed. First Lieutenant John L. Brady claimed he was in command. Ladd, *Bachelder Papers,* 3: 1334.
20. Sherrill was mortally wounded on July 3, 1863. *OR,* 27/1: 473. Shot through the bowels. Ladd, *Bachelder Papers,* 2:343. He died at the George Spangler Farm, 11th Army Corps Hospital.
21. He was wounded in action July 3, 1863. Raus, *A Generation on the March,* 61; *New York at Gettysburg,* 1: 285.
22. He was wounded on July 3, 1863 by a gunshot wound to the left forearm. *Bachelder Papers,* 3: 1762.
23. The units listed here for the Third Corps for the most part were in place at the left center of the Union line on July 3, 1863 during the attack. In many cases it is unknown as to what extent they played in the defense and/or repulse of the attack.
24. This regiment moved to Cemetery Ridge at 3:00 p.m. to support a battery in Doubleday's Division. *OR,* 27/1: 497.
25. At 3:00 p.m. on July 3, 1863 this regiment moved to the left center. *OR,* 27/1: 498.
26. This regiment supported a battery on July 3, 1863 at the left center of the Union line. *OR,* 27/1: 499; Raus, *A Generation on the March,* 116.
27. *OR,* 27/1: 501.
28. This regiment arrived at the left center on the afternoon of July 3, 1863. The regiment supported Cowan's Battery. *OR,* 27/1: 114.
29. This regiment supported a battery with Webb's Brigade on July 3, 1863. *OR,* 27/1: 506.
30. The regiment was ordered to the left center at 11:00 a.m. *OR,* 27/1: 506.
31. Lakeman claims in his official report that his regiment arrived on July 3, 1863 at Webb's front after the enemy was repulsed. *OR,* 27/1: 509.
32. The 4th Maine supported the Second Division of the Second Corps. *OR,* 27/1: 510.
33. This unit assisted in removing damaged guns of Cushing's Battery after the cannonade. *OR,* 27/1: 513-514.
34. This New York regiment supported a battery in the center of the Union line. *OR,* 27/1: 512.
35. On July 3, 1863 this regiment occupied a spot behind the Union battle line just north of Pleasonton Avenue as identified by a memorial to the regiment commemorating the action on July 3.
36. While both regiments of "Berdan's" Sharpshooters were assigned to Ward's Brigade they often worked independently as a division and/or corps level asset. It appears seven companies of the 1st regiment of sharpshooters supported the 9th MI Light Artillery Battery under the command of Captain Jabez J. Daniels during Pickett's Charge. Three companies were with the Fifth Corps. *OR,* 27/1: 517.
37. At least some portion of the eight companies of this regiment were engaged on July 3, 1863. Twelve volunteers did make an effort to silence Confederate artillery west of the Emmitsburg Road. They lost one man killed and one man wounded in the mission. *OR,* 27/1: 519.
38. This regiment supported the 9th MI Battery. *OR,* 27/1: 522.
39. This regiment was sent to support the Second Division of the Second Corps. No casualties were reported. *OR,* 27/1: 524.
40. The 5th MI moved at 2:00 p.m. on July 3, 1863 to the center of the Union line.
41. Two men were wounded July 3, 1863. *OR,* 27/1: 529.

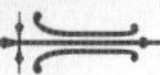
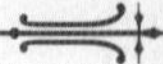

ENGAGED UNION ARTILLERY [1]

I UNION ARMY CORPS
ARTILLERY BRIGADE
Colonel Charles S. Wainwright

Battery B, 1st PA Light Artillery Regiment
Captain James H. Cooper
four 3" Rifles [2]

Battery B, 4th US Light Artillery Regiment [3]
2nd Lieutenant James Stewart
six Napoleons

II UNION ARMY CORPS
ARTILLERY BRIGADE
Captain John G. Hazard

Battery B, 1st NY Light Artillery Regiment
Captain James McKay Rorty [4]
four Parrott Rifles [5]

Battery A, 1st RI Light Artillery Regiment
Captain William A. Arnold
six 3" Rifles

Battery B, 1st RI Light Artillery Regiment
1st Lieutenant Walter S. Perrin [6]
six Napoleons [7]

Battery I, 1st US Light Artillery Regiment
1st Lieutenant George A. Woodruff [8]
six Napoleons

Battery A, 4th US Light Artillery Regiment
2nd Lieutenant Alonzo H. Cushing [9]
six 3" Rifles

V UNION ARMY CORPS
ARTILLERY BRIGADE
Captain Augustus P. Martin

Battery D, 5th US Artillery Regiment [10]
1st Lieutenant Benjamin F. Rittenhouse
six Parrott Rifles

Battery L, 1st OH Light Artillery Regiment
Captain Frank C. Gibbs [11]
six Napoleons

VI UNION ARMY CORPS
ARTILLERY BRIGADE
Colonel Charles H. Tompkins

Battery A, 1st MA Artillery
Captain William H. McCartney [12]
six Napoleons

1st NY Independent Battery
Captain Andrew Cowan
six 3" Rifles [13]

XI UNION ARMY CORPS
ARTILLERY BRIGADE
Major Thomas Osborn

13th NY Independent Battery
1st Lieutenant William Wheeler [14]
four 3" Rifles

Battery G, 4th US Artillery Regiment
1st Lieutenant Eugene A. Bancroft [15]
six Napoleons [16]

Battery I, 1st NY Light Artillery Regiment
Captain Michael Wiedrich [17]
six 3" Rifle

CAVALRY CORPS, FIRST BRIGADE,
HORSE ARTILLERY
Captain James M. Robertson

9th MI Light Artillery Battery
Captain Jabez J. Daniels
six 3" Rifles

ARTILLERY RESERVE
Brigadier General Robert O. Tyler

FIRST REGULAR BRIGADE
Captain Dunbar Ranson [18]

Batteries F and K,
3rd US Artillery Regiment
1st Lieutenant John G. Turnbull
six Napoleons [19]

Battery C, 4th US Artillery Regiment
1st Lieutenant Evan Thomas
six Napoleons

Battery C, 5th US Artillery Regiment
1st Lieutenant Gulian V. Weir
six Napoleons

Battery H, 1st US Artillery Regiment
2nd Lieutenant Philip D. Mason [20]
six Napoleons

FIRST VOLUNTEER BRIGADE
Lieutenant Colonel Freeman McGilvery

9th Battery Massachusetts Light Artillery
1st Lieutenant Richard S. Milton
six Napoleons [21]

Battery H, 3rd Pennsylvania
Heavy Artillery [22]
Captain William D. Rank
two 3" Rifles

Battery E, 5th MA Light Artillery
Captain Charles A. Phillips [23]
six 3" Rifles

15th NY Independent Battery
Captain Patrick Hart [24]
four Napoleons

Independent Batteries C and F,
PA Light Artillery
Captain James Thompson [25]
five 3" Rifles

SECOND VOLUNTEER BRIGADE
Captain Elijah Taft

5th NY Independent Battery
Captain Elijah Taft [26]
six 20-pounder Parrott Rifles

2nd CT Independent Light Artillery Battery
Captain John W. Sterling
four 6-pounder James Rifles,
and two 12-pounder Howitzers

THIRD VOLUNTEER BRIGADE
Captain James F. Huntington

Battery A, 1st NH Artillery
Captain Frederick M. Edgell
four 3" Rifles

Battery H, 1st OH Light Artillery Regiment
1st Lieutenant George W. Norton
six 3" Rifles

Batteries F and G, 1st PA Light Artillery
Captain R. Bruce Ricketts
six 3" Rifles

Battery C, 1st WV Light Artillery Regiment
Captain Wallace Hill
four Parrott Rifles

FOURTH VOLUNTEER BRIGADE
Captain Robert H. Fitzhugh

Battery F, 6th ME Artillery
1st Lieutenant Edwin B. Dow
four Napoleons

Battery A, 1st NJ Light Artillery
1st Lieutenant Augustin N. Parsons
six Parrott Rifles

Battery G, 1s NY Light Artillery Regiment
Captain Nelson Ames
six Napoleons

Battery K, 1st NY Light Artillery Regiment
Captain Robert H. Fitzhugh [27]
six 3" Rifles

NOTES:

1. This order of battle attempts to list all federal Union artillery units which fired in the cannonade, attack, and/or repulse of Pickett's Charge.
2. One of Cooper's guns was dismounted in the fighting on July 1, but apparently was remounted and used in the action on July 3. *OR*, 27/1: 365. This battery reported for duty 3:00 p.m. on July 3.
3. In a postwar account, Stewart claimed the battery did fire in the cannonade. Stewart stated after July 1 the battery had four serviceable guns. Brady and Freeland, *The Gettysburg Papers*, 373-377.
4. This battery was transferred from the artillery reserve to the Second Corps on July 1. The 14th New York Battery was attached to Rorty's command. Rorty was killed in action on July 3, 1863 having commanded the battery but a single day. *OR*, 27/1: 480. The nature of his mortal wound is not exactly known. "James McKay Rorty A Worthy Officer, A Gallant Soldier, An Estimable Man" by Brian C. Pohanka. Battery B, 1st NY Light Artillery File, ALBG, GNMP.
5. All Parrott Rifles are 10-pounder models unless otherwise stated.
6. The assigned commander of this battery, 1st Lieutenant T. Fred Brown, was wounded in the neck on July 3, 1863 and Lieutenant Perrin took command. *OR*, 27/1: 481.
7. All Napoleons listed are 12-pounder models. Two guns of this battery were sent to the rear on July 2 with four guns in action on July 3. *OR*, 27/1: 478.
8. Woodruff was mortally wounded by a gunshot wound to his back on July 3, 1863. He died the next day at the Granite School House not far from the front. *OR*, 27/1: 480-481; Busey, *Union Casualties at Gettysburg*, 2: 1075.
9. Cushing was killed in action July 3, 1863 by a gunshot wound through the mouth. *OR*, 27/1: 480; Testimony of Frederick Fuger, *Supreme Court of Pennsylvania*, 129. Of the six guns in action that day with the battery, two were placed on the wall and used during the attack. It appears four disabled guns, damaged in the cannonade, were removed by the 99th Pennsylvania when they reported for duty near the Union center. *OR*, 27/1: 514.
10. Captain Martin says in his report, "On the 3d instant the battery opened upon the enemy at intervals throughout the day." *OR*, 27/1: 659. In a postwar account, Rittenhouse says all his guns participated at some time during the assault. Brady and Freeland, *The Gettysburg Papers*, 526.
11. While the brigade commander of this battery, Augustus Martin, wrote in his report that this battery was not engaged on July 3, 1863, Captain Gibbs noted that artillerymen of his unit were "... occasionally working the battery." *OR*, 27/1: 662.
12. This battery was engaged but only fired four rounds of solid shot on July 3. *OR*, 27/1: 689.
13. The battery was split with five guns going into action south of the Copse of Trees and one gun just north. *OR Supplement*, Part I, Reports, Vol. 5, Serial 5, 212. For more detail as to this battery's participation in the defense see Cowan's complete account 211-216.
14. This battery was detached from Cemetery Hill to aid the Second Corps and arrived in time to fire in the attack and repulse. *OR*, 27/1: 753.
15. The center and right section of this battery, four total guns, were in action to repulse Pickett's Charge. *OR*, 27/1: 756-757.
16. This battery had six total guns with only four in action on July 3.
17. This battery fired in the cannonade from Cemetery Hill. *New York at Gettysburg*, 3: 1247.
18. Ransom was wounded in the right leg in action on July 2, 1863. It is not known who succeeded him to command for July 3. Busey, *Union Casualties at Gettysburg*, 2: 1079.
19. Four of these guns were lost on July 2 but retaken. It is not known to what extent this battery participated on July 3. *OR*, 27/1: 873.
20. Mason stated the entire battery was "... engaged throughout the whole day." *OR Supplement*, Part I, Reports, Vol. 5, Serial, 225. It appears three guns fired at a time then being relieved by the other three Napoleons of the battery.
21. This battery suffered terribly July 2. The battery lost four of its' guns to the Confederates that day, but the guns were later recovered on July 2. Two guns were brought to the center of the Union line on July 3. It is unclear to what extend the battery participated in the action, if at all, on July 3. *OR*, 27/1: 886; Ladd, *Bachelder Papers*, 3: 1973; Eric A. Campbell editor, *"A Grand Terrible Dramma," From Gettysburg to Petersburg" The Civil War Letters of Charles Wellington Reed* (New York, 2000), 117-121.
22. This battery was normally part of John B. McIntosh's First Brigade, Second Division of the Calvary Corps. On July 3, battery, really just one section of two guns, was serving as light artillery under the immediate supervision of Colonel McGilvery. *OR*, 27/1: 166, 883; *Pennsylvania at Gettysburg*, 2: 934.
23. This battery repulsed the Florida Brigade. *OR*, 27/1: 885. Also has the 10th New York Battery attached.
24. Wounded in action July 3, 1863. *OR*, 27/1: 888. Hart described this wound as "slight."
25. This unit lost one gun to the enemy on July 2, 1863. *OR*, 27/1: 890.
26. Taft exercised command of the brigade with one of his officers commanding his battery. At the beginning of the cannonade at least two of his guns fired to the west. These guns were later relieved by three more of Taft's battery. *New York at Gettysburg*, 3: 1297; *OR*, 27/1: 891.
27. The 11th New York Battery was attached. Fitzhugh was the senior officer and commanded the combined battery. The commander of the two guns attached to Fitzhugh from the 11th were under the command of 1st Lieutenant John E. Burton. Ladd, *Bachelder Papers*, 1: 573-574; *New York at Gettysburg*, 3: 1250.

CONFEDERATE INFANTRY FORCES

FIRST ARMY CORPS
Lieutenant General James Longstreet

PICKETT'S DIVISION
Major General George E. Pickett

KEMPER'S BRIGADE
Brigadier General James L. Kemper [1]

1st VA Volunteer Infantry Regiment
Colonel Lewis B. Williams [2]

3rd VA Volunteer Infantry Regiment
Colonel Joseph Mayo, Jr. [3]

7th VA Volunteer Infantry Regiment
Colonel Waller Tazewell Patton [4]

11th VA Volunteer Infantry Regiment
Major Kirkwood Otey [5]

24th VA Volunteer Infantry Regiment
Colonel William R. Terry [6]

GARNETT'S BRIGADE
Brigadier General Richard B. Garnett [7]

8th VA Volunteer Infantry Regiment
Colonel Eppa Hunton [8]

18th VA Volunteer Infantry Regiment
Lieutenant Colonel Henry A. Carrington [9]

19th VA Volunteer Infantry Regiment
Colonel Henry A. Gantt [10]

28th VA Volunteer Infantry Regiment
Colonel Robert C. Allen [11]

56th VA Volunteer Infantry Regiment
Colonel William D. Stuart [12]

ARMISTEAD'S BRIGADE
Brigadier General Lewis A. Armistead [13]

9th VA Volunteer Infantry Regiment
Colonel John C. Owens [14]

14th VA Volunteer Infantry Regiment
Colonel James G. Hodges [15]

38th VA Volunteer Infantry Regiment
Colonel Edmund C. Edmonds [16]

53rd VA Volunteer Infantry Regiment
Colonel William Aylett [17]

57th VA Volunteer Infantry Regiment
Colonel John B. Magruder [18]

THIRD ARMY CORPS
Lieutenant General Ambrose Powell Hill

HETH'S DIVISION
Brigadier General James J. Pettigrew [19]

DAVIS'S BRIGADE
Brigadier General Joseph R. Davis [20]

2nd MS Volunteer Infantry Regiment
Lieutenant Colonel David W. Humphreys [21]

11th MS Volunteer Infantry Regiment
Colonel Francis M. Green [22]

42nd MS Volunteer Infantry Regiment
Colonel Hugh R. Miller [23]

55th North Carolina Volunteer Infantry Regiment
Captain George A. Gilreath [24]

BROCKENBROUGH'S BRIGADE
Colonel John M. Brockenbrough [25]

40th VA Volunteer Infantry Regiment
Captain Thomas E. Betts [26] or *Captain Richard B. Davis*

47th VA Volunteer Infantry Regiment
Colonel Robert M. Mayo

55th VA Volunteer Infantry Regiment
Colonel William S. Christian [27]

22nd VA Volunteer Infantry Battalion
Lieutenant Colonel Edward P. Tayloe [28]

ARCHER'S BRIGADE
Colonel Birkett D. Fry [29]

13th AL Volunteer Infantry Regiment
Successor to Colonel Birkett Fry not verified.

5th AL Volunteer Infantry Battalion
Major Albert S. Van de Graff

1st TN (Provisional Army) Infantry Regiment
Lieutenant Colonel Newton J. George [30]

7th TN Volunteer Infantry Regiment
Colonel John A. Fite [31]

14th TN Volunteer Infantry Regiment
Lieutenant Colonel James W. Lockert [32]

PETTIGREW'S BRIGADE
Colonel James K. Marshall [33]

11th NC Volunteer Infantry Regiment
Captain Francis W. Bird [34]

26th NC Volunteer Infantry Regiment
Major John T. Jones [35]

47th NC Volunteer Infantry Regiment
Colonel George H. Faribault [36]

52nd NC Volunteer Infantry Regiment
Lieutenant Colonel Marcus J. Parks [37]

PENDER'S DIVISION
Major General Isaac R. Trimble [38]

LANE'S BRIGADE
Brigadier General James H. Lane

7th NC Volunteer Infantry Regiment
Major J. McLeod Turner [39]

18th NC Volunteer Infantry Regiment
Colonel John D. Barry

28th NC Volunteer Infantry Regiment
Colonel Samuel D. Lowe [40]

33rd NC Volunteer Infantry Regiment
Colonel Charles M. Avery [41]

37th NC Volunteer Infantry Regiment
Colonel William M. Barbour [42]

SCALES'S BRIGADE
Colonel William Lee J. Lowrance [43]

13th NC Volunteer Infantry Regiment
Second Lieutenant Robert L. Moir [44]

16th NC Volunteer Infantry Regiment
Captain Abel S. Cloud [45]

22nd NC Volunteer Infantry Regiment
Colonel James Conner [46]

34th NC Volunteer Infantry Regiment
Lieutenant Colonel George T. Gordon [47]

38th NC Volunteer Infantry Regiment
Captain William L. Thornburg [48]

ANDERSON'S DIVISION
Major General Richard H. Anderson

PERRY'S BRIGADE
Colonel David Lang [49]

2nd FL Volunteer Infantry Regiment
Captain Charles S. Fleming [50]

5th FL Volunteer Infantry Regiment
Captain John W. Holleyman [51]

8th FL Volunteer Infantry Regiment
Lieutenant Colonel William Baya [52]

WILCOX'S BRIGADE
Brigadier General Cadmus M. Wilcox

8th AL Volunteer Infantry Regiment
Lieutenant Colonel Hilary A. Herbert

9th AL Volunteer Infantry Regiment
Captain Joseph H. King [53]

10th AL Volunteer Infantry Regiment
Lieutenant Colonel James E. Shelley [54]

11th AL Volunteer Infantry Regiment
Lieutenant Colonel George E. Tayloe [55]

14th AL Volunteer Infantry Regiment
Lieutenant Colonel James A. Broome [56]

NOTES:

1. Wounded in the groin. Robert A. Bright, "Pickett's Charge at Gettysburg," *Confederate Veteran* XXXVIII (1930), 266. See also Jack Welsh, M.D., *Medical Histories of Confederate Generals* (Kent, OH, 1995), 125. "He was struck by a minie ball on the inside cavity of the left thigh, near the femoral artery. The ball glanced up the femur, passed through the cavity of the body, and lodged near the spine."

2. Mortally wounded when Federal fire struck him in the shoulder and he fell on his own sword, impaling himself. *Richmond Times Dispatch*, December 13, 1903.

3. Wounded in the hand. Richard M. McMurry, *Virginia Military Institute Alumni in the Civil War* (Lynchburg, VA, 1999), 171; Handwritten biography, undated, no author, Joseph Mayo, Jr., Student File, VMI Archives, Lexington, VA.

4. Mortally wounded at the Emmitsburg Road by a gunshot wound, which passed through both his jaws. He died at Pennsylvania (Gettysburg) College on July 21, 1863. See biographical sketch of Patton in Walker, *Memorial, Virginia Military Institute,* 425-425; McMurry, *VMI Alumni,* 175.

5. Wounded in the shoulder. *OR Supplement*, Part I, Reports, Vol. 5, Serial 5, 328; Hilary V. Harris to Father, July 7, 1863, Hilary V. Harris Papers, 1863, Pearce Civil War Collection, Navarro

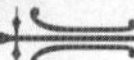

College, Corsicana, TX; McMurry, *VMI Alumni,* 182.

6. Some accounts list Terry as wounded in the attack but there are currently no contemporary primary sources to support the claim.

7. Killed in action in front of the Union works by a bullet to the head. R. H. Irvine, "Brig. Gen. Richard B. Garnett," *Confederate Veteran* XXIII (1915), 391; *OR Supplement*, Part I, Reports, Vol. 5, Serial 5, 313.

8. Wounded in right leg just below the knee. *OR Supplement*, Part I, Reports, Vol. 5, Serial 5, 309.

9. This officer was wounded and captured. Henry T. Owen to Henry A. Carrington, January 27, 1878. A copy of this correspondence is in the 18th VA Volunteer Infantry Regiment File, ALBG, GNMP; "Autographs from an old Album," *Confederate Veteran,* XXXII (1924), 130; Henry A. Carrington, CMSR, RG 109, M 324, Roll 599; George C. Cabell, "Colonel H. A. Carrington," *Southern Historical Society Papers,* Vol. 32, 217; *Richmond Times-Dispatch*, February 28, 1904.

10. Wounded in the face. Had his teeth shot out. Also wounded in left arm. Henry A. Gantt, CMSR, RG 109, M 324, Roll 360; War Record of Colonel Henry Gantt given to his niece Mrs. W. D. Patterson by Private William P. Londeree of Company D, 19th Virginia, March 1910, Henry A. Gantt, Student File, VMI Archives, Lexington, VA; Handwritten biographical sketch by Thomas P. Gantt, undated, Henry Gantt, Student File, VMI Archives, Lexington, VA.

11. Killed in action. Allen was shot twice in the head and once in the shoulder. "Echoes from Gettysburg," *Confederate Veteran* XXI (1913), 430; *Richmond Times Dispatch*, date unknown; Robert C. Allen, Student File, VMI Archives, Lexington, VA; Miss Gates Moffett, "Colonel Robert Allen," Robert C. Allen, Student File, VMI Archives, Lexington, VA.

12. Mortally wounded at the onset of the advance. George W. Finley, "Bloody Angle, "*Buffalo Evening News*, May 29, 1894; Wm. Couper, Colonel, Executive Officer & Historiographer to Mr. J. A. Stuart, Buena Vista, CA states time of death was at 3:50 a.m. on July 29, 1863, William D. Stuart, Student File, VMI Archives, Lexington, VA.

13. Armistead was hit by two bullets inside the angle. One bullet struck him in the left leg and another hit him in the right arm. He died on July 5, 1863. Ladd, *Bachelder Papers,* 1: 358-359. Contrary to other sources, and according to one of the doctors who treated him, Armistead was not wounded in the chest as often depicted.

14. While Owens is listed on the Order of Battle after Gettysburg as a major, his rank in Pickett's Charge was colonel. James J. Phillips to Francis H. Smith, July 18, 1863, VMI Archives, Lexington, VA. Owens was mortally wounded in the groin and died July 4, 1863. Clement A. Evans ed., *Confederate Military History Extended Version* (Wilmington, NC, 1987), Vol. 4, 288-289.

15. Killed in action within a few feet of the stonewall on Cemetery Ridge. James F. Crocker, "James Gregory Hodges," *Southern Historical Society Papers,* Vol. 37, 193-195. Colonel Hodges' body was never recovered.

16. Killed in action by a Union rifle bullet, which pierced his skull. *OR Supplement,* Part I, Reports, Vol. 5, Serial, 333. Edmonds was followed in command of the regiment by Lieutenant Colonel Powhatan Whittle and then Major Joseph Cabell.

17. Wounded in action during the cannonade, and subsequently did not make the charge. John C. Timberlake to the editor of *the Richmond Times Dispatch*, October 29, 1887, Virginia Historical Society, Richmond, VA. Lieutenant Colonel Rawley W. Martin led the regiment in the attack. He was wounded in both legs and captured inside the famous "Angle."

18. Mortally wounded by two rifle bullets in the chest and arm. He died as a prisoner of war on July 5, 1863. William H. Stewart, "Col. John Bowie M'Gruder," *Confederate Veteran* VIII (1900), 329; William H. Stewart, "Colonel John Bowie Magruder," *Southern Historical Society Papers,* Vol. 27, 205-210.

19. Wounded in hand. *OR*, 27/2: 321-362; *OR*, 27/2: 640-641. T. J. Cureton of the 26th North Carolina Infantry stated that Pettigrew was wounded in the arm. *OR Supplement*, Part I, Reports, Vol. 5, Serial 5, 430.

20. Two sources claim that Davis was wounded in the attack on July 3, but this is questionable. Welsh, *Medical Histories of Confederate Generals,* 51; John C. Rietti, *Military Annals of Mississippi*, 148. Davis's CMSR indicates he was furloughed from Hospital # 4 in Richmond, VA on July 30, 1863 suffering from engorgement of the liver and general disability. Joseph R. Davis, CMSR, NARA, RG 109, M 331, Roll 72.

21. The Colonel of the 2nd Mississippi, John Marshall Stone was wounded in the side by shrapnel on July 1. *OR*, 27/2: 648; Ladd, *Bachelder Papers*, 1: 329; T. P. Williams, *The Mississippi Brigade of Brig. Gen. Joseph R. Davis* (Dayton, OH, 1999), 86. It appears that despite being wounded on July 1, Stone viewed Pickett's Charge but did not lead his regiment in the assault. Stone was wounded again on July 3 near the front while he was attempting to return to a Confederate field hospital. See *Biographical & Historical Memoirs of Mississippi.* Vol. 2 (Spartansburg, SC, 1978), 650-653. With Colonel Stone out of action the regiment was led on July 3 by Lieutenant Colonel David W. Humphreys. He was killed in action on July 3. David W. Humphreys, CMSR, RG 109, M 269, Roll 117.

22. Wounded in action on July 3. Baxter M'Farland, "Casualties of the Eleventh Mississippi Regiment at Gettysburg," *Confederate Veteran* XXIV (1916), 410-411. McFarland was not at Gettysburg although he was a member of the regiment until June 1863.

23. Miller was mortally wounded in the left breast and right knee on July 3. He was captured and died in captivity July 19, 1863. Rev. Dr. T. D. Witherspoon, "Prison Life at Fort McHenry," *Southern Historical Society Papers,* Vol. 8, 77; Hugh R. Miller, CMSR, RG 109, M 269, Roll 396; Williams, *Davis's Brigade*, 225; Coco, *Wasted Valor*, 119-121.

24. Killed in action on July 3. On July 1, Colonel John Kerr Connally was severely wounded, succeeded by Lieutenant Colonel Maurice Thompson Smith who was killed, succeeded by Major Alfred Horatio Belo who was also wounded, leaving Captain Gilreath in command on July 3. Walter B. Clark ed., *Histories of the Several Regiments and Battalions from North Carolina in the Great War 1861-'65*, Vol. 3 (Wilmington, NC, 1996), 299-301; Jordan, *North Carolina Troops*, 13: 386 and 444. Upon Gilreath's death, command passed to 1st Lieutenant Marcus C. Stevens.

25. Colonel Robert M. Mayo, commander of the 47th Virginia filed the official report of the brigade for the action at Gettysburg. A former subordinate H. H. Walker replaced Brockenbrough very shortly after Gettysburg. Brockenbrough was present and in command on July 3. J. M. Brockenbrough to Jefferson Davis, July 27, 1863, John M. Brockenbrough, Student File, VMI Archives, Lexington, VA; H. J. Horner, *Confederate Veteran* VI (1898), 68; William S. Christian to John W. Daniel, October 24, 1904, John W. Daniel Papers, University of Virginia, Richmond, VA.

26. Betts was wounded at Gettysburg and later captured July 5, 1863. Date of wound is unknown therefore either he or Davis commanded in the charge. Thomas E. Betts, CMSR, RG 109, M 347, Roll 852.

27. Captured during the retreat from Gettysburg, July 14, 1863 at Falling Waters. James Dinkins, "The Negroes as Slaves," *Southern Historical Society Papers,* Vol. 35, 62; "Colonel William Steptoe Christian," *Confederate Veteran* XIX (1911), 350.

28. While the *OR* lists Major John S. Bowles in command of this unit on July 3, it was actually under the leadership of Tayloe. Jaquelin M. Meredith, "The First Day at Gettysburg Tribute to Brave General Harry Heth who Opened the Great Battle," *Southern Historical Society Papers,* Vol. 3, 24, 185.

29. Fry was the commander of the 13th Alabama Infantry. When General Archer was captured on July 1, Fry assumed command of Archer's Brigade. During Pickett's Charge on July 3, Fry was wounded in the right shoulder by a shell during the artillery barrage preceding the advance. He remained in command, however, until he was shot in the thigh (fracturing the bone) and captured. *OR*, 27/2: 608; *OR*, 27/2: 65; Fry, "Pettigrew's Charge," 7: 91-93. The successor to brigade command

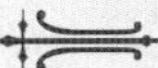

was **NOT** Lieutenant Colonel S. G. Shepard as stated in the *OR*. Shepard did write the report for the brigade's actions at Gettysburg on August 10, 1863, and clearly states "I beg leave to state that, although I was not in command of the brigade, yet I was in each of the engagements, and upon my own observation and the testimony of the officers of each of the regiments I predicate my statements," *OR*, 27/2: 646-648.

30. Wounded and captured July 3, 1863. Reports differ on whether he was wounded or not, but Colonel Birkett Fry states George was wounded by Fry's side. *OR*, 27/2: 289 lists Major Felix G. Buchanan as in command, but George's CMSR and multiple sources including *OR*, 27/1: 467-468, identify him as being captured on July 3; Ladd, *Bachelder Papers*, 1: 516-520; Fry, "Pettigrew's Charge," 7: 92-93.

31. *OR*, 27/2: 289 lists Shepard in command but he was not. Colonel Fite was in command and captured on July 3. *OR*, 27/1: 467-468; Evans, *Confederate Military History*, 8: 201; Gustavus W. Dyer and John Trotwood Moore, *The Tennessee Civil War Veterans Questionnaires* (Easley, SC, 1985), 816-819. This source is Fite's own account. See also John Fite, CMSR, RG 109, M 268, Roll 144; *OR*, 27/1: 467-468.

32. Wounded in thigh and captured in Pickett's Charge, July 3 while crossing the wall. *OR*, 27/2: 289 lists Captain B. L. Phillips as in command, but Lockert was senior, present, and in command until wounded. Krick, *Lee's Colonels*, 241; F. S. Harris, "Heroism in the Battle of Gettysburg," *Confederate Veteran* IX (1901), 16; James Lockert, CMSR, RG 109, M 268, Roll 175.

33. Killed instantly by two bullets in the forehead. Jennings Cropper Wise, *The Military History of the Virginia Military Institute from 1839 to 1865* (Lynchburg, VA, 1915), 450; F. Lewis Marshall to Uncle, October 6, 1863, VMI Archives Manuscript # 0165, Lexington, VA. Available online at www.vmi.edu/archives/manuscripts/ms0165.html.

34. Francis W. Bird, CMSR, RG 109, M 270, Roll 191.

35. Wounded by a shell fragment on July 1, but remained on the field. Knocked down by a shell and stunned on July 3. Jordan, *North Carolina Troops*, 7: 463; Evans, *Confederate Military History*, 4: 189.

36. Severely wounded in the shoulder and foot, July 3. *OR*, 27/2: 645; Jordan, *North Carolina Troops*, 11: 244. Nathaniel L. Brown of the 47th North Carolina says in a letter that Faribault was "…slightly wounded in the right arm." See Don Ernsberger, *Also For Glory The Pettigrew Trimble Charge* (No City, 2008), 172.

37. Wounded in both thighs July 3, and captured. *OR*, 27/1: 467-468; Jordan, *North Carolina Troops*, 12: 415.

38. Major General William D. Pender was mortally wounded on July 2, 1863. James H. Lane assumed command of the division on the evening of July 2, Trimble took command from Lane on July 3. Trimble was wounded by a Federal bullet, which struck him in the left leg near the Emmitsburg Road. Ladd, *Bachelder Papers*, 2: 934; Isaac R. Trimble, "Civil War Diary of I. R. Trimble," *Maryland Historical Magazine* (1922), 1-2.

39. Wounded in action July 3 with a "ball through the body" and received a contusion on the "…instep of his foot…" *OR Supplement*, Part II, Records of Events, Vol. 48, Serial 60, 476; *OR Supplement*, Part I, Reports, Vol. 5, Serial 5, 447. He spent time at the Lutheran Theological Seminary Hospital and Camp Letterman. On September 21, 1863, Turner arrived at a hospital in Baltimore. J. McLeod Turner, CMSR, RG 109, M 270, Roll 178. After Turner was disabled the command of the regiment fell to Captain James Gilmer Harris. See *OR Supplement*, Part I, Reports, Vol. 5, Serial, 5, 454.

40. Wounded in action in left thigh. *OR*, 27/2: 668.

41. Wounded in action bruised by an artillery fragment. *OR*, 27/2: 668.

42. Wounded in action. H. A. Brown, "Col. W. M. Barbour," *Confederate Veteran* VII (1899), 30.

43. General Scales was wounded on July 1. Lowrance was wounded in action on July 1 but reported for duty and commanded the brigade during the attack. *OR*, 27/2: 659; Evans, *Confederate Military History*, 15: 518.

44. Wounded in action. Clark, *NC Regiments*, 1: 698.

45. While the *OR* lists Captain Leroy Stowe in command of this regiment at Gettysburg, Stowe was wounded in action on September 1, 1862 and was not present at Gettysburg. See *OR*, 27/2: 290; Leroy W. Stowe, CMSR, RG 109, M 270, Roll 247. Captain Cloud was in command of the regiment and captured on July 3, 1863. See Abel S. Cloud, CMSR, RG 109, M 270, Roll 242; *OR Supplement*, Part I, Reports, Vol. 5, Serial 5, 468-469; Jordan, *North Carolina Troops*, 6: 46-47.

46. Colonel Conner was wounded at the Battle of Mechanicsville in 1862. While absent for some time, according to his CMSR, he is back with the regiment on April 1, 1863 and signs for stationary through the period of June 30, 1863. He resigned from the service on account of his wound on August 13, 1863. James Connor, CMSR, RG 109, M 270, Roll 286. While there is some question, he appears to be present at Gettysburg with his command.

47. Wounded in the leg. Jordan, *North Carolina Troops*, 9: 251; George T. Gordon, CMSR, RG 109, M 270, Roll 388. According to his CMSR the wound was in his left leg.

48. Captain Thornburg was acting major of the regiment on July 3. He was wounded in action on July 1, but was present on July 3. As senior officer, he assumed command of the regiment on July 3. During the assault, Thornburg was severely wounded in the face which resulted in the destruction of his right eye. See *OR Supplement*, Part I, Reports, Vol. 5, Serial 5, 464-465; Clark, *NC Regiments*, 2: 692; Jordan, *North Carolina Troops*, 7: 10; George W. Flowers, "The Thirty-Eighth N. C. Regiment," *Southern Historical Society Papers*, Vol. 25, 259-260.

49. Lang commanded Perry's Brigade as General Edward A. Perry was absent sick with Typhoid. Evans, *Confederate Military History*, 7: 150.

50. Fleming was in command on July 3 as Major Walter R. Moore, commanding, and Captain Ballantine, second in command, were both wounded on July 2. Walter R. Moore, CMSR, RG 109, M 251, Roll 39; Evans, *Confederate Military History*, 16: 152, 155, 219, and 262.

51. Holleyman (also spelled as Hollyman) was in command on July 3 as Captain Richmond N. Gardner, commanding, was wounded (lost an arm) on July 2. Richard N. Gardner, CMSR, RG 109, M 251, Roll 62; Evans, *Confederate Military History*, 16: 155. One source mentions that a Captain Bryan commanded between Gardner and Holleyman, but this is not verified elsewhere; Francis S. Fleming, *Memoir of Capt. C. S. Fleming, of the Second Florida Infantry, C. S. A.* (Alexandria, VA, 1985), 87.

52. Baya was in command as Colonel Lang was temporarily commanding the brigade. Baya, anglicized from Balla, was the only Spanish-American to command a Confederate unit at Gettysburg. Biography found in Evans, *Confederate Military History*, 16: 221-222; David W. Hartman and David Coles compilers, *Biographical Roster of Florida's Confederate and Union Soldiers, 1861-1865*, Vol. 2 (Wilmington, NC, 1985), 808.

53. Wounded, finger shot off on July 2. Remained in command. *OR*, 27/2: 619-621.

54. Shelley succeeded to the command of the 10th Alabama after Colonel William H. Forney was severely wounded on July 2. *OR*, 27/2: 619-620.

55. Tayloe commanded on July 3 as Colonel J. C. C. Sanders was wounded in the knee by a minie ball on July 2. W. Brewer, *Alabama: Her History, Resources, War Record, and Public Men. From 1540 to 1872* (Tuscaloosa, AL, 1872), 268-269; *OR*, 27/2: 619-62.

56. Broome commanded on July 3 as Colonel Lucius Pinckard had been wounded (right arm broken) on July 2. Coincidentally, both Broome of the 14th Alabama and Tayloe of the 11th were graduates of the Virginia Military Institute. Evans, *Confederate Military History*, 7: 520.

ENGAGED CONFEDERATE ARTILLERY

FIRST ARMY CORPS (LONGSTREET)
HOOD'S DIVISIONAL ARTILLERY

HENRY'S BATTALION
Major Mathis [1] *W. Henry*

Palmetto Artillery (SC)
Captain Hugh R. Garden
two Napoleons, and two Parrott Rifles [2]

Branch Artillery (NC)
Captain Alexander C. Latham
one 6-pounder, one 12-pounder Howitzer, and three Napoleons [3]

MCLAWS' DIVISIONAL ARTILLERY

CABELL'S BATTALION
Colonel Henry C. Cabell [4]

Pulaski Artillery (GA) Artillery
1st Lieutenant William J. Furlong [5]
two Parrott Rifles

First Richmond Howitzers (VA)
Captain Edward S. McCarthy
two Napoleons, and two 3" Rifles

Troup Artillery (GA)
Captain Henry H. Carlton [6]
two 12-pounder Howitzers, and two Parrott Rifles [7]

Battery A, First Artillery (NC)
Captain Basil C. Manly
two Napoleons, and four 3" Rifles [8]

PICKETT'S DIVISIONAL ARTILLERY
38th Battalion Virginia Light Artillery

DEARING'S BATTALION
Major James Dearing

Fauquier Artillery (VA)
Captain Robert M. Stribling
four Napoleons, and two 20-pounder Parrott Rifles [9]

Hampden Artillery (VA)
Captain William H. Caskie
two Napoleons, one 3" Rifle, and one Parrott Rifle

Richmond Fayette Artillery (VA)
Captain Miles C. Macon
two Napoleons, and two Parrott Rifles

Lynchburg Virginia Battery (VA)
Captain Joseph G. Blount
four Napoleons

FIRST ARMY CORPS (LONGSTREET) ARTILLERY RESERVE
Colonel James B. Walton
(Chief of Artillery for Longstreet's Corps) [10]

ALEXANDER'S BATTALION
Colonel Edward Porter Alexander [11]

Ashland Artillery [12] (VA)
1st Lieutenant James Woolfolk [13]
two Napoleons, and two 20-pounder Parrott Rifles

Bedford Artillery (VA)
Captain Tyler C. Jordan
four 3" Rifles

Brooks Artillery (SC)
2nd Lieutenant William W. Fickling [14]
four 12-pounder Howitzers [15]

Richmond Virginia Battery (VA)
Captain William W. Parker
3-3" Rifles, and one Parrott Rifle [16]

Bath Virginia Battery (VA)
Captain Osmond B. Taylor
four Napoleons

Madison Light Artillery (LA)
Captain George W. Moody
four 24-pounder Howitzers

ESHLEMAN'S BATTALION
(LA Washington Artillery)
Major Benjamin F. Eshleman

First Company (LA)
2nd Lieutenant Charles H. C. Brown [17]
one Napoleon

Second Company (LA)
Captain John B. Richardson
two Napoleons, and one 12-pounder Howitzer [18]

Third Company (LA)
Captain Merritt B. Miller
three Napoleons [19]

Fourth Company (LA)
Captain Joseph Norcom, Jr. [20]
two Napoleons, and one 12-pounder Howitzer [21]

SECOND ARMY CORPS (EWELL)
RODES'S DIVISIONAL ARTILLERY

CARTER'S BATTALION
Lieutenant Colonel Thomas H. Carter

Jeff Davis Artillery (AL)
Captain William J. Reese
four 3" Rifles

King William Artillery (VA)
Captain William P. P. Carter
two Parrott Rifles [22]

Orange Artillery (VA)
Captain Charles W. Fry
two Parrott Rifles, and two 3" Rifles

ATTACHED TO THIS BATTALION
2nd Maryland Battery
(Baltimore Artillery)
Captain Wiley H. Griffin [23]
four Napoleons [24]

SECOND ARMY CORPS (EWELL) ARTILLERY RESERVE
Colonel J. Thompson Brown
(Acting Chief of Ewell's Corps Artillery) [25]

DANCE'S BATTALION
First Virginia Artillery
Captain Willis J. Dance

Second Richmond Howitzers (VA)
Captain David Watson
four Parrott Rifles

Third Richmond Howitzers (VA)
Captain Benjamin H. Smith, Jr.
three 3" Rifles [26]

Powhatan Artillery (VA)
1st Lieutenant John M. Cunningham [27]
four 3" rifles

Rockbridge Artillery (VA)
Captain Archibald Graham, Jr.
four 20-pounder Parrott Rifles [28]

Salem Artillery (VA)
1st Lieutenant Charles B. Griffin [29]
two 3" Rifles [30]

NELSON'S BATTALION
Lieutenant Colonel William Nelson [31]

Georgia Battery (GA)
Captain John Milledge, Jr.
one Parrott Rifle, and two 3" Rifles

THIRD ARMY CORPS (HILL) [32]
ANDERSON'S DIVISIONAL ARTILLERY

11TH GEORGIA ARTILLERY BATTALION
Sumter Artillery Battalion
Major John Lane [33]

Company A (GA)
Captain Hugh M. Ross
one 12-pounder Howitzer, one Napoleon, one 3" Navy Parrott Rifle, and three Parrott Rifles [34]

Company C (GA)
Captain John T. Wingfield [35]
two 20-pounder Parrott Rifles, and three 3" Navy Parrott Rifles

PENDER'S DIVISIONAL ARTILLERY

POAGUE'S BATTALION
Major William T. Poague

Albemarle Artillery (VA)
Captain James W. Wyatt
one 12-pounder Howitzer, two 3" Rifles, and one Parrott Rifle

Charlotte Artillery (NC)
Captain Joseph Graham [36]
two 12-pounder Howitzers, and two Napoleons

Madison Light Artillery (MS)
Captain George Ward
one 12-pounder Howitzer, and three Napoleons

Virginia Battery (VA)
1st Lieutenant Addison W. Utterback [37]
two 12-pounder Howitzers, and two Napoleons

THIRD ARMY CORPS (HILL) ARTILLERY RESERVE
Colonel Rueben L. Walker
(Chief of Hill's Corps Artillery)

MCINTOSH'S BATTALION
Major David G. McIntosh

Danville Artillery (VA)
Captain Robert S. Rice
four Napoleons

Hardaway Artillery (AL)
Captain William B. Hurt [38]
two 3" Rifles, and two Whitworth Cannons

2nd Rockbridge Artillery (VA)
1st Lieutenant Samuel Wallace
two Napoleons, and two 3" Rifles [39]

Virginia Battery (VA)
Captain Marmaduke Johnson
two Napoleons, and two 3" Rifles

PEGRAM'S BATTALION
Major William J. Pegram [40]

Crenshaw's Battery (VA)
1st Lieutenant Andrew B. Johnston [41]
two Napoleons[42]

Pee Dee Artillery (SC)
Captain Ervin B. Brunson [43]
four 3" Rifles [44]

Fredericksburg Artillery (VA)
Captain Edward A. Marye
two Parrott Rifles, and two 3" Rifles [45]

Purcell Artillery (VA)
Captain Joseph McGraw
four Napoleons

Letcher Artillery (VA)
Captain Thomas A. Brander
two Napoleons,[46] and two Parrott Rifles

NOTES:

1. Frequently given as Mathias, Henry's first name was actually Mathis. *Proceedings of the Clarke County Historical Association*, Vol. VI, 1946, 53-60.
2. Hereafter all Parrott cannon are 10-pounder models unless otherwise stated. A post-war source states this battery also had 12-pounder Howitzer. "Hugh Garden's Battery," *Sumter Herald*, August 29, 1902.
3. Latham received two captured Parrott Rifles from Smith's 4th NY Independent Battery. Two of his original guns were disabled July 2, 1863.
4. During Pickett's Charge Colonel Cabell had two horses shot from beneath him and he was slightly wounded in the left side. He did, however, remain in command. See S. Basset French, *Biographical Sketches*, Archives Division, Library of Virginia; "The Cabells and Their Kin," *Confederate Veteran* XVI (1908), 562-563.
5. Captain John C. Fraser, the battery commander, was mortally wounded on July 2 and died July 11. John C. Fraser, CMSR, RG 109, M 266, Roll 104. This battery was so crippled on July 2, 1863, that Colonel Cabell took two 3" Rifles and attached them to Basil Manly's battery. Lieutenant John C. Payne, one of Manly's subordinates, commanded these guns on July 3, 1863. The remaining Parrott Rifles were left under the immediate command of 1st Lieutenant William J. Furlong of Fraser's battery. *OR*, 27/2: 375.
6. Carlton was severely wounded. *OR*, 27/2: 384. Columbus Motes takes command.
7. Only the two Parrott Rifles were engaged in the cannonade on July 3. All four guns were moved to the Emmitsburg Road during the advance and fired in support of the assault. See *OR*, 27/2: 384.
8. On July 3, Manly had six total guns under his command with two 3" Rifles assigned to him from the crippled Pulaski Artillery (Furlong's battery).
9. The armament of this battery is disputed. The war department plaque on the battlefield states this battery had two 20-pounder Parrott Rifles. Michael J. Andrus, *The Brooke, Fauquier, Loudoun, and Alexandria Artillery* (Lynchburg, VA, 1990), 77 states the battery received six new Napoleons May 16, 1863. An extract dated July 1, 1863 also states this battery had six Napoleons at Gettysburg. *OR Supplement*, Part I, Reports, Vol. 5, Serial 5, 341. Dearing says Alexander gave him a 20-pounder Parrott Rifle, and in exchange, Dearing gave Alexander a 12-pounder Howitzer. *OR*, 27/2: 391.
10. While Walton was the senior artillery officer in Longstreet's command, Colonel E. Porter Alexander exercised defacto control of all of Longstreet's artillery on July 3, 1863. Alexander noted he was third in seniority, with Colonel Cabell's date of rank prior to his. Gallagher, *Fighting for the Confederacy*, 224.
11. On July 3, 1863 Major Frank Huger commanded the battalion while Alexander exercised command over all of Longstreet's guns.
12. Operated separate from the rest of the battalion on July 3, 1863. See *OR*, 27/2: 430.
13. Captain Pichegru Woolfolk, was wounded in action on July 2, and the battery command fell to his brother. *OR*, 27/2: 430.
14. This battery is also known as Rhett's battery. The battery's commander S. Capers Gilbert was wounded in the left knee at Gettysburg, most likely July 2. *OR*, 27/2: 431; S. Capers Gilbert, CMSR, RG 109, M 267, Roll 94.
15. Two of these guns were dismounted on July 2, 1863. Gallagher, *Fighting for the Confederacy*, 240. James Dearing finds another howitzer on July 4 and states it was Alexander's. *OR*, 27/2: 391.
16. One gun was defective July 3, 1863 and not used in the cannonade. *OR Supplement*, Part I, Reports, Vol. 5, Serial 5, 367.
17. Captain Squires, this battery's commander, held a staff position at Gettysburg, and his one gun was attached to the Third Company during

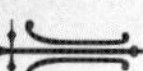

the fighting. *OR*, 27/2: 434; Charles W. Squires, "My Artillery Fire Was Very Destructive," *Civil War Times Illustrated*, June 1975, 20. Brown was wounded on July 3, and later taken prisoner at Gettysburg. Squires reassumed command of the battery afterwards. Charles H. C. Brown, CMSR, RG 109, M 320, Roll 63.

18. To add to these cannons, on the morning of July 3, 1863, Captain Richardson ordered off the field an abandoned 3" Ordnance Rifle from Consolidated Battery C & F, Independent Pennsylvania Artillery, Captain James Thompson commanding. *OR*, 27/2: 434. The one howitzer of this company was held in reserve under 1st Lieutenant George E. Apps and did not fire in the cannonade. Both 12-pounder Howitzers of the battalion (Second and Fourth Company) did fire after the Confederate infantry was repulsed. Lieutenant Apps commanded both these howitzers and was wounded at Gettysburg on July 3 as well as had a horse shot from under him. George E. Apps, CMSR, RG 109, M 320, Roll 62.

19. The Third Company also had and additional gun from Squires (Brown's Fourth Company).

20. Norcom was wounded July 3 by a piece of shell and left the field. Command of the battery fell to 1st Lieutenant Henry A. Battles. *OR*, 27/2: 434.

21. The 12-pounder Howitzer was held in reserve on July 3, 1863, and did not fire in the cannonade. *OR*, 27/2: 434-435. It did, however, fire after the repulse. See footnote # 18.

22. This battery had four total guns but the two Napoleons did not fire on July 3. *OR*, 27/2: 603.

23. Griffin's first name is often incorrectly listed as William. "Capt. Wiley Hunter Griffin," *Confederate Veteran* V (1897), 247-248; "Hunter Griffin's Career," *The Galveston Daily News*, November 25, 1896.

24. The armament for this battery is disputed. Major Latimer ordered this battery, which was normally part of the horse artillery, to the Confederate center. W. W. Goldsborough, *The Maryland Line in the Confederate Army 1861-1865* (Gaithersburg, MD, 1987), 285.

25. Brown replaced the wounded Stapleton Crutchfield, Jr., who lost his leg at Chancellorsville.

26. While this battery did have four total guns only three where in action on July 3. On gun was sent to the rear because of the lack of men and ammunition to service rifled guns. White, "*Contributions to the Richmond Howitzer Battalion,*" 206-207.

27. This battery is Dance's battery.

28. This battery was detached from the battalion and sent to Benner's Hill where it fired on July 3, 1863. *OR*, 27/2: 604-5.

29. This was Captain Abraham Hupp's battery.

30. Two Napoleons of this battery were held in reserve on July 2 and 3 and not engaged. *OR*, 27/2: 604.

31. Nelson's battalion was composed of three batteries at Gettysburg. According to the war department plaques only Milledge's battery of the battalion fired on July 3. Colonel Nelson stated in his report that the battalion fired only "…20 or 25 rounds…." *OR*, 27/2: 606.

32. Given the extended range of the Third Corps batteries to the Union defensive line it is doubtful any smoothbore howitzer assigned to A. P. Hill's Corps fired in the cannonade on July 3, 1863.

33 The battalion's permanently assigned commander was Lieutenant Colonel Allen S. Cutts. Cutts was absent during the Battle of Gettysburg and did not report back to the organization until July 15, 1863. *OR*, 27/2: 636. Some sources refer to this organization as Cutts's battalion.

34. The howitzer was detached and sent to General Wilcox on July 2, 1863. It is not known if it fired on July 3, 1863. *OR*, 27/2: 635.

35. Captain Wingfield's leg was bruised by a Union shell fragment on July 3, but he stayed in command of his battery. *OR*, 27/2: 636.

36. This battery was new to the battalion, being assigned to the command on June 21, 1863 at Berryville, VA. For detail related to the action of this battery at Gettysburg see the letter of Joseph Graham in "An Awful Affair," *Civil War Times Illustrated*, April 1984, 46-49.

37. The regular captain of this battery was James V. Brooke. He was not present at Gettysburg. Brooke resigned his commission on July 24, 1863 on account of an injury he received in 1862. He was also elected a representative from Fauquier County to the Virginia House of Delegates in May 1863. James V. Brooke, CMSR, RG 109, M 324, Roll 347.

38. Captain Hurt was wounded at Gettysburg but the specific day and nature of the wound is unknown. See Evans, *Confederate Military History*, 8: 317-318; Brewer, *Alabama: Her History, Resources, War Record, and Public Men*, 697. One Whitworth gun was damaged on July 1, 1863, by enemy fire and repaired. The gun broke again on July 3 after firing and was removed from the field. *OR*, 27/2: 675.

39. One 3" Rifle was damaged on July 1, 1863 and sent to the rear. *OR*, 27/2: 675.

40. Major William J. Pegram was ill right before the battle, but arrived for duty and assumed command of the battalion on June 30, 1863. Pegram's second in command, Captain Ervin B. Brunson, exercised command of the battalion during Pegram's absence, and filed the official report of the action at Gettysburg. *OR*, 27/2: 610, 639, 652.

41. Captain Crenshaw was in Europe at the time of the battle. 1st Lieutenant John H. Chamberlayne was in command of the battery until he was captured right before the battle of Gettysburg. John H. Chamberlayne, CMSR, RG 109, M 324, Roll 291. Chamberlyane was succeeded by 1st Lieutenant Andrew B. Johnston. "Annual Reunion of Pegram's Battalion," May 21, 1886, *Southern Historical Society Papers*, Vol. 14, 34.

42. Two 12-pounder Howitzers of this battery were not engaged on July 3. One gun of this battery was permanently disabled during the battle. *OR Supplement*, Part II, Record of Events, Vol. 70, Serial 82, 419.

43. When Pegram reported for duty June 30, 1863, it is likely Captain Brunson returned to his battery. Brunson was wounded at Gettysburg but the date is not known. Joseph Woods Brunson, *Pee Dee Light Artillery of Maxcy Gregg's (Later McGowan's) Brigade, First South Carolina Volunteers (Infantry) C.S.A. A Historical Sketch* (Auburn, AL, 1983), 28. On July 3, 1863 it is possible that Lieutenant William E. Zimmerman commanded this battery.

44. One gun was disabled on July 1, 1863. It may or may not have been repaired for July 3. *OR*, 27/II: 678.

45. The armament for this battery is disputed. According to the war department plaque located on the battlefield it contained the four guns listed above. The Battery may have used 3" Rifles instead of the Parrott Rifles at Gettysburg. It seems accounts vary on the types of rifles this battery possesses. See Robert K. Krick, *The Fredericksburg Artillery* (Lynchburg, VA, 1986), 51.

46. Sometime during the fighting at Gettysburg, "…one Napoleon gun [was] disabled and afterwards captured by the enemy while it was with the wagon train." *OR Supplement*, Part II, Record of Events, Vol. 70, Serial 82, 379.

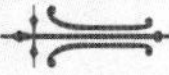

Notes

INTRODUCTION

1. "The Battle," *Compiler*, June 7, 1887.
2. Kathryn Jorgensen, "Gettysburg 150th Brings Thousands to Programs, Battlefield, Reenactments," *Civil War News* (August 2013), 10.

TOUR 1: CONFEDERATE BATTLE LINE

1. A.L. Long, *Memoirs of Robert E. Lee* (Secaucus, NJ, 1983), 292. A note regarding our use of unit designations (division, brigade, etc.) within this book. We have elected to capitalize the names of Confederate units when it refers to their formal designation and typically includes the name of the commanding officer (i.e. Pickett's Division, Armistead's Brigade.) Exceptions are made for artillery batteries that often had different official designations or when used differently in contemporary quotations. Official designations for the Army of the Potomac were typically numeric (i.e. Second Division) and we have not capitalized when we use an unofficial designation with an officer's name (i.e. Gibbon's division.)

STOP C1: General Robert E. Lee's Headquarters

2. The War of the Rebellion: A Compilation of the Official Records of the Union and Confederate Armies, 128 vols. (Washington, DC, 1880-1901), Series 1, Vol. 27, pt. 2, 318. Hereafter cited as *OR*. All references are to series 1 unless otherwise indicated.
3. James Longstreet, "Lee's Invasion of Pennsylvania," in Robert Underwood Johnson and Clarence Clough Buel, ed., *Battles and Leaders of the Civil War* (New York, 1956), Vol. 3, 246-247.
4. James Longstreet to Lafayette McLaws, July 25, 1873. Lafayette McLaws Papers #472, Southern Historical Collection, Wilson Library, University of North Carolina at Chapel Hill; William Allan, "Memoranda of Conversations with General Robert E. Lee," in Gary Gallagher, ed., *Lee: The Soldier* (Lincoln, NE, 1996), 15.
5. James Longstreet, "Lee's Right Wing at Gettysburg," in Robert Underwood Johnson and Clarence Clough Buel, ed., *Battles and Leaders of the Civil War (New York)*, Vol. 3, 339. It should be noted that Longstreet's recollections of this Seminary Ridge conversation are the only versions known to exist.
6. Several accounts besides Longstreet's support the notion that Lee was unusually "agitated" at Gettysburg. For example see the letter from Prussian observer Justus Scheibert, "Letter from Maj. Justus Scheibert, of the Prussian Royal Engineers," *Southern Historical Society Papers*, Vol. 5, 92. Also see Long, *Memoirs of Robert E. Lee*, 275. Colonel Armistead Long, Lee's military secretary, commented on Lee's "uneasiness" and he "exhibited a degree of anxiety and impatience, and expressed regret at the absence of the cavalry."
7. *OR*, 27/2: 318.
8. Ibid.
9. *OR*, 27/2: 320.
10. Douglas Southall Freeman, *Lee's Lieutenants: A Study in Command* (New York, 1944), Vol. 3, 140.
11. For example, Lee allegedly told William Allan in 1868, "victory would have been won if he could have gotten one decided simultaneous attack on the whole line. This he [Lee] tried his utmost to effect for three days, and failed. Ewell he could not get to act with decision…Then Longstreet & Hill & c. could not be gotten to act in concert." See Allan, "Memoranda of Conversations with General Robert E. Lee," 14.
12. *OR*, 27/2: 320. Artillerist Edward Porter Alexander argued that Lee's insistence upon continuing the attack showed that "the strongest features of the enemy's position were not yet apprehended." See Edward Porter Alexander, *Military Memoirs of a Confederate* (New York, 1907), 414.
13. *OR*, 27/2: 320.
14. Freeman, *Lee's Lieutenants*, 3: 144.
15. *OR*, 27/2: 359.
16. James Longstreet, "General James Longstreet's Account of the Campaign and Battle," reprinted from the *Philadelphia Weekly Times* in *Southern Historical Society Papers*, Vol. 5, 68.
17. James Longstreet, *From Manassas to Appomattox* (1992), 385-386.
18. *OR*, 27/2: 447.
19. Walter Taylor, "Memorandum by Colonel Walter H. Taylor, Of General Lee's Staff," *Southern Historical Society Papers*, Vol. 4, 84.
20. Edward Porter Alexander, "The Great Charge and Artillery Fighting at Gettysburg," *Battles and Leaders of the Civil War*, 3: 360-361.
21. David Callihan, "Neither Villain Nor Hero," *Gettysburg Magazine 26* (July 2002), *16*.
22. Long, *Memoirs of Robert E. Lee*, 287-288; Arthur Fremantle, *Three Months in the Southern States* (Lincoln, NE, 1991), 262.
23. Historians have debated how and when Lee learned of Wright's perceived success, but it is logical to assume Lee was aware of it. See Paul Cooksey, "The Plan for Pickett's Charge," *Gettysburg Magazine 22* (January 2000), 69-70 for a discussion.
24. Longstreet, "General James Longstreet's Account of the Campaign and Battle," 5: 68.
25. Ibid.
26. Longstreet, *From Manassas to Appomattox*, 387.
27. Long, *Memoirs of R.E. Lee*, 288.
28. *OR*, 27/2: 321.
29. *OR*, 27/2: 359.
30. Long, *Memoirs of Robert E. Lee*, 287-288.
31. *OR*, 27/2: 320; Long, *Memoirs of Robert E. Lee*, 293-294.
32. *OR*, 27/2: 320.
33. Ibid. Several other participant accounts support this understanding. For example, see the report of Brig. General William N. Pendleton, C. S. Army, Chief of Artillery, *OR*, 27/2: 352.

Sidebar C1: The Role of Confederate General J.E.B. Stuart's Cavalry

1. Henry Brainerd McClellan, *The Life and Campaigns of Major-General J.E.B Stuart, Commander of the Cavalry of the Army of Northern Virginia* (New York, 1885), 337.
2. William Brooke-Rawle, *Gregg's Cavalry Fight at Gettysburg. Historical Address Delivered October 15, 1884, Upon the Dedication of the Monumental Shaft Erected Upon the Site of the Cavalry Engagement on the Right Flank of the Army of the Potomac, July 3d, 1863, During the Battle of Gettysburg* (Philadelphia, 1884), 13.
3. *OR*, 27/2: 308-309.
4. *OR*, 27/2: 322.
5. *OR*, 27/2: 697.
6. *OR*, 27/2: 724.
7. For a thorough discussion on the fighting for East Cavalry Field, refer to Eric Wittenberg's *Protecting the Flank at Gettysburg: The Battles for Brinkerhoff's Ridge and East Cavalry Field, July 2-3, 1863* (Savas Beatie, 2013.)
8. McClellan, *Life and Campaigns of Major-General J.E.B. Stuart*, 338.
9. Mark Nesbitt, *Saber and Scapegoat: J.E.B. Stuart and the Gettysburg Controversy* (Mechanicsburg, PA, 1994), 96.
10. Eric J. Wittenberg and J. David Petruzzi, *Plenty of Blame to Go Around: Jeb Stuart's Controversial Ride to Gettysburg* (New York, 2006), 177, 276.
11. Wittenberg, *Protecting the Flanks*, 150; John W. Busey and David G. Martin, *Regimental Strengths and Losses at Gettysburg* (NJ, 2005), 245.
12. McClellan, *Life and Campaigns of Major-General J.E.B. Stuart*, 338-339.
13. William Styple, ed., *Generals in Bronze: Interviewing the Commanders of the Civil War* (Kearny, NJ, 2005), 258-259.

STOP C2: The Confederate Left Flank (David McMillan Farm)

1. Gregory A. Coco, *A Vast Sea of Misery* (Gettysburg, PA, 1988), 7; *Adams Sentinel*, August 25, 1863; Abdel Ross Wentz, *History of the Gettysburg Theological Seminary* (Philadelphia, PA, 1926), 204.
2. Margaret McMillan account, January 6, 1941, McMillan Farm File, Association of Licensed Battlefield Guides (ALBG), Gettysburg National Military Park (GNMP); "McMillan Woods Earthworks: Update," www.Gettysburgdaily.com, April 28, 2011.

C2A: Hill and Ewell's Artillery

3. *OR*, 27/2: 610.
4. Monroe F. Cockrell, ed. *Gunner with Stonewall: Reminiscences of William Thomas Poague* (Jackson, TN, 1957), 74. Poague's memoirs were written for family in 1903 and were clearly influenced by other post-war accounts and controversies. For example, Poague insisted Longstreet should have attacked "early in the morning" on July 2, echoing post-war claims of an anti-Longstreet faction comprised of artillery chief William N. Pendleton and others.
5. Captain Archibald Graham's battery of four 20-pounder Parrotts from Capt.

Willis Dance's battalion was detached here on both July 2 and July 3. Per Dance's report, Graham fired "occasionally upon the enemy with good effect." *OR*, 27/2: 604-605. Lt. Colonel William Nelson, who commanded a battalion in Ewell's reserve, reported that his batteries, "in connection" with Graham, fired "about 20 or 25 rounds" during the third afternoon. *OR*, 27/2: 605-606. These rounds were fired by Capt. John Milledge's Georgia Battery of three guns as per their War Department battlefield tablet. Finally, the tablet to Capt. Charles Raine's battery (also on Benner's Hill) states that their two 20-pounder Parrotts "were actively engaged in the great cannonade." Battalion commander R. Snowden Andrews did not record any firing from Raine in his report, and only acknowledged that Raine spent the morning in reserve and was ordered "to the front" during the "evening." *OR*, 27/2: 544. It should be noted, however, that Snowden Andrews was not actually present at Gettysburg.

6. *OR*, 27/2: 675.
7. *OR*, 27/2: 603. Carter's battalion consisted of four batteries under William P. P. Carter, R. C. M. Page, C. W. Fry, and William J. Reese. *OR*, 27/2: 545. Page's battery was not engaged and two additional Napoleons from William Carter were also held in reserve and not used. See *OR*, 27/2: 603.
8. McClellan, *Life and Campaigns of Major-General J.E.B. Stuart*, 338-339. Maryland artillerist Henry Haw Matthews told early Gettysburg National Park Commissioner William McKenna Robbins in 1903 that McClellan mistook the Baltimore Light for Jackson's Virginia Battery on East Cavalry Field. See Jaime Boyle and Robert Rehr, editors, *Journal of William McKenna Robbins* (Gettysburg, PA), 174. For information on Matthews, see Robert J. Trout, editor, *Memoirs of the Stuart Horse Artillery Battalion* (Knoxville, TN, 2010.)
9. W.W. Goldsborough, *The Maryland Line in the Confederate Army* (Baltimore, MD, 1900), 285; David and Audrey Ladd, editors, *The Bachelder Papers: Gettysburg in Their Own Words* (Dayton, OH, 1995), Vol. 2, 1250-1251, 1289. John F. Hayden told John Bachelder that they arrived on the evening of July 2 and were placed "about 200 yards" from the "left" of the pike. See Ladd, *Bachelder Papers*, 2: 1289.
10. Freeman, *Lee's Lieutenants*, 3: 178-179; Alexander, *Military Memoirs*, 419. Carter did assert that he successfully softened the Federal artillery: "The effect of this concentrated fire on that part of the line was obvious to all. Their fire slackened, and finally ceased. It was feebly resumed from a few guns when Pickett's and Hill's troops advanced, but the most destructive fire sustained by these troops came from the right and left of this salient." See *OR*, 27/2: 603. Alexander lamented Ewell and Hill's failure to place more batteries "in and near the town" to enfilade the Federal position but did not offer any suggestions on where such favorable positions might have been located. See Alexander, *Military Memoirs*, 419.
11. William S. White, *Contributions to a History of the Richmond Howitzer Battalion, Pamphlet No.2, A Diary of the War or What I Saw of It*, (Baltimore, MD, 2000), 206. Also see Philip Laino, *Gettysburg Campaign Atlas* (Dayton, OH, 2009), 317; John Michael Priest, *Into the Fight: Pickett's Charge at Gettysburg* (Shippensburg, PA, 1998), 186.
12. Colonel Alexander wrote that Walker had 60 Third Corps guns on Seminary Ridge to the Hagerstown (Fairfield Road), plus the two Whitworth rifles further north. Alexander added another 20 pieces and had four more positioned northeast of Cemetery Hill for Ewell. In Alexander's estimate, 41 rifles and Napoleons of the Second Corps and 15 in the Third Corps went unused. See Alexander, *Military Memoirs*, 419.

C2B: A.P. Hill's Infantry Left Flank

13. *OR*, 27/2: 666.
14. George Newton, "Brockenbrough's Virginia Brigade at Gettysburg," *Blue & Gray Magazine* (Vol. XXVII, No. 4), 44.
15. Newton, "Brockenbrough's Virginia Brigade at Gettysburg," 43-44; Larry Tagg, *The Generals of Gettysburg* (Cambridge, MA, 2003), 346-347.
16. Bradley M. Gottfried, *Brigades of Gettysburg* (Cambridge, MA, 2002), 621-623; Newton, "Brockenbrough's Virginia Brigade at Gettysburg," 45.
17. *OR*, 27/2: 669-670.
18. Gottfried, "To Fail Twice: Brockenbrough's Brigade at Gettysburg," *Gettysburg Magazine 23* (July 2000), 71.
19. *OR*, 27/2: 638.
20. Gottfried, "To Fail Twice,"72.
21. Newton, "Brockenbrough's Virginia Brigade at Gettysburg," 46.
22. *Supplement to the Official Records of the Union and Confederate Armies* (Wilmington, NC, 1995), Vol. 5, Serial 5, 415. Hereafter cited as *OR Supplement*. Richard Rollins cited Mayo as reporting "not more than 500 muskets." See Richard Rollins, *Pickett's Charge: Eyewitness Accounts* (Redondo Beach, CA, 1994), 259.
23. The debate amongst historians is not over whether Brockenbrough was present at Gettysburg (he was), but whether he led his troops in combat on July 3. In submitting the report, Mayo wrote that Brockenbrough "commanded" the brigade "in the recent engagements... at Gettysburg" but does not record any further specific actions by Brockenbrough on July 3. (In contrast, Mayo does reference Brockenbrough on the field on July 1.) See *OR Supplement*, Part I, Reports, Vol. 5, Serial 15, 415. Douglas Southall Freeman wrote, "On the 3rd, for reasons that do not appear in the records, the Brigade was commanded by Col. Robert Mayo of the 47th Virginia." Freeman was aware of Mayo's report, but apparently did not physically see it since it was not published as part of the ORs. See Freeman, *Lee's Lieutenant's*, 3: 185, including n. 83. Also see Newton, "Brockenbrough's Virginia Brigade at Gettysburg," 46.
24. Newton, "Brockenbrough's Virginia Brigade at Gettysburg," 44-46.
25. *OR Supplement*, Part I, Reports, Vol. 5, Serial 15, 415; Rollins, *Eyewitness Accounts*, 258; Newton, "Brockenbrough's Virginia Brigade at Gettysburg," 46.

Sidebar C2: Longstreet's Command of Hill's Troops

1. *OR*, 27/2: 666.
2. Longstreet, *From Manassas to Appomattox*, 388.
3. Donald Bridgman Sanger, *General James Longstreet and the Civil War* (Chicago, 1934), 19.
4. Thomas W. Cutrer, ed., *Longstreet's Aide: The Civil War Letters of Major Thomas J. Goree* (Charlottesville, VA, 1995), 168; Freeman, *Lee's Lieutenants*, 3: 147, 185.
5. Jeffry D. Wert, *Gettysburg Day Three* (New York, 2001), 128; Sanger, "General James Longstreet," 18.
6. Callihan, "Neither Villain Nor Hero," 18-19.

STOP C3: Pettigrew and Trimble's Battle Line (North Carolina State Memorial)

1. Frederick W. Hawthorne, *Gettysburg: Stories of Men and Monuments As Told by Battlefield Guides* (Gettysburg, PA, 1988), 36.
2. *OR*, 27/2: 320.
3. *OR*, 27/2: 608.
4. T.M.R. Talcott, "The Third Day At Gettysburg," *Southern Historical Society Papers*, Vol. 41, 40.
5. Cockrell, *Gunner with Stonewall*, 70; Tagg, *Generals of Gettysburg*, 343-344.
6. Birkett Fry, "Pettigrew's Charge at Gettysburg," *Southern Historical Society Papers*, Vol. 7, 92. Capt. Benjamin Little of the 52nd North Carolina wrote that Lee, Longstreet, Hill, and several other officers "met in a shady bottom near a little branch. Lee sat on a stump, was reading a paper of some kind a long time before the action." See Little account, 52nd North Carolina Infantry File, ALBG, GNMP.
7. *OR*, 27/2: 666.
8. Tagg, *The Generals of Gettysburg*, 328-330.
9. Rollins, *Eyewitness Accounts*, 251; Trimble quoted in James Lane, "Letter from General James H. Lane," *Southern Historical Society Papers*, Vol. 5, 43.
10. Marshall was born April 17, 1839. Charles D. Walker, *Biographical Sketches of the Graduates and Eleves of the Virginia Military Institute Who Fell During the War Between the States* (Philadelphia, PA, 1875), 369.
11. *OR*, 27/2: 650.
12. *OR*, 27/2: 671.
13. Rollins, *Eyewitness Accounts*, 269; Freeman, *Lee's Lieutenants*, 3: 150.
14. Michael C. Hardy, *North Carolina Remembers Gettysburg* (Gettysburg, PA, 2011), 68.
15. *OR*, 27/2: 621.
16. *OR*, 27/2: 633-634.
17. A.T. Watts, "Something More About Gettysburg," *Confederate Veteran* VI (1898), 67.
18. *OR*, 27/2: 663, 668-669.
19. Busey and Martin, *Strengths and Losses*, 302.
20. William H. Swallow, "The Third Day at Gettysburg," *Southern Bivouac*, Vol.1, No. 9, 565.
21. Ibid.
22. Rollins, *Eyewitness Accounts*, 270.
23. Fry, "Pettigrew's Charge," 7: 93.
24. Lt. Colonel S. G. Shepard, 7th Tennessee Infantry, reported for Archer's Brigade: "There was a space of a few hundred yards between the right of Archer's brigade and the left of General Pickett's division when we advanced," and the lines were not "an exact continuation of each other." See *OR*, 27/2: 647.

C3B: 11th Mississippi Infantry Regimental Monument

25. Busey and Martin, *Strengths and Loses,* 299. Busey and Martin's study arrived at a much higher total strength of 592. Sources are unclear on the precise regimental alignment of Davis's Brigade. Modern secondary sources most frequently cite Baxter McFarland, who was a member of the 11th Mississippi regiment until June 1863 and by his own admission was not at Gettysburg. McFarland wrote that the 11th Mississippi was on the brigade's left, the 55th North Carolina on the right, and "the 2nd and 42nd Mississippi regiments in the center." McFarland did not specify, however, which of the two regiments was in the left center and which was in the right center. See Baxter McFarland, "The Eleventh Mississippi Regiment at Gettysburg," *Publications of the Mississippi Historical Society* (Jackson, MS, 1918), 549 – 550.
26. Steven R. Davis, "Ole Miss' Spirited University Greys Left Their Quiet University Campus for the War's Worst Battlefields," *America's Civil War* (March 1992), 71-72.

C3C: Tennessee State Memorial

27. The Maryland State Monument was dedicated in 1994 and although they contributed troops to both sides at Gettysburg, Maryland never joined the Confederacy and are not counted as such here.

Sidebar C3: Strength of Pettigrew and Trimble's Divisions?

1. *OR*, 25/2: 798-799. Also see Wayne Motts, "A Brave and Resolute Force," *North & South* (June 1999), 28-34 for another discussion regarding July 3 strengths and losses.
2. All strength and casualty figures are from Busey and Martin, *Strengths and Losses*, 297-300 unless noted otherwise.
3. *OR*, 27/2: 667. Lane reported 660 total casualties.
4. *OR*, 27/2: 671.
5. Busey and Martin, *Strengths and Losses*, 304-305.
6. William Swallow estimated 7,500 men. See Swallow, 565. John Michael Priest, in his modern study, created some controversy by estimating Pettigrew's strength downward to 3,819 and Trimble's to 1,916 for a total of 5,735. This broke down by brigade-level as follows: Fry (900), Marshall (1,205), Davis (1,143), Brockenbrough (500), Lane (1,076), and Lowrance (840) with each summing to some negligible differences from the grand totals. See Priest, 199. As will be discussed again with Pickett's strengths, researcher John Busey has also acknowledged nearly all estimates of engaged Confederate strengths and losses are purely speculative for a variety of reasons. See Busey and Martin, 159-168.

STOP C4: Virginia State Memorial

1. Hawthorne, *Stories of Men and Monuments*, 38.
2. Kathy Georg Harrison and John W. Busey, *Nothing But Glory: Pickett's Division at Gettysburg* (Gettysburg, PA, 1993), 119-120.
3. Walter Harrison, *Pickett's Men: A Fragment of War History* (Baton Rouge, LA, 2000), 86-88. Charles Loehr, 1st Virginia later wrote: "Pickett's men could have gone into battle on the previous evening, when they reached Gettysburg. They were in fine condition. The march from Chambersburg did not fatigue them at all. Anyone who will visit Gettysburg battlefield will see the truth of these views." See Charles Loehr, "The Old First Virginia at Gettysburg," *Southern Historical Society Papers*, Vol. 32, 40. John Dooley wrote that the men understood Pickett had made "representations…regarding the jaded condition of his men, we are allowed a respite of a few hours…" See Joseph T. Durkin, ed., *John Dooley Confederate Soldier: His War Journal* (1963), 101.
4. *OR*, 27/2: 320. At least one writer, and probably others, has taken the extreme position that the July 3 assault and Pickett's selection were specifically undertaken because "Lee thought that it would be dishonorable and disgraceful to his native state of Virginia if her troops were not prominent in this battle." Henry J. Greenberg, "Pickett's Charge: The Reason Why," *Gettysburg Magazine 5* (July 1991), 104.
5. Longstreet, *From Manassas to Appomattox*, 385-386.
6. *OR Supplement*, Part I, Vol. 5, Serial 5, 332; *OR*, 27/2: 999.
7. Harrison, *Pickett's Men*, 90-91.
8. *OR*, 27/2: 359.
9. *OR*, 27/2: 385. Little of note must have occurred during the morning halt as Southern accounts often short-hand or ignore this stop completely. See, for example, John Holmes Smith, "Captain John Holmes Smith's Account," *Southern Historical Society Papers*, Vol. 32, 190.
10. Harrison, *Nothing But Glory*, 13-14.
11. Wayne Motts, *Trust in God and Fear Nothing (Gettysburg, PA, 1994)*, 42.
12. Harrison, *Pickett's Men*, 92. One may reasonably question the accuracy of Harrison's recollections and whether Longstreet actually intended for Pickett's three brigades to advance in one line.
13. Harrison, *Nothing But Glory*, 17.
14. Harrison, *Pickett's Men*, 91.

Sidebar C4.1: Major General George Pickett

1. Longstreet quoted in LaSalle Corbell Pickett, *Pickett and his Men* (Philadelphia, PA, 1913), IX.
2. Moxley G. Sorrel, *At the Right Hand of Longstreet: Recollections of a Confederate Staff Officer* (Lincoln, NE, 1999), 54.
3. Harrison, *Pickett's Men*, 64; Edward G. Longacre, *Pickett: Leader of the Charge* (Shippensburg, PA, 1995), 3-6.
4. Sorrell, *At the Right Hand of Longstreet*, 54.
5. Harrison, *Pickett's Men*, 64; Pickett, *Pickett and His Men*, 6; Longacre, *Pickett: Leader of the Charge*, 26.
6. Longacre, *Pickett: Leader of the Charge*, 30, 40-41, 45-49; Pickett, *Pickett and His Men*, 22-25. Information on James Pickett contained in "Pickett" file, ALBG, GNMP. An undated copy of records from Riverview Cemetery (Portland, Oregon) lists James Pickett's birth date as December 31, 1857 and his date of death as August 28, 1889. Also see correspondence of Mrs. James Tarte to Barbara Schutt, October 31, 1972 and *Shelton-Mason County Journal*, October 28, 1976 in "Pickett" File, ALBG, GNMP.
7. One account, whose credibility has been questioned by some, had him "bewailing himself" and declaring the wound to be mortal. Longacre, *Pickett: Leader of the Charge*, 85-87; Pickett, *Pickett's Men*, 93-94.
8. *OR*, 19/2: 683; Longacre, *Pickett: Leader of the Charge*, 91-93.
9. Sorrell, *At the Right Hand of Longstreet*, 54.
10. Richard F. Selcer, *Lee vs. Pickett: Two Divided by War* (Gettysburg, PA, 1998), 20-24, 27; *OR*, 18: 1090-1091.
11. Longacre, *Pickett: Leader of the Charge*, 111.
12. John B. Jones, *A Rebel War Clerk's Diary* (Philadelphia, PA, 1866), Vol. 2, 196-197.
13. Eppa Hunton, *Autobiography of Eppa Hunton* (Richmond, VA, 1933), 126; Selcer, *Lee vs. Pickett*, 1, 4-6.
14. Longacre, *Pickett: Leader of the Charge*, 31-33.
15. Sorrel, *At the Right Hand of Longstreet*, 155-156.
16. Hunton, *Autobiography*, 127.
17. Pickett, *Pickett and His Men*, 37-38; Longacre, *Pickett: Leader of the Charge*, 6-7. LaSalle published a collection of Pickett's alleged letters in 1913 under the title, *The Heart of a Soldier*. For an assessment on why these letters are considered to be unreliable and not the work of General Pickett himself, see Gary Gallagher, "A Widow and Her Soldier," *The Virginia Magazine of History*, Vol. 94, No. 3 (July 1986), 329-344.
18. Jan Vanderheiden, "Who Buried the Children?" *The Longstreet Society*, http://www.longstreet.org/children.html.
19. Longacre, *Pickett: Leader of the Charge*, 125-127; George R. Stewart, *Pickett's Charge: A Microhistory of the Final Attack at Gettysburg, July 3, 1863* (Boston, MA, 1959), 256. For a discussion of the reported variances in Pickett's reply see Selcer, *Lee vs. Pickett*, 115, n. 35.
20. *OR*, 27/3: 986-987.
21. Loehr, "The Old First Virginia at Gettysburg," 32: 36-38.
22. *OR*, 27/3: 1075. For discussions of Pickett's "lost" report, see Richard E. Selcer, "Re-Creating Pickett's Lost Gettysburg Report," *Columbiad: A Quarterly Review of the War Between the States* (1998), Vol. 1, no. 4, 93-121; Henry Clay McDougal, *Recollections, 1844-1909* (Kansas City, MO, 1910), 376-377.
23. See Hunton, *Autobiography*, 126-127. Hunton "unquestionably" thought Pickett had been relieved based on information obtained from Taylor and Fitzhugh Lee. Mosby wrote that he had heard the story of Pickett being ordered under arrest from Charles Venable in 1892. See John S. Mosby, "Personal Recollections of General Lee," *Munsey's Magazine*, Vol. 45, No. 1, 68-69.
24. LaSalle Corbell Pickett, *What Happened to Me* (New York, 1917), 281.
25. Mosby, "Personal Recollections of General Lee," 68-69.

Sidebar C4.2: Strength of Pickett's Division?

1. Before engaging in further speculation on the number of Confederates engaged, it may be useful to recall the work of noted researcher John Busey. Busey and David Martin's work in estimating Gettysburg's strengths and losses are considered to

be as nearly definitive as possible by most serious students. In determining the Confederate strengths engaged at Gettysburg, Busey was forced to deal with incomplete returns and missing records and then applied a standard ratio to calculate available strength engaged based on one actual existing ratio from Doles's Brigade of Rodes's Division. The intent of this is not to criticize Busey's methodology, but to remind readers that certain questions will never be answered with definitive certainty when the original data is simply lost. Diligent researchers can often only apply their best theories. See Busey and Martin, *Strengths and Losses*, 159-165.

2. Ibid., 167.
3. *OR*, 27/3: 910.
4. Harrison, *Pickett's Men*, 90.
5. Fremantle, *Three Months in the Southern States*, 263.
6. James Longstreet, "The Mistakes of Gettysburg," in *The Annals of the War: Written by Leading Participants North and South* (Dayton, OH, 1988), 632.
7. Rollins, *Eyewitness Accounts*, 139.
8. David E. Johnston, *The Story of a Confederate Boy in the Civil War* (Portland, OR, 1914), 202.
9. *OR*, 27/2: 387.
10. *OR*, 27/2: 291.
11. *OR*, 27/2: 363.
12. Busey and Martin, *Strengths and Losses*, 159-165.
13. Stewart, *Pickett's Charge*, 90-91. Stewart believed that 10,500 men comprised Pickett, Pettigrew, and Trimble's columns with another 1,400 for Wilcox and Perry.
14. Busey and Martin, *Strengths and Losses*, 184.
15. Harrison, *Nothing But Glory*, 4.
16. Ibid., 451-467. Busey acknowledged that his *Strengths and Losses* estimate of 5,474 engaged was simply too low based on continued analysis. See *Nothing But Glory*, 172-173. Our strength estimates table for Busey's *Nothing But Glory* does not include 10 men assigned to division staff.
17. For examples of the 5,830 number put forward in recent battle histories: Stephen Sears wrote that Pickett could "put but 5,830 men on the battle line." Stephen Sears, *Gettysburg*, (New York, 2003), 383. Jeffry Wert's "slightly more than 5,800 officers and men in the ranks." Wert, *Gettysburg Day 3*, 106. Noah Trudeau came to 5,820 infantrymen. Noah Andre Trudeau. *Gettysburg: A Testing of Courage* (New York, 2002), 584. John Michael Priest also noted 5,820 "present." Priest, *Into the Fight*, 199. All are referencing the same sources: Busey and Harrison. See notes for Sears, 578 (n. 9), Priest, 252 (n. 1-3), and Wert, 344 (n. 49) as examples.
18. A more generous 1,300 yard continuous front for Garnett and Kemper would bring the infantry to 5,400 plus 325 skirmishers for a total of 5,725. But this would require a nearly continuous line from the fence that currently runs north of the Virginia monument to the Sherfy farm. Some allotment needs to be made for a break in the lines between Garnett and Kemper's two brigades.
19. Johnston, *A Confederate Boy*, 207.
20. Scott Bowden and Bill Ward, *Last Chance for Victory: Robert E. Lee and the Gettysburg Campaign* (Cambridge, MA, 2001), 38, 44.
21. *OR*, 27/3: 910.
22. *OR*, 27/3: 944-945. See *OR*, 27/3: 925-926, 931 for examples of Lee's attempts to obtain more men from Richmond. Also see Bowden and Ward, *Last Chance for Victory*, 99-101.

STOP C5: Support of Wilcox and Lang's Brigades (Wilcox Brigade Tablet and Florida State Memorial)

1. *OR*, 27/2: 359.
2. Stuart Dempsey, "The Florida Brigade at Gettysburg," *Blue & Gray Magazine* (Vol. XXVII, No. 4), 25.
3. *OR*, 27/2: 619-620. Wilcox wrote in an 1877 letter: "About 10 A.M. Pickett's Division arrived and formed in line nearly parallel with the pike, his center brigade [sic] directly in rear of Wilcox's Brigade." See Cadmus Wilcox, "Letter from General C. M. Wilcox, March 26th, 1877," *Southern Historical Society Papers*, Vol. 4, 116.
4. *OR*, 27/2: 632.
5. Dempsey, "Florida Brigade at Gettysburg," *Blue & Gray*, 25.
6. *OR*, 27/2: 620.
7. Totals in the accompanying table are from Busey and Martin, *Strengths and Losses*, 307-308. Lang wrote in his report that 300 of his 455 reported casualties were actually suffered on July 2. See *OR*, 27/2: 632-633. Wilcox's estimate of 1,200 on July 3 would then also presume that the majority of his losses occurred on the second.
8. Rollins, *Eyewitness Accounts*, p. 154; Alexander, *Military Memoirs*, 425-432.
9. Fremantle, *Three Months in the Southern States*, 265-266; Rollins, *Eyewitness Accounts*, 142. Fremantle was a captain in the Coldstream Guards and brevet lieutenant colonel in the British army. See Gallagher intro to *Three Months in Southern States*, viii.
10. Rollins, *Eyewitness Accounts*, 142.
11. Ibid.; *OR*, 27/2: 619-620.
12. Wilcox, "General C. M. Wilcox Letter," 4: 117. Author Richard Rollins supposed that Wilcox's delay was intentional and their lag, in fact, was perfectly within the definition of "reinforcement." See Richard Rollins, "The Second Wave of Pickett's Charge," *Gettysburg Magazine* 18 (January 1998), 102.
13. *OR*, 27/2: 632.
14. Dempsey, "Florida Brigade at Gettysburg," 26.
15. Edward Porter Alexander, "Letter from General E. P. Alexander, March 17, 1877," *Southern Historical Society Papers*, Vol. 4, 109.
16. Edward Porter Alexander, "The Great Charge and Artillery Fighting at Gettysburg, " in Robert U. Johnson and Clarence C. Buel, *Battles and Leaders of the Civil War*, Vol. 3, 366-367.
17. *OR*, 27/2: 620.

C5B: Dearing's Artillery Battalion

18. Joseph Mayo, "Pickett's Charge at Gettysburg," *Southern Historical Society Papers*, Vol. 34, 329.
19. Ezra J. Warner, *Generals in Gray: Lives of the Confederate Commanders* (Baton Rouge, LA, 1959), 69-70.

C5C: Eshleman's Artillery Battalion

20. Hawthorne, *Men and Monuments*, 40.

Sidebar C5: Connected with the Rebel Army

1. "Gettysburg History of Town Lots," Adams County Historical Society (ACHS), Lot #72E, Eliza Harper (1863), n.p. Also see William Frassanito, *Early Photography at Gettysburg* (Gettysburg, 1995), 370. Frank is listed as being 8 years-old on the 1850 census and his tombstone in Culpeper, VA, lists his birth date as May 13, 1842. The Hoffman's Gettysburg residence was torn down about 1940. At the time of this writing, the property was the site of a Credit Union at 105 Chambersburg Street.
2. Francis W. Hoffman, Compiled Military Service Record (CMSR), Record Group (RG) 109, Microfilm (M) 382, Roll 27. All references to CMSR are from the National Archives, Washington, DC; Michael J. Andrus, *The Brooke, Fauquier, Loudoun and Alexandria Artillery* (Lynchburg, VA, 1990), 112.
3. Busey and Martin, *Strengths and Losses*, 275.
4. Frassanito, *Early Photography*, 370; Robert N. Hoffman, CMSR, RG 109, M 324, Roll 376.
5. "Gettysburg History of Town Lots," ACHS, Lot #72E; Frassanito, *Early Photography*, 370.
6. Emily G. Ramey and John K. Gott, *The Years of Anguish: Fauquier County, Virginia, 1861-1865* (Fauquier, VA, 1965), 196; "Frank W. Hoffman Dead," *The Culpeper Eaponent*, October 14, 1920.

STOP C6: The Peach Orchard

1. *OR*, 27/2: 320.
2. James Longstreet, "Letter from General Longstreet," *Southern Historical Society Papers*, Vol. 5, 52-53. This letter was addressed to Colonel Walton and dated November 6, 1877. Brigadier General William N. Pendleton, Confederate Chief of Artillery, noted in his report that Alexander was "placed here in charge [of Confederate batteries on the right] by General Longstreet." *OR*, 27/2: 352.
3. Alexander, "Artillery Fighting at Gettysburg," 3: 360.
4. Ibid. Richardson's battery monument on West Confederate Avenue gives some insight into these movements. It states: "The Napoleons took position before daylight north of the Peach Orchard but moved at dawn further northward and West of Emmitsburg Road."
5. *OR*, 27/2: 351-352.
6. Alexander, "Artillery Fighting at Gettysburg," 3: 360-362; Alexander, *Military Memoirs*, 420. Alexander added fuel to historians who debate Lee's objectives as the clump of trees vs. Cemetery Hill when he wrote in *Military Memoirs* (418): "A clump of trees in the enemy's line was pointed out to me as the proposed point of our attack, which I was incorrectly told was the cemetery of the town."
7. Our principal source for placement of Confederate batteries is John Bachelder's "July 3 Troop Position Map," but see our "Engaged Confederate Artillery Order of Battle" for additional comments and adjustments.
8. Alexander, "The Great Charge and Artillery Fighting," 3: 362.
9. Longstreet, *From Manassas to Appomattox*, 390.

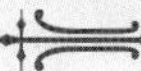

10. Miller quoted in Alexander, "The Great Charge and Artillery Fighting," 3: 362. A note in the William Storrick Collection, Box 1, A-D, Artillery at Gettysburg Folder, ACHS, states that Miller's battery position was "275 feet at right angles from the centre of the Emmitsburg Road at a point near John [sic] Sherfy's barn. 570 feet north-easterly from the centre of the Wheatfield Road near the 68th Pa. monument. 445 feet from the iron marker U.S. marker [sic.] Said marker being 350 feet S.E. of the 105th Pa. monument. Authority of Lieut. Hero. General Alexander marks this position 40 feet in advance, 6 A.M. to 1 P.M. July 3rd, 1863."
11. Harrison, *Nothing but Glory*, 132-133.
12. Fremantle, *Three Months in the Southern States*, 262; John P. Nicholson, ed., *Pennsylvania at Gettysburg* (Harrisburg, PA, 1914), Vol. 2, 606, 612; Kathleen Georg, "The Sherfy Farm and the Battle of Gettysburg" (NPS, 1977), 25.
13. Thomas Desjardin, *Stand Firm Ye Boys From Maine* (Gettysburg, PA, 1995), 102.

TOUR 2: PETTIGREW – TRIMBLE CHARGE

1. Rollins, *Eyewitness Accounts*, 277.

STOP PT1: North Carolina State Memorial

2. Swallow, "Third Day at Gettysburg," 564.
3. Rollins, *Eyewitness Accounts*, 257.
4. Ibid., 277.
5. Ibid., 269-270.
6. Hardy, *North Carolina Remembers Gettysburg*, 31.
7. Ibid., 40.
8. *OR*, 27/2: 644, 651; Rollins, *Eyewitness Accounts*, 277; Swallow, "Third Day at Gettysburg," 567.
9. Fry, "Pettigrew's Charge," 7: 92-93.
10. *OR*, 27/2: 643-644, 650-651.
11. Stewart, *Pickett's Charge*, 179-180. Author George R. Stewart speculated rather directly that Davis's men had lost their nerve. See Stewart, 180.
12. Ibid., 180.
13. Ladd, *Bachelder Papers*, 3: 1800.

STOP PT2: Bliss Farm

1. Charles D. Page, *History of the Fourteenth Regiment, Connecticut Vol. Infantry* (Meriden, CT, 1906), 144.
2. New Jersey Gettysburg Battlefield Commission, *Final Report of the Gettysburg Battlefield Commission of New Jersey* (Trenton, NJ, 1891), 108.
3. John Archer, *Fury on the Bliss Farm* (Gettysburg, PA, 2012), 43, 48-49.
4. Ibid., 50-51.
5. Page, *History of the 14th Regiment*, 144-145; Archer, *Fury on the Bliss Farm*, 56-57.
6. *OR*, 27/1: 454; Page, *History of the 14th Regiment*, 146-147.
7. *Battlefield Commission of New Jersey*, 108. There was, not surprisingly, controversy over who burned the property before Bachelder accorded the honor to the 14th Connecticut. See Page, *History of the 14th Regiment*, 147-148. Also see the detailed account of the 14th's Theodore Ellis in *Bachelder Papers*, 1: 406-407. Major Hill, 12th New Jersey, for example insisted it was artillery fire from Arnold's battery that set the structures ablaze. For several eyewitness accounts from members of the 12th New Jersey regarding the Bliss farm, see *Battlefield Commission of New Jersey*, 108-117.
8. Elwood Christ, "Struggle for the Bliss Farm," http://www.gettysburgdaily.com/?page_id=4475.

PT2A: Bliss Farm Monuments to the 12th New Jersey, 14th Connecticut, and 1st Delaware

9. Hawthorne, *Stories of Men and Monuments*, 126.
10. Christ, "Struggle for the Bliss Farm," http://www.gettysburgdaily.com/?page_id=4475.
11. Archer, *Fury on the Bliss Farm*, 38.
12. *Battlefield Commission of New Jersey*, 22-23.
13. Christ, "Struggle for the Bliss Farm," http://www.gettysburgdaily.com/?page_id=4475.
14. *Battlefield Commission of New Jersey*, 108.
15. *OR*, 27/1: 750.
16. *OR*, 27/2: 666.

STOP PT3: Long Lane

1. Archer, *Fury on the Bliss Farm*, 35.
2. Newton, "Brockenbrough's Virginia Brigade at Gettysburg," 46.
3. Hardy, *North Carolina Remembers Gettysburg*, 45; Rollins, *Eyewitness Accounts*, 254.
4. Hardy, *North Carolina Remembers Gettysburg*, 31.
5. Turner is referred to as a lieutenant in some accounts, however he was appointed a major on May 3, 1863 and transferred to a Field and Staff position. Weymouth T. Jordan, compiler, *North Carolina Troops 1861-1865: A Roster* (Raleigh, NC, 2004), Vol. IV, 405.
6. Rollins, *Eyewitness Accounts*, 261. It has been argued that the 7th North Carolina's position on the right of Lane's line would have been too far to the right to have been impacted by Brockenbrough's men and that Turner was witnessing other stragglers from Pettigrew's front. See Bruce Trinque, "Confederate Battle Flags in the July 3rd Charge," *Gettysburg Magazine 21* (July 1999), 111.
7. Rollins, *Eyewitness Accounts*, 259. Christian was aware of criticism "that we gave back too quickly" and thought it "would be far more correct if it had been that we delayed starting too long."
8. Ibid.
9. Busey and Martin, *Strengths and Losses*, 289, 291-293, 303. Note that if we use the casualties as reported in *OR*, 27/2: 338-346, we achieve approximately 500 less casualties or 500 more men available.
10. *OR*, 27/2: 556, 598.
11. Rollins, "The Second Wave of Pickett's Charge," 105.
12. *OR*, 27/2: 668-669.
13. Rollins, *Eyewitness Accounts*, 254.
14. *OR*, 27/2: 663.
15. Page, *History of the 14th Regiment*, 145.
16. Both accounts, along with portions of the 35th Georgia Regimental History and including the passage quoted above, are on file in the 35th Georgia Infantry File, ALBG, GNMP. Also see Rollins, "The Second Wave of Pickett's Charge," 106.
17. *OR*, 27/2: 556-557. See also the reports of Brig. General S. D. Ramseur, Col. J. M. Hall, and Maj. Eugene Blackford which describe the day's artillery and skirmish activity in Rodes's front. *OR*, 27/2: 588, 596, 598.

STOP PT4: 8TH Ohio

1. Franklin Sawyer, *The Eighth Ohio at Gettysburg* (OH, 1887), 4-6.
2. Rollins, *Eyewitness Accounts*, 296.
3. Sawyer, *8th Ohio at Gettysburg*, 5-6.
4. *OR*, 27/1: 461-462.
5. Sawyer, *8th Ohio at Gettysburg*, 7.
6. Rollins, *Eyewitness Accounts*, 296.
7. Sawyer, *8th Ohio at Gettysburg*, 7.
8. Newton, "Brockenbrough's Virginia Brigade at Gettysburg," 46.
9. Ibid.
10. Newton, "Brockenbrough's Virginia Brigade at Gettysburg," 46; Laino, *Gettysburg Campaign Atlas*, 343; New York Monuments Commission for the Battlefields of Gettysburg and Chattanooga, *Final Report on the Battle of Gettysburg* (Albany, NY, 1902), Vol.2, 907-908. Hereafter cited as *New York at Gettysburg*.
11. Sawyer, *8th Ohio at Gettysburg*, 7-8; *OR*, 27/1: 462; Busey and Martin, *Strengths and Losses*, 42.
12. Sawyer, *8th Ohio at Gettysburg*, 1, 9.
13. Ibid., 9.
14. See Keith Snipes, "The Improper Placement of the 8th Ohio Monument," *Gettysburg Magazine 35* (July 2006), 68-93.
15. Ibid., 79.
16. Ladd, *Bachelder Papers*, 2: 1132-33; Snipes, "The Improper Placement of the 8th Ohio Monument," 87.
17. Francis A. Walker, *History of the Second Army Corps* (New York, 1887), 294; also in Thomas M. Aldrich, *The History of Battery A: First Regiment Rhode Island Light Artillery in the War to Preserve the Union 1861-1865* (Providence, RI, 1904), 218.

STOP PT5: 26th North Carolina Regimental Monument

1. Bruce Trinque, "Arnold's Battery and the 26th North Carolina," *Gettysburg Magazine 12* (January 1995), 62-67; Trinque, "Confederate Battle Flags," 110.
2. Busey and Martin, *Strengths and Losses*, 298.
3. Robert Himmer, "Col. Hugh Reid Miller, 42nd Mississippi Volunteers, and the Pickett-Pettigrew-Trimble Assault," *Gettysburg Magazine 35* (July 2006), 58, 60; Terrence J. Winschel, "Heavy Was Their Loss: Joe Davis' Brigade at Gettysburg," *Gettysburg Magazine 3* (July 1990), 83; *OR*, 27/2: 651.
4. F. Lewis Marshall Letter, VMI Archives Manuscript #0165; Hardy, *North Carolina Remembers Gettysburg*, 33. Marshall may have been struck by two bullets. Walker, *Biographical Sketches*, 372.
5. *OR*, 27/2: 647-648.
6. Fry, "Pettigrew's Charge," 7: 93.
7. Rollins, *Eyewitness Accounts*, 251.
8. Hardy, *North Carolina Remembers Gettysburg*, 44-45.
9. Ibid., 31.
10. Ibid., 51; Rollins, *Eyewitness Accounts*, 261-262.
11. Hardy, *North Carolina Remembers Gettysburg*, 46, 56.
12. *OR*, 27/2: 666-667. In another account, Lane claimed that a staff officer from

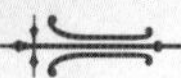

Longstreet arrived with orders to "move by brigade rapidly to the left, as the enemy had thrown out a flanking force in that direction." Lane gave the order but a colonel in the 33rd North Carolina replied, "My God General, do you intend rushing your men into such a place unsupported, when the troops on the right are falling back?" Lane agreed it would be a "useless" sacrifice and ordered his men to fall back. See Rollins, *Eyewitness Accounts*, 254.

13. Rollins, *Eyewitness Accounts*, 252.
14. Ibid., 271.
15. Trinque, "Confederate Battle Flags," 111-112, 116-118.

Sidebar PT5: Farthest to the Front at Gettysburg

1. Robert A. Bright, "Pickett's Charge at Gettysburg," *Confederate Veteran* XXXVIII (1930), 264.
2. Hunton, *Autobiography*, 93-94.
3. Rollins, *Eyewitness Accounts*, 148.
4. Carol Reardon, "Pickett's Charge: The Convergence of History and Myth in the Southern Past," in Gary Gallagher, ed., *The Third Day at Gettysburg and Beyond* (Chapel Hill, NC, 1994), 62.
5. Edward A. Pollard, *The Second Year of the War* (New York, 1864), 282; Reardon, "Pickett's Charge," 65.
6. Edward A. Pollard, *The Lost Cause: A New Southern History of the War of the Confederates* (New York, 1867), 410.
7. William Swinton, *Campaigns of the Army of the Potomac* (New York, 1882), 358-359. Swinton had obtained Longstreet's cooperation in his reconstruction of the campaign, and it is interesting to speculate if Swinton was also relaying Longstreet's opinions regarding the charge. For Swinton's acknowledgements to Longstreet, see notes on 340, 358.
8. "Obituary: Gen. George E. Pickett," *New York Times*, July 31, 1875.
9. Walter Taylor, "Second Paper by Walter Taylor," in *Southern Historical Society Papers*, Vol. 4, 132-135.
10. Hardy, *North Carolina Remembers Gettysburg*, 60-61.
11. Newton, "Brockenbrough's Virginia Brigade at Gettysburg," 47.
12. William R. Bond, *Pickett or Pettigrew? An Historical Essay* (Scotland Neck, NC, 1900), 10-14, 18, 34, 36, 60, 64.
13. Reardon, "Pickett's Charge," 70, 77, 79.
14. William Faulkner, *Intruder in the Dust* (New York, 1972), 194-195.
15. Regarding the actual distances covered by each command, for Pettigrew it is roughly 1,152 yards from the modern North Carolina State Memorial to the Brien farm, and 1,243 yards from the same monument to the 26th North Carolina advance marker. For Pickett, it is roughly 1,200 yards from the left-center of Spangler's Woods to the wall in front of the modern 72nd Pennsylvania memorial. Kemper's right on the Spangler farm to the Copse of Trees is approximately 1,550 yards.
16. Hardy, *North Carolina Remembers Gettysburg*, 31.

STOP PT6: 11th Mississippi Advance Monument

1. See J. Walter Coleman to Mrs. Calvin (Maud) Brown, February 28, 1941 and related correspondence in 11th Mississippi Infantry File, ALBG, GNMP.
2. McFarland, "The Eleventh Mississippi Regiment at Gettysburg," 549, 567.
3. Terrence J. Winschel, "The Gettysburg Diary of Lieutenant William Peel," *Gettysburg Magazine 9* (July 1993), 104-106; Winschel, "Heavy Was Their Loss," 82-83; Himmer, "Col. Hugh Reid Miller, 42nd Mississippi Volunteers," 56-57, 59.
4. *Star and Sentinel*, May 10, 1887; *Compiler*, Undated May 1887, Erik Dorr Collection. Special thanks also to Timothy Smith, Adams County Historical Society.

Sidebar PT6: Expected to be a Bloody Contest

1. George W. Cullum, *Biographical Register of the Officers and Graduates of the U.S. Military Academy, from 1802 to 1867* (New York, 1879), Vol. 2, 260.
2. Cullum, *Biographical Register*, 2: 260; William T. Magruder, CMSR, RG 109, M 331, Roll 162; Francis B. Heitman, *Historical Register and Dictionary of the United States Army, From Its Organization, September 29, 1789 to March 2, 1903* (Washington, D.C., 1903), Volume 2, 183. It was reported that Magruder resigned following issuance of the Emancipation Proclamation. Andrew J. Baker, "Tribute to Capt. Magruder and Wife," *Confederate Veteran* VI (1898), 507. While this is possible since Lincoln issued his Preliminary Emancipation Proclamation on September 22, 1862, and Magruder resigned on October 1, Magruder had been on leave since August and it seems likely his loyalties were conflicted prior to issuance of emancipation.
3. Field Diary of Capt. Magruder, July 3, 1863 entry, William T. Magruder Family Archives. The authors wish to thank Sam Magruder for permitting use of this material.
4. Baker, "Tribute to Capt. Magruder and Wife," 507.
5. Letter of Capt. W. D. Nunn, July 9, 1863, Magruder Family Archives; Gregory Coco, *Wasted Valor: The Confederate Dead at Gettysburg* (Gettysburg, PA, 1990), 130; Baker, "Tribute to Capt. Magruder and Wife," 507.

STOP PT7: Camp Colt and Other Developments

1. See Jim Weeks, *Gettysburg: Memory, Market, and an American Shrine* (Princeton, NJ, 2003) for a discussion.
2. Snipes, "The Improper Placement of the 8th Ohio Monument," 80, 87.
3. See Maj. Laurence Thomas, Commander Third Service Command, "Location of the Prisoner of War Camp on the Gettysburg Battlefield during World War II – 1944-1945," in WW II German POW Camp File, ALBG, GNMP; also Sarah Fuss, "Gettysburg's WWII Prisoner of War Camp," Emmitsburg Area Historical Society, www.emmitsburg.net/archive_list/articles/history/gb/war/ww2_prisoner_camp.htm.

PT7A: Camp Colt Tree

4. "Field Marshal Montgomery Comes to Gettysburg with President Eisenhower," *Gettysburg Times*, May 11, 1957; "President, Montgomery Tour Battlefield Sunday," *Gettysburg Times*, May 13, 1957.

TOUR 3: PICKETT'S CHARGE

1. Longstreet, "Lee's Right Wing at Gettysburg," 3: 345.

STOP PC1: Point of Woods

2. Alexander, "Artillery Fighting at Gettysburg," 3: 362.
3. Ibid.
4. Ibid.
5. Longstreet, "Lee's Right Wing at Gettysburg," 3: 345.
6. Longstreet's later public writings omitted the fact that he tried to defer responsibility to Alexander to call off the attack. In *Battles and Leaders*, Longstreet wrote, "I sent word to Alexander that unless he could do something more, *I* [emphasis added] would not feel warranted in ordering the troops forward." See Longstreet, "Lee's Right Wing at Gettysburg," 3: 345.
7. Alexander, "Artillery Fighting at Gettysburg," 3: 362.
8. Ibid., 3: 363.
9. Ibid.
10. Alexander, *Military Memoirs*, 419-420; Alexander, "Artillery Fighting at Gettysburg," 3: 363.
11. Alexander, "Artillery Fighting at Gettysburg," 3: 364.
12. Pendleton noted in his report that he went to see "about the anticipated advance of the artillery, delayed beyond expectation…" telling us in one sentence that the artillery was expected to move (presumably with the infantry) and both were delayed longer than expected. See *OR*, 27/2: 352.
13. Alexander, *Military Memoirs*, 423.
14. Alexander, "Artillery Fighting at Gettysburg," 3: 364.
15. Paul Cooksey, "Forcing the Issue: Brig. Gen. Henry Hunt at Gettysburg on July 3, 1863," *Gettysburg Magazine 30* (January 2004), 81.
16. Alexander, "Artillery Fighting at Gettysburg", 3: 364. Also see Alexander, *Fighting for the Confederacy*, 258-259; Cooksey, "Forcing the Issue," 81-82.
17. Longstreet, "Lee's Right Wing at Gettysburg," 3:345; Alexander, "Artillery Fighting at Gettysburg," 3: 364-365.
18. Longstreet, "Lee's Right Wing at Gettysburg," 3: 343-345; Alexander, "Artillery Fighting at Gettysburg," 3: 365. By Alexander's count, it was about 1:40 p.m. when he met with Longstreet. Both Alexander and Longstreet wrote that this conversation coincided with Pickett's first steps forward, and the implications for the day's overall timeline will be discussed later in our narrative.
19. Cooksey, "Forcing the Issue," 85.
20. Alexander, "Artillery Fighting at Gettysburg," 3: 365.

Sidebar PC1: A Most Terrific Artillery Duel

1. *OR*, 27/2: 352.
2. *OR*, 27/2: 389.
3. Rollins, *Eyewitness Accounts*, 148.
4. *OR*, 27/2: 610.
5. *OR*, 27/2: 435.
6. Cooksey, "Forcing the Issue," 84-85. Also see Alexander, *Fighting for the Confederacy*, 246.
7. Priest, *Into the Fight*, 194-195.
8. Jones Report, 7th Virginia Infantry File, ALBG, GNMP.

9. Meade: *OR*, 27/1: 117; Hancock: *OR*, 27/1: 372-373; Hunt: *OR*, 27/1: 239. Hunt explained in *Battles and Leaders* that after the Confederates ceased fire "almost immediately his infantry came out of the woods and formed for the assault." See Henry Hunt, "The Third Day at Gettysburg," in *Battles and Leaders of the Civil War*, Vol. 3, 374.
10. *OR*, 27/1: 883-884.
11. Michael Jacobs, *The Rebel Invasion of Maryland & Pennsylvania and Battle of Gettysburg* (Philadelphia, PA, 1864), 41-42.
12. *OR*, 27/2: 376.
13. Longstreet, "Lee's Right Wing," 3: 343.
14. *OR*, 27/2: 434-435.
15. Alexander, "Artillery Fighting at Gettysburg," 3: 364-365. In *Military Memoirs*, 424, Alexander added that it was "doubtless 1:50 or later, but I did not look at my watch again." In *Fighting for the Confederacy*, 251, Alexander noted that "many writers" mistook the 11:00 a.m. artillery firing along Hill's front as part of the cannonade that preceded the charge, although this seems unlikely to have fooled the likes of Generals Meade, Hunt, Hancock, and Colonel Cabell, especially since several of them specifically recorded the opening as occurring around 1:00 p.m.
16. *OR*, 27/2: 352.
17. Alexander, "Artillery Fighting at Gettysburg," 3: 363.
18. Alexander, *Military Memoirs*, 425-428. Although there are several Confederate reports that refer to the intended forward movement of Confederate batteries, no reports describe it actually occurring. When noted, they refer instead to covering actions taken as the Southern infantry was retreating. For example, Colonel Cabell's report indicated: "After Pickett's Division was ordered back from their assault on the Cemetery Hill, Captain McCarthy and Lieutenant Motes were ordered to move forward, and came in position immediately on the road [Emmitsburg] above mentioned, occupying the left flank of the line extended, upon which were placed the sections commanded, respectively, by Lieutenants Anderson, Payne, and Furlong. One of Lieutenant Furlong's guns being entirely out of ammunition, was ordered to the rear. The other piece was placed about 300 yards on the left of his previous position." See *OR*, 27/2: 376.

STOP PC2: Armistead's Brigade

1. George K Griggs, "From Diary of Colonel George K. Griggs," *Southern Historical Society Papers*, Vol. 14, 253.
2. Cooksey, "Forcing the Issue," 77.
3. Rawley Martin, "Rawley Martin's Account," *Southern Historical Society Papers*, Vol. 32, 188 and "Armistead at the Battle of Gettysburg," *Southern Historical Society Papers*, Vol. 39, 186.
4. James T. Carter, "Flag of the Fifty-Third VA. Regiment," *Confederate Veteran* X (1902), 263; Martin, "Rawley Martin's Account," 32: 186; Martin, "Armistead at the Battle of Gettysburg," 39: 186.
5. John H. Lewis, *Recollections from 1860-1865* (Portsmouth, VA: 1893), 79.

Sidebar PC2.1: Armistead and Hancock

1. Harrison, *Pickett's Men*, 33. Armistead was not expelled, but resigned in February 1836.
2. James E. Poindexter, "General Armistead's Portrait Presented," *Southern Historical Society Papers*, Vol. 37, 144; Motts, *Trust in God and Fear Nothing*, 14-15.
3. Almira Russell Hancock, *Reminiscences of Winfield Scott Hancock* (New York, 1887), 69-70.
4. Michael Shaara, *The Killer Angels* (New York, 1974), 258-259.
5. Hancock, *Reminiscences of Winfield Scott Hancock*, 69-70.
6. Armistead's letter of December 2, 1861 in W. Keith Armistead, CMSR, RG 109, M 324, Roll 62.

Sidebar PC2.2: The Son of a Brave Soldier

1. See Motts, *Trust in God and Fear Nothing*, 17-33. Cecilia's mother, Eliza Love, was very fond of her grandson Keith. She complained bitterly that then- Brevet Major Armistead took Keith to live with Lewis's family, ignoring Cecilia's "known wishes." She also claimed that Lewis had not let her see Keith for ten years. "The Lord forgive him for his cruelty." Eliza M. Love, *Recollections of Eliza Matilda Love*, Unpublished Typescript (Wayne Motts Collection), 12, 17.
2. W. Keith Armistead, CMSR, RG 109, M 324, Roll 62.
3. Ibid.
4. *Coupland R. Page Memoir*, Typescript in Possession of Robert K. Krick (Fredericksburg, VA), 27.
5. Cazenove Gardner Lee, *Lee Chronicle: Studies of the Early Generations of the Lees of Virginia* (New York, 1957), 306 (n.1); W. Keith Armistead, CMSR, RG 109, M 324, Roll 62.
6. "Death of W. Keith Armistead," *Newport Daily News*, March 30, 1896. A third son had been killed previously in a firearms accident.

STOP PC3: Garnett's Brigade

1. Harrison, *Pickett's Men*, 18; Robert K. Krick, "Armistead and Garnett: The Parallel Lives of Two Virginia Soldiers," in Gary Gallagher, ed., *The Third Day at Gettysburg and Beyond* (Chapel Hill, NC, 1994), 95, 97, 100; Tagg, *Generals of Gettysburg*, 246.
2. Krick, "Armistead and Garnett," 95-97; Matthew W. Burton, *The River of Blood and the Valley of Death: The Lives of Robert Selden Garnett and Richard Brooke Garnett, C.S.A.* (Columbus, OH, 1998), 149-154.
3. Krick, "Armistead and Garnett," 104; Richard Hardoff, *The Surrender and Death of Crazy Horse* (Spokane, WA, 1998), 24-58. See Hardoff (24) for a photograph of Billie Garnett and a lengthy interview with him.
4. Harrison, *Pickett's Men*, 19.
5. Krick, "Armistead and Garnett," 113-115; Stephen Davis, "The Death and Burials of General Richard Brooke Garnett," *Gettysburg Magazine* 5 (July 1991), 108; Harrison, *Pickett's Men*, 21.
6. Davis, "Death and Burials," 108.
7. Harrison, *Pickett's Men*, 20.
8. Davis, "Death and Burials," 110; Krick, "Armistead and Garnett," 122. See Davis, note 13, regarding disputes surrounding the date of Garnett's injury.
9. Alexander, "Artillery Fighting at Gettysburg," 3: 365; Davis, "Death and Burials," 110.
10. *OR*, 27/2: 385-386.
11. Rollins, *Eyewitness Accounts*, 181.

STOP PC4: Henry Spangler Farm

1. *Historic American Buildings Survey: Spangler Farm* (Gettysburg, 1985), n.p.
2. Smith, "John Holmes Smith's Account," 32: 190; Hilary V. Harris to Father, July 7, 1863. Harris (Hilary Valentine) Papers, 1863. Pearce Civil War Collection, Navarro College, Corsicana, Texas.
3. Laino, *Gettysburg Campaign Atlas*, 328.
4. Rollins, *Eyewitness Accounts*, 156.
5. Mayo, "Pickett's Charge at Gettysburg," 34: 328-329.
6. Johnston, *A Confederate Boy*, 207.
7. Rollins, *Eyewitness Accounts*, 156.
8. Charles T. Loehr, *War History of the Old First Virginia* (Richmond, 1884), 36 and "The Old First Virginia at Gettysburg," *Southern Historical Society Papers*, Vol. 32, 34.
9. Durkin, *John Dooley*, 103.
10. Ladd, *Bachelder Papers*, 2: 1191.
11. Mayo, "Pickett's Charge at Gettysburg," 34: 331-332.
12. Johnston, *A Confederate Boy*, 207.
13. Smith, "John Holmes Smith's Account," 32: 190.

STOP PC5: Emmitsburg Road (West Side) Across from Codori Farm

1. See the previously unpublished OR of Capt. William W. Bentley in Rollins, *Eyewitness Accounts*, 176. Kemper's movements have been of interest to historians- was it a distinct change of front or a series of left obliques? Captain John Holmes Smith described it as: "There was no distinct change of front; but 'close and dress to the left' was the command, and this gave us an oblique movement to the left as we pressed ranks in that direction." See Smith, "John Holmes Smith's Account," 32: 191.
2. Martin, "Rawley Martin's Account,"32: 186.
3. *OR Supplement*, Part I, Reports, Vol. 5, Serial 5, 332.
4. Loehr, *War History of the Old First Virginia*, 36.
5. James Francis Crocker, *Gettysburg-Pickett's Charge, Address by James F. Crocker, November 7, 1894* (Portsmouth, VA, 1906), 18.
6. Rollins, *Eyewitness Accounts*, 179.
7. For example, John Bachelder's 1863 Isometric Map shows an orchard west of the road and the Codori house. The 1868-69 Warren Map clearly places an orchard east of the house and the Emmitsburg Road. William Tipton images taken in 1876-1877 also suggest an orchard east of the road and behind the house. See Frassanito, *Early Photography at Gettysburg*, 237.
8. Loehr, "The Old First Virginia at Gettysburg," 32: 40.
9. Mayo, "Pickett's Charge at Gettysburg," 34: 332-333.

PC5A: Nicholas Codori Farm

10. "Shocking Accident," *Star and Sentinel*, July 11, 1878; "Death of Mr. Codori," *Star and Sentinel*, July 18, 1878; Timothy H. Smith, *Farms at Gettysburg: The Fields of Battle* (Gettysburg, PA, 2007), 15.

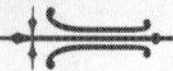

PC5B: Daniel Klingle Farm

11. Smith, *Farms at Gettysburg*, 16.
12. Ibid., 16-17.

Sidebar PC5: Emmitsburg Road Fences

1. Bond, *Pickett or Pettigrew?*, 67.
2. Swallow, "The Third Day at Gettysburg," 568.
3. Martin, "Rawley Martin's Account," 32: 188.
4. V.A. Tapscott, "One of Pickett's Men," in Richard A. Sauers, ed. *Fighting Them Over: How the Veterans Remembered Gettysburg in the Pages of the National Tribune* (Baltimore, MD, 1998), 413.
5. Crocker, *Gettysburg-Pickett's Charge*, 18.
6. *Philadelphia Press*, July 4, 1887; also in Wert, *Gettysburg Day Three*, 221-222.
7. Mayo, "Pickett's Charge at Gettysburg," 34: 332.
8. *OR*, 27/2: 386.
9. See account of Samuel Roberts, Ladd, *Bachelder Papers*, 2: 967.
10. Styple, *Generals in Bronze*, 154.
11. Rollins, *Eyewitness Accounts*, 179.
12. Ibid., 181.
13. Snipes, "The Improper Placement of the 8th Ohio Monument," 88.
14. Rollins, *Eyewitness Accounts*, 261-262.
15. Ibid., 303-304.

STOP PC6: Emmitsburg Road (East Side) West of Stone Wall

1. *OR*, 27/2: 386.
2. Ibid.
3. Mayo, "Pickett's Charge at Gettysburg," 34: 333. Mayo's reference was to Garnett having been "seriously ill a few days before."
4. *OR*, 27/2: 387.
5. Ladd, *Bachelder Papers*, 1: 519.
6. Davis, "Death and Burials," 113.
7. Rollins, *Eyewitness Accounts*, 149-150.
8. Krick, "Armistead and Garnett," 122.
9. Swallow, "The Third Day at Gettysburg," 568.
10. Harrison, *Pickett's Men*, 185.
11. Rollins, *Eyewitness Accounts*, 149-150.
12. Krick, "Armistead and Garnett," 123.
13. See accounts of Lt. Wyatt Whitman of the 53rd Virginia in Rollins, *Eyewitness Accounts*, 183; Carter, *Confederate Veteran* X, 263 (1904); Mayo, "Pickett's Charge at Gettysburg," 34: 332. Martin, "Armistead at the Battle of Gettysburg," 39: 186, recalled Kemper's appeal as, "General, hurry up, my men can stand no more."
14. Mayo, "Pickett's Charge at Gettysburg," 34: 333.
15. Smith, "Captain John Holmes Smith's Account," 32: 192-193; H.V. Harris to Father, Harris Papers, Pearce Civil War Collection, Navarro College. Unfortunately for Smith's historical credibility, he also made the fantastic claim that "to my surprise and disgust, the whole line [broke] away in flight…Unmolested from the front or on either side, and with nothing to indicate that we would be assailed, we thus remained for fully twenty minutes" waiting for reinforcements. "Seeing no sign of coming help, anticipating that we would soon be attacked, and being in no condition of numbers or power to resist any serious assault, we soon concluded… to send the men back to our lines, and we so ordered." Even decades after the fact, some ex-Rebels refused to admit that they had simply been overwhelmed and forced back. See Smith 32: 192-193.
16. Ladd, *Bachelder Papers*, 2: 1192.
17. Harrison, *Pickett's Men*, 103; H.V. Harris to Father, Harris Papers, Pearce Civil War Collection, Navarro College. Harris wrote his father on July 7 that Kemper "was brought off the field and was alive yesterday morning but there was no hope of his recovery."
18. Carter, "Flag of the 53rd VA Regiment," 263; Martin, "Armistead's Brigade at Gettysburg," 39: 186.
19. Carter, "Flag of the Fifty-Third VA. Regiment," 263.
20. Rollins, *Eyewitness Accounts*, 179-180.
21. Rollins, *Eyewitness Accounts*, 163, 183, 193; Martin, "Rawley Martin's Account," 32: 187; Poindexter, "General Armistead's Portrait," 37: 149; Motts, *Trust in God and Fear Nothing*, 45.

Sidebar PC6.1: To Die in a Foreign Land

1. Williams was born September 13, 1833. Walker, *Biographical Sketches*, 536; Robert K. Krick, *Lee's Colonels: A Biographical Register of the Field Officers of the Army of Northern Virginia* (Dayton, OH, 1992), 4th edition, 400.
2. Mayo, "Pickett's Charge at Gettysburg,"34: 333; Bright, "Pickett's Charge at Gettysburg," 264; Krick, *Lee's Colonels*, 400; *Richmond Times Dispatch*, December 13, 1903.
3. Allen was born June 22, 1834. Krick, *Lee's Colonels*, 32; Walker, *Biographical Sketches*, 26.
4. Walker, *Biographical Sketches*, 27-28.
5. Hunton, *Autobiography*, 78.
6. Walker, *Biographical Sketches*, 29; *Confederate Veteran* XXI (1913), 430.
7. Walker, *Biographical Sketches*, 425; Krick, *Lee's Colonels*, 300.
8. Walker, *Biographical Sketches*, 426; Krick, *Lee's Colonels*, 300.
9. Walker, *Biographical Sketches*, 427.

Sidebar PC6.3: Where was Pickett?

1. Styple, *Generals in Bronze*, 154.
2. Bond, *Pickett or Pettigrew?*, 57.
3. Hunton, *Autobiography*, 98-99.
4. Harrison, *Nothing But Glory*, 131-132.
5. Ibid., 130.
6. Ibid., 132-133, 162 n. 14.
7. Sorrel, *At the Right Hand of Longstreet*, 172-173.
8. Martin, "Rawley Martin's Account," 32: 187-188.
9. J.H. Stine, *History of the Army of the Potomac* (Washington DC, 1893), 538-539.
10. Bright, "Pickett's Charge at Gettysburg," 265.
11. Harrison, *Nothing But Glory*, 129, 132.
12. Bond, *Pickett or Pettigrew?*, 57; Bright, "Pickett's Charge at Gettysburg," 266.

TOUR 4: UNION BATTLE LINE

1. John Gibbon, "The Council of War on the Second Day," *Battles and Leaders of the Civil War*, Vol. 3, 313-314.

STOP U1: Major General George Meade's Headquarters

2. Her sister Catherine was married to John Slyder, whose farm was near the Round Tops. Frassanito, *Early Photography at Gettysburg*, 224; Smith, *Farms at Gettysburg*, 40; 1860 United States Federal Census, Census Place: Cumberland, Adams, Pennsylvania, Roll: M653_1057, Page: 63, Image: 67, Family History Library Film: 805057. Leister's age on the 1860 census is 49, making her birth year about 1811, but Leister did not know with certainty how old she or her children were. See Smith, 41. Historians have been careless in relaying the age of Leister's children, often using their 1860 census ages as their ages at the time of the battle. For example, several sources state that Leister's youngest child was 3 years old in 1863, however, the youngest (Matilda A. Leister) was 3 on the 1860 census, actually making her about 6 years old in 1863. The oldest, Eliza then 24, may not have been living at home in 1863.
3. *OR*, 27/1: 72.
4. OR, 27/1: 73; Gibbon, "The Council of War on the Second Day," 3: 313. For a discussion about Meade's relationship with Hooker and chief of staff Dan Butterfield, refer to James Hessler, *Sickles at Gettysburg: The Controversial Civil War General Who Committed Murder, Abandoned Little Round Top, and Declared Himself the Hero of Gettysburg* (New York, 2009), 44-48, 63-76.
5. Gibbon, "The Council of War on the Second Day," 3: 314; George Meade, *The Life and Letters of George Gordon Meade* (New York, 1913), Vol. 2, 97.
6. Bill Hyde, ed., *The Union Generals Speak: The Meade Hearings on the Battle of Gettysburg* (Baton Rouge, LA, 2003), 127.
7. Meade, *Life and Letters*, 2: 105; Frank Haskell, *The Battle of Gettysburg* (Wisconsin, 1908), 90-93.
8. Meade, *Life and Letters*, 2: 105-106.
9. *OR*, 27/1: 74.
10. Haskell, *Battle of Gettysburg*, 94-96.
11. Meade, *Life and Letters*, 2: 106-107.
12. Ladd, *Bachelder Papers*, 3: 1360-1361.
13. Smith, *Farms at Gettysburg*, 41.
14. Meade, *Life and Letters*, 2:107, 111. As we will discuss in our sidebar regarding Meade's counter-attack, the emphasis clearly seemed to be on defensively preventing a Confederate breakthrough and no clear orders were given to mass for a counter-assault.
15. Meade, *Life and Letters*, 2: 107-108.
16. Ibid., 2:112.
17. Frassanito, *Early Photography*, 225-229. The deteriorated house and shed were torn down in 1989.
18. Smith, *Farms at Gettysburg*, 41. Also see Ladd, *Bachelder Papers*, 3: 1360.
19. Frassanito, *Early Photography at Gettysburg*, 224. The GBMA purchase of the Leister property was noted in the *Compiler*, January 3, 1888. In order to bring the home's appearance back to 1863, the GBMA removed a two story structure that Leister had added in the 1870s.

U1A: Peter Fry (Frey) Farm

20. Coco, *A Vast Sea of Misery*, 63.
21. Ibid., 63.
22. See Biggs Family File and Leander Warren, "Recollections of the Battle of Gettysburg," ACHS; Smith, *Farms at Gettysburg*, 37; "Leading Colored Citizen,"

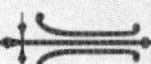

Compiler, June 13, 1906; James M. Paradis, *African Americans and the Gettysburg Campaign* (Lanham, MD, 2013), 8.

STOP U2: Wright and Howe Avenues

1. Longstreet, "General James Longstreet's Account of the Campaign and Battle," 5: 68.
2. *OR*, 27/1: 665, 675.
3. Busey and Martin, *Strengths and Losses*, 71.
4. *OR*, 27/1: 661, 675, 678.
5. *Monuments at Gettysburg. Report of the Vermont Commissioners* (Rutland, VT, 1888), 8.

STOP U3: Little Round Top

1. *OR*, 27/2:320.
2. Garry E. Adelman, *The Myth of Little Round Top* (Gettysburg, PA, 2003), 69.
3. Paul Cooksey, "The Union Artillery at Gettysburg on July 3," *Gettysburg Magazine 38* (January 2008), 74.
4. Benjamin F. Rittenhouse, "The Battle Seen From Little Round Top," in Ken Bandy and Florence Freeland, ed. *The Gettysburg Papers, Two Volumes in One* (Dayton, OH, 1986), 526.
5. Mayo, "Pickett's Charge at Gettysburg," 34: 331.
6. *OR*, 27/2: 386.
7. *OR*, 27/1: 239.
8. Adelman, *The Myth of Little Round Top*, 44.
9. Hyde, *The Union Generals Speak*, 111.

STOP U4: Lieutenant Colonel Freeman McGilvery's Artillery Line

1. *OR*, 27/1: 883.
2. Ibid.
3. See Laino, *Gettysburg Campaign Atlas*, 384, note 13, for a discussion. McGilvery's report claimed command of the following batteries: "Ames' battery, six light 12-pounders; Dow's Sixth Maine Battery, four light 12-pounders; a New Jersey battery, six 3-inch guns; one section New York [Pennsylvania] Artillery, Lieutenant Rock [Captain Rank], two 3-inch guns; First [Second] Connecticut, four James rifled and two howitzers; Hart's Fifteenth New York Independent Battery, four light 12-pounders; Phillips' Fifth Massachusetts, six 3-inch rifled guns; Thompson's battery, F and C, consolidated Pennsylvania Artillery, five 3-inch rifled guns; total, thirty-nine guns." *OR*, 27/1: 883. Thompson had lost one cannon to capture on July 2. *OR*, 27/1: 890.
4. Cooksey, "The Union Artillery at Gettysburg on July 3," 81-82; *OR*, 27/1: 896, 899-900. Lieutenant Parsons, however, wrote in 1889 that he unlimbered in an open space "between Fitzhugh's and McGilvery's batteries," with Fitzhugh on the right and McGilvery on the left. See New Jersey Gettysburg Battlefield Commission, *Final Report*, 122, 124.
5. Laino, *Gettysburg Campaign Atlas*, 318-319.
6. Cooksey, "The Union Artillery at Gettysburg on July 3," 76; *OR*, 27/1: 586.
7. *OR*, 27/1: 238-239.
8. Cooksey, "The Union Artillery at Gettysburg," 89-90. In Cooksey's estimate, the batteries commanded by Hart, Phillips, Thompson, Thomas, and Daniels complied with Hancock's orders. Those batteries under Ames, Dow, Sterling, and Rank obeyed Hunt and McGilvery's directives to not fire.
9. *OR*, 27/1: 883-884.
10. Hunt, "The Third Day at Gettysburg," 3: 372-373.

Sidebar U4.1: Who Ordered the Cease-Fire?

1. Cooksey, "Forcing the Issue," 86-88.
2. *OR*, 27/1: 239.
3. Hunt, "The Third Day at Gettysburg," 3: 374.
4. Ladd, *Bachelder Papers*, 1: 431. In the later debate with Hancock over who had the ultimate control of the artillery on July 3, Hunt pointed to the fact that Meade had sent an order (through one of Hancock's aides, no less) for Hunt to stop firing; demonstrating that Meade recognized Hunt as being the one accountable. See 1873 account of Hunt, *Bachelder Papers*, 1: 431.
5. Meade, *Life and Letters*, 2: 107-108.
6. Cooksey, "Forcing the Issue," 80-81. Most historians give Hunt the credit for initiating the order based on his popular post-war writings, but Hunt's contemporary report only states that he intended to first "report to" Meade and is therefore potentially ambiguous in determining whether Hunt decided to cease fire before or after riding along the Union lines.

Sidebar U4.2: How Little an Infantry Officer Knows About Artillery

1. *OR*, 27/1: 238-239; Hunt, "The Third Day at Gettysburg," 3: 372; Cooksey, "Forcing the Issue," 80.
2. *OR*, 27/1: 117, 417.
3. Ladd, *Bachelder Papers*, 2: 802.
4. Ibid., 2: 807, 811.
5. Francis A. Walker, "General Hancock and the Artillery at Gettysburg," *Battles and Leaders of the Civil War*, Vol. 3, 385-386.
6. Ladd, *Bachelder Papers*, 3: 1361.
7. Ibid., 2: 802-803.
8. Cooksey, "The Union Artillery at Gettysburg on July 3," 81.
9. *OR*, 27/1: 884.
10. Ladd, *Bachelder Papers*, 2: 826-827; *OR*, 27/1: 888.
11. *OR*, 27/1: 885.
12. Ladd, *Bachelder Papers*, 1: 169.
13. *History of the Fifth Massachusetts Battery* (Boston, MA, 1902), 652, 654.
14. Cooksey, "The Union Artillery at Gettysburg on July 3," 81.
15. *OR*, 27/1: 884.
16. Ladd, *Bachelder Papers*, 1:169.
17. Dempsey, "Florida Brigade at Gettysburg," 26.
18. *OR*, 27/1: 373.
19. Hunt, "The Third Day at Gettysburg," 3: 375.
20. *OR*, 27/1: 366.
21. Ladd, *Bachelder Papers*, 2: 815. Anyone who questions the depths of the Hunt-Hancock feud beyond the semi-polite public exchanges that appeared in *Battles and Leaders* should read Hunt's lengthy letter to Sherman in Ladd, *Bachelder Papers*, 2: 790-828.

STOP U5: Stannard's Brigade Counterattacks

1. Ladd, *Bachelder Papers*, 1: 52.
2. Ibid., 1: 54, 58. Also see postwar account of Colonel Asa Peabody Blunt of the 12th Vermont in *OR Supplement*, Part I, Vol. 5, Serial 5, 153.
3. Ibid., 1: 59. Most accounts such as Stannard's *OR* imply that the entire 16th Vermont was on picket. Lieutenant George G. Benedict, on the other hand, wrote in a December 1863 account that only part of the regiment skirmished. See Ladd, *Bachelder Papers*, 1: 48-50.
4. Rollins, Eyewitness Accounts, 208.
5. Ladd, *Bachelder Papers*, 1: 55-56.
6. Rollins, *Eyewitness Accounts*, 156.
7. *OR*, 27/1: 349-350.
8. Ladd, *Bachelder Papers*, 1: 55-56.
9. George G. Benedict, *Army Life in Virginia* (Burlington, VT, 1895), 178.
10. Rollins, Eyewitness Accounts, 208.
11. Ladd, *Bachelder Papers*, 1: 56; OR, 27/1: 349-350.
12. Ladd, *Bachelder Papers*, 1: 62.
13. *OR*, 27/1: 349-350.
14. Ladd, *Bachelder Papers*, 1: 62.
15. Benedict, *Army Life*, 180-181.
16. Ladd, *Bachelder Papers*, 1: 56.
17. Dempsey, "Florida Brigade at Gettysburg," 26.
18. Ladd, *Bachelder Papers*, 1: 57.

U5A: Vermont State Memorial

19. *Report of Vermont Commissioners 1888*, 8.
20. Hawthorne, *Men and Monuments*, 109.

U5B: 13th Vermont Regimental Monument

21. Ibid., 110-111.

U5C: 16th Vermont Regimental Monument

22. *Gettysburg Stone Sentinels*, http://www.gettysburg.stonesentinels.com/VT/16Vt.php. Thanks to Steve Floyd for sharing his research on the 16th Vermont monument, including clarifying the date as 1907 and not 1901 as has been printed elsewhere.
23. *Report of the Vermont Commissioners 1888*, 4.

STOP U6: Monument to the Wounding of Major General Winfield Hancock

1. Hancock, for example, credited himself and his staff as issuing the order in his name. See Ladd, *Bachelder Papers*, 3: 1949.
2. Benedict, *Army Life*, 182-183.
3. Ladd, *Bachelder Papers*, 3: 1949; Hancock, *Reminiscences*, 214.
4. Benedict, *Army Life*, 183-184; Ladd, *Bachelder Papers*, 1: 56.
5. Steven J. Wright, "'Don't Let Me Bleed to Death.' The Wounding of Maj. Gen. Winfield Scott Hancock," *Gettysburg Magazine 6* (January 1992), 91.
6. Benedict, *Army Life*, 183.
7. Hancock, *Reminiscences*, 216-217.
8. John M. Vanderslice, *Gettysburg Then and Now* (New York, 1897), 256.
9. Hancock, *Reminiscences*, 214-215.
10. *OR*, 27/1: 366.
11. Hancock, *Reminiscences*, 215.
12. Ibid., 98.
13. Hancock, *Reminiscences*, 99; Benedict, *Army Life*, 184; Winfield S. Hancock to William G. Mitchell, August 24, 1863, Ed and Faye Max private collection. Used with permission.

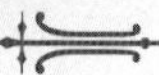

14. *Report of the Vermont Commissioners*, 8.
15. Wright, "Don't Let Me Bleed to Death," 87.
16. Ladd, *Bachelder Papers*, 2: 1162-1163.
17. Wright, "Don't Let Me Bleed to Death," 87. Also see Hancock to Bachelder, December 20, 1885: "I saw no great boulders in front of the Vermont brigade or about it, and therefore I am satisfied that the position indicated where I was shot is incorrect. It was established in 1866 [in the presence of several people including Stannard and Benedict] but is not placed as indicated on that field, on my last visit by a sign-board"; Ladd, *Bachelder Papers*, 3: 1949.
18. See Timothy H. Smith, *Gettysburg's Battlefield Photographer- William H. Tipton* (Gettysburg, PA, 2005), 47 for a before and after perspective.
19. It was said that he was near Company "K" of the 13th Vermont when hit, although this monument is in front of the 14th Vermont and some distance away from the 13th's monument. See Wright, "Don't Let Me Bleed to Death," 89.
20. "After Thirty Years," *Compiler*, July 4, 1893.

STOP U7: Monuments South of the High Water Mark

U7A: Brigadier General John Gibbon Statue and "The Gibbon Tree"

1. Nathaniel Cheairs Hughes Jr., *Yale's Confederates: A Biographical Dictionary* (Knoxville, TN, 2008), 81.
2. John Gibbon, *Personal Recollections of the Civil War* (Dayton, OH, 1988), 9.
3. Lardner Gibbon, CMSR, RG 109, M 331, Roll 105; Edward W. Callahan, ed. *List of Officers of the Navy of the United States and of the Marine Corps from 1771 to 1900* (NY, 1901), 216; "Lardner Gibbon's Explorations in South America," *Bulletin of the International Bureau of the American Republics* (Washington, DC, 1910), 448-458.
4. John Gibbon to William Seward, Case Files of Applications from Former Confederates for Presidential Pardons ("Amnesty Papers"), NARA, RG 94, M 1003, Roll 45.
5. Robert Gibbon, CMSR, RG 109, M270, Roll 345 and RG 109, M 331, Roll 105; Hughes, *Yale's Confederates*, 81.
6. Nicholas Gibbon, CMSR, RG 109, M 270, Roll 345 and RG 109, M 331, Roll 105.
7. Tagg, *Generals of Gettysburg*, 45.
8. Fred Hawthorne, "140 Places Every Guide Should Know," http://www.gettysburgdaily.com/?p=9080.
9. Ladd, *Bachelder Papers*, 1: 260.
10. Rollins, *Eyewitness Accounts*, 319. John Bachelder likewise thought that an officer, presumably Gibbon, was wounded while amongst the 19th Maine. The officer discharged his pistol into the air, ordered a "charge," and was then struck. See *Bachelder Papers*, 3: 1987.
11. Ladd, *Bachelder Papers*, 2: 1163.
12. Ibid., 2: 1162-1163.

U7B: 1st Minnesota Secondary Monument (July 3)

13. Kathy Georg Harrison, *The Location of the Monuments, Markers, and Tablets on Gettysburg Battlefield* (Gettysburg, PA), 6. There is not universal consensus on how Union regiments in this area were deployed. For example, the historical sketch of the 82nd New York in *New York at Gettysburg* stated that the 1st Minnesota was posted on the left of the 82nd New York. The placement of the two regiments' monuments is exactly the opposite. See *New York at Gettysburg*, 2: 664.
14. Nathan Messick's exact birth date in unclear but he was born about 1827 in New Jersey. He relocated to Indiana in the 1840s (from where he enlisted in the 4th Indiana), before later moving to Minnesota. Nathan Messick, CMSR, RG 94, M 616, Roll 25 (4th Indiana, Mexican War); Nathan Messick, Pension Record, RG 15. All pension file references are to the National Archives in Washington, DC in Record Group (RG) 15. See also Travis W. Busey and John W. Busey, *Union Casualties at Gettysburg: A Comprehensive Record* (Jefferson, NC, 2011), Vol. 1, 320; James Cole and Roy Frampton, *Lincoln and the Human Interest Stories of the Gettysburg National Cemetery* (Gettysburg, PA, 1995), 43.
15. Busey, *Union Casualties at Gettysburg*, 1: 320; *OR*, 27/1: 425. How many men were in the 1st Minnesota's ranks on July 3? The traditional version of July 2, as replayed on the primary monument, is that eight companies of 262 men participated in the July 2 counter-attack, and 47 returned unscathed. It is sometimes misinterpreted or implied that only these 47 then faced Pickett on July 3. See Richard Moe, *The Last Full Measure: The Life and Death of the First Minnesota Volunteers* (New York, 1993), 281 and T.J. Mosher, "The 1st Minn. Losses, " in Richard Sauers, ed., *Fighting Them Over: How the Veterans Remembered Gettysburg in the Pages of The National Tribune* (Baltimore, MD, 1998), 330. The secondary monument, however, then indicates that 330 total men were engaged during the battle. Colonel Colvill, in an 1866 letter to John Bachelder, implied that actually three companies were detached on July 2 and "all joined the command the next morning, raising it to upwards of 100 men which came in at the final melee." See Ladd, *Bachelder Papers*, 1: 258. Busey and Martin (129, 358) likewise accept a total engaged of 330, implying that 68 detached men rejoined the 47 survivors on July 3. The regimental history estimated "about 140 officers and men." R.I. Holcombe, *History of the First Minnesota Volunteer Infantry* (Gaithersburg, MD, 1987), 364. One then wonders how many fell as casualties on July 3. The secondary monument states that 17 fell on July 3 (for a battle total of 232 k/w/c), yet Busey and Martin, *Strengths and Losses*, 129 only tally 224 casualties for the total battle. In Ladd, *Bachelder Papers*, 3: 1987, 35 men killed and wounded are computed as causalities for July 3. In the absence of definitive conclusions on the subject, we accept the secondary monument's estimate of 17 casualties for July 3.
16. Holcombe, *History of the First Minnesota Volunteer Infantry*, 364; Moe, *The Last Full Measure*, 283.
17. *OR*, 27/1: 425.
18. Moe, *The Last Full Measure*, 289.
19. Ibid., 290.
20. *OR*, 27/1: 425.
21. Nathan Messick, Pension Record, RG 15; Busey, *Union Casualties at Gettysburg*, 1: 320; Cole and Frampton, *Lincoln and the Human Interest Stories*, 43.
22. Cole and Frampton, *Lincoln and the Human Interest Stories*, 43.

U7C: 20th Massachusetts Regimental Monument

23. Hawthorne, *Men and Monuments*, 112. Captain, later Major, Henry Abbott wrote that Paine was 17-years-old, but his birth date was May 10, 1845, which would make him 18 at Gettysburg. See Robert Garth Scott, ed. *Fallen Leaves: The Civil War Letters of Major Henry Livermore Abbott* (Kent, OH, 1991), 186 and *Harvard Memorial Biographies* (Cambridge, MA, 1867), Vol. 2, 453. The youngest known officer in the Union army leading men at Gettysburg was 17-year-old Edward R. Geary who commanded a section of Knap's Battery on Culp's Hill. See James P. Brady, *Hurrah for the Artillery!: Knap's Independent Battery "E", Pennsylvania Light Artillery* (Gettysburg, PA, 1992), 12-15.
24. *Harvard Memorial Biographies*, 2: 453.
25. Ibid., 2: 454.
26. Ibid., 2: 455.
27. Scott, *Fallen Leaves*, 186.
28. Busey, *Union Casualties at Gettysburg*, 1: 209.
29. Vanderslice, *Then and Now*, 301, 411; Hawthorne, *Men and Monuments*, 112.

U7D: 19th Massachusetts Regimental Monument

30. Ladd, *Bachelder Papers*, 3: 1609; *OR*, 27/1: 443. Hancock also mentioned this incident in his own *OR*, 27/1: 374 and together these accounts help create a timeline in which Webb's front was threatened before, or at least concurrently with, Stannard's flank attack and then Hancock's wounding.
31. Joseph H. DeCastro, Pension Record, RG 15; *OR*, 27/1: 444. Devereux added in his report that his regiment had a fifth enemy flag but gave it to Webb upon protests from the latter that his brigade had actually captured the colors.
32. *Original Battle Report of Col. Arthur Devereux*, National Archives, Record Group 94; Ladd, *Bachelder Papers*, 3: 1610 and 3: 1879-1880.
33. After the war, DeCastro served in the 6th U.S. Cavalry from 1870-1874. He died in New York City in 1892 at the age of 47; Joseph DeCastro, Pension Record, RG 15.

STOP U8: Copse of Trees / High Water Mark and 69th Pennsylvania Regimental Monument

1. Alexander S. Webb, *An Address Delivered at Gettysburg, August 27, 1883 by Gen. Alexander S. Webb at the Dedication of the 72nd PA. Vols. Monument* (Philadelphia, PA, 1883), 3.
2. Samuel Roberts, "The 72d PA," *Fighting Them Over: How the Veterans Remembered Gettysburg in the Pages of the National Tribune*, 417.
3. *OR*, 27/1: 428. In later testimony, Webb modified his opinion to: "The concentration of the artillery fired from the rebel side upon the ground about the clump of trees had made known to us that there was to be the point of attack." See Rollins, *Eyewitness Accounts*, 316.
4. *OR*, 27/1: 428, 434; Rollins, *Eyewitness Accounts*, 316.
5. Scott Hartwig, "It Struck Horror to Us All," *Gettysburg Magazine 4* (January 1991), 89-90; Michael H.

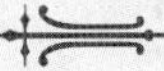

Kane, "The Court Martial of Dennis O'Kane," n.p., 69th Pennsylvania Infantry File, ALBG, GNMP.

6. John H. Rhodes, *The History of Battery B. First Regiment Rhode Island Light Artillery* (Providence, RI, 1894), 207.
7. Hartwig, "It Struck Horror to Us All," 90, 92, 94; Ladd, *Bachelder Papers*, 2: 1146, 3: 1403; Rollins, *Eyewitness Accounts*, 316.
8. *OR*, 27/1: 318-319. Also see Stewart, *Pickett's Charge*, 67 and Hartwig, "It Struck Horror to Us All," 90.
9. Ladd, *Bachelder Papers*, 1: 19.
10. Ladd, *Bachelder Papers*, 3: 1410-1411; Hartwig, "It Struck Horror to Us All," 96-97.
11. Ladd, *Bachelder Papers*, 2: 1156-1157. Also see R.L. Murray, "Cowan's, Cushing's, and Rorty's Batteries in Action during the Pickett-Pettigrew-Trimble Charge," *Gettysburg Magazine 35* (July 2006), 50.
12. Hartwig, "It Struck Horror to Us All," 97.
13. Ladd, *Bachelder Papers*, 3: 1410.
14. Ibid., 1:19.
15. Ladd, *Bachelder Papers*, 2: 1157, 3: 1411; Hartwig, "It Struck Horror to Us All," 98. In the typically warm afterglow of monument dedication speeches, General Webb (at the 72nd PA dedication) said: "the right of those who guarded the wall on the left of Cushing was pressed to the rear, but not penetrated or driven to the rear. They were better for defense in their new position." See Webb, *Dedication of the 72nd PA.*, 15.
16. Hartwig, "It Struck Horror to Us All," 98; Ladd, *Bachelder Papers*, 3: 1414; Kane, "The Court Martial of Dennis O'Kane," n.p.
17. *OR*, 27/1: 439.
18. Haskell, *Gettysburg*, 123-125.
19. *OR*, 27/1: 420.
20. Ladd, *Bachelder Papers*, 1: 393.
21. *OR*, 27/1: 318-319. Gates's 80th New York was also referred to as the 20th Militia.
22. Ladd, *Bachelder Papers*, 3: 1414-1415, 1656; Hartwig, "It Struck Horror to Us All," 99. McDermott added: "The 69th has never claimed that no other troops came to their assistance for we always allow that Hall's brigade came up and were followed by the 72nd, also that the 71st Penna. aided on our right [and then names numerous other regiments] all aided on our left in repulsing Pickett, but we claim that no troops came to the wall at our position…Not one of the 11 regiments you [Bachelder] mention came to the wall as such at any time, notwithstanding their official reports say so." The 69th veterans all "solemnly" insisted that no other regiments reached the wall. See Ladd, *Bachelder Papers*, 3: 1655.

U8A: 1st Rhode Island Artillery, Battery B

23. Rhodes, *History of Battery B*, 189.
24. Rhodes, *History of Battery B*, 204; George Newton, "Gettysburg Artillery, Part 10," http://www.gettysburgdaily.com/?p=5461.
25. Rhodes, *History of Battery B*, 209. Cowan said Battery B was "almost annihilated by the heavy cannonade." See Ladd, *Bachelder Papers*, 2: 1146.
26. Rhodes, *History of Battery B*, 209-210, 379-380, 386; Hawthorne, *Men and Monuments*, 114-115.
27. Rhodes, *History of Battery B*, 211, 214.
28. Ibid., 213.

U8B: Cowan's 1st New York Independent Battery

29. *OR*, 27/1: 690; Ladd, *Bachelder Papers*, 1: 281; Cowan, "How Cowan's Battery Withstood Pickett's Great Charge," *Washington Post*, July 2, 1911; Murray, "Cowan's, Cushing's, and Rorty's Batteries in Action," 46-47; *New York at Gettysburg*, 3: 1276.
30. Ladd, *Bachelder Papers*, 2: 1146, 1: 282.
31. *OR*, 27/1: 690.
32. Ladd, *Bachelder Papers*, 2: 1155-1157; Styple, *Generals in Bronze*, 157; Murray, "Cowan's, Cushing's, and Rorty's Batteries in Action," 48.
33. Ladd, *Bachelder Papers*, 1: 282.
34. Murray, "Cowan's, Cushing's, and Rorty's Batteries in Action," 51-52.
35. *OR*, 27/1: 690.
36. *OR*, 27/1: 690; Murray, "Cowan's, Cushing's, and Rorty's Batteries in Action," 53.
37. Ladd, *Bachelder Papers*, 2: 1157.
38. Cowan, "How Cowan's Battery Withstood Pickett's Great Charge." Also see Webb's *OR*, 27/1: 428.
39. George Newton, *Silent Sentinels: A Reference Guide to the Artillery at Gettysburg* (New York, 2005), 110.

Sidebar U8.1: John Bachelder and the High Water Mark

1. Ladd, *Bachelder Papers*, 1: 9.
2. John Bachelder, *The Story of the Battle of Gettysburg and Description of the Painting of the Repulse of Longstreet's Assault* (Boston, 1904), 29.
3. Ibid.
4. Vanderslice, *Gettysburg Then and Now*, 395; Ladd, *Bachelder Papers*, 1: 9-11. Bachelder resigned as Superintendent of Tablets and Legends on September 16, 1887. See Vanderslice, *Gettysburg Then and Now*, 379.
5. Bachelder, *Story of the Battle of Gettysburg*, 5. Also in Frassanito, *Early Photography*, 239.
6. Longstreet, "Lee in Pennsylvania," 429.
7. Longstreet, "Lee's Right Wing at Gettysburg," 3: 342.
8. Longstreet, *From Manassas to Appomattox*, 388-394.
9. Ladd, *Bachelder Papers*, 3: 1854-1855; Frassanito, *Early Photography*, 239-240.
10. Harrison, *Pickett's Men*, 176.
11. Ibid., 183. As esteemed historian William Frassanito noted, Harrison had curiously not included this commentary in his original sketch of the third day's activities, but instead added it to an almost appendix-like chapter about his visit. See Frassanito, *Early Photography*, 240.
12. John Bachelder, *Gettysburg: What to See and How to See it* (Boston, MA, 1878), 54; Frassanito, *Early Photography*, 239.
13. Webb, *Dedication of the 72nd PA.*, 11, 13; Harrison, *Location of the Monuments*, 13.
14. Ladd, *Bachelder Papers*, 3: 1855; Vanderslice, *Gettysburg Then and Now*, 375, 388; Frassanito, *Early Photography*, 240; Thomas Desjardin, *These Honored Dead: How the Story of Gettysburg Shaped American History* (Cambridge, MA, 2003), 98.
15. Hawthorne, *Men and Monuments*, 116.
16. Ladd, *Bachelder Papers*, 3: 1858; Frassanito, *Early Photography*, 240.

Sidebar U8.2: Murder and Mayhem in the Philadelphia Brigade

1. Frank H. Taylor, *Philadelphia in the Civil War* (Philadelphia, PA, 1913), 85-86; Gary Lash, "The Philadelphia Brigade at Gettysburg," *Gettysburg Magazine 7* (July 1992), 97; Jim Heenehan, "Philadelphia Defends the Wall: The Philadelphia Brigade during 'Pickett's Charge,'" *Gettysburg Magazine 38* (January 2008), 93.
2. Taylor, *Philadelphia in the Civil War*, 85-86; Charles H. Banes, *History of the Philadelphia Brigade* (Philadelphia, PA, 1876), 3, 9-10; Lash, "The Philadelphia Brigade at Gettysburg," 98.
3. Taylor, *Philadelphia in the Civil War*, 86. Charles Banes tap-danced over the issue in the brigade history, saying only that there had been a "misunderstanding" between the state and the War Department concerning the regiments' muster. See Banes, *History of the Philadelphia Brigade*, 33.
4. Heenehan, "Philadelphia Defends the Wall: The Philadelphia Brigade During 'Pickett's Charge,'" 92.
5. Lash, "The Philadelphia Brigade," 99; Wert, *Gettysburg: Day Three*, 149-150.
6. Lash, "The Philadelphia Brigade at Gettysburg," 98.
7. Kane, "The Court Martial of Dennis O'Kane," n.p.
8. Lash, "The Philadelphia Brigade," 98-99; Ladd, *Bachelder Papers*, 2: 968; Banes, *History of the Philadelphia Brigade*, 173-174. Why was Owen dismissed? Reasons given have included lax discipline, drunkenness, and arrest for allowing civilians to cross his picket line. See Heenehan, 93, note 9 for a good discussion.
9. Gary Lash, "The Cases of Pvt. Jesse Mayberry and Capt. Bernard McMahon, 71st Pennsylvania Infantry," *Gettysburg Magazine 22* (January 2000), 88-89; Banes, *History of the Philadelphia Brigade*, 168. Then Lieutenant McMahon had been arrested in the fall of 1862 for levying taxes on store keepers and sutlers in Harpers Ferry. McMahon's defense: "I was drunk." He was soon thereafter promoted to captain of Company "C" anyways. McMahon was wounded during the Fredericksburg campaign. See Lash, 88-89.
10. Lash, "The Cases of Pvt. Jesse Mayberry and Capt. Bernard McMahon," 89.
11. Ibid., 91, 94. For a very brief account of McMahon working one of Cushing's guns; Ladd, *Bachelder Papers*, 3: 1628.
12. Ibid., 94-95.
13. *OR*, 27/1: 432; Ladd, *Bachelder Papers*, 1: 294-295, 3: 1359; Harry W. Pfanz, *Gettysburg: Culp's Hill and Cemetery Hill* (Chapel Hill, NC, 1993), 220-221; Wert, *Gettysburg: Day Three*, 149-150; Lash, "The Philadelphia Brigade," 101. Banes wrote in the brigade history that Smith withdrew from Culp's Hill due to the "strong force" of the enemy, darkness, unfamiliarity with ground, and the capture of the regiment's skirmishers. See Banes, *History of the Philadelphia Brigade*, 186.

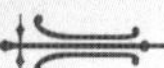

STOP U9: The Angle

1. "The Battle," *Compiler*, June 7, 1887; Banes, *History of the Philadelphia Brigade*, 194.
2. "The Battle," *Compiler*, June 7, 1887; Lash, "Philadelphia Brigade at Gettysburg," 104; *OR*, 27/1: 428; Edwin B. Coddington, *The Gettysburg Campaign: A Study in Command* (New York, 1984), 511; Roberts, "The 72d PA," 417. Stockton said that one gun was at the Angle and worked entirely by the men of the 71st and none of Cushing's battery mates. See Rollins, *Eyewitness Accts*, 339. As we discuss in the tour stop for Cushing's battery, many modern historical accounts accept that two of Cushing's pieces were rolled forward although there were discrepancies amongst eyewitness accounts.
3. *OR*, 27/1: 432; Coddington, *The Gettysburg Campaign*, 511. For some of the differing accounts regarding whether eight companies or two were in front, see Sgt. Major William Stockton in Rollins, *Eyewitness Accounts*, 339; A. McDermott in *Bachelder Papers*, 3: 1657; and Lash, "The Philadelphia Brigade," 104, including n. 25. Some accounts suggest that there were two companies in front and eight in the rear. Capt. Charles Banes, brigade asst. adjutant general, is typical of the conflicts: "There were not over three and I think only two companies at the front. The rest of the Company was with Colonel Smith over on what is known as the Ridge." See *Bachelder Papers* 3: 1707 and also 3: 1701. Colonel Smith, while vague on the exact numbers, specifically said that Banes was "entirely mistaken" in assuming only two companies at the front wall. See "The Battle," *Compiler*, June 7, 1887. Still other historians have tried to address the distance issues by suggesting a five and five deployment. Esteemed chronicler John Bachelder, who interviewed many of the veterans and should have been more equipped than any modern historian to answer the question, actually left a blank space for the number of front-line companies in a circa. 1875 account. Clearly at one point he was not even sure! See Ladd, *Bachelder Papers*, 3: 1989. Banes's brigade history states only that "one wing" was at the fence while the other was in the rear. See Banes, *History of the Philadelphia Brigade*, 187. Like so many "facts" that Gettysburg enthusiasts accept, the accounts of those who were here on July 3 are simply not conclusive enough to make a definite decision.
4. William J. Burns, *Civil War Diary*, 59-60, in 71st Pennsylvania Infantry File, ALBG, GNMP.
5. "The Battle," *Compiler*, June 7, 1887.
6. *OR*, 27/1: 428.
7. *OR*, 27/1: 428; Ladd, *Bachelder Papers*, 1:19. Curiously, Webb told sculptor James Kelly in 1905 that "the mass in my immediate front was forced to surrender…became a mob- threw down their arms and rushed in as prisoners. And have ever since claimed that they pierced the line and went over two lines of earthworks that never existed." See Styple, *Generals in Bronze*, 155.
8. Coddington, *The Gettysburg Campaign*, 516.
9. Ladd, *Bachelder Papers*, 3: 1657.
10. Roberts, "The 72d PA," 418.
11. Rollins, *Eyewitness Accounts*, 339.
12. Banes, *History of the Philadelphia Brigade*, 190-191.
13. Ladd, *Bachelder Papers*, 3: 1706. Author George Stewart described the 71st's retreat fairly directly in his seminal work *Pickett's Charge*, asserting that the regiment's "color-bearers and officers too- broke in wild flight, all but a few of them." Stewart did accept that the regiment's forward position was faulty to begin with. Stewart, *Pickett's Charge*, 207-208, 212-213. John Bachelder acknowledged that the regiment's retro-movement was necessitated by the fact that they had "no connection on its right." See Ladd, *Bachelder Papers*, 3: 1901.
14. Ladd, *Bachelder Papers*, 1: 19.
15. Burns, *Civil War Diary*, 59-60.
16. *Pennsylvania at Gettysburg*, 412-414; Hawthorne, *Men and Monuments*, 120.

U9A: 72nd Pennsylvania Regimental Monuments

17. Banes, *History of the Philadelphia Brigade*, 11-13.
18. Jonathan D. Neu, "The 72nd Pennsylvania Monument Controversy," *Gettysburg Magazine 40* (January 2009), 84.
19. Rollins, *Eyewitness Accounts*, 316-317.
20. Ibid., 317.
21. Ibid., 317. In Webb's battle report, he wrote: "The Seventy-second Pennsylvania Volunteers fought steadily and persistently, but the enemy would probably have succeeded in piercing our lines had not Colonel Hall advanced with several of his regiments to my support." *OR*, 27/1: 428.
22. Rollins, Eyewitness Accounts, 328.
23. Ibid., 317.
24. Roberts, "The 72d PA," 418.
25. Ladd, *Bachelder Papers*, 3: 1609-1610.
26. Ibid., 3:1628, 1649.
27. Haskell, *Gettysburg*, 128-129.
28. Ladd, *Bachelder Papers*, 3: 1701, 1704, 1706.
29. Roberts, "The 72d PA," 418.
30. Rollins, *Eyewitness Accounts*, 328.
31. Ibid., 337; Fuger to Sylvester Byrne, May 13, 1888, 72nd Pennsylvania Infantry File, ALBG, GNMP.
32. Busey and Martin, *Strengths and Losses*, 129. The 72nd's casualties were 50.5% on 380 engaged vs. 137 losses and 48.2% for the 69th and 98 losses and 37.5% for the 71st Pennsylvania.
33. Harrison, *Location of the Monuments*, 13.
34. Webb, *Dedication of the 72nd PA*, 15. Both Webb and Banes testified that the regiment had been "near" or a "little in front" of the monument. It has been proposed that part of the confusion in interpreting the court testimony is that there were numerous references to an east-west "hill" near the Copse that is often confused with the north-south Cemetery "Ridge." See David Trout, "The Seventy-second Pennsylvania Monument Controversy," *Baxter's 72nd Pennsylvania Infantry*, http://baxters72ndpenninfantry.blogspot.com.
35. Vanderslice, *Then and Now*, 376; Letter of Samuel Roberts, June 22, 1888, 72nd Pennsylvania Infantry File, ALBG, GNMP.
36. Neu, "72nd Pennsylvania Monument Controversy," 82.
37. "Circular No. I. 72nd Regt, P.V. vs. Gettysburg Battle-field Asso'n," 72nd Pennsylvania File, ALBG, GNMP; *Pennsylvania at Gettysburg*, 1: 416.
38. *Pennsylvania at Gettysburg*, 1: 416.
39. Letter from Sylvester Byrne to Samuel Harper, July 11, 1888, 72nd Pennsylvania Infantry File, ALBG, GNMP.
40. "History of the Case" extract, 72nd Pennsylvania Infantry File, ALBG, GNMP; Neu, "72nd Pennsylvania Monument Controversy," 82.
41. Neu, "The 72nd Pennsylvania Monument Controversy," 82-83, 88-89, 91.
42. *Pennsylvania at Gettysburg*, 1: 416-417; Desjardin, *These Honored Dead*, 163; Neu, "The 72nd Pennsylvania Monument Controversy," 89.
43. "Storm Topples Monument," *Gettysburg Times*, June 27, 2013.

U9B: Lieutenant Alonzo Cushing's Battery A, 4th US Artillery

44. Kent Masterson Brown, *Cushing of Gettysburg: The Story of a Union Artillery Commander* (KY, 1993), 53.
45. Frederick Fuger, "Cushing's Battery at Gettysburg," *Journal of the Military Service Institution of the United States*, Vol. 41 (1907), 407.
46. Frederick Fuger, "Battle of Gettysburg and Personal Recollections of that Battle," Typed manuscript, 22, in Alexander Stewart Webb Papers, MS 684, Box 7, Folder 110, Manuscripts and Archives, Yale University Library; Fuger, *Cushing's Battery*, 407.
47. Both quoted in Murray, "Cowan's, Cushing's, and Rorty's Batteries in Action," 43.
48. Brown, *Cushing of Gettysburg*, 237.
49. Fuger, *Personal Recollections*, 23 and *Cushing's Battery*, 408. In *Personal Recollections*, Fuger wrote that the canister was placed behind both guns but in *Cushing's Battery*, he wrote that all canister was piled in rear of gun number two. Also see Rollins, *Eyewitness Accounts*, 336-337; Murray, "Cowan's, Cushing's, and Rorty's Batteries in Action," 48.
50. *OR*, 27/1: 428.
51. Rollins, *Eyewitness Accounts*, 316.
52. Ladd, *Bachelder Papers*, 3: 1978, 1989.
53. Rollins, *Eyewitness Accounts*, 336-337; Fuger, *Personal Recollections*, 23 and *Cushing's Battery*, 408. For modern support of two guns, see Laino, *Gettysburg Campaign Atlas*, 343; Brown, *Cushing of Gettysburg*, 249-250; Sears, *Gettysburg*, 448-449. However, the esteemed Edwin Coddington (who relied heavily on Bachelder's papers) went with three guns at the wall. See Coddington, 511. As noted in our 71st Pennsylvania tour stop, it is possible that two guns were initially rolled forward and that a third was later moved in amongst the space occupied by the forward portion of the 71st regiment.
54. Ladd, *Bachelder Papers*, 3: 1411, 1649. Charles Banes (1890) testified that a portion of the battery was run to wall but couldn't say how many. See *Bachelder Papers*, 3: 1705.
55. Fuger, *Personal Recollections*, 23 and *Cushing's Battery*, 408.
56. Brown, *Cushing of Gettysburg*, 249.
57. Fuger, *Personal Recollections*, 24 and *Cushing's Battery*, 408. Pickett's men would also have been getting hit with canister from Cowan's batteries. See Murray, "Cowan's, Cushing's, and Rorty's Batteries in Action," 48.

58. Ladd, *Bachelder Papers*, 2: 1146, 1157; Scott Hartwig, "Lieutenant Cushing," *From the Fields of Gettysburg* (June 21, 2002), http://npsgnmp.wordpress.com/2012/06/21/lieutenant-cushing/.
59. Roberts, "The 72d PA," 417. Roberts's account does not say how many guns were still in service.
60. Ladd, *Bachelder Papers*, 3: 1978.
61. Fuger, *Personal Recollections*, 24 and *Cushing's Battery*, 408-409. According to Fuger, Armistead and Cushing fell only about seven yards apart.
62. Thomas Moon, *Reminiscences of Thomas Moon*, Battery A, 4th US Artillery Regiment File, ALBG, GNMP, n.p.
63. Busey and Martin, *Strengths and Losses*, 442, 444, 446-448.
64. Moon, *Reminiscences*; also quoted in Brown, *Cushing of Gettysburg*, 259-260.
65. Brown, *Cushing of Gettysburg*, 12.
66. *Fuger Family Book*, 16-17, Battery A, 4th US Artillery Regiment File, ALBG, GNMP.
67. Dirk Johnson, "Winning a Battle to Honor a Civil War Hero," *New York Times*, June 11, 2010; Kathryn Jorgensen, "Alonzo Cushing May Yet Be Awarded the Medal of Honor," *Civil War News*, July 2012; Peter Baker, "Civil War Hero Awarded the Medal of Honor at Last," *New York Times*, November 7, 2014.

U9C: Brigadier General Lewis Armistead Fell Here

68. Martin, "Rawley Martin's Account," 32: 187; Poindexter, "General Armistead's Portrait," 37: 149; Rollins, *Eyewitness Accounts*, 163, 183, 193.
69. Tapscott, "One of Pickett's Men," 413.
70. Fuger, *Recollections*, 24.
71. *OR*, 27/1: 428; Earl J. Hess, *Pickett's Charge: The Last Attack at Gettysburg* (Chapel Hill, NC, 2001), 261-265, 438, n.33; Michael Halleran, "'The Widow's Son.' Lewis Armistead at Gettysburg," *Gettysburg Magazine 43* (July 2009), 96.
72. Harrison, *Nothing But Glory*, 107.
73. Rollins, *Eyewitness Accounts*, 337-338. Fuger's accounts become more confusing when he frequently fails to differentiate whether or not Cushing's entire battery or only part was at the wall. Also see Heenehan, "Philadelphia Defends the Wall," 105, n.72.
74. Ladd, *Bachelder Papers*, 3: 1989.
75. Roberts, "The 72d PA," 418.
76. Ladd, *Bachelder Papers*, 1: 19.
77. Ibid., 3: 1704-1705. Also see Motts, *Trust in God and Fear Nothing*, 45.
78. A higher-end estimate of four to five feet per pace would equate 33 paces as being from the Armistead marker to slightly east side of Hancock Avenue.
79. D.B. Easley, "With Armistead When He Was Killed," *Confederate Veteran* XX (1912), 379. Easley misidentified the cannon as being "brass."
80. Easley, "With Armistead When He Was Killed," 379; Rollins, *Eyewitness Accounts*, 190-191. In a separate 1913 account, Easley problematically identified the position of the Union squad that shot Armistead as being "about where" the 71st Pennsylvania monument is located. See Rollins, 192.
81. *OR*, 27/1: 514; Brown, *Cushing of Gettysburg*, 242.
82. Tapscott, "One of Pickett's Men," 413.
83. Ladd, *Bachelder Papers*, 3: 1412-1413.
84. Ibid., 3: 1647.
85. Sheldon A. Munn, *Freemasons at Gettysburg* (Gettysburg, PA, 1993), 16; Halleran, "'The Widow's Son'," 93.
86. Banes, *History of the Philadelphia Brigade*, 192.
87. Ladd, *Bachelder Papers*, 3: 1705, 3: 1901. Capt. John C. Brown, 20th Indiana, wrote John Bachelder a lengthy 1887 letter in which he claimed to have found a wounded Rebel officer near the spot of Armistead's fall who introduced himself as a Mason. Brown never learned the name of this officer and later wondered if it was Armistead. Some historians have accepted Brown as Armistead's first rescuer while others are skeptical of the account. See Ladd, *Bachelder Papers*, 3: 1494-1497. The soldier who heard this signal may have been a Pvt. Jacob Wildemore of the 72nd Pennsylvania. See Halleran, "'The Widow's Son'," 106 and Glenn Tucker, *High Tide at Gettysburg* (Gettysburg, PA, 1995), 431, n. 53
88. Ladd, *Bachelder Papers*, 1: 351-352.
89. Ibid., 1: 351. For a fanciful tale of the wounded Armistead meeting Hancock himself, see Martin, "Armistead's Brigade at Gettysburg," 39: 187. As Martin is an otherwise often used primary source, his inclusion of the Hancock-Armistead meeting highlights the troubling challenges faced in evaluating "reliable" sources.
90. Abner Doubleday, *Chancellorsville and Gettysburg* (New York, 1882), 195.
91. Haskell, *Gettysburg*, 132-133.
92. James A. Stevens, "Do You Believe It?" *Confederate Veteran* XXVIII (1920), 356; Holland, "With Armistead at Gettysburg," 62.
93. Loehr, "The Old First Virginia at Gettysburg," 32: 34.
94. Coco, *A Vast Sea of Misery*, 105-106.
95. Ibid., 106-107.
96. Ladd, *Bachelder Papers*, 1: 358-359. Descriptions of Armistead's wounds by others vary, but as an attending physician, Brinton's recollections carry the most weight. Justus Silliman, 17th Connecticut, said Armistead was "wounded in the breast and leg." Coco, *A Vast Sea of Misery*, 105. John Irvin, 154th New York, recalled two wounds in the body and one in the thigh. A Dr. Hovey said Armistead was shot in the chest. Doctor Henry Van Aernam found no fatal wounds, implying no body wounds. John M. Irvin and Henry Van Aernam interviews in Edwin Dwight Northrup Papers, #4190, Department of Manuscripts and University Archives, Cornell University Libraries, Ithaca, NY. Thank you to Mark H. Dunkelman for transcribing and providing the Northrup material.
97. *Star and Sentinel*, July 11, 1893.
98. Coco, *A Vast Sea of Misery*, 105; Irvin and Van Aernam Interviews, Northrup Papers, Cornell University Libraries; Storrick, "General Armistead Was Only Southern Leader to Cross Wall at 'Angle' in Pickett's Charge," *Gettysburg Times*, March 23, 1939; Holland, "With Armistead at Gettysburg," 62; Motts, *Trust in God and Fear Nothing*, 48. Co-author Wayne Motts has corresponded with medical doctors on Armistead's death and believes that the general died of a pulmonary embolism. (A blood clot that went from Armistead's leg to his heart.) The facts that Armistead died quickly and had no indication of infection support this theory.
99. Ladd, *Bachelder Papers*, 3: 1128.
100. Ibid.; Storrick, "General Armistead Was Only Southern Leader to Cross Wall at 'Angle' in Pickett's Charge"; Wayne Motts and Silas Felton, "In Their Words: Recollections of Visitations at Gettysburg After the Great Battle in July 1863," *Gettysburg Magazine 46* (January 2012), 112.
101. Vanderslice, *Gettysburg Then and Now*, 376, 379; Carol Reardon, *Pickett's Charge in History and Memory* (Chapel Hill, NC, 1997), 93-95.
102. Munn, *Freemasons at Gettysburg*, 8-15.
103. Mayo, "Pickett's Charge," 34: 334-335.

U9D: Brigadier General Alexander Webb Monument

104. New York Monuments Commission for the Battlefields of Gettysburg and Chattanooga, *In Memoriam: Alexander Stewart Webb, 1835-1911* (Albany, NY, 1916), 93-94.
105. Ibid., 11-12.
106. Ibid., 54.
107. Ibid., 12, 95.
108. Lash, "The Philadelphia Brigade," 98-99; Ladd, *Bachelder Papers*, 2: 968; Banes, *History of the Philadelphia Brigade*, 173-174.
109. Styple, *Generals in Bronze*, 151.
110. Stine, *History of the Army of the Potomac*, 531.
111. Styple, *Generals in Bronze*, 144, 147, 151, 159.
112. New York Monuments Commission, *In Memoriam*, 13. However, Webb told monument sculptor James Kelly an interesting post-Gettysburg story in which Meade on one occasion "allowed his tongue to run away with him" and presumably insulted Webb, after which Webb refused to share his commander's mess. See Styple, *Generals in Bronze*, 149-150.
113. New York Monuments Commission, *In Memoriam*, 12, 104-105; Tagg, *Generals of Gettysburg*, 51.
114. New York Monuments Commission, *In Memoriam*, 11-12, 14, 16; Tagg, *Generals of Gettysburg*, 51.
115. New York Monuments Commission, *In Memoriam*, 106.
116. Ibid., 18, 27.
117. Ibid., 19; Styple, *Generals in Bronze*, 152.

Sidebar U9.1: There Was a Great Boulder

1. Ladd, *Bachelder Papers*, 3: 1411. Some accounts believe that this flight was caused by confusion that resulted from the company's captain becoming an early casualty.
2. *OR*, 27/2: 386.
3. Harrison, *Nothing But Glory*, 85.
4. Testimony of William S. Stockton, *Supreme Court of Pennsylvania*, 243-244. Also see "The Battle," *Compiler*, June 7, 1887; Rollins, *Eyewitness Accounts*, 339. Stockton was born April 12, 1841, in Philadelphia and enlisted in May 1861 at Burlington, New Jersey. Occupation listed as "dentist." William S. Stockton, Pension Record, RG 15.

5. Fred Hawthorne, "140 Places Every Guide Should Know," http://www.gettysburgdaily.com/?p=8821.
6. Stockton Testimony, *Supreme Court of Pennsylvania*, 244. Anthony McDermott of the 69th Pennsylvania told John Bachelder that Stockton "claims to have remained at the wall right at the 'Angle' after the Rebels crossed, a sort of prisoner, and was of course there until the enemy gave up." Ladd, *Bachelder Papers*, 3: 1648.
7. William S. Stockton, Pension Record, RG 15; "Obituary Notice," *Public Ledger* (Philadelphia, PA), August 30, 1913; *Pennsylvania at Gettysburg*, 412; "Friends Not Foes," *The Atlanta Constitution*, July 3, 1887.

Sidebar U9.2: Hazardous Service

1. Busey and Martin, *Strengths and Losses*, 486-487. Wainwright and Randolph's brigades were tied for second with 106 losses and McGilvery's was second in rate at 24.2%.
2. Ladd, *Bachelder Papers*, 2: 1157.
3. All Hazard quotes from *OR*, 27/1: 477-481.
4. Register of Enlistments of the United States Army, NARA, RG 94, M233, Roll 27; Busey, *Union Casualties at Gettysburg*, 2: 1075.
5. "Veteran Dies Fighting To Prove He Was Alive," *Oakland Tribune*, June 13, 1926.

Sidebar U9.3: Why Don't They Come?

1. Rollins, *Eyewitness Accounts*, 157; also Rollins, "The Second Wave of Pickett's Charge," 96.
2. Mayo, "Pickett's Charge," 34: 334.
3. *OR*, 27/2: 360.
4. *OR*, 27/2: 320.
5. *OR*, 27/2: 614-615.
6. *OR*, 27/2: 621.
7. Private Joseph Folkes of the 41st Virginia and Westwood Todd of the 12th Virginia both left similar accounts of Mahone advancing briefly before being told to halt. Rollins, "The Second Wave of Pickett's Charge," 104-105.
8. Walter H. Taylor, *Four Years with General Lee* (New York, 1878), 107-108.
9. Taylor, "Memorandum," 4: 84-85.
10. Long, *Memoirs of R.E. Lee*, 294; Rollins, "The Second Wave of Pickett's Charge," 108.
11. Long, *Memoirs of R.E. Lee*, 294.
12. Longstreet, "Longstreet's Account of the Campaign and Battle," 5: 71.
13. Longstreet, *From Manassas to Appomattox*, 393.

Sidebar U9.4: One Female in Rebel Uniform

1. See Eileen F. Conklin, *Women at Gettysburg* (Gettysburg, PA, 1993) for a discussion.
2. *OR*, 27/1: 378.
3. Martha Keller, "The Hero of Pickett's Old Brigade. By the Author of 'Love and Rebellion,'" *Confederate Veteran*, Vol. I (1893), 174.
4. Conklin, *Women at Gettysburg*, 134-135.

STOP U10: The "Inner Angle" and the Abraham Bryan Farm

1. *OR*, 27/1: 454-455.
2. George T. Fleming and Gilbert Adams Hays, *General Alexander Hays at the Battle of Gettysburg* (Pittsburgh, PA, 1913), 19.
3. *OR*, 27/1: 454.
4. *OR*, 27/1: 465.
5. *OR*, 27/1: 706.
6. Rollins, *Eyewitness Accounts*, 285-286.

U10A: Captain William Arnold's Battery A, First Rhode Island

7. Aldrich, *History of Battery A*, 215.
8. Ladd, *Bachelder Papers*, 1: 399.
9. Busey and Martin, *Strengths and Losses*, 442-444.
10. Ladd, *Bachelder Papers*, 1: 341.
11. Hunt, "The Third Day at Gettysburg," 374.
12. *OR*, 27/1: 480.
13. Ladd, *Bachelder Papers*, 1: 79 and 1: 407.
14. Aldrich, *History of Battery A*, 215-216.
15. Trinque, "Arnold's Battery," 64-66.
16. Rollins, *Eyewitness Accounts*, 326. Weir's recollections that he started with shorter range canister before using longer-range case and shot is counter-intuitive unless he used the longer range rounds on retreating Confederates.
17. Aldrich, *History of Battery A*, 217.
18. Ibid., 218-219.
19. Harrison, *The Location of the Monuments*, 17.

U10B: 1st Massachusetts "Andrew" Sharpshooters

20. Hawthorne, *Men and Monuments*, 121; Ladd, *Bachelder Papers*, 2: 1101.
21. Ladd, *Bachelder Papers*, 2: 964.
22. *OR*, 27/1: 311.
23. Rollins, *Eyewitness Accounts*, 291-292; Ladd, *Bachelder Papers* 2: 964; 3; 1902. Capt. Armstrong of the 125th New York likewise described the "charge" and "great execution" of the sharpshooters. See Ladd, *Bachelder Papers*, 2: 1001.
24. Ladd, *Bachelder Papers*, 2: 986-987.

U10C: 14th Connecticut Regimental Monument

25. Page, *History of the 14th*, 143.
26. Ibid., 151; Busey and Martin, *Strengths and Losses*, 130.
27. Page, *History of the 14th*, 149.
28. Ladd, *Bachelder Papers*, 1:79.
29. *OR*, 27/1:467.
30. Page, *History of the 14th*, 152. Federal accounts often conflict on how many Confederate lines appeared to be coming. Charles Page wrote: "There were three lines, and a portion of a fourth line, extending a mile or more. It was, indeed, a scene of unsurpassed grandeur and majesty…As far as eye could reach could be seen the advancing troops." See Page, *History of the 14th*, 151.
31. Rollins, *Eyewitness Accounts*, 268.
32. Trinque, "Confederate Battle Flags," 114.
33. Page, *History of the 14th*, 155-156. Elijah Bacon and Christopher Flynn were also awarded Medals for their July 3 valor.
34. Harrison, *Location of the Monuments*, 1.

U10D: 12th New Jersey Regimental Monument

35. Busey and Martin, *Strengths and Losses*, 130.
36. Hawthorne, *Men and Monuments*, 126; Samuel Toombs, *New Jersey Troops in the Gettysburg Campaign from June 5 to July 31, 1863* (Orange, NJ, 1888), 294-295.
37. Rollins, *Eyewitness Accounts*, 288-289.
38. From the Address of Col. William Potter in Toombs, *New Jersey Troops*, 298.
39. Ibid., 284.
40. New Jersey Gettysburg Battlefield Commission, *Final Report*, 107.
41. Hawthorne, *Men and Monuments*, 127.

U10E: Abraham Bryan Farm

42. Smith, *Farms at Gettysburg*, 13-14.
43. Frassanito, *Early Photography*, 229, 232-233. Bachelder described it in his 1873 guidebook as Hays's headquarters.

U10F: Bryan Tenant House

44. Christ, "Struggle for the Bliss Farm, Part 3," *http://www.gettysburgdaily.com/?p=4574*.
45. Paradis, *African Americans and the Gettysburg Campaign*, 60.
46. Frassanito, *Early Photography*, 234.
47. Peter Vermilyea, "The Effect of the Confederate Invasion on Pennsylvania's African American Community," *Gettysburg Magazine 24* (July 2001), 113-119.
48. Paradis, *African Americans and the Gettysburg Campaign*, 9.

U10G: Willard / Sherrill's Brigade

49. *Dedication of the New York Auxiliary State Monument on the Battlefield of Gettysburg* (Albany, NY, 1926), 136.
50. Eric Campbell, "'Remember Harper's Ferry': The Degradation, Humiliation, and Redemption of Col. George L. Willard's Brigade," *Gettysburg Magazine 7* (July 1992), 73-75.
51. *New York at Gettysburg*, 2: 907; Laino, *Gettysburg Campaign Atlas*, 346.
52. Ezra Dee Frest Simons, *A Regimental History: The One Hundred and Twenty-fifth New York State Volunteers* (New York, 1888), 136, 138; *OR*, 27/1: 477.
53. *OR*, 27/1: 476.
54. Edith Armstrong Talbot, *Samuel Chapman Armstrong: A Biographical Study* (New York, 1904), 92.
55. Ladd, *Bachelder Papers*, 2: 1000-1001; Talbot, *Samuel Chapman Armstrong*, 92-93.
56. Simons, *125th New York State Volunteers*, 136-138.
57. *OR*, 27/1: 473.
58. *New York at Gettysburg*, 2: 907-908.
59. Ibid., 2: 907; *Dedication of the New York Auxiliary State Monument*, 137.
60. *OR*, 27/1: 473.

STOP U11: Ziegler's Grove

1. Frassanito, *Early Photography*, 180; Harmon, *Cemetery Hill*, 117-131.
2. Frassanito, *Early Photography*, 180; Christ, "Struggle for the Bliss Farm," http://www.gettysburgdaily.com/?p=4289.
3. *Cyclorama Building, Historic American Buildings Survey* (National Park Service), 5-6.; *GNMP Commission Reports*, 31.
4. *Cyclorama Building HABS*, 3-4, 8-10. The cyclorama painting had been displayed in a building along the Baltimore pike since 1913. See HABS, 6.
5. Ibid., 8-10.
6. Ibid., 4.
7. Sarah Allaback, *Mission 66 Visitor Centers: The History of a Building Type* (Washington, DC, 2000), n.p.
8. *Cyclorama Building HABS*, 44.

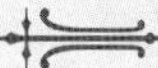

9. Robert Housch, "National Cemetery Parking and North Cemetery Ridge Updates," *Gettysburgdaily.com* (February 24, 2012), http://www.gettysburgdaily.com/?p=13420. Thanks to Gettysburg National Military Park Historian John Heiser for providing updated information regarding the monuments' return to their original positions.

U11A: Lieutenant George Woodruff's Battery I, First U.S. Artillery and 108th New York

10. Rollins, *Eyewitness Accounts*, 291.
11. Ibid.
12. Coco, *A Vast Sea of Misery*, 73; Rollins, *Eyewitness Accounts*, 291.
13. Toombs, *New Jersey Troops*, 282.

U11B: Brigadier General Alexander Hays Monument

14. Tagg, *The Generals of Gettysburg*, 53; Fleming, *Hays at the Battle of Gettysburg*, 3.
15. Fleming, *Hays at the Battle of Gettysburg*, 14.
16. Tagg, *The Generals of Gettysburg*, 53.
17. Fleming, *Hays at the Battle of Gettysburg*, 13.
18. Ibid., 20. Hays reportedly lost two horses at Gettysburg. See Tagg, *Generals of Gettysburg*, 54.
19. Fleming, *Hays at Battle of Gettysburg*, 22-23.
20. Harrison, *The Location of the Monuments*, 41; Wayne Manhood, *Alexander "Fighting Elleck" Hays: The Life of a Civil War General from West Point to the Wilderness* (NC, 2005), 173; Swift, "Gettysburg Monument to be Dedicated," *The Daily Item*, August 11, 2007. One may note stylistic similarities between the Hays statue and several others on the field: President Lincoln, David M. Gregg and Alfred Pleasonton from the Pennsylvania State Monument, William Wells on South Confederate Avenue, John Geary on Culp's Hill, and Andrew Humphreys along the Emmitsburg Road. All of these were the work of the same man: Swiss-born sculptor J. Otto Schweitzer.

STOP U12: Major General George Meade Equestrian Monument

1. Haskell, *The Battle of Gettysburg*, 137; Meade, *Life and Letters*, 2: 109-110. Meade's *Life and Letters*, 2: 109 claimed Meade rode "straight to the front, arrived on the crest at the point where the enemy were making their attack, and rode among the batteries and troops encouraging the men by his voice and presence. He remained on the ridge throughout the attack, and until the enemy was repulsed."
2. *OR*, 27/1: 74-75.
3. Harrison, *Location of the Monuments, Markers, and Tablets*, 41. On the Federal side, Reynolds's statue was dedicated in 1899, Slocum in 1902, Sedgwick in 1913, and Howard in 1932. Amongst Confederates, Lee received his (via the Virginia memorial) in 1917 and Longstreet in 1998. John Bachelder wrote in 1890 that he secured 70,000 pounds of bronze to make equestrian statues of Meade, Hancock, Sykes, Sedgwick, and Warren, "and while I would erect those of the Corps Commanders with their commands I would place General Meade on the crowning summit of Cemetery Hill." See Ladd, *Bachelder Papers*, 3: 1906.
4. "Meade and Hancock," *Compiler*, June 9, 1896; Vanderslice, *Gettysburg Then and Now*, 451. Also see "Meade and Hancock Statues," *Compiler*, June 2, 1896.
5. "Meade and Hancock," *Compiler*, June 9, 1896.
6. Meade, *Life Letters*, 2: 125; Hawthorne, *Men and Monuments*, 125.

Sidebar U12.1: Did General Meade Counterattack?

1. Alexander, "Letter from General E. P. Alexander, March 17th 1877," 4: 109.
2. Alexander, *Military Memoirs*, 432.
3. *OR*, 27/2: 321.
4. *OR*, 27/2: 361-362.
5. "Meade's Great Mistake," *New York Times*, July 4, 1888. Longstreet continued the notion in his memoirs, writing that a combined cavalry and infantry operation "pushed with vigor…could have reached our line of retreat." See Longstreet, *From Manassas to Appomattox*, 396.
6. Bond, *Pickett or Pettigrew?*, 61. Bond considered Longstreet to be personally "honest" but was "so largely imaginative, that his statement of facts is rarely worthy of credence."
7. *OR*, 27/1: 75.
8. See *OR*, 27/1: 117. "This terminated the battle, the enemy retiring to his lines, leaving the field strewn with his dead and wounded, and numerous prisoners in our hands…Kilpatrick's division, that on the 29th, 30th, and 1st had been successfully engaging the enemy's cavalry, was on the 3d sent on our extreme left, on the Emmitsburg road, where good service was rendered in assaulting the enemy's line and occupying his attention. At the same time, General Gregg was engaged with the enemy on our extreme right, having passed across the Baltimore pike and Bonaughtown road, and boldly attacked the enemy's left and rear."
9. Hyde, *The Union Generals Speak*, 111.
10. *OR*, 27/1: 366.
11. Hyde, *The Union Generals Speak*, 218.
12. *OR*, 27/1: 593.
13. *OR*, 27/1: 654-655. As it was actually Colonel McCandless, and not General Crawford, who led this movement, refer also to McCandless's *OR*, 27/1: 657-658. Regarding his orders, McCandless wrote: "I was ordered to advance and clear the woods on my front and left, to do which the command had to cross an open field about 800 yards wide."
14. *OR*, 27/1: 654-655, 657-658.
15. Hyde, *The Union Generals Speak*, 345-348.
16. Ibid., 139-140. Pleasonton's own report was considerably less dramatic. "General Kilpatrick did valuable service with the First Brigade, under General Farnsworth, in charging the enemy's infantry, and, with the assistance of Merritt's brigade and the good execution of their united batteries, caused him to detach largely from his main attack on the left of our line." See *OR*, 27/1: 916.
17. *OR*, 27/1: 992- 993. The report of Col. Nathaniel Richmond, First West Virginia Cavalry, described the assault: "General Farnsworth was ordered to charge the enemy's right, which he at once did, making one of the most desperate, and at the same time most successful, charges it has ever been my lot to witness, and during which that gallant officer (General Farnsworth) was killed while in the thickest of the fight." See *OR*, 27/1: 1005.
18. *OR*, 27/1: 992- 993.
19. See Eric J. Wittenberg, *Gettysburg's Forgotten Cavalry Actions* (New York, 2011), 145 for commentary on the lack of coordination between the infantry and cavalry.
20. Hyde, *The Union Generals Speak*, 170. Warren did add that casualties in the officers' ranks contributed to a "shattered" feeling within the army.
21. Doubleday, *Chancellorsville and Gettysburg*, 202-203. Abner Doubleday, another of Meade's critics, proposed that the VI and portions of the XII Corps should have been moved into Gibbon's rear at the moment Pickett's Division was seen emerging from the woods.
22. Hunt, "The Third Day at Gettysburg," 376 and "The Second Day at Gettysburg," 302.
23. Hyde, *The Union Generals Speak*, 119.
24. Ibid., 170.
25. Meade, *Life and Letters*, 2: 125.

Sidebar U12.2: Piles of Dead and Thousands of Wounded

1. Page, *History of the 14th Regiment*, 156.
2. *OR*, 27/1: 428.
3. *OR*, 27/1: 454.
4. *OR*, 27/1: 440.
5. Haskell, *Gettysburg*, 131.
6. Ibid., 140.
7. "The Great Battles," *New York Times*, July 4, 1863; "The Battle of Gettysburg," *Burlington Weekly Hawk-Eye*, July 11, 1863. The *New York Times* of July 4 headlined that both Generals Longstreet and Hill had been killed.
8. Ladd, *Bachelder Papers*, 1: 19.
9. *OR*, 27/1: 440.
10. Hartwig, "It Struck Horror to Us All," 99.
11. Fleming, *Hays at Battle of Gettysburg*, 13, 18.
12. Burns, *Civil War Diary*, 59-60.
13. Coco, *Vast Sea of Misery*, 67.
14. Harrison, *Location of the Monuments*, 34.
15. Busey and Martin, *Strengths and Losses*, 129.
16. Davis (69th Pennsylvania) estimated 121 of 149 casualties on July 3. See *OR*, 27/1: 431. Colonel Smith approximated 100 of 117; *OR*, 27/1: 432. Colonel Hall estimated that "about 150 men" were killed or wounded on July 2 and subtracting from Busey's estimated 377 total losses yields 227 on the third day. *OR*, 27/1: 437 and Busey and Martin, *Strengths and Losses*, 129.
17. In Hays's division, Maj. Theodore Ellis, 14th Connecticut, claimed all of the regiment's 66 reported casualties were on July 3, save one injury on July 2, a captain "who was seriously injured accidentally by a runaway horse." See *OR*, 27/1: 467-468. Lieutenant John Dent, First Delaware Infantry, estimated 32 lost on July 2, leaving about 45 (or 60% of total losses) on July 3. See *OR*, 27/1: 469 and Busey and Martin, *Strengths and Losses*, 130.
18. Harrison, *Pickett's Men*, 101-102; H.V. Harris to Father, Harris Papers, Pearce Civil War Collection, Navarro College. Capt. Bright similarly claimed: "5,000 in the morning; 1,600 were put in camp that night; 3,400 killed,

wounded, and missing." Bright, "Pickett's Charge at Gettysburg," 266.

19. See *OR*, 27/2: 363. Medical Director Lafayette Guild's initial estimate was 214 killed and 1,152 wounded. See *OR*, 27/2: 329-330. An addendum to Guild's report estimates the total loss at 2,888. See *OR*, 27/2: 339.
20. Harrison and Busey, *Nothing But Glory*, 170, 467.
21. Ibid., 170 - 171, 451, 467. In this analysis, Busey tallied 1,476 total wounded of which 833 were also captured. An additional 681 of the captured were not wounded. See Harrison and Busey, *Nothing But Glory*, 170 – 171, 467. For our purposes here, we have included the 833 wounded and the 681 non-wounded to arrive at the total missing / captured of 1,514.
22. *OR Supplement*, Part I, Reports, Vol. 5, Serial 5, 333-334.
23. Busey and Martin, *Strengths and Losses*, 299.
24. Coco, *Vast Sea of Misery*, 148.
25. Ibid., 135-136.
26. Ibid., 140-141.
27. *Adams Sentinel*, August 25, 1863.
28. Harrison and Busey, *Nothing But Glory*, 468, 494, 496-497.
29. Ibid., 501-503.

Sidebar U12.3: My Country Called, I Came to Die

1. Beth Swift, "Captain Blinn," *Dear Old Wabash*, February 5, 2009; Gregory Coco, *Killed in Action* (Gettysburg, PA, 1992), 103-105.
2. A.H. Nickerson, "Personal Recollections of Two Visits to Gettysburg," *Scribner's Magazine*, Vol. 4, Issue 1 (June 1893), 25.
3. Swift, "Captain Blinn," *Dear Old Wabash*.
4. "Letter from Dorthea Blinn to Amory Blinn," July 29, 1863, Blinn Papers, Cincinnati Historical Society, Box 5, Folder / Letter 667. His mother applied for and received a pension of $20 per month. John Blinn, Pension Record, RG 15. There is dispute over Blinn's date of death, as it has alternately been reported as July 14 or July 18. See Busey, *Union Casualties at Gettysburg*, 22. Blinn's mother placed the date as July 14 and we would assume that a mother, who was present, would know the date of her son's death. The authors wish to acknowledge Martha Brogan for assistance with materials related to John Blinn.
5. Nickerson, "Personal Recollections of Two Visits to Gettysburg," 26-28.
6. "Col. A.H. Nickerson," *The Reports of Committees of the House of Representatives for the Second Session of the 52nd Congress 1892-1893, 2nd Session* (Washington, DC, 1893), Report 2579, 1-6.

CONCLUSION: More Criticized and is Still Less Understood

1. Alexander, *Military Memoirs*, 425-426.
2. Fremantle, *Three Months in the Southern States*, 268-269.
3. Rollins, *Eyewitness Accounts*, 143.
4. Loehr, "The Old First Virginia at Gettysburg," 32: 36-38.
5. *OR*, 27/2: 299.
6. *OR*, 27/2: 309.
7. *OR*, 27/2: 321.
8. Robert E. Lee, *Recollections and Letters of General Robert E. Lee* (Garden City, NY: 1924), 102.
9. Allan, "Memoranda," 17-18.
10. William Allan, "Letter from Colonel William Allan, of Ewell's Staff," *Southern Historical Society Papers*, Vol. 4, 79-80.
11. Imboden, "Lee after Gettysburg," *The Petersburg Index*, March 25, 1871.
12. Rollins, *Eyewitness Accounts*, 149.
13. *OR*, 27/2: 360.
14. Longstreet, "The Mistakes of Gettysburg," 627.
15. Long, *Memoirs of Robert E. Lee*, 292.
16. Numerous published works have recounted Longstreet's post-war trials regarding his politics and war performance, notably the voluminous *Southern Historical Society Papers*, compiled primarily by Jubal Early and J. William Jones.
17. Jubal Early, "The Campaigns of Gen. Robert E. Lee. An Address by Lieut. General Jubal A. Early, before Washington and Lee University, January 19th, 1872," in Gary Gallagher, ed., *Lee the Soldier* (Lincoln, NE, 1996), 37-73; Swinton, *Campaigns of the Army of the Potomac*, 340.
18. Wilcox, "Letter," 4: 117. Wilcox also added as a primary reason: "Absence of the cavalry, and failure to report promptly when the Federal army had crossed the Potomac, and the line of direction of their march."
19. Alexander, "Letter," 4: 110.
20. Martin, "Rawley Martin's Account," 32: 189.
21. Freeman, *Lee's Lieutenants*, 3: 178.
22. Ibid., 3: 178-180.
23. Ibid., 3: 181.
24. Ibid., 3: 182-186.
25. See Callihan, "Neither Villain nor Hero," 18-19 for a similar viewpoint.

Sidebar Co1: Onslaught of Peace

1. "It's Again a Tented Field," *New York Times*, July 1, 1888; Undated newspaper article, Folder #190, Battle of Gettysburg: 25th Anniversary, ACHS.
2. "It's Again a Tented Field," *New York Times*; Undated newspaper article, Folder #190, Battle of Gettysburg: 25th Anniversary, ACHS; *Star and Sentinel*, July 17, 1888.
3. "Meade's Great Mistake," *New York Times*, July 4, 1888.
4. *Public Ledger*, July 1, 1913, Gettysburg 50th, PA State Archives; "Old Soldiers Defy Heat," *New York Times*, July 2, 1913; Stan Cohen, *Hands Across the Wall: The 50th and 75th Reunions of the Gettysburg Battle* (1982), 13.
5. Cohen, *Hands Across the Wall*, 13, 36; "Old Soldiers Defy Heat," *New York Times*, July 2, 1913; "Son and Grandsons of Gen. Longstreet," *Atlanta Constitution*, June 30, 1913; "Will Dedicate New Monument," *Gettysburg Times*, June 28, 1913.
6. "Lincoln Abused; 7 Men Are Stabbed," *Raleigh News and Observer*, July 3, 1913.
7. "Old Soldiers Defy Heat," *New York Times*, July 2, 1913.
8. "Limping Gray Men Once More Charge Up Cemetery Ridge," *The Atlanta Constitution*, July 4, 1913; Cohen, *Hands Across the Wall*, 13.
9. "Crowd of More than 35,000," *Gettysburg Times*, July 3, 1963.
10. "Colorful Re-Enactment of Pickett's Charge Attracts Huge Crowd," *Gettysburg Times*, July 5, 1963.
11. "Battle Hero's Son Here for Re-Enactment," *Gettysburg Times*, July 5, 1963.
12. Jorgensen, "Gettysburg 150th Brings Thousands," 1, 10.
13. Gast, "150th Anniversary of Battle of Gettysburg Provides a Bigger Story," *CNN.com*, June 30, 2013.
14. "Gettysburg 150th- July 3 Battlefield Experience Programs," From the Fields of Gettysburg, http://npsgnmp.wordpress.com/2013/05/17/gettysburg-150th-july-3-battlefield-experience-programs/.
15. Jorgensen, "Gettysburg 150th Brings Thousands," 1.

Bibliography

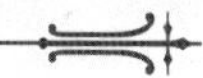

Archival Sources

Adams County Historical Society (Gettysburg, PA)

Battle of Gettysburg 25th Anniversary Folder

Biggs Family File

Gettysburg History of Town Lots

William Storrick Collection

Leander Warren, "Recollections of the Battle of Gettysburg"

J. Howard Wert Gettysburg Battlefield Scrapbook

Cincinnati Museum Center (Cincinnati, OH)

Blinn Papers

Cornell University Libraries (Ithaca, NY)

Edwin Dwight Northrup Papers, #4190, Department of Manuscripts and University Archives

Gettysburg College (Gettysburg, PA)

Special Collections, Musselman Library

Gettysburg National Military Park (GNMP) (Gettysburg, PA)

Association of Licensed Battlefield Guides (ALBG) Regimental and Misc. Files:

Battery A, 4th U.S. Artillery (7-U1L)

35th Georgia Infantry (7-CS4w)

11th Mississippi Infantry (7-CS8b)

11th North Carolina Infantry (7-CS9j)

26th North Carolina Infantry (7-CS9t)

47th North Carolina Infantry (7-CS9dd)

52nd North Carolina Infantry (7-CS9ee)

69th Pennsylvania Infantry (6-P69)

71st Pennsylvania Infantry (6-P71)

72nd Pennsylvania Infantry (6-P72)

1st Virginia Infantry (7-CS13a)

3rd Virginia Infantry (7-CS13c)

7th Virginia Infantry (7-CS13g)

8th Virginia Infantry (7-CS13h)

18th Virginia Infantry (7-CS13o)

19th Virginia Infantry (7-CS13p)

28th Virginia Infantry (7-CS13w)

40th Virginia Infantry (7-CS13bb)

42nd Virginia Infantry (7-CS13ff)

53rd Virginia Infantry (7-CS13kk)

55th Virginia Infantry (7-CS13LL)

56th Virginia Infantry (7-CS13mm)

WWII German POW Camp (11-40)

Boyle, Jaime and Robert Rehr, editors. *Journal of William McKenna Robbins: Commissioner, Gettysburg National Military Park, 1898-1905.* Gettysburg, PA: Gettysburg National Military Park.

Burns, William J. Co 'G', 1st Cal Regt. (71st PA), Civil War Diary, September 27, 1861 - December 31, 1863.

Georg, Kathleen. "The Sherfy Farm and the Battle of Gettysburg." National Park Service Environmental & Interpretive Planning, Research & Curatorial Division, January 1977.

Historic American Buildings Survey, Cyclorama Building, National Park Service.

Historic American Buildings Survey, Henry Spangler Farm, National Park Service.

Kane, Michael H. *The Court Martial of Dennis O'Kane.*

McMillan, Margaret. Historical account, January 6, 1941, McMillan Farm Vertical Files.

Monuments and Tablets in Gettysburg National Military Park.

Moon, Thomas. *Reminiscences of Thomas Moon, Battery A, 4th US.*

Pohanka, Brian C. *James McKay Rorty: An Appreciation. On the Occasion of the Unveiling of a Memorial First Cavalry Cemetery, Queens, New York, May 29, 1993.*

Webb, Alexander S. *An Address Delivered at Gettysburg, August 27, 1883 by Gen. Alexander S. Webb at the Dedication of the 72nd PA. Vols. Monument.* Philadelphia: Porter & Coates, 1883.

Harvard University Archives (Cambridge, MA)

HUP carte-de-visite, Paine, Sumner

Library of Congress, Manuscripts Division (Washington, DC)

Jubal Early Papers

Cadmus Wilcox Papers

Minnesota Historical Society (St. Paul, MN)

Copy Image of Nathan Messick by John J. Phillips

National Archives Records Administration (NARA), Compiled Military Service Record (CMSR)

Armistead, W. Keith. RG 109, M 324, Roll 62 (6th Virginia Cavalry)

Blackburn, Leander. RG 109, M 324, Roll 944 (53rd Virginia)

Gibbon, Lardner. RG 109, M 331, Roll 105 (Generals and Staff Officers)

Gibbon, Nicholas. RG 109, M 270, Roll 345 (28th North Carolina)

Gibbon, Robert. RG 109, M 270, Roll 345 (28th North Carolina)

Hoffman, Francis W. RG 109, M 382, Roll 27 (38th Battalion, Virginia Light Artillery)

Hoffman, Robert N. RG 109, M 324, Roll 376 (2nd Virginia Infantry)

Magruder, William T. RG 109, M 331, Roll 162. (General and Staff Officers, CSA)

Messick, Nathan. RG 94, M 616, Roll 25 (4th Indiana, Mexican War)

Page, Coupland Randolph. RG 109, M 324, Roll 317 (Amherst Artillery)

National Archives Record Administration (NARA)

Case Files of Applications from Former Confederates for Presidential Pardons, Record Group 94, M 1003, Roll 45 (Lardner Gibbon)

Original Battle Report of Col. Arthur Devereux, Record Group 94

Pension Record of John P. Blinn, Record Group 15

Pension Record of Joseph H. DeCastro, Record Group 15

Pension Record of Nathan Messick, Record Group 15

Pension Record of William S. Stockton, Record Group 15

Register of Enlistments of the United States Army, 1798-1914, Record Group 94, M 233, Roll 27

National Civil War Museum (Harrisburg, PA)

Blinn, John (Image)

Cushing, Alonzo (Image of Belt)

Garnett, Richard (Image)

Navarro College (Corsicana, TX)

Harris (Hilary Valentine) Papers, 1863, Pearce Civil War Collection

Pennsylvania State Archives (Harrisburg, PA)

50th Anniversary of the Battle of Gettysburg

U.S. Army Heritage and Education Center (Carlisle, PA)

Armistead, Lewis (Image)

Brake, Robert L. Collection

Kemper, James (Image)

Sanger, Donald Bridgman. "General James Longstreet and the Civil War." Ph.D. dissertation, University of Chicago, 1934

University of North Carolina at Chapel Hill, Southern Historical Collection, Wilson Library

Lafayette McLaws Papers

University of Virginia

John W. Daniel Papers

Virginia Historical Society

John C. Timberlake Papers

Virginia Military Institute (Lexington, VA)

F. Lewis Marshall Letter, October 6, 1863. Manuscript #0165, VMI Archives.

Student Files

Yale University Library

Alexander Stewart Webb Papers (MS 684). Manuscripts and Archives.

Fuger, Frederick. "Battle of Gettysburg and Personal Recollections of that Battle." Typed manuscript, Box 7, Folder 110.

Books, Articles, and Maps

Adelman, Garry E. *Little Round Top: A Detailed Tour Guide.* Gettysburg: Thomas Publications, 2000.

----. *The Myth of Little Round Top.* Gettysburg: Thomas Publications, 2003.

Aldrich, Thomas M. *The History of Battery A: First Regiment Rhode Island Light Artillery in the War to Preserve the Union 1861-1865.* Providence: Snow & Farnham, 1904.

Alexander, Edward Porter. *Fighting for the Confederacy: The Personal Recollections of General Edward Porter Alexander.* University of North Carolina Press, 1989.

----. "The Great Charge and Artillery Fighting at Gettysburg." *Battles and Leaders of the Civil War,* edited by Robert U. Johnson and Clarence C. Buel, 3: 357-368.

----. "Letter from General E. P. Alexander, March 17, 1877." *Southern Historical Society Papers,* 4: 97-111.

----. *Military Memoirs of a Confederate.* New York: Charles Scribner's Sons, 1907.

Allaback, Sarah. *Mission 66 Visitor Centers: The History of a Building Type.* Washington, DC: U.S. Department of the Interior, 2000.

Allan, William. "Letter from Colonel William Allan, of Ewell's Staff." *Southern Historical Society Papers,* 4:77-80.

----. "Memoranda of Conversations with General Robert E. Lee." *Lee the Soldier,* edited by Gary Gallagher, 7-24.

Andrus, Michael J. *The Brooke, Fauquier, Loudoun and Alexandria Artillery.* Lynchburg, VA: H.E. Howard, 1990.

"Annual Reunion of Pegram Battalion Association in the Hall of House of Delegates, Richmond, Va., May 21st, 1886." *Southern Historical Society Papers,* 14: 34.

Archer, John. *Fury on the Bliss Farm at Gettysburg.* Gettysburg: Ten Roads Publishing, 2012.

"Autographs from an old Album." *Confederate Veteran* XXXII (1924): 130.

Bachelder, John. *Gettysburg: What to See and How to See it.* Boston: 1878.

----. *Position of Troops, Third Day's Battle.* New York: Office of the Chief of Engineers, U.S. Army, 1876.

----. *The Story of the Battle of Gettysburg and Description of the Painting of the Repulse of Longstreet's* Assault. Boston: Historical Art Company, 1904.

Baker, Andrew J. "Tribute to Capt. Magruder and Wife." *Confederate Veteran* VI (1898): 507.

Bandy, Ken and Florence Freeland, editors. *The Gettysburg Papers, Two Volumes in One.* Dayton, OH: Morningside Bookshop, 1986.

Banes, Charles H. *History of the Philadelphia Brigade.* Philadelphia: J.B. Lippincott & Co, 1876.

Baumgartner, Richard A. *Buckeye Blood: Ohio at Gettysburg.* Huntington, WV: Blue Acorn Press, 2003.

Benedict, George G. *Army Life in Virginia.* Burlington: Free Press Association, 1895.

Biographical & Historical Memoirs of Mississippi. 2 Volumes. Spartansburg, SC: The Reprint Company, 1978. A reprint of the 1891 edition.

Bond, William R. *Pickett or Pettigrew? An Historical Essay.* Scotland Neck, NC: W.L.L. Hall, 1900. Second edition.

Bowden, Scott and Bill Ward. *Last Chance for Victory: Robert E. Lee and the Gettysburg Campaign.* Da Capo Press, 2001.

Bowen, James L. *Massachusetts in the War 1861-1865.* Springfield, MA: Clark W. Bryan & Company, 1889.

Brady, James P. *Hurrah for the Artillery! : Knap's Independent Battery "E", Pennsylvania Light Artillery.* Gettysburg, PA: Thomas Publications, 1992.

Brewer, W. *Alabama: Her History, Resources, War Record, and Public Men. From 1540 to 1872.* Tuscaloosa, AL: Willo Publishing Company, 1872.

Bright, Robert A. "Pickett's Charge at Gettysburg." *Confederate Veteran,* Vol. XXXVIII (1930): 263-266.

Brooke-Rawle, William. *Gregg's Cavalry Fight at Gettysburg. Historical Address Delivered October 15, 1884, Upon the Dedication of the Monumental Shaft Erected Upon the Site of the Cavalry Engagement on the Right Flank of the Army of the Potomac, July 3d, 1863, During the Battle of Gettysburg.* Philadelphia: 1884.

Brown, Kent Masterson. *Cushing of Gettysburg: The Story of a Union Artillery Commander.* The University Press of Kentucky, 1993.

Brunson, Joseph Woods. *Pee Dee Light Artillery of Maxcy Gregg's (Later McGowan's) Brigade, First South Carolina Volunteers (Infantry) C.S.A. A Historical Sketch.* Auburn, AL: Confederate Publish Company, 1983. Reprint of the 1905 edition.

Burton, Matthew W. *The River of Blood and the Valley of Death: The Lives of Robert Selden Garnett and Richard Brooke Garnett, C.S.A.* Columbus, OH: The General's Books, 1998.

Busey, John W. and David G. Martin. *Regimental Strengths and Losses at Gettysburg.* New Jersey: Longstreet House, 2005.

Busey, Travis W. and John W. Busey. *Union Casualties at Gettysburg: A Comprehensive Record.* Jefferson, NC: McFarland & Company, 2011.

Cabell, George C. "Colonel H. A. Carrington." *Sothern Historical Society Papers,* 32: 217.

Callahan, Edward W., editor. *List of Officers of the Navy of the United States and of the Marine Corps from 1771 to 1900.* New York: L. R. Hamersly & Co., 1901.

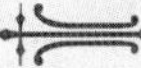

Callihan, David. "Neither Villain Nor Hero: A Reassessment of James Longstreet's Performance at Gettysburg." *Gettysburg Magazine 26* (July 2002): 6-19.

Campbell, Eric editor, *"A Grand Terrible Dramma," From Gettysburg to Petersburg" The Civil War Letters of Charles Wellington Reed*, New York: Fordham University Press, 2000.

----. "'Remember Harper's Ferry': The Degradation, Humiliation, and Redemption of Col. George L. Willard's Brigade." *Gettysburg Magazine 7* (July 1992): 50-75.

"Capt. Wiley Hunter Griffin." *Confederate Veteran* V (1897), 247-248.

Carter, James T. "Flag of the Fifty-Third VA. Regiment." *Confederate Veteran*, Vol. X (1902): 263.

Clark, Walter B. ed., *Histories of the Several Regiments and Battalions from North Carolina in the Great War 1861-'65.* 5 Volumes. Wilmington, NC: Broadfoot Publishing Company, 1996. Reprint of the 1901 edition.

Cockrell, Monroe F., editor. *Gunner with Stonewall: Reminiscences of William Thomas Poague.* Jackson, Tenn.: McCowat-Mercer Press, 1957.

Coco, Gregory A. *Killed in Action: Eyewitness Accounts of the Last Moments of 100 Union Soldiers Who Died at Gettysburg.* Gettysburg, PA: Thomas Publications, 1992.

----. *A Vast Sea of Misery.* Gettysburg: Thomas Publications, 1988.

----. *Wasted Valor: The Confederate Dead at Gettysburg.* Gettysburg: Thomas Publications, 1990.

Coddington, Edwin B. *The Gettysburg Campaign: A Study in Command.* New York: Charles Scribner's Sons, 1984. Reprint of the 1979 edition.

Cohen, Stan. *Hands Across the Wall: The 50th and 75th Reunions of the Gettysburg Battle.* Pictorial Histories Publishing Co., 1982.

Cole, James and Roy Frampton. *Lincoln and the Human Interest Stories of the Gettysburg National Cemetery.* Gettysburg, PA: 1995.

"Colonel William Steptoe Christian." *Confederate Veteran* XIX (1911), 350.

Conklin, Eileen F. *Women at Gettysburg.* Gettysburg: Thomas Publications, 1993.

Cooksey, Paul. "Forcing the Issue: Brig. Gen. Henry Hunt at Gettysburg on July 3, 1863." *Gettysburg Magazine 30* (January 2004): 77-88.

----. "The Plan for Pickett's Charge." *Gettysburg Magazine 22* (January 2000): 66-79.

----. "The Union Artillery at Gettysburg on July 3." Gettysburg Magazine 38 (January 2008): 72-90.

Crocker, James Francis. *Gettysburg- Pickett's Charge, Address by James F. Crocker, November 7, 1894.* Portsmouth VA: W.A. Fiske, 1906.

----. "James Gregory Hodges." *Southern Historical Society Papers*, 37: 193-195.

Cullum, George W. *Biographical Register of the Officers and Graduates of the U.S. Military Academy, from 1802 to 1867.* Volume 2. New York: James Miller, 1879.

Cutrer, Thomas W., editor. *Longstreet's Aide: The Civil War Letters of Major Thomas J. Goree.* Charlottesville: University Press of Virginia, 1995.

Davis, Stephen R. "The Death and Burials of General Richard Brooke Garnett." *Gettysburg Magazine 5* (July 1991): 107-116.

----. "Ole Miss' Spirited University Greys Left Their Quiet University Campus for the War's Worst Battlefields." *America's Civil War* (March 1992): 10-12, 70-72.

Dawson, Francis W. *Reminiscences of Confederate Service, 1861-1865.* Louisiana State University Press, 1980.

Dedication of the New York Auxiliary State Monument on the Battlefield of Gettysburg. Albany: J.B. Lyon Company, 1926.

Dempsey, Stuart. "The Florida Brigade at Gettysburg." *Blue & Gray Magazine* (Vol. XXVII, No. 4): 6-42.

Desjardin, Thomas. *Stand Firm Ye Boys From Maine: The 20th Maine and the Gettysburg Campaign.* Gettysburg: Thomas Publications, 1995.

----. *These Honored Dead: How the Story of Gettysburg Shaped American History.* Cambridge, MA: Da Capo, 2003.

Dinkins, James. "The Negroes as Slaves." *Southern Historical Society Papers*, 35: 62.

Doubleday, Abner. *Chancellorsville and Gettysburg.* New York: Charles Scribner's Sons, 1882.

Durkin, Joseph T. editor. *John Dooley Confederate Soldier: His War Journal.* University of Notre Dame Press, 1963.

Early, Jubal. "The Campaigns of Gen. Robert E. Lee. An Address by Lieut. General Jubal A. Early, before Washington and Lee University, January 19th, 1872." *Lee the Soldier*, edited by Gary Gallagher, 37-73.

Easley, D.B. "With Armistead When He Was Killed." *Confederate Veteran* XX (1912): 379.

"Echoes from Gettysburg." *Confederate Veteran* XXI (1913).

Elliott's Map of the Battlefield of Gettysburg, Pennsylvania. Made from an accurate survey of the ground by transit and chain. Philadelphia: S. G. Elliott & Co., 1864.

Ernsberger, Don. *Also for Glory: The Petigrew-Trimble Charge At Gettysburg July 3, 1863.* Xlibris Corporation, 2008.

Evans, Clement A. ed., *Confederate Military History Extended Version.* 17 Volumes. Wilmington, NC: Broadfoot Publishing Company, 1987. Reprint of the 1899 edition.

Faulkner, William. *Intruder in the Dust.* New York: Vintage Press, 1972.

Fiftieth Anniversary of the Battle of Gettysburg: Report of the Pennsylvania Commission. Harrisburg: Wm. Stanley Ray, 1914.

Fleming, Francis S. *Memoir of Capt. C. S. Fleming, of the Second Florida Infantry, C. S. A.* Alexandria, VA: Stonewall House, 1985. Reprint of the 1881 edition.

Fleming, George T. and Gilbert Adams Hays. *General Alexander Hays at the Battle of Gettysburg.* Pittsburgh: 1913.

Flowers, George W. "The Thirty-Eighth N. C. Regiment." *Southern Historical Society Papers*, 25: 259-260.

Frassanito, William. *Early Photography at Gettysburg.* Gettysburg: Thomas Publications, 1995.

Freeman, Douglas Southall. *Lee's Lieutenants: A Study in Command.* New York: Scribner Classics, 1944.

Fremantle, Arthur J.L. *Three Months in the Southern States.* Lincoln: University of Nebraska Press, 1991. Reprint of the 1864 edition.

Fry, Birkett. "Pettigrew's Charge at Gettysburg." *Southern Historical Society Papers*, 7: 91-93.

Fuger, Frederick. "Cushing's Battery at Gettysburg." *Journal of the Military Service Institution of the United States*, Vol. 41 (1907): 405-410.

Gallagher, Gary, editor. *Lee: The Soldier.* Lincoln: University of Nebraska Press, 1996.

----. *The Third Day at Gettysburg and Beyond.* Chapel Hill, NC: University of North Carolina Press, 1994.

----. "A Widow and Her Soldier: LaSalle Corbell Pickett as Author of the George E. Pickett Letters." *The Virginia Magazine of History and Biography*, Vol. 94, No. 3 (July 1986): 329-344.

Gibbon, John. "The Council of War on the Second Day." *Battles and Leaders of the Civil War*, 3: 313-314.

----. *Personal Recollections of the Civil War.* Dayton, OH:

Morningside Bookshop, 1988. Reprint of the 1928 edition.

Goldsborough, W.W. *The Maryland Line in the Confederate Army.* Gaithersburg, MD: Olde Soldier Books, 1987. Reprint of the 1900 edition.

Gottfried, Bradley M. *Brigades of Gettysburg.* Cambridge, MA: Da Capo Press, 2002.

----. "To Fail Twice: Brockenbrough's Brigade at Gettysburg." *Gettysburg Magazine 23* (July 2000): 66–75.

Graham, Joseph. "An Awful Affair." *Civil War Times Illustrated,* April 1984.

Greenberg, Henry J. "Pickett's Charge: The Reason Why." *Gettysburg Magazine 5* (July 1991): 103-106.

Griggs, George K. "From Diary of Colonel George K. Griggs." *Southern Historical Society Papers,* 14: 250-257.

Halleran, Michael. "'The Widow's Son.' Lewis Armistead at Gettysburg." *Gettysburg Magazine 43* (July 2009): 93-106.

Hancock, Almira Russell. *Reminiscences of Winfield Scott Hancock.* New York: Charles L. Webster and Company, 1887.

Hardoff, Richard. *The Surrender and Death of Crazy Horse.* Spokane: The Arthur H. Clark Company, 1998.

Hardy, Michael C. *North Carolina Remembers Gettysburg.* Gettysburg: Ten Roads Publishing, 2011.

Harris, F. S. "Heroism in the Battle of Gettysburg." *Confederate Veteran* IX (1901), 16.

Harrison, Kathy Georg. *The Location of the Monuments, Markers, and Tablets on Gettysburg Battlefield. Markers.* Gettysburg National Military Park.

---- and John W. Busey. *Nothing But Glory: Pickett's Division at Gettysburg.* Gettysburg: Thomas Publications, 1993.

Harrison, Walter. *Pickett's Men: A Fragment of War History.* Baton Rouge: Louisiana State University Press, 2000. Reprint of the 1870 edition.

Hartman, David W. and David Coles compilers. *Biographical Roster of Florida's Confederate and Union Soldiers. 1861-1865. 6* Volumes. Wilmington, NC: Broadfoot Publishing Company, 1985.

Hartwig, Scott. "It Struck Horror to Us All." *Gettysburg Magazine 4* (January 1991): 89-100.

Harvard Memorial Biographies. Volume 2. Cambridge, MA: Sever and Francis, 1867.

Haskell, Frank. *The Battle of Gettysburg.* Wisconsin History Commission, 1908.

Hawthorne, Frederick W. *Gettysburg: Stories of Men and Monuments As Told by Battlefield Guides.* Gettysburg: The Association of Licensed Battlefield Guides, 1988.

Hazelwood, Martin W. "Gettysburg Charge." *Southern Historical Society Papers,* 23: 229-238.

Heenehan, Jim. "Philadelphia Defends the Wall: The Philadelphia Brigade during 'Pickett's Charge.'" *Gettysburg Magazine 38* (January 2008): 91-106.

Heitman, Francis B. *Historical Register and Dictionary of the United States Army, From Its Organization, September 29, 1789 to March 2, 1903. Volume 2.* Washington, D.C.: Government Printing Office, 1903.

Hess, Earl J. *Pickett's Charge: The Last Attack at Gettysburg.* Chapel Hill, NC: University of North Carolina Press, 2001.

Hessler, James A. *Sickles at Gettysburg: The Controversial Civil War General Who Committed Murder, Abandoned Little Round Top, and Declared Himself the Hero of Gettysburg.* New York: Savas Beatie, 2009.

Hewett, Janet B., editor. *The Roster of Confederate Soldiers 1861-1865.* Wilmington, NC: Broadfoot Publishing Co., 1996.

Himmer, Robert. "Col. Hugh Reid Miller, 42nd Mississippi Volunteers, and the Pickett-Pettigrew-Trimble Assault." *Gettysburg Magazine 35* (July 2006): 54-67.

History of the Fifth Massachusetts Battery. Boston: Luther E. Cowles, 1902.

Holcombe, R.I. *History of the First Regiment Minnesota Volunteer Infantry.* Gaithersburg, MD: Ron R. Van Sickle Military Books, 1987. Reprint of the 1916 edition.

Holland, T.C. "With Armistead at Gettysburg." *Confederate Veteran* XXIX (1921): 62.

Hughes, Nathaniel Cheairs Jr. *Yale's Confederates: A Biographical Dictionary.* Knoxville, TN: The University of Tennessee Press, 2008.

Hunt, Henry. "The Third Day at Gettysburg." *Battles and Leaders of the Civil War,* edited by Robert U. Johnson and Clarence C. Buel, 3: 369-385.

Hunton, Eppa. *Autobiography of Eppa Hunton.* Richmond: The William Byrd Press, 1933.

Hyde, Bill, editor. *The Union Generals Speak: The Meade Hearings on the Battle of Gettysburg.* Baton Rouge: Louisiana State University Press, 2003.

Irvine, R. H. "Brig. Gen. Richard B. Garnett." *Confederate Veteran* XXIII (1915): 351.

Jacobs, Michael. *The Rebel Invasion of Maryland & Pennsylvania and Battle of Gettysburg.* Philadelphia: J.B. Lippincott & Co., 1864.

Johnson, Robert U., and Clarence C. Buel, editors. *Battles and Leaders of the Civil War.* New York: Castle Books. Reprint of the 1887-1888 edition.

Johnston, David E. *The Story of a Confederate Boy in the Civil War.* Portland, OR: Glass & Prudhomme Co., 1914.

Jones, John B. *A Rebel War Clerk's Diary,* 2 Volumes. Philadelphia: J.B. Lippincott & Co. 1866.

Jones, John William. *Army of Northern Virginia Memorial Volume.* Richmond: J.W. Randolph & English, 1880.

Jordan, Weymouth T. *North Carolina Troops 1861-1865: A Roster.* 19 Volumes. Raleigh: North Carolina Office of Archives and History, 2004.

Kane, Michael H. "The Irish Lineage of the 69th Pennsylvania Volunteers." *The Irish Sword: The Journal of the Military History Society of Ireland.* Vol. XVIII, No. 72 (Winter, 1991): 184-198.

Keller, Martha. "The Hero of Pickett's Old Brigade. By the Author of 'Love and Rebellion.'" *Confederate Veteran* I (1893): 174.

Krick, Robert K. "Armistead and Garnett: The Parallel Lives of Two Virginia Soldiers." *The Third Day at Gettysburg and Beyond,* edited by Gary Gallagher, 93-131.

----. *The Fredericksburg Artillery.* Lynchburg, VA: H. E. Howard, 1986.

----. *Lee's Colonels: A Biographical Register of the Field Officers of the Army of Northern Virginia.* 4th Edition. Dayton, OH: Morningside, 1992.

Ladd, David and Audrey, editors. *The Bachelder Papers: Gettysburg in Their Own Words.* 3 Volumes. Dayton, OH: Morningside, 1995.

Laino, Philip. *Gettysburg Campaign Atlas.* Dayton, OH: Gatehouse Press, 2009.

Lane, James. "Letter from General James H. Lane." *Southern Historical Society Papers,* 5: 43.

"Lardner Gibbon's Explorations in South America." *Bulletin of the International Bureau of the American Republics* (March 1910): 448-458.

Lash, Gary. "The Cases of Pvt. Jesse Mayberry and Capt. Bernard McMahon, 71st Pennsylvania Infantry." *Gettysburg Magazine 22* (January 2000): 85-95.

----. "The Philadelphia Brigade at Gettysburg."

Gettysburg Magazine 7 (July 1992): 97-113.

Lee, Cazenove Gardner. *Lee Chronicle: Studies of the Early Generations of the Lees of Virginia.* New York: Vantage Press, 1957.

Lee, Robert E. *Recollections and Letters of General Robert E. Lee.* Garden City, New York: Garden City Publishing Co., 1924.

Lewis, John H. *Recollections from 1860-1865.* Portsmouth, VA: 1893.

Loehr, Charles T. "The 'Old First' Virginia at Gettysburg." *Southern Historical Society Papers*, 32: 33-40.

----. *War History of the Old First Virginia Infantry Regiment, Army of Northern Virginia.* Richmond: Wm. Ellis Jones, 1884.

Long, A.L. *Memoirs of Robert E. Lee.* Secaucus, N.J.: Blue and Grey Press, 1983.

Longacre, Edward G. *Pickett: Leader of the Charge.* Shippensburg, PA: White Mane Publishing, 1995.

Longstreet, James. *From Manassas to Appomattox.* Da Capo Press, 1992. Reprint of the 1895 edition.

----. "General James Longstreet's Account of the Campaign and Battle." *Southern Historical Society Papers*, 5:54-85. Originally published in the *Philadelphia Weekly Times.*

----. "Lee's Invasion of Pennsylvania." *Battles and Leaders of the Civil War*, edited by Robert U. Johnson and Clarence C. Buel, 3: 246-247.

----. "Lee's Right Wing at Gettysburg." *Battles and Leaders of the Civil War*, edited by Robert U. Johnson and Clarence C. Buel, 3: 339-354.

----. "Letter from General Longstreet." *Southern Historical Society Papers*, 5: 52-53.

----. "The Mistakes of Gettysburg." *The Annals of the War: Written by Leading Participants North and South.* Dayton OH: Morningside House, 1988. 619-633. Originally published in the *Philadelphia Weekly Times.*

Manhood, Wayne. *Alexander "Fighting Elleck" Hays: The Life of a Civil War General from West Point to the Wilderness.* North Carolina: McFarland & Company, 2005.

Martin, Rawley. "Armistead at the Battle of Gettysburg." *Southern Historical Society Papers*, 39: 186-187.

----. "Rawley Martin's Account." *Southern Historical Society Papers*, 32: 183-189.

Mayo, Joseph. "Pickett's Charge at Gettysburg." *Southern Historical Society Papers*, 34: 327-335.

McClellan, Henry Brainerd. *The Life and Campaigns of Major-General J.E.B Stuart, Commander of the Cavalry of the Army of Northern Virginia.* New York: Houghton, Mifflin and Company, 1885.

McDougal, Henry Clay. *Recollections, 1844-1909.* Kansas City, MO: Franklin Hudson Publishing Co., 1910.

McFarland, Baxter. "The Eleventh Mississippi Regiment at Gettysburg." *Publications of the Mississippi Historical Society.* Jackson, Mississippi: 1918. 549-568.

----. "Casualties of the Eleventh Mississippi Regiment at Gettysburg." *Confederate Veteran* XXIV (1916), 410-411.

McMurry, Richard M. *Virginia Military Institute Alumni in the Civil War.* Lynchburg, VA: HE Howard, 1999.

Meade, George. *The Life and Letters of George Gordon Meade.* New York: Charles Scribner's Sons, 1913.

Meredith, Jaquelin M. "The First Day at Gettysburg Tribute to Brave General Harry Heth who Opened the Great Battle." *Southern Historical Society Papers,* 3: 24, 185.

Moe, Richard. *The Last Full Measure: The Life and Death of the First Minnesota Volunteers.* New York: Avon Books, 1993.

Monuments at Gettysburg. Report of the Vermont Commissioners 1888. Rutland: The Tuttle Company, 1888.

Moore, John Trotwood. *The Tennessee Civil War Veterans Questionnaires.* Easley, SC: Southern Historical Society Press, Inc., 1985.

Mosby, John S. "Personal Recollections of General Lee." *Munsey's Magazine.* Vol. 45, No. 1 (April, 1911). 65-69.

Mosher, T.J. "The 1st Minn. Losses." *Fighting Them Over: How the Veterans Remembered Gettysburg in the Pages of The National Tribune*, edited by Richard A. Sauers, 330.

Motts, Wayne E. "A Brave and Resolute Force." *North & South*, Vol. 2, No. 5 (June 1999): 28-34.

----. *Trust in God and Fear Nothing: Gen. Lewis A. Armistead, CSA.* Gettysburg: Farnsworth House Military Impressions, 1994.

---- and Silas Felton. "In Their Words: Recollections of Visitations at Gettysburg After the Great Battle in July 1863." *Gettysburg Magazine 46* (January 2012): 106-124.

Munn, Sheldon A. *Freemasons at Gettysburg.* Gettysburg: Thomas Publications, 1993.

Murray, R.L. "Cowan's, Cushing's, and Rorty's Batteries in Action during the Pickett-Pettigrew-Trimble Charge." *Gettysburg Magazine 35* (July 2006): 39-53.

Nesbitt, Mark. *Saber and Scapegoat: J.E.B. Stuart and the Gettysburg Controversy.* Mechanicsburg, PA: Stackpole Books, 1994.

Neu, Jonathan D. "The 72nd Pennsylvania Monument Controversy." *Gettysburg Magazine 40* (January 2009): 79-93.

New Jersey Gettysburg Battlefield Commission. *Final Report of the Gettysburg Battlefield Commission of New Jersey.* Trenton, NJ: John L. Murphy Publishing Co., 1891.

Newton, George. "Brockenbrough's Virginia Brigade at Gettysburg." *Blue & Gray Magazine* (Vol. XXVII, No. 4): 43-48.

----. *Silent Sentinels: A Reference Guide to the Artillery at Gettysburg.* New York: Savas Beatie LLC, 2005.

New York Monuments Commission for the Battlefields of Gettysburg and Chattanooga. *Final Report on the Battle of Gettysburg.* Albany, NY: J.B. Lyon Company, 1902.

----. *In Memoriam: Alexander Stewart Webb, 1835-1911.* Albany, NY: J.B. Lyon Company, 1916.

Nicholson, John P., editor. *Pennsylvania at Gettysburg.* Harrisburg, PA: 1914.

Nickerson, A.H. "Personal Recollections of Two Visits to Gettysburg." *Scribner's Magazine*, Vol. 4, Issue 1 (June 1893): 19-28.

Page, Charles D. *History of the Fourteenth Regiment, Connecticut Vol. Infantry.* Meriden, Conn.: The Horton Printing Co., 1906.

Paradis, James M. *African Americans and the Gettysburg Campaign.* Lanham, MD: Scarecrow Press, 2013.

Pfanz, Harry W. *Gettysburg: Culp's Hill and Cemetery Hill.* Chapel Hill: University of North Carolina Press, 1993.

Pickett, LaSalle Corbell. *Pickett and his Men.* Philadelphia: J.B. Lippincott Company, 1913.

----. *What Happened to Me.* New York: Brentano's, 1917.

Poindexter, James E. "General Armistead's Portrait Presented." *Southern Historical Society Papers*, 37: 144-151.

Pollard, Edward A. *The Lost Cause: A New Southern History of the War of the Confederates.* New York: E.B. Treat & Co., 1867.

----. *The Second Year of the War.* New York: Charles B. Richardson, 1864.

Priest, John Michael. *Into the Fight: Pickett's Charge at Gettysburg.* Shippensburg, PA: White Mane Books, 1998.

Proceedings of the Clarke County Historical

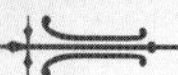

Association. Volume VI, 1946, 53-60.

Ramey, Emily G. and John K. Gott. *The Years of Anguish: Fauquier County, Virginia, 1861-1865.* Fauquier, VA: The Fauquier County Civil War Centennial Committee and the Board of Supervisors, 1965.

Raus, Edmund J., Jr. *A Generation on the March: The Union Army at Gettysburg.* Gettysburg, PA: Thomas Publications, 1996.

Reardon, Carol. "Pickett's Charge: The Convergence of History and Myth in the Southern Past." *The Third Day at Gettysburg and Beyond,* edited by Gary Gallagher, 56-92.

----. *Pickett's Charge in History and Memory.* Chapel Hill: University of North Carolina Press, 1997.

Rhodes, John H. *The History of Battery B. First Regiment Rhode Island Light Artillery.* Providence: Snow & Farnham, 1894.

Rice, Edmund. "Repelling Lee's Last Blow," *Battles and Leaders of the Civil War,* 3: 391-392.

Rietti, John C. *Military Annals of Mississippi.* Spartanburg, SC: The Reprint Company, 1976. Reprint of 1895 edition.

Rittenhouse, Benjamin F. "The Battle Seen From Little Round Top." *The Gettysburg Papers, Two Volumes in One,* edited by Ken Bandy and Florence Freeland, 517-529.

Roberts, Samuel. "The 72d PA." *Fighting Them Over: How the Veterans Remembered Gettysburg in the Pages of the National Tribune,* edited by Richard Sauers, 415-418.

Rollins, Richard. *Pickett's Charge: Eyewitness Accounts.* Redondo Beach, California: Rank and File Publications, 1994.

----. "The Second Wave of Pickett's Charge." *Gettysburg Magazine 18* (January 1998): 96-113.

Sauers, Richard A., editor. *Fighting Them Over: How the Veterans Remembered Gettysburg in the Pages of the National Tribune.* Baltimore: Butternut and Blue, 1998.

Sawyer, Franklin. *The Eighth Ohio at Gettysburg. (Unveiling of the Ohio Monuments. September 14, 1887.)* Privately published.

Scheibert, Justus. "Letter from Maj. Justus Scheibert, of the Prussian Royal Engineers." *Southern Historical Society Papers,* 5: 90-93.

----. Edited by Wm. Stanley Hoole. *Seven Months in the Rebel States during the North American War, 1863.* Confederate Publishing Company, 1958.

Scott, Robert Garth, editor. *Fallen Leaves: The Civil War Letters of Major Henry Livermore Abbott.* Kent, OH: Kent State University Press, 1991.

Sears, Stephen W. *Gettysburg.* New York: Houghton Mifflin, 2003.

Selcer, Richard F. *Lee vs. Pickett: Two Divided by War.* Gettysburg: Thomas Publications, 1998.

----. "Re-Creating Pickett's Lost Gettysburg Report." *Columbiad: A Quarterly Review of the War Between the States* (Winter 1998), Vol. 1, Number 4: 93-121.

Seville, William P. *History of the First Regiment of Delaware Volunteers.* Baltimore, MD: Gateway Press for Longstreet House, 1986. Reprint of the 1884 edition.

Shaara, Michael. *The Killer Angels.* New York: Ballantine Books, 1974.

Simons, Ezra Dee Frest. *A Regimental History: The One Hundred and Twenty-fifth New York State Volunteers.* New York: 1888.

Smith, John Holmes. "Captain John Holmes Smith's Account." *Southern Historical Society Papers,* 32: 189-195.

Smith, Timothy H. *Farms at Gettysburg: The Fields of Battle.* Gettysburg: Adams County Historical Society, 2007.

----. *Gettysburg's Battlefield Photographer- William H. Tipton.* Gettysburg: Adams County Historical Society, 2005.

Snipes, Keith. "The Improper Placement of the 8th Ohio Monument: A Study of Words and Maps." *Gettysburg Magazine 35* (July 2006): 68-93.

Sorrel, G. Moxley. *At the Right Hand of Longstreet: Recollections of a Confederate Staff Officer.* University of Nebraska Press, 1999. Reprint of the 1905 edition.

Squires, Charles W. "My Artillery Fire Was Very Destructive." *Civil War Times Illustrated,* June 1975.

Stevens, James A. "Do You Believe It?" *Confederate Veteran* XXVIII (1920): 356.

Stewart, George R. *Pickett's Charge: A Microhistory of the Final Attack at Gettysburg, July 3, 1863.* Boston: Houghton Mifflin, 1959.

Stewart, William H. "Col. John Bowie M'Gruder." *Confederate Veteran* VIII (1900), 329.

----."Colonel John Bowie Magruder." *Southern Historical Society Papers,* 27: 205-210.

Stine, J.H. *History of the Army of the Potomac.* Washington, D.C.: Gibson Bros., 1893.

Styple, William B. editor. *Generals in Bronze: Interviewing the Commanders of the Civil War.* Kearny, NJ: Belle Grove Publishing Company, 2005.

Supplement to the Official Records of the Union and Confederate Armies. 100 Volumes. Wilmington, NC: Broadfoot Publishing, 1995.

Swallow, William H. "The Third Day at Gettysburg." *Southern Bivouac,* Vol.1, No. 9 (February 1886): 562-572.

Swinton, William. *Campaigns of the Army of the Potomac.* New York: Charles Scribner's Sons, 1882. Revision and reprint of the 1866 edition.

Tagg, Larry. *The Generals of Gettysburg.* Cambridge, MA: Da Capo Press, 2003.

Talbot, Edith Armstrong. *Samuel Chapman Armstrong: A Biographical Study.* New York: Doubleday, Page & Co., 1904.

Talcott, T.M.R. "The Third Day At Gettysburg." *Southern Historical Society Papers,* 41: 37-46.

Tapscott, V.A. "One of Pickett's Men." *Fighting Them Over: How the Veterans Remembered Gettysburg in the Pages of the National Tribune,* 413-414.

Taylor, Frank H. *Philadelphia in the Civil War.* Philadelphia: 1913.

Taylor, Walter H. *Four Years with General Lee.* New York: D. Appleton and Company, 1878.

----. "Memorandum by Colonel Walter H. Taylor, Of General Lee's Staff." *Southern Historical Society Papers,* 4: 80-87.

----. "Second Paper by Walter Taylor." *Southern Historical Society Papers,* 4: 132-135.

Toombs, Samuel. *New Jersey Troops in the Gettysburg Campaign from June 5 to July 31, 1863.* Orange, NJ: The Evening Mail Publishing House, 1888.

Trimble, Isaac R. "Civil War Diary of I. R. Trimble." *Maryland Historical Magazine* (1922), 1-2.

Trinque, Bruce. "Arnold's Battery and the 26th North Carolina." *Gettysburg Magazine 12* (January 1995): 61-67.

----. "Confederate Battle Flags in the July 3rd Charge." *Gettysburg Magazine 21* (July 1999): 108-125.

Trout, Robert J., editor. *Memoirs of the Stuart Horse Artillery Battalion, Volume 2.* Knoxville, TN: University of Tennessee Press, 2010.

Trudeau, Noah Andre. *Gettysburg: A Testing of Courage.* New York: Harper Collins, 2002.

Tucker, Glenn. *High Tide at Gettysburg.* Gettysburg: Stan Clark Military Books, 1995. Reprint of 1958 edition.

Vanderslice, John M. *Gettysburg Then and Now.*

New York: G.W. Dillingham, 1897.

Vermilyea, Peter C. "The Effect of the Confederate Invasion on Pennsylvania's African American Community." *Gettysburg Magazine 24* (July 2001): 113-119.

Walker, Charles D. *Biographical Sketches of the Graduates and Eleves of the Virginia Military Institute Who Fell During the War Between the States.* Philadelphia, PA: J.B. Lippincott & Co., 1875.

Walker, Francis A. "General Hancock and the Artillery at Gettysburg." *Battles and Leaders of the Civil War*, edited by Robert U. Johnson and Clarence C. Buel, 3:385-386.

----. *History of the Second Army Corps.* New York: Charles Scribner's Sons, 1887.

Warner, Ezra J. *Generals in Gray: Lives of the Confederate Commanders.* Baton Rouge: Louisiana State University Press, 1959.

Watts, A.T. "Something More About Gettysburg." *Confederate Veteran* VI (1898): 67.

Webb, Alexander S. *An Address Delivered at Gettysburg, August 27, 1883 by Gen. Alexander S. Webb at the Dedication of the 72nd PA. Vols. Monument.* Philadelphia: Porter & Coates, 1883.

Weeks, Jim. *Gettysburg: Memory, Market, and an American Shrine.* Princeton, NJ: Princeton University Press, 2003.

Welsh, Jack M.D., *Medical Histories of Confederate Generals.* Kent, OH: Kent State University Press, 1995.

Wentz, Abdel Ross. *History of the Gettysburg Theological Seminary.* Philadelphia: The United Lutheran Publication House, 1926.

Wert, Jeffry D. *Gettysburg Day Three.* New York: Simon & Schuster, 2001.

White, William S. *Contributions to a History of the Richmond Howitzer Battalion, Pamphlet No.2, A Diary of the War or What I Saw of It.* Baltimore, MD: Butternut & Blue, 2000. Reprint of the 1883 edition.

Wilcox, Cadmus. "General C. M. Wilcox. Letter, Baltimore, MD. March 26th, 1877." *Southern Historical Society Papers*, 4: 111-118.

Williams, *T. P. The Mississippi Brigade of Brig. Gen. Joseph R. Davis.* Dayton, OH: Morningside Books, 1999.

Winschel, Terrence J. "The Gettysburg Diary of Lieutenant William Peel." *Gettysburg Magazine 9* (July 1993): 98-107.

----. "Heavy Was Their Loss: Joe Davis' Brigade at Gettysburg." *Gettysburg Magazine 3* (July 1990): 76-85.

Wise, Jennings Cropper. *The Military History of the Virginia Military Institute from 1839 to 1865.* Lynchburg, VA: J. P. Bell Company Inc., 1915.

Witherspoon, Rev. Dr. T. D. "Prison Life at Fort McHenry." *Southern Historical Society Papers,* 8: 77.

Wittenberg, Eric J. *Gettysburg's Forgotten Cavalry Actions.* New York: Savas Beatie, 2011.

----. *Protecting the Flank at Gettysburg: The Battles for Brinkerhoff's Ridge and East Cavalry Field, July 2-3, 1863.* New York: Savas Beatie, 2013.

---- and J. David Petruzzi. *Plenty of Blame to Go Around: Jeb Stuart's Controversial Ride to Gettysburg.* New York: Savas Beatie, 2006.

Wright, Steven J. "'Don't Let Me Bleed to Death.' The Wounding of Maj. Gen. Winfield Scott Hancock." *Gettysburg Magazine 6* (January 1992): 87-92.

Government and Court Documents

1860 United States Federal Census. Census Place: Cumberland, Adams County, Pennsylvania.

Annual Reports of the Gettysburg National Military Park Commission to the Secretary of War (1893-1904). Washington: Government Printing Office, 1905.

The Reports of Committees of the House of Representatives for the Second Session of the 52nd Congress 1892-1893, 2nd Session. Washington: Government Printing Office, 1893.

Supreme Court of Pennsylvania. Middle District. May Term, 1891, Nos. 20 and 30. *Appeal of the Gettysburg Battlefield Memorial Association from the Decree of the Court of Common Pleas of Adams County.*

The War of the Rebellion: A Compilation of the Official Records of the Union and Confederate Armies. Washington: Government Printing Office, 1880-1901.

Typescripts and Unpublished Accounts

Hancock, Winfield S. Correspondence to William Mitchell. Private Collection of Ed and Faye Max.

Love, Eliza M. *Recollections of Eliza Matilda Love.* Typescript in Possession of Wayne Motts.

Magruder, William T. Family Archives
William Magruder *Field Diary*
Letter of Capt. W. D. Nunn. July 9, 1863.

Page, Coupland. *Coupland R. Page Memoir.* Unpublished Typescript in Possession of Robert K. Krick (Fredericksburg, VA.)

Newspapers

Adams Sentinel (Gettysburg, PA), August 25, 1863.

"After Thirty Years." *Compiler* (Gettysburg, PA), July 4, 1893.

Baker, Peter. "Civil War Hero Awarded the Medal of Honor at Last." *New York Times*, November 7, 2014.

"The Battle." *Compiler* (Gettysburg, PA), June 7, 1887.

"Battle Hero's Son Here for Re-Enactment." *Gettysburg Times*, July 5, 1963.

"The Battle of Gettysburg." *Weekly Hawk-Eye* (Burlington, IA), July 11, 1863.

"Colorful Re-Enactment of Pickett's Charge Attracts Huge Crowd." *Gettysburg Times*, July 5, 1963.

Compiler (Gettysburg, PA), January 3, 1888.

Cowan, Andrew. "How Cowan's Battery Withstood Pickett's Great Charge." *Washington Post*, July 2, 1911.

"Crowd of More than 35,000." *Gettysburg Times*, July 3, 1963.

"Death of Mr. Codori." *Star and Sentinel* (Gettysburg, PA), July 18, 1878.

"Death of W. Keith Armistead." *Newport Daily News* (Newport, RI), March 30, 1896.

"Field Marshal Montgomery Comes to Gettysburg with President Eisenhower." *Gettysburg Times*, May 11, 1957.

Finley, George W. "Bloody Angle." *Buffalo Evening News* (Buffalo, NY), May 29, 1894.

"40,000 Will View Pickett's Charge at Gettysburg." *The Daily Courier* (Connellsville, PA), July 3, 1963.

"Frank W. Hoffman Dead." *The Culpeper Eaponent* (Culpeper, VA), October 14, 1920.

"Friends Not Foes." *Atlanta Constitution*, July 3, 1887.

"Gettysburg Generalship Poor Say Ike and Monty." *Sarasota Herald-Tribune*, May 13, 1957.

"Hugh Garden's Battery." *Sumter Herald* (Sumter, SC), August 29, 1902.

"Hunter Griffin's Career." *The Galveston Daily News* (Galveston, TX), November 25, 1896.

Imboden, John D. "Lee after Gettysburg," *The Petersburg Index*, March 25, 1871.

"It's Again a Tented Field." *New York Times*, July 1, 1888.

Johnson, Dirk. "Winning a Battle to Honor a Civil War Hero." *New York Times*, June 11, 2010.

Jorgensen, Kathryn. "Alonzo Cushing May Yet Be Awarded the Medal of Honor." *Civil War News*, July 2012.

----. "Gettysburg 150th Brings Thousands to Programs, Battlefield, Reenactments." *Civil War News*, August 2013.

"Leading Colored Citizen." *Compiler* (Gettysburg, PA), June 13, 1906.

"Limping Gray Men Once More Charge Up Cemetery Ridge." *The Atlanta Constitution*, July 4, 1913.

"Lincoln Abused; 7 Men Are Stabbed." *Raleigh News and Observer* (Raleigh, NC), July 3, 1913.

"Meade and Hancock." *Compiler* (Gettysburg, PA), June 9, 1896.

"Meade and Hancock Statues." *Compiler* (Gettysburg, PA), June 2, 1896.

"Meade's Great Mistake." *New York Times*, July 4, 1888.

New York World, July 4, 1888.

"Obituary: Gen. George E. Pickett." *New York Times*, July 31, 1875.

"Obituary Notice (William Stockton)." *Public Ledger* (Philadelphia, PA), August 30, 1913.

"Old Soldiers Defy Heat." *New York Times*, July 2, 1913.

The Philadelphia Press, July 4, 1887.

"President, Montgomery Tour Battlefield Sunday." *Gettysburg Times*, May 13, 1957.

Richmond Times Dispatch, December 13, 1903.

"Shocking Accident." *Star and Sentinel* (Gettysburg, PA), July 11, 1878.

"Son and Grandsons of Gen. Longstreet." *Atlanta Constitution*, June 30, 1913.

Star and Sentinel (Gettysburg, PA), May 10, 1887.

Star and Sentinel (Gettysburg, PA), July 17, 1888.

Star and Sentinel (Gettysburg, PA), July 11, 1893.

"Storm Topples Monument." *Gettysburg Times*, June 27, 2013.

Storrick, William C. "General Armistead Was Only Southern Leader to Cross Wall at 'Angle' in Pickett's Charge." *Gettysburg Times*, March 23, 1939.

Swift, R.B. "Gettysburg Monument to be Dedicated." *The Daily Item* (Sunbury, PA), August 11, 2007.

"Veteran Dies Fighting To Prove He Was Alive." *Oakland Tribune* (Oakland, CA), June 13, 1926.

"Veteran Found Dead in Tent." *New York Times*, July 1, 1913.

"Will Dedicate New Monument." *Gettysburg Times*, June 28, 1913.

Internet

Christ, Elwood. "Struggle for the Bliss Farm." *Gettysburgdaily.com*. June 2009. http://www.gettysburgdaily.com/?page_id=4475.

Fuss, Sara. "Gettysburg's WWII Prisoner of War Camp." *Emmitsburg Area Historical Society*. http://wwww.emmitsburg.net/archive_list/articles/history/gb/war/ww2_prisoner_camp.htm.

Gast, Phil. "150th Anniversary of Battle of Gettysburg Provides a Bigger Story." *CNN.com*. June 30, 2013. http://www.cnn.com/2013/06/28/travel/gettysburg-anniversary/.

"Gettysburg 150th- July 3 Battlefield Experience Programs." *From the Fields of Gettysburg*. May 17, 2013. http://npsgnmp.wordpress.com/2013/05/17/gettysburg-150th-july-3-battlefield-experience-programs/.

Hartwig, Scott. "Lieutenant Cushing." *From the Fields of Gettysburg*. June 21, 2002. http://npsgnmp.wordpress.com/2012/06/21/lieutenant-cushing/.

Hawthorne, Fred. "140 Places Every Guide Should Know, Part 2. The Stockton Rock." *Gettysburgdaily.com*. October 6, 2010. http://www.gettysburgdaily.com/?p=8821.

----. "140 Places Every Guide Should Know, Part 3. The Gibbon Tree." *Gettysburgdaily.com*. November 1, 2010. http://www.gettysburgdaily.com/?p=9080.

Housch, Robert. "McMillan Woods Earthworks: Update." *Gettysburgdaily.com*. April 28, 2011. http://www.gettysburgdaily.com/?p=10688.

----. "National Cemetery Parking and North Cemetery Ridge Updates." *Gettysburgdaily.com*. February 24, 2012. http://www.gettysburgdaily.com/?p=13420.

Lechak, Phil. "Gettysburg Hospitals, Part 5. George Spangler Farm." *Gettysburgdaily.com*. June 14, 2011. http://www.gettysburgdaily.com/?p=11221.

Newton, George. "Gettysburg Artillery, Part 10. Brown's Battery." *Gettysburgdaily.com*. October 1, 2009. http://www.gettysburgdaily.com/?p=5461.

Stone Sentinels: The Battle of Gettysburg. http://www.gettysburg.stonesentinels.com.

Swift, Beth. "Captain Blinn." *Dear Old Wabash*. February 5, 2009.

Trout, David and Cheri James. "The Seventy-second Pennsylvania Monument Controversy at Gettysburg." *Baxter's 72nd Pennsylvania Infantry*. September 3, 2012. http://baxters72ndpenninfantry.blogspot.com.

Vanderheiden, Jan. "Who Buried the Children?" *The Longstreet Society*. http://www.longstreet.org/children.html.

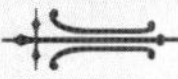

Index

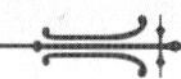

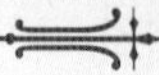